Divided into five major sections, this handbook stresses principles and fundamentals of strategic management in early chapters, and specific on-the-job techniques in later chapters. Always realistic, this storehouse of down-to-earth guidance is illustrated with real-world case studies, tables, and graphs to help you guide your company's future. It is an invaluable tool for corporate presidents and vice presidents, and for division, corporate planning, and marketing managers... indeed, for any concerned executive on the move.

The business world is changing rapidly, both domestically and internationally. In this survival of the fittest environment, businesses must adapt to change or suffer the consequences. This book tells managers where they should be headed, and even more important, exactly how to get there.

ABOUT THE EDITOR IN CHIEF

Kenneth J. Albert is a veteran industrial marketing and business strategy consultant who maintains an independent consulting practice in the San Francisco Bay area. He is the author or editor of several McGraw-Hill business books, including THE HANDBOOK OF BUSINESS PROBLEM SOLVING. Mr. Albert holds an M.B.A. degree from the University of Chicago, an M.S. degree from Rensselaer Polytechnic Institute, and a B.S. degree in engineering from the University of Illinois.

The Strategic Management Handbook

KENNETH J. ALBERT Editor in Chief
Strategy Consultant and Author

MCGRAW-HILL BOOK COMPANY
New York St. Louis San Francisco Auckland
Bogotá Hamburg Johannesburg London
Madrid Mexico Montreal New Delhi
Panama Paris São Paulo Singapore
Sydney Tokyo Toronto

Library of Congress Cataloging in Publication Data
Main entry under title:

The Strategic management handbook.

Includes index.
1. Corporate planning. 2. Management.
I. Albert, Kenneth J., date.
HD30.28.S732 1983 658.4'01 82-17110
ISBN 0-07-000954-6

1 2 3 4 5 6 7 8 9 0 KGP/KGP 8 9 8 7 6 5 4 3 2

ISBN 0-07-000954-6

The editors for this book were William R. Newton and Olive H. Collen, the designer was Naomi Auerbach, and the production supervisor was Thomas G. Kowalczyk. It was set in Baskerville by Waldman Graphics.

Printed and bound by The Kingsport Press.

To the contributing authors.
You made this book possible,
and you made this book good.

About the Editor in Chief

KENNETH J. ALBERT *is a veteran industrial marketing and business strategy consultant who maintains an independent consulting practice in the San Francisco Bay area. He is the author or editor of several McGraw-Hill business books, including* The Handbook of Business Problem Solving. *Mr. Albert holds an M.B.A. degree from the University of Chicago, an M.S. degree from Rensselaer Polytechnic Institute, and a B.S. degree in engineering from the University of Illinois.*

Contents

Contributors

MICHAEL G. ALLEN *President, Michael G. Allen Company, New York, New York.* (CHAPTERS 7 AND 18)

J. SCOTT ARMSTRONG *Associate Professor of Marketing, The Wharton School, University of Pennsylvania, Philadelphia, Pennsylvania.* (CHAPTER 2)

WALTER P. BLASS *Director of Corporate Planning, New York Telephone, American Telephone & Telegraph.* (CHAPTER 6)

GEORGE CALHOUN *Managing Director, The Philadelphia Consulting Group, Wynnewood, Pennsylvania.* (CHAPTER 25)

MARV EISTHEN *President and Chief Executive Officer, OPI, Limited, Dallas, Texas.* (CHAPTER 16)

LIAM FAHEY *Assistant Professor of Policy and Environment, J. L. Kellogg Graduate School of Management, Northwestern University, Evanston, Illinois.* (CHAPTER 21)

LYNN H. GLENNEY *Director of Corporate Planning, Lear Siegler, Inc., Santa Monica, California.* (CHAPTER 5)

JOHN M. HARRIS *Senior Vice President, Booz·Allen & Hamilton, Inc., New York, New York.* (CHAPTER 20)

BRUCE D. HENDERSON *Chairman of the Board, The Boston Consulting Group, Inc., Boston, Massachusetts.* (CHAPTER 1 AND APPENDIX)

WALTER J. KRUEL *Vice President, Corporate Planning and Development, Lear Siegler, Inc., Santa Monica, California.* (CHAPTER 5)

ROBERT E. LIENHARD *Vice President, The Boston Consulting Group, Inc., Boston, Massachusetts.* (CHAPTER 12)

W. WALKER LEWIS *President, Strategic Planning Associates, Inc., Washington, DC.* (CHAPTER 24)

JAMES F. LYONS *Vice President, Strategic Planning, United Technologies Corporation, Hartford, Connecticut.* (CHAPTER 3)

THOMAS F. MANDEL *Senior Strategic Analyst, Business Intelligence Program, SRI International, Menlo Park, California.* (CHAPTER 10)

CHESTER D. MARKS *Manager, Strategic Planning, Dow Chemical USA, Midland, Michigan.* (CHAPTER 4)

KENNETH G. MARTIN *Director, Hay Associates, Philadelphia, Pennsylvania.* (CHAPTER 17)

J. ERNEST MITCHELL *Director, Corporate Planning, The Dow Chemical Company, Midland, Michigan.* (CHAPTER 4)

EDWARD W. MORSE *Director, Hay Associates, Philadelphia, Pennsylvania.* (CHAPTER 17)

V. K. NARAYANAN *Assistant Professor of Organization and Management, School of Business, University of Kansas, Lawrence, Kansas.* (CHAPTER 21)

MICHAEL E. NAYLOR *Strategic Planning Department, General Motors Corporation, Warren, Michigan.* (CHAPTER 22)

ALEXANDER R. OLIVER *Vice President, Booz·Allen & Hamilton, Inc., San Francisco, California.* (CHAPTER 18)

THEODORE E. POLLOCK *Manager, A. T. Kearney, Inc., Chicago, Illinois.* (CHAPTER 14)

ALLAN J. PRAGER *Vice President and Director, Cresap, McCormick and Paget Inc., San Francisco, California.* (CHAPTER 8)

JOHN D. C. ROACH *Vice President and Managing Officer, Strategic Management Group, Booz·Allen & Hamilton, Inc. Houston, Texas.* (CHAPTER 7)

RUSSELL G. ROBERTS *Director, Hay Associates, Chicago, Illinois.* (CHAPTER 15)

THOMAS S. ROBERTSON *Professor and Chairperson, Department of Marketing, The Wharton School, University of Pennsylvania, Philadelphia, Pennsylvania.* (CHAPTER 11)

JOHN E. ROBSON *Executive Vice President, G. D. Searle & Co., Skokie, Illinois.* (CHAPTER 19)

ROBERT H. ROCK *Partner, Hay Associates, Strategic Management Group, Hay Associates, Philadelphia, Pennsylvania.* (CHAPTER 16)

JOSEPH D. ROMANO *Vice President, A. T. Kearney, Inc., Chicago, Illinois.* (CHAPTER 13)

WLADIMIR M. SACHS *Managing Director, The Philadelphia Consulting Group, Wynnewood, Pennsylvania.* (CHAPTER 25)

SIDNEY SCHOEFFLER *Managing Director, The Strategic Planning Institute, Cambridge, Massachusetts.* (CHAPTER 23)

EDWARD H. SCHWALLIE *Senior Vice President, Booz·Allen & Hamilton, Inc., San Francisco, California.* (CHAPTER 18)

MARY BETH SHEA *Managing Consultant, Cresap, McCormick and Paget Inc., San Francisco, California.* (CHAPTER 8)

IAN WILSON *Senior Management Consultant, International Development Center, SRI International, Menlo Park, California.* (CHAPTER 9)

YORAM WIND *Professor of Marketing and Director, Center for International Studies, The Wharton School, University of Pennsylvania, Philadelphia, Pennsylvania.* (CHAPTER 11)

MARTIN G. WOLF *Senior Principal, Hay Associates, Philadelphia, Pennsylvania.* (CHAPTER 15)

ALAN J. ZAKON *Chief Executive Officer, The Boston Consulting Group, Inc., Boston, Massachusetts.* (APPENDIX)

Preface

The past decade has not been an easy one for business decision makers. We've been through a period of unprecedented change, increased competition, and growing uncertainty.

Unfortunately, the years ahead, very likely, will bring even more change, more competition, and more uncertainty. Technological and social change will no doubt accelerate. Competition will become even more global, moving us toward a worldwide economy, and this trend will have an impact on all types and sizes of businesses. As for uncertainty, well, the only certainty is that uncertainty is likely to become epidemic. All too often, an unanticipated change in the competitive environment of a company will turn an apparently masterful business strategy into fodder for a "what went wrong" cover story in *Business Week*.

Strategic Management

Some companies will prosper in the years ahead, and others will fall back. Luck (that is, being in the right market, with the right product, at the right time, and at the right price) will surely shine on some businesses. But most successes will result from a sound strategy and the ability of the leaders and managers of an organization to think and perform in concert with that strategy. This is the essence of strategic management. And that is what this book is all about. It thoroughly treats each of the important aspects of strategic management:

- Strategy formulation
- Strategy for major business functions
- Anticipating and responding to change in the competitive environment
- Leading and motivating the organization
- Structural and human considerations
- Effective implementation
- Measuring results and making adjustments
- Useful techniques and resources

This Book

This book brings together the best in contemporary thought, principle, and practice in all aspects of strategic management.

The list of individual contributors and the organizations they represent constitute a veritable "Who's Who" of leading strategic advisers and practitioners. Almost all the world's leading management consulting firms are represented. The industrial organizations represented are, in most people's judgment, among the best-managed companies in the world. And some top business schools round out this impressive group.

All the chapters in *The Strategic Management Handbook* emphasize pragmatic, usable, how-to material. Most are illustrated with actual case histories.

This book is, of course, a reference book; thus each chapter is a complete treatment of a particular topic. But since many topics are interrelated, it is advisable to consult the index for material throughout the book that may be helpful. Also, a comprehensive bibliography of business strategy references is included at the end of Chapter 2.

People filling many different roles in the business community will benefit from this book:

- Corporate executives
- Planners and strategists
- Divisional managers
- Functional managers
- Entrepreneurs
- Consultants
- Professors
- Students, especially in graduate business schools

Acknowledgments

One group of people was most instrumental in making this book possible. They, of course, are the authors of the individual chapters. All are very busy senior people with untold demands on their time. I sincerely appreciate the special effort each has made to contribute to this book.

Aptos, California KEN ALBERT

Section One

Strategic Thoughts and Actions

Chapter 1
THE CONCEPT OF STRATEGY

BRUCE D. HENDERSON
Chairman of the Board, The Boston Consulting Group, Inc.

THE BEGINNING OF NATURAL COMPETITION

Competition existed long before strategy. Competition began with life itself. The first one-cell organisms required certain resources for maintenance of life. When those resources were adequate, then each generation became greater in number than the preceding one. If there had been no limitation on required resources, then exponential growth would have led to infinite numbers.

But as life evolved, the single-cell life form became a food resource for more complex life. With increasing complexity, each level became the resource for the next higher level. When two competitors were in perpetual competition, one inevitably displaced the other, unless something prevented it. In the absence of some counterbalancing force to maintain a stable equilibrium between the two competitors by giving each an advantage in its own territory, only one competitor survived.

In this way a very complex web of competitive interaction developed. It required millions of years. Now there are more than a million distinct species which have been catalogued, and there are believed to be millions more such variations of species as yet unclassified. Each has a unique advantage in competition for its required resources within its particular niche of the environment.

Since each of these competitors must be unique, the abundance of variations must match an equal variation in potential factors which define an environmental niche, and the varied characteristics in the environment which make each combination effective. The richer the environment, the more severe the competition is and the greater the number of competitors. Likewise, the richer the environment, the smaller the differences between competitors.

This is quite consistent with recent biological research. Experimental laboratory ecologists discovered in the 1930s and 1940s that if one puts two similar species of small organisms together in a bottle with food and uniform substrate, only one species can persist.[1]

The observation that coexisting species in nature do differ ecologically and that species must differ ecologically to coexist in bottles led to Gause's Competitive Exclusion Principle: "No two species can coexist who make their living in the same way."

For millions of years natural competition involved no strategy. It was natural selection, adaptation, and survival of the fittest. Random chance determined the mutations and variations which survived and succeeded to compound their numbers. Those who left relatively fewer offspring became displaced. Those who adapted best displaced the rest. Physical and structural characteristics adapted, but behavior adapted also and became embedded in their instinctual reactions.

The awareness of natural competition as a systematic effect is centuries old. Thomas Malthus quoted Benjamin Franklin's observation about the crowding out of natural competition. Charles Darwin himself credited Malthus with the insight. Alfred Wallace and Darwin, separated by thousands of miles, simultaneously developed the concept of natural selection by competition. Darwin emphasized repeatedly the overriding importance of competition. It is awesome in its potential for evolution.

As far as we know, only primates possess imagination and the ability to reason logically. But without these qualities, behavior and tactics are either intuitive or the result of conditioned reflexes. Without these capabilities, strategy is impossible. Strategy depends upon the ability to foresee the future consequences of present initiatives.

THE BEGINNING OF STRATEGIC COMPETITION

Strategy in its most elementary form most likely developed when the hunting party was formed by early humans to capture large game which could not have been handled by a single individual. But this was hardly true strategy. The quarry itself could have no counterstrategy, only its instinctive behavior. True strategy was probably first practiced by one tribe attempting to take over the hunting grounds of another tribe.

For strategy to be possible, it is necessary to be able to imagine and evaluate the possible consequences of alternate courses of action. But imagination and reasoning power are not sufficient. There also must be knowledge of competition and the higher-order effects that are characteristic of alternative actions. That knowledge must reach a critical mass before it becomes really significant. Until enough knowledge has been integrated to see the whole pattern, knowledge is no more than the individual pieces of a jigsaw puzzle. The basic requirements for strategy development are:

- A critical mass of knowledge
- Ability to integrate all of this knowledge and examine it as an interactive dynamic system
- Skill at system analysis sufficient to understand sensitivity, time lags, and immediate and future possibilities and consequences
- Imagination and logic to choose between specific alternatives
- Resource control beyond immediate needs
- The will to forgo current benefits in order to invest in the future potential

Simple as these requirements may seem, they are absent in natural competition. Strategic competition requires an ability to understand the dynamics of the complex web of natural competition. The value of strategy in competition comes from developing the potential to intervene in a complex system with only a limited input and thereby produce a predictable and desired change in the system's equilibrium.

Strategy, as a concept, probably emerged in connection with military operations. All the elements that make strategy valuable are present in military encounters:

- Finite resources
- Uncertainty about an adversary's capability and intentions
- Irreversible commitment of resources
- Necessity of coordinating action over time and distance
- Uncertainty about control of the initiative
- The critical nature of the adversaries' mutual perceptions of each other

History books tend to tell us the sequence of events and who won a war. They tell us less about why the initiator thought it was worth taking the risk and even less about the strategy of each adversary. Strategy is often not clear or obvious even with the benefit of hindsight. Sun Tsu, a general in 500 B.C., said it well: "All men can see the tactics whereby I conquer, but what none can see is the strategy out of which victory is evolved." The history of strategy is rarely more than rationalization.

There are many analogies between business and military strategy. One in particular is quite important: visible conflict is only a periodic symptom of a continuing effort on the part of each to manage a dynamic equilibrium between adversaries.

Visible "hot" wars are the result of instability in the competitive relationship. This instability is subtle and complex. It is not easily seen or easily understood. There are two basic reasons for this instability. First, no one logically starts a war unless the inevitable destruction to both adversaries is more than offset by the combination of favorable odds and potential positive net payoffs. Second, many of the events that lead to a progressive destabilization of equilibrium are emotional and not necessarily logical.

The aggression which is inherent in warfare is unavoidably destructive, but the outcome may seem to be potentially valuable enough to at least one party to justify the initiative.

The relationships of geopolitical strategy are more comparable to business strategy than the battles which usually mark the turning points in military conflict. The ideal ultimate objective for both participants is stability with peace and greater prosperity on a sustainable basis.

THE UNDERLYING PRINCIPLES AND OBJECTIVES OF STRATEGY

Many of the basic principles of strategy have been distilled from warfare. Liddell Hart, the military historian, stated some basic principles:[2]

> The true aim is not so much to seek battle as to seek a strategic situation so advantageous that if it does not of itself produce the decision, its continuation by a battle is sure to achieve this.
>
> But we can at least crystallize the lessons into two simple maxims—one negative, the other positive. The first is that, in face of the overwhelming evidence of history, no general is justified in launching his troops to a direct attack upon an enemy firmly in position. The second, that instead of seeking to upset the enemy's equilibrium by one's attack, it must be upset before a real attack is, or can be successfully launched.
>
> The principles of war, not merely one principle, can be condensed into a single word—"concentration." But for truth this needs to be amplified as the "concentration of strength against weakness."

Others have spoken on the subject:

> The whole art of war consists in a well-reasoned and extremely circumspect defensive, followed by a rapid and audacious attack. NAPOLEON

> Supreme excellence consists in breaking the enemy's resistance without fighting. Thus the highest form of generalship is to baulk the enemy's plans; the next best is to prevent the junction of the enemy's forces; the next in order is to attack the enemy's army in the field; the worst policy of all is to besiege walled cities. SUN TSU

> In all fighting, the direct method may be used for joining battle, but indirect methods will be needed in order to secure victory. SUN TSU

> The most complete and happy victory is this: to compel one's enemy to give up his purpose, while suffering no harm oneself. BELISARIUS

The underlying concepts of strategy involve the allocation and concentration of resources, the need for communication and mobility, the element of surprise, and the advantage of the defense.

However, military strategy concepts revolve around the assumption that open battle has already begun. Hart introduced the concept of "grand strategy"—the plan for securing and stabilizing the peace for which the war is fought. This is an aspect of strategy which is of the greatest importance to business. Business strategy must manage a constantly shifting dynamic equilibrium with multiple competitors.

For business, as for nations, continued coexistence is the ultimate objective. It is not the elimination of the competitor. The purpose of the strategy in both peace and war is a future stable relationship with respect to the competitors on the most favorable possible terms and conditions.

The emergence of grand strategy concepts for business has been severely handicapped by the lack of a comprehensive general theory of dynamic competition. Only in game theory has a systematic and methodical approach been developed. But a general theory of competition now appears possible and imminent.

THE BEGINNING OF A GENERAL THEORY OF COMPETITION

There has always been conflict and competition for scarce resources. Strategy has been practiced whenever an advantage was gained by planning the sequence and timing of the deployment of resources while simultaneously taking into account the probable capabilities and behavior of competition. But the insight about this experience has rarely been integrated conceptually as a competitive system.

Many aspects of competition were explored in great depth but rarely as a dynamic system in equilibrium. The natural field of study which should have been expected to generate such insight was economics. For whatever reason, philosophical constraints on assumptions and their implications were biased, and economics earned the name of the "dismal science." It remained for a most unlikely discipline, biology, to develop the foundation of a general theory of competition. However, this began to emerge after considerable progress had already been made in the field of business strategy development.

TRIALS AND ERRORS OF CONCEPTUAL DEVELOPMENT

The history of conceptual insight of the general public in the United States into the economic system can, to some extent, be judged by the evolution of the antitrust laws and the implicit assumptions embedded in them.

The antitrust laws were precipitated around the turn of the century by Standard Oil's efforts to integrate. Their tactics were to concentrate on a local competitor and undersell until it capitulated. In the absence of competition, Standard Oil could thereafter charge higher prices to recoup its losses. As strategy, it was excellent short-term. As grand strategy, it was flawed. It caused second-order effects which were very damaging.

Since the turn of the century, the antitrust laws have been interpreted and reinterpreted by the courts in the light of past and current concepts of competition. The evolution of theory represented the gradual development of generally accepted models of competitive behavior. Unfortunately, these competitive models were highly theoretical and simplistic. They were also based on untested and dogmatic assumptions.

Semantics played an important role. "Perfect competition" became a goal. Perfect competition was meant to describe an idealized situation in which all competitors were so small that no one individual competitor could have any perceptible effect on supply or demand and therefore on price. No situation of this kind has ever existed except for very short periods. Such a situation is inherently unstable. But all alternate models were labeled "imperfect competition."

The conceptual model developed through court interpretation was quite simplistic. Although scale effects and their inherent instability were recognized, they were brushed aside. A never-tested assumption that optimum scale is only a fraction of industry size was necessary for the presumption that multiple competitors are in stable equilibrium. The assumption that all cost-versus-scale curves are L-shaped or U-shaped was also a fundamental premise for competitive equilibrium to exist without monopoly. Assumptions were made that within a generalized industry all competition is essentially head to head.

These assumptions were further compounded by confusion as to whether the objective was to protect competitors from each other or to protect competition as a concept. And, of course, all of the assumptions were made within the constraints imposed by legal concepts of property and social organization.

Such constraints were simplistic enough to sharply distort a realistic view of the nature of competition. As a consequence, substantial inhibitions were created in the business community toward the usage of certain words and phrases like "dominate," "preempt share," "capture market," and "match price."

In and of itself this was minor compared to the inhibitions created with respect to the thinking about competitive interaction between specific pairs of competitors. Yet the interaction between specific pairs of competitors who vie for specific needed and scarce resources is the essence of strategy.

This is a generic problem inherent in any strategy. Characteristically for any competitor there are many such pairs of competitors to be dealt with simultaneously. The realities of competition forced business leaders, often as a matter of course, to think in such terms. But the effect was to suppress open discussion and conceptual development of business strategy except in a peripheral way.

THE EMERGENCE OF EXPLICIT BUSINESS STRATEGY

Strategy, by its very nature, is like a poker game and not subject to accurate reconstruction by either kibitzers or historians. However, there are a few classic examples such as the General Motors segmentation strategy developed by Alfred P. Sloan against Ford's Model T. But this occurred in the early 1930s. Soon after, the focus was centered on war efforts. To a considerable extent, the emergence of concepts of business strategy can be traced to the late 1950s and the early 1960s.

Several streams of thought converged to produce the focus on business strategy that blossomed in the 1970s. These included:

- The problems of strategy development within a complex organization
- The problems of strategy execution within a complex organization
- The problems of information in a complex organization
- The problems of control in a multiple business organization sharing common resources

Many of these were foreshadowed by the development of the giant organizations and trusts of the early twentieth century which precipitated the antitrust laws. In the United States many of these were monolithic, single-industry, narrow-range product organizations. The conspicuous examples were the oil and steel companies. The automobile companies were close behind. Characteristically, scale was a critical factor.

However, the multiproduct companies were simultaneously beginning to emerge. The electrical manufacturing companies which had their birth in the latter part of the nineteenth century were inherently multiproduct.

Although examples of large multiproduct companies had emerged in Europe even earlier, the European environment was different from the American environment. Consequently, the multiproduct companies in Europe had different characteristics.

When small countries are constrained by trade barriers at their boundaries, then the trade market area is inherently small. Large scale could only come from multiple product companies in small countries. Banks and banking institutions constituted the only source of capital for most concerns. Frequently such financial institutions were large equity owners.

In such countries, the interaction among the financial institutions and between them and the government tended to inhibit freewheeling competition. In such small markets specialization produced very small scale. The generalist had an advantage. Short distances prevented the growth of regional competitors who were isolated initially but who, with increasing infrastructure and transportation capability, later became competitors in other regions.

In the early twentieth century, when Japan abandoned its policy of self-imposed isolation, the same pattern emerged. However, in the United States a quite different pattern developed which, instead of inhibiting competitive strategy, required it.

A vast and growing market without barriers or regulation except logistics, the U.S. market favored the generalist initially but forced specialization as the market density increased. A large and dense market offers economies of scale to the specialist. But increased specialization on a national scale also means increased competition with finer and finer subdivisions of the market into competitive segments. The ability to define those competitive segments, determine who sets the boundaries, appraise the potential within those boundaries, and assess the opportunity for redefinition of boundaries becomes ever more valuable. In the United States, the need for strategy increased even though the understanding of it did not.

Unlike those in Europe and Japan, the banking institutions of the United States were often unstable and highly fragmented until well into the twentieth century. This removed a major influence from the development of competitive growth patterns and imposed much of the responsibility for financing growth or success back upon the earnings retained in the business. The absence of an income tax on corporate earnings greatly increased the degree of competition and the need for internal financial resources. In some measure, this laid the foundation for multiproduct companies such as Westinghouse and General Electric, which, in turn, presaged the conglomerates that developed following World War II.

In all strategy the ultimate objectives tend to be access to and control of the required resources. For business this almost always includes money, supplies, markets, and recruits. Money, or its equivalent, comes first. This may have been the underlying cause of the development of the multiproduct or conglomerate form of company.

The multiproduct form of organization is particularly well suited for continual growth of a business organization in the same way that a multigeneration family pattern is well suited to propagation of the species over time. The impact of this is almost entirely in capital formation and reallocation rather than in marketing, manufacturing, or technology. Those business areas which succeed and reach full potential are characteristically unable to reinvest in themselves at rates equal to their capital generation. Conversely, they are well positioned to finance the young, rapidly growing segments of their company which offer investment potential far in excess of any possible capital self-generation.

An additional area of potential for the multiproduct company was sharing of experience and scale across related but not identical products and services even though the competitive segments served by the products were different. This, too, was greatly facilitated by the absence of any income tax complications on the internal expense financing as well as the lack of the inherent overhead in external financing and other supply interfaces.

FROM STRATEGY TO STRUCTURE

All of these factors made the United States a seedbed for productivity increase. But this very dynamism and complexity increased the importance of a conceptual framework for strategy development rather than an intuitive base for resource deployment and management. Tactics can be learned from experience, but strategy cannot. Strategy is nonobvious management of a system over time. Good strategy must be based primarily on logic, not primarily on experience derived from intuition.

Perhaps the greatest insight into the complexity of the management of the large corporation was provided by Chester Barnard in his book *The Functions of the Executive* (Harvard University Press, 1968). Alfred D. Chandler and Stephen Salsbury later provided additional insight into the relationships between strategy and structure in *Pierre S. Du Pont and the Making of the Modern Corporation* (Harper & Row, 1971). Alfred P. Sloan also revealed some of his strategy concerns in *My Years with General Motors* (Doubleday, 1972).

The foundation of Sloan's success with General Motors' management was divisional autonomy with central control combined with the separation of policy and operations. However, the emergence of structural and organizational problems and their connection with strategy were foreshadowed prior to World War II.

Both Westinghouse and General Electric changed from functional control by central management to profit center management prior to World War II. But it was not until the early 1950s when General Electric, under Ralph Cordiner, carried the profit center concept to extremes, and General Electric became identified publicly as the pioneer and leader of this structural architecture which rapidly became widespread.

However, profit center organization soon began to reveal some problems. Carried to one extreme, there was no function for central management except as an interface between the company and the banks and tax collector. At the opposite extreme, the profit center was only a symbol. The proliferation of corporate staff and the leverage of its influence effectively wiped out the independent profit center as a functioning unit. The parallel with the king and his troubles with the barons suggests that the problem is not a new one.

THE DILEMMA OF DECENTRALIZED STRATEGY

In large-scale, diversified, multiproduct companies it was impractical for central management to be familiar in depth with each business, each product, each competitive segment, and each unit's implied strategy. This led to more and more reliance on short-term financial control measures. This, in turn, rapidly led toward more short-term suboptimization of results.

The inevitable short-range viewpoint induced by quarterly profit measurements as the prime control often confined profit center management to tactical resource management only. In such a context, there also was little real management judgment possible at the corporate level with respect to overall strategy except with regard to financial policy. This conflict between strategy and structure may account for a company such as Westinghouse having been a pioneer and technical leader in products that ranged from automobile generators to television tubes to silicon transistors and integrated circuits yet enjoying no success in these products. On the other hand, when the developments were clearly strategic enough to threaten the core business of the company, Westinghouse became a world leader in such developments as alternating current machinery and, later, atomic power.

By the late 1950s it was becoming obvious that something more than profit centers or profit centers with large corporate functional staffs were needed. The corporate staffs tended to regard themselves as the real source of policy and direction in much the same way that government agencies do. In the same fashion, large corporate staff represented a heavy drain on the time, energy, and initiative of operating unit management.

Later this dilemma was to encourage the development of long-range planning and then strategy development. Before that period, however, the "five-year plan" became the centerpiece of performance measurement and control. The use of such a forecast became widespread.

Although five-year plans provided a basis for discussion, they were almost a charade. The budgetary process and the five-year plan became almost inseparable. In the absence of an integrated, coherent strategy based on system analysis and coordinated planning, it was inevitable that five-year plans could be no more than forecasts which were then frozen into budgets.

The characteristic five-year plan promised results that were based on a somewhat higher price realization forecast, a somewhat higher market share forecast, and a somewhat lower cost forecast. They were revised annually to reduce the forecasted performance overall, yet to maintain a trendline forecast of ever higher achievement.

Such a pattern was inevitable in the absence of a fundamental strategy as the basis of the plan. There is no reason to expect a change in competitive equilibrium without a plan to cause it to happen. Incremental improvement in costs can be expected on the basis of the experience curve phenomenon. Most companies have long records of such reductions. So do their competitors. How can an improvement in long term performance be forecast in the absence of a prediction of a *differential* change in competitive capability?

Five-year plans evolved into hoped-for goals rather than significant shifts in competitive relationships. This was the common situation when the concept of long-range planning first emerged.

In spite of all the research into business administration and the functional aspects of business, all of the exploration of competitive situations by consulting firms, and a few books on the planning process such as those by George Steiner, there were no organized efforts to explore and develop an approach to the subject until Stanford Research Institute developed the Long Range Planning Service in the early 1960s.

The SRI Long Range Planning Service was in no sense a strategy approach for a given company; nor was Arthur D. Little's Service to Investors, which was quite similar. In both cases the firms drew on their breadth of knowledge of technical process to evaluate the development of the market itself. To do this well required some assessment of the competitive system as a whole and its behavior for specific sectors.

At about the same time, the word "development" came into rather common usage. The corporate staff position of director of corporate development began to appear in announcements in the press. The duties and responsibilities of such positions were highly variable. But the duties were apparently to evaluate the position and direction of the company as a whole in order to develop alternatives which held promise of leading to more desirable scenarios.

Another title, director of planning, soon appeared. Then in some companies the title director of strategic planning emerged. This somewhat ambiguous and redundant title served a purpose. It was an indication of a focus gradually shifting toward strategy as a concept. Although the role itself has never been clear, the value of staff work in preparation for strategy development has achieved increased recognition.

THE APPROACH TO A CRITICAL MASS OF KNOWLEDGE

By the mid-1960s, many of the pieces needed for the development of business strategy were in place. Although Morgenstern and von Neumann's studies of game theory[3] were directly applicable when published in 1953 and Jay Forrester's studies of the feedback loops and higher-order effects of dynamic systems[4] were very substantial insights into the possibility of quantitative modeling of competitive interaction, these studies were somewhat before their time in terms of being integrated with other concepts. There was still nothing resembling a general theory of competition. Acceptance of the "perfect competition" theory of microeconomics was still widespread.

In the mid-1960s observations by The Boston Consulting Group brought into question some of the underlying assumptions of "perfect competition." BCG made the first presentation to a client of projections and recommendations based on the experience curve effect in 1966.[5] During the next fifteen years, this characteristic cost-behavior pattern became conventional wisdom in business in most of the developed countries. Even government regulators, whose policies had been based on incompatible assumptions, conceded its validity although they continued to argue about its eventual application.[6]

The experience curve theory postulated that in complex products and services, costs corrected for inflation typically decline about 20 to 30 percent each time total accumulated experience doubles. This was a statement of pragmatic observation easily observable and testable. The simplicity of the statement, however, did not reveal the complexity of the interaction. Nor, if this were typical, did the far-reaching implications become obvious at first.

The learning curve had first been observed in the 1920s. During World

War II it had been observed repeatedly in the labor hours required for building aircraft. However, the characteristic cost declines from learning applied to labor hours were far less than the observed cost declines in the total cost as expressed in the experience curve.

Some reflection makes it obvious that all cost components do not go down in cost at equal rates. This means they follow different cost decline rates. They share different amounts of experience with other uses. The end products for different uses have differing elasticities. Substitution of cost elements is not only possible, it is also inevitable. That is probably why the experience curve is so much steeper in its cost decline than the learning curve. There were many years between the recognition of the learning curve phenomenon and the far-reaching implications of the same pattern with respect to overall cost as seen in the experience curve.

All costs and cost effects, except inflation, are included in the experience curve. This includes cost of capital and scale effects. Ordinarily these effects are obscured by accounting conventions which try to match expenditures with revenue over long time spans. The experience curve is an exponential smoothing of the ratio of cash flow to output.

Conventional accounting treatment of experience-related costs such as R&D, advertising, and staff development is impossible to couple with cash flow because of the uncertainty of the effect both on timing and in the amount of output that eventually leads to revenue. All accounting is consequently either a forecast or a smoothing model. The experience curve, however, is the rate of change in cash flow expenditures plotted against accumulated units of output. In this form it, too, is an exponentially smoothed curve.

The significant facts have far-reaching implications:

- The experience curve costs are a reasonably accurate approximation of cash flow versus volume.
- These curves apparently never turn upward in cost.
- Market share soon becomes a direct surrogate for experience.
- If the growth rate is constant, so is the rate of cost decline.
- Individual competitors tend to follow parallel, but not congruent, cost slopes if their market shares remain stable.

The experience curve is only a schematic pattern for normative behavior. But if the experience curve is representative, then the stability of competitive relationships postulated in the concept of "perfect competition" could never exist; nor could the basic assumption of conventional microeconomic theory that all cost-versus-volume curves are L- or U-shaped and turn up far below available market volume.

The strong and long-held convictions about "perfect competition" and "cost curve shape" had a reason. Without those assumptions, competitive stability would be very improbable under any circumstances. The whole foundation for public policy and conventional strategy analysis would otherwise disappear.

There is nothing to take the place of such theory without acceptance of the idea that every competitor is uniquely superior and dominates his competitive segment as a virtual monopolist. Later insights from other sources were to demonstrate that this was probably literally true. But acceptance of such radical notions takes time. It was a dozen years before understandable and acceptable alternatives for business use came into the open.

There is, or should be, a direct functional relationship between market share and cost which is, in effect, a relationship between cash generation and market share, of which the following are true:

- A business requires cash to invest in its assets as it grows.
- A rapidly growing business will require very large amounts of investment, usually more than it can finance from retained earnings.
- A slowly growing successful business cannot continually reinvest in itself faster than it grows.

The simple implication is that a corporation is a portfolio of businesses, each of which has differing cash needs and differing cash generation capabilities. But the corporation as a whole must be consistently within certain bounds in its cash flows.

The growth-share matrix developed by BCG led to a whole category of colloquial expressions for differing combinations such as "star," "cash cow," "question mark," and "dog," which became part of the business vocabulary.

Several other consulting firms developed their own versions of the relevant tradeoffs and combinations. The best-known was McKinsey's tradeoff of industry attractiveness versus the company's own competitive strength. This more generalized matrix accurately reflected the large number of variables which needed to be integrated into a realistic analysis. However, it gave no indication or guidance on the relationships or how they integrated, but contented itself with pointing out the implications of certain combinations of appraisals.

The BCG model was based on a far more logical and quantitative set of relationships. But it too was dependent upon accuracy and precision in defining relevant markets and evaluation of market shares.

Neither of these displays was really useful except as a guide to a logical way of thinking about competitive relationships. But they were a step toward the concept of a model of competition as an interactive dynamic system.

All of these hypotheses and constructs were the subject of considerable discussion which eventually included the academic community and particularly the leading graduate schools of business. While these ideas were still controversial, they were included in case materials and class discussions and argued in academic journals.

Harvard Business School meanwhile became deeply involved in a project which had originated at General Electric under Dr. Sidney Schoeffler. Professor Robert Buzzell and Dr. Schoeffler succeeded in using computerized data from multiple sources to correlate the relationship between various factors and profitability. The system became widely known as PIMS, an acronym for Profit Impact of Market Strategy. (See Chapter 23, "The PIMS Program.")

The PIMS program provided many interesting insights and the basis for a number of hypotheses. One in particular was quite timely. The correlation between market share and profitability was demonstrated beyond any reasonable doubt.

Even in the late 1970s, however, no general theory of competition had been developed. There was no integrating concept.

THE INTEGRATION OF STRATEGIC KNOWLEDGE

There was not even a credible hypothesis to replace the suspect reference provided by traditional concepts of "perfect competition." However, a potentially revolutionary conceptual insight was about to become the subject of general discussion. Its source was a most unexpected one: biology—and more specifically, sociobiology.

In retrospect, it is clear that a number of books had been published during the preceding period which cast a great deal of light on the potential of a general theory of strategy and competition. Some of these, such as Antony Jay's *Management and Machiavelli* (Holt, Rinehart & Winston, 1968), Robert Ardrey's *African Genesis* (Atheneum, 1971), and Desmond Morris's *The Naked Ape* (McGraw-Hill, 1967), seemed more like popular bestsellers than the cutting edge of the state of the art.

However, some were quite relevant to the hypothesis of the disciples of ethology, an emerging branch of biology. The significance of this inquiry was emphasized when Konrad Lorenz, author of *On Aggression* (Bantam, 1967) and *Studies in Animal and Human Behaviour* (Harvard University Press, 1970), received a Nobel Prize. His fellow Nobel laureate, Nikolaas Tinbergen, was working in the same field. Their writing and research, as well as the more popularized versions by Ardrey and Morris, were concerned with aspects of evolution and behavior. Inevitably all of this tended to include a large component of competitive behavior.

In 1975, after the expiration of the required thirty years, the British War Office opened the classified files concerning World War II. Serious readers of these descriptions of "war by other means" may feel inclined to revise their entire concept of what happened in World War II.[7]

The evidence was clear that the outcome of visible conflict depended upon highly subjective evaluations of intentions, capabilities, and behavior which would be invisible to all except those involved. This behavioral component of strategy is fundamental to its development and its execution.

All of the developments, insight, and theories of strategy up until 1975 were useful but merely part of a jigsaw puzzle in which the relationships of the parts were still unknown.

The advantage of hindsight may someday cause business historians to feel that 1975 was the turning of the tide: the beginning of the integration of a general theory of strategy and competition.

In 1975 Edward O. Wilson, a Harvard professor, published a landmark book entitled *Sociobiology* (Harvard University Press). In this book he attempted to synthesize all that is known about population biology, zoology, genetics, and social behavior. The resulting foundation of a conceptual framework was based on the social behavior of species which were successful because of that behavior. Since the whole structure of the biological community is determined by competition for resources, this kind of analysis has many parallels for business.

Mankind as a species is at the top of the ecological chain, but is still a member of the biological community. Economics is only a subset of the behavior pattern of this species. Alfred Marshall pointed this out in his 1920 text, *The Principles of Economics,* when he said, "Economics has no near kinship with any physical science. It is a branch of biology broadly interpreted."

Wilson's synthesis is the closest approach to a general theory of competition which has yet been achieved. Business competition is a specialized form of this, but nevertheless it is subject to the same principles and part of the same conceptual framework. The parallels may lead to a further insight into a general theory of business competition.

> There is, however, a special link between economics and sociobiology over and above the mere fact that economics studies a subset of the social behavior of higher mammals. The fundamental organizing concepts of the dominant analytical structures employed in economics and in sociobiology are strikingly parallel.
>
> HIRSHLEIFER[8]

The traditional core of compartmentalized economics is characterized by models that:

- Postulate rational self-interest behavior on the part of individuals who have preferences for goods and services.
- Attempt to explain these interactions among such individuals through the form of market exchanges under a fixed legal system of property and free contract.

Only a very limited portion of human behavior can be adequately represented by such self-imposed constraints. In recent years economics has begun to break through these self-imposed barriers. Hirshleifer[8] suggests this when he says, "From one point of view the various social sciences devoted to the study of mankind, taken together, constitute but a subdivision of the all-encompassing field of sociobiology."

The factors of sociobiological analysis have proceeded so far that much of the results of research has become quite suitable for computerized analysis. There is considerable promise that within the next generation or so these sociobiological factors can be so well defined and quantified that analysis can be far more predictive than ever before. This is the hope and expectation that Wilson holds out.

The mathematical descriptions of niches by G. Evelyn Hutchinson in 1958, Richard Levins in 1963, and Robert H. MacArthur in 1968, 1970, and 1972 made the analysis of niches quantitative. These authors considered a resource spectrum with the niche for each species defined by its utilization function distribution along the axis of the resource it consumes.

Biological study of competition has a long history. But that history was punctuated with a flash of brilliant insight in 1859 by Darwin and Wallace, and then followed by more than three-quarters of a century of data gathering, and apparently little progress, until all of this knowledge began to come together in the third quarter of this century.

When Darwin delivered his paper *On the Origin of Species* to the Royal Academy of Science in London in 1859, it was a perspective from a mountain peak. It would be a long time before the outlines would be examined in detail. But some of his remarks can readily be translated from biological competition to business competition:

> Some make the deep-seated error of considering the physical conditions of a country as the most important for its inhabitants; whereas it cannot, I think, be disputed that the nature of the other inhabitants, with which each has to compete, is generally a far more important element of success.
>
> When we reach the arctic regions, or snowcapped summits, or absolute deserts, the struggle for life is almost exclusively with the elements. . . . When we travel southward and see a species decreasing in numbers, we may feel sure that the cause lies quite as much in other species being favored, as in this one being hurt.

> As species of the same genus have usually, though by no means invariably, some similarities in habits and constitution, and always in structure, the struggle will generally be more severe between species of the same genus, when they come into competition with each other, than between species of distinct genera.

The biologists began to focus on relationships between species in the mid-twentieth century. There are millions of species, and they are all unique in their particular niche. This very fact raises the question about the nature of the forces that keep them in equilibrium with each other. Inevitably there is perpetual competition because many species use the same resources. In addition, many of the resources for one species are other species below them in the ecological chain.

Gradually a whole series of patterns of behavior and characteristic relationships emerged from this intensive research. The analogies to business competition are striking. In the absence of strategy, it *is* biological competition. As Marshall and Hirshleifer pointed out, economics is only a subset of the sociobiology of one species of the primates. However, the ability to use strategy is the ability to manage the natural competitive system by calculated intervention in order to produce predictable shifts in competitive equilibrium. For that to be possible, the characteristics of natural competition must first be understood.

Natural competition in the strict sense, as it is defined by Darwinian natural selection and evolution, contains no element of strategy. It is pure expediency—almost mindless at some stages. Instinctive needs that are urgent serve as the motivation. Day-to-day survival and cyclical procreation are the ultimate objectives.

This kind of competition by natural selection is glacially slow. It is trial and error: more mistakes than improvements will prove to be fatal. Over time, the more successful patterns must be immortalized and multiplied by the genes, while the mistakes must be diminished in future generations by the same process. It must be a slow process to succeed at all.

Natural competition can and does eventually evolve exquisitely complex and effective forms. Humanity itself is such an end result. But unmanaged change takes many thousands of generations. Sometimes, perhaps often, change is too slow to cope with the combination of a changing environment and the adaptation of competitors.

TIME COMPRESSION BY STRATEGY

By contrast, strategic competition is revolutionary, not just evolutionary. It is capable of extreme time compression. However, to accomplish this revolution, the preparation must be conservative, careful, precise, and all-inclusive. The environment itself must be well understood. The competitors who are critical or even important to the change must be equally well identified and understood. Then uncertainties in the environment must be carefully assessed and evaluated. The systematic interaction of competitors with each other and with the environment must be modeled and tested for sensitivity. This meticulous staff work must be continued until cause and effect become sufficiently predictable to justify the massive commitment of nonrecoverable resources.

The wild expediency of natural competition leads to glacial evolution. The meticulous conservatism of strategic competition leads to time compression and revolutionary change because strategy is the management of natural competition.

The biological model of natural competition provides illustrations of relationships which are of importance in business competition:

- Every species (business) must be uniquely superior to all others in its chosen combination of characteristics which define its competitive niche or segment.
- The boundaries of a competitive niche are determined by the points where competitors are equivalent.
- At any given boundary line, there will always be a specific competitor who determines that boundary.
- The number of boundary competitors is determined by the number of possible tradeoffs between behavioral characteristics and capabilities which will provide a differential advantage over other competitors in that environment.
- The more variable the environment, the more combinations that may become critical.
- The more distinctly different resources needed, the more possible critical combinations exist.
- If any one factor is overwhelmingly important, only one competitor will survive.

If the biological pattern of natural competition is useful as a model, then the reality of the competitive system is quite different from traditional microeconomic models:

- Every competitor, whatever the role in the competitive system, requires certain resources to enable it to persist.
- In the absence of some constraint on those resources, every competitor would tend to grow to infinity.
- In almost every case the limit on growth, or size, is set by the ability of some competitor to preempt a significant part of the supply.
- No two competitors can coexist who make their living in the same way. Their relationship is unstable. One will displace the other. This is Gause's Principle of Mutual Exclusion.

- Except for the most elementary forms of life, the required resources are other forms of life or activity. This establishes a form of vertical equilibrium. The higher levels prey on the lower levels but cannot live without them. Excessive success is self-defeating.
- The horizontal competition between organisms or organizations combined with the vertical dependency on an ecological chain constitutes a community or web of relationships which is in dynamic equilibrium, but in which competition in all dimensions is perpetual.
- A stable relationship which permits both competitors to coexist requires each competitor to have a combination of characteristics in some segment or sector of the environment which permits it to be uniquely superior in that "competitive segment."
- The source of virtually all resources is elementary natural material. The conversion of these to the form of end use must necessarily be an ecological chain in which each link is the resource for the next higher level which is dependent on the continuation of all the lower-level links.

Some analogies between sociobiology and business lead to testable and reasonable hypotheses:

- Pure chance provides an initial advantage to the first competitor to enter or define a competitive segment. The initial competitor becomes a part of the environment to be coped with by the next competitor who chooses to enter that specific arena.
- Definition of a new competitive segment requires that the differences between the specific competitors involved be sufficient to provide a distinct advantage for one of the competitors compared to all others in the competitive niche which is erected.
- If competitors are alike and equally capable, they cannot coexist. One will displace the other.
- Competitors who have distinctly different capabilities cannot coexist in the same competitive segment, but they can and will be in perpetual competition along the boundary lines where their respective competitive segments come into contact (the line of zero advantage).
- If there are few competitors and the market is thin, then the generalist has the advantage. The generalist can obtain a small amount of resources from multiple sources, but the thin market will support few specialists on an adequate scale to be effective competition for the generalist.
- Conversely, rich markets tend to eliminate generalists since the market can be subdivided into competitive segments, each of which can be dominated by specialists of significant scale and scope.
- The ability to grow rapidly when conditions are favorable, and to survive long periods of adversity when conditions are unfavorable, can

be a critical combination that offsets superiority in many other respects if the environment is cyclical.

- Since size or scale often provides a significant advantage and size or scale is incompatible with many other characteristics, then an orderly distinction from small to large size is predictable when there is a diversity of factors that are important in a market or environment.
- Since distance and logistics are often critical factors, then both scale and total market size are factors that determine the number, size, distribution, and competitive segment boundaries where these factors are important.
- Since the variety of characteristics among competitors is matched by an equal or greater variety in desired or required resources, then every significant difference in customer preferences provides the possibility of subdivision into multiple competitive segments. This is dependent upon the capability to serve both segments simultaneously being incompatible with optimization of both.
- The characteristic fundamental resource segments for business are sources of:

  Money, either in capital or in ongoing revenue
  Suitable skills, abilities, and individuals on an ongoing basis
  Materials, supplies, energy, and components not contained within the organization
  Knowledge and communication capability with respect to all external resources and factors affecting their availability

- Since multiple resources are always required, there will always be multiple competitors, each of which has characteristics that cause it to be the constraint on that specific resource availability.
- Each competitor for each resource will require a different combination of capabilities to be in stable equilibrium with competition.
- Adaptation to meet a specific competitor will often reduce the capability to offset another competitor.
- Any change in the environment will require adaptation of all competitors either to the environment, or to each other, or both. The equilibrium points between competitors will be shifted for all members of the community web of relationships.

This is the logic which describes the competitive system's major constraints. The complexity should be obvious, since it is inherent in millions of unique competitors in a moving but stable dynamic equilibrium.

For any specific individual competitor to use strategy, that competitor must be able to visualize the system's behavior and the competitor's own relationship to it. The fundamental requirements for such strategy development are:

- A critical mass of knowledge
- The ability to relate this knowledge in the form of an interactive system
- The capability of system analysis adequate to determine the probabilities of cause and effect for inputs that result in delayed higher-order effects
- The orderly analysis of alternatives and tradeoffs to determine the optimum sequence and timing of reallocation of available resources
- An adequate excess of resources beyond current needs to permit reallocation and the capability of tolerating deferral of benefits in order to compound them

In business these basics must be converted into an analytical process which permits development of a specific strategy. There are six steps:

1. Self-examination to determine what is needed to achieve the organization's purposes and implicit goals. This will determine the combination of resources which will be required on a continuing basis.
2. Determination of which competitors are the obstacles to those specific resources.
3. Determination of the differences between a given competitor and each of those specific competitors which make each superior within its own competitive segments.
4. Determination of which combinations of what factors produce those differences in capability.
5. Mapping of the boundaries of "zero advantage" which determine the individual competitive segments.
6. Mapping of the competitive characteristic resources, behavior patterns, and alternatives.

At this point the strategy development process becomes highly analytical in an effort to assess the available alternative payoffs, risks, and odds. Because the possible combinations are nearly infinite, however, the final choice, like many business decisions, is essentially an intuitive one.

In spite of the enormous effort and attention devoted to this process, procedure, and conceptual framework during the past twenty years, it is still very much in an early stage of development. The task is even more complex than it appears to be.

Almost every corporate organization is composed of multiple businesses. This requires multiple but compatible strategies. The strategies must be compatible because, for a given company, all the business units draw upon a common base of resources. The different businesses may share certain capabilities in a synergistic fashion or in an incompatible or preemptive fashion. The company as a whole may have purposes and goals which override or are incompatible with those of the units.

The defender of a competitive segment normally has a significant advantage if alert and entrenched. The result of this is usually a "cold war" stable equilibrium between most competitors. This kind of equilibrium is conditionally unstable, that is, stable unless disturbed beyond a certain point. Skirmishing and testing of limits occurs continually on the boundary line.

Such a cold war stability depends on the acceptance by both parties that the odds of winning a hot war are insufficient to offset the inevitable losses and destruction of a "negative sum" payoff from such an escalation.

A company with multiple businesses has a multiple of the total resources available to a single business. However, it loses that advantage if the strategies of the individual businesses are not coordinated to preserve adequate uncommitted reserves if any individual business strategy contemplates escalation.

STRATEGY AND THE FUTURE

Strategy development is still embryonic. But the rate of development of the conceptual base is very rapid and holds forth the promise of precision, elegance, and power within a reasonable time period.

Sociobiologist Wilson foresees the probability of the quantification of sociobiological behavior, even the computerization of analysis, within the next decade or so. In the same way, business strategy development should soon go through a period of rapid development.

As this happens, the problems of strategy execution will emerge as even more formidable and challenging. Here, too, there is promise that sociobiology will provide guides that will compress the time of accomplishment.

It seems almost certain that exponential growth in insight with respect to business competitive strategy will result in time compression for change. Those companies who are not able to learn, adapt, and apply these emerging insights at an accelerated rate are subject to Darwinian natural selection. In this context, the race will be won by the swift.

NOTES

[1]G. F. Gause, *The Struggle for Existence,* Williams & Wilkins, 1934; A. C. Crombie, "Further Experiments on Insect Competition," *Proc. Roy. Soc. London,* B. 133:76–109, 1946.

[2]B. H. Liddell Hart, *Strategy,* Praeger, New York, 1954, pp. 164, 347, 365.

[3]Oskar Morgenstern and John von Neumann, *Theory of Games and Economic Behavior,* Princeton University Press, Princeton, 1953.

[4]Jay W. Forrester, *Industrial Dynamics,* MIT Press, Cambridge, 1961.
[5]Bruce D. Henderson, *Perspectives on Experience,* The Boston Consulting Group, Inc., Boston, 1968.
[6]The Conference Board, *Strategic Planning and the Future of Antitrust,* Bulletin no. 90, 1980.
[7]William Stevenson, *A Man Called Intrepid,* Harcourt Brace Jovanovich, New York, 1976; Anthony Cave Brown, *Bodyguard of Lies,* Harper & Row, New York, 1975; James M. Gavin, *On to Berlin,* Viking, New York, 1978.
[8]Jack Hirshleifer, "Economics from a Biological Viewpoint," *Journal of Law and Economics,* vol. 20, no. 1, April 1977.

This chapter has been reprinted by permission of The Boston Consulting Group, Inc.

Chapter 2

STRATEGIC PLANNING AND FORECASTING FUNDAMENTALS

J. SCOTT ARMSTRONG*

Associate Professor of Marketing, The Wharton School, University of Pennsylvania

Individuals and organizations have operated for hundreds of years by planning and forecasting in an intuitive manner. It was not until the 1950s that formal approaches became popular. Since then, such approaches have been used by business, government, and nonprofit organizations. Advocates of formal approaches (for example, Steiner, 1979) claim that an organization can improve its effectiveness if it can forecast its environment, anticipate problems, and develop plans to respond to those problems. However, formal planning and forecasting are expensive activities; this raises questions about their superiority over informal planning and forecasting. Furthermore, critics of the formal approach claim that it introduces rigidity and hampers creativity. These critics include many observers with practical experience (for example, Wrapp, 1967).

This chapter presents a framework for formal planning and forecasting which shows how they interact with one another. Suggestions

*With acknowledgments to Richard C. Hoffman IV, Spyros Makridakis, Deepak Mehta, and Robert Fildes, who provided useful comments on various drafts of this chapter. Support for this paper was provided by IMEDE in Lausanne, Switzerland.

are presented on how to use formal planning for strategic decision making. (For simplicity, references to planning and forecasting in this chapter will mean *formal* strategic planning and forecasting.) Planning is not expected to be useful in all situations, so recommendations are made on when planning is most useful. Descriptions of forecasting methods are then provided. Finally, suggestions are made on which forecasting methods to use when developing plans for a company.

Where possible, the advice on planning and forecasting is supported by relevant research. In some areas much research exists. (For a review of the psychological literature on forecasting and planning, see Hogarth and Makridakis, 1981.) In many areas, however, little research has been done.

Various aspects of formal planning and forecasting are illustrated here by using the strategic decision by Ford to introduce the Edsel automobile in 1957. In this situation, formal planning and forecasting would have been expected to be useful. Judging from published accounts by a participant at Ford (Baker, 1957) and an observer (Brooks, 1969), Ford did not use formal planning and forecasting for the strategic decisions involved in the introduction of the Edsel. (Of course, having decided intuitively to proceed, they did carry out operational planning for the production of the car.) The introduction of the Edsel is regarded as one of the largest business errors of all time. Ford itself lost $350 million. Their dealers also lost a substantial amount. Is it possible that formal planning and forecasting might have protected Ford from such a large strategic error?

Figure 2-1 provides a framework to conceptualize strategic planning within a company. A scanning of the environment yields relevant data for the "Data Bank." This data bank (or information system) would contain such data as government regulations, demographic indicators, industry sales, the resources of the company and of its competitors, and information on available technologies for production. Ideally, these data would be assembled in a central location, such as in a filing cabinet, chart room, or computer.

The left-hand side of Figure 2-1 examines planning. A variety of planning processes can be used. These will be described in more detail below. The planning processes draw upon information from the data bank (evidence on the current situation) and also upon the forecasts (evidence on what will happen in the future). The two-way arrow from "Data Bank" to "Planning Processes" indicates that the planning process, to a large extent, dictates what information is required. *It is recommended that formal planning start with the planning process rather than with the data.*

The planning process produces a set of plans. These describe objectives and alternative strategies. One strategy is selected as a basis for action. In practice, the actions actually taken by the company can deviate substantially from the intended strategy. The actions lead to results, both intended and unintended. A record of these results is kept in the data bank.

The right-hand side of Figure 2-1 examines forecasting. To make forecasts for a company, it is necessary to have information about the company's proposed strategies (thus the arrow from "Plans" to "Forecasting Methods"). An examination of the forecasting methods, then,

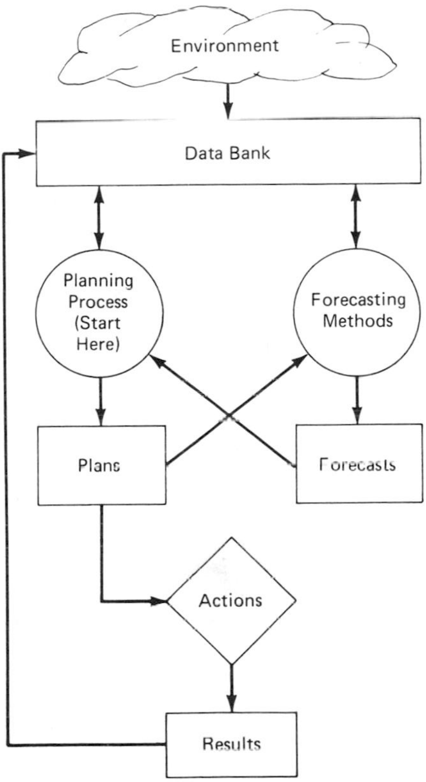

FIGURE 2-1
Framework for formal planning and forecasting.

will help determine what data are required (thus the two-way arrow from "Data Bank" to "Forecasting Methods"). The forecasting methods, to be described in more detail below, yield a set of forecasts. What will happen if the company attempts strategy A and environment X occurs? How likely is environment X? How much confidence can we have in the forecast? These forecasts are then used as inputs to the planning process.

Note the distinctions between forecasting and planning. Planning provides the strategies, given certain forecasts, whereas forecasting estimates the results, given the plan. Planning relates to what the firm *should do*. Forecasting relates to *what will happen* if the firm tries to implement a given strategy in a possible environment. Forecasting also helps to determine the likelihood of the possible environments.

The remainder of this chapter discusses the items in the two circles on Figure 2-1, the Planning Process and Forecasting Methods.

DESCRIPTION OF THE STRATEGIC PLANNING PROCESS

Formal strategic planning calls for an explicit *written process for determining the firm's long-range objectives, the generation of alternative strategies for achieving these objectives, the evaluation of these strategies, and a systematic procedure for monitoring results. Each of these steps of the planning process should be accompanied by an explicit procedure for gaining commitment.* This process is summarized in Figure 2-2. The arrows suggest the best order in which to proceed. The need for commitment is relevant for all phases. The

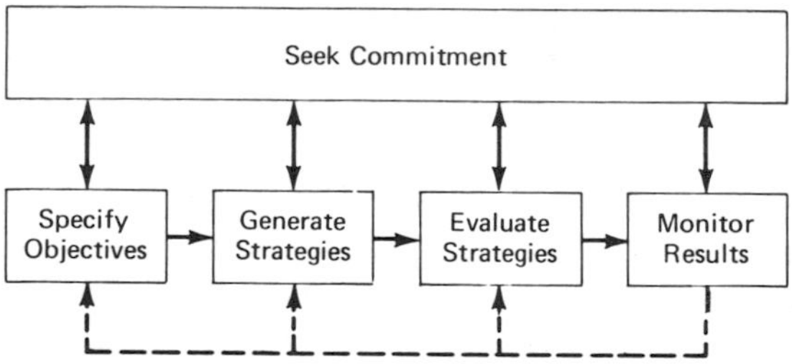

FIGURE 2-2
The planning process.

specification of objectives should be done before the generation of strategies which, in turn, should be completed before the evaluation. The monitoring step is last. The dotted line indicates that, to some extent, the process is iterative. For example, the evaluation may call for going back to the generation of new strategies, or monitoring may require a new evaluation of strategies.

The various steps of the planning process are described below along with some formal techniques that can be used to make each step explicit. (Although commitment is the first step, it is easiest to discuss this last.) This discussion is prescriptive; it suggests how planning *should* be done. Numerous accounts are available of how formal strategic planning *is* done (for example, see Wood, 1980, and the extensive review of the descriptive research by Hofer, 1976).

Specify Objectives

Formal planning should start with the identification of the ultimate objectives of the organization. Frequently, companies confuse their objectives (what they want and by when) with their strategies (how they will achieve the objectives). For example, suppose that a company desires to make money for its stockholders. To do this, it decides to build a tunnel through a mountain in order to charge tolls to automobiles. They plan to complete the tunnel in five years. On the way through the mountain, they strike gold. To mine the gold, activities on the tunnel must be suspended. Does the company pursue its objective of making money or does it stay with its strategy of tunnel building? What would your organization do?

The analysis and setting of objectives has long been regarded as a major step in formal strategic planning. Informal planners seldom devote much energy to this step. For example, in Baker's (1957) summary of the Edsel, less than 1 percent of his discussion concerned objectives.

Unfortunately, the identification of objectives is a difficult step for organizations. It is even difficult for individuals. The simplest way to demonstrate this is the following: Ask yourself to set objectives for your use of this chapter. Write your objectives. Be specific. Find measurable objectives. Set time deadlines for implementing changes. It *is* possible (for example, you could have as an objective that you will take action within the next month on at least one technique to improve the strategic planning of your organization), but it is stressful.

The difficulties in setting objectives have led some observers to recommend that formal planners ignore this step. The recommendation here is just the opposite. Significant time and money should be allocated to the analysis of objectives. This difficult step might be aided by use of an outside consultant to help the group focus only upon the objectives. The question can also be attacked by asking what results would define successful performance by the company over the next twenty years. At this stage, no concern should be given as to how to achieve the objectives.

Companies pursue many objectives and planners should explicitly recognize all of the important objectives of the system. One way to help ensure that the analysis of objectives is comprehensive is to use the *stakeholder* approach. This calls for a listing of all groups that contribute resources to the firm. Then a description is provided of the objectives of each of these stakeholders.

Applying the stakeholder approach in the Edsel case, the following groups would be included: creditors, stockholders, employees, consumers, suppliers, dealers, and the local community. In many cases, these groups will have conflicting objectives. The planners would write out the objectives for each group, for example, return on investment (ROI) for stockholders; stability, good wages, and good working conditions for employees; safe and reliable products at a low price for consumers; ROI for the dealers. Specific measures would then be established for each objective (for example, ROI should exceed 10 percent per year after taxes in real dollars). In contrast to this stakeholder approach, Ford's informal approach led to a narrow objective: "to obtain 3.3 percent to 3.5 percent of the auto market" (Baker, 1957). Explicit consideration was not given to other stakeholders.

A *strengths and weakness analysis* should then be conducted. This calls for an inventory of the organization's resources (such as financial, marketing, production). What do they have now and what do they plan to have? The objectives would then be drawn from what is desired (stakeholder analysis) and what is feasible (strengths and weakness analysis).

The written statement of objectives should start with the ultimate objectives. These general objectives would then be translated into more specific objectives so that each decision maker can see how to contribute to the overall objectives. In addition to being specific, the objectives should be measurable (Latham and Kinne, 1974). The objectives would include statements on *what* is desired and *when.* Thus, the marketing department can refer to the planning manual to determine its role in meeting the overall company objectives.

One danger in planning is that the objectives may become confused with the strategies. For example, a company might decide that one strategy to better meet the needs of its stakeholders is to increase its market share during the next five years. But this strategy might falsely be regarded as an objective by the marketing department. Five years later, the department might still pursue market share—even if it is detrimental to the company's objectives. (They continue to build the tunnel and ignore the gold.)

Advocates of informal planning argue that specific written objectives create political problems within the organization. Vague objectives allow for the greatest flexibility in actions. Politically oriented leaders often prefer that the objectives be unstated. But evidence from studies in organizational behavior suggests that explicit and specific objectives are of substantial benefit, especially when used in conjunction with the other planning steps (see reviews of this research in Latham and Yukl, 1975; Tolchinsky and King, 1980; and Locke et al., 1981).

Once the objectives have been specified, the planners can proceed to the generation of strategies. If the objective setting was successful, the remaining steps will be easier.

Generate Alternative Strategies

A strategy is a statement about the way in which the objectives should be achieved. Strategies should be subordinate to objectives. That is, they are relevant only to the extent that they help to meet the objectives.

This advice is obvious but often ignored. The generation of *alternative* strategies helps to avoid this problem. It recognizes explicitly that the objectives may be achieved in many different ways.

Strategies should first be stated in general terms. The more promising strategies should be explained in more detail.

The planning process is not complete until the company has at least one (and preferably more than one) operational strategy. An operational strategy describes:

1. What tasks must be done
2. Who is responsible for each task
3. When each task must be started and completed
4. The resources (time and money) available for each task
5. How the tasks relate to one another

This operational strategy becomes the basis for action by various functions in the firm: finance, personnel, production, and marketing.

Alternative strategies can improve the adaptability of the organization in two ways. First, by explicitly examining alternatives, it is likely that the organization will find some that are superior to their current strategy. Second, the environment might change; if alternative (contingency) plans have been prepared, the organization is in a better position to respond successfully. Alternatively, they can select a strategy that performs well even if the environment changes.

Organizations sometimes have difficulty developing alternative strategies to deal with unfavorable environments (threats). One technique that can help organizations with this problem is the use of scenarios. This involves having decision makers write stories about the future of their company. They can write a scenario describing what will happen to their company if the threat occurs, given their current strategy. Then, they could write about a desired future. What would they want the company to be like? The question then becomes, "What must we do to achieve this type of future?" Consideration can be given to changing the organization's resources or to the use of alternative strategies.

The development of scenarios calls for creativity within the organization. To bring out this creativity, it is helpful to use brainstorming. Key stakeholders for the organization can be asked to consider alternative *strategies,* alternative *resources,* and alternative *environments* by following these rules for brainstorming:

1. Gain agreement within the group to use brainstorming.
2. Select a facilitator. The facilitator:
   a. Records ideas as they are mentioned

b. Encourages quantity of ideas
c. Reminds the group not to evaluate (either favorably or unfavorably)
d. Encourages wild ideas
e. Does *not* introduce ideas

For a more complete description of scenarios, see Armstrong (1978a, pp. 38–43), Ackoff (1970, pp. 24–29), and Chapter 10.

It is difficult to say how many alternative strategies should be listed. Certainly more than one! But the number could quickly get out of hand considering the vast number of possible combinations. Try to list strategies to deal with dramatically different yet likely environments. After this larger list has been developed, screen the list to determine which strategies should be developed in more detail.

Two guidelines appear to be of particular importance for the development of a strategy. The strategy should be *comprehensive* and it should provide *slack.*

To ensure that strategies are comprehensive, planners have typically suggested the use of flow charts. These list each of the key tasks that must be accomplished and show how each task relates to the others. Numerous publications have offered advice in this area (for example, Ansoff, 1965; Steiner, 1979). Slack means that resources (time, money, facilities) should not be fully committed to the recommended strategy. Some resources should be held in reserve; these can be used to relieve stress if parts of the plan break down. Slack is analogous to the use of inventories. *The use of slack adds flexibility to the plan.*

The Edsel case illustrated the informal approach to strategic planning. Ford decided to build a large, powerful, and ornate automobile. They did not report that they examined alternatives. Their plan did not appear to be comprehensive, and no mention was made of provision for slack. The environment changed prior to the introduction. Ornate cars were not so popular, small foreign cars were capturing a growing market segment, large powerful engines were the subject of much criticism, and a small recession was under way when the first Edsels came onto the market. But Ford had no contingency plans. In retrospect, low-cost contingency plans could have been introduced. For example, the distribution of the cars could have been done primarily through existing dealers rather than through the new Edsel dealer network. (This recommendation was proposed by management students who developed a plan for a disguised version of the Edsel case. Most of these students, who had been asked to try formal planning, decided to use the existing dealer network.)

Evidence from studies in organizational behavior suggests that, in general, the generation of ideas should be separated from the evaluation of ideas (Maier, 1963); they cannot be done together with much effectiveness. Thus, this step of generating alternatives should be completed before the next step is begun.

Evaluate Alternative Strategies

Once sufficient strategies have been proposed, the evaluation of alternatives can begin. This requires a procedure by which each alternative plan is judged for its ability to meet the objectives of the organization. Such a process is not simple, because conflicting objectives usually exist among stakeholders. Furthermore, the presence of uncertainty complicates the choice of a strategy. For example, one should consider not only how well the strategy does for the most likely situation, but also how well it does against other possible situations, especially those that are dramatically different.

One procedure for the evaluation of alternatives is the *Delphi technique.* Various strategies (for a given environment) are presented to the key stakeholders. Each person works independently to rank these alternatives. A summary of the group rankings is then presented to these same stakeholders, and they are asked to provide a second ranking, still working independently. This procedure can be repeated for a number of "rounds." As a variation, group discussion can be used to exchange information between rounds. The Delphi technique provides a more efficient and less biased way to use the information held by the key decision makers than that provided by informal methods (for more on Delphi see Linstone, 1975).

The use of scenarios is also relevant to evaluation, particularly when dealing with negative evidence from the environment. Much research suggests that organizations avoid unpleasant information. As an example of this tendency to reject negative evidence, Griffith and Wellman (1979), in a study of expansion plans in six hospitals, found that forecasts of decreasing demand were ignored. As a result, the hospitals overbuilt. The use of scenarios might have identified the reactions to unfavorable forecasts prior to investing money on these forecasts. The hospitals could then have canceled the proposed expenditures on forecasting if they could not decide how the forecasts might affect their decision making.

Other formal procedures for evaluation can also be used. For example, structured rating sheets can be used to evaluate the *general* strategies against the stakeholders' objectives and to gauge the extent to which negative information was considered. Also, one could rate each *operational* strategy on the extent to which it succeeded in the following areas: provided adequate resources, allowed adequate slack, set reasonable time deadlines, presented a comprehensive strategy, and presented an operational strategy. The use of the devil's advocate, when a person argues against a favored alternative, can help to ensure that both sides of a plan are considered (Cosier, 1978).

The major point for evaluation is to use formal procedures and to not use informal ones, such as the traditional group meeting. The latter provides one of the poorest ways to evaluate strategies. Janis (1971) examined a number of major failures in strategy evaluation, such as the Bay of Pigs, and concluded that much of the blame was due to the lack of formal processes for evaluation. He provided a checklist that groups can use to improve their ability to generate and evaluate alternative strategies.

The evaluation step concludes with the selection of an operational strategy. This is the strategy the company will attempt to implement. (This strategy should contain contingency plans also.) But will the strategy really meet the objectives? To assess this, the next step of the planning process, monitoring results, is taken. This step is prepared *prior* to the implementation of the strategy.

Monitor Results

The value of feedback has been well established in laboratory studies, especially when combined with the setting of objectives (Tolchinsky and King, 1980; Ilgen, Fisher, and Taylor, 1979). Field studies have also demonstrated the value of explicit feedback (for example, Becker, 1978). It seems important, then, to provide feedback to the organization on how well they are meeting their objectives. In other words, specific procedures should be developed to "monitor results."

The monitoring system should allow for corrective action. To do this, the following items should be measured in a systematic way:

1. Changes in the environment (sometimes called "environmental scanning")
2. Changes in the organization's capabilities (and in their competitors' capabilities)
3. Actions that were actually taken by the organization (did they implement the desired strategy?)
4. Actions by major competitors
5. Results

Planning involves a trade-off between consistency and flexibility. Formal planners try to develop a strategy so that a complex organization can operate in a coordinated manner. The members of the organization must sacrifice flexibility in order to follow a consistent strategy. However, changes in any of items 1 to 5 above could suggest a change in strategy. Thus, the monitoring system should signal when a change in strategy should be considered.

Fixed review times should be selected in advance. Many firms conduct a review once a year. At these times, decisions should be made whether to continue with the original strategy, revise the strategy, or switch to a contingency plan. For very large changes, it is best to view the strategy as being experimental and to schedule more frequent review periods, perhaps quarterly.

In addition to fixed review times, the monitoring system should also have control limits. These would be upper and lower bounds for each of the above five areas. When the system goes outside of these limits, a planning review would be conducted whether or not it was time for the fixed review.

The monitoring of outcomes should relate back to the objectives for each stakeholder. This should allow for a comparison to be made between results and objectives in order to decide whether the strategy is successful for each stakeholder.

The monitoring system is expected to have a greater impact if it is tied into the organization's incentive system. This helps to ensure that the participants are committed to the objectives described in the plan. Companies sometimes develop comprehensive plans, but then focus solely on the stockholders or the managers. The monitoring system should focus on the long-range impact of the plan on all of its stakeholders. For example, to recognize the interests of its customers, IBM uses consumer-satisfaction surveys to help determine management's compensation.

In the Edsel case, no monitoring procedure had been developed. Substantial confusion seemed to occur when the initial results were examined. What results constituted a failure? This had not been defined in advance. Some months after what seemed to be a disastrous introduction, Ford told its dealers that there was no cause for alarm (Brooks, 1969). Apparently, Ford was unable to respond rapidly to evidence that their strategy was failing.

The Edsel monitoring procedure, or lack of it, is apparently not unusual. Horovitz (1979), in a survey of the planning practices of 52 large firms in Great Britain, France, and West Germany, found that virtually none of them had a formal procedure for monitoring results of their long-range plans.

One way to improve the monitoring of results is to have an evaluation performed each year by an independent auditor. The following questions could be addressed: Is the monitoring system comprehensive? Is the planning process adequate? Is the forecasting process adequate? (A procedure for the auditing process for forecasting is provided in Armstrong, 1982a.)

Seek Commitment

Business plans and forecasts are frequently ignored; at other times they are used to rationalize a course of action previously decided. What can be done to develop commitment to the planning process? What can be done to ensure that the various stakeholders will cooperate and try to implement the chosen strategy? Attention should be given to commitment throughout each of the above steps in planning.

Formal planning calls for an explicit procedure for gaining commitment to the plan. A first condition is that key stakeholders should be involved in the planning process. This would mean, *at least,* that information should be obtained from these stakeholders.

Publicly stated objectives are a requirement if the objectives are expected to have an impact on behavior. Each stakeholder group and each key decision maker should be aware of the objectives. This can help to achieve consensus.

Commitment to objectives is expected to be higher if those who are affected by the strategic decisions participate in the objective-setting process. In other words, self-set objectives are more likely to be attained than objectives set by others. This generalization is based on laboratory studies (for example, Bass, 1977) and on field studies. Participation is not necessary in all situations; however, it generally helps, and seldom does it make things worse.

Participation by stakeholders is also helpful in the generation and evaluation of alternative strategies (Van de Ven, 1980). This is most important where the strategy involves large changes, because the threat to the various stakeholders is reduced if they have some control over these changes.

Commitment can be maintained more effectively if the monitoring system provides quantitative feedback on success in meeting each objective. Key decision makers can then use this feedback to make tactical changes. Stakeholders can see how the strategy is meeting their objectives.

Rather than seeking commitment to the plan, top management sometimes uses planning as a way to gain control over others. They may use it to reduce the authority of subordinate managers and unilaterally to reduce the ability of these managers to act. This may help to explain why planning is more popular among top management. For example, in a survey done by Ang and Chua (1979), 80 percent of top management reported that they were "very favorable" toward long-range planning; 30 percent of the operating managers agreed. If plans are imposed on others, their impact might be detrimental. Operating management could feel less responsible for the success of strategic decisions. They might even feel threatened by the strategic decisions and attempt to reduce their effectiveness.

To avoid having the monitoring system used to control others, it is best to provide managers with information about how their *group* has performed, not the individuals within their group. Their subordinate managers, in turn, would receive information only about their group. Overall, then, sufficient feedback is received, but it is used to guide one's own actions as a manager. "How can I help my group to perform?" is the issue, not "How can I control the managers under me?"

SITUATIONS FAVORING THE USE OF STRATEGIC PLANNING

Consider a simple example: planning for lunch on a workday. Generally, you need not do much. When you are hungry, you may send for a sandwich, or you may walk to the nearest restaurant. What happens, however, when a group of managers from corporate headquarters comes for a meeting that includes lunch? You obtain input to decide what type of atmosphere and food would be appropriate. After deciding on a restaurant, you ask your secretary to make reservations and arrangements for transportation to and from the restaurant. Obviously, you will charge the luncheon to the company's expense account.

As implied by this example, some everyday activities can benefit from planning. In particular, planning is most helpful in situations that involve more complexity (a fancy meal), change (a large increase in the number of people to be fed), uncertainty (what do our guests like? how will everybody get to the restaurant?), and an inefficient market (expense account).

Planning is also expected to be very useful for organizations facing major strategic decisions as these generally involve high task complexity, change, uncertainty, and inefficient markets. These characteristics are summarized below:

1. High complexity of the task means that there is a greater need for explicit plans to ensure that the various bits and pieces fit together. The production and marketing of an automobile, for example, is a complex task.

2. Large changes create a need for planning because organizations are designed to deal primarily with repetitive situations. The changes could come from the environment (an economic recession), from competitors (foreign competition in automobiles), or from the firm itself (a

decision to introduce a new line of automobiles). For large changes, the standard bureaucratic responses would be less useful. Large changes call for planning rather than merely reacting.

3. Uncertainty can lead to a waste of resources. Organizations must be prepared to meet different environments. Planning can address "what if" questions so that the firm can develop ways to respond. As uncertainty increases, the need for planning also increases. Ford faced an uncertain economy when it introduced the Edsel.

4. Inefficient markets call for planning because the price system does not dictate the organization's actions. The organization has much flexibility in how it acts. Thus, planning is expected to be more relevant to government organizations, nonprofit organizations, regulated sectors, and protected industries. Ford, for example, received some protection from foreign imports. (Managers in competitive markets may feel that planning is more important as competition *increases.* This is because poor planning could lead to the failure of the company. However, failure is a natural event in competitive markets. An efficient market would inform stakeholders and would help to ensure that their needs are met, no matter what an individual company does. If they plan poorly, another company will replace them.)

Planning is expected to be most relevant when all four of these conditions hold. Ford faced this situation when introducing the Edsel. A more extreme example of a company that meets all four conditions would be a utility deciding whether to build an atomic reactor. It has a complex task, large changes are involved, uncertainty is high (for example, what if the law is changed so that the company must bear the full costs of waste disposal?), and the market is inefficient (huge subsidies are paid by the government and the local community bears the costs of disasters).

One industry that has been moving toward the above four conditions is banking. According to Wood (1980), change and uncertainty have increased in this industry during the 1970s. During this period, the use of formal strategic planning increased from 6 percent of the banks prior to 1970 to 80 percent by the end of 1977.

Another example that met the above four conditions was Ford's introduction of the Edsel. The market inefficiencies in this case, however, were not large.

At the other extreme would be a company that meets none of the conditions. Here formal planning would be of little value. An example would be the normal operations for an existing middle-priced restaurant in New York City.

An investment in formal planning might be considered like an insurance policy: It *might* be needed. But in situations where the risk is small, the investment in insurance may not be necessary.

The above conditions are inferred from research in organizational behavior (see review in Armstrong, 1982b). Perhaps there are other conditions that are more important. A survey of the empirical *field research* on the value of strategic planning yielded twelve studies: Van de Ven (1980), Ansoff et al. (1970), Thune and House (1970), Herold (1972), Wood and LaForge (1979), Karger and Malik (1975), Harju (1981), Kudla (1980), Leontiades and Tezel (1980), Grinyer and Norburn (1975), Kallman and Shapiro (1978), and Fulmer and Rue (1974). A systematic analysis of results from these studies concluded that the evidence was consistent with the position that planning is useful for organizations (Armstrong, 1982b). But the studies provided little useful data on "how to plan" and on "when to plan" because few of them provided adequate information on the planning processes used or on the situations in which the planning was used.

THE FORECASTING METHODS

Forecasting methods, as defined here, are *explicit procedures for translating information about the environment and the company's proposed strategy into statements about future results.* What would be the results if the environment were favorable and we did A? What if it were unfavorable and we did A? What if it were unfavorable and we did B?

Before discussing how the forecasting methods can be used in strategic planning, a general description is provided here on the various methods that can be used in forecasting.

A number of schemes exist for classifying forecasting methods (see, for example, Chisholm and Whitaker, 1971; Chambers, Mullick, and Smith, 1974). These schemes are based upon the type of data used, the type of people doing the forecasting, or the degree of sophistication of the methods used to analyze data. The scheme used below is based upon the methods used to analyze the data.

Research on methods for analyzing data has historically been organized along three continuums: subjective versus objective, naive versus causal, and linear versus classification methods. The discussion below considers the fictitious end points of each continuum.

Subjective versus Objective Methods

Subjective methods are those in which the processes used to analyze the data have not been well specified. These are also called implicit, informal, clinical, or intuitive methods. They may be based on simple or complex processes. They may use objective data or subjective data as inputs. Subjective methods may be supported by much formal analysis or by none. But the critical point is that the analyst makes the forecast in his or her head. For example, executives could be asked to make annual forecasts of automobile sales for the next five years. They would be provided with any information they request, but they would produce the final forecasts by thinking.

Objective methods are those that use well-specified processes to analyze the data. Ideally, they have been specified so well that other analysts can replicate them and obtain identical forecasts. These are also called explicit, statistical, or formal methods. They may be based on simple or complex processes. They may use objective data or subjective data as inputs. They may be supported by much formal analysis or none. But the critical factor is that the inputs are translated into forecasts using a process that can be replicated by other analysts. Furthermore, the forecasting process could be programmed on the computer. An example would be an econometric model to forecast industry automobile sales.

The choice between subjective and objective methods is an important one. Most forecasts are made using subjective methods (Rothe, 1978). It also seems that the more important the forecast, the greater is the likelihood that subjective methods will be used. (But the popularity of a method is a poor guide in determining which method is most useful.)

Naive versus Causal Methods

A continuum of causality exists in forecasting models. At the naive end, no statements are made about causality (automobile sales can be plotted against time and the trend can be projected); at the causal end, the model may include many factors (the real income per capita, the real price of gasoline, the real price of automobiles, the population, and the real price of substitute forms of transportation).

Causal methods are more complex than naive methods. First, data must be obtained on the causal factors. Estimates of causal relationships are obtained from these data. These estimates of the causal relationships should be adjusted so that they are relevant over the forecast horizon. Next, one must forecast the changes in the causal variables. Finally, the forecasts of the causal variables and the relationships are used to calculate the overall forecast.

Causal methods are of more obvious value in planning. They can be used in any phase of planning. However, naive methods can be used in some phases. For example, naive methods can provide forecasts of environmental factors.

Linear versus Classification Methods

Methods that are objective and that rely upon causality can be categorized according to whether they use linear or classification methods.

This decision generally has only a small impact on accuracy. It depends mostly upon convenience and the availability of data (classification methods typically require much data).

The linear method is based upon the usual way we think about causality: "If *X* goes up, this will cause *Y* to go up by so much." An attempt is made to find linear relationships between *X* and *Y*. Linear methods are used because it is easier to work with models where the terms can be combined by using simple arithmetical operations. Thus, one might try to predict automobile sales by forecasting changes in income and price, and then multiplying by the relationships of these factors to auto sales.

The classification approach groups similar behavioral units. These groups or segments would be expected to respond in a similar fashion. For example, to forecast automobile sales, one segment might be "family size of two, age of head of household 65 to 75, low income, living in apartment in a large city, near mass transportation." Another segment might be "family size of five, age of head of household 25 to 35, high income, living in house in a suburb, not near mass transportation." The people *within* each segment would be expected to have similar behavior with respect to the purchase of automobiles, but the segments differ substantially from one another (low automobile purchases in the first group and high in the second group). To make a prediction using the classification method, forecasts would be made of the population of each segment and also of their behavior. These are then combined to get a forecast of auto sales for each segment. By summing across segments, an overall forecast is obtained (for example, total industry sales). The classification approach is most useful when the groups differ substantially from one another.

The Methodology Tree

The methodology tree (Figure 2-3) is used to summarize the above discussion on the choice of a forecasting method. The first decision to be made is whether it is most appropriate to use a subjective or objective method. The subjective branch leads to the "judgment" leaf. An extension of this is called "bootstrapping." This involves the development of an objective method to replicate the judgmental forecasts. This can be done by asking the judges to specify the rules they used to make forecasts. Alternatively, one can statistically analyze the judgmental forecasts and the data used by the judges to infer what rules were used. The bootstrapping model can then be used to make the forecasts.

The objective branch offers a number of approaches to forecasting. One must decide whether it is most appropriate to use naive or causal methods. The naive branch leads to the "extrapolation method."

Use of the causal branch requires an additional decision. Should you use linear or classification methods? The linear branch leads to "econometric methods" and the classification branch leads to "segmentation methods."

The thickness of the branches of the methodology tree indicates which decisions are most important in the selection of a forecasting method. The "leaves" of the tree (boxes) can be used as a checklist for selecting a method.

The methods will be discussed in a somewhat more detailed fashion below. For a more in-depth description, many sources exist (e.g., Wood and Fildes, 1976; Wheelwright and Makridakis, 1980).

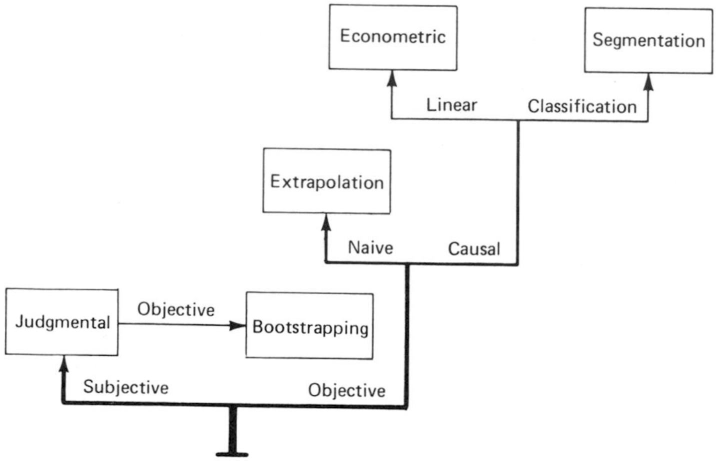

FIGURE 2-3
Forecasting methodology tree.

MATCHING THE FORECASTING METHOD TO THE SITUATION

Formal forecasting methods help to improve planning in two ways. First, they can increase accuracy over what would occur with informal methods and, thus, reduce uncertainty. Second, they can provide better estimates of the degree of uncertainty (risk).

Improved accuracy and better estimates of risk are needed for various phases of the forecasting and planning processes. These needs are described below, starting with the environmental forecast.

Environmental forecasts are useful as an input to strategic planning. The identification of possible states of the environment and a forecast of their likelihood can provide ideas on what strategies should be considered by your company.

Environmental forecasts also can help to provide better industry forecasts (the total demand for a product class in a given market). Industry forecasts can be made for each of the possible states of the environment and also for various assumptions about the future behavior of the companies in this industry. Forecasts would be required for each of the company's major products and markets.

The company then can forecast what actions it will actually take. Ideally, the company's optimal strategy would be translated directly into actions. However, the actual strategy (actions) frequently departs from the proposed strategy due to communication problems, lack of interest, resistance to the strategy by those in the company, insufficient resources within the company, or a decision to abort the strategy because of environmental changes (such as a change in available technology).

Actions by the company are also influenced by the actions of its competitors. Thus, it is helpful to forecast how the competitors will react to environmental changes. For industries that are not highly competitive (that is, for most situations), you should also try to forecast how competitors will react to major strategy changes by your company.

Forecasts of the actions (and reactions) by a company and its competitors can help to forecast the company's market share. Sales forecasts can then be calculated by multiplying the forecast market share times the industry forecast. This should be done for each major product market.

Costs should also be forecast. These depend primarily upon environmental changes, the actions taken by your company, and the level of your company's sales.

The company is then in a position to forecast results. The sales and cost forecasts allow for a forecast of profits. It would also be possible to examine the forecast costs and benefits to each of the company's stakeholders.

This list of the forecasting needs in company planning is summarized in Figure 2-4. The exhibit elaborates on the "Forecasts" box of Figure 2-1. It starts with environmental forecasts and then proceeds downward through the other areas until forecasts are obtained from results in the organization. The larger arrowhead indicates the preferred sequence. The smaller arrowhead indicates that some backtracking will probably be needed. Below, a discussion is provided on techniques that can be used for each of the areas listed in Figure 2-4. In some cases, existing knowledge on the most useful techniques is scarce. Thus, an open-minded use of the methodology tree (Figure 2-3) is advised.

Environment

Environmental forecasts are needed to help the company formulate its strategy. It is important that the forecasting methods first identify the *possible* states of the future. For this, brainstorming among a variety of experts would be useful.

Particular attention would be given to the more important of these possible states. Importance should be judged not only by the likelihood

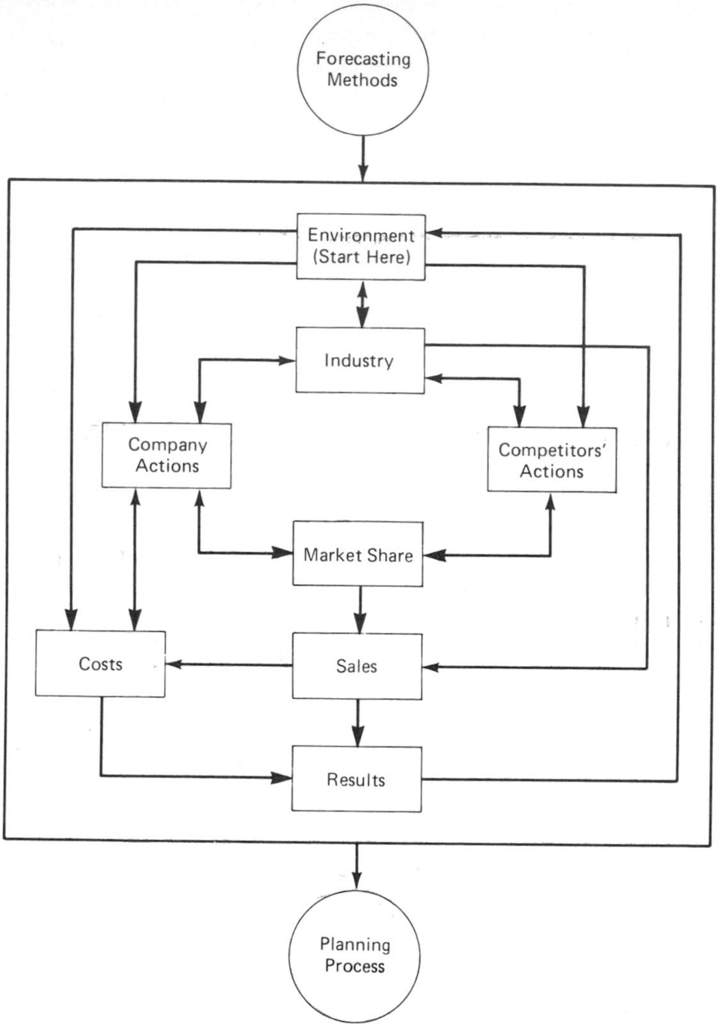

FIGURE 2-4
Need for forecasts in company planning.

of the environmental change, but also by its potential impact on the company if it does occur. The use of structured judgmental methods provides an obvious starting point to assess the likelihood of the events.

However, extrapolation from analogous events in history can also be useful.

An environmental change can directly affect company actions (e.g., a change in export laws), or it can indirectly affect the company by its impact on the industry (e.g., increased energy costs).

Surprisingly, the accuracy of industry forecasts is not highly sensitive to the accuracy of the environmental forecast (evidence on this point is summarized in Armstrong, 1978a, pp. 219, 241, 378). It is expected that this generalization will not hold for extremely large environmental changes such as wars, depressions, shortages, government controls, or major technological innovations. But, generally, highly accurate environmental forecasts are not required for industry forecasts.

It *is* important to determine which are the important factors in the environment that might affect the industry. It is also important to predict the direction of change in the important factors, and to then get "approximately correct" predictions of the magnitude of the changes in these factors. For the direction of change in environmental factors, only general trends, not cycles, should be considered. Other than recurrent events owing to the seasons of the year (seasonality), cycles have been of little value for improving the accuracy of forecasts. The reason? One must also predict the phases (timing) of the cycles. If the timing is off, large errors can occur.

Ample data exist on trends in the environment. The more important factors are published in magazines, newspapers, and financial newsletters. The problem is not a lack of data; rather, it is how to use the data. Companies often spend much time and money seeking information from the environment that will confirm their beliefs. Frequently they ignore negative or "disconfirming" information that is easily available. It seems useful, therefore, to severely limit the budget for the collection of environmental data. Seldom is the additional information expected to have a strong positive impact on decision making. (Most of the evidence in this area is from studies in psychology; Goldberg, 1968, provides a summary of this research.)

This advice on environmental forecasts is counterintuitive. People typically expect that better environmental forecasts are of great value to the company. Thus, much time and money are spent by firms to obtain "better forecasts." For example, many companies purchase econometric forecasts to obtain short-range forecasts of GNP, inflation rates, and unemployment. This practice is widespread despite the fact that little evidence exists to suggest that these forecasts are superior to other, cheaper alternatives such as extrapolations or forecasts by a panel of experts (Armstrong, 1978b).

Industry

After preparing the environmental forecasts, the company should prepare industry forecasts. In some cases, these have been prepared by others. For example, Predicasts, Inc. of Cleveland, Ohio, summarizes the U.S. forecasts in a quarterly publication called *Predicasts*. They publish forecasts for other countries in their *Worldcasts*. The disadvantages of using forecasts prepared by others are that:

1. They may not use the product-market definitions that are relevant to your company
2. A time lag exists from the time the forecast was made until it was published
3. Forecasts are not updated frequently
4. The original sources (as cited in *Predicasts* and *Worldcasts*) often do not provide sufficient information on the assumptions behind the forecasts

For these reasons, medium-sized and large firms are best advised to develop their own industry forecasting models.

Much of the error in industry forecasts is due to errors in estimating the current status. What are the industry sales now? Thus, some useful (though often ignored) advice is to break the forecasting problem into two subproblems. First, estimate the current sales level. Then use methods to forecast change over the forecast horizon. The forecast is the sum of the current sales plus the change in sales over the forecast horizon.

Judgmental methods are often appropriate for estimating current sales. Experts, such as sales people, are likely to have up-to-date information on the current sales. In contrast, objective data are often reported after much delay.

To obtain judgmental estimates of current sales, use structured methods such as the following: First, provide those concerned with up-to-date information in an easy-to-read format (such as tables or graphs). Then, replace the group meeting with a survey. After each person makes his or her best estimate, an average of their forecasts is calculated. A refinement, helpful when there may be ambiguities in the question, is the Delphi technique, described earlier in this chapter.

Although judgment might be useful for estimating current sales, it is not so relevant in forecasting *change*. For this task, objective methods are more appropriate (see Armstrong, 1978a, pp. 363–372 for a summary of the evidence leading to this conclusion).

If experts are used to forecast change, there is no need to obtain the "best" experts (Armstrong, 1980). According to the research, sufficient expertise in the area of interest can be obtained in a few months. Thus, it is advisable to obtain inexpensive experts.

Of the objective methods available to forecast change, econometric methods are perhaps the most useful. The econometric model should aim at two desirable, but conflicting, goals in industry forecasting: (1) include all important factors, and (2) keep it simple. Research in this area suggests that little complexity is needed. Often, "near optimal" results have been obtained with the use of only two or three variables.

The magnitude of the causal relationships in an industry-forecasting model can be estimated judgmentally. However, for most situations it is safer to obtain estimates from historical data or from experiments. Regression analysis provides a common and useful way of estimating these relationships. In some cases, these estimates can be obtained from published studies using regression analyses of similar products. Surprisingly, accurate estimates of regression coefficients are often not necessary (Dawes, 1979), although exceptions to this generalization do occur (Remus and Jenicke, 1978). A reasonable approach, recommended in econometrics, is to start with judgmental (a priori) estimates of causal relationships, then update these by use of regression analysis.

Another objective method relevant to long-range market forecasting is the segmentation model. This approach is expected to be accurate, but it requires much data. Furthermore, it is difficult to use when examining changes in the company's strategies or in competitive responses.

The resulting industry forecasts can be used as an input to the planning process. For example, different strategies might be required depending on whether the organization is in a growing or declining industry.

Company Actions

Forecasts for the environment and the industry can then be considered along with the company's proposed strategies to predict what actions would actually be taken. In other words, what will the strategy look like in practice? Forecasting is aided if the company considers well-defined and operational strategies, if the people in the company will be firmly committed to implementing the strategy, and if the company will have adequate resources.

But will all of the stakeholders be successful at implementing the strategy? One way to forecast the actual actions by the company is to survey these stakeholders. They would be presented with a description of a strategy and would be asked how successful they would be in carrying out their part. Perhaps a given strategy is not realistic from their viewpoint.

In some situations, such as when negative effects would be encountered by the company, it may be difficult to forecast stakeholder actions by direct questioning. Here, "group depth interviews" may be useful. To do this, groups of key decision makers in the organization meet with a consultant. The consultant presents scenarios with different strategies and environments. The decision makers are then asked how they would act in these situations. The reason for meeting in a group is because the decisions of these people are interdependent. A similar procedure could be followed with the stakeholders.

Forecasts should also be made of the company's resources. Will financial resources, supplies of raw materials, and personnel be adequate for a given strategy? Forecasts of labor-management relations might be important at this stage.

Competitors' Actions

A company's strategy is often dependent on the actions of its competitors. But the competitors are unlikely to tell you about their intentions. In many cases, it may be sufficient to forecast the competitors' actions using expert judgment. In doing this, it may be helpful to consider a forecast of the competitors' resources.

If a substantial amount of historical data exists, it may be possible to find analogous situations. Summaries of how competitors reacted in past situations may allow for a forecast of how they will respond to changes in the environment or to different strategies that your company might use. For example, how do your major competitors react to new product introductions?

One technique that is useful in forecasting competitors' actions is *role playing*. This involves having some members of your management team act as if they were in their current role while others play the role of competitors. Role playing can be used to test various strategies. It is especially useful for analyzing unusual strategies when secrecy is important (such as with new products). It is also useful when it would be impractical to test out a strategy with a field experiment.

Role playing is relatively easy to carry out. The following rules are suggested:

1. Assign people to roles of key decision makers for the company and its major competitors. Provide a short description of the role, the environment, the firm's capabilities, and the selected strategy. Use four pages, one for each of these four topics.
2. The role players should not step out of their roles; that is, once they meet, they should "be" that person at all times. Ask the role players to prepare individually and then return to the meeting place when they are ready to stay with their roles.
3. The players should improvise as needed.
4. The players should act as they themselves would act in that role, asking themselves, "What would *I* do, given this strategy?"

Role playing has been popular in political science and in the military, where it is called gaming. The use of role playing in business has been limited. Busch (1961) said that the Lockheed Corporation used role playing to forecast the behavior of their customers. IBM used a form of role playing to forecast the reactions of a jury in a trial (*The Wall Street Journal,* February 3, 1977). Armstrong (1977) used it to forecast the actions by members of the board of directors of the Upjohn Corporation in a case in which the government tried to force Upjohn to remove one of its drugs from the market.

Forecasts from role playing may differ greatly from those provided by other methods. Four studies have contrasted the accuracy of role playing with judgmental forecasts. In three studies, role playing was superior, and there was no difference in the fourth. Armstrong (1978a, pp. 118–121) summarized this evidence.

In the Edsel case, it would have been useful to identify the key competitors of the Edsel and to conduct role playing to predict their reactions. For example, one of the key competitors was Ford's Mercury division. Role playing might have predicted what happened. (What actually happened, according to Brooks, 1969, was that Mercury launched a large advertising campaign in retaliation against the introduction of the Edsel. Furthermore, Mercury production workers apparently sabotaged the Edsel cars that were being produced in the same plants.)

Market Share

Given the forecast actions by the company and by its competitors, what market share can the company expect? Research in this area has provided few generalizations on which methods are most effective. However, a number of techniques seem reasonable.

For small changes in strategy, it may be sufficient to extrapolate the company's market share. Alternatively, you might employ the judgment of a group of experts using structured methods to obtain these forecasts. In most situations it is better to first obtain forecasts independently with both extrapolation and judgment methods, and then use the average of these forecasts.

For large changes in strategy, the use of econometric methods is desirable. This assumes that one has data on the dependent variable (for example, sales) and on the key aspects of the strategy. If significantly different strategies were used in the past (such as the use of different prices) and if this led to substantial differences in sales, the econometric model may be useful in identifying the effects due to changes in the strategy.

In some cases (such as with new products), data are not available for the sales variables. Here the use of bootstrapping can be considered.

The bootstrapping model is developed from management's judgment and from the data they use. Typically, the model is estimated by regression analysis. An example of such a model would be:

$$M = c + b_p P + b_a A$$

where M is management's *forecasted* market share
c is a constant
P is the product's price relative to its competition
A is the product's advertising relative to its competition
b_p and b_a are coefficients reflecting the relationships used by management

The bootstrapping model offers some advantages. First, it applies management's beliefs in a consistent manner. Thus, it can evaluate a large set of alternative strategies in a consistent way. Second, bootstrapping can provide insight to management's current forecasting beliefs, and this may foster learning. Finally, bootstrapping is slightly more accurate than the judges themselves (evidence is summarized in Armstrong, 1978a, pp. 251–259, and in Camerer, 1981). Thus the name: It is like lifting oneself up by the straps on one's boots. An application of this model for new product forecasting is described by Montgomery (1975).

Costs

The company is now in a position to forecast its costs. An explicit forecast should be made of the costs of a given strategy to each of the important stakeholders. For example, in the Edsel case, how much would Ford's strategy cost the employees, the dealers, the customers, the local community, and the stockholders? The formal approach is expected to produce better forecasts of the costs to each member of the system than would be obtained by informal forecasting methods.

Forecasts of costs can be used in the evaluation of the strategies (thus the two-way arrow from "Costs" to "Company Actions" in Figure 2-4). Where will the company's future costs be low relative to its competitors?

The cost forecasts depend upon the environment, the actions taken by the company, and its sales. Thus, forecasts of these other areas should be made before making the cost forecasts.

The best methods for forecasting costs will depend upon the industry, the strategy, and stakeholders. It is difficult to provide generalizations on what method is best in which situation. A logical starting point, however, is the use of extrapolations. For example, learning curves can be used to forecast decreases in manufacturing costs. The simplest way to do this is to estimate a straight line on log paper to reflect what is typically a constant percentage decrease in manufacturing costs as volume increases. Experience curves attempt the same thing using the decrease in *total costs* as volume rises. But large changes in technology or in supplies can lead to significant departures from this extrapolation. In view of the potential for errors, it seems reasonable to base the forecast on two or more different methods.

Sales Forecasts

Completion of the market share and industry forecasts allows for a calculation of the sales forecast. If uncertainty has been estimated for both the industry and market share forecasts, these can be used to estimate the uncertainty in the sales forecast.

Results

By using forecasts from the preceding steps, calculations can then be made of the forecasted costs and benefits of each strategy for each of the major stakeholders. For example, profit and loss statements could be prepared for the stockholders, environmental impacts could be summarized for the local community, and the effects of product usage could be summarized from the consumer's point of view.

The forecasts should examine not only the expected results for a given strategy, but also the uncertainty. What are the most favorable and least favorable results that might occur? Furthermore, they should describe how the strategy performs in different environments.

These forecasts of results provide the basis for selecting among the various strategies. How do they each perform against the original objectives? If none of the strategies is acceptable, it is useful to go back to the planning process for the generation of additional strategies.

SUMMARY

A framework was presented to show the relationship between strategic planning and forecasting (Figure 2-1). To make forecasts, it is necessary to consider the strategies; to plan, it is helpful to have good forecasts of the environment and of the impact of various strategies.

A description of the planning process was then provided (see Figure 2-2). This stressed the need for commitment-seeking in all steps of the planning process. Some of the major guidelines for planning were:

1. For objective setting, start with the ultimate objectives for each stakeholder. Translate these into specific, challenging, and measurable

objectives by considering the comparative strengths and weaknesses of the company.

2. Develop alternative strategies for each of the more important possible states of the environment. Particular attention should be given to unfavorable situations; scenarios and brainstorming can be used here to increase creativity and openness within the organization. The plans should be comprehensive and they should contain slack. The more promising strategies should be specified in operational terms. Contingency plans should also be prepared for alternative environments.

3. Evaluate alternative strategies explicitly. The Delphi technique can be used here as well as group depth interviews, scenarios, rating sheets, and the devil's advocate.

4. Establish a monitoring system to obtain information on:

   a. Environmental changes
   b. Changes in the company's capabilities and in the capabilities of its competitors
   c. Actions taken by the organization
   d. Actions taken by major competitors
   e. Results

This information should be compared with predetermined standards to indicate when the strategy should be reexamined. Furthermore, fixed review periods should be scheduled.

Participation of the company's stakeholders in each of the above four steps should help to increase the commitment of these stakeholders to making the strategy a success.

This advice on formal strategic planning is summarized in the checklist of Figure 2-5. Although it may help to use some of the planning techniques separately, it seems best to use them in combination with one another.

Formal planning is expected to be most useful in situations where:

1. The task is complex
2. Large changes occur (in the environment, by competitors, or by the company itself)
3. Uncertainty is high
4. The market is inefficient

When one or more of these conditions do not hold, an investment in formal planning would be expected to yield a smaller return.

Various forecasting methods were described. They were classified using the forecasting methodology tree (see Figure 2-3). This described the methods as subjective or objective, naive or causal, and linear or classification. The tree can be used as a checklist in selecting a method for a given forecasting problem.

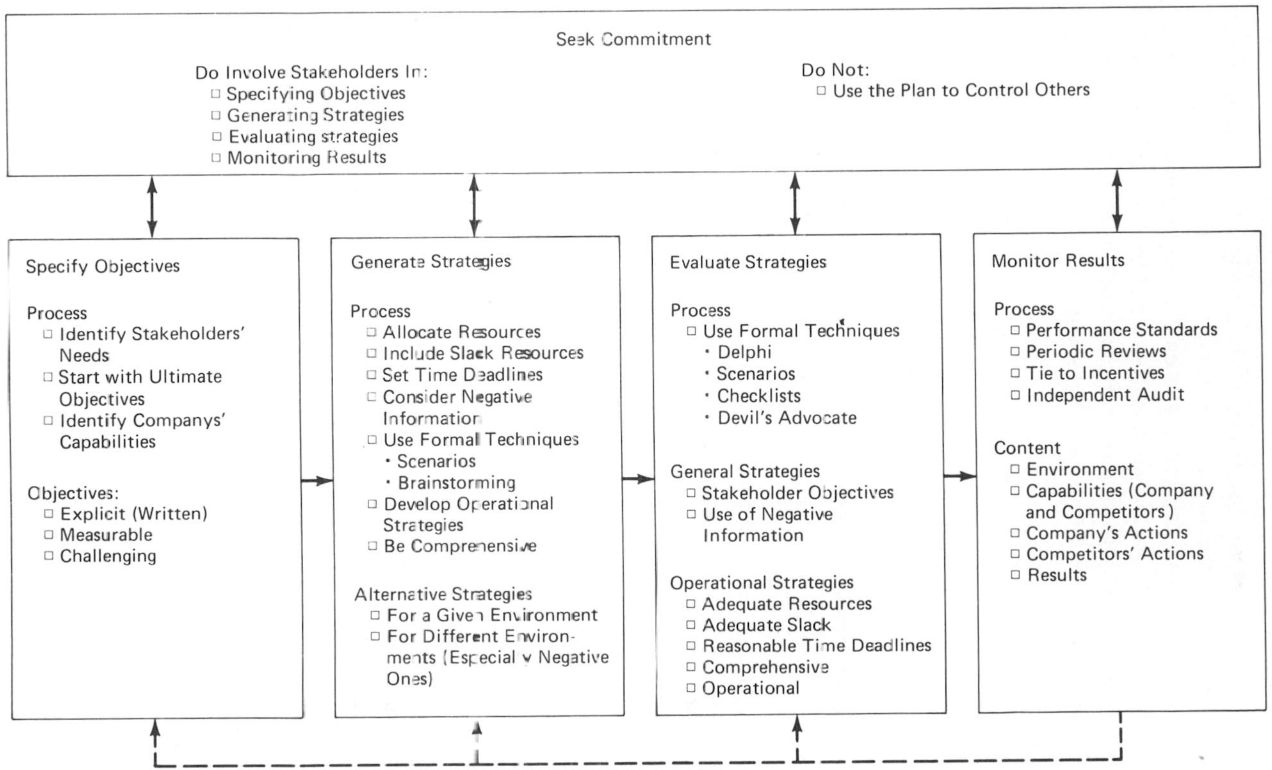

Seek Commitment
Do Involve Stakeholders In:
□ Specifying Objectives
□ Generating Strategies
□ Evaluating strategies
□ Monitoring Results
Do Not:
□ Use the Plan to Control Others
Specify Objectives
Process
□ Identify Stakeholders' Needs
□ Start with Ultimate Objectives
□ Identify Companys' Capabilities
Objectives:
□ Explicit (Written)
□ Measurable
□ Challenging
Generate Strategies
Process
□ Allocate Resources
□ Include Slack Resources
□ Set Time Deadlines
□ Consider Negative Information
□ Use Formal Techniques
• Scenarios
• Brainstorming
□ Develop Operational Strategies
□ Be Comprehensive
Alternative Strategies
□ For a Given Environment
□ For Different Environments (Especially Negative Ones)
Evaluate Strategies
Process
□ Use Formal Techniques
• Delphi
• Scenarios
• Checklists
• Devil's Advocate
General Strategies
□ Stakeholder Objectives
□ Use of Negative Information
Operational Strategies
□ Adequate Resources
□ Adequate Slack
□ Reasonable Time Deadlines
□ Comprehensive
□ Operational
Monitor Results
Process
□ Performance Standards
□ Periodic Reviews
□ Tie to Incentives
□ Independent Audit
Content
□ Environment
□ Capabilities (Company and Competitors)
□ Company's Actions
□ Competitors' Actions
□ Results

FIGURE 2-5
Planning process checklist.

Suggestions were made for the use of forecasting methods for the various needs in the company's planning (see Figure 2-4). This included methods for forecasting the environment, industry, company actions, competitors' actions, market share, and costs. These forecasts allow one to calculate sales forecasts and then to examine the costs and benefits for each stakeholder. Some of the more important suggestions were:

1. Use structured judgmental methods to forecast the possible environmental states, their likelihood, and their potential effect on the company and the industry. As an input to the industry forecast, concentrate on identifying the important factors and their direction of change. Generally, only approximately correct predictions are needed for the magnitude of change. Do not forecast long-range cycles.
2. To obtain industry forecasts, first estimate current sales, and then forecast changes. Judgmental forecasts are often appropriate for estimating current sales. Simple econometric and segmentation methods are useful to forecast changes.
3. Organizations do not always have operational strategies. When they do have such strategies, they do not always follow them. To forecast what actions the company will actually take, use surveys or group depth interviews with the key decision makers and stakeholders. Group depth interviews seem especially useful for dealing with situations that could be unfavorable to the organization.
4. Competitive reactions to large changes in the environment or to changes in your company's strategy can be forecast by historical analogies or by role playing.
5. Market share can be forecast by extrapolation or by judgment. If large changes in strategy are considered, econometric models are appropriate. However, when data are lacking on actual results, bootstrapping can be used.
6. Forecast the costs for each stakeholder by using forecasts of the environment, company actions, and sales levels. Try to obtain forecasts using different methods in order to compensate for errors inherent in a single method.

This chapter has summarized the current state of the art in formal planning and forecasting. The evidence to date suggests that formal planning and forecasting are valuable for organizations.

BIBLIOGRAPHY

Ackoff, Russell L.: *A Concept of Corporate Planning,* John Wiley, New York, 1970.

Ang, James S., and Jess H. Chua: "Long-Range Planning in Large United States Corporations—A Survey," *Long-Range Planning,* vol. 12, 1979, pp. 99–102.

Ansoff, H. Igor: *Corporate Strategy*. McGraw-Hill, New York, 1965.
——— et al.: "Does Planning Pay? The Effect of Planning on Success of Acquisitions in American Firms," *Long-Range Planning*, vol. 3, 1970, pp. 2–7.
Armstrong, J. Scott: "Social Irresponsibility in Management," *Journal of Business Research*, vol. 5, 1977, pp. 185–213.
———: *Long-Range Forecasting: From Crystal Ball to Computer*, John Wiley, New York, 1978a.
———: "Forecasting with Econometric Methods: Folklore versus Fact," *Journal of Business*, vol. 51, 1978b, pp. 549–564.
———: "The Seer-Sucker Theory: The Value of Experts in Forecasting," *Technology Review*, vol. 83, June–July, 1980, pp. 18–24.
———: "The Forecasting Audit," in Spyros Makridakis and Steven C. Wheelwright (eds.), *The Handbook of Forecasting: A Manager's Guide*, John Wiley, New York, 1982a.
———: "The Value of Formal Planning for Strategic Decisions: Review of Empirical Research," *Strategic Management Journal* (forthcoming), 1982b.
Baker, Henry G.: "Sales and Marketing Planning of the Edsel," in *Marketing's Role in Scientific Management*, American Marketing Association, Chicago, 1957, pp. 128–144.
Bass, Bernard M.: "Utility of Managerial Self-Planning on a Simulated Production Task with Replications in Twelve Countries," *Journal of Applied Psychology*, vol. 62, 1977, pp. 506–509.
Becker, Lawrence J.: "Joint Effect of Feedback and Goal Setting on Performance: A Field Study of Residential Energy Conservation," *Journal of Applied Psychology*, vol. 63, 1978, pp. 428–433.
Brooks, John N.: *Business Adventures*, Weybright and Talley, New York, 1969.
Busch, G. A.: "Prudent-Manager Forecasting," *Harvard Business Review*, vol. 39, 1961, pp. 57–64.
Camerer, Colin: "General Conditions for the Success of Bootstrapping Models," *Organizational Behavior and Human Performance*, vol. 27, 1981, pp. 411–422.
Chambers, John C., S. Mullick, and D. D. Smith: *An Executive's Guide to Forecasting*. John Wiley, New York, 1974.
Chisholm, Roger K., and Gilbert R. Whitaker, Jr.: *Forecasting Methods*, Irwin, Homewood, Ill., 1971.
Cosier, Richard A.: "The Effects of Three Potential Aids for Making Strategic Decisions on Prediction Accuracy," *Organizational Behavior and Human Performance*, vol. 22, 1978, pp. 295–306.
Dawes, Robyn M.: "The Robust Beauty of Improper Linear Models in Decision Making," *American Psychologist*, vol. 34, 1979, pp. 571–582.
Fulmer, Robert M., and Leslie W. Rue: "The Practice and Profitability of Long-Range Planning," *Managerial Planning*, vol. 22, May–June, 1974, pp. 1–7.
Goldberg, Lewis R.: "Simple Models or Simple Processes? Some Research on Clinical Judgments," *American Psychologist*, vol. 23, 1968, pp. 483–496.
Griffith, J. R., and B. T. Wellman: "Forecasting Bed Needs and Recommending Facilities Plans for Community Hospitals," *Medical Care*, vol. 17, 1979, pp. 293–303.
Grinyer, P. H., and D. Norburn: "Planning for Existing Markets: Perceptions of Executives and Financial Performance," *Journal of the Royal Statistical Society (A)*, vol. 138, 1975, pp. 70–97.
Harju, Paavo: *Attitude of Strategic Managers toward Formalized Corporate Planning*, School of Economics, Turku, Finland, 1981.
Herold, David M.: "Long-Range Planning and Organizational Performance: A Cross-Validation Study," *Academy of Management Journal*, vol. 15, 1972, pp. 91–102.
Hofer, Charles W.: "Research on Strategic Planning: A Survey of Past Studies and Suggestions for Future Efforts," *Journal of Economics and Business*, vol. 28, 1976, pp. 261–286.
Hogarth, Robin M., and Spyros Makridakis: "Forecasting and Planning: An Evaluation," *Management Science*, vol. 27, 1981, pp. 115–138.
Horovitz, J. H.: "Strategic Control: A New Task for Top Management," *Long-Range Planning*, vol. 12, 1979, pp. 2–7.
Ilgen, Daniel R., C. D. Fisher, and M. S. Taylor: "Consequences of Individual Feedback on Behavior in Organizations," *Journal of Applied Psychology*, vol. 64, 1979, pp. 349–371.

Janis, Irving L.: "Groupthink," *Psychology Today,* November 1971, pp. 43–77.
Kallman, Ernest J., and H. Jack Shapiro: "The Motor Freight Industry—A Case Against Planning," *Long-Range Planning,* vol. 11, February 1978, pp. 81–86.
Karger, Delmar W. and Zafar A. Malik: "Long-Range Planning and Organizational Performance," *Long-Range Planning,* vol. 8, 1975, pp. 60–64.
Kudla, Ronald J.: "The Effects of Strategic Planning on Common Stock Returns," *Academy of Management Journal,* vol. 23, 1980, pp. 5–20.
Latham, Gary P., and Sydney B. Kinne: "Improving Job Performance through Training in Goal Setting," *Journal of Applied Psychology,* vol. 59, 1974, pp. 187–191.
——— and G. A. Yukl: "A Review of Research on the Application of Goal Setting in Organizations," *Academy of Management Journal,* vol. 18, 1975, pp. 824–845.
Leontiades, Milton, and Ahmet Tezel: "Planning Perceptions and Planning Results," *Strategic Management Journal,* vol. 1, 1980, pp. 65–75.
Linstone, Harold: *The Delphi Method: Techniques and Applications,* Addison-Wesley, Reading, Mass., 1975.
Locke, Edwin A., K. N. Shaw, L. M. Saari, and G. P. Latham: "Goal Setting and Task Performance: 1969–1980," *Psychological Bulletin,* vol. 90, 1981, pp. 125–152.
Maier, Norman R. F.: *Problem-Solving Discussions and Conferences,* McGraw-Hill, New York, 1963.
Montgomery, David B.: "New Product Distribution: An Analysis of Supermarket Buyer Decisions," *Journal of Marketing Research,* vol. 12, 1975, pp. 255–264.
Remus, William E., and Lawrence O. Jenicke: "Unit and Random Linear Models in Decision Making," *Multivariate Behavioral Research,* vol. 13, 1978, pp. 215–221.
Rothe, James T.: "Effectiveness of Sales Forecasting Methods," *Industrial Marketing Management,* vol. 7, 1978, pp. 114–118.
Steiner, George A.: *Strategic Planning,* Free Press, New York, 1979.
Thune, Stanley S., and Robert J. House: "Where Long-Range Planning Pays Off," *Business Horizons,* vol. 13, 1970, pp. 81–87.
Tolchinsky, Paul D., and Donald C. King: "Do Goals Mediate the Effects of Incentives on Performance?," *Academy of Management Review,* vol. 5, 1980, pp. 455–467.
Van de Ven, Andrew H.: "Problem Solving, Planning, and Innovation. Part 1: Test of the Program Planning Model," *Human Relations,* vol. 33, 1980, pp. 711–740.
Wheelwright, Steven C. and S. Makridakis: *Forecasting Methods for Management,* 3d ed., John Wiley, New York, 1980.
Wood, D. Robley, Jr.: "Long Range Planning in Large United States Banks," *Long-Range Planning,* vol. 13, 1980, pp. 91–98.
——— and R. L. LaForge: "The Impact of Comprehensive Planning on Financial Performance," *Academy of Management Journal,* vol. 22, 1979, pp. 516–526.
Wood, Douglas and Robert Fildes: *Forecasting for Business—Methods and Applications,* Longman, London, 1976.
Wrapp, H. Edward, "Good Managers Don't Make Policy Decisions," *Harvard Business Review,* vol. 45, 1967, pp. 91–99.

Chapter 3
STRATEGIC MANAGEMENT AND STRATEGIC PLANNING IN THE 1980s

JAMES F. LYONS
Vice President, Strategic Planning, United Technologies Corporation

In ecology, *diversity* means the variety of complementary species of plants and animals within an ecosystem. To ecologists, the richness of such variety has a vital, inherent value: it promotes stability. The more species that are interacting, the more stable the ecosystem will be; the more difficult it is to disrupt the ecosystem, the less it will fluctuate. Thus diversity and biological productivity are clearly dependent.

In corporate performance, too, diversity promotes stability. It can be a source of strength and profitability. Complementary businesses, technologies, and resources within a total business organization tend to promote predictability and stability. As in ecology, the rich variety (for example, counter-cyclicality or sources of cash versus growth) within a business organization is vital.

Corporations, like ecosystems, have thresholds of limitations in their ability to withstand threat and external change. The broader the context of complementary and reinforcing businesses, the more likely the corporation is to withstand periods of economic instability, geopolitical change in its major international markets, and major substitution-technology threats. As in an ecosystem, diversity in its basic business areas is important to the corporation's growth and stability. Emphasis should, however, be on complementary and reinforcing businesses as opposed to pure diversity. This is a distinction between a conglomerate and a corporation. Although a corporation is, in fact, a multimarket, multi-industry, multitechnology business organization, it has complementarity and major opportunities for technical and capital resource transfer.

A corporation may be the sum of its parts. Its strengths, however, may not lie only in the sum of those parts but in their complementarity and their ability to sustain growth and profitable performance in a number of different economic and geopolitical contexts. The common denominator of that diversity is technology.

Such business organizations create unique management and planning challenges. This is especially true in the context of discontinuous change and worldwide competition. As a result, the corporation of the future will be more planning-intensive. It will not be enough to maintain professional planners at the top of the corporation and engage in annual planning exercises which, more often than not, are rigid, constricting, and regarded by the staff and line alike as a waste of time. As decision making moves downward and mission orientation becomes more prominent, more responsible and more focused planning must take place at lower levels in semiautonomous divisions or businesses. These lower levels will be provided with resources and held accountable for performance.

THE NEED FOR STRATEGIC MANAGEMENT AND PLANNING

In this context, the objective of strategic management is the effective management of change. The focus of planning is the resource allocation process. The emphasis is on investing in strategies, not simply approving capital projects. The process is analytical as well as qualitative. The end results are strategic decisions on the timing, priority, and context for deploying capital, technical, and human resources to assure attainment of the growth and profit objectives of the corporation.

Strategic management will increasingly gain acceptance as the best vehicle for improving the performance of large, complex companies. Effective strategic management can pull together a diverse organization, communicate clear objectives and values, and achieve the creative integration of capital, technical, and human resources. Communication is an absolute necessity—it is frequently overlooked and almost always frustrated. Large corporations must clearly articulate corporate goals and objectives throughout the organization, and ensure that they are continually understood and interpreted in the context of short-term decisions. As indicated above, there will be more management decentralization in order to move the planning process and the strategic decisions down to the firing line. Another critical form of communication is management development. It must continually stress strategic management and planning concepts and techniques and develop within management the ability to challenge the status quo and conventional wisdom.

Strategic management, then, can change and create a new corporate culture in many organizations. But this process will demand vision because the strategic management system must be an effective vehicle for change; thus the planning system must evolve, and management at all levels must understand this process of evolution.

Ineffectual or erroneous planning will be increasingly visible as major corporations and business strategies fail. Discontinuous change and worldwide markets increase the risks of errors in strategic judgment and impose a greater penalty for such errors on the organization's success; indeed, its very survival is at risk.

One key to protecting corporate strategy from blind spots is to make sure that the planning system clearly identifies critical assumptions about the environment and competition. As has been said frequently, the role of strategy is in some way to change or affect the competitive environment in order to optimize the strength and opportunities of a given corporation. Planning systems, therefore, should be dedicated to perceptive analysis and insight and not to control.

In response to these challenges, threats, changes, and opportunities, planning must increasingly be integrated across a broad analytical spectrum of business and function. Integrated long-range planning will include the direction of strategic planning, the proximate short-term impact of financial plans and budgets for control purposes (midcourse corrections and specific actions such as acquisitions and divestitures), and priorities and strategies on resource allocation for technical, capital, and human resources.

In addition, strategic management will be integrated from a time standpoint. It will not be a two-year operating plan plus three or seven years of long-range planning extrapolation. Emphasis will be placed on the implicit assumptions for the long term in support of short-term resource commitments.

As indicated earlier, not only must that planning be integrated, it must be decentralized. Within corporations, the emphasis must be on the transition from strategic planning to strategic management. Resource allocation priorities can be established on a broad corporate portfolio basis. However, the deployment of those resources must be left to the operating unit managers and their staffs. The situation is similar to a military campaign in which decisions on the deployment of personnel and materiel are left to the commanders in the field, who are in turn responding to broad objectives and a general battle strategy.

The Common Threat Is Change

For many companies in the United States the idea of a battle plan is especially appropriate since they all will be fighting for their survival in the face of an increased scale of world competition by foreign manufacturers and the impact of major substitution technologies that structurally and permanently alter industries. Much of this substitution will have its genesis in very large scale integrated (VLSI) electronics, electrooptics, and communications well beyond the twisted pair and telephony as we know it.

One word on the need for planning and the transition the American corporation will face: These threats and opportunities can be discerned only if the corporation moves out far enough to clearly test its assumptions against emerging technology, changes in competitive structures, and its own strengths and weaknesses. If these threats and opportunities are perceived too late, the corporation will not be able to effectively manipulate its human, capital, and technical resources to either counter or capitalize on them. No industry can assume that it will not be subject to major structural change either within its component businesses or in the end markets it serves.

The Common Response Is Planning

Never has the need for planning and a better understanding of the futurity of current decisions been greater. Seldom has the penalty for the wrong decision been so severe. Seldom has there been a need for more intellectual value added in planning and less sterile methodology. Seldom has there been a greater need for managers to plan rather than for planners to manage. Seldom has there been a greater need for the word *plan* to be a verb and not a noun.

Let's take a look at this concept and process of integrated long-range business planning. And then let's interpret that process in a specific situation and see its implementation in fostering a strategy for long-range growth and investment in a large corporation.

Planning is the most basic of all management functions. It deals with the impact of today's decisions on tomorrow. It is key to effective corporate performance. A planning process should provide a framework for addressing change and should improve not only decision making but communications as well. One of the results of effective planning is a consistent set of objectives. Nothing is more dangerous than inconsistency in the context of discontinuous and permanent change; it is like a ship that continually resets its direction and recharts its course based on random reactions to short-term events.

Planning must be sequential and iterative. The process used for such planning should match with the cultural context of that organization. Companies are managed and planned very differently. The process and philosophy of one corporation may be absolutely inappropriate for another because of the dynamics of its marketplace or the unique culture of its management and organization.

The most significant determining variable for successful long-range business planning is the involvement and commitment of the chief executive officer—the chief planner, the chief strategic officer. If that is in hand, the second most important variable will follow, and that is involvement by line management on an active and committed basis. The third important variable is that planning must be integral with the total management process of decision making and resource allocation. These cannot be discrete functions. If they are, the process will wither.

Finally, the planning process should provide a consistent data base to provide flexibility, rather than rigid dogma or methodology, in response to change.

THE STRATEGIC MANAGEMENT PROCESS

The strategic management process must evolve to keep pace with the changing needs and complexities of corporations and specific product businesses as they emerge from a traditional manufacturing or marketing position to an environment in which they must offer broader product mix, develop more advanced technology, and successfully respond to world competitive threats.

During the 1980s, most corporations' long-range plans must provide a continuing shift to strategic management, changes in their long-term investment priorities, and a greater emphasis on emerging technologies and international competition. Technologies have, for the most part, been considered in the context of product development. In the 1980s, however, technology will be important to process and manufacturing management. The major forces will be building office and factory automation, and it is those technologies as well as the product development technologies that long-range plans must focus on. If corporations are to become functionally supportive and anticipate the impact of technological opportunities for increased productivity and for cost leadership in manufacturing, marketing, and distribution, their long-range plans must emphasize these emerging technologies. For a number of current businesses, particularly in the United States, incremental growth will come in response to the growth of world markets outside of North

America. This accentuates the need for more intense international business planning and effective organization management.

The diversity of products, technologies, and markets which began to emerge in the 1970s should awaken most business organizations to the realization that no single corporate-wide organizational solution is adequate for effective international marketing and operations. Each domestic, regional, and national market presents its own business opportunity.

As a consequence, corporations will move away from a highly centralized approach to planning. In its place, an integrated multilevel business process will be instituted that spreads planning throughout the corporation. The process will fully recognize both the needs of and the contributions to be made by each group, division, and subsidiary as a part of the overall corporate entity. (Corporate management will move more toward the portfolio concept, but not with its rigid methodology or its generalized investment profiles. It will be more of a corporate venture in that each business will be viewed in the context of a specific investment strategy and both capital and R&D spending will support that strategy rather than follow discrete functional plans, projects, and tasks.) Additionally, the process will acknowledge that important interrelationships among strategic, technical, financial, and human resource aspects of planning must be established and nurtured if maximum benefits are to be realized.

The process is strategy-oriented. It focuses on maintaining a viable match between the organization and its environment. It will result in a continuous search for competence and resources, from within and outside the corporation, to better adapt internal structures and operations. It will lead to the development of products and services to serve changing markets.

This changing process and evolution will dramatically alter the way planning staffs are perceived. It will also alter the skills profile and resource requirements for most planning staffs. It should reduce the size of corporate staffs and decentralize the resources. No corporate staff, particularly for large corporations, can be adequately staffed to anticipate the myriad number of new technologies, threats, opportunities, and analyses that will be encountered. As a result, there will be an increased emphasis on data bases, the use of consultants for specific tasks based on their special competence, and a decentralization of the strategic analysis to the operating units.

Utility and Relevance Will Guide Strategic Management Process Development

In the development of the strategic management process, emphasis must be placed on obtaining the high degree of relevance and utility for managers of all levels in the organization. The process will be structured to provide an accurate and consistent planning base for business assessment and performance measurement at division, group, and corporate levels.

At the business-area level, the process and the plan must become tools which assist line managers in managing their resources and in anticipating changes in their specific industries and end markets. The usefulness of the process at these levels will be facilitated by encouraging operating units to adopt the planning approaches, within the framework of a single corporate planning process, that are best suited to their particular markets, operations, and management styles.

Focus on Business Areas, Markets, and Industries

To facilitate a realistic approach to managing diverse businesses, it will be necessary for the planning process to focus on individual business opportunities, competition, and long-term business strengths and needs. There will be an increasingly higher level of economic rather than accounting data in the analysis of long-range business plans.

The concept of the strategic business units (SBU), for example, will be widespread. (Sectors will be similar "summing points" for those SBUs at the corporate level.) Divisions will identify the smallest real or potential organizational unit that can be considered as a separate business capable of serving a market and having a specific set of competitors, at a business level where long-term business decisions can be effectively made and resource priorities can be established. These somewhat "pure" businesses become the business areas or SBUs which are the building blocks of the planning process. The SBU is where most of the economic and competitive analysis should be focused.

Identification not only of these business areas but also of the end markets and industries they serve is critical. Meaningful assessments of market attractiveness and business-area strengths and performance can be made only by categorizing each business into an appropriate market and industry. Evaluations of infrastructure, driving forces, competition, growth expectation, and performance standards can be made and measured after categorizing. This segmentation permits in-depth evaluations of the microeconomics of each business. It provides the capability to identify broad-gauged environmental trends so that actions can be taken in advance to offset threats or capitalize on emerging opportunities.

To aid in this planning process, an industry-end market matrix (which bears a striking resemblance to the IO matrix of the 1960s) will be developed to better visualize all of the diverse businesses which must be addressed. (This matrix has another use and that plays to the increasing emphasis on planning for accountability and action. In acquisitions and divestitures, this matrix can facilitate not only the development of specific acquisition criteria and objectives but also the assessment of the impact of acquisitions and specific operations on the total corporation. See Figure 3-1.)

Top Down versus Bottom Up—Balance

One of the major functions of the strategic management process is to provide a set of objectives and strategies that are realistic, consistent, and understood throughout the organization. Because planning takes place at all levels in the organization, distinctly different planning tasks must be recognized.

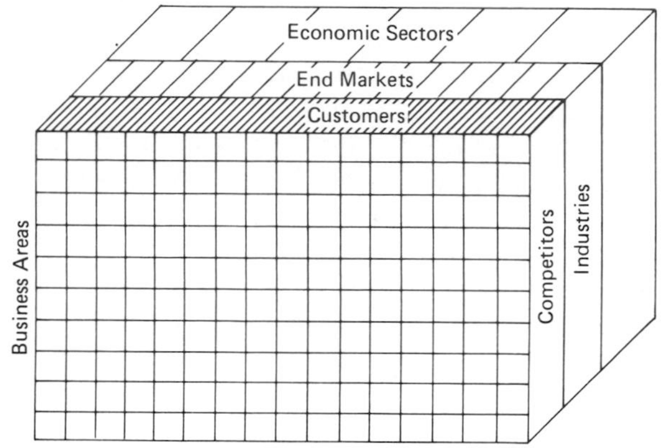

FIGURE 3-1
Business matrix.

At the corporate level, the task is to develop a portfolio strategy which delineates the role of each group in terms of its basic businesses and operating scope, and to allocate necessary resources. At the group level, the principal task is delineating the role for each division and optimizing investments and returns. At the division level, the challenge is to develop a business strategy and to deploy resources in a manner which best ensures success within the unit's designated role. The task at the functional level is to formulate supportive programs to implement business strategies.

The division of responsibility in labor calls for a *top-down* corporate input in the planning process, not only to identify the roles of each subunit but also to set tentative financial objectives, identify the resources available, and provide general guidance for group and division strategies. This process also calls for a *bottom-up* response from the operating units, in the form of a business plan drawing upon the specialized skills and insights of those managers closest to a particular business scene.

The top-down–bottom-up element of a corporation's strategic management process is an effective communications device because it is both interactive and iterative. It permits managers at each organizational level to contribute a particular perspective and ultimately reconcile differences which may exist between senior management's top-down portfolio strategy and group and divisional bottom-up specialized business approaches. The exchange results in agreed-upon strategies which are thoroughly understood, and a commitment on the part of each manager.

This organization hierarchy is important because senior managers, staff planners, and line operating executives all add value to the total planning process. Subordinate plans require more than just synthesizing. They must be evaluated and revised or approved in view of the division or group manager's broader business perspective and responsibilities. A lower-level plan to add resources or to diversify into an unserved market may be contrary to the best interests of a senior manager's total business portfolio. Redirection of the subordinate plan, based upon recommendations in favor of a more optimal position, would constitute adding value to the strategic management process. See Figure 3-2.

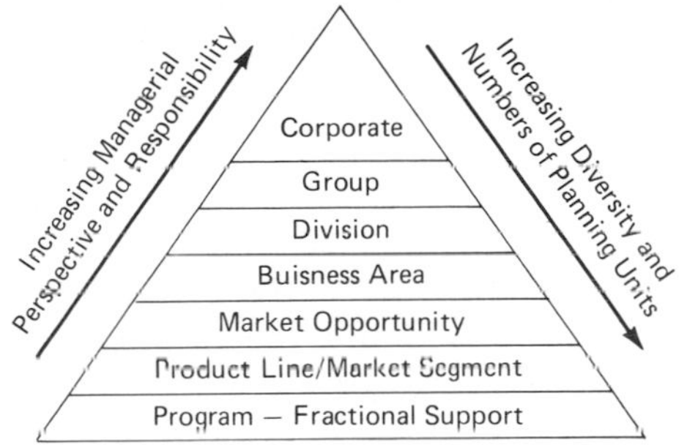

FIGURE 3-2
Organization hierarchy.

FLEXIBLE PROCESS BUT DISCIPLINED SCHEDULE

The success of a strategic management process lies in the committed involvement of key executives and planners throughout the organization in an annual planning cycle. The cycle should be coupled to a scheduled periodic review of operations and financial performance on either a monthly or a quarterly basis for each of the major operating units. Feedback on short-term operating performance is important in terms of testing strategies and monitoring investments and progress.

The planning cycle sets the timing and pace of planning events and acts as a vehicle for interaction among the various units of a corporation. Although the planning process involves numerous and formal meetings among managers and planners, and presentations of the results of special studies, a considered effort should be made to ensure that submittal dates for specific plans are met and that these dates tie in to a reevaluation of investment priorities, capital appropriation hurdle rates, and so on.

For example, in one corporation, the strategic plan for each division, group, and subsidiary is due on July 1. Capital, technical, and human resource plans consistent with the strategic plan are due on October 1. The financial plan, with limited strategic, technical, and capital updates, is due on December 1. The final integrated long-range plan is approved during the month of December.

Although these are separate submission dates, each plan represents a part of an integrated business plan and requires coordinated support from all managers and staff planners in each of the functional disciplines.

Scheduled periodic review and planning meetings among key executives are vital to the process. These meetings can represent the communications forum for developing plans, and the medium for reviewing current operating performance and testing the reasonableness of longer-term strategic direction.

For example, in one corporation, there are four quarterly reviews each year. The focus of each review differs but is consistent with the planning cycle. In the first quarterly review, the current year's profit assurance programs and next year's profit and cash-flow targets are analyzed.

In the second quarterly review, the strategic plan is reviewed in detail, with special emphasis on periodic programs that can deal with productivity leadership, managing in the high inflation environment, and so on.

In the third quarter, capital, technical, and human resource plans are reviewed together with a preliminary financial outlook for the next year's performance and the coming five years in summary.

In the final, fourth-quarter review, the short-term financial plan is approved, and any key strategic issues still outstanding are assigned to both staff and operating management for resolution in the following year. Frequently the resolution and prioritization of the strategic issues are part of the incentive-compensation plan based on nonfinancial performance objectives.

The strategic planning process, explained in more detail, begins early during the first quarter, when management meetings focus on key planning challenges for the coming years and conduct a review of strategies being shaped and investments being made on the basis of previous plans. Major questions of corporate and business strategy are addressed in the context of recent performance and the influence of competitive and macroenvironmental issues which could affect future business. The output of these meetings provides input with which to test objectives and strategies at the first quarter meeting. The management meetings serve as a background upon which to begin reviews and preparations of plans at the various organizational levels.

In the early summer, the review meetings with each group and division describe the planning situation and respond to the planning challenges identified earlier. Long-range objectives are presented, along with

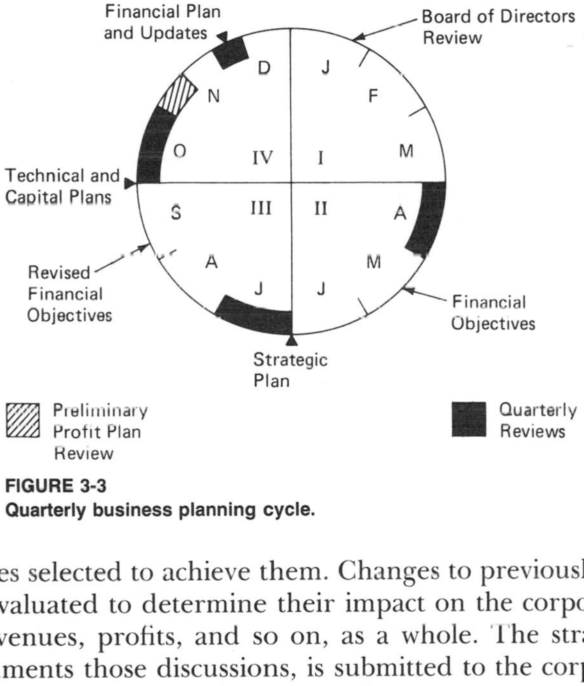

FIGURE 3-3
Quarterly business planning cycle.

the strategies selected to achieve them. Changes to previously proposed plans are evaluated to determine their impact on the corporation's resources, revenues, profits, and so on, as a whole. The strategic plan, which documents those discussions, is submitted to the corporation on July 1. See Figure 3-3.

After the capital, technical, and human resource plans are submitted by the various operating units, the corporate planning staff integrates the requirements and implications of all of these major plans, identifies important key issues, couples these resource plans to specific business strategies and objectives, and assesses corporate capabilities, competitive changes, and environmental issues. Feedback is provided to the operating units, and revisions may be made to the plans as appropriate.

In the fall, the formal capital, human resource, and technical plans are submitted. The resource allocations that are identified in these plans must relate closely to the unit's strategic objectives previously agreed upon. At the same time, a tentative overview of the financial plan and the implication of these resource allocations is completed.

In sum, the cycle begins with a macro look at the environment, the possible impact of change, and the corporation's current and projected business strategies; moves to specific business objectives and the strategies to achieve them; identifies and reviews the resources required, the short- and long-term financial results, and the major planning challenges to be met; and finally produces an approved budget.

INTEGRATING THE LONG-RANGE BUSINESS PLAN

The long-range business plan is really the integration of strategic, financial, capital, technical, and human resource plans. Because these plans are all elements of the planning process, they depend upon each other for continuity and consistency. Each plan should clearly establish resource-allocation priorities and long-term growth objectives. Each plan should be prepared in a manner that permits it to be fully integrated with the other plans.

The Strategic Plan

The strategic plan is a product that emerges from all the planning efforts of the corporation. It is derived from the organization's assessment of its internal competencies and shortcomings, anticipated changes in its environment, and contingent moves by competition. The plan identifies and supports the organization's priorities for resource allocations and integrates major goals, policies, and actions into a cohesive whole. It is organized around strategic business units or business areas, identified opportunities in specific markets, and product line definitions.

For example, the strategic plan of one business is simply the result of eight exhibits utilizing standard formats that create an organizational structure not only for the strategic plan but also for the supporting financial- and resource-allocation plans.

Four exhibits that are directed to the business area raise questions of charter, functional support strategies, resource-allocation priorities, contingency plans, and selected operating data. These exhibits address the business as if it were a stand-alone investment opportunity and a separate corporation. A broad definition of the basic business and operating scope, incremental resource requirements, objectives, and major competitors are contained in these summary exhibits. Also included is a succinct statement of strategy, projected sales, profits, growth margins, and other selected operating data, along with contingency plans for critical planning assumptions which are most sensitive to probable change.

The fifth exhibit addresses each generic or available market opportunity identified within the business area. Historical and forecast market size and share, along with a marketing-strategy summary of the business area's plans for competitively marketing its products to specific groups, are contained in the exhibit. The last three exhibits address specific product-line market segments that are served by the business area. Market size and share, product strategies, major competitors and customers, historical and projected sales, gross margin and profit, and other selected financial data are provided in the exhibits.

Technical Planning

Technical planning should be based on the premise that R&D plans must be prepared and evaluated within the context of the current and future technical environments. Accordingly, technical planning is an integral and iterative part of the total planning process.

Technical plans enable divisions, groups, and the corporation to test whether the technical activities are adequately supporting business objectives and strategies. The critical test is whether or not the R&D spending is actually relevant and is offering adequate strategic and financial return on investment.

Innovation and knowledge building are expensive. Technical risk is a cost of doing business in today's high-technology marketplace. R&D spending today is the best guarantee of market leadership tomorrow. But management must insist that risks taken be relevant to the long-range business objectives for the enterprise and the specific business area.

One technique for ensuring relevant technical activities is called research management. Its premise is that the R&D capability in a corporation is a resource to help the corporation achieve its goals and, therefore, should have relevance.

One of the primary planning tools used to achieve this kind of R&D management overview is a matrix that couples R&D plans and business objectives. This detailed coupling analysis creates a new perspective that enables technical planners and corporate managers to look ahead at the anticipated payoffs of R&D spending.

The kinds of questions that a matrix such as this answers are: Do planned R&D projects support corporate strategy? Do they reflect strategic decisions and marketing plans? Are those company activities that need technical support receiving it? Are important R&D projects being postponed or overlooked? Is there a proper balance among R&D projects that will build new knowledge, develop new products, improve existing ones?

This business-technical portfolio is a key element in the plan providing the basis for a thorough assessment of technical efforts. Technical activities are arranged in the matrix in categories that represent the type

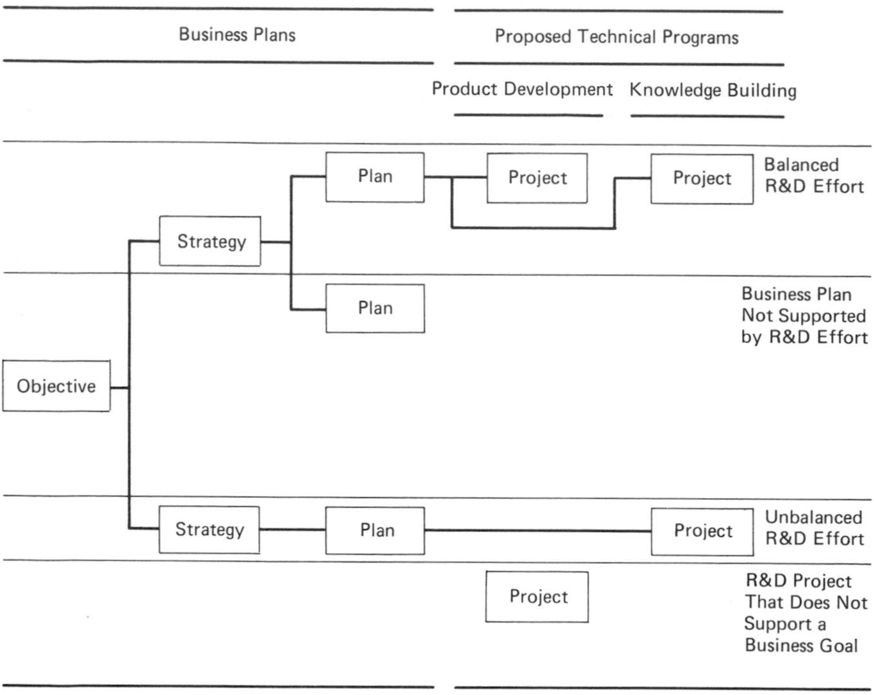

FIGURE 3-4
Matrix that couples R&D plans and business objectives.

of support work they entail. The category *current products* concerns R&D work to carry out slight modifications in products currently being manufactured in order to make them attractive in the marketplace, to extend product life, or to reduce manufacturing costs. The term *product-line* extensions refers to major technical efforts performed on an established product in order to broaden demand. *New products* is a category in which the technical efforts are associated with the development and/or testing of new products intended for either new or existing markets. *Knowledge building* consists of technical activities leading to generic advances and/or the maintenance of a competitive posture for the business area. This category is further divided into manufacturing processes, engineering methodology, and basic technology.

When completed, the matrix provides a display which links business plans, action plans, and technical programs in a manner in which gaps between objectives and supportive programs become apparent. See Figure 3-4.

Capital Planning

The planning of capital expenditure should be similarly coupled to long-range strategic plans and business objectives. The thrust should be that capital investments are made in strategies, not discrete projects. It is only by understanding those strategies that capital expenditures can be effectively analyzed, their timing understood, and their priorities clearly established.

In addition, capital planning should balance risk and returns so that there is an intelligent time-phasing of expenditures and cash flows. This is especially true in periods of high capital costs, when poor timing or premature execution of capital plans based on anticipated demand that does not materialize causes serious capital imbalances, high interest expense, and in some cases a total mismatch of strategy and market.

Balance also should be sought between tactical and strategic allocations. Tactical allocations maintain the cash flow and profitability of core businesses by adding capacity or by replacing or overhauling equipment to improve productivity. Strategic allocations may be necessary to support marketing, R&D, and new or changed products for longer term growth. The investability and the investment timing for each of the business areas and their specific product markets are carefully examined during the planning process to discern those investments which can be deferred without impairing either current market positions or long-term growth.

The capital plan should contain a summary of planned appropriation expenditures for each year and the long-range planning period. A long-range narrative should be included in the plan, and it should address major operations and manufacturing objectives, strategies and assumptions, and their relationships to business objectives.

Human Resource Planning

The integration of human resource planning with the formulation of all long-range plans is fundamental. Increasingly, in the 1980s, personnel planning must be reflected in the strategic, technical, capital, and financial plans of each business unit if the unit is to properly anticipate substitution or new technologies, potential competition, and issues such as international markets which will become a major source of growth as opposed to opportunities which will arise in traditional domestic markets.

Knowledge of present capabilities, along with a completed set of functional plans, permits human resource requirements to be anticipated in advance of their needs. Thus, action programs for recruitment, education, management development, and training can be designed and implemented.

As new technologies, particularly in microelectronics, are implemented in product and business strategies, it will be increasingly important to understand the human resource implications of these strategy and technology changes. For those businesses that have been heavily mechanical or electromechanical, an increasing use of solid-state electronics means the requirement for new service strategies with advanced service training and new approaches to equipment service diagnostics and (perhaps) manufacturing. Perhaps significant changes will also occur in market and distribution channels because of a high electronics value added. In some cases the need may also arise to work with customers before a blueprint is created rather than responding on a produced-to-print basis.

This is especially true in commodity-type businesses, in which in the past there have been little product differentiation and a decreasing value based on new technology. For many of those businesses, that will change—with a vengeance. The critical impact of those changes will be in the area of human resource planning. It will not be enough to understand technology.

The Financial Plan

The final component in the integrated long-range business plan—the financial plan—translates the results of the various activities in the planning process into a common financial framework in which historical and current performance can be reported and future performance projected.

The best-laid strategies must have control points in the short term in order to monitor the resources committed to those strategies and the extent to which those strategies (both short- and long-term) are proving viable in the competitive world marketplace.

As with the strategic plan, a financial plan narrative establishes the context in which the plan has been developed. A review of the current year briefly summarizes the estimated performance of each operating unit in the light of the current plan, with an emphasis on significant events, changes, and accomplishments.

In addition, assumptions made about specific factors that have an impact on division or business-unit performance should be clearly identified in order to properly understand the environment in which the operating unit is adhering to specific strategies and the extent to which the divisions are measuring their competitive strengths and weaknesses against identified world competition.

After the Planning—Analysis and Review

Analysis of business-unit plans is a crucial element in the planning process. After the individual plans are submitted, corporate planners and staff executives as well as managers should consolidate and assess information in the documents to ensure that planned actions are compatible with corporate objectives and capabilities and are consistent with the overall corporate financial, technical, and market strategy.

The sequence in which the plans are submitted requires that timely strategic evaluations be conducted throughout the planning cycle. These evaluations cross a number of organizational and business dimensions. Business areas, divisions, and groups are viewed individually and in the aggregate to determine where the business is and where the plan indicates it is going. The adequacy of the plans in view of the potential impact of critical trends and issues on the market served, and the comparisons to economic and competitive data bases, are only some of the many factors considered in the overall critique.

The business matrix is another basis for analyzing the plan. Through it, focus can be directed on sources of growth and investments by industry and market sectors. Critical issues such as investment timing versus economic cyclicality, portfolio balance in terms of durables industries versus soft or service industries can be distinguished.

The results of these evaluations often prompt new rounds of iterations, with the efforts directed toward setting more suitable resource-allocation priorities, and improving the timing of those investments as well as the leverage of the overall corporate competencies.

MEASURING THE EFFECTIVENESS OF THE STRATEGIC MANAGEMENT AND STRATEGIC PLANNING PROCESS

Business challenges will persist. Energy and geopolitical issues will continue to loom large in the planning horizons of most U.S. corporations. Those changes will have significant long-term influences on all businesses. Domestic political issues will reach into the core of many activities. Inflation throughout the decade will continue to be a significant economic problem both within and outside the United States.

The challenge to planners is to assess these negative trends and turn them into positive opportunities. As business patterns undergo change, the planning process of the organization will continue to evolve, as will the realization that the best way to mobilize all resources to meet future challenges is through a systematic and comprehensive approach to raising and addressing problematic issues.

The effectiveness of the planning process must ultimately be measured by the value it adds to management thinking and action, that is, the impact it has on the resource-allocation process and the resultant level of achievement of long-range corporate objectives. The final result of strategic management should be viable strategies that improve the corporation's opportunities. A plan is useless unless it makes something happen.

CONCLUSION

In summary, *plan* should be thought of as a verb, not a noun. The goal is strategic management. The means is the strategic plan. The impetus for planning is change. Change is the only permanence. The adjective *strategic* connotes creativity, not control (auditing plans and performance are control functions, not planning). Planning facilitates the implementation of strategy. The value added by strategic planning systems is the clear and objective identification of critical assumptions. Long-range business planning may be an extrapolation that ends in numbers, but it is not strategic planning (the data bases for strategic plans are frequently economic but not accounting in nature). Planning must challenge and stimulate. As a result, it requires not only intelligence but intuition. There is no one solution. There is no textbook. There is no boilerplate. The strategic management process must evolve and must be especially sensitive to the culture, the needs, and the context of the corporation.

In many corporations in the early stage of planning evolution, the strategic management process is really one of management development. In large, diverse corporations, more than one planning process may be needed in order to accommodate various worldwide businesses. The overall corporate planning process should be able to account for these differences. If the strategic management process is to aid in the management of diversity, its strength must lie in accommodating diversity rather than attempting to impose uniformity.

Chapter 4

STRATEGY FORMULATION—A COMPREHENSIVE ILLUSTRATION

J. ERNEST MITCHELL
Director, Corporate Planning, The Dow Chemical Company

CHESTER D. MARKS
Manager, Strategic Planning, Dow Chemical U.S.A.

Strategic planning is hardly a new discovery. Nor can it be an isolated specialty. Strategic planning is merely the process of exploring:

- Where you *need* to go—and when
- Whether you are prepared for the trip
- What kind of trip it will probably be
- Whether there will be suitable rewards when you arrive

All of this is an integral part of good management. Nothing is so demoralizing to an organization as superb implementation of a bad idea. Strategic planning, properly employed, should help greatly in making the whole effort effective.

Superior managers in smaller successful companies are instinctively good strategic planners unless they happen to be unusually lucky. They may not have read the literature or attended formal seminars, but they have the instincts to position their businesses. And positioning is what strategy is all about.

In the larger institutions of the 1980s, the chief executive officers

(CEOs) are subject to many pressures which their predecessors did not feel. Current economic, social, and political urgencies preempt so much time that longer-term strategic planning can easily get squeezed out. If this vital strategic activity is to be maintained with reasonable continuity, it must be set up separately as a full-time activity. Once this bridge has been crossed, a very delicate relationship must be established and maintained among the professional planners, the CEO, and the rest of the organization. No planning system can work well without the continuing involvement and visible backing of the top person in the organization.

The chief planner cannot exist for long as a pushy autocrat. Persuasion through "the logic of the situation" is the planner's most powerful tool—both with the CEO and with the rest of the organization. The planner must never adversely disturb the close relationship between the CEO and the organization. The planner can identify issues, question direction discreetly, obtain new information, and help to sell ideas and programs, but should never try to assume the role of the boss. The whole organization knows that the planner is not the boss, and will quickly turn on the pretender. In fact, it has been said that the only profession with a shorter job expectancy than a major league baseball manager is that of corporate planner.

The successful planner must appear to be an integrator. This is an acceptable role to other members of the organization. The planner cannot be a second-guesser, a tattletale, or a bureaucrat. Above all, the planner must work visibly for the whole organization and sincerely try to make its managers look good. If a planner has a wealth of new ideas, it should be arranged so that the ideas are proposed by line managers.

STRATEGIC PLANNING AND THE CORPORATE PERSONALITY

Organizations, like people, develop distinct personalities which guide their objectives and style. It is clear that strategic planning activities must mirror this personality. The following considerations are vital when developing a strategic plan:

- Centralized or decentralized?
- Formal or informal internal communications?
- Flexible or inflexible?
- Risk takers or conservative?
- Where is the real power?
    - In functions?
    - In geographical groupings?
    - In product groups?
    - Or in an accepted matrix?

- Relationship between management and board of directors
- Scientific innovators or copiers?
- Where are greater strengths?
    - R&D?
    - Marketing?
    - Manufacturing?
    - Purchasing?
    - Public relations?
    - Financial?
- Active or passive position in politics?
- Personnel policies:
    - Hiring
    - Remuneration
    - Opportunities for personal growth
    - Short-term or long-term emphasis
    - Ethical standards

Above all, the planner must have a feeling for what is acceptable, who makes policy, and how to sell ideas.

The strategic planning approaches described here have been adapted to fit the needs of Dow Chemical, a $10 billion corporation selling in most of the countries of the world and having 115 manufacturing locations in twenty-nine countries. Products are chemicals, plastics, metals, films, foams, petroleum production services, oil and gas production, agricultural chemicals, pharmaceuticals, and consumer products, with about half of sales in the United States.

The management personality could be described as decentralized with highly informal internal communications. A flat organization, minimizing the problem of multilevel communication and action, is favored. Flexibility and short response time are always stressed over tight bureaucratic procedure. *Appropriate risk* would be a generally descriptive term except for safety programs and product stewardship. In these areas of industrial health and safe and effective use of products, maximum caution is the norm.

Dow Chemical long ago decided that all three dimensions of the organization must be recognized and optimized. Consequently, a matrix organization is presently employed to guarantee appropriate contributions of functions, geographical management, and product line management. A high percentage of the members of the board of directors is in active management.

New products are based on both scientific innovation and rapid adaptation to the good developments of others. All the major functions are in reasonably good balance.

In politics, it is customary for a corporation to take a reasonably active position in the United States. Outside the United States, the view is quite different. A company knows that it is a guest in a foreign country—invited there for the mutual benefit of guest and host. It is the company's job to help in the economic development of the host country, and to create jobs. It seems inappropriate for a corporation to be active in promoting political or social change.

Personnel policies are clear. Dow believes in a lean organization. This approach necessitates hiring only the highest-quality people and giving them superior compensation and job opportunity. Turnover is low, and very few new hires take place at management levels. Thus a manager has absorbed a real sense of the company's personality while growing up, which minimizes the need for handbooks and formal training. The headquarters is located in a small city with a population of 40,000, which contributes greatly to close understanding and communication of company objectives. The first paragraph of the published objectives of The Dow Chemical Company follows:

> To seek maximum long-term profit growth as the primary means to ensure the prosperity and well-being of our employees, stockholders and our customers by making products that the people of the world need, and to do so better than anyone else.

This goal of serving customers, employees, suppliers, and society is, more simply stated, to maximize physical growth over the long term while maintaining a return on investment (ROI) which will supply needed cash. In goal setting and in planning, we try to heed the words of Henry David Thoreau: "Our life is frittered away by detail. Simplify, simplify." In understanding and formulating business strategy, there are seldom more than four or five *really significant* variables. Many additional minor factors exist, but the strategic effort cannot risk being diluted by trivia. It is better to deemphasize these minor considerations and concentrate on the few make-or-break factors which really matter.

The organization is unusual in that a small corporate organization, under 400 people, ties together the activities of nearly 60,000 employees around the world. The corporate management is almost entirely separate from the management of the U.S. Area.

This extended explanation of the basic corporate personality is a necessary preamble to a description of strategic planning methods. The system which works for one company may be completely unsuited to another. It can be categorically stated that no one standard system should be blindly copied. Every system must be tailored specifically to the unique personality and objectives involved.

Our strategic planning must blend the product line and geographic objectives around the world. Operations management is divided into the following geographic areas: United States, Europe (including Africa and the Middle East), Canada, Latin America, Pacific, and Brazil. It is predictable that planning methods used must be very different as we go from the United States with $5 billion of sales to Brazil with $300 million and a limited product line. A system which is ideal for the United States would be entirely unsuited to the smaller areas. We must search for the really significant threads which are important to *all* areas and build a corporate system which is a "least common denominator" for all parts of the world.

Detailed numbers systems are not very friendly and ordinarily fail to motivate people properly. The minimum basic measures which can define a strategic direction are:

- Physical growth rate
- ROI
- A brief statement of strategic intent

Emphasizing these factors results in a very simple numbers system, easy to understand and easy to remember.

For strategic purposes, these three simple factors are surprisingly complete. Our time perspective on major existing product lines extends to seven years ahead. Experience has shown that five years is too short and ten years too long. Obviously, entirely new product lines or energy planning must encompass a much longer period—sometimes up to twenty years.

Table 4-1 Strategy Alternatives

Basic strategy	Action
A. Maintain present strong position	Hold present market share.
B. Fertilize heavily to penetrate market	Increase market share by aggressive selling and strong technical backup. Sacrifice some ROI short term to achieve acceptable position.
C. Diligent normal management	Maintain or slightly increase market share—make this product line self-sufficient or better on cash flow. Employ tight price and cost control. Improve process aggressively.
D. Harvest	Since the long-term picture appears questionable, maximize near-term cash flow while giving up market share. Minimize backup technical and marketing effort. License technology aggressively.
E. Share risk	Sell a share of operation.
F. Prune	Go out of business gracefully.
G. Opportunistic sales	Sell available material without heavy support or promotional program.

There are not very many *basic* strategies available for managing product lines (which we call *planning units*). The items listed in Table 4-1 have been found to describe the alternatives ordinarily employed regardless of the specific product line.

The application of Table 4-1 can be summarized in a seven-year grid as follows:

	United States		Europe		Canada		Latin America		Pacific		Total	
Product A	7 / 30	C	5 / 30	C	30 / 20	B	0 /	G	13 / 20	B	6 / 30	C
Product B	8 / 24	B/C	17 / 25	B/C	8 / 20	B/C	10 / 26	B/C	15 / 18	B/C	11 / 25	B/C

A Maintain leadership
B Penetration
C Normal balanced management
D Harvest
E Share risk
F Prune
G Opportunistic sales

The top number in the box is the targeted physical growth rate. The lower number is the ROI before taxes. Discounted cash flow or net present value could be employed, but we have found that a simple ROI on all capital employed works better for generalized seven-year strategic purposes.

According to the seven-year grid, in this case, product A in the United States would have a goal of growing at 7 percent per year during the next seven years to achieve an ROI before taxes of 30 percent while employing a basic strategy of diligent normal management. The 7 percent growth rate would parallel expected growth of the total market. Activity would center around process and cost improvements to guarantee that the product line generates enough cash to maintain or exceed its own capital investment needs.

It should be clear that this system of representation is not designed for auditing performance except in a general way. Its chief purpose is to facilitate agreement on meaningful differentiated goals for each major planning unit (MPU) in each geographical area of the world.

Product line management develops product strategies according to a specific process. Product line management begins by understanding the present market for a product in the given country. We must know the current physical volume, the current price level, past growth rates, and projected future growth rates. We must objectively evaluate our strengths and weaknesses, in regard to both technology and acceptance by customers. We must evaluate competitive strengths and weaknesses as well as probable actions. (Not always do these actions logically follow strengths and weaknesses.) We must determine the optimum market share objective, the best balance between growth and ROI. This, of course, is just about the most difficult and sophisticated business decision we encounter.

We must define the projected future unit capital requirements, since we always intend to grow in healthy product lines. We must know whether this optimum product strategy supplies cash or requires cash from the rest of the organization. We can then target the unit margin goal which must be maintained on this product in day-to-day management. We then develop concise statements to describe the management approach on critical factors. We try to limit these strategies to one written page plus one page of charts. And then, most important of all, we must implement these plans aggressively. Strategies are reviewed at least every year—more often if necessary.

The whole approach is to determine where we *need to be* in seven years and then define the strategy and action required to arrive there successfully. Product management teams made up of R&D, manufacturing, and marketing representatives operate within the individual geographic areas. Global product planning meetings bring together product business managers from each area. This type of activity takes place when needed—as near to "real time" planning as we can make it. We do not believe in yearly strategic planning orgies during which decisions are arrived at through personal boredom and fatigue.

The foregoing has described the bottom-up aspects of strategic product planning as practiced by each product management group in each area. It also describes the methods used to develop an overall interrelated global product strategy. Obviously, no good management system can be purely bottom-up or top-down. It must involve a dynamic combination of both.

A detailed financial simulation model of the whole company has been employed since the early 1960s to test various alternatives—the most important being physical growth rate and ROI for the whole corporation. Varying operating and financial policies can be tested until a reasonable combination is developed. Then corporate planning integrates overall goals with the buildup of the separate MPUs, or product lines. Similarly, the growth and ROI goals of geographical areas are developed to match the corporate goal. Cutting and fitting in both the geographical and the product dimensions develop the needed capital program, including needed diversification.

At the corporate level, the strategic planning approach is largely qualitative with the use of simple numbers and codes. It stresses examination, introspection, and integrated, meaningful direction. It is not designed to provide a basis for tight performance measures. These are provided through a separately administered one-year profit plan and a five-year capital plan.

Each operating area is free to develop its own detailed strategic planning system as required. The particular system designed for the U.S. Area follows.

STRATEGIC PLANNING IN THE U.S. AREA

The previous discussion dealt with the broader corporate issues. This section will describe the planning process as it is practiced in the U.S. Area. The U.S. Area is the largest area, and the most complex. As befits a truly international company, in a typical year, the international areas will account for about half of total corporate sales and profits, while the U.S. Area provides more than half of the production capacity of the company—as domestic plants produce products for export sale. As a consequence, the U.S. Area must manage an asset base that is about 65 percent of the corporate total. The U.S. Area has also, by design, retained basic R&D responsibility for the company.

As a result, the U.S. Area remains responsible not only for its own domestic sales and profits but also for a larger portion of corporate assets and R&D resources, which must be managed in concert with overall corporate goals in support of the global system.

This discussion will touch on the following elements of the planning process in the U.S. Area:

- Organizational environment
- Planning system overview
- Product planning
- Capital planning
- U.S. Area strategy statement

A generalized product strategy example, based on actual practice, is included.

Organization

Each Dow geographic area has a different objective and a different cultural environment in which to achieve those objectives. This results in each area having its own unique organizational structure. Planning needs also vary by area, and each area organizes its planning activity to suit its requirements. The various areas do have a responsibility to be responsive to corporate goals and information requirements. A common accounting system is used around the world, and so far as possible, a common planning vocabulary and data base.

U.S. Area Management Structure The U.S. Area is large and extremely complex, with over 30,000 employees, sales in 1980 of over $5 billion, five major integrated production sites, many satellite plant locations, and a capital base of over $6 billion. The planning challenge is to establish and maintain a movement in the desired strategic direction while pushing decision making down as far in the organization as possible, and allowing maximum flexibility so that each business can set and meet its own specific objectives.

This need for executive control, coupled with decentralized decision making, is met through a matrix of strong functional management overlaid with a business and product management organization. Figure 4-1 outlines this concept.

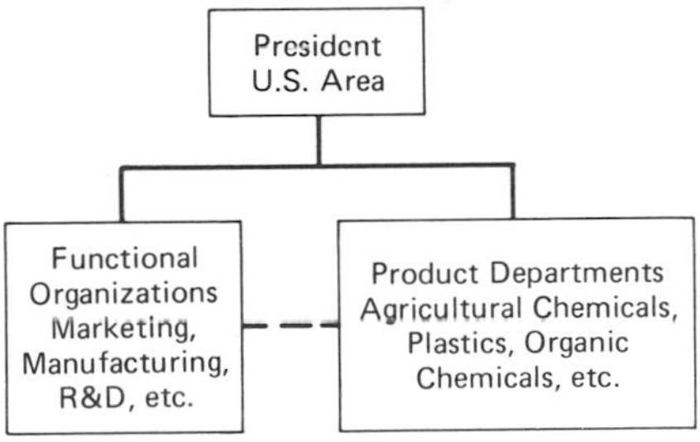

Area Organization Is a Matrix.
Matrix Consists of Functions and Products.
Functions and Products Have Own Line Organizations.
Functions and Products Are Coordinated by Operating Board (Top Managers) and Business Teams (Representatives of Products and Key Functions).
Functions Are Cost Centers While Products Are Profit Centers.
All Budgets Approved by Functions and Product Departments.

FIGURE 4-1
Outline of U.S. Area management structure.

The intent is to ensure that functional expertise and responsibility for operational results are maintained, while at the same time, functional activity is integrated toward the accomplishment of defined product goals and objectives. Functional management is carried on through a generally conventional line organization; the product management is accomplished through the product department organization, which has its own line organization.

Figure 4-2 fills in a few more boxes, and shows graphically how functional integrity is maintained while business and product integration across the functions is achieved through business and product management teams operating at the product level.

Business integration is achieved at the business team level. Business management teams (BMTs) are composed of functional representatives from marketing, R&D, and manufacturing, and chaired by a business manager. The business manager for each business is responsible for integrating the functional activity toward optimizing short- and long-term profitability.

The typical business is further divided into product management teams (PMTs) composed of functional representatives, with specific responsibility for a product, which perform the same integration function at the product level. Any team member designated by the business manager may chair a PMT. The PMT is responsible to the BMT for the profit performance of its particular portion of the business. The individual functional team members are, of course, responsible to their management for the execution of their functional responsibility.

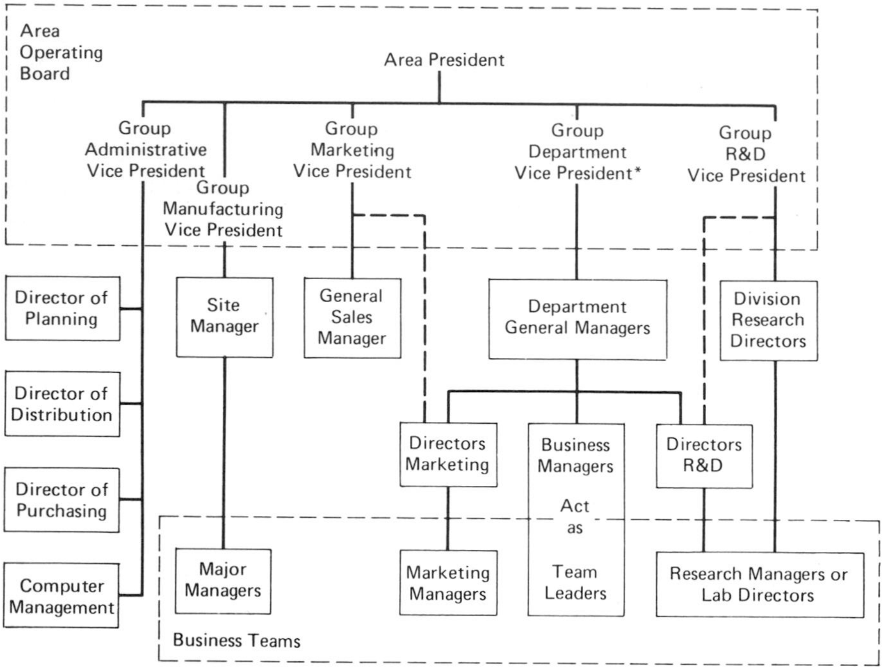

*Eleven department general managers; three report to group department vice president; the others report to area president, or group administrative vice president and group manufacturing vice president.

FIGURE 4-2
Detailed U.S. Area management structure.

Organizational Environment An organization of this type will not work universally in all corporate cultures. Its use requires an organization which is comfortable with shared responsibility and teamwork. It works best in an environment as free as possible from ingrained bureaucracy—in a lean organization in which everyone is challenged and stretched to expand his or her job to encompass whatever needs to be done.

The U.S. Area organization can be characterized by several descriptive traits:

- "Home-grown" management
- Teamwork and consensus
- Broad management experience
- People-oriented philosophy
- Matrix management and controlled friction
- Organizational commitment
- Informal style and easy communication

With very few exceptions, management at all levels has worked together for years, everyone having joined the company at entry level and grown up together. This results in an informal atmosphere that leads to the development of the high trust level that is necessary for teamwork and a consensual approach to work—and ensures that the inevitable friction is in fact controlled. The organization's commitment to people and their development leads to a high degree of commitment to the company; it results in middle and senior management with typically broad management experience obtained through a number of job assignments over the years.

An organization such as this will tend to do its planning and set its direction through a process of consensus, in which there is seldom a "final" direction imposed by executive management. There is a process of evolution in which, as circumstances change and the organization responds to it, the right direction emerges. The strategic direction, when it is finally articulated, will tend to be a *confirmation* rather than a call for a radical new course.

The matrix organization provides the means for taking this consensual approach to planning activity, while allowing for strong functional organizations at the product line level which can, and do, make and implement operating decisions on very short notice as circumstances dictate.

This does not at all imply a passive planning role for senior management. As explained later on, the general approach is toward the establishment of a general direction, with specific performance objectives by the operating board. This leaves room for flexibility at the individual business level for each to plan those strategic actions appropriate for that business. These, in turn, are reviewed by the responsible senior management and recycled as necessary until the "pieces" are compatible both with the overall general direction and with each other.

This process is continuous, without a beginning or an end. The formal planning process is meant to provide a format for and systematic approach to this continuous examination of alternatives. The actual planning is done by the responsible business management, and the responsibility for execution and results remains with them.

Planning System Overview

Role of the U.S. Planning Department Planning, both short- and long-term, is an integral part of management at all levels. A central planning group, regardless of size or expertise, cannot effectively plan the activities of a large and complex organization. Effective planning, from short-term operating plans to long-range strategic planning by top management, can be done only by those responsible for the results.

The primary function of a central planning group is to *create an environment* conducive to effective planning, and to *provide a structure* which will maximize the benefits obtained from planning activity, while allowing maximum freedom of action and approach throughout the organization.

The small professional central group *designs* planning systems, *administers* those systems on a consistent basis throughout the area, and *provides information* of an aggregate nature (such as economic forecasts) which helps *define the environment* in which the organization operates. Further, it acts as the *focal point for aggregating data* from sources throughout the organization and for *presenting it* in meaningful form to management.

The department has a specific responsibility for these systems and programs:

- U.S. Area strategy statement
- Capital planning system
- Product strategy system
- Economic forecasting
- Economic planning
- Operational (production) planning system
- Special projects and reports
- Functional leadership

All these activities interrelate so that, when combined with the annual profit planning cycle, they provide an overall framework for the planning effort, from the setting of overall area objectives to the detailed annual profit planning in support of those objectives.

To carry out these activities, the department has a small group of professionals (fewer than twenty), organized as shown in Figure 4-3.

Profit Planning versus Strategic Planning Most business organizations prepare an annual profit plan. A great deal of time is spent on this, and since the overall process is known generally as *profit planning*, a significant part of the organization assumes, that by completing the cycle, they have engaged in planning. In reality, they have completed a budgeting exercise; the profit plan really represents a monthly operating budget for each function. The primary and essential purpose of a one-year profit plan is to allocate people and expense resources for the next year, and provide management with a basis for exception reporting throughout the organization. The completion of the profit planning cycle does not ensure that what was planned was what should have been planned, or that the overall effort will take the organization where it wants to go. In fact, annual repetitions of a one-year budgeting horizon will inevit-

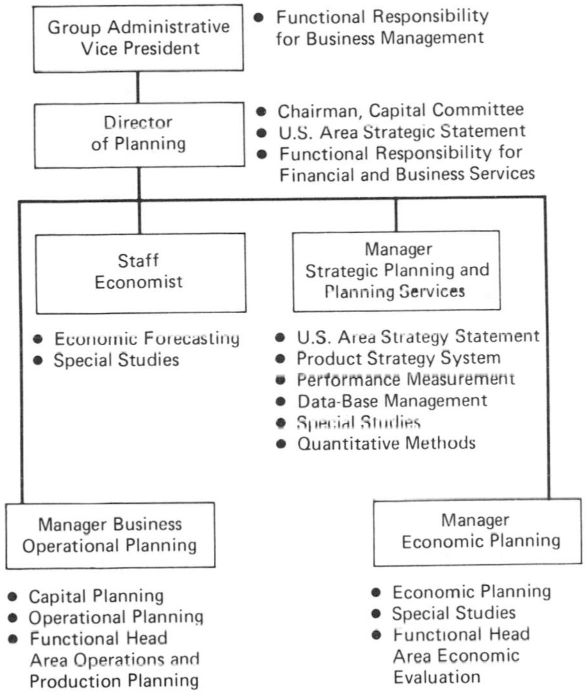

FIGURE 4-3
Organization of small professional group.

ably result in an organization going in circles, completely analogous to people caught in a snowstorm who, without landmarks, will always walk in a circle while believing that they are moving directly toward a distant but unseen goal.

The secret, of course, is to ensure that the annual budgeting process does not take place in a vacuum. The strategic planning process is designed to provide a framework for viewing the future so that each succeeding one-year plan is a step toward an identified goal. A five-year plan should be done in the same highly detailed way as a one-year budgeting plan; the emphasis must be more qualitative as we attempt to identify direction and position as opposed to numerical precision. A highly structured numerical approach will actually work against the development of a viable longer-term plan, for the organization eventually becomes bogged down in numerical detail.

Strategic Planning Process: An Overview The strategic planning process consists of three components: the product strategy cycle, capital planning, and the area strategy statement. In practice, these three components are intertwined in such a way that there is no "correct" order for discussion; at various times, each provides input to and utilizes output from the others as part of an ongoing process.

Many discussions of possible planning approaches focus on the organizational flow of planning information and decisions, and characterize a bottom-up process in which planning activity takes place at the lowest possible level and flows upward, as opposed to a top-down process in which the activity and directional decisions are determined at the executive level and flow downward for execution. Unfortunately, many such discussions imply that the two approaches are mutually exclusive when, in fact, they can and should be *mutually supportive.*

For the mechanically inclined, the process can be viewed as a fluid coupling, driven on one end by the bottom-up product strategy cycle, and on the other by the top-down strategy statement. During part of the process the system is driven by the many individual financial and product strategy inputs from the product strategy cycle, as described in the Planning by Product section which follows. After some aggregation and analysis, the system may be driven by the strategic statement, which outlines executive management's expectation, as *tempered* by product input and capital opportunities and constraints (see the U.S. Area Strategy Statement section later in this chapter). There is not a requirement that there be an *exact* meshing with area total at the product plan level, nor that the reverse be true for area totals, hence the fluid coupling analogy. The two components can work together and absorb some slippage while moving in a common direction.

Since there is no "in the beginning" in an ongoing regenerative process, a more detailed explanation can start with any component. For present purposes, the discussion of the process will arbitrarily follow this order:

- Planning by product: The product strategy cycle
- Capital planning: Setting priorities
- U.S. Area strategy statement: Overall direction

Planning by Product: The Product Strategy Cycle

In a large commercial organization with a diversified product portfolio, it is easy to forget that the marketplace ultimately determines the degree of success the company will have. But, the marketplace is not monolithic any more than the company is. Each product must successfully compete in its own market against its own set of competitors. It is essential that attention be focused on the health and prospects of each product line to ensure that we are not only optimizing the contribution of each product but are also optimizing the overall use of resources by setting appropriate product and capital priorities.

To accomplish this we:

- Identify our relevant product portfolio by establishing MPUs.
- Establish a format for qualitative information and display quantitative data.
- Encourage the development of product strategies at the product management team and business team level.
- Aggregate the data in a central data base to provide a basis for capital planning, area strategic analysis, and recycle and feedback to the various businesses. (This section will describe the process in more detail.)

MPU Definition: What Are We Managing? The selection and definition of business units is key to the overall product planning process. The product portfolio for the U.S. Area consists of about eighty MPUs. In general, MPUs should meet these criteria:

1. Sufficient size to warrant commitment to planning
2. Managed by a single business or product team
3. Identifiable capital base
4. Reasonably similar market segments

There is no fixed set of quantitative criteria, other than a reasonably strict guideline for size as measured by sales dollars. Figure 4-4 illustrates some considerations.

The primary guideline in MPU definition is whether a single strategy makes sense for the entire business unit. In most cases, the definition logically falls along naturally occurring organizational lines. The exceptional cases require the greatest effort and must be continually reevaluated.

As competitive product differentiation in the marketplace increases, more emphasis must be put on the end-use markets in defining an MPU. Commodity products will tend to be managed on the basis of their capital base, while more specialized products will need more strategic emphasis on the market in which they are competing.

Strategic Format The qualitative and quantitative data required for each MPU should be kept to a minimum of perhaps eight one- or two-page

Product Type	Strategy Concepts	MPU Organization
"Building blocks"	▪ Capital planning ▪ Make versus buy ▪ Cost control ▪ Integration of derivatives	Should include all plants within the area—dedicated precursors as well.
"Coproducts"	▪ Cost allocation ▪ Balanced output	Should be included in the same MPU to avoid inconsistent strategies and cost conflicts.
Merchant products	▪ Demand forecast ▪ Profitability ▪ Integration of functions ▪ Competition ▪ Cost and product strategies	Should include unique capital base and relatively homogeneous markets. Should be split if market definition does not allow a consistent strategy.

FIGURE 4-4
Major Planning Unit Definition.

components. Each component should address a specific decision-making process.

A typical individual product strategy will consist of:

- Product strategy
- Supply and demand balances
- Competitive analysis
- Inventory management
- Financial plan
- Strategic summary

A complete generalized product strategy is presented on pp. 4-20 to 4-27. The following discussion will describe the content and use of the individual components.

▪ *Product Strategy.* This one- to two-page written strategy highlights the important qualitative considerations, objectives, and functional actions that are considered key to the product's future development. In addition, the strategy summarizes the important business and competitive assumptions affecting the strategy. See pp. 4-20 and 4-21 for an example.

▪ *Supply and Demand Balances.* The purpose of this analysis is to estimate the physical volume growth in specific areas with the following strategy implications:

Shifts in relative market position among competitors

Anticipated industry growth rates
Anticipated Dow and industry operating rates
Timing of anticipated expansions
Relative export and import levels

The bases used in these documents should be consistent with those in other documents—particularly the competitive analysis.

Three balances are prepared: a global internal Dow balance showing the global impact on the product, a U.S. industry balance, and an internal U.S. Area balance (see pp. 4-24, 4-25, and 4-26).

- *Competitive Analysis.* An analysis of the relative positions of competitors is essential to the development of a realistic strategy. The competitive evaluation must be brutally impartial to be meaningful. Specific strategy implications include:

Relative positions and trends in the competitive market place
Relative strengths and weaknesses among competitors
Alternative uses of products and pricing implications
The attractiveness of the marketplace itself

A completed competitive analysis is shown on p. 4-22.

- *Inventory Management.* This one-page section summarizes the inventory plans for the product and focuses attention on the working capital required to support the business (p. 4-23).

- *Financial Plan.* This one-page summary represents the quantitative outcomes of the product strategy, and compares the forecast values with recent history. The implications of these documents include:

Impact of physical volume changes
Capital requirements (including working capital)
Profitability trends
Impact of pricing and costs changes
Deployment of resources
Changes in market position

(See p. 4-26.)

- *Strategic Summary.* This one-page section summarizes the whole document, and includes:

The objective
Competitive environment
Strengths and weaknesses
Key plans
Price and volume trends
Major capital projects

(See p. 4-27.)

Strategy Implications In general, successful MPUs tend to have the following characteristics:

1. A sufficient critical mass ratio[1] is attainable within the time frame of the strategy.
2. Historical profitability and future profitability are consistent and at acceptable levels.
3. Physical volume growth rates are higher than average.
4. Relative competitive strength is high, and a significant competitive advantage exists.
5. The industry is an attractive place for investment.
6. Sustainable differentiated position within the industry and/or cost position that is better than competition.

The fundamental elements of the business are generally more revealing than specific profit objectives.

Analytical Relationships The communication of aggregate MPU data is an important part of the planning process. The relationship of forecast change in "Competitive Strength" versus "Critical Mass" (p. 4-27) tends to characterize the strategic positions of Dow and the other firms in that industry. [On a more subjective basis, the industry environment grid (p. 4-27) is a useful means of communicating the relative attractiveness of the industry for future investment as well as the specific elements affecting this appraisal.] The financial plan (p. 4-26) is a specific statement regarding performance objectives.

Aggregate trends are also useful. Cumulative values for operating margin and sales for product types (commodities, differentiated commodities, and specialties) and cash generators, as well as other organizational groups, provide a necessary perspective. Variations in relative concentration and strength also provide insight into competitive strategies.

Strategy Development Process The strategy development process can be described as a *bottom-up process with recycle*. The historical data are part of the normal accounting process. The initial forecasts result from a consensus of the PMTs using benchmark inputs from the hydrocarbons department, financial groups, and others. While the individual groups may vary in their relative level of optimism, the common bases serve to tie the forecasts together in a meaningful way.

The PMT strategies are then reviewed by the business team, business manager, department general manager, legal department, and finally approved by the U.S. Area group vice president responsible for the

[1]Critical mass ratio is the firm's domestic market share divided by the aggregate of the top three suppliers in the relevant market.

product department. All product strategies are reviewed by the U.S. Area operating board during scheduled oral presentations by the product department general managers. This process serves as an excellent communications network, and provides a single, fundamental view of the MPU's prospects.

Product Strategy Cycle The *product strategy cycle* is the time frame in which the strategy development process takes place. The process begins in January, when the format instructions and forecast bases are sent to the business managers responsible for each MPU. The updating of history and the initial cost forecasts are developed by the accounting and financial services functions. By early March, the PMTs are beginning to develop detailed forecasts for price and volume, competitor evaluations, and so on. By mid-April, the strategies are refined to a state at which the business team can provide its input, and the recycle begins. In May, the strategies are complete and have passed through the entire approval process, including formal presentations to area executives.

The one-year budgeting and profit planning process begins in June. With the strategic process completed, we can now approach the one-year planning cycle as the first step in a five-year program.

Product Strategy Example As noted earlier, a complete product strategy example is presented on the following pages (4-20 to 4-27). This example is based on actual practice, but has been generalized. The items in this example are:

PRODUCT STRATEGY - DOWPROD

I. Objectives and Goals:

Continue to penetrate fast growing "high tech" market segment while maintaining ROS at approximately 26% (ROI at 21%). Maintain market position with timing of expansions and product differentiation rather than price. Physical volume should increase 11%/year during 1980-85 compared with 8% for the industry thereby regaining historical market position.

II. Strategy (Plans):

A. Research and Development

1. Develop "high activity" Dowprod for electronic component applications and convert Midland Train C for commercial production (120 MM#/year) by 1Q82. (2 man years)

2. Develop new "HTA" catalyst system to increase yields from 96% to 98% (1Q 1981) (3 man years).

3. Expand Product Stewardship program to include 1 day seminar to all major customers and distributors.

4. Monitor performance of Marco Manufacturing's "high tech" products.

5. Maintain R&D expenditures at approximately 2.5% of trade sales.

B. Manufacturing

1. Start up 245 MM lb expansion (Train C-Texas Div.) by 1Q 1983 and shut down 120 MM lb Train A in Midland.

2. Start up 505 MM lb grass roots plant (Train A - Western) by 2Q 1984. HTA technology - 25% reduction in conversion costs.

3. Expand "finishing capacity" (Train A - Central) and increase capacity from 120 to 175 MM lbs by 1985.

4. Shut down three trains (Texas Train A and Midland Trains A & B) for maintenance (2 months) during 1981 taking advantage of lower operating rate. (Effective 93% Dow operating rate). Add an additional 65 MM lbs of attainable capacity through equipment modifications.

C. Marketing

1. Increase prices an average of 14.3% per year during 1980-85 period to maintain ROS at approx. 26%. Sacrifice less profitable business in "low tech" segment to maintain ROS.

2. Increase trade demand 10% per year during 1980-85.

3. Concentrate resources in "high tech" market segment. Deploy 1 man year for market development in electronic component segment.

4. Increase percentage of business covered by multi-year contracts from 42% to 60%.

5. Explore co-producer sales to smooth out capacity additions. (Especially Consolidated).

6. Maintain marketing expenses at approximately 2% of trade sales.

D. Scenario

The product strategy assumes an industry merchant volume growth rate of 8% per year. It assumes an average inflation rate of 10% for non-hydrocarbon items and an average 16% per year for hydrocarbon based raw material (year to year values consistent with Hydrocarbons Department forecasts). The "reinvestment" net unit return for new facilities is estimated to be $0.368 per pound. Assume pricing of purchased MJ-5 will increase 14.5% per year with no anticipated availability problems.

III. Competitive Environment (Tri-Pol Industry):

It is assumed that Marco Manufacturing will continue an aggressive penetration strategy in the "low tech" and "mid tech" market segments causing a profitability decline of about 3 ROS points. Consolidate chemicals is expected to lose position due to its commitment to the derivatives (ESSM) business and its substantially higher cost position (process and raw material). U.S. Petrochemical does not appear to be strongly committed to the Tri-Pol market place and perceives it to be one of several outlets for its domestic ES business. New products will be a major competitive factor. Products designed for the "high tech" market will provide a selling price premium of 6-15% over "mid-tech" products and 15-20% premium over "low tech" products. Technical support will be another major competitive element with "high tech" customers willing to pay a premium for Dow technical support.

MPU Dowprod

DATE 1/29/81

EVALUATION -- COMPETITIVE SITUATION -- TRI-POL

COMPETITORS

	WT	DOW	Consolidated Chem	U.S. Petrochemical	Marco Manufacturing
US CAPACITY MM#		1485 (32.8%)	1800 (39.7%)	700 (15.4%)	550 (12.1%)
% 1980 TR DEM		29.7% (CM = 0.350)*	28.9% (CM = 0.363)*	20.2% (CM = 0.254)*	21.1% (CM = 0.178)*
% 1985 TR DEM		34% (CM = 0.409)*	24% (CM = 0.287)*	17% (CM = 0.203)*	25% (CM = 0.329)*
'80-85 % CGR (Trade Vol)		11.0% per year	4% per year	4.3% per year	12% per year
PROCESS TECHNOLOGY		Continuous Reactor (MMJ type)	Semi Batch	Continuous (MMJ type)	Continuous (Marco technology)
RM POSITION		Makes 100% ES Makes 40% MJ-85 Makes 100% Ethylene	Buys 100% ES Makes 40% MJ-85 Buys 100% Ethylene	Makes 100% ES Buys 100% MJ-85 Makes 100 Ethylene	Makes 100% ES* Makes 100% MJ-85 Makes 100% Ethylene *Announced ES expansion of 1 billion lbs.
PRODUCT LINE: PERFORMANCE COMPLETENESS		High quality and full product line. Excellent position in "high tech" market segments.	High quality and full product line. Large % of sales in "high tech" market segments.	Most products in "low tech" and "mid tech" markets	Good product quality. Beginning to penetrate some of the "high tech" market segments.
INTERNAL USES: (% TOTAL PROD)		DOWRET 150 MM #'s ESSM 100 MM #'s Use is approx 25% of production	ESSM = 1000 MM #'s Use is approx 56% of production	No known internal uses.	Developing ESSM Capabilities (20 MM #'s) Use approx 5%
FACTOR	WT				
Prod Perform	20	A-	A	C	B
Process Tech	15	A	C	A	A
RM Position	25	B+	C	B	A
Pricing	25	A+	B	D	C
TS&D	5	A	A	C	A
Mkting	5	B+	B	C	C
Plant Loc	5	A	B	C	A
TOTAL	100	A	B-	C+	B+

*CM = Critical Mass Ratio (firm's % of U.S. Trade Demand/Sum of the top three firms in the industry).

CDM 1/29/81

INVENTORY MANAGEMENT

PRODUCT Dowprod

MM UNITS

	'79	'80	'81	'82	'83	'84	'85
MINIMUM	67.4	65.8	75.2	81.3	88.1	103.3	112.4
MAXIMUM	112.3	109.8	125.4	135.5	146.8	172.2	187.4
AVERAGE	89.8	87.8	100.3	108.4	117.5	137.8	149.9

MM DOLLARS

	'79	'80	'81	'82	'83	'84	'85
MINIMUM	13.8	15.5	19.6	24.5	30.1	40.9	51.3
MAXIMUM	23.0	25.8	32.7	40.8	50.2	68.2	85.5
AVERAGE	18.4	20.6	26.2	32.6	40.2	54.6	68.4

I/D

	'79	'80	'81	'82	'83	'84	'85
MINIMUM	.73	.76	.65	.65	.65	.65	.65
MAXIMUM	1.48	1.36	1.20	1.40	1.20	1.20	1.20
AVERAGE	.97	.92	.90	.90	.85	.85	.85

Notes: (1) Min., Max., Ave., refer to month end inventories during year shown.

(2) Provide units only if the unit consistent within product family.

(3) Use standard costs from the financial plan for the year shown to determine dollar projections.

(4) I/S refers to month end inventory divided by the month's trade export, and internal use demand on a standard cost basis (consistent with Financial Plan).

RATIONALE : (Comment as appropriate on desired service level, seasonality, fixed/variable portions of inventory, building to delay capital spending or cover annual shortfall, etc.)

Desired level no less than 0.65, with maximum at 1.20 during forecast period. Decreasing I/D ratios result from lower operating ratio during 1983-85. Maximum inventory levels will occur as trains are shut down for significant maintenance.

CDM 1/27/81

INDUSTRY SUPPLY/DEMAND BALANCE - TRI-POL

	1976	1977	1978	1979	1980	1981	1982	1983	1984	1985
US TRADE DEMAND	1650	1833	1929	2270	2420	2655	2720	2910	3210	3565
CAPTIVE USE	1150	1200	1200	1350	1270	1372	1481	1600	1728	1866
EXPORT	250	276	283	350	275	367	390	429	472	519
TOTAL US MFG	3050	3309	3412	3970	3965	4394	4591	4939	5410	5950
TOTAL CAPACITY	3302	3368	3580	4270	4270	4535	4885	5130	5515	6370
INDUSTRY BALANCE	252	59	168	300	305	141	294	191	105	420
OPERATING RATE	92.4	98.2	95.3	93.0	92.9	96.9	94.0	96.3	98.1	93.4
PRODUCERS/CAPACITY (ADJUSTED NAME PLATE):										
Dow	902	968	980	1420	1420	1485	1485	1730	2115	2170
Consolidated Ind.	1500	1500	1700	1800	1800	1800	1800	1800	1800	2100*
US Petro Chem	500	500	500	500	500	700*	700	700	700	900*
Marco Manuf.	400	400	400	550	550	550	900*	900	900	1200*
	3302	3368	3580	4270	4270	4535	4885	5130	5515	6370
Dow's % of total	27.3	28.7	27.4	33.3	33.3	33.7	30.4	33.7	38.3	34.1

* anticipated expansions

DOW GLOBAL SUPPLY/DEMAND BALANCE - DOWPROD

- MM Pounds (Prime) -

	1976	1977	1978	1979	1980	1981	1982	1983	1984	1985
Demand	1278	1399	1532	1678	1837	2012	2203	2478	2788	3137
Supply	1332	1465	1595	2035	2150	2290	2401	2646	3031	3366
Balance	54	66	63	357	323	278	198	168	243	229
% Operating Rate	96	95.5	96.1	82.5	85.1	87.9	91.8	94.7	92.0	93.2
Planned Additions:										
USA	0	66	12	440	0	65	0	245	385	55
EUROPE	0	0	65	0	0	0	14	0	0	140
PACIFIC	0	67	0	0	70	0	0	0	0	0
CANADA	0	0	53	0	0	0	0	0	0	140
LATIN AMERICA	0	0	0	0	55	65	0	0	0	0
	0	133	130	440	125	130	111	245	385	335

CDM 01/15/81

FINANCIAL PLAN / DOWPROD

02/16/81 @ 15:51

	1976	1977	1978	1979	1980	1981	1982	1983	1984	1985	GTH H	GTH F
DEMAND (MM LBS)												
TRADE DEMAND	509.9	546.2	540.1	715.1	718.7	796.5	843.2	931.2	1059.3	1212.1	9.0	11.0
SUB DEMAND	156.0	173.0	170.0	215.0	173.0	232.0	250.0	298.0	411.0	305.0	2.6	12.0
USE	200.0	210.0	225.0	238.0	250.0	275.0	316.0	348.0	402.0	432.0	5.7	11.6
TOTAL DEMAND	865.9	929.2	935.1	1168.1	1141.7	1303.5	1409.2	1577.2	1872.3	1949.1	7.2	11.3
SUPPLY (MM LBS)												
EXISTING	902.0	968.0	980.0	1420.0	1420.0	1485.0	1485.0	1485.0	1365.0	1365.0		
AUTHORIZED	.0	.0	.0	.0	.0	.0	.0	245.0	245.0	245.0		
PLANNED	.0	.0	.0	.0	.0	.0	.0	.0	505.0	560.0		
IMPORTS	.0	.0	.0	.0	.0	.0	.0	.0	.0	.0		
PURCHASES	.0	.0	.0	.0	.0	.0	.0	.0	.0	.0		
TOTAL SUPPLY	902.0	968.0	980.0	1420.0	1420.0	1485.0	1485.0	1730.0	2115.0	2170.0	12.0	8.9
% OPERATING RATE	96	96	95	82	80	88	95	91	89	90		
CAPITAL (MM$)												
DIRECT FIXED	63.0	69.0	70.5	121.0	123.0	154.0	164.0	205.0	292.0	298.0	18.2	19.4
ALLOCATED FIXED	111.5	122.1	124.8	214.2	217.7	272.6	290.3	362.9	516.8	527.5	18.2	19.4
WORKING	23.9	27.2	29.0	46.6	52.5	65.0	77.0	98.1	131.7	172.5	21.8	26.9
TOTAL CAPITAL	198.4	218.3	224.3	381.7	393.2	491.6	531.3	666.0	940.5	998.0	18.7	20.5
TOTAL CAPITAL FOR SALES	154.4	170.9	172.8	317.8	324.0	400.6	418.2	532.0	761.7	799.3	20.4	19.8
AVG. NUR($/LBS)												
TRADE NUR	.213	.226	.244	.296	.332	.371	.415	.479	.565	.647	11.7	14.3
SUB NUR	.192	.203	.220	.266	.299	.334	.374	.431	.509	.582	11.7	14.3
UNIT STANDARD COST	.146	.157	.173	.205	.235	.261	.301	.342	.396	.456	12.6	14.2
SALES REVENUE(MM$)												
TRADE SALES	108.6	123.4	131.8	211.7	238.6	295.5	349.9	446.0	598.5	784.2	21.8	26.9
SUB SALES	29.9	35.2	37.3	57.3	51.7	77.5	93.4	128.5	209.0	177.6	14.7	28.0
TOTAL SALES	138.5	158.6	169.1	268.9	290.3	373.0	443.3	574.5	807.5	961.8	20.3	27.1
COST FOR SALE(MM$)												
MANUFACTURING COST	99.2	115.2	125.3	194.5	213.8	273.8	335.6	428.8	593.9	705.6	21.2	27.0
RESEARCH & DEVELOPMENT	2.7	3.1	3.3	5.3	6.0	7.4	8.7	11.2	15.0	19.6	21.8	26.9
SELLING	2.2	2.5	2.6	4.2	4.8	5.9	7.0	8.9	12.0	15.7	21.8	26.9
ADMINISTRATIVE	2.5	2.9	3.0	4.8	5.2	6.7	8.0	10.3	14.5	17.3	20.3	27.1
TOTAL COST OF SALES	106.5	123.6	134.3	208.8	229.7	293.8	359.4	459.2	635.4	758.2	21.2	27.0
OPERATING MARGIN (MM $)	32.0	35.0	34.8	60.1	60.6	79.1	83.9	115.3	172.1	203.6	17.3	27.4
PBT (MM$)	.0	.0	.0	.0	.0	.0	.0	.0	.0	.0		
% ROS	29	28	26	28	25	27	24	26	29	26	-3.6	.4
% ROI												
BOOK ROI	21	21	20	19	19	20	20	22	23	25	-2.5	6.4
TRADE ROI	23	23	23	21	20	22	23	24	26	28	-2.7	6.4
CRITICAL MASS RATIO	.425	.390	.360	.409	.377	.380	.376	.383	.395	.409		
% OF U S TRADE SALES	31	30	28	32	30	30	31	32	33	34		
INDUSTRY VOLUME GROWTH												

DOW USA STRATEGY SUMMARY

Bus.Mgr: S. E. Mehlberg   MPU: Dowprod   Date: 1/29/81

Objective: Low cost and High Product Performance Strategy. Continue penetration of "high tech" segments. Maintain ROS at 26% and ROI at 21%. Maintain market position with product differentiation and timing of capital projects. Continue position as lowest cost producer.

Industry Environment

FACTOR	WT	RATE
Size	.15	+
Technol	.25	+
SD Bal	.15	-
Growth	.25	++
RM/Price	.20	0
Total/Ave	1.0	0.75
Scale is -2 to +2		

Competitive Strength

FACTOR	WT	DOW	Consol	USP	Marco	
Prod Perform	20	A-	A	C	B	
Process Tech	15	A	C	A	A	
RM Position	25	B+	C	B	A	
Pricing	25	A+	B	D	C	
Other	15	A	B	C	B	
TOTAL/AVERAGE	100	A	B-	C+	B+	
1980 % TD VOL*	-	29.7	28.9	20.2	21.1	
1985 % TD VOL*	-	34	24	17	25	

* % of U.S. Trade Demand (Volume)

CRITICAL MASS

COMPETITIVE STRENGTH	>0.25	0.25-0.20	<0.20
HIGH	Dow		Marco
MID	Consol US Pet		
LOW			

Dow Strengths:

1. Raw material position and cost
2. Product line and customer base
3. Freight advantage over Marco & USP ($0.008)
4. Major position in sub sales and derivatives (37%)
5. Leader in development of applications technology

Dow Weaknesses/Vunerability:

1. Penetration pricing by Marco manufacturing
2. Customer resistance to RM/Price pressure
3. Purchase 60% of MI-5 requirements
4. Increasing competition in "high tech" segments
5. Some incursions by "replacement products" into "low tech" and "high tech" segments.

KEY PLANS:

1. Concentrate on new markets in electronic components segment.
2. Develop "HTA" Catalyst system and implement in 1984 capital project.
3. Explore co-producer sales to smooth out Dow operating rate.
4. Expand "Product Stewardship" program.
5. Maintain market position at 34% of US trade sales.
6. Increase prices an average of 14.3% per year during 1980-85 periods.

PRICE/VOLUME (% CHANGE/YEAR)

Trade Sales:	1972-80	1980-85
Price	8.2%	14.3%
Volume: Dow	7.6%	11.0%
Industry	8.0%	8.0%

OPERATING RATE (%)

U.S.A.:	'80	'81	'83	'85
Dow	80.4	87.8	88.3	89.8
Industry	92.9	96.9	96.3	93.4

MAJOR CAPITAL PROJECTS (>$1MM):

1. Train C (Texas Div.) $38MM (TEX 277648). Approved.
2. Modernize Train A (Texad Div) and Trains B & C (Midland) $8MM. Approved. (TEX 277921 and MID 929664).
3. New "grass roots" 505MM lbs. (Train A-Western Div). To be submitted 3 Q 1981.
4. Increase "finishing capacity" (Train A Central Div.) $3MM. To be submitted 1Q 1982.

Capital Planning

The objective of the capital planning system is to ensure that our capital expenditures are directed into the products and projects that are consistent with the strategic objectives of the area, and eliminate a "first-come, first-served" approach to capital investment.

The area's capital planning system integrates the *need* for capital, and

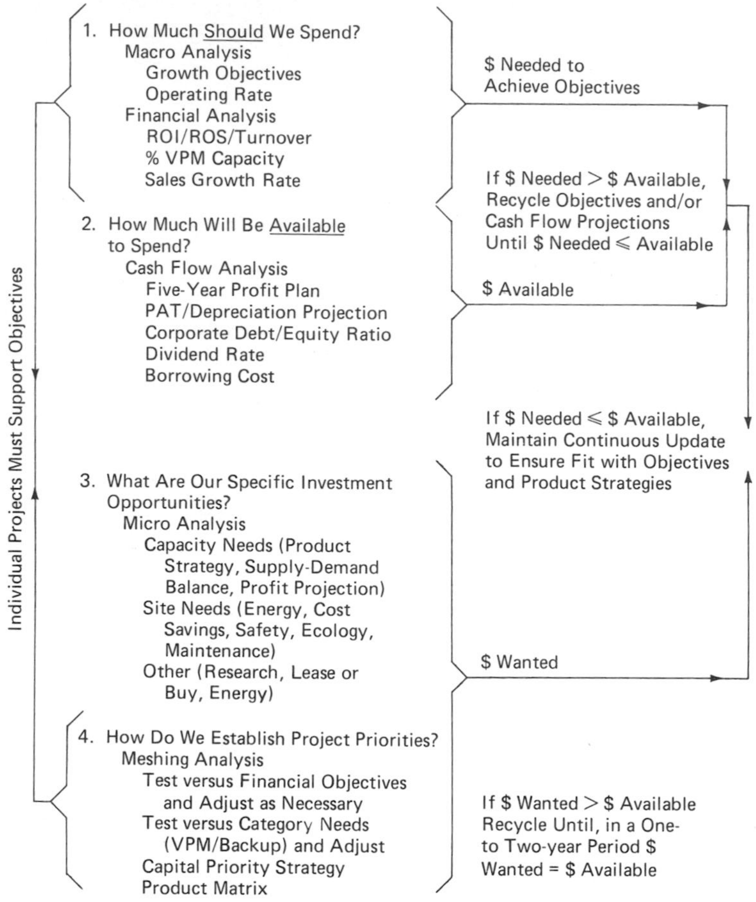

FIGURE 4-5
Integrated capital planning system.

the overall *availability* of cash to meet those needs, with specific project opportunities. A schematic of the system is shown in Figure 4-5.

The first question—*How much should we spend?*—is approached by a strategic analysis of the area as a whole. This approach forces attention to the organization's real objectives and performance goals, and provides a basis for estimating the money needed to achieve those objectives and goals. The strategic analysis includes the determination of growth and operating rate objectives, and the financial parameters, such as ROI in relation to the return on sales, turnover ratios, sales growth, and operating rate necessary to meet those objectives.

The second question—*How much is available to spend?*—is approached on an overall corporate cash flow basis, and is rooted firmly in today's reality. A profitability projection based on our performance expectations will give us an approximation of the cash that our current and intermediate term operations will provide. The net availability of cash will be further influenced by the overall corporate debt/equity ratio, dividend rate, and the cost of borrowing. The U.S. Area is, of course, only one of several geographic areas competing for capital resources. The U.S. share of the available investment capital is dependent upon many factors, the most significant of which are overriding corporate, as opposed to area, objectives.

Since the *need* for capital and the *availability* of cash are functions of entirely separate variables, there must be a resolution between the two. The strategic analysis of the area's need for capital and/or the corporate view of the cash available to the area must be recycled, perhaps by modifying our objectives, until there is a reasonable balance between them.

The third question—*What specific investment opportunities are available to us?*—is the most visible part of the capital planning process, and is often mistaken *for* the total process. This is a project-by-project compilation of additional capacity requirements as determined through the product strategy process; our site needs for such things as energy savings, maintenance, safety, and ecology; and our other requirements such as transportation equipment, and buildings.

The last question—*How do we establish project priorities?*—is perhaps the most crucial. An objective set of criteria should be developed which can be applied to a given project to measure its contribution to the overall goals of the organization. This is basically approached through a meshing analysis in which our project list is tested against the financial objectives, and against the need for a proper balance between new capacity and backup capital.

The capital project list is in a state of continual flux as new opportunities are identified and other projects dropped or modified, and there will normally be an allocation program in effect since, it is hoped, the opportunities available will exceed the available cash.

Left unrestrained, most of the emphasis will drift toward questions two and three—the availability of cash and the specific investment opportunities. Continuous effort must be placed on the first consideration—what we should spend to meet our strategic objectives—and the last consideration—the establishment and application of capital priorities. Our purpose is to optimize the use of our resources; we work toward meshing the system together to ensure that what we are doing on a product and project basis will take the area where we want it to go. The discussion below covers the system in more detail.

How Much Do We Need to Spend? This question is answered in the context of the organization's strategic objectives, and the economic and business environment in which we expect to be operating. If the performance goals defined by the objectives represent our definition of *success,* then we should be able to define, in macro terms, the capital resources needed to achieve success.

It is important, at this point, not to confuse the issue with the second question—How much do we have to spend? This can come later. Initially we are concerned only with the resources needed to achieve our stated objectives.

Every company will have a different set of resource parameters that are important to it. A consumer products company will need to cope with rapid product turnover, new product development and introduction, massive marketing investment, and relatively low manufacturing capacity investment. By contrast, a large, integrated, basic chemical manufacturer will find that most of its growth resources are needed for capacity additions and asset base maintenance.

The capital model, then, for the U.S. Area is based primarily on the required growth of the manufacturing base and the need for noncapacity site capital. The general logic sequence looks like this:

1. The need for *capacity* growth is a function of:

   Trade volume growth + export volume growth
   + abandonments of existing facilities

2. Then, the need for *new capacity capital* is a function of:

   Capacity growth (point 1 above)
   Present operating rate
   Future operating rate (limiting case)
   Capacity turnover ratio ($sales/$capacity capital)
   Capital inflation rate

3. The need for noncapacity site capital is a function of:

   Manufacturing capital base ($ of plant on replacement basis)
   Site spending ratio (annual site spending/manufacturing capital base)

Note again that the question of *profitability* does not enter into this analysis. Profits will be a key determinant of *availability* of capital, not the *need* for capital to meet stated objectives.

There are other capital demands that will not be defined by this model: nonmanufacturing capacity for service businesses such as the oil well service division, research capital, and specific hydrocarbon and energy projects needed for specific strategic reasons.

Computerization of this macro approach is not required in principle, but the complexity of the solution encouraged the development of an interactive simulation model which will allow on-line goal setting and "what if" analysis of a number of alternative scenarios. This reiterative capability is particularly useful when what we need is compared to what we have to spend.

How Much Will Be Available to Spend? Capital availability is a corporate question beyond the scope of a geographic operating unit. The capital spending budget for the corporation as a whole is a function of current and projected cash flow. Cash flow for our purpose here can be roughly approximated by:

Profit after tax + depreciation = cash flow from operations

The net available for a capital spending program is given by:

Capital budget = cash flow from operations − dividends
± working capital ± external borrowings

Clearly, the most important factor is current and anticipated profitability, but there are a number of important management decisions and philosophical principles which impact heavily on the amount of money which will be spent on new projects.

The dividend rate, both in absolute terms and desired growth, and the corporate philosophy on the use of leverage as measured by the debt/equity ratio goal, are important factors in determining the amount of cash available.

In any event, the overall corporate cash availability and corporate decisions as to dividend policy and financing methods are beyond the scope of any one area operating unit. Each area will make its representations as to the capital each needs to be able to achieve its objectives, and, just as the intra-area project demands will be more than is available, the total will inevitably be more than is available.

An allocation of available capital will be made to each area, based on corporate objectives. For this purpose we can focus our attention on the practical result. A capital availability budget for the U.S. Area is, after appropriate consultation, established. When an unbalance exists between the amount of capital available, and the amount previously determined to be *needed* to meet area objectives, some recycling must occur to bring the two into balance. If the corporate allocation is inflexible, then the area objectives must be modified to conform with the availability of resources.

The recycle process is neutral—neither good nor bad—so long as, during the process, both area and corporate management achieve a *mutual* understanding of what is given up—or gained—by a given allocation of resources.

What Are Our Opportunities?: Project Identification and Planning This part of the capital planning process is the most visible. Each product department and manufacturing division identifies its investment opportunities, screens them for reasonableness, and ends with a listing of specific capital projects defined in terms of direct fixed capital, authorization and spending schedules, and capacity changes. Such a listing could include *new capacity projects* which will result in raw materials for use and end products for sale; *site capital* such as energy conservation, cost savings, maintenance, safety, and ecology, which, while necessary, does not produce new sales; and *others* such as research, energy, and administrative.

The capacity projects are developed by each business taking into consideration the product opportunities existing in their particular marketplace, the area overall strategy, area and global supply and demand balances, and relative product profitability.

Site capital projects, which do not generate new capacity, are developed by each manufacturing division and represent all those things we must do to operate efficiently and safely while maintaining the asset base.

The relative split between these two broad categories varies according to the area and the size and age of its manufacturing base.

This project listing is not a static view of our opportunities. At a minimum, the entire list is updated and reviewed quarterly. New projects are added and others dropped as each moves through the authorization screening process.

The "raw" project listing will invariably add up to more money than is available, and may or may not have an appropriate split between capacity and noncapacity projects. A final step is needed to "close the loop" by establishing and applying product and project priorities to ensure that, in aggregate, the implementation of individual projects will result in the achievement of our profit objectives.

How Do We Establish Priorities?: Tying It Together with Product Strategy and Portfolio Analysis The U.S. Area has adopted a product matrix approach which categorizes products in accordance with two criteria—profitability (the quality and quantity of profits) and competitiveness (cost performance and product performance). The nine-block matrix (Figure 4-6) currently in use contains five levels of product classifications:

GROUP 1 Products in attractive markets with excellent track records of profitability and earnings growth. Strategic emphasis is on ensuring capacity for anticipated growth.

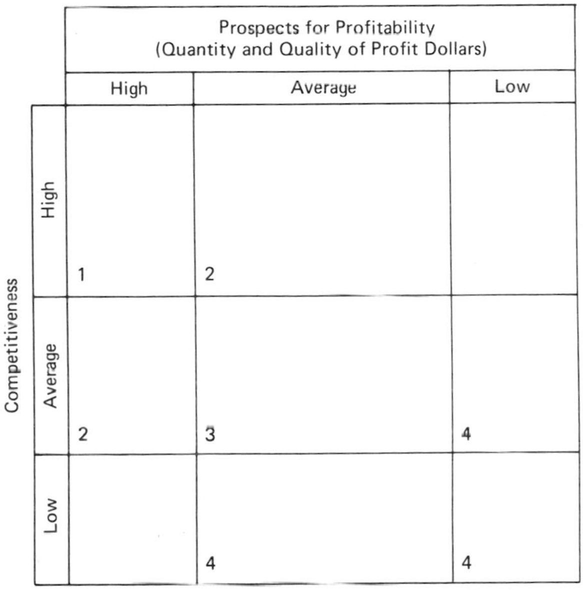

Group 5: New Products Which Will Require Capital for Development.

FIGURE 4-6
Nine-block product matrix.

GROUP 2 Products strong on balance, but average in either profitability, competitiveness, or market attractiveness. Strategic emphasis is on growth but excess capacity should be avoided.

GROUP 3 Products with average profitability, prospects, and competitive position and/or market attractiveness. Strategic emphasis will be on maximizing operating margin with some risk of being short of capacity.

GROUP 4 Products with serious competitive and/or market weakness; perhaps with environmental or health hazard threats, leading to an unacceptable profitability level (or an unacceptable profit growth rate). Strategic emphasis is on maximizing cash generation or developing technical improvements or new markets which will alter its prospects. If there is no prospect for a change in technology or markets, no new capacity capital will be spent.

GROUP 5 New or developing products. These products are not positioned in the matrix. Strategic emphasis is on identifying the opportunity and appropriately funding potential winners.

A clear distinction needs to be made between *resource* allocation—research and marketing resources particularly—and capital allocation. The product matrix should be considered a snapshot in time; new product or process developments and/or marketing efforts may, and do, cause movement in relative positioning. That movement, in turn, may trigger a capital investment that was previously not supported by reasonable performance expectations.

After the major products are positioned relative to one another in this matrix, we have a base from which priorities for capital can be applied to our raw project list. The U.S. Area has established the following capital priority scheme:

	Capacity	Noncapacity*	R&D†
High priority	Groups 1 and 5 products Group 2 products Raw materials (good economics and security of supply)		
Medium priority	Group 3 products		
Low priority	Group 4 products		

*Noncapacity spending will include maintenance, cost savings, oil and gas exploration, energy programs, terminals, distribution equipment, computers, office buildings, and so on.

†R&D spending will include pilot plants and semiplants, offices, and labs.

It is not intended that the sum of the capital project list will match the projected budget exactly year by year. History shows that some projects drop out, and others appear—sometimes unexpectedly. The system must be flexible enough to provide capital for new opportunities. As a rough guideline, we aim at project lists totaling no more than 125 percent of the target three years out, 110 percent two years out, and 100 percent for current year spending.

The end result of the application of this system is a capital project list that should support those projects which will contribute the most toward achieving our overall objectives and maintain an appropriate split between new capacity and site capital.

U.S. Area Strategy Statement: Taking a Broader Perspective

The analogy of fluid coupling was used earlier in describing the balance between the bottom-up and top-down approaches to planning. The product strategy cycle provides an opportunity for the people running the individual businesses to communicate their own strategies and plans, and a portfolio analysis based on the product data helps provide a basis for capital allocation toward our best opportunities.

There is a need occasionally to "drive" the system from the top down, and provide a perspective for the organization as its members go about running their own specific business on a day-to-day basis. In the U.S. Area, this is accomplished by the publication, early in each year, of the U.S. Area Strategy Statement.

The purpose of the document is to provide overall guidance and direction for the organization, while allowing for the flexibility needed for each business to establish and execute its own unique strategies and objectives.

The statement is brief—at least in the context of a guiding document for a multibillion dollar business. It typically runs about twenty pages in length: six or seven pages of text with the remainder being financial and product displays which amplify and tie together the text. The statement covers the next five years specifically, and the next ten to twenty years for product development. Typically, the content would be outlined as:

- *Area objective statement.* A brief statement outlining the business we expect to be in and the direction of growth and diversification.
- *Area performance goals, growth assumptions, and planning assumptions.* An outline of the financial performance goals of the area, given against a background of expected physical volume growth and macroeconomic assumptions. The text is supported by a five-year goal-setting model displaying area performance *given the achievement* of our objectives and goals.
- *Business management.* An overview of our product portfolio, and the general strategic direction we expect over time.
- *Interarea supply strategy.* The U.S. Area is both a major exporter supplying to the rest of the Dow world and an importer from overseas sites. This section helps define our expectations for new capacity and export activity for the next five years.

- *Hydrocarbons and energy.* Hydrocarbon raw materials and power are vital to our future. This section outlines our emphasis and action to protect our base.
- *Capital program.* The capital program objectives and needs, in terms of portfolio management (matrix approach described earlier), capital priorities, and five-year capital plan, are outlined here in text and exhibits.
- *Research.* The new product potentials and process emphasis are outlined in brief text and exhibits.
- *Functional.* Manufacturing, marketing, and support statements of the functional objective are needed.

The finished document is widely used by area management within their own organizations to help establish a background for their own people, and as a check that we are all moving in the same general direction. The statement tends to be a *confirmation* of direction; by design, there are seldom, if ever, any "surprises" as the general approach is articulated.

We do not, at any time, try to "lock" the overall area expectations into a one-number system either by forcing the area to match the aggregation of the prices, or by unilaterally forcing each product piece to fit a preconceived area expectation. The whole process is a continuous and regenerative one, which, when running smoothly, has neither a beginning nor an end, but can be measured, producing an assessment as to progress achieved.

The Chinese have two proverbs—of the many correctly or incorrectly attributed to them—which are appropriate in closing:

> If you don't know where you are going, any road will take you there.

and

> It is difficult to prophesy with accuracy, particularly with respect to the future.

We think that our system will allow us to keep our eye on where we want to go, recognizing that our forecasts will often be wrong and that we can flexibly respond to changing conditions with appropriate new strategies and tactics.

Chapter 5
BUSINESS UNIT STRATEGY

WALTER J. KRUEL
Vice President, Corporate Planning and Development, Lear Siegler, Inc.

LYNN H. GLENNEY
Director of Corporate Planning, Lear Siegler, Inc.

The development of business unit strategy is a dilemma that has faced businesspeople since the beginning of entrepreneurship and industrialization. In the sole proprietorship, strategies are developed by the owner on the basis of knowledge, experience, and perhaps intuition. As a firm becomes more complex, the problem of business unit strategy becomes more difficult because there are so many factors that can bear upon the strategy decision. Concurrently, the range of backgrounds and experiences of the managers becomes diverse. Each person will approach a strategy decision in a different way, based on personal background.

At Lear Siegler, Inc., a complex company with 48 divisions located around the world and 224 product lines, an attempt has been made to bring some order to the strategy development process. We have designed a system whereby the variations in the general market environment, market position, competitive factors, and managerial experiences may all be dealt with in a consistent manner throughout the company. Another aim is to ensure that the pertinent factors that bear on the success or failure of any strategy are identified and dealt with logically.

Obviously, there is no single consistent strategy for all of the company's various lines of business. Each product has its own unique set of characteristics which influences decision making. Consequently, there is no single set of questions that will provide all of the proper information on which to base decisions.

In view of this condition, we developed a broad set of questions which we believed were appropriate in determining product-line strategies. Over several years, we reviewed and changed the questions and finally winnowed them down to a few that are truly important in determining strategic direction.

This discussion will explain the identification of product lines, then describe how meaningful information about them is developed, and finally, define the way strategic postures and goals for the products were set.

KNOWLEDGE: KEY TO STRATEGY DEVELOPMENT

Knowledge is the foundation to the decision-making process. Decisions about our current actions that change our future performance are strategies. They are implemented through allocation of resources to the alternate choices within the business.

Allocations can be made without a precept of strategy, but once made, a strategy has been launched. Decisions can be made without knowledge, but they always result in a strategy. Only the quality of the decision varies.

While the prudent decision maker would demand information and knowledge before making a move, there is never adequate knowledge on which to base decisions. The truism "dealing with the future is filled with uncertainties" always applies, and therefore it is important to develop systems which can help identify the factors that are significant in decision making, and to concentrate on them.

Since plans never become reality, at least not in the way that was forecast, there are those who say that there is no reason to spend time on planning. Apparently, many businesspeople feel that since perfect knowledge is not attainable, there is no reason to seek any knowledge. The chaotic outcome of this attitude is fairly obvious.

To overcome this attitude, we developed a set of questions and a format for synthesizing a base of knowledge that everyone can use within our company, and on which decisions can be based. In addition, this technique provides a terminology that greatly improves communication.

Because of differences in background, individual managers tend to evaluate different business factors as foundations for developing their plans. In many cases, these varying approaches to evaluation will not necessarily lead to the proper decision. In view of this, we have provided standards for business analysis for the operating units of the company. At the same time, considerable flexibility is allowed in the application of the process, so that it can be applied to the highly divergent businesses that operate within the corporation.

The key to developing meaningful information within our planning system is called the market/business audit. This evaluation consists of three parts:

- Product factors analysis
- Product performance analysis
- Business operations audit

This audit produces an assessment of the business environment in which each of the operating units, or businesses, operates—past, present, and projected future—and includes factors both internal and external to the division. The market/business audit is considered the starting point for developing goals which will guide the division in its planning effort. The audit evaluates the strengths and weaknesses of each of the product lines in relationship to its markets. The market/business audit helps to identify the required actions that develop into strategies and tactics to be employed in achieving the desired goals.

Since the audit deals with the product line, the foundation of our planning system is the identification of that basic element of the business. (We use the terms *product line* and *line of business* more or less interchangeably even though the term *line of business* connotes a greater breadth of function.) Whatever term is used, the product line must be a distinguishable part of the business that has its own competitors, its own set of customers, and its own features of product performance. It is a separable part of the business where costs are incurred and where prices are established.

The actual naming of a product line is not a simple task, and the outcome is not as obvious as it seems at first glance. Experience and knowledge of the marketplace are essential in taking this step, which sets the basic course of the journey into the future.

Product Factors Analysis

The product factors section of the market/business audit is a qualitative evaluation of each significant product line and its markets. The evaluation is directed toward making a comparative evaluation between the line of business and all competitive products. It concludes by identifying the threats and opportunities incumbent to the product line during the planning period.

The product factors are analyzed by the four primary functional areas of the business, and competition is reviewed. The findings of this analysis are summarized in terms of threats and opportunities for each product line. The audit is done in these six steps:

- Marketing considerations
- Competitive considerations
- Technical considerations
- Operational considerations
- Financial considerations
- Threats and opportunities

In order to develop facts about the relative position of each product line, specific questions are posed within each of these steps. For instance, the marketing considerations are divided into three sections and deal with market factors, the market environment, and marketing operations. Market factors are categories of specific data that are believed to be basic to strategy formulation, and they pose questions that must be answered for all product lines throughout the company.

The four market factors are:

1. The current size of the served market for this line of business
2. The annual compound growth rate of this served market for the past three years
3. The current share of the served market
4. The internal sales growth rate compounded for the past three years for this line of business

In addition, more than seventy-five general questions concerning market environment and marketing operations are posed. The division management may respond to these questions and others that they may develop depending on what information they feel is significant to strategy formulation for the product line. The information provided will vary from product to product depending on division management's judgment.

In the competitive considerations section, we also have developed four competitive factors to which all divisions must respond in developing their plans. The four competitive-factor questions that require response are:

1. How many competitive producers including ourselves account for 80 percent of the sales in our served market?
2. What is our relative market share as compared to the size of our largest competitor?
3. What is the number of entries by producers to this marketplace during the last five years? How many competitors have left this market during the past five years?

4. What position changes in market shares have occurred during the past five years?

Some of the questions dealing with general competitive considerations concern the financial status of competitors, the degree of vertical integration of competitors, and the pricing policies that are utilized in this market. Again, the subjects addressed in this section are left to the judgment of operating management.

Technical considerations deal with technical factors and general technical considerations. The four technical factors requiring specific response from all operating units are:

1. What are the maturity and volatility of technology for this line of business?
2. What particular technical skills do we possess that contribute to the marketplace?
3. What is our relative technical position as compared to that of our competitors?
4. What is the primary technical advantage possessed by competitors in this marketplace?

Technical considerations are an extremely important part of the whole strategic and competitive framework of the product lines. It is the one area in which product differentiation can be exploited. Some specific technical actions make it possible to lengthen the product life cycle, increase reliability, improve maintainability and/or reduce maintenance requirements, increase the performance characteristics of the product, expand standardization of parts and components, or reduce the operational skills required to operate the equipment. The market/business audit reviews all of these and other points to develop strategic information.

In "make-to-print" operations, technical skills lose their importance as a way of differentiating product lines. Efficiency of production becomes the major factor in maintaining competitive position and must be emphasized in developing strategies for this type of business. This is usually the case in other service industries also.

The question-and-answer format allows us to make these switches in emphasis and respond to features that are important to the given product line.

Operational considerations deal with the manufacturing and logistical functions of the business. They include all elements from the purchase of raw materials and the movement through production to storage and distribution of the finished product. Operational factors which must be examined are:

1. What is the gross margin for this line of business?
2. What is the rate of productivity growth for this line of business?
3. What is the average age of capital equipment used to produce this product?
4. What is the specific production advantage that we possess as compared with competitors?

General operational considerations include the evaluation of the labor and material content of the product line in absolute and comparative terms. Other considerations deal with inventory, quality control, availability of material, warranty costs, order processing and scheduling, facility adequacy, and the future availability of people, energy, floor space, and control systems to assure the continuation of the operation.

Financial considerations explore financial and economic factors which impact the profitability and the competitive position of the product line. The four required financial factors are:

1. What is our aftertax return on sales and return on assets for this product line?
2. What proportion of total costs do fixed costs represent for this line of business?
3. What is the rate of capacity utilization for this product?
4. What barriers to entry exist in this served market?

General financial considerations deal with information like the distribution of significant direct and allocated costs for each product line, as well as the profile of overhead expenses such as cost of sales and general and administrative costs.

The most important single financial consideration for a product line is the cash flow it produces. We can best evaluate the effectiveness of our performance for a product line by comparing cash flow to such performance measures as sales levels, sales growth rates, changes in assets utilized, and profitability measures.

Experience indicates that few companies have the ability to make an accurate determination of the actual cash flow for their product lines. Accounting systems often are not designed to develop that information readily. This is a major problem because of the primary importance of this financial measure.

Once the functional product factors are developed, the competitive and market position of each line of business is well understood. All the pertinent current strengths and weaknesses of each product line have been reviewed and reduced to writing. Trends are also revealed in this summary, and between the knowledge of what has happened and what is likely to happen in the future, we can express these conditions in terms of threats and opportunities for the future. It is imperative that managers honestly assess the critical issues that will impact the future viability of each product line. These issues become the foundation for the product line goals, strategies, and tactics that are developed during the following stages of the planning process.

Product Performance Analysis

The product performance analysis is a quantitative assessment of each significant product and its market. It assists in analyzing the critical performance elements of the past and those projected for the future of the product, rates the product on the basis of maturity within the life cycle, and compares its performance with appropriate standards.

The product performance analysis starts with a critique of several measures of performance during the past three years. Historical performance figures are developed for all product lines and for each division as a whole. After the strategies and tactics are complete and their impact on future performance is evaluated, the expected results for each year of the planning period are also projected. It is an iterative process that requires several steps from start to finish.

The specific data categories included in this quantitative presentation are product identification, product maturity, market size, market growth rate, product sales volume, average net current assets employed, purchases, earnings after tax, and aftertax cash flow. Using the above information, performance measures are calculated for each year of the planning period. They include market share, annual product sales growth, return on sales, asset turnover, return on assets, and cash return on assets.

Business Operations Audit

The business operations audit is the last part of the market/business audit. It reviews the overall operations of the division as seen from the standpoint of the five functional areas: financial performance, marketing operations, technical operations, operations and manufacturing performance, and general management.

In this part of the audit, the basic questions considered are similar to those used in the product factors analysis, but the scope of the evaluation is division-wide as opposed to only dealing with the individual product lines that make up the business. In the case of single product-line divisions, the results of the specific product evaluation will be essentially the same as the evaluation for the overall division. Typically, there are significant strengths and weaknesses within a business unit concerning its personnel, its organization, and the systems that are used to control the business. None of these would be specific to a given product line but could greatly influence the product's performance. These characteristics are extremely important because they will have major impact on the ability of the organization to implement specific product-line strategies, achieve the divisional goals, and exploit specific market opportunities.

General management is a significant functional category that requires continual scrutiny in the planning process. Every operating unit is asked to review in detail such management concerns as people and their skills, quality and utilization of physical resources, effectiveness of control systems, and responsibilities to the public, the government, suppliers, employees, and customers.

The market/business audit lays the foundation upon which the plan is built. It is the window through which we can best view the future and develop strategies which are the essence of planning. It provides the means to determine goals which will facilitate achievement of maximum results from the business. Most important, it assists in identifying required actions that become the strategies and tactics used to achieve these goals.

STRATEGIC POSTURE

The concept of strategic posture was developed in response to the need for specific pointed directions for companies under common sets of business conditions. Strategic posture allows us to test strategies quickly and easily, challenge strategies that vary from those suggested by the strategic posture, and decide which actions should be implemented.

The Conditions That Determine Strategic Posture

The market/business audit provides diverse information about the business unit and its revenue-generating product lines. Data are greatly reduced and focused in the audit but are still too complex to be interpreted easily and consistently for strategy creation. For years, we struggled with the problem of selecting the items that should be considered in strategic positioning. We knew that we had to develop some easily understood factors to assist in these decisions. The research and presentations of the prime consulting firms indicated that there were a few environmental conditions that were most important in decision making. Redundancy made this clear: more and more people were saying the same things. In addition, we had our own years of business experience that we believed we should not ignore. We had strong feelings about some conditions and how they affected our business performance. For instance, we had seen that there was a lot of opportunity for growth when the market was growing. All that had to be done was aggressively exploit the situation. On the other hand, whenever we had tried to be aggressive in nongrowth markets, poor results had almost always followed. Further, we knew that we did not have much confidence in any businesses that were losing money, and we always felt good about businesses that were very profitable. Finally, we had experienced bad results whenever we directly competed with a company that was much larger than ourselves. When the competitors were small, particularly smaller than we, we usually had good outcomes from our business moves.

When we listed these reactions to business circumstances and compared them to the utterances of all of the management pundits, we saw a pattern that was valuable because it represented what really happens in the business world. The main problem was that we had literally thousands of other experiences that confused the issue because they distorted the focus of our thinking. We had to subdue this "clutter" factor continually so that we could concentrate on the problem. Finally, we accepted the fact that the most important ingredient to strategic posturing is the rate of growth of the market. The other components that we isolated as important were the profitability of the line of business and its market share in the served market.

As we had perceived informally, high market growth provides an opportunity for expansion, but it also limits the ability to reposition when market growth is slow. In a growth market, which by definition has demand expanding at a rate greater than the industry's ability to fill it, there is likely to be minimal competition for the marginal increases of a product's sales volume. The volume gain is taken from the market, not from competitors. On the other hand, in a slow or no-growth market, the competitive positions are established and any growth that is achieved must be taken away from a competitor. Such diversion will eventually result in a drastic reaction from the competitor that is losing the business. The violence of the reaction depends on how critical the volume loss is to the competitor's well-being. Experience shows that the violence of competitors' reactions is not influenced much by whether or not the market is highly structured. When it starts to pinch, all competitors will react with vigor when their sales volumes are seized.

The primary competitive strategy used by firms in slow-growth, mature markets often degenerates to price competition. This apparently results because technology is well developed and product features have become quite standard. Second, distribution systems are generally well developed by this stage, and production-cost benefits resulting from experience have all been realized. Consequently, managers feel that there is very little opportunity to differentiate their products from competitive products by any other means.

When price-cutting tactics are used, and no cost advantage exists for the perpetrator, competitors will most likely react to the price changes almost instantly.

We laughingly say that it takes about twenty minutes for key customers to announce your price decrease to all competitors across the country. Unfortunately, it's not funny, because they can quickly respond, usually by meeting or beating the price that you set. This often leads to a price war which is usually won by the company that has the greatest financial staying power. It rarely benefits any competing party.

We will view an attempt to grow in a no-growth market with skepticism unless the operating unit can show specific and real contributions to the customer that change the competitive position and *win* market share.

A specific example of attempting price competition while disregarding other market variables occurred in one of our divisions many years ago. This case has had a great influence on our thinking. New division management had been placed in the unit because of declining financial performance. One of the division's primary products was the stretch press, a machine which formed aluminum plates into specific shapes that were used in aircraft fuselages. The volume of sales of stretch presses was declining steadily, and prices had been cut to stimulate demand. The product line was highly unprofitable, and the sales department was insisting on further price reductions to "turn the tide." The new management took a hard stand and instead raised the price to a level that would make the product line profitable. The sales department was shocked, insisting that they would never be able to sell another unit. The division president stood firm, however, stating that he would rather leave the market and sell no units than continue to sell any units at a loss.

The results were mystifying at first, but with a little market analysis they were proved to be not only logical but predictable. Unit sales did not change at the new price level. The only change was that the product was being sold at a profit. The market situation was caused by the lack of demand for the shaped aluminum plates. Jet aircraft, which had recently made their commercial entry, required stronger and more exotic materials in their skins because of the speeds and altitudes at which they flew. Stretch presses could not form those materials.

Since producers of the fuselage panels had experienced large declines in demand for their product, they bought presses only to replace worn-out equipment. If they owned the equipment we produced, they would buy ours only as a replacement because of maintenance and spare parts problems. Their purchases were practically insensitive to price. The buying decision was based purely on the requirement for a few replacement units that had to be compatible with the presses they already owned.

We had waged a price war, with the full participation of our competitors, for no practical reason.

As a decision factor, the concept of profitability must be dealt with in a broader sense than its obvious function as a financial measure. Contribution to the marketplace is a feature that we try to identify for each product line, and we believe that profitability is a prime indicator that a contribution is being made.

We use the broad term *contribution* because it can come from any functional area and, of course, represents some differentiation that our product line possesses as compared to competitors' products. Contribution may be superior quality, fast response to customer requests, reliable after-sales service, low price, or many other things that customers need and demand.

Profitability can be equated to excess coverage of both fixed and variable costs. Sales volume which more than allows us to recover all out-of-pocket costs and absorb fixed costs implies a contribution for which customers are willing to exchange their money. On the other side of the coin, we believe that profitability also implies an ability on our part to produce a given volume of business with efficiency and control. Therefore, we believe that profitability can be used as a fiat to represent both contribution to the marketplace and managerial capabilities, the combination of which rewards us with profits. The higher the profit, the greater our confidence in our ability to maintain our competitive position because of the implied business strengths.

Another measure of contribution is revealed by the market share of the product line. The concept of the served market is used here as it is in the Profit Impact of Market Strategy (PIMS) project. This idea defines the served market as that market segment where our product functionally competes and, concurrently, is reached by our distribution network.

Knowledge of the size of the market in which a product line is actually competing is extremely important. Rarely do we cover a national market in its entirety. Therefore, we must do quite a bit of analysis to determine the size of the market, identify our competitors, and determine our true market share.

False market-share numbers often lead to errant decisions about the future of the product line.

Operating managers commonly tend to overestimate the size of the served market for their products because they think that corporate management will be highly impressed by large markets. They presume that their superiors will envision a chance for growth through the capture of market share. Since we have built a fund of knowledge about the importance of market share within the company, corporate managers tend to reject funding for product lines showing low market shares. Today, any attempt to develop "politically acceptable" plan numbers seems to backfire because of misinterpretations of what is "desired." The manipulations end up being contrary to the division's best interests in the long term. For instance, when plans show a large share of the served market but have relatively low levels of profitability, we usually impose a maintenance strategy which results in reduced funding and, in turn, limits opportunity for future growth.

The above reactions indicate a requirement of accuracy in estimating market sizes and market shares rather than any attempt to "tell them what they want to hear."

Market share determination is extremely difficult in most industrial markets, particularly where regional fragmentation occurs. Also, comparisons to competitors can be deceiving because of regional competitors who have varying strengths within different geographical markets. Attention to the development of reasonably accurate market size within each segment of the served market is worth the effort, even though some errors will always exist, because the information is so vital to the construction of strategies.

Analysis of the three measurements, market growth, market share, and profitability, results in the selection of a strategic posture for every product line of the company. The conditions that determine each of the strategic postures are shown in Table 5-1. Each of the three measurements is divided into three parts, high, medium, and low, with specific dividing lines between each. For real market growth we use 20 percent as the line of demarcation between high and medium growth rates. Five percent divides medium growth from low. High profitability is defined as aftertax return on assets of over 15 percent and low return is under 5 percent. High market share is considered to be 20 percent of the served market, or more, while low market share is less than 10 percent.

Over the years, conditions in the environment change, as do internal rates of return change. In the future, we will undoubtedly raise our expectations for earnings and raise the thresholds for high and medium ratings. Since economic growth has slowed over the past years, we may lower our estimates of what constitutes high rates of growth.

It is imperative that each company determine its own dividing lines to define high, medium, and low performance in each of the factors that determine strategic posture. They will vary from industry to industry as the profit expectations of corporate management vary for each firm. The concept of high, medium, and low performance measures is vital in selecting the appropriate strategic postures for each product line.

Characteristics of Strategic Postures

Once we developed a process for determining the conditions which define the various strategic postures and had selected names for the postures, the next task was to define the actions that should be taken once a strategic posture was selected. A good deal of what was to be done was already suggested by the titles that were selected for each posture.

The strategic postures shown in Table 5-1 are listed in sequence from the most aggressive, in terms of investment and growth, to the opposite extreme of leaving the marketplace. The posture of "critical review," which has a specific meaning in our company, is placed in the seventh position. A review of each posture's characteristics follows.

Table 5-1 Strategic Positions and Their Determining Conditions

Strategic posture	Conditions
Invest I	High real market growth; medium-to-high market share; any level profitability
Invest II	High market growth; low market share; low-to-medium profitability
Protect	Medium market growth; medium-to-high market share; high profitability
Improve	Medium market growth; medium profitability; any share of market—or medium market growth; high market share; and low profitability
Maintain	Low market growth; medium-to-high market share; medium-to-high profitability
Cash out	Low market growth; any market share; low profitability—or low market growth; low market share and medium-to-high profitability
Critical review	Medium market growth; low-to-medium market share; low profitability

Invest I Invest I implies a building strategy designed to increase market share. It includes such actions as increasing production capacity, expanding the distribution network, and spending heavily on engineering efforts that will lead to the product-capturing market share. The posture is usually accompanied by negative cash flow with varying degrees of aftertax return on sales and assets sometimes including heavy losses. The critical element for this strategic posture is the high rates of real market growth. If the product is truly in the growth stage of the life cycle, then this strategic posture is essentially a "no-holds-barred" investment program. Increases in market share give the only significant measurement of performance when this path is taken. Even high increases in our sales volume are meaningless unless they represent gains in market share. No financial performance measure applies unless negative cash flow threatens the welfare of the whole corporation. If that becomes a problem, poor planning is indicated because such investment requirements should have been foreseen and this posture should not have been undertaken without being able to "cover all bets." This strategic posture cannot condone profligacy, however. The growth will end someday, and only the most efficient producers will survive. Remember the case of CB radio manufacturers in the mid-1970s.

The ability to separate cyclical swings in demand from long-term secular growth is an important element in making strategic investments. As a case in point, one of our divisions (one which came to us recently through merger, we hasten to point out) which supplies capital equipment to the forest products industry made a strategic error by responding improperly to a short-term swing in demand for its products. During the early 1970s, when housing construction was at all-time highs, the sales of our product were above our capacity to produce. The founding management of the division had always resisted expansion because they understood the cyclical nature of the business. Upon the retirement of these managers, the new division president convinced the corporation to invest in order to accommodate the exuberant market demand. The plant capacity was trebled just before the energy crisis and credit crunch of 1973–1974. The impact of these economic changes backed up through the supply system to cause the forest products industry to cease capital purchases. We were left with a huge capacity problem which made our business unprofitable because of the overhead costs. Even during more recent upsurges in demand, we have never used more than 50 percent of the plant capacity.

Highly cyclical industries are tantalizing during their rapid upswings and seem to induce a degree of amnesia that blocks out any recollection of past declines and sluggish nadirs. The message is clear that a corporation must be realistic about growth rates when setting out to strategize. Be sure that growth rates are long-term before investing to support them.

Invest II This posture calls for investment to increase market share, but with a degree of caution. Because we are concerned with our weak market position, we are reserved about committing to heavy investments. We carefully analyze the risk-reward relationship to determine whether future returns warrant the financial exposure. If, after taking this cautious approach, we prove that we have a competitive product, we can move into an invest I mode. Market share is the most important performance measure for this strategic posture.

Protect The protect posture indicates investment in ongoing operations to assure continued product leadership. Upgrading product features on a continuing basis, investing in productivity improvement and providing after-sales product support are all indicated. This strategic posture is accompanied by positive cash flow, but not to the degree that we sacrifice our ability to produce future earnings and cash generation for short-term earnings. Maximization of long-term profitability is the goal of this posture. The protect strategic posture is doubtlessly the most important posture in the United States today. Most industries are mature, and competitive relationships are established. Protection of a position of leadership is imperative once the position has been achieved. Protection results only from positive action, not from inactivity.

One of our old-line divisions produces an aircraft component that is respected as the industry standard around the world. Production volumes have been high for decades, and it has been a very lucrative business. During the last ten years of inflation, we have been able to pass our cost increases along to the customers with minimal resistance. Finally, a few years ago, a new producer entered the market, producing a duplicate of our highest-volume model. By using new production equipment, eschewing all design efforts, and maintaining minimal overhead expenses, this new producer was able to enter the market and divert some volume from us on the basis of price.

This competitor's market entry caused us to evaluate our past protective actions, and we were alerted to the fact that we had allowed our production equipment to become outdated through limited investment. Further, we had not continued to upgrade the designs of our basic high-volume models. Luckily, we had stayed familiar with the latest advances in production techniques, so that we quickly purchased new capital equipment to regain the position of low-cost producer. Concurrently, we redirected a portion of our engineering effort back to this basic product so that we will eventually displace our own product, and therefore the competitor, through technological advances.

Continuous and conscious actions are required to truly protect a position of leadership. The alternative is decline and decay as the Roman Empire has verified by its very demise.

Improve This strategic posture concentrates on an increasing return on assets. Emphasis is on asset management, productivity gains, and/or cost-reduction programs. This is essentially an efficiency strategy that is aimed at improving returns to the point at which they at least equal the corporate averages. It indicates a continuing commitment to the product line; but we expect it eventually to move to a protect posture, unless market growth declines, in which case it would become a "maintain" product.

Maintain This is a harvesting strategy aimed at achieving high short-term earnings and high positive cash flow. Some fast payback investments in production equipment will be entertained if they promote profitability in the next couple of years. We strive for profitability rather than market position.

Cash Out This is also a harvesting strategy, but the pace of liquidation is much faster than it is with maintain products. Here we liquidate the product line in exchange for cash by permitting market share to decline while we achieve increased cash flow.

Some products that are relegated to a cash-out position refuse to die. We have several component-part products which we have priced to levels that we felt would stop the demand for them. Profits and cash flow are high, but the demand for them continues unabated. When this occurs, as we saw earlier in the stretch-press case, we merely continue the harvest. We prepare ourselves for their imminent demise, however, because nothing is more dangerous than becoming dependent on cash-out products. We remain flexible and reap our rewards as long as the product represents an economic benefit to both ourselves and the customer.

Critical Review Critical review is a transitory strategic posture. It calls for careful scrutiny of the product line to determine whether or not reasonable opportunity for improvement exists. If it does, we take actions to improve its financial performance. If not, we divest the product.

We would prefer to continue all our businesses as long as they provide compensatory returns. Over the years, however, one of the most plaguing business problems has been the continuation of poorly performing products in low-growth markets. This is often rationalized on the basis that they absorb burden or that something positive is bound to happen if we wait long enough.

An important point regarding strategic postures should be made before closing this discussion. Not every strategy can be evaluated on the basis of today's situation and a presumed continuation of the status quo. Sometimes, through dramatic action, the business situation can be greatly altered. For instance, several years ago one of our divisions made a significant change to restructure its segment of the consumer-durable industry. The situation was one in which market growth was equal to GNP growth, ten competitors of roughly equal size shared the market, and all were returning low profits. The industry had all the markings of a fragmented and stagnant business. In the face of all this, we made a sizable investment in equipment that greatly automated the production function. The direct cost of manufacturing the product dropped by more than 20 percent and the savings was passed on to the customer through price reduction. The competitors immediately met our price but could not afford the investment to equal our costs. Slowly, they dropped out of the market until today only a few remain. We have assumed their share, and this greatly increased volume has made it a very profitable business for us.

This case illustrates the ability to change an undesirable situation through aggressive action. When you can make a contribution that restructures the competitive position, good results can occur. You must be able to project the competitor's ability to respond, however. In this case, a key point was our recognition that the competitors did not have the financial resources either to duplicate our investment or to survive a prolonged period of losses resulting from price competition.

Strategic posture has been used in our company for several years, and we have applied it to all our product lines through good times and bad. In hundreds of individual applications, we have never found the strategic posture to be "wrong." In many cases its use led to lengthy arguments and lots of rationalization about our true position, but these experiences have been helpful and educational. Strategic posture has helped us focus our plans and activities in a manner that has contributed to the company's improved market and financial performance.

The concept of strategic posture has not done two things, however. It has not replaced managerial judgment in the decision-making process, although it has assisted in the application of judgment. Also, it has not identified the specific actions to be taken in order to achieve the intended results. We are trying to summarize the actions indicated by each strategic posture, but the number of variables affecting specific strategy selection is still too great for us to reduce it to a working tool.

Finally, one last caveat: The best managers analyzing and planning their divisions' futures, applying strategic postures, and seeking ways of defeating their competitors will eventually do the things that reward them financially. If the incentive or bonus system rewards only current profitability, all strategic postures will gravitate toward a maintain posture. Opportunities will be bypassed and advantages will be dissipated in the name of current profitability. Many other barriers arise within a business to restrict managers from doing the "right" things. In the end, all the management systems and controls must support the optimization of the business over the long term, or optimization will not occur.

In today's complex world we will never develop that "perfect" system, but we will continue to develop tools that lead to that end.

Section Two

Strategy Management

Chapter 6
OPTIMIZING THE CORPORATE PLANNING FUNCTION

WALTER P. BLASS*
Director of Corporate Planning, New York Telephone, American Telephone & Telegraph

At times, one wonders why, if corporate planning is so important, it did not surface anywhere in the Bible. Certainly Moses seems to have been able to carry out an immense task over a long period of time without the hint of either plan or planner. Consider, however, how clearly the elements of good planning were present.

- He had a goal, clear and unconditional. (Exodus 3:17)
- He was so well acquainted with the environment that he could predict it with ease and change it on command. (Exodus 7–14; 14:21)
- He developed the ultimate strategy: *If you can't change them, leave them.* (Exodus 12:37)
- He was not deaf to the feedback from the people he was leading. (Exodus 15:24)

In the absence of providential guidance, we ordinary mortals seem to find it necessary to create something mundane to replace such insight and God-given help. This chapter deals with how the corporate plan-

*The views expressed are those of the author and not necessarily those of New York Telephone.

ning task is accomplished without a prophet or supernatural intervention. It may not lead a corporation into the promised land, but enough experience among a large number of American corporations in the past twenty years suggests that this process can accomplish worthwhile results.

EVOLUTION OF THE CORPORATE PLANNING FUNCTION

In a seminal article,[1] three members of McKinsey & Company laid out a conceptual development of the function of corporate planning (see Figure 6-1). Their approach is useful to understanding precisely what planning is because it sees planning as a *learning process,* rather than as a state of being, like learning to ride a bicycle as opposed to producing a year's balance sheet. The article also reflects the historical development of planning as a discipline to embrace longer-range as well as broader views.

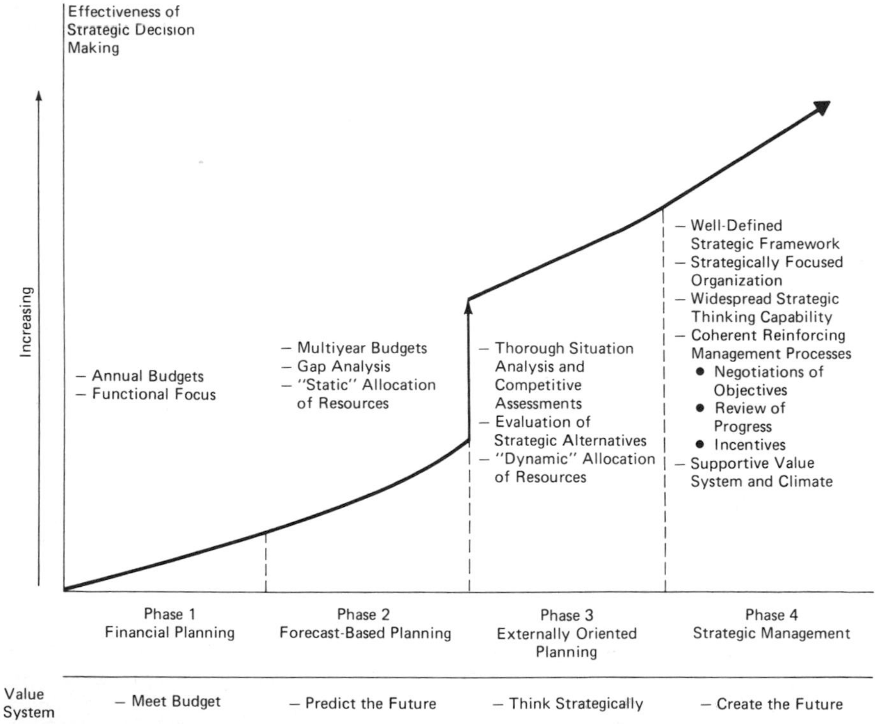

FIGURE 6-1
Phases in the evolution of strategic planning.
(*From Gluck, Kaufman, and Walleck, 1978.*)

Phase 1—Financial Planning

Most divisions, if not companies as a whole, can recognize themselves today in phase 1. A target, usually financial in nature, is set out for the year and limits are placed on what a division manager and his or her people are expected to spend in expenses or capital to reach the desired bottom line. Some companies even restrict themselves to a monthly review of these early results, though most operate on quarterly stocktaking of how closely they are hewing to the program. Such efforts are often tied to corporate targets regarding annual capital budgets, desired rates of return on investment or equity, and, not accidentally, to the annual report to shareowners or the speech of the chairman to the securities analysts' luncheon. Likewise, activities such as employment, training, appraisals, and compensation of management are closely tied to this annual cycle.

Of course, few human activities conform to the astronomical standard of 365 days to a year, and it doesn't surprise students of management that companies, like people, take time to grow to maturity, or competence, or decline into old age and eventually death. Thus, it is evident that some standard time period other than one year is needed to accomplish some significant goals.

In fact, both the goal and the context in which the goal is to be accomplished need reconsideration. Sales of a given quantity of a product clearly are not the ultimate achievement. A return on investment or other financial measurement over a single year can be manipulated. Companies that feel the need to move out of phase 1 are looking not merely for a multiyear period in which to accomplish a goal, but a different goal altogether.

Market share, market *leadership,* development of new technologies, entry into a different industry—all these aspects of future results begin to enter into management consciousness as organizations enter phase 2.

Phase 2—Forecast-Based Planning

As the goals change, so do the time frames. Now, several years, in some cases even a decade, are clearly needed to reach a major goal. For example:

- When General Electric entered the jet engine business, it realized that perhaps ten or fifteen years might be required to establish a market position equal to that of Pratt & Whitney or Rolls Royce.
- When Castle and Cook decided to diversify into real estate and leisure markets, it was aware that it would be years before the development of the land and access roads was completed, and the consciousness of buyers was ready.

- Ralston-Purina developed the Keystone resort in Dillon, Colorado, in part as an offset to seasonal cash flows but also to take advantage of a massive change in American tastes regarding leisure time activities (winter skiing) and the ample possibilities of cashing in on convention—plus spouse and children—attendance at a winter-summer resort ninety minutes from Denver. Having already explored the fast food market and higher-priced restaurants, they felt ready to use their expertise in feeding a more affluent market.

These examples suggest obvious marketing principles, but they also involve more subtle changes in corporate *outlooks.* The McKinsey & Company observers detected a curious phenomenon in phase 2. The more companies deliberately shift themselves into phase 2, the clearer become the shortcomings of the various elements within the corporate structure, such as the following:

- A multiyear goal quickly runs up against the wall of the management appraisal system's clear signal to produce short-term annual results.
- A multiyear budget exposes the company to risks with respect to inflation, shifts in consumer preferences, competitive actions, and governmental acts which appear immense because no one has seen fit to examine or measure them in advance.
- A multiyear enterprise within a division or corporation requires changes in personnel policies (management continuity, bonus-on-performance pay, contract hiring), nonfinancial measurements (market share statistics, foreign trade estimates, learning-curve productivity, and state-of-the-art technology), and even management style (management grid, theory Z, matrix management, ad-hocracy) that are alien to the established ways of running, for example, Ford Motor Company or General Dynamics.

The upshot of this unease within companies undergoing these changes makes phase 2 a fairly unstable environment. Many managers either prefer to go back to the old rules which are consistent with the unspoken or implicit ways of management, or want to move to a far more universal way of arranging the affairs of the corporation than the mere extension of annual budgets, appraisals, inventories, and so on, into multiyear efforts.

Phase 3—Externally Oriented Planning

This change of heart brings another several hundred companies to formal corporate planning and what McKinsey & Company called the beginnings of strategic planning. Now formal schedules of goal definition, environmental scanning, strategy formulation, and newly devised feedback systems to afford management adequate information are required. A new bureaucracy develops: the corporate planner must have a staff, access to top management, and communication with middle management through training sessions, reports, and continual face-to-face meetings.

Division managers find themselves asked to respond with "strategic" answers to questions based on an environment they have never considered important. During the early 1960s and 1970s, managers were asked to come up with solutions to continuing inflation problems not merely in Brazil and Argentina, but in New York and London as well. A consulting firm was asked to come up with a decision matrix to evaluate political risks in ten countries to enable an electrical manufacturer to balance economic opportunities with total risk.

More important, however, than the creation or institution of specific instruments to make possible some of these desired means is the general change in management style. One consulting firm specializing in these changes informed its client that the officers of the company should give up day-to-day operational management to their subordinates and devote the majority of their time to planning for the future. The officers were even told to schedule deliberately significant amounts of time away from the in basket and the telephone so that thinking and anticipation would replace rushing and reaction.

Another aspect of the change in management style in phase 3 has to do with an openness of communication. In phase 1, the style is autocratic, usually one of following short-term orders, be they to cut expenses, to add inventory or promote sales, or to hire or fire. Management employees in phase 1 know only what their immediate supervisor tells them, and can learn more from a 10K Securities and Exchange report or an annual report (not to mention the water cooler rumor mill) than they can from official internal communication channels.

Not so in phase 3: here, top management seeks channels to transmit broad goals and strategies to all management, takes time to give feedback on bottom-up planning, and encourages middle and upper management to question and test existing plans. Through these mechanisms, top management seeks to broaden the perspective of management from the current quarter or annual target to broad-based, long-range objectives and policies.

Phase 4—Strategic Management

In phase 4, these trends seem to merge organically into a strategic planning framework. Here the few companies that have arrived at this stage (for example, General Electric and Texas Instruments) are characterized by three elements that interact to push the organization into a more than adequate response to a changing environment:

- *Widespread Strategic Thinking.* Not only do the planners have this capability, but through training and rotation of personnel, all strategic business unit (SBU) managers *and their line supervisors* do so.
- *Coherent Reinforcing Management Processes.* In contrast with the earlier phases, in which long-range planning and strategy formulation are at odds with market goals, budget cycles, appraisals, and management incentives, all these processes operate in phase 4 as a mutually reinforcing beneficial circle.
- *Supportive Value System and Climate.* Just as the formal aspects of management processes operate to support widespread sensitivity to the changing environment and appropriate responses, architecture, office layout, diversity in life styles, reliance on theory Y or Z, Quality of Work Life (QWL) programs, or quality control circles all contribute to management's *Weltanschauung* (world view).

PRESENT ACTIVITIES COVERED BY CORPORATE PLANNING

Ever since corporate planning started to burgeon as an activity, researchers have been curious about what is actually covered by the term. In the early 1970s, emphasis seemed to lie in the start-up of a planning process. Table 6-1 is typical of this era. A more recent survey[2] (1980) emphasized increased responsibilities:

- More responsibility for, or addition of, acquisition activities and other corporate development activities
- Generally broader role and scope of activities
- More responsibility for and/or more involvement in linkage of plans to operations through involvement in business group and unit planning, and monitoring and analysis of operations
- More responsibility for capital program and allocation
- More emphasis on strategic planning (or addition of such responsibilities) and less emphasis on budgeting
- Addition of a broad range of miscellaneous functions reporting to the chief planner, including legislative analysis, federal government affairs, internal consulting, corporate communications, data processing, management information systems, and some line business.

What conclusions can be drawn from these changes? Leading corporations in the United States seem to be moving in the direction of phase 4 as outlined earlier, but it is evident that many still have a piecemeal approach. Furthermore, although there is an awareness that everything from the parking lot (hierarchy versus first come, first served) to the accessibility of management (executive dining room versus cafeteria for all) affects the total enterprise, this still has not made a major dent in U.S. practice.

In part, changes such as those implied in McKinsey & Company's view of corporate planning take decades to accomplish. General Electric first started in the 1950s to train its managers at Crotonville, New York, for fifteen weeks in the new processes; decade by decade, it shortened the course and changed the concepts of planning. While some U.S. com-

Table 6-1 Corporate Planning Responsibilities in the 1970s

Responsibility for ongoing businesses	Number of mentions
Proposing, or participating in the formulation of, corporate objectives	106
Proposing, or participating in the formulation of, corporate strategy	102
Developing, revising, and monitoring the proper functioning of the planning system	101
Serving as an "idea" person for the chief executive and other members of top management as they think about the future	100
Counseling operating management about planning issues and problems	100
Educating top and operating management about planning techniques	91
Investigating the socioeconomic-technological environment and formulating assumptions or making forecasts about it	84
Evaluating operating management's plans	82
Identifying new opportunities for internal development	80
Monitoring performance against plans	75
Consolidating and editing written plans prepared by operating management for top management	71
Serving on a management planning committee	71
Proposing, or participating in the formulation of, operating-unit (divisions, subsidiaries) and/or functional-unit (marketing, production) objectives	64
Proposing, or participating in the formulation of, strategy of operating units and/or functional units	64
Developing and maintaining computer-based models of the company, industry, and so on	54
Sales or market forecasting	38
Other (including guidance of related research; catalyst to line management; implementing new ideas for internal development; problem solving; organization planning)	18

SOURCE: The Conference Board, *Planning and the Corporate Planning Director,* Rep. 627, 1974, p. 2.

panies caught on to the skills of the Japanese, most continued through the 1970s in the belief that the Japanese were still blindly copying the lessons that Americans had taught them after World War II.

The use of mathematical modeling gives another insight into managerial perceptions. During the 1950s much attention was given to macroeconomic models of the firm, embodying simplified concepts of *the* production function and total factor productivity. By the mid-1960s, Gershevski's Sun Oil model, with hundreds of equations for inputs and intermediate stages, was the envy of planners. In the latter 1960s, with the Vietnamese War wreaking its havoc on price stability and hierarchical order and respect, modeling came to have a bad name precisely because it neglected those "externalities" to which no one had paid much attention. In the 1980s, modeling seems to be staging a comeback as it tackles partial aspects of corporations—providing insight into the "black box" of what really happens in a division's operations and developing sensitivity to inflation, raw material substitutability, and changes in technology. Line managers with more training in quantitative analysis are more comfortable with listening to assumptions and caveats, and distinguishing degrees of error. Planners who are not kept apart in some exurban think tank are more willing to use day-to-day operating measurements in lieu of conventional academic aggregate concepts.

All told, the corporate planning function seems to be evolving into the kind of synthesis of the firm for which planning was originally designed, but without the "Wizard-of-Oz-magician-pretending-to-run-the-world" ambience. Rather, corporate planning as a function seems to serve as a central processing unit for information: listening, sensing, and searching on the one hand; and transmitting broad guidelines, goals, strategies, and directions on the other hand.

PRESENT ORGANIZATION

The changes described above can also be seen in the movements of the planning function in the organization chart of the firm. Table 6-2 shows a survey of the reporting relationships between chief planners and other executives in 1972.

By 1981, when a sample roughly twice as large was used,[3] the reporting relationship was not much changed overall, but some changes were perceptible:

Chairman of the board	22%
President	21%
Other line or operating officer including vice chairman, executive vice president, and so on	61%*

*Does not add up to 100 percent due to multiple reporting.

In 1981, about 15 percent of those 200 companies in the Fortune 500 that had a full-time corporate planning executive changed the reporting relationship of this person. In two-thirds of the instances in which the relationship changed, the planner reported to a person higher up in the corporate hierarchy.

Table 6-2 To Whom Does the Chief Planning Executive Report?

Position title	Number of mentions
President and chief executive officer (CEO)*	39†
Chairman and CEO	25‡
President or chairman not designated as CEO	12
President who is not CEO (chairman is)	6
Vice chairman§	3
Senior vice president	6
Executive vice president¶	6
Other vice presidents (designations include group, corporate, administration, operations, corporate affairs, and development)	14
Total	111

*Includes a vice president and general manager of a cooperative who is "equivalent to a president."
†Includes one planner who reports both to the president (CEO) and the vice president—finance.
‡Includes one planner who reports both to the chairman (CEO) and the president; one planner who reports to the Office of CEO (3 people); and one planner who reports to the chairman and president (1 person).
§Includes one who is also chief financial officer.
¶Includes one who is also general manager.
SOURCE: The Conference Board, *Planning and the Corporate Planning Director,* Rep. 627, 1974, p. 2.

CORPORATE PLANNING STAFF

Among the more difficult questions that the planner must face is the question of the size of the staff required to get the job done. This depends to a great extent on two considerations: how much work the planner(s) should take on, and how much of it should be on nonplanning tasks—for example, requests from top management that can be turned down only at great political cost.

The answer to the size question seems to be surprisingly uniform as Table 6-3 shows.

Table 6-3 Size of Corporate Planning Staffs*
(Excluding the chief planning executive and clerical and stenographic help)

Number of professionals on staff	Number of companies
0	12
1–5	65
6–10	17
11–20	7
21–30	6
Over 30†	2
Total	109

*Fifty chief planning executives have, in addition, separate staffs to assist them with other functions for which they are responsible. These separate staffs are not included in the table.
†The size of one staff is 46; of the other, 60.
SOURCE: The Conference Board, *Planning and the Corporate Planning Director,* Rep. 627, 1974, p. 37.

Nor does this seem to have changed appreciably over time. In 1981, a survey[4] of 300 companies revealed an average of 7.6 professional personnel in corporate planning, although commercial banks, transportation, energy, and manufacturing all had more than 12 professionals, putting them on the high end of the scale.

Much of the actual planning work in large companies is dispersed throughout the line divisions, most of which usually have a planning staff of their own to conduct the annual planning cycle. In one national company, about forty professionals are in corporate headquarters, but 130 other management people do planning in the regional and functional divisions.

With respect to the second issue, it is clear that most planning staffs do quite a few things other than planning, as illustrated both below and in Table 6-4.

Functional area	% respondents
Corporate strategic planning	93
Acquisitions, divestitures	55
Plans analysis and programs	55
Mergers	45
New business development	40
Capital coordination	32
Operations analysis	27
Division, subsidiary planning	27
Joint ventures	45
Economics, economic analysis	57
Market analysis, market research	31
Business information center, library, archives, business research	27

SOURCE: Johnson, Smith & Knisely, 1981, p. 35.

The upshot of this table and Table 6-4 is that it ill behooves planners to turn down all tasks save those in their job descriptions. Indeed, one planner at a major manufacturer found out to his dismay that in being

Table 6-4 Time Spent on Planning by Seventy Corporate Planning Staffs

Percent of time spent on planning	Corporate planning staffs	
	Number	%
100	12	17
75–99	25	36
50–74	20	29
10–49	13	18
Total*	70	100

*Not tabulated, in addition to the 29 who did not offer this information, are the 12 companies whose chief planning executives have no planning staffs.

SOURCE: The Conference Board, *Planning and the Corporate Planning Director,* Rep. 627, 1974, p. 37.

a purist, he had sufficiently alienated his fellow vice presidents to the point at which, in the first serious recession to hit the firm during his tenure, he was abruptly fired.

FUTURE DIRECTIONS

Up to this point the discussion has focused on the ontogeny of planning. What must be more important to the student of this subject is where it is going in the future. What tasks lie ahead? What skills will be needed? What will be the reporting relationship of the planner in the future?

Perhaps the most useful starting point lies in the question of accountability—in its broadest sense—of the firm to its stakeholders. The concept of stakeholder (as distinguished from shareowner) management holds as its main tenet that an organization such as a corporation is actually more akin to a governmental entity in a democracy; that is, it has a diversity of constituents who must be "satisficed" (satisfied-sufficed) so that, at worst, they will not vote against proposals by that entity and, at best, they will go out and campaign or lobby for them.[5]

Such a process of looking at the firm's stakeholders is not the traditional approach, which is worrying first and foremost about the bottom line. On the contrary, this process starts with the definition of a stakeholder as "any group whose collective behavior can directly affect the organization's future but which is not under management's direct control, e.g., suppliers, customers, competitors, government, neighbors, employees and their families, special interest groups. . . . Stakeholder management will not help manipulate or control external groups but it will foster an atmosphere of cooperation and negotiation to help create a more favorable public climate than most business organizations operate in today."[6]

This is not the place to describe this technique at length. The *approach,* however, is critical to the planner's conception of the firm he or she is helping to lead and consequently to the conduct of the planning function. If the operative phrases in stakeholder management are "cooperation and negotiation" as contrasted to "manipulation and control," then the style of planning will accordingly have to move from the postulation and establishment of corporate goals ordained by a top management which is concerned by the bottom line alone to a set of goals consistent with the negotiated requirements of these "outside" groups.

For example, Shell Oil (USA) has set a policy that none of its products or purchases may travel in tankers that fail to meet acceptable safety standards, or to utilize ships that have a history of accidents. This policy is an outgrowth of a concern for Shell's "neighbors" in the broadest sense of the term. The result is, naturally, higher initial costs of shipment, but an extraordinary absence of oil spills as contrasted to the experience of much of the industry.

By contrast, New England Telephone discovered the hard way that failure to consult and negotiate in advance with the union representing information operators was a serious mistake. It resulted in a bill being passed (overriding the veto of the governor of Massachusetts) that banned the practice of charging for directory assistance calls. This occurred despite the fact that the company (belatedly) offered to guarantee the jobs of all affected operators.[7]

From today's experience of widespread negotiations with internal constituencies (controller, division X, personnel, international operations, and so on), future corporate planners will find themselves at the vortex of what Woodrow Wilson called "open commitments openly arrived at" with external stakeholders. Previously, the public relations vice president frequently was the corporation's proxy for the many publics the corporation had to deal with, too often as an apologist in print after the fact.

In the future, the planner will have to anticipate the technological, ideational, and sociological environments and find the negotiated consensus that embodies the desiderata of all affected parties. Needless to say, such anticipation and negotiation by the planner are in addition to the changes described at the beginning of the chapter.

PLANNING AND GOVERNMENT

One of the most important stakeholders for U.S. companies is the federal government. Yet, in contrast to many companies in other countries, most U.S. firms regard Washington as the enemy and any process of accommodation as a defeat for the company. When will the lessons of Japan, France, and Germany percolate to U.S. management? We need not buy into the *dirigiste* atmosphere of the French *Grandes Ecoles,* or into the power of German banks, and through them the monetary and other federal governmental authorities, to obtain the sense of mutual gain that pervades foreign corporate managements' thinking and stance vis-à-vis the world.

Contrast the following two examples:

- As early as May 1978, newspaper reports told of rising numbers of consumers complaining about medical hazards related to formaldehyde materials exuding toxic fumes in their homes, especially from blown insulation foam. Instantly, the industries involved contended that "no significant health hazard existed."

By December 1978 insulation sales generally were seriously down, one contractor reporting a 70 percent drop. A year later (November 1979), legislation was being introduced in California to ban the use of foam insulation until regulations were adopted to protect consumers.

In July 1980, the State Public Health Department of Massachusetts announced that homeowners whose houses were insulated with urea formaldehyde foam were entitled to have the foam removed at the manufacturer's expense at a cost of $20,000 each; the industry screamed that the program, if instituted nationally, could bankrupt the large foam makers and the thousands of small contractors who installed it.

In December 1980, the Formaldehyde Institute cautioned the Consumer Product Safety Commission (CPSC) against banning foam insulation on the grounds that a ban was premature; a month later, the CPSC did propose a ban on a party line three-to-two vote, with the minority suggesting warning labels. On February 23, 1982, the CPSC ordered, by a four-to-one vote, a total ban on the sale of formaldehyde foam for home insulation.

- In 1976, the Environmental Protection Agency (EPA) proposed new regulations on diesel engine emissions. At Cummins Engine Co., Columbus, Indiana, these regulations were perceived as removing any economic basis for diesel engines for trucks, the mainstay of the company. After a short time spent considering how to block EPA from making the proposed regulations effective, Cummins turned to its newly appointed director of ethical responsibility, Charles Powers, and asked him to spearhead a task force to deal with this problem.

Rather than work on mechanisms designed to block the EPA, Powers and Cummins Engine took the motives of EPA as being honorable and set about designing regulations that were within the bounds of developing technology and likely economic conditions, but that would still massively reduce emissions. Finding that this task was indeed practicable, they approached General Motors with a view to a common approach to EPA and the relevant Congressional committees. In time, the Cummins proposals, with some modifications, proved acceptable to all parties and were subsequently promulgated by EPA.

When will other U.S. companies learn what benefits IBM, Burroughs, Bechtel, and Merck have derived from choosing senior executives with Cabinet-level experience in Washington, or at least with nonbusiness mind-sets? An executive exchange program at lower levels has been a feature in a number of corporations, but few have seen the light regarding deliberate "acquisition" of such negotiating talent.

DIVERSITY AND PLANNING

As the conglomerate form of enterprise has spread in American corporations, the planning process has adapted to it with a number of wrinkles, including The Boston Consulting Group matrix form of portfolio management, Profit Impact of Market Strategy (PIMS), scenario-writing, Synectics, and Futures Wheel.

Still, the organization and underlying technical expertise of corporate planning have not changed dramatically to keep pace. Mostly backgrounds in engineering and financial analysis, M.B.A.s, and a combination of line and staff experience in the firm seem to comprise the usual planning staff.

Compare that with the background of Pierre Wack, Chief Strategist for Royal Dutch Shell (London): Pierre Wack is an economist by training, having studied at the prestigious *Ecole des Sciences Politiques* in Paris as well as at the Universities of Heidelberg and Frankfurt. Subsequent to his government service, he became the publisher of an art magazine which brought him wide critical acclaim. Subsequently, he spent ten years as a management consultant specializing on the interface between macro- and micro-economics. He then joined Shell Francaise as head of planning and economics.

During his tenure at Shell, he has spent a sabbatical year in Japan focusing on what can be learned from Japanese companies and how they do their planning. Anyone listening to a lecture by M. Wack would think he was listening to a Montesquieu, so widely read and informed a man is he.

Given the diversity of business, constituencies, and stakeholders, won't the planner of tomorrow have to broaden the analytic base of the corporate planning staff from the typical left-brained activities to a variety of different personality types, processes, or even temporary resources?

Wack, to give but one example, has had government planners from the governments of the countries in which Shell operates seconded to his staff for a year, both to contribute their particular insights into the planning process and to carry away some personal experience with private sector planning. According to Wack, there is no substitute for the *mix* of host-country nationals in a planning staff of a multinational firm.

In an article in *Managerial Planning,* I have speculated on how the awareness that differences in personality types are mutually complementary will influence changes in senior management selection and organization.[8] For example, one senior Bell Laboratories scientist once told me of his sense that five different people were necessary for a successful invention:

- The discoverer of the idea
- The person to whom the discoverer brings the idea for a reaction
- The company critic, who is always ready to knock an idea down, but is useful as a proxy for the cold world outside

- The "stone" to the discoverer's flint—the person who gets all sorts of secondary ideas from the initial thrust by the discoverer
- The individual who edits or even writes up the idea in patent or publishable form, a skill frequently lacking in the original discoverer

Compensation schemes should reflect all five contributors if the laboratories were interested in continuing progress, he told me.

In yet another instance, an oil industry executive, observing the diversification of his company into other minerals, coyly commented that the company needed to invest in some commodity broker types instead of staying with the successful—if traditional—petroleum engineering types from Houston. The future planner, therefore, might well require outlooks and experiences far removed from the patterns of today in an M.B.A. course or in the company's traditional management rotation program.

THE PLANNER AND THE CEO

Of all the internal relationships, the one most important to effective corporate planning is certainly the relationship between the planner and the CEO. It is no accident nor is it necessarily a disaster that the partnership between Mary Cunningham and William Agee, planner and chairman respectively at Bendix Corporation, became so intense that they were suspected of having a romance. Said John Thackeray in the *Financial Times* (London): "The real value of the corporate planner is the catalytic effect that he can have on a corporation."[9] That can only be done by the kind of openness and understanding between the two principals that comes from almost daily contact. David Mahoney, chairman of Norton-Simon Inc., put it this way: "The planner's role isn't to make policy. It's almost like a psychiatrist. . . . He's supposed to be a mirror, saying, what do you want to be when you grow up, David? Where do you want to move the company?"[10]

Indeed, an informal correlation between the involvement of the CEO in the planning process, as measured by the distance in reporting relationship clearly shows that impact on the bottom line (see Figure 6-2).

In the future, that link will likely increase, but from the planner's standpoint it needs careful management. As in the Cunningham-Agee case, too close a relationship may become a serious liability, especially when great changes with massive negative implications for certain jobs are involved. Another common instance is that in which a close tie has been established over a period of years, and the CEO departs, leaving the planner as vulnerable as a holdover political appointee in Washington after an upset election.

George Steiner, professor of management and public policy at the Graduate School of Management at UCLA, has this to say about the developing relationship in the 1980s: "The importance of the planner to the chief executive officer will grow in the eighties to the point where the planner may become truly the right-hand man to the CEO. Relative compensation will rise as top management comes to realize that fact. From concern with today's results and next quarter's balance sheet and profit and loss statement, CEOs will use their planner more and more to help them set the direction of the firm ten or so years out."[11]

Since George Steiner spoke these words in 1978, both CITICORP and J. C. Penney used their strategic planners to draft major changes and goals in the operation of these companies. In the case of J. C.

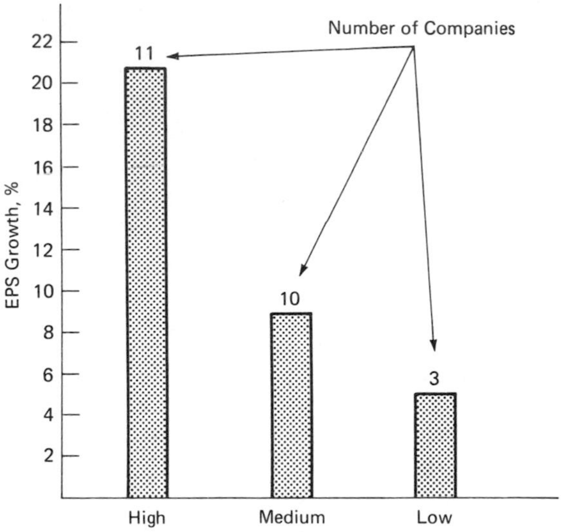

FIGURE 6-2
CEO involvement in planning and profitability.
(*From R. Jagannathan, Corporate Profitability and Planning Effort, New York Telephone, 1979, unpublished.*)

Penney, the outgoing chairman, William Batten, used his planner to draft a set of goals for the board to hold his replacement as CEO accountable to. It is not coincidental, perhaps, that Penney's has done as well in comparison to other retailers as a result of such top management planning.

All this should not be construed as suggesting that the planner neglect other internal constituencies. One of my colleagues, Robert Jaeger, has suggested the simile of two overlapping ovoids. The upper one is the executive suite, the lower one middle and upper management, and the planner and the planning staff occupy the space of the overlap. Proper judgment in the conduct of the planning function implies an awareness of the critical nature of this overlap, both as the source of information and power for the planner, and as the source of the negative aspects—conflict of interest with and vulnerability to both segments.

CONCLUSION

In summary, the planning function may be seen as an evolving process to bring together the disparate parts of a large organization. Starting with fairly simple statements of multiyear goals and how given resources are to be allocated in the pursuit of these goals, the planning function generally spreads into an encyclopedic view of the total organization:

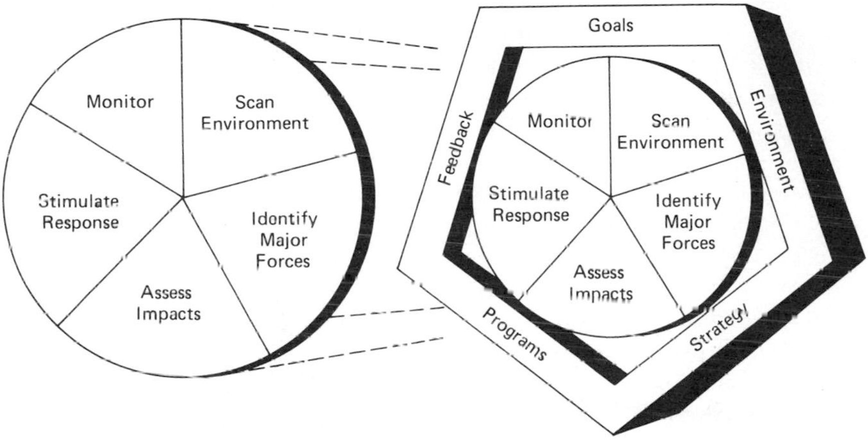

FIGURE 6-3
Planning for a turbulent environment.

new goals, corporation environments, the issues that are important to its managers, the strategies that are to be used in reaching the goals, the specific programs underlying the strategies, and ultimately the feedback information loops that allow management to make corrections in any of these elements.

Aspects of the process, though not the entire process, may be conveniently diagrammed as shown in Figure 6-3.

Gradually, as the entire management group becomes familiar with the techniques, the encyclopedic size and detail of the early planning formats can and should be dispensed with. One of the worst traps corporate planning can get caught in is an intermediate stage of massive paperwork, where all of the major thrusts of the corporation are lost like needles in haystacks of useless extrapolations of past events. Like a Gresham's law in reverse, the progressive organization sheds its plentiful but bad planning for the good and scarce coin of clear strategic statements buttressed with as few figures as necessary. General Electric's corporate plan can be gleaned from only eleven pages of data on fifty SBUs, five years back and five in the future. Naturally, top management will question both the results and the logic, but as a result of the evolution described in the beginning of this chapter, it can rely on thoroughly defensible and thought-through plans.

A wise management will avoid making the planning function into a competitive fifth wheel that continually gets in the way of the relationship between the CEO and those who are responsible to the CEO. As close as the relationship between CEO and planner should be, it should not be allowed to develop into an office of a Cardinal Richelieu, insulated and autonomous from the stresses and realities of the total organization. Again, the planner who plays the role of the Rogerian psychotherapist,[12] teasing out the latent priorities and goals of the top management, helping to crystallize the means to those ends and to reject dysfunctional behavior, and then quietly pulling back into the background is to be greatly preferred over the headline grabber, the ambitious fair-haired boy, or the self-appointed guru.

In outlining that persona, there must be added the caution of not allowing excessive additional functions to be grafted onto the basic function. Such additional tasks as forecasting, operations research, special R&D, and so on, lead to a diversion of the energies and character of a group which probably should number between four and twenty professionals. Some companies will allow a corporate planning group to assume characteristics of an ongoing corporate staff operation, numbering in the hundreds, with the inevitable result that some other very much smaller group closer to the CEO runs off with the strategic brass ring.

Finally, the corporate planner should perceive the changes not only in the outside environment but also in the very governance of the organization. A management style appropriate to a massive homogeneous production may have to be changed to take account of technological and marketing revolutions that overtake the industry. Cultural determinism of the single country may have to give way to multinational decision making with all the uncertainties which such expansion brings. The corporate planner should help the CEO and quite possibly the board and other powerful publics to recognize these changes as they are building and to anticipate responses rather than bemoan "the snows of yesteryear."

In a word, the planner is the alter ego of the CEO, not in the sense of a deputy, but in the sense of Marley's ghosts of the past, present, and future. Played well, this role is a rewarding one for corporation and individual alike.

NOTES

[1]Frederick W. Gluck, Stephen P. Kaufman, and Stephen Walleck, "The Evolution of Strategic Management," McKinsey staff paper, McKinsey & Company, New York, October 1978. Also appeared in abridged form in *Harvard Business Review,* July–August 1980, pp. 154–161.

[2]Johnson, Smith & Knisely Inc., "The Corporate Planner: Compensation, Staffing, and Activities," New York, 1981, p. 20.

[3]Johnson, Smith & Knisely, p. 14.

[4]Johnson, Smith & Knisely Inc., "The Corporate Planner: Career Development Comprehension and Staffing," *1981 Survey,* New York, 1981, p. 30.

[5]Herbert A. Simon, *The New Science of Management Decision,* Harper, New York, 1960, p. 98.

[6]Emshoff and Freeman, "Who's Butting into Your Business?" *Wharton Magazine,* Fall 1979, p. 46.

[7]Ibid., p. 48.

[8]Walter P. Blass, "Corporate Planning as Psychotherapy: Guiding Your Company to Self-knowledge," *Managerial Planning,* July–August 1980, p. 11.

[9]John Thackeray, "Planning Is More Important Than the Plan," *Financial Times,* London, December 13, 1972.

[10]David Mahoney, "Frustration and Turmoil Plague a Marketing Prodigy: Norton-Simon Inc.'s," *Business Week,* April 7, 1980, p. 74.

[11]George A. Steiner, Address to Bell System Planning Coordinators' Conference, San Diego, October 1978.

[12]Walter P. Blass, p. 12.

Chapter 7

STRENGTHENING THE STRATEGIC PLANNING PROCESS

JOHN D. C. ROACH
Vice President and Managing Officer, Strategic Management Group, Booz·Allen & Hamilton, Inc.

MICHAEL G. ALLEN
President, Michael G. Allen Company

The strategic planning process (SPP) is ideally the product of the best minds inside and outside the corporation (management consultants and other advisors). Inside the corporation every management echelon helps to develop and implement the SPP.

The best SPP allows for various scenarios and possibilities, for feedback and midcourse correction, while still adhering to its basic goals. Such a plan, while financially sophisticated, is more activity-oriented than money-oriented.

The strategic plan must be as meaningful and workable on the shop floor, from which it derives some of its wisdom, as it is within all the management ranks above.

Given the numbers involved—of people to inform, of projects to conduct, of results to achieve, of revenues to gain—forming the strategic plan is necessarily complex. It must make solid sense to a lot of people and interests, creating a vital network of responsibility and coordination.

The strategic plan, of course, begins to age from the minute the ink dries on the paper. Achieving the goals it states is the prime challenge of the corporation. Otherwise the strategic plan, for all the resources that went into it, becomes little more than a process mistaken for a product.

An effective strategic plan envisions the mechanism for its own fulfillment, setting forth the courses of specific action that will endow the corporation with strength in the years to come. In itself, the strategic plan is optimistic: a statement of belief tempered by faith and intuition in the good things that can emerge from the impending future.

But the pitfalls are many and failures are numerous. The purpose of this chapter is to set forth some of the ground rules for strategic planning in terms of a process that will enlist the best minds available to confront the biggest of all corporate challenges: the time to come.

Strategic planning amounts to making real progress too slowly for the general American mood. But top management must rise to the occasion, nonetheless. The best of all beginnings is the planning structure that makes planning move, the better to accommodate and drive home the ideas that are the essence.

Achievement thus becomes the payoff—even if the payoff is years away. Strategic planning—the process and the results—calls for top management reeducation, indeed, for a reeducation of everyone interested in the future viability of American enterprise.

SPP: ITS ROLE IN THE MANAGEMENT SYSTEM

How It Works

SPP is the beginning of strategic planning. Strategy per se determines the use of company resources to achieve competitive success in attractive markets of the future. Figure 7-1 deals with SPP terms and concepts. In brief, SPP:

1. Considers the future implications of current decisions
2. Adjusts plans to the emerging business environment on a continuing basis
3. Manages the business through analytic understanding of the business situation as it evolves over time
4. Links, directs, and controls complex business enterprises through a practical, working management system.

Thus SPP must become an integral part of the total management system, infusing every part of the corporation, both anticipating and reacting to change while setting forth the basic and detailed procedures the corporation will follow in years to come.

It amounts to methodical long-range thinking that is at the same time flexible and adaptable to both the pace of the age and the periodic emergence of challenges barely forecast and often downright unexpected—such as the social and environmental concerns of the 1960s, the energy crunch of the 1970s, the interest rate pressures of the early 1980s, and an assortment of other "surprises" within recent memory, ranging from the onslaught of foreign competition to the changing role of government in business affairs.

The scope of SPP is well-nigh total: it infuses the entire corporation both as a process and as the plan that emerges from it.

Making the company's SPP work effectively becomes, by its very nature, a multiyear activity—arguably even a permanent, ongoing effort of revision and adjustment that the best corporate minds, contemplating the changing business environment, will direct.

TERM	BASIC DEFINITIONS	EVOLUTION
Planning	Setting goals and programs to achieve them, typically at the functional and subfunctional level	Used by thought leaders of industrial engineering, like F. W. Taylor Emerged with concept of professional management in the 1950s Embodied in systems of management by objective in the 1960s
Business planning	Combining the plans of each function into a business plan	Followed the establishment of decentralized organization structure in the 1950s by GM, DuPont, GE Popularized and documented by leading academics like George Steiner in the 1960s
Strategic business planning	Focusing the business plan on the utilization of resources to achieve competitive success in attractive markets of the future	Emphasis of business planning changed in the early 1970s by leadership of several corporations (Texas Instruments, GE) and consulting firms
Corporate strategic planning	Integrating business strategic plans so that the performance of the whole is greater than the sum of the parts	Portfolio analysis concepts stimulated by consultants in the late 1970s Corporate planning staffs shape content and role of corporate plan in the late 1970s

FIGURE 7-1
Evolution of planning terms and concepts.

So, if SPP is an ongoing part of the corporation's activities, how do we get our arms around it?

SPP Agenda and Caveats SPP must deal with the foreseeable company challenges of the future. It is a top management responsibility that depends upon adequate planning resources—human and otherwise—and an environment in which the planners have both the ability and the energy to probe the furthermost reaches and details of company activity.

No planning system can work off-the-cuff, on the instant, to resolve immediate problems. It must be medium-term at least, but more likely long-term, and will almost undoubtedly require sacrificing certain short-term values (such as an impressive quarterly or annual bottom line) for longer-term benefits.

Nor can a planning system in itself compensate for management system weaknesses, such as unsuitable personnel, ineffective information and communication, weak organization around strategic aspects of the business, and the attitude that past success necessarily assures future accomplishments.

The issues SPP must address include:

- Market selection and evaluation
- Competitive strategies
- Financial strategy, including return on assets, risk, and debt structure
- Development strategy, including business diversity, stability, growth policies, acquisition and divestiture feasibilities, R&D

Some of the considerations that will inevitably arise in varying priority include capital acquisition, productivity, energy, profit planning, new product development, rapid technological change, social and environmental considerations, government impact on the business (including taxes, regulatory matters, and pension and benefit planning).

Addressing these problems, the corporation will be wise to enlist a range of the best minds available—both inside and outside the corporation.

All concerned must be aware that they themselves will be the most likely implementers of the strategic plan as it moves from the drawing board toward reality. SPP must draw upon both the analytical and the intuitive talents of the corporation; it may sometimes verge upon the estimated and even the theoretical possibilities of the future. It may engage several scenarios, from "worst case" on up. But the strategic plan, once again, is essentially pragmatic and optimistic. At heart it is a can-do blueprint for the company in times to come.

Two Dominant Management Styles Two management styles dominate SPP.

One style tends to make the corporation, like any other institution, Emerson's "lengthened shadow of one man," thus harkening back to an entrepreneurial vein in American corporate culture that is still substantial.

This style, which could be termed *sensor-feeler,* implies strong interpersonal relationships and a heavy dose of hunch and intuition as inputs to decision making, tends to dislike statistics, data, and analysis.

Managers in this style, however, often tend to have a good strategic grasp of the power politics of the corporation, the ways in which plans can be made to work. Such managers believe that leaders shape the plans—not staff analysts or other "noncombatants" in the competitive fray.

Conversely, the *analyst-thinker* management style—often based on financial, legal, and/or analysis-based training and experience—tends to favor a planning system designed around information systems and rigorous business analysis. The instincts are distrusted; the internal logic of analysis tends to overrule all else.

The sensor-feeler manager may tend to oversimplify problems. The analyst-thinker manager may tend to overcomplicate them.

In recent years a certain symbiosis has developed between these two types of managers. Each type tends to respect the occasional virtues of the other without losing sight of the shortcomings of the other. Sometimes the same manager may exhibit definite signs of deploying both styles at once to attack a given problem.

The planning challenge resides in utilizing both styles selectively and appropriately, strengthening the virtues of both and minimizing the occasional tendency to stress the stylistic approach to a problem rather than the nature of the problem itself.

Some Guidelines for the Planning System The planning system must evolve certain characteristics of its own, the styles of the individual planners notwithstanding. Among these characteristics are:

1. Recognition of complementary management responsibilities at each level of concern and authority.
2. Independence from centralized corporate control, approval, and decision making, the better to evaluate corporate control itself in terms of specific parts of the business.
3. Avoidance of overdeterministic "road maps" that may not yield to changing times and circumstances, thus quickly becoming obsolete.
4. Due emphasis (but not overemphasis) on detailed forecasts and budgets.
5. Issue orientation, the better to help management confront the major business challenges facing the company.
6. Stress on strategic performance (market and competitive positioning) rather than financial performance (Figure 7-2).
7. Allowance for updating strategies as conditions change (see point 3, above).

8. Facilitation of decisive resource deployment.

9. Coordination of functional and/or regionally related activities.

10. Simplification rather than complication of the general management task at each level.

11. The scope and the room to move around for managers at every level, allowing them to make their own decisions over as wide a range as possible.

12. Competent management! None of the foregoing is logical or practical otherwise. Help management by clearly conceiving and spelling out roles, responsibilities, and expectations. Choose the right manager for the right strategy, in terms of both the manager's own style and the "corporate culture" that manager must serve.

Planning Hierarchy Planning, like management, has its rank and station in terms of principles and priorities, wherein the upper reaches of the

	Strategic Leadership	EPS Growth, % Year for 10 Years (1970–1980)	Price/Earnings Ratio (July 1981)
3M	High	13.1	11
GE	High	13.8	9
Esmark	Medium	28.4	7
United Technologies	Medium	14.0	8
ITT	Low	6.9	5
Westinghouse	Low	11.9	6
Gulf & Western	Low	16.8	4

FIGURE 7-2
Strategic performance versus financial performance.

corporate hierarchy naturally take broader strategic approaches than those below.

Each level, however, must plan strategically within its own scope and purview. The entire purpose of strategic planning must be to add value to subordinate units beyond that achievable through their own strategic planning.

Such added value may include ideas, funds, facilities, and personnel, anything that adds competitive strength to the units below.

A typical hierarchy of planning tasks in a large, decentralized, multibusiness corporation:

1. CORPORATE STRATEGY. Essentially the chief executive officer's (CEO's) plan for the enterprise, as approved by the board of directors, it identifies the specific issues and challenges the company will confront.

Planning at this level indicates the industries or business arenas in which the company will focus its efforts in terms of competition, markets, finance, and development (such as R&D, acquisition and divestiture, and growth).

Planning at this level sets forth strategic objectives for the major business units of the enterprise, specifies investment priorities, and sets up the structure and function for communicating these ideas and receiving feedback up and down the corporate ranks as the planning evolves and goes into effect.

Corporate strategic planning on this highest level determines what mix of business activities will enhance the value of the shareowners' investment.

2. SECTOR STRATEGY. Many Fortune 500 (and, indeed, Fortune 1000) companies are sufficiently complex to justify a structure of sectors or groups which in turn contain strategic business units (SBUs), so called because they are distinctive businesses in their own right, dealing with products, markets, and problems different from those of other SBUs within their own and other sectors of the company.

Many of these SBUs, in fact, represent corporate acquisitions of once-independent businesses and may well tend to retain their entrepreneurial, smaller-scale outlooks even under the present corporate umbrella. Indeed, some of the top personnel, including the former CEO, may be managing a given SBU.

The possibilities for differences of opinion and outlook between an SBU and its governing sector or group—quite apart from those of the sector or group vis-à-vis top company management—give sector planning its special challenge, even a certain relish. Meshing the SBUs within the sector, and then fitting the sector into the corporate strategy, is second-level strategic planning, but nonetheless a first-rate challenge.

Within its narrower scope, sector planning parallels corporate planning, but sector planning may well call upon the broader resources of the corporation to achieve its particular goals or to take advantage of special opportunities, such as employing rapid investment to confront an emerging market opportunity.

Direction setting, business development priorities, and resource allocation priorities govern the sector's strategy, often combining SBU approaches to achieve competitive advantage. Such approaches might include pooled advertising to create a common image for the SBUs, a pooled distribution strategy, or a common R&D effort.

3. STRATEGIC BUSINESS STRATEGY. The SBU, as noted, is one of the component building blocks of the sector and indeed of the corporation through the sector. It is self-contained and functional in its own right.

Citing the military analogy, the SBU's *strategy* would be the corporation's *tactics*—but even at the lower level of the SBU, the challenge properly deserves the grander concept of strategy. This encompasses such strategic issues as product market segmentation, analysis of the competition, development and allocation of business resources—all within the sector strategy.

4. BUSINESS SEGMENT STRATEGY. This is the smallest part of the SBU deserving a specialized strategy, focusing on product strategy, pricing, marketing plans, focused production, quality control, and productivity.

One could almost call this level of strategy the hands-on approach. Ideas move upward from the shop floor, burst forth in the engineering lab, crop up from the sales force. Good ideas should keep moving, in an ideal corporate capillarity, to the point at which they influence strategy at every level. Ideas also move inward to the company—from the marketplace, from suppliers, from customers, from outside consultants.

Indeed, the upward flowability of ideas—not merely the downward thrust from on high—may well determine the true viability of overall company strategy. It is all-important in strategic planning to make certain that the view from the thick-carpeted corporate offices is in touch with the view from the front lines. At this level the company meets head-on with competition and the marketplace, where concepts undergo the definitive test of the real world.

While the "one-over-one" review applies from the higher to the lower level, the trick remains to improve what may already be good without blunting the labors of those most closely responsible for performance. Thus an SBU manager will review pricing strategies by business segment, but the entire system will become self-defeating if segment-pricing strategies are reviewed at the corporate level.

The company, after all, has little need of SBUs that do not add value to the company as a whole—nor does the SBU need the overall corporate umbrella if the company cannot add value to it. The levels are distinctly different, but the responsibilities are mutual.

Generic Types of Planning Process SPP principles apply everywhere, but the design of the SPP system varies greatly from company to company, largely in the combination of three planning procedures.

Each of these procedures must be periodically reviewed to make certain they are producing results:

- *Analytic planning procedure.* Three examples of this procedure are shown in Figure 7-3. Note the modes of analysis: business companywide planning, gap analysis, and market strength and attractiveness are three examples of the analysis "agenda" in SPP.

- *Assignment of responsibilities procedure.* Assigning responsibility varies among differing corporate structures—the decentralized multibusiness company, the centralized functional company, the matrix-structured company—but in each case the analytical tasks are assigned by level within the organization and, or course, by functional expertise.
- *Integration procedure.* Some corporations require matrix integration of product-market strategies across functions or regions. This will be discussed in more detail later in the chapter. (See Making the Planning System Work: General Approach.)

EVOLUTION OF PLANNING SYSTEMS

Evolving Companies, Ergo Evolving Planning

Strategic planning systems vary as companies vary, and they must evolve as companies evolve. Many companies grow faster and, indeed, change faster than the strategic planning systems that generated the growth and the change.

Such companies regress in their planning and thus in their management control, which poses a potential danger to future progress.

A given company has already evolved to a certain point where it can actually choose a strategic planning evolutionary stage if it hasn't done so already. Which stage should be chosen depends on two major forces:

1. *Complexity,* as determined by:
a. Size as measured by sales
b. Business and product diversity
c. Technological intensity
d. International scope
e. Special situations, such as government regulation, licensing, social and environmental considerations, and energy and raw material considerations
2. *Performance Trajectory,* as determined by:
a. Earnings per share growth
b. Return on investment
c. Market valuation
d. Bond rating

The best possible planning is needed at every evolutionary stage. But, clearly, more sophisticated planning is required for larger, more complex companies. A multinational company requires a much more elaborate SPP than a regional real estate company or a retail store.

In terms of performance trajectory, the first two considerations are objective, that is, they are measurable in actual dollars and cents. The final two considerations are both objective and subjective—objective be-

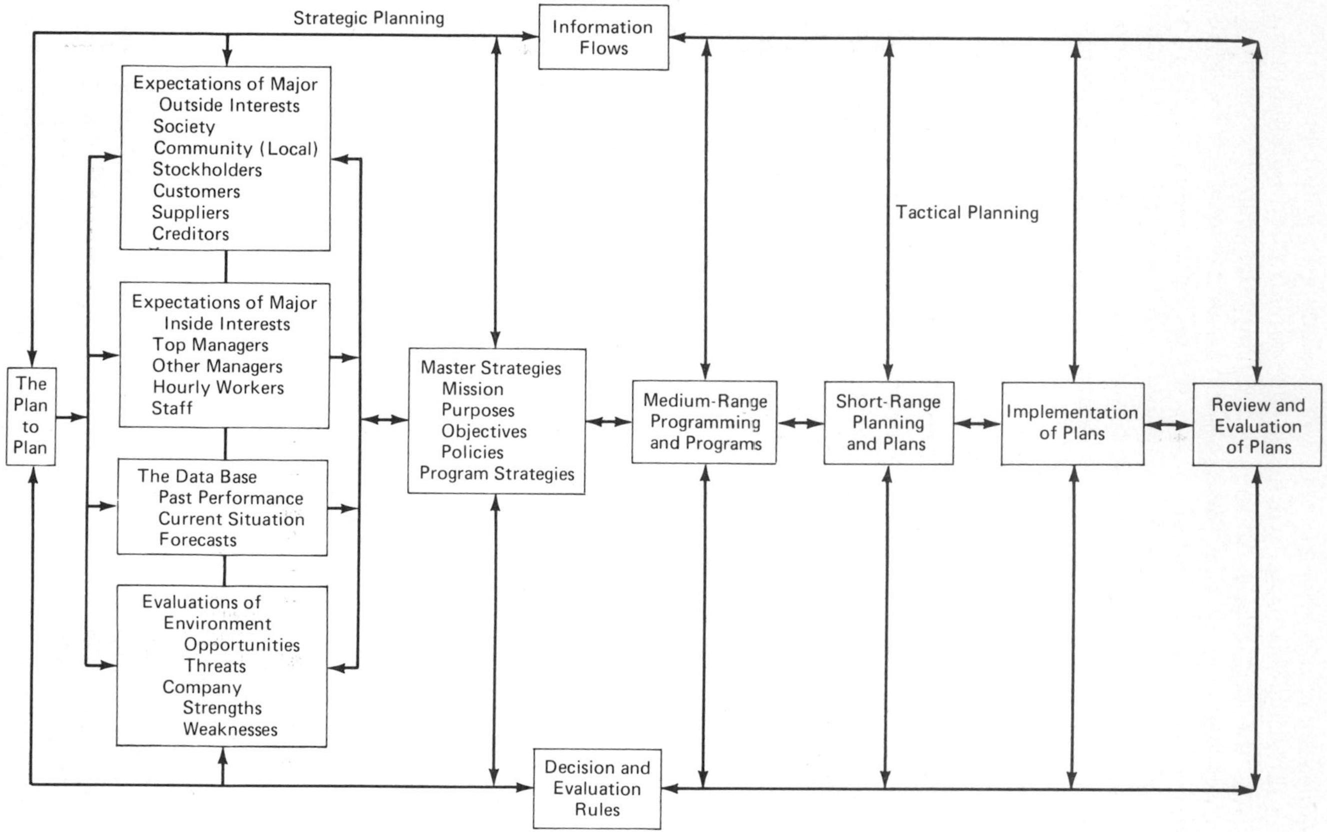

FIGURE 7-3
Analytic planning procedure. (*a*) Structure and process of business companywide planning.

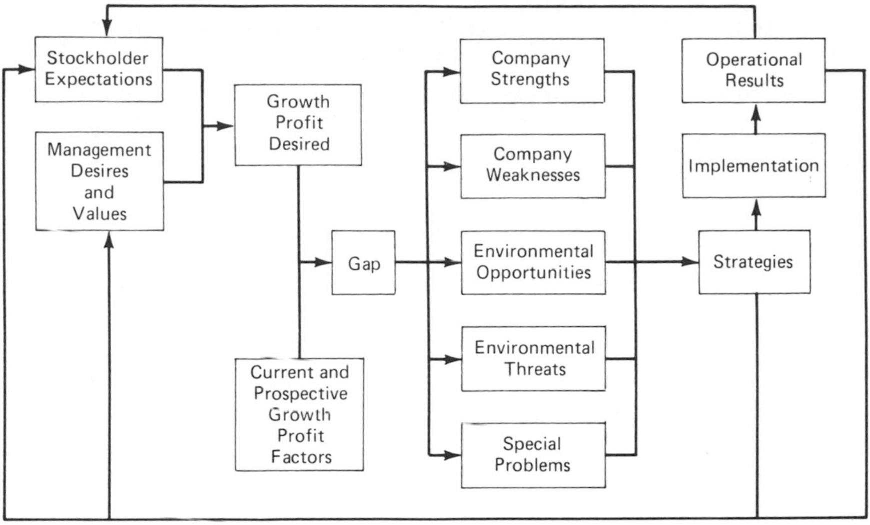

FIGURE 7-3
Analytic planning procedure (continued). (*b*) A strategic planning model centered on gap analysis.

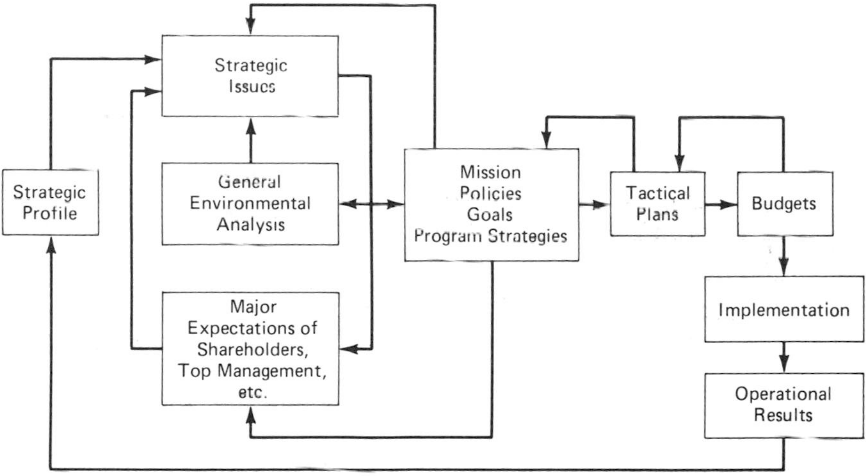

FIGURE 7-3
Analytic planning procedure (continued). (c) A strategic planning model with market strength and attractiveness as the central focus.

cause they actually exist, but subjective because they depend upon a human consensus. Market valuation depends upon both hard-nosed and emotional factors, often in the same investor at the same or at different times. Bond rating depends upon a more blasé appraisal of seasoned market observers, based on objective criteria but nonetheless subjective because of the judgmental factor.

All these performance criteria are practical realities the strategic planner must take into account, the better to improve them in the course of time. Figure 7-4 shows the four stages of SPP evolution as both the complexity and the performance standards of a company increase.

Planning Evolution: Stage A. Financial Planning and Control Companies in this stage are the least complex, having relatively modest financial

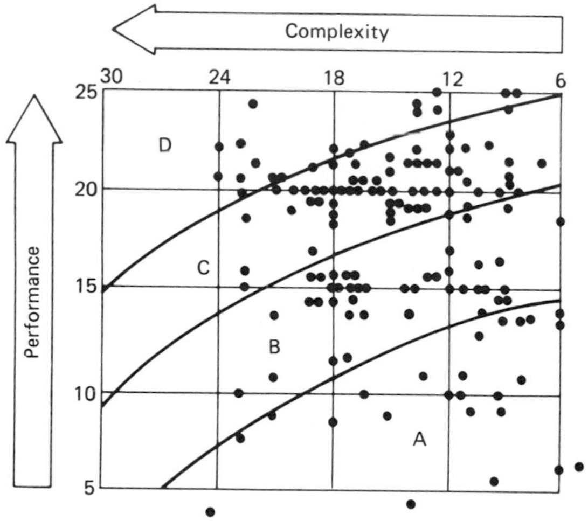

FIGURE 7-4
Four stages of planning evolution. (*a*) Financial planning and control. (*b*) Business strategy control. (c) Corporate strategy development. (*d*) Multilevel strategic management.

performance objectives and needing a relatively simple system of financial planning and control. Some typical aspects of this planning stage are:

- *Three- to Four-Month Planning Cycle.* This takes place at the end of the fiscal year and emphasizes financial budgets, financial forecasts, financial performance controls, and capital investment plans.
- *Numerical Plans Predominating.* In the financial planning and budgeting cycle, each profit center projects its profit and loss statements for the coming year, possibly even for three to five years. Such projections

assume the best possible prediction of future market conditions and the operating programs to confront them, and are reflected in present rates of sales growth, cost trends, demographic changes, and social and economic forces—as far as one can reasonably foresee these in terms of present trends. How the projected numbers will be achieved is determined by one or more budgeting discussions.

- *Capital Investment Program.* This is part of the budget. Individual spending items require specific analysis, review, and approval against corporate hurdle rates during the year to come. Discounted cash-flow evaluation is usually made. Capital requests are often accompanied by discussions of market assumptions, facility plans, and so on.
- *Financial Measurement and Control.* A detailed financial reporting system by profit center is put in place. Performance may be measured

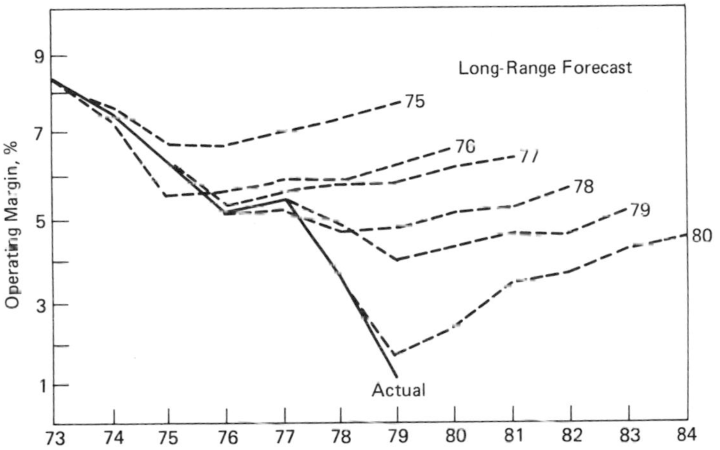

FIGURE 7-5
Failure of financial forecasts: Typical hockey stick projections of operation margins. (*From a top fifty U.S. multinational.*)

in numerous dimensions against predetermined monthly budgets. Management review tends to focus on historical variances and the reasons for them. Control is exercised on an exception basis.

Such stage A financial planning and control systems, standing alone, provide only a partial picture of today's business environment. They tend to refer largely to historical performance, a measure no longer valid in the fast-changing business environment of the 1980s that has blunted the effectiveness of financial forecasting. (See Figure 7-5 for an example of the hockey stick configuration of such financial forecasting.)

Planning Evolution: Stage B. Business Strategy Control This higher stage in company evolution toward complexity and performance standards is actually the first stage of true strategic planning because it goes beyond the dollars, that is, beyond financial numbers as the sole measurement of company goals.

This stage looks at the operations, concentrates more on profit-making activities than on the profits per se, and nourishes strategic perspectives in running the business. Characteristics of this stage:

- *Definition of Strategic Business Units.* Stage B thinking is inimical to profit centers based on span of control. The SBU is more manageable and is defined in terms of a clear set of competitors and a complete strategic plan in its own right.
- *Basic Business Planning Process.* Each SBU utilizes its own planning system to develop and update its strategic plan every year, according to a specified plan format. The idea is to set business goals and to improve

1. STRATEGIC BUSINESS ANALYSIS
   - Environmental Assessment
   - Market Assessment and Segmentation
   - Competitive Assessment
   - Resource Assessment
2. IDENTIFICATION AND ANALYSIS OF STRATEGIC ISSUES
3. STRATEGY DEVELOPMENT
   - Mission, Objectives, and Goals
   - Strategy Elements and Priorities
   - Operating Programs
   - Contingencies
4. FINANCIAL EXPRESSION
   - Projection of Results
   - Projection of Resource Requirements
   - Sensitivity Analysis
   - Triggers for Replanning

FIGURE 7-6
Contents of a business strategic plan.

the plan as time and experience dictate. A typical format for a business-strategic plan is shown in Figure 7-6.

- *Business Strategy Review.* Corporate management shifts time and attention away from financial forecasting and control in favor of business analysis, strategic issue identification, and strategy approval.
- *Development of Planning-Resource Skills.* SBU managers, charged with responsibility for strategy development and results, work with dedicated planning staffs to assist them. Training programs, consulting assistance, and improved planning information sources are funded and heeded to improve actual performance.

- *Investment Approvals Based on Strategy Approvals.* Specific capital appropriation requests require more thorough discussion and approval of the business strategy itself.

Inherent in this stage of planning evolution is a changing management style that moves away from control of financial results toward the control of business strategy.

Business objectives and strategies—not budget discussions—are the main agenda between management levels. But management at every level recognizes that effective business strategy is a prerequisite for superior financial performance.

Planning Evolution: Stage C. Corporate Strategy Development The more complex multibusiness enterprise requires appropriately more sophisticated stage A and stage B systems. But it also requires a corporate strategy framework to guide business development and resource allocation.

At this stage the company has the following characteristics:

- *Corporate Strategic Plan.* A dedicated staff and the proper protocol facilitate the development of a corporate strategy framework to set forth corporate objectives, assess major corporate opportunities and perils, analyze the corporate portfolio, and examine corporate resources such as R&D, marketing, finance, and even the corporate strategic plan itself, that is, the corporate strategic plan should embody a system for its own periodic evaluation and review.
- *Corporate Planning Challenges.* As each planning cycle begins, major issues, opportunities, and threats facing the company are denoted planning challenges. Each SBU will address these in its own planning within sector planning.
- *Portfolio Strategy Differentiation.* Every company business is evaluated in terms of market attractiveness and competitive strength. Its strategic objectives and investment requirements are reviewed against the portfolio analysis framework.
- *Corporate Business Development.* Planners analyze the portfolio and achievement gaps (the shortfalls between performance goals and performance results) to determine the need for and direction of business development through acquisition, divestiture, and/or closure of specified businesses. These options, while reviewed and approved at the corporate level, may be identified at any planning level.

In this stage of SPP evolution, a further shift in management style and activity takes place. Corporate management, no longer merely a reviewer and approver of business plans, begins to take the initiative in active strategy development and leadership. It challenges the organization to develop plans that address specific corporatewide interests. See Figure 7-7 for an outline of such a corporate plan.

The transition to stage C is often slow and difficult, but it is essential that top management make this move despite all obstacles. One hurdle is the stage B mind-set that tends to feel that corporate planning is antithetical to the concepts and principles of decentralization.

This is wrong. The idea in stage C is to enjoy the best of both centralized and decentralized thinking, making the most of the company's talents on every level of management. Blending all this together is *the* strategic planning challenge in stage C.

OVERVIEW

1. Mission and Objectives
   - *a.* Summary mission statement
   - *b.* Progress toward achievement of corporate objectives
2. Environmental Outlook
   - *a.* Macroenvironment: drivers, constraints, system changes, discontinuities
   - *b.* Microenvironment: sales indicators, inflation outlook
   - *c.* Summary environmental outlook
3. Corporate Position Assessment
   - *a.* Sales earnings profile
   - *b.* Operating sources of income
   - *c.* Financial position
   - *d.* International position
   - *e.* Technology position
   - *f.* Human resources position
   - *g.* Competitive position
   - *h.* Corporate investment priorities
   - *i.* Summary position assessment
4. Sector Strategies and Programs
   - *a.* Overview: Inferred strategies/commitments
   - *b.* Sector performance profiles and strategic thrusts
5. Corporate Strategic Issues and Challenges
   - *a.* Response to 1980 challenges
Productivity improvement
Growth profile
Business development
   - *b.* 1981–1982 issues and challenges
Business development
International growth and integration
Productivity improvement
Technology

FIGURE 7-7
Corporate plan illustration.

The corporation, after all, pays for management wisdom and expertise at every level of command. If it fails to respond to its human resource, it is wasting it and the other resources that depend on it.

Planning Evolution: Stage D. Multilevel Strategic Management In the previous stage C the SPP emphasis was at the corporate level—with due reference and counsel from other levels. Here, for the most complex companies, strategic planning becomes the basic management style on every level of the corporation as part and parcel of ongoing operations.

This is necessary to sustain high levels of performance in a company dealing with many kinds of business in many different operating environments at home and abroad.

Some of the features of this multilevel strategic management are as follows:

- *Organization Structure.* A strategic planning organization has replaced a financial organization. In other words, business activity plans have superseded profit management and control plans as the main corporate focus. The strategic planning organization deals with sectors, SBUs, and business segments, in contrast to the financial organization that tends to deal in terms of groups, divisions, and departments.

GENERAL ELECTRIC
Consumer Products and Services Sector
Industrial Products and Components Sector
Technical Systems Sector
Power Systems Sector
International Sector
Utah International
ITT
Telecommunications and Electronics
Engineered Products
Consumer Products and Services
Natural Resources
Insurance and Finance
SHELL
Oil
Gas
Chemicals (including Agricultural Chemicals)
Coal
Metals
3M
Industrial and Consumer Sector
Life Sciences Sector
Electro and Communications Technologies Sector
Imaging Science Sector

FIGURE 7-8
Sector structures of some highly complex organizations.

Figure 7-8 shows the sector structures of some highly complex organizations.

- *Multilevel Planning.* Each level in the organization hierarchy—corporate, sector, SBU, business segment—knows its planning role and executes it skillfully. This planning system evaluates, discusses, and adjusts the fit of strategic plans as necessary at each of these levels.
- *Strategic Management Systems.* Management systems, apart from planning systems, are designed to put the strategy to work. Among these

are systems embracing compensation, information, performance appraisal, and promotion.

- *Strategic Management Perspectives.* The ultimate change in the company at this stage is in the skills, qualities, and outlook of top management itself. Until recently, the main concerns of the CEOs and their immediate confreres have been financial, accounting, and legal matters—at the expense of R&D, manufacturing, and marketing.

There is now evidence that the CEO of the 1980s is again tending to remember the basic purposes of an enterprise as a producer of goods and services, realizing that strategic development should be directed more toward market-oriented rather than finance-oriented activities.

Management Assessment	Stage A. Centralized Financial Performance Management	Stage D. Multilevel Strategic Management
Organizational Structure		
Control Span	Group Division	Sector, SBU, Segment
Business Unit Linkage	Most Autonomous	Cross-fertilization
Communications	Number-Oriented	Issue-Directed
Investment Procedures	Request-Approved	Strategy-Approved
Management System Design		
Purpose	Reduce Error	Add Value
Major Approach	Financial or Budgetary	Strategy Development
Time Horizon	Short	Short, Medium, and Long
Business Unit Thrust	Profitability Maintenance	Competitive Position
Corporate Strategy	Financial Performance	Strategic Performance
Management Orientation		
Style	Theory X	Theory Y
Administration Style	Control-Directed	Change-Oriented
Management Type	Individualistic	Multidisciplined
Procedures	Structural and Uniform	Flexible and Tailored
Skills	Experience-Based	Analysis-Based
Decision Making	Reactive	Proactive

FIGURE 7-9
Characteristics of strategic management.

Nonetheless, while it remains "cheaper to buy than to build," all top corporate management must face the reality as well as the ideal in the strategic development of the company.

Questions of technology, productivity, and competition are now tending to rise above the status of buzz words as factories automate and even robotize, as corporations recognize the thrust of competition to be worldwide, and as the customer becomes ever more sophisticated.

A company evolving to stage D has changed profoundly from its stage A period. See Figure 7-9 for a summary of these changes.

BASIC PLANNING SYSTEMS: PHASES, ELEMENTS, STATUS, GAP

The Basic Planning System: Phases and Elements

Four phases in the basic SPP—generally applicable to all plans in all four stages of evolution—are depicted in Figure 7-10. Note that each has ten steps, a checklist of the key features that make SPP work:

- Corporate situation assessment: strategic direction
- Business strategy development: SBU planning
- Corporate integration of plans: top management review
- Plan implementation: moving SPP to operating plans and budgets

The checklists are by no means comprehensive. But each of the listed elements amounts to a substantial activity in its own right.

A decentralized multibusiness company would require an SPP along these general lines:

- Corporate direction and business strategy—the first two steps—should be established in the first half of the cycle. Operating plans, budgets, and implementation—the final two steps—should be established in the second half of the cycle.
- Strategic and financial planning should be combined into a single system. If either were separate, neither would be in touch with the other on the dynamic, continuing basis the times require. The company, while duly cognizant of financial planning aspects, must be activity oriented.
- Short-range plans are permissible only in the context of medium- and long-term plans. Isolated short-range planning is ipso facto contradictory to the idea of SPP.
- The SPP must be continuing, ongoing, both up and down the management hierarchy to keep all interested, knowledgeable parties informed and participating. While SPP is inherently a responsibility of top management, it becomes a total involvement of every level of management in the corporation.
- Every SPP step and timetable is adjustable to the company and general business situation. An SPP too rigorously set forth to adapt to changing circumstances would amount to an SPP belying the requirements of the age. In other words, the SPP—through scenario options and contingency planning—must allow for its own changes as these become appropriate.

Status Report: Company Planning Systems

A recent survey of 145 companies by the Michael Allen Company showed strategic planning system development falling far short of the need in almost 90 percent of cases studied.

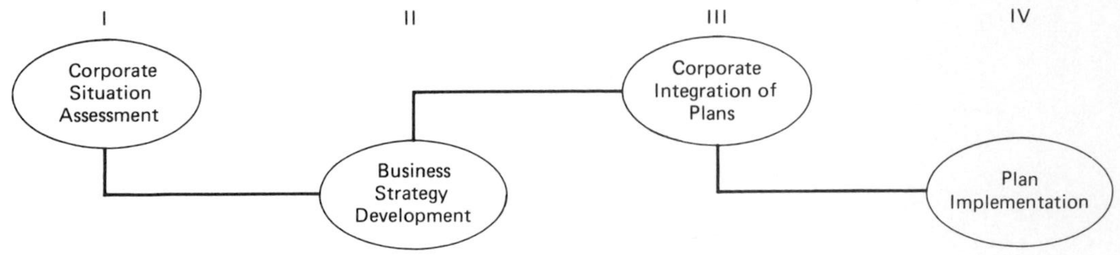

I

1. Financial objectives and goals
2. Strategy toward earnings quality
3. Development of new businesses and markets
4. Goals for improving competitive position
5. Anticipation of key corporate risks
6. Anticipation of key corporate opportunities
7. Developing and protecting key resources
8. Formulating corporate strategy framework
9. Pinpointing corporate strategic issues
10. Articulating major planning challenges

II

1. Planning data base
2. Product-market segmentation
3. Analysis of keys to competitive success
4. Competitive analysis to assess position
5. Definition of critical strategic issues
6. Measurable objectives and goals
7. Creative strategies to improve position
8. Innovation and venture management
9. Resource strategies — production and technology people
10. Financial resource strategy

III

1. Review of business plans for analytic consistency
2. Review of plans to pinpoint strategic issues
3. Review of plans for fit with corporate strategy
4. Review of strategic resource expenditures
5. Methodology for resource allocation
6. Tradeoffs between short- and long-term results
7. Support of new business development
8. Integration of acquisitions and divestitures
9. International integration of plans
10. Feedback on business objectives and strategy

IV

1. Board of directors involvement in planning
2. Top management involvement in planning
3. Middle management involvement in planning
4. Caliber of and investment in planning resources
5. Coupling of strategic performance with pay and promotion
6. Organization for effective strategy implementation
7. Management selection linked to strategic task
8. Linkage of strategic priorities with budgets
9. Toughness of operating plans to execute strategy
10. Degree of implementation and impact of strategy

FIGURE 7-10
Steps and elements of basic planning system.

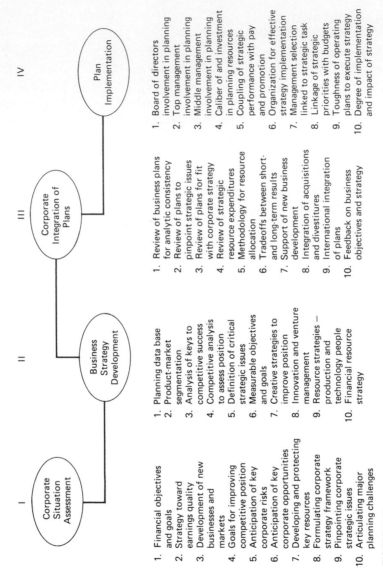

Figure 7-11 shows companies in each of the four stages of planning-system evolution in descending order of complexity.

The upper part of the exhibit shows the distribution of companies in terms of planning *need*. More than half require at least stage C planning systems based on their complexity and performance trend.

The lower part of the exhibit shows that most companies fall short of their needed planning capability. The chart indicates the relative strengths and weaknesses of each phase of the company's planning system, according to the four steps in the basic planning system:

SURVEY DATA—NEED FOR PLANNING

	Companies Responding: Number	Companies Responding: Percent of Total
D. Multilevel Planning	14	9.6
C. Corporate Strategy Development	58	40.0
B. Business Strategy Control	45	31.0
A. Financial Control	28	19.4
	145	100.0

SURVEY DATA—STATUS OF PLANNING
(SUMMARY OF RELATIVE STRENGTHS AND WEAKNESSES)

	I	II	III	IV
A.	−23	−22	−27	−41
B.	−12	−23	−26	−43
C.	0	−2	−18	−35
D.	+7	+7	−7	0
Total	−7	−13	−23	−34

FIGURE 7-11
Companies in each of the four stages of planning system evolution, in descending order of complexity. (*The Michael Allen Company, 1979.*)

- Stage A companies are weak in all planning phases.
- Stage B companies are stronger in corporate strategy development but weaker in other planning phases.
- Stage C companies provide adequate corporate direction and business strategy control but are weak in corporate strategy development.
- Stage D companies (representing only about 10 percent of the sample) are adequate in every planning phase and thus make strategic planning work.

Planning, as a system of activities, depends on the effective working of its components. Otherwise, the system breaks down.

MAKING THE PLANNING SYSTEM WORK: GENERAL APPROACH

Strategic Planning Premises

Strategic planning remains a prime area for corporate improvement, even in the largest, most complex, and best-managed enterprises. Yesterday's apparent planning sophistication is forever vulnerable to the planning needs of today and tomorrow.

How to approach the planning challenge at each stage in planning evolution, to keep it appropriately evolving upward from stage A, is the subject of this section.

The planning system:

- Exists to harness and give full rein to the creative business talents of the organization, the ultimate test of its effectiveness. A planning system that stifles creativity is self-defeating.
- Must have many elements working harmoniously together on a formal, scheduled basis. But each element must work toward specific objectives of its own.
- Needs constant redesign and reorientation to new problems, challenges, and circumstances as they occur or evolve in the course of time.
- Must deal with specific planning challenges, not purely theoretical standards or concepts. These should be considered in terms of various possible scenarios.
- Must be an integral part of the total management system and style—a regular, ongoing part of the business itself.
- Must allow for assistance from outside the company, such as new personnel as needed in both the planning and the implementation stages, that is, new management to suit the strategies and/or counseling personnel during both planning and implementation stages.

Phases in the Planning System

As the planning system takes shape and as the planning process moves forward, it is important to set interim goals and objectives, periodically measuring these against actual progress in the planning at every management level. The following discussion will explain the several phases of the planning system.

The eventual credibility of strategic planning rests on top management support and commitment. Planning that lapses generally becomes planning that fails—a reflection on management and on the company.

In such an event it is difficult to renew the planning process. A vital management imperative thus becomes compromised and delayed to the damage and demoralization of the company and its people.

Phase I: *Assessment of the Need for Stronger Planning* Among the broad performance and environmental indicators of the need for stronger planning are those that provide what amounts to circumstantial evidence in themselves. The following prima facie conditions call for a strategic planning program:

- *Weak Financial Performance.* Total bottom-line performance for investors is measured by relative investors' gain: the combination of current yield and stock price appreciation. The trend and/or discontinuity in financial performance should be examined. See Figure 7-12.
- *Eroding Strategic Performance.* Strategic performance indicates the proportion of company sales and investment in attractive markets and in strong competitive positions. Eroding performance is a sign of weakness of corporate and/or business strategy. (Refer to Figure 7-2 to note the impact of strategic performance on shareholders' appraisal of the stock in the relationship of strategic leadership to earnings per share and the price/earnings ratio.)

			Investor Return	
	Dividend Yield, %	Stock Price Increase, %	Total, %	Average %/Year
1966–1971	11.8	76.7	88.5	17.7
1971–1976	12.0	18.8	30.8	6.1
1976–1980	20.0	−27.4	−7.4	−1.8

FIGURE 7-12
Discontinuities in total investor returns. (*Emery Air Freight.*)

- *Mounting Environmental Challenges.* Even before actual performance begins to erode, signs of an increasingly difficult operating environment will be visible in terms of marketplace, technology, regulation, and competition. Even to sustain current performance levels or trends will require revised, improved strategic planning.

Most companies at the stage A (financial planning and control) evolutionary position display hockey stick financial forecasts (see Figure 7-5). Analysis of these will demonstrate the need for improved strategic planning.

Typically, both the general environment and the competition will be tougher. To the extent that new factors affect circumstances and trends for better or worse, the new condition is a discontinuity (which can be favorable or unfavorable).

An unfavorable discontinuity is shown in Figure 7-12. Note the 1966–1980 trends in dividend yield compared to stock price increase and total investor return (the unfavorable discontinuity).

Favorable and unfavorable discontinuities belong on the SPP agenda, for examination in terms of how these are now trending. Generators of discontinuities include both favorable and unfavorable changes in technology, market share, regulation, resource availability, competition, and, indeed, any aspect of the business environment.

A favorable discontinuity is achievable in one or more of the following ways (Figure 7-13):

- *Better Environment.* Environmental changes can improve market position and growth, inflationary pressures, cost trends, productivity, and so on.
- *Less Competition.* As a business matures, some competitors may withdraw entirely or narrow their scope to limited market segments, reducing head-on competition. Competitors may also shift strategies from price to service, significantly affecting growth and profitability.
- *Improved Strategy.* Strategy per se has proved to have a strong, often controllable impact on performance. Both growth and profitability often stem from better market selection, product-oriented strategy, competitive success, and better utilization of resources.
- *Stronger Management.* Matching the manager to the strategy, experience shows, often generates a considerable performance turnaround. Managers vary greatly in style. Some are better at planning than at implementation. There are great variances in ability and experience vis-à-vis marketing, technology, R&D, and indeed in terms of personal characteristics such as creativity; initiative; willingness to take risks; relationships to suppliers, customers, and other managers, and much else that defies precise measurement—especially new, often unrealized management characteristics that emerge in new jobs and circumstances.

Thus the managerial personality, as it impacts the company's activities at every level in the changing business environment, becomes a tremendous influence on the effectiveness of the SPP at every level and in every planning phase.

Phase II: *Making the SPP Fit the Company* The corporate planning team, having pondered the foregoing, must cut and shape the SPP to the unique needs of the company.

To do this, the planners narrow their sights from the general prin-

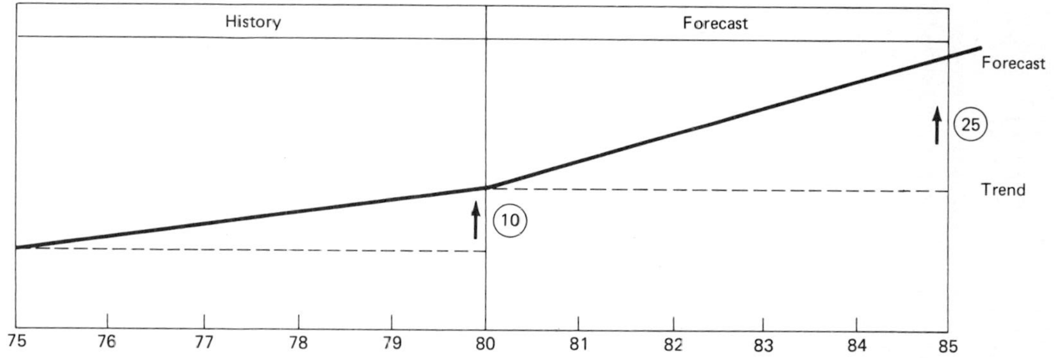

	History	Impact 75–80	Forecast	Impact 80–85
Environment →	– Market growth with GNP at 5% per year – Inflation recovery 95 percent owing to price controls	15	– Market erratic with growth 2 percent per year – No price controls – Mix shift to cheaper standardized products	10
Competition →	– Share eroded 1 percent per year owing to price leadership strategy – Regional competitors gained	–6	– Halt erosion of share to regionals – Anticipate Japanese entry	0
Strategy →	– Achieve full product line for United States and export – Expand independent distribution and service – Improve U.S. manufacture in Midwest	–4	– Modernize product line – Direct sales to key segments – Bring offshore plans on stream and increase sourcing	7
Management →	– Experienced in business, with engineering background – Average twenty-five years with company	5	– New general manager with marketing background – Strengthen sales, marketing, and planning functions	8
	Performance increment	10		25

FIGURE 7-13
Analyzing the hockey stick.

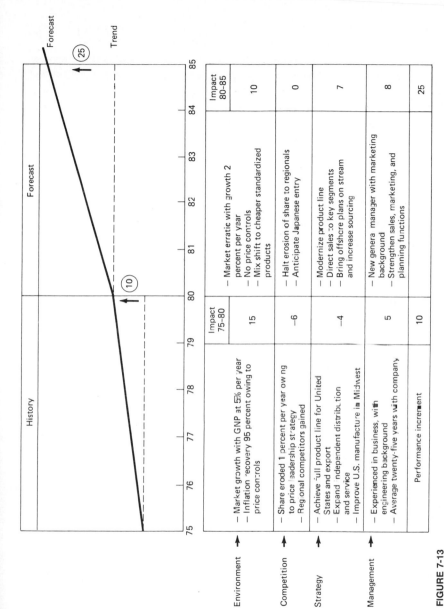

ciples to the individual case at hand: company size, business type, business structure, key business element, or environmental situation.

Each of these factors provides a working arena in which the planner will further delineate and tailor the planning process to the particular enterprise.

Well-executed planning basics are the *sine qua non* of sustained performance. This depends on clear corporate direction, competitive business strategy, concentration and integration of resources, and linkage of strategy to operations.

But the routes to these destinations differ according to the size, type, structure, key business element, and environmental situation for each business. The planning system for a corporation will require custom-tailored:

- Organization
- Procedure
- Formality
- Time horizon
- Frequency
- Documentation
- Meetings
- Information

Company Size Every company, whatever its size, requires strategic planning—but strategic planning is partly dependent on dimensions and magnitudes, namely the size of the company and the sizes of the business sectors, units, and segments within it.

Indeed one company's single product—WATS, Kodak 35mm Kodachrome II, Kleenex, Coca-Cola, and others, for example—can amount to many times the size of entire corporations.

The strategic planning process requires a design and methodology that can adapt to different magnitudes in coordination, information and communication, flexibility, and adaptability of larger and smaller organizations.

The "smaller company" (a term which defines all but the largest companies) must plan more formally, rigorously, analytically, and thus more strategically than the larger company—if only because it has fewer human and material resources to work with.

More to the point, it can probably afford fewer mistakes. Business failures among the top 500 companies are so few that they make headlines; their incidence is observably much more frequent as the listing moves down the top 1000 toward the thousands of companies that are little noted as they come and go.

Implicit in the planning challenge, especially for smaller companies, is the upgrading of the professionalism of management at all levels. Planning development for such companies should emphasize:

- *Planning by the management team, not just by the CEO.* The CEO knows more about the smaller company but does not have the time for unassisted planning. More to the point, the CEO needs more advice than his or her own counsel.
- *Strategy by outline, not by detailed action steps.* Parameters rather than specific steps give the smaller company more flexibility.
- *Improving the market and competitive information base.* Smaller companies tend to lack marketing and environmental details but generally know operating and financial details better.
- *Management education in business analysis tools.* Smaller company management tends to lack the sophisticated level of formal business management of the larger enterprise, relying more on intuitive, "seat-of-the-pants" decisions.
- *Serial, not parallel, plan development.* In smaller companies management tends to look at one area or issue at a time before proceeding to the next. In larger companies, the need for substantial coordination and corporate-level planning requires that all parts of the company conform to a more structured format and schedule—usually involving a simultaneity of planning processes at every level and examining several areas and/or issues at a time.

As noted, the planning process in the smaller company tends to become a more intensive educational process at the same time. As management plans, so it rises professionally.

But, as companies grow in size, developing a more complex mix of businesses, organizational hierarchies develop. These put a strain on information and communication. As management decentralizes, bureaucracy expands. Narrower, more specialized perspectives emerge, raising the likelihood of the proverbial peril: "The expert is one who learns more and more about less and less until he knows everything about nothing."

The information-communication barrier is discussed by Stafford Beer in his milestone work on management cybernetics, *Decision and Control* (Wiley, New York, 1966). He terms this barrier "vertical opaqueness." Figure 7-14 shows how a message sent upward through the organizational hierarchy from department head to CEO falls prey to miscommunication more than half the time—despite good communication and understanding at each step.

Communicating—getting a message through as intended—is one of management's most fundamental problems. Top management, frustrated at the seeming failure of the organization to be alert to both problems and opportunities, tries to compensate by requesting even more information for control—or more detailed plans for decision making.

The idea is to check up on subordinate operations. But the very process exacerbates vertical miscommunication because lower-level management now tends to vary the information by holding back a more or less significant portion of it. The upshot of this is that top management tends

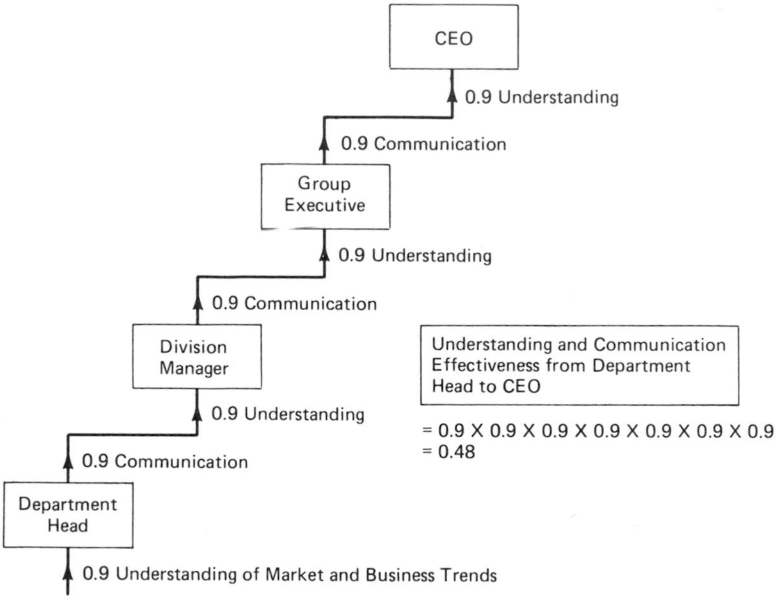

FIGURE 7-14
Vertical opaqueness of organizational hierarchies.

to receive ever poorer information; that is, the original misinformation becomes even more misleading.

A well-designed planning system can help to minimize the problems of such a vicious cycle in several ways:

- *Establish a simpler, shorter SPP hierarchy.* Figure 7-15 shows the differences between a financial organization and reporting hierarchy, and a strategic organization and planning structure. Bear in mind that the former is generally inadequate in our era (see Evolution of Planning Systems earlier in this chapter) because of their backward- rather than forward-looking posture.

- *Review planning at several levels.* Three to four levels of management are involved in periodic planning reviews. This puts the CEO directly in touch with a department manager, for example, and drives home the imperative for strategic planning throughout the management hierarchy.
- *Require written plans and business analyses.* Here, too, the CEO sees the department manager's information, but the CEO must also overcome the hierarchy's tendency to screen the information before it is passed on.

Larger organizations—as analyzed by outside consultants on numerous occasions, and even as analyzed by their own management—are

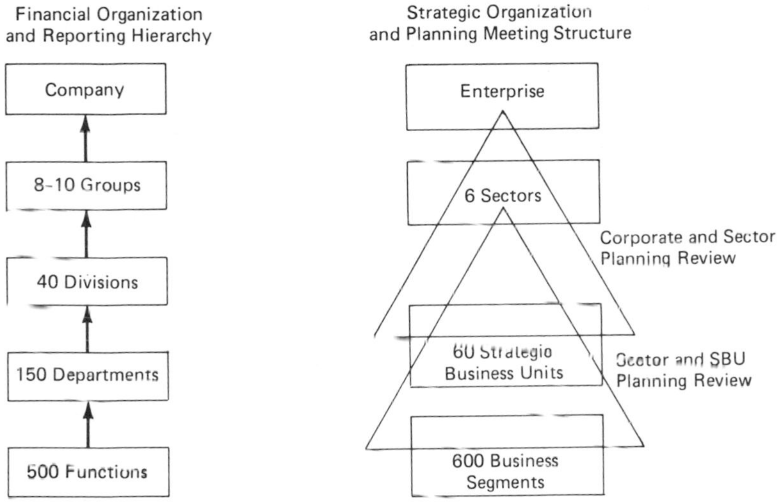

FIGURE 7-15
Using planning to shorten the organizational hierarchy.

found to face acute problems of sensitivity, adaptability, and alertness to changing opportunities and challenges.

The essence of the problem is the inevitable spillage of information in the vertical communication structure; it is as if the communicators were water carriers trying to carry water in their hands, transmitting it up a long line.

Business Type Clearly, planning must be tailored to a specific type of business because the critical management questions and freedoms differ profoundly, as indicated:

- *Natural Resources.* Highly centralized strategic planning dominates these businesses, in which relatively few large decisions determine the course of the company. Property acquisitions, exploration, extraction, production, and pricing are among such big questions, all of which, except for pricing, tend to involve large investments and long-range time periods. In such companies the planning system must be tailored to confront these few big, fairly infrequent questions.

Unfortunately, natural resource companies tend to overemphasize the one phase of their activities in which leverage is least effective: operational planning.

- *Manufacturing.* Formal strategic planning that is written out in detail, reviewed, and approved on a regular cycle is well suited to most manufacturing business. These tend to be mature and slow-moving, requiring frequent multifunctional decisions and coordination. They involve product design, plant addition, and pricing decisions at a significant cost, but with a five- to ten-year payout.
- *Services.* The proliferation of a single activity that has been tried out and proved successful in one or a few places is the dominant characteristic of larger service businesses. Franchise retailing (such as fast-food stores), chain stores, branch banks, field service operations (maintenance calls for machinery), car rental agencies, American Express, and the like typify service businesses that have mastered the art of providing much the same service in scores, even hundreds, of locations throughout the nation and the world. The idea is to multiply a single success in one place, to obliterate failure before it can multiply. Planning thus tends to be pragmatic and experimental, at least at first. Management controls are exercised through tailored compensation systems, often with substantial incentives, rather than through planning review and approval.

Larger-scale service businesses often utilize a network of interacting units such as car rental and hotel-motel systems, and/or pooled activities, such as purchasing and data processing. Centralized strategy for these functions must complement the highly decentralized planning of the service-delivery unit.

See Figure 7-16 for a summary of the different planning needs of these three business types.

Business Structure For discussion purposes we can group the four generic organization structures of business—functional, product, regional, and matrix—into the three strategic planning categories below to set forth three different planning methods.

A key problem everywhere in business is the need to inform and involve all management simultaneously in planning along several dimensions—the need to ponder many interlocking problems that cross organizational lines and that must therefore be considered both together and simultaneously.

In each of the following cases, the SPP informs and involves the several organizational units whose cooperation is vital to the planning.

- *Matrix Information.* Matrix organization forms have become a common way to address the problem of integrating product, market, and region, but they suffer from divided accountability. Figure 7-17 shows how the most minimal planning system should provide planning information on each cell of the matrix. All too often, however, the information is inadequate for planning. For example, pooled functions, such as sales, usually segment results by region but not by product; production may show costs and investment by plant or product but not by market, and so on.

Business Type	Investment Size	Time Horizon	Decision Similarities and Repetition	Degree of Operating Freedom	Need for Centralized Coordinator	Need for Decentralized Informational Flexibility
Natural Resources	Greatest	Greatest	Least	Least	Least	Mixed
Manufacturing	Mixed	Least	Least	Greatest	Mixed	Mixed
Services — Network	Mixed	Mixed	Mixed	Least	Greatest	Mixed
Services—Distribution	Least	Least	Greatest	Greatest	Least	Greatest

Greatest Mixed Least

FIGURE 7-16
Impact of business type on planning needs.

- *Matrix Integration.* The planning cycle in a matrix organization tends to differ from that of a purely product-oriented structure. Figure 7-18 shows the three-part planning cycle system for a bank: business planning, integration (for example, for pooled data-processing operations or for new multiregion product developments), and traditional operating plan–budget cycles. But many financial service institutions lack the integration cycle system, thus creating a nonintegrated (disconnected) planning cycle: segment and function strategies move on one track while resource conflicts remain unresolved on the second, disconnected track.
- *Functional-Regional-Product Integration.* Where integration is the key

factor, it is important to design a planning protocol with several integration iterations as shown in Figure 7-19. This prevents a last-minute rush to pull all functional plans together. It also avoids the problem of product and/or marketing plans being presented to operations, not for consideration, but as *faits accomplis*.

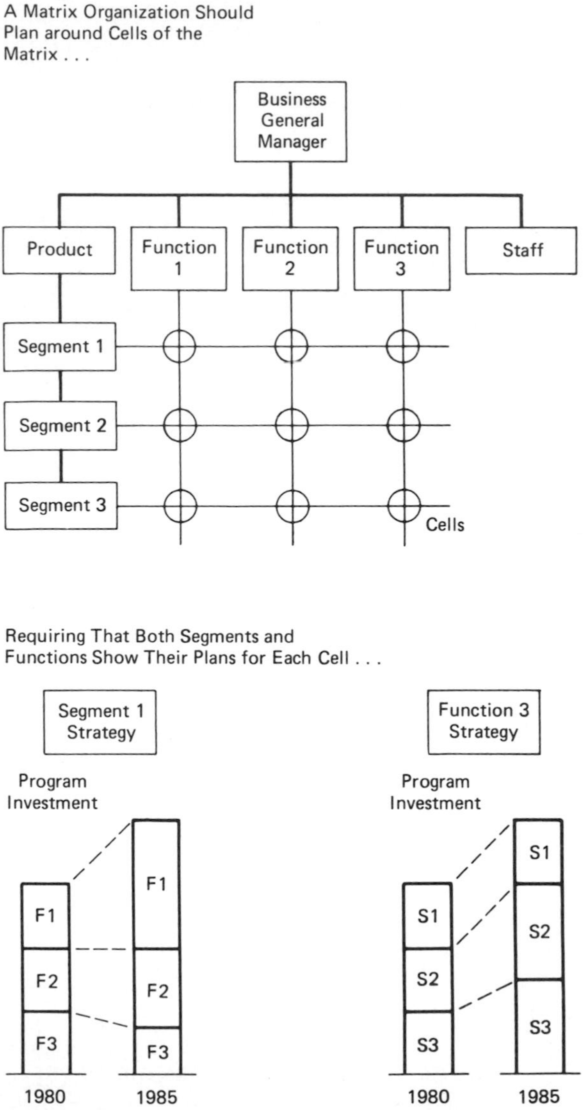

FIGURE 7-17
Matrix planning information: minimal planning system.

Key Business Element Strategic planning must accommodate the dominant characteristic of the enterprise, around which all other characteristics tend to become peripheral in terms of planning.

The key business element shapes the emphasis and focus of planning and usually demands highly specialized skills, a potential peril if business strategy basics are preempted.

The following businesses have chosen different planning system approaches to accommodate their key elements:

- *Investment Intensive.* Businesses with high fixed-capital intensity are especially sensitive to the relationship between market demand and capacity, relative competitive costs, transportation costs, and regulatory restrictions. Among these businesses are utility, process, chemical, and transportation industries. Major capital planning must be long-range, usually using scenario evaluation. Planning often utilizes detailed microeconomic models to project production-transportation economics. The SPP requires widespread management integration and information on sophisticated analyses of major decisions. The challenge resides in keep-

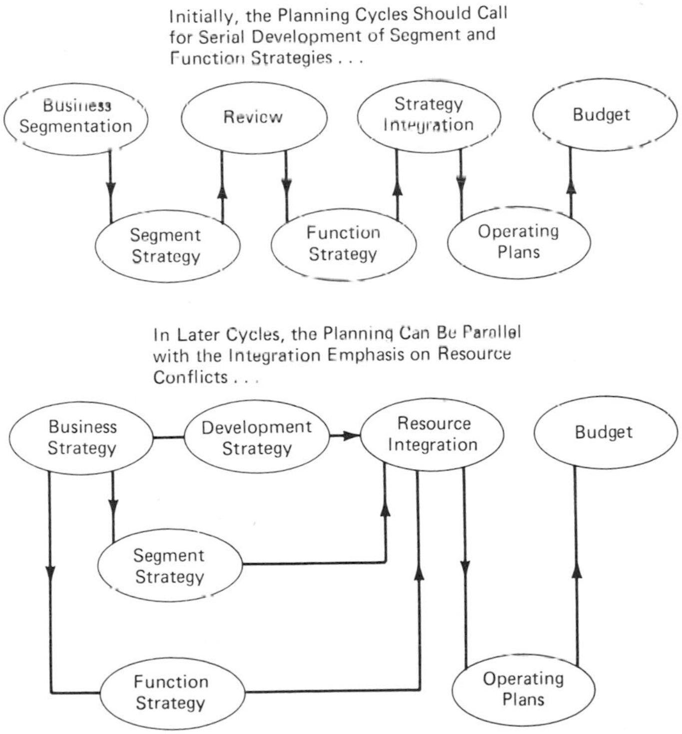

FIGURE 7-18
Matrix planning information: three-part planning cycle.

ing the capital planning strategic rather than predominantly operational or financial.

▪ *Multinational.* Investment-intensive businesses often require multinational production and product development (aircraft, pharmaceuticals), or they may be sensitive to local market idiosyncracies (food). They

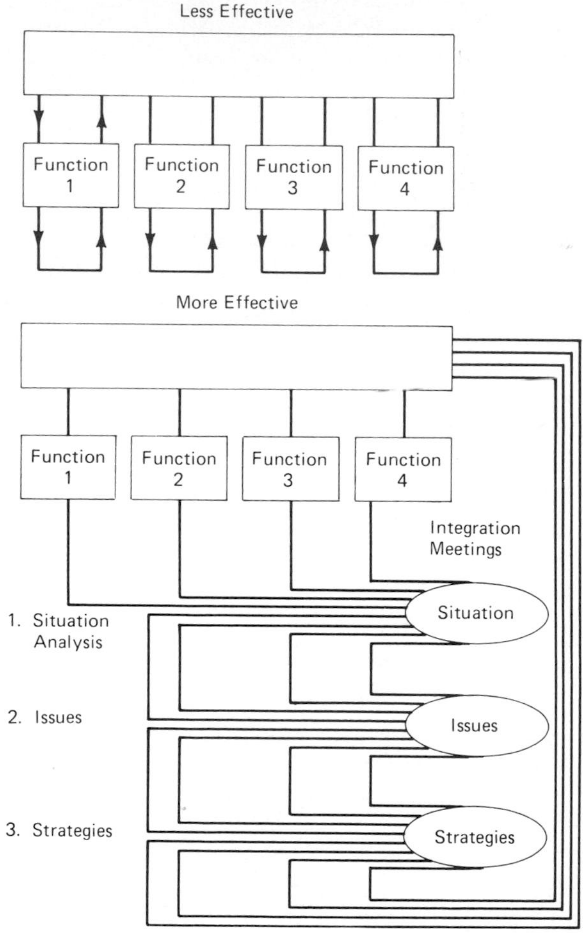

FIGURE 7-19
Planning protocols to achieve functional integration.

may, also, represent a mixture of the two concerns (automobiles, coffee). Multinational companies require a special type of matrix planning to combine expertise on local market conditions and worldwide technology and sourcing options. The SPP, therefore, requires a specific international integration procedure or mechanism.

- *Technology Intensive.* Technology-dominated companies cope with the functional-integration planning problem: they tend to understand the performance of a product better than they do its marketability. Similarly, the marketing organization tends to understand the market but not its elasticity to a technological breakthrough. Consumer electronics, one highly conspicuous example, represents an almost unending flow of technological innovation—from electronic games to home computers—that is fraught with innovational-cum-competitive difficulties.

Many companies play the risky innovation game as leaders, others as followers, some as both, depending on the product and the circumstances. Innovations and improvements, some of them cosmetic or even illusory, tend to make even new products obsolete or discontinued models within a year or two in such products lines as audio equipment, cameras, smaller computers, and word processing equipment.

The planning approach depends on the governing corporate "style" or "culture." The *innovation leader* corporation, when small, plans around the execution of the ideas of a few key individuals or even one key individual (for example, Polaroid). When larger, such a company tends toward a more formal new-venture planning system (3M), while still recognizing the key role of the creative individual in innovation. Some, like 3M, are proud of the speed and the leanness of the planning systems that support the policy "At 3M we make all kinds of tape except red tape."

Large R&D resources and extensive production skill and capacity allow many companies to take a wait, watch, and see approach to higher-technology businesses. Called a *me-too* or *leapfrog follower,* a company of this sort allows others to take the risks, and then imitates, emulates, or even surpasses them. This planning system approach must be alert, quick, project-oriented, and precisely targeted to the desired market position (for example, IBM's late entry into the home computer business).

All this focuses planning in the technology-intensive enterprise on key individuals and ventures. It searches for ways to link the specializing technologist and the marketer. Such planning moves at a fast pace, often with a three-month rather than twelve-month cycle. It is team-driven and project-oriented, and often takes a zero-base approach to program priorities.

Above all else, planning in such technology-intensive companies highlights the level and allocation of strategic expenditures for technology and the innovation that keeps it competitive in the market. Texas Instruments (see Figure 7-20) is a good example of this planning approach.

▪ *Marketing Intensive.* The consumer products business demands superior planning and strategy in the marketing realm. Branded goods—food, cosmetics, housewares, clothing—require innovative flair in product concepts, advertising, promotion, and even distribution (paperback books in supermarkets, or health insurance via credit card companies, for example). But all these potentially overenthusiastic thrusts to the marketplace are tempered and screened through rigorous consumer market and distribution analysis, from current and historical research to selective market testing. Leading consumer packaged goods companies, notably Procter and Gamble and Pepsico, utilize superior market analysis and research to remove as much risk as possible from the risk inherent in all innovation.

▪ *Overhead Intensive.* Overhead literally hangs over service-intensive business—banking, retailing, insurance, hotels, transportation, and others. Costs tend to be heavy, margins narrow. Escalating administrative costs push up break-even points rapidly, making overhead-cost control a key strategic issue. Such companies require fundamental value analysis of every administrative function to improve overhead costs. Strategic planning helps define the mission and the program elements of every overhead operation to determine its need, cost effectiveness, and relevance.

PROFIT AND LOSS STATEMENT				ZERO-BASED STRATEGIC PROGRAM EXPENSES		
		$000s			$000s	
	1980	1981	V %	Program	1980	1981
Revenues	$100	$110	10	1.	5	7
Variable Cost	30	33	10	2.	2	2
Period Cost	40	44	10	3.	1	2
Operating Profit	30	33	10	4.	1	1
Strategic Expenses	10	15	50	5.	0.5	1
Taxes	4	6	50	6.	0.5	—
Net Profit	$ 16	$ 12	−25	7.	10	—
				8.		1
				9.		15

FIGURE 7-20
Focus on strategic expenditures in the planning system of Texas Instruments.

Environmental Situation *Environmental situation,* of course, refers to the business-operating rather than physical environment of land, water, and air; but the business environment also deploys a varying topography, climate, and supporting meteorology for corporate planners.

In the following four cases, the environmental effects on the strategic planning system differ in terms of time scale and time horizon, the degree of centralization, the required skills, and the focus of the corporation.

- *Market Growth versus Maturity.* The high-growth company enjoys plentiful opportunities but suffers from scarce resources. The planning system must therefore focus on functional resource development. But the mature company tends to have more resources than opportunities. Here the planning system must focus on opportunity identification and development.
- *Regulation.* Regulatory change is a prime influence for better or worse, in an increasing number of industries—better (that is, less regulation), for airlines, worse (more regulation) for chemicals. Strategic planning to improve performance must work out numerous contingencies and scenarios. The planning system itself should be utilized to influence regulatory policy on an active, ongoing basis.
- *Uncertainty.* Many managers believe that planning is obsolete and unworkable because environmental uncertainty has undermined forecasting capability and, indeed, credibility. But the essence of strategic planning is not dependent so much on forecasting results as it is on understanding how to maintain competitive position in a wide variety of situations. Shell Oil, as one example, uses scenario planning to test the effectiveness of various strategies in a variety of environmental situations. Thus strategic planning must posit a range of possibilities rather than risking everything on hardened forecasts.
- *Crisis.* Profit collapse and critical cash shortages define the business crisis that may catch a mature business unaware and unprepared for an adverse environmental shift and/or competitive attack. The crisis may stem from underinvestment in prior years, a situation calling for the end of the "regular" planning system and the beginning of a crisis planning approach. This will be more centralized, objective, and self-critical. It must be action-oriented, favoring the good offense as the proverbial best defense. It must identify and concentrate on competitive weakness. The crisis is no time to be frantic, only determined.

Phase III: *Implementation of the Basic Planning System* The following are time-tested ground rules of SPP:

1. Simplify the process wherever and whenever possible.
2. Staff with proven doers, not with administrators.
3. Give management as much scope and freedom as possible.
4. Avoid forms, agendas, and overcoordination; in other words, be specific but stay loose.

The corporate plan will represent a consensus of top management and the board on the following:

The business profile of the company
The broad strategic objectives to be pursued in each business
Arenas for new business and technology development
The level of financial commitment the company will undertake
Key measures of operating performance
Principal financial results to be achieved

Accordingly, the corporate plan will *not* be a "blueprint" or "road map" preempting all key business decisions for the next five years. It will be the result of a dynamic and ongoing planning system. *This process is likely to be iterated each year.* The purpose of the corporate plan is to achieve a dynamic equilibrium among changing business strategy options, emerging corporate diversification opportunities, shifting financial markets, and variations in operating performance and financial results.

FIGURE 7-21
Purpose and definition of a corporate plan.

5. Identify action opportunities to keep SPP moving.

6. Keep talking, conferring, and listening to general management—and to suppliers and customers, too.

7. Reward results periodically, not just over the longer term.

8. Press for strategies to address both near-term and longer-term issues.

9. Don't expect perfection in the first go-through. Repeat, fine-tune, repeat again.

10. Build on success: provide models or pilot programs that can be copied, emulated, and applied throughout the company—but allow room for management creativity and variation at every level.

11. Keep in touch with all concerned as they progress.

Phase IV: *Some Important Planning System Strategies* It is important to match the strategy to the area of interest, whether it's a problem area or a successful one where improvement is desired. A good beginning is the corporate strategy framework.

This framework must embody certain key concepts and objectives (see Figure 7-21). It should also set forth an analytic procedure for the SPP (see Figure 7-22) that makes definitions, concepts, and processes clear to management, separating them from one another to set up an orderly agenda for consideration.

The problem, as ever, is to translate the abstract and the conceptual into the concrete and specific. The idea is to cut through the haze (or mystique), to break big challenges into their smaller, more digestible components. Such a no-nonsense, "brass tacks" approach increases management confidence and involvement, generates ideas, and lends the resulting strategic plan the status of a credo worth everyone's contribution.

The appropriate planning system strategy should be developed with a company's individual area of interest in mind, as in the following examples:

- *Production-Technology Resource Strategies.* Few strategic plans are integrated with innovative technology and production strategies. Manufacturing has long been termed the missing link in corporate strategy, perhaps as a result of a latter-day propensity to explore almost everything in the business except what it makes. Often enough the technological side of a company knows little about corporate strategies it is supposedly serving—and vice versa.

To overcome this lag, corporate plans must focus on the actual specifics of manufacturing techniques. Gaining this knowledge may well require shorter or longer courses of management familiarization and reinforcement, often to make up for long neglect.

Strategic plans must be specific to the point of synchronizing the manufacturing, production, and marketing procedures; buying influences

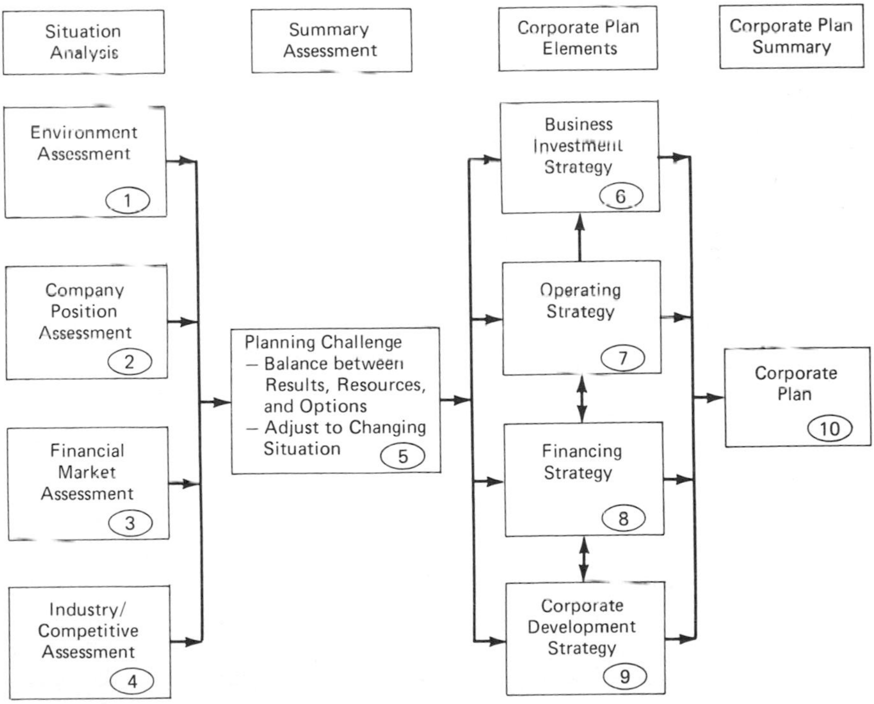

FIGURE 7-22
The corporate planning process.

by customer segment (a key to productivity strategy); and conducting "value analysis" of products in terms of technology-innovation potential.

These approaches demand clarity of communication, best achieved by actual demonstration—from the shop floor of the factory to the R&D labs, from the sales office to the marketplace.

A management failing to see these relationships and act upon them is a management forgetting the true business of the corporation. What the company makes and sells is what corporate strategic planning is essentially *about*—quite apart from all else that is relevant.

▪ *Budgeting Strategies.* Tying resource allocation priorities to budgets is corporate portfolio analysis spelled out and ready for implementation. Portfolio analysis that doesn't shape budgets is academic. Figure 7-23

STRATEGIC PORTFOLIO ANALYSIS	INVEST AND GROW	BUILD POSITION	DEFEND POSITION	HARVEST
BUDGET ELEMENT		YEAR-TO-YEAR VARIANCE, %		
Sales	20	15	10	0
Gross margin	25	15	12	5
Programs	30	20	15	0
Overhead	15	10	5	−10
Net profit	30	20	15	10
Working capital	20	15	5	−10
Fixed investments	30	15	10	−20
Cash flow	Negative	Balanced	Positive	Positive

FIGURE 7-23
Strategic budgets.

shows how operating budgets must have differing profiles depending on the strategic mission of the business unit or segment.

▪ *Management Selection Strategies.* A business, like any other institution, becomes (to quote Emerson) "the lengthened shadow of one man." The choice of the general manager at any level may be the greatest single strategic influence for success or failure. All too often the basis for such choice rests on personality, success in a different business, or administrative skill. Rarely, indeed, does top management make a serious effort to assess a potential manager's strategic leadership skills, the driving force of the business. Figure 7-24 charts these skills in terms of the strategic mission.

Phase V: *Auditing the SPP* The effective communications cited above tend to project a kind of ongoing audit to the SPP, but a separate periodic audit will allow management to keep the SPP on course. Such an audit, whether performed internally and/or utilizing the services of outside consultants, must reveal what steps in the SPP are working properly and what are not.

Two auditing methods allow management to recognize SPP elements that need the most attention:

- *Questionnaire.* Top management conferees ask one another to rate each element of the SPP system on a scale of 1 to 5. Typical responses are shown in Figure 7-25.
- *Management Interviews.* The questionnaire then becomes an agenda for management interviews based on problem areas the questionnaire may indicate. Management participation in these interviews often generates further management thinking about the planning system. An extract of typical management comments is shown in Figure 7-26.

Business Strategic Mission	Managerial Type	Strategic Management Skills
Invest and Grow	Entrepreneur	Change Maker Leader Risk Analyzer
Selectivity and Earnings	Sophisticate	Discriminator Judge Business Analyzer
Harvest and/or Divest	Retrencher	Negotiator Controller Asset Analyzer

FIGURE 7-24
Management for selection.

Such self-appraisal leads to self-correction of SPP system weaknesses—even if the improvement takes several years (see Figure 7-27).

Phase VI: *Counseling on SPP Problems* Strategic planning is not simply one of the greater management challenges in terms of importance to the enterprise—it is also commensurately and inherently difficult because the assumptions and even the successes of the past rarely provide a sound basis for the future.

Up until the late 1960s, the general business environment—from regulation to inflation—tended to progress toward steadily larger numbers, without such interruptions (discontinuities) as double-digit inflation, energy and other resource shortages, regulatory changes, capital acquisition problems, and the like.

The enterprise may well need the experience and perspective of outsiders. Management consulting can often provide analysis, insight, and objectivity to help the corporation's SPP move from the conceptual through the implementational stages.

Planning System Element	Major Strengths		Major Weaknesses	
Stage 1. Clarity of corporate direction	Financial objectives	+50	Planning challenges	−8
	Emphasis on competitive position	+50	Corporate issues	−11
			Corporate risks	−14
			Corporate strategy	−40
	SUMMARY: What is the corporate plan to meet objectives?			
Stage 2. Strength of business planning	Financial strategy	+8	Innovation strategy	−44
	Business objectives	+16	Planning data base	−11
	Product/market segmentation	+16	Resource strategies	−25
			Creative strategies to improve share	−22
	SUMMARY: Business planning is finance-driven and deterministic—not innovative.			
Stage 3. Corporate review and integration	Review of plans for analytic consistency	+5	Resource allocation	−55
			Short-term–long-term trade-offs	−55
			Integration of acquisitions	−50
			International integration	−36
			Feedback on strategy	−28
	SUMMARY: Top management does little with the plans it receives.			
Stage 4. Linkage of plans with operations	Top management involvement	+33	Organization for strategy	−58
			Management fit with strategy	−55
			Pay and promotion for strategy	−50
			Linkage of budgets to strategy	−55
	SUMMARY: Strategy is not linked to key management systems.			

FIGURE 7-25
Questionnaire on planning used in a consumer packaged-goods company.

Indeed, the SPP can well utilize a kind of consulting ombudsman at every level, who will help to keep management in solid control of the SPP as it progresses.

Often important problems emerge that must affect the SPP, especially during years 3 to 10 in the planning cycle. Among these are:

- Company organization changes after major acquisition, divestiture, and/or closure

Issues Covered in Audit	Typical Management Responses
Need for stronger planning	Top management "We are pinpointing issues." "Do plans exist or merely issues?" Middle management "A corporate strategy is urgently needed." "Plans need to be more strategic."
Effectiveness of planning process	Top management "Planning is not a process, it's form-filling." "Planners don't have sufficient stature." "Line people are untrained." Middle management "The process is a farce, a joke." "We need clearer direction on how to allocate resources." "We need deeper strategic analysis."
Linkage with operating management systems	Top management "The budgeting process gets the upper hand." "We must differentiate compensation." Middle management "There is no linkage of performance appraisal to longer term." "Plans aren't specific enough to translate into functional tactics."

FIGURE 7-26
Management interview audit of planning system in a financial services company.

Timing	Key Steps
YEAR 1	1. Audit and planning improvement program 2. Conference and seminar series on strategic planning 3. Decisive move on key corporate issue 4. SBUs defined 5. Ten percent of SBUs to begin thorough strategy analysis
YEAR 2	1. Broaden education program 2. Strengthen SBU and corporate planning staffs 3. Extend SBU strategy development 4. Make initial corporate portfolio reviews 5. Initiate strategic budgeting
YEAR 3	1. Shape corporate plan 2. Focus SBUs on key challenges and innovation 3. Modify pay and promotion system 4. Adjust organization and management assignments

FIGURE 7-27
Planning development program.

- Decline in calibre of planning staff
- Overemphasis on functional planning work
- Operating crisis and overhead reductions
- Reduced management attention and involvement

SUMMARY

Strategic planning is essentially the business of all managers, whether or not they are actually called into the ranks of strategic planners per se. Every manager's experience is a corporate resource that the best strategic planners will put to good use.

The lines of information and communication comprise a network of knowledge that strategic planning must process (the SPP) into future-directed wisdom. This is the basic management challenge.

The future of the enterprise depends on the long-term thoughtfulness that guides its various ways; beyond the immediate, pressing imperatives of the moment, the apparently distant years are approaching faster than management tends to realize.

In our era of rapid change—including rapid top-management and other personnel change—the SPP sometimes begins to be seen as someone else's responsibility. This point of view is a major disincentive to thinking and planning beyond the next quarterly and annual reports.

But all management is most likely to outlive any strategic planning, witnessing its legacy and thus being associated with its results—wherever the planners may be when the plan comes to fruition, however much the plan may vary from the original and subsequent intents.

The SPP thus amounts to more than the duty of corporate management: it becomes a moral as well as an occupational, ex officio task.

The times we live in tend to cloud the aspect of the future more than any previous era—in the widest perspectives of the nation and the world, in the narrower ones of the industry and the enterprise, and certainly in the narrowest perspective of all: that of the individuals responsible for the strategic planning that determines the course of our economy.

In this sense the strict duty to plan strategically—honoring the obligation inherent in management—becomes imbued with a certain noblesse oblige: to honor the long-term needs of the enterprise, of its owners and constituent communities, in the best traditions of leadership.

Chapter 8
THE STRATEGY AUDIT

ALLAN J. PRAGER
Vice President and Director, Cresap, McCormick and Paget Inc.

MARY BETH SHEA
Managing Consultant, Cresap, McCormick and Paget Inc.

Since the beginning of recorded history, strategy has been associated primarily with military action. In business, strategy as a concept and strategic planning as a formal activity or a process came into their own during the 1970s. During this time strategy became the target of intense scrutiny: innumerable articles and books were written, seminars and other educational programs held, new positions and departments created, and new business-planning processes established. In short, significant amounts of time and money have been expended in pursuit of "strategy."

An important question arises for the business community as a whole and for any given firm in particular: namely, how well is a strategy working? What are the key variables? How can strategy be evaluated? The purpose of this chapter is to provide a framework within which strategy can be evaluated and specific answers to these questions developed.

Most of the attention paid to strategy during the past 10 or 15 years has focused on the process of strategic planning, but very little on how to evaluate a strategy once you have one. Strategy, however, has four characteristics that argue strongly for periodic review and evaluation.

First, strategic decisions determine what a company as a whole is trying to achieve and to become. As such, they are the most fundamental and important decisions a company makes.

Second, a strategy often takes years to unfold. Time thus provides the ultimate answer as to whether or not a particular strategy was successful, that is, whether the company in question achieved its strategic goals and objectives. While this time is passing, considerable resources will be expended, and opportunities to pursue alternative courses of action will be missed. With so much at risk, few companies can afford the test of time as the only means to determine if a strategy is viable. A systematic review of a firm's strategy and its ability to carry it forward can alert management to problems and to opportunities. In either case, the need to take corrective action can be pinpointed before definitive results are determined.

Third, because strategy is prospective in orientation and rests heavily on assumptions about the external environment, a strategy is inherently uncertain and subject to change. And yet failure to detect indicators of environmental shifts that may profoundly influence the course of a strategy is not uncommon. A periodic strategy "checkup" will help to ensure that the plan remains in concert with reality.

Fourth, a strategy is typically not a neat, integrated package produced all at once. Rather, a strategy tends to be a pattern of objectives, goals, policies and resource-allocation decisions. From time to time, it is useful for a company to step back and make an objective appraisal of the integrity of strategic decisions and how well or poorly the organization, its people, and its processes support and reinforce the decisions. A strategy audit is a vehicle for carrying out such an appraisal.

WHEN AND WHY SHOULD A STRATEGY AUDIT BE CONDUCTED?

The existence of any of a number of conditions or factors may suggest the need for a strategy audit. For example:

- Performance indicators suggest the strategy is not working or is producing unexpected, negative side effects.
- Things are not getting done; what people seem to be spending time on is inconsistent with priorities identified in the strategic plan.
- A shift or change occurs in the external environment; for example, the competition announces a technology breakthrough or a new competitor enters the market.

Aside from specific warning signals that suggest a problem with either strategy formulation or strategy implementation, a strategy audit can also be useful to top management:

- To fine-tune a strategy that is already successful
- To ensure that a strategy that has worked in the past continues to be in tune with subtle internal or external changes that may have occurred

STRATEGY AUDIT: FRAMEWORK FOR EVALUATING STRATEGY

The success of a strategy is a function of both its formulation and implementation; that is, how well it is put together and how well it is executed. The evaluation of strategy is problematic in that so many factors contribute to its relative effectiveness. Good plans can fail through poor implementation. Assumptions based on erroneous forecasts can negate the best of strategies; assumptions that prove to be on target can be offset through poor planning. The most brilliant strategy can be undermined when communication breaks down between strategic decision makers and those who must carry out the strategy.

There are three principal components of what might be termed the strategic system of a company. The three components are:

1. *Planning,* which involves an iterative process of setting objectives, making assumptions about conditions that will affect the business, identifying critical contingencies, and developing policies and programs to achieve the objectives in light of the assumptions and contingencies
2. *Implementation,* which involves the tangible and intangible elements that enable a company to get things done, including how it is organized, its resources, internal systems and processes, management style and employee culture, and agreement among employees as to what is to be accomplished
3. *Results,* which can be measured in various ways and which, when properly evaluated, provide continuous feedback to the planning and implementation components.

This strategic system in turn provides a framework for the systematic evaluation of strategy. As illustrated in Figure 8-1, a strategy audit focuses on the key elements of strategy formulation, implementation, and results as well as on the interrelationships among the elements.

AUDITING STRATEGY FORMULATION

Auditing strategy formulation requires an approach different from that used to develop a strategy in the first place. Strategy development usually begins with situation analysis and proceeds through various iterations that involve formulation and testing of mission statements, objectives, assumptions, and alternatives, and evaluation of resources available and required. The process culminates, of course, in a strategic plan.

Auditing this process, however, starts from a different point, as indicated in Figure 8-2. Since the company, by definition, already has not only a strategic plan but also some performance data from the period since the plan was developed, the logical starting place is the performance data. Working from the results of the strategic plan, the strategy audit goes through the strategy formulation process in reverse, identifying and tracing the various elements of performance back to their underpinnings in the analysis that produced the plan. In so doing, the strategy audit addresses the following key questions:

- Is there evidence that the strategy is working?
- Is the strategy practical?
- Are corporate objectives and goals, policies, and major programs clearly articulated and internally consistent?
- Are the underlying assumptions valid?
- Have contingencies been recognized and assessed?
- Does the strategy continue to be appropriate?

Is There Evidence That the Strategy Is Working?

Quantitative and qualitative indicators should be identified and examined to gain a preliminary estimate of:

- The company's current position in relation to its competitors
- Performance trends
- Degree to which short- and long-term goals and objectives are being met

Quantitative performance indicators include sales volume, earnings, stock price, leverage, return on equity, return on assets, profit margins,

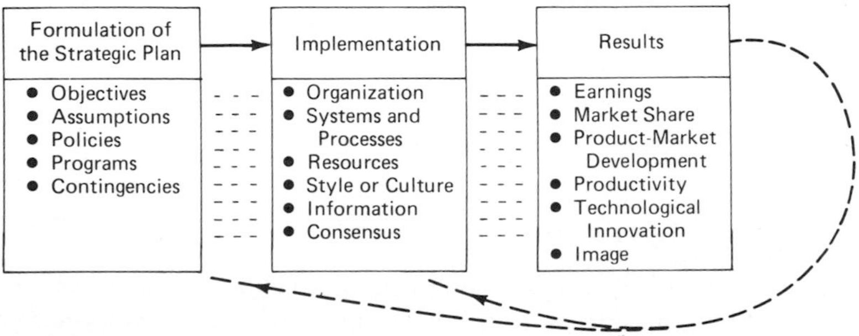

FIGURE 8-1
Components of a strategic system.

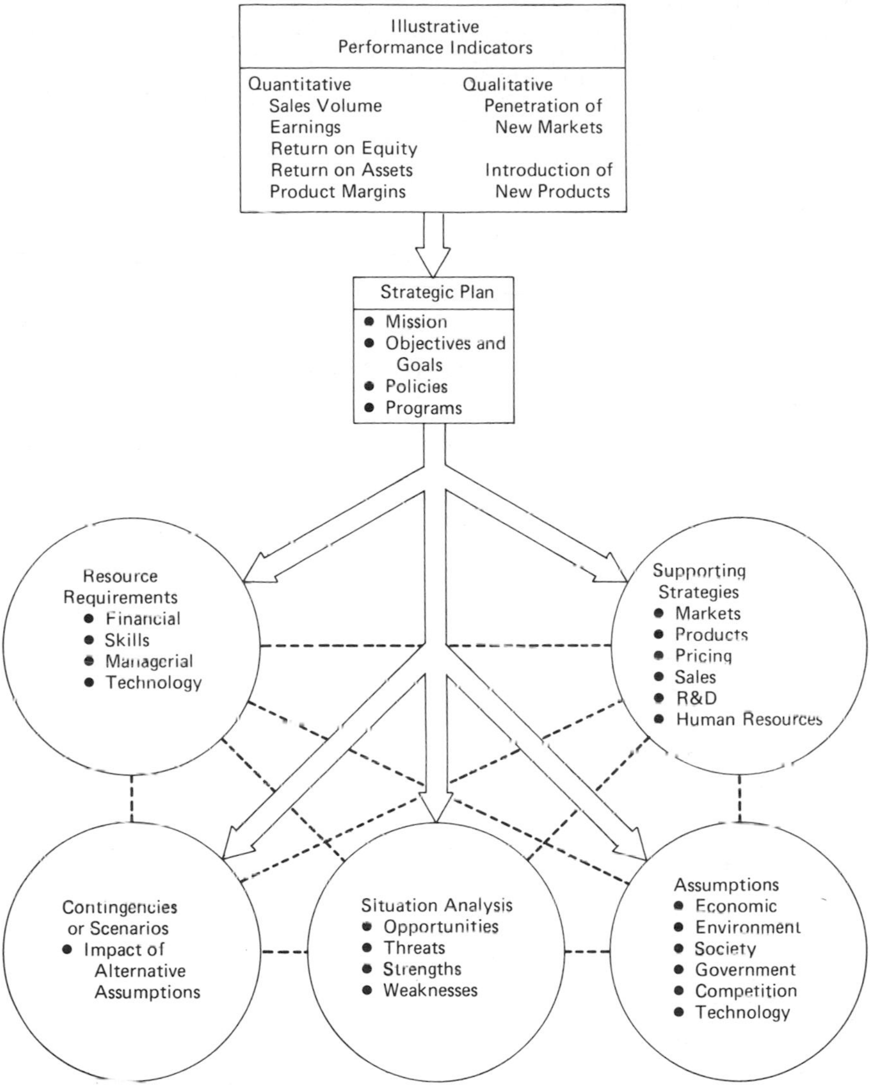

FIGURE 8-2
Auditing strategy formulation.

market share, and productivity measures. Qualitative indicators may include factors such as penetration of new markets, introduction of new products or product enhancements, process improvements, and so forth. Of particular interest is the identification of early warning indicators that provide visibility over unfavorable performance trends that have yet to impact overall financial results.

Is the Strategy Practical?

A strategy must be realistic with respect to the company's ability to carry it out. An assessment of the practicality of a strategy will include the extent to which:

- The strategy builds on proved strengths and recognizes any real or potential weaknesses or deficiencies that must be addressed
- The resources required to implement the strategy, including capital, human, physical and technological, have been identified and either are available or can reasonably be obtained.

A key challenge in strategy formulation is estimating correctly what it will take to implement the strategy. While the initial estimate upon which the decision to proceed is based is critical, it is equally important to reassess that initial estimate frequently. Resource requirements may be greater than expected, thus requiring top management to make adjustments if the strategy is to be successful, or they may be less than expected, thus affording the opportunity to reallocate excess resources.

The abortive attempts of three corporate giants to enter the computer mainframe business in the late 1950s and early 1960s reflect fundamental miscalculations of the resources required to compete. Similarly, the strategy of a fast-food restaurant chain to expand quickly in prime areas to promote long-term growth in advance of the competition was sound in every respect except for the fact that half of the new restaurants could not be opened on schedule for lack of experienced managers to run them.

Are Corporate Objectives and Goals, Policies, and Major Programs Clearly Articulated and Internally Consistent?

Three elements—objectives and goals, policies, and major programs—provide the basic direction to all actions taken in support of the company's strategy. Without clearly defined objectives and measurable goals, the company does not know where it is going or what it is trying to accomplish. Many companies have developed a concept of strategy, but fail to articulate objectives and goals. Consequently, there is no benchmark against which to measure overall progress. Moreover, the company lacks a common frame of reference to serve as a rallying point.

Once goals are defined, major policies must be defined or reexamined to ensure consistency. For example, a traditionally conservative bank, facing intense competitive pressures and a declining market share, decided to adopt a more aggressive strategy to increase its deposit base and loan portfolio. However, the bank's traditional credit policies were not reexamined in the course of strategy formulation. They remained in force, severely limiting the ability of the loan officers to adopt the more aggressive posture in their interactions with customers and prospects.

Major programs must also be reassessed to ensure that they support the strategy. A major retailer, for example, established an aggressive goal of opening 28 new properties within several years. The goal was widely known among all levels of management, but progress toward achieving it lagged because management was slow to recognize that the internal processes related to the store development program would have to change substantially if a rate of expansion significantly higher than three or four units per year were to be achieved.

Are the Underlying Assumptions Valid?

In a dynamic environment, a key, generic success factor for any company is the ability to understand the assumptions upon which strategic decisions are based and to revise them in a timely manner. Many companies fail in this regard because:

- Their assumptions are implicit and perhaps not well understood
- Developing assumptions becomes a mechanical, not a creative process
- Certain assumptions attain the status of sacred beliefs which no one in the company thinks to challenge

A strategy audit involves an objective appraisal of the critical assumptions that underlie the firm's current strategy, focusing on four essential issues:

- Have all important or potentially important trends and impacts been identified and assessed?
- Are the assumptions consistent with external data? If not, are inconsistencies known and justified?
- Is the data base consistent and integrated with all planning activities? (Is everyone making decisions on the basis of the same information?)
- Are critical assumptions monitored routinely and revised as appropriate?

Strategy is based on facts about the past and the present and on assumptions about the future. How a company's strategic decision makers think about the future is a critical influence on strategy formulation. The depth and breadth of that thinking and the degree to which top management can think creatively about traditional assumptions will vitally affect a company's ability to adapt to changing conditions.

Business history is replete with examples of strategies (and sometimes companies) that failed because of faulty assumptions, where faulty assumptions are defined not simply as those that prove to be wrong *in time,* but those that do not hold up under scrutiny *at the time.* Many companies cling tenaciously to basic assumptions about, for example, consumer preferences, supply of natural resources, technology development, growth patterns, and so forth, even in the face of emerging counterevidence.

The U.S. auto industry seriously weakened its dominant position in the domestic market by being slow to recognize the fundamental nature of the shift in consumer preference toward smaller, more fuel-efficient cars. Following a significant decline in sales, automakers are in the process of redesigning and retooling their entire lines, a massive and time-consuming undertaking. Meanwhile, foreign competitors who could meet the demand gained record market share.

Similarly, many utilities refused to believe that the decline in demand for energy following the 1973–1974 oil embargo was any more than a temporary aberration. At the same time, they failed to recognize the long-term potential of conservation. Seeing instead the continuation of historical demand and usage trends, many companies followed old patterns and committed themselves to build huge amounts of new generating capacity. In many instances, these construction projects were to become financial albatrosses, severely limiting the flexibility of the sponsor companies to adjust when the changes that had been foreshadowed became fact.

Have Contingencies Been Recognized and Assessed?

In formulating a strategy, a company must make decisions about how the future environment will affect the fundamental strategic elements such as supply, demand, regulation, and technology. Each decision is subject to some probability that it will be wrong. Strategy formulation is not complete unless the key contingencies have been recognized and the impact of one or more contingent events occurring has been assessed. Examples of contingencies that could impact strategic assumptions follow.

Key strategic assumptions	Examples of contingencies
Critical resources	Cost
	Availability
Regulation and legislation	Supportive
	Restrictive
Competition	Industry concentration
	Product and/or service differentiation
	Productive capacity
Technology	New developments and breakthroughs
	Delays and/or failure

The sensitivity of projected results to the assumptions on which they are based must be measured. For example, if the cost of debt is a critical assumption, has the sensitivity of output parameters, such as operating income or coverage ratios, to changes in the assumption been evaluated? Do decision makers have information on the risk profile of projected results? Too often, strategy is based on a scenario deemed "most likely" without any attempt to assess the probability of occurrence and, more importantly, without an understanding of the probability of other results that could have serious consequences.

Changes in regulation can have dramatic impact on the strategy of any company. By identifying alternative regulatory scenarios and assessing the relative effect of each on projected results, a company can facilitate rapid adjustment if a critical contingency occurs. Long before the Brazilian government began to talk about requiring local manufacturers to produce alcohol-fueled cars, at least one manufacturer had "on the shelf" a set of detailed engineering drawings, cost estimates, and procurement plans to produce the motors that the government later required.

A strategy audit would identify and confirm the contingencies which could impact a strategic plan. It would evaluate the extent to which appropriate "what if . . ." questions have been asked, and alternative scenarios developed and assessed during the formulation process. Finally, a strategy audit would examine whether mechanisms were in place to reassess the relative merits of alternative scenarios frequently as the strategy is implemented.

The goal of an audit of strategy formulation is essentially to ascertain the original and continuing validity of the strategic plan. The second phase of a strategy audit focuses on the ability of the company to carry out its strategy.

AUDITING STRATEGY IMPLEMENTATION

A strategy must be consistent with the internal—as well as external—environment and requires support systems that will stimulate and reinforce the behavior necessary to carry it out. The success of strategy implementation depends on a synthesis of those factors that determine the fundamental character of the firm and how it operates. Implementation will be facilitated in proportion to the degree of synchronization between the strategy and these factors as reflected in the following:

- Is the strategy congruent with management style, values, and risk preferences?
- Is the organization structured to achieve strategic objectives?

- Do management systems and processes support overall strategic direction and key programs?
- Does the information system monitor strategic implementation?
- Is there an appropriate balance between preparing for the future and maximizing the present?
- Is there a consensus within the company as to strategy?

Is the Strategy Congruent with Management Style, Values, and Risk Preferences?

Every firm can be described in qualitative terms just as it can be described in terms of sales, assets, return on equity, and so forth. The qualitative description can cover relatively objective factors such as products or services provided, types of customers served, modes of distribution, and so forth. In addition, however, every firm can be described along much more subjective dimensions, such as whether it is tightly or loosely controlled, conservative or progressive, risk-averse or risk-seeking, entrepreneurial or bureaucratic. In effect, these factors define the personality of the company. In planning and implementing strategy, corporate personality is a subtle factor, often overlooked, but a critical determinant of success, nonetheless. For example, it accounts to a large degree for the difficulty that large, highly structured companies experience in fostering innovation.

Is the Organization Structured to Achieve Strategic Objectives?

Organization structure is a tool that can either enhance or impede strategy implementation. For example, a key element in the strategy of a large bank was to develop total banking relationships with retail customers by providing a full range of consumer-oriented financial services. And yet, responsibility for consumer services was fragmented into four separate departments. Unless responsibility is integrated at an operational level, a critical strategic goal may well not be met.

Organizational arrangements have symbolic as well as real implications. For example, by elevating the status of the exploration function in the organization and by giving it direct access to the board, a major oil company signaled that exploration had become a corporate priority. As a result of this and related actions, the company was able to improve its performance from the worst major oil company in exploration to the best.

Do Management Systems and Processes Support Overall Strategic Direction and Key Programs?

In any company, the major functions of the business are linked, formally or informally, by management systems and processes. In a manufacturing company, the major functions may include, for example, research and development, procurement, manufacturing, marketing, and finance. Key management systems and processes, including business or operational planning, budgeting and control, as well as rewards for performance, should provide the linkage among these functions to ensure that taken together they reflect and support the company's strategy. Examples of problems that can occur include the following:

- Planning and budgeting are not synchronized. For example, the budgeting process may allocate insufficient funds to maintenance of current businesses, while at the same time investing heavily to achieve longer-term strategic objectives, or, conversely, provide adequate funding for business in the coming year, but fail to invest to meet strategic objectives with long lead times.
- Specific operational objectives are incompatible with corporate strategic direction.
- Reporting systems measure actual short-term results, but do not adequately capture progress toward longer term goals and/or do not monitor variances from events, actions, or conditions assumed in a strategic plan.
- The rewards system emphasizes short-term performance.

In practice, the thrust of management systems and processes is often separated from overall strategic direction. An industrial equipment manufacturer, in an attempt to rejuvenate a product line, added microprocessor controls. No provision was made, however, to ensure smooth integration of the product strategy with production. Consequently, new lead times took production managers by surprise, causing severe production foul-ups and parts shortages. Similarly, a consumer-textile products company markedly changed its strategy when competitors introduced fashion concepts to sheets and towels. Marketing programs were designed accordingly, but implications on production were not assessed. In fact, the implications, which included significant product line expansion and shorter product life cycles, had enormous repercussions on production scheduling and inventory planning, as well as on ingrained behavior patterns. Because none of these factors was anticipated, the company learned by trial and error, suffering cost increases and critical delays in the process.

The strategic plan of a financial institution called for development of sophisticated financial services in order to retain and attract corporate customers. In-house development of a cash-management system was identified as a top priority. The data processing organization, however, had its own priorities. The result: three years later, the company had produced a manual cash-management system.

Does the Information System Monitor Strategic Implementation?

Information tools must be available and adequate to allow strategic decision makers to monitor progress toward strategic goals and objectives, track actual performance, pinpoint accountability, and, most importantly, provide early warning of any need to adjust the strategy.

Two common problems, one systemic and the other cultural, exist with respect to strategic information. First, information systems tend to focus on financial results and furnish only minimal visibility over variances from assumptions underlying operating plans and the strategy. Take, for example, the handling of information to top management on the progress of a major product development project. At the time approval is requested, a complete project report is usually prepared, documenting market opportunities, facility costs, added gross profit, cumulative cash flow, return on investment, and so on. Once approval has been obtained, however, the reporting tends to become fragmented. For example, there may be regular reporting of commitments, expenditures, and even physical progress, but usually there is no consolidated project reporting which regularly pulls together the latest assumptions concerning all key factors, such as consumer trends, competitive action, anticipated sales, gross profit, facility costs, and cash flow. Consequently, management often finds it difficult to recognize problems or opportunities until the project is completed and adjustment of plans is no longer possible.

The second problem relates to a "shoot the messenger" atmosphere which often pervades a company. Managers and corporate staff analysts feel a disincentive to report negative indicators or other bad news. For example, the vice president, construction, of a major utility company perceived that top management did not want to know about an impending overrun on major capital projects. Consequently, overruns were reported after the fact. On the other hand, the culture in other companies serves to encourage a "no-surprises" atmosphere. A major multinational company, for example, has strong incentives to report even subtle environmental changes that could impact corporate strategy.

Is There an Appropriate Balance between Preparing for the Future and Maximizing the Present?

Many companies exhibit the pendulum problem, that is, focusing on the present at the expense of the future, or vice versa. Sometimes this situation is precipitated by seeming expediency. For example, a manufacturer of computer peripheral equipment and data storage products, in a successful attempt to improve its weak financial position, among other actions, slashed the R&D budget. Five years later the company found itself paying the price of a short-lived recovery strategy that made too little provision for the future in a business that depends on technological innovation.

At the opposite end of the spectrum are companies that pursue the future with too little regard for the present. An office machines company, in an attempt to atone for failure to adapt quickly enough to the electronic age, committed itself to a strategy of intensive acquisition and growth. The problem: failure to safeguard a steady stream of profits to provide funding for the new programs.

The American preoccupation with the bottom line is well known. It results from the extensive reliance of U.S. industry on capital markets and, more specifically, from the pressure induced by the constant scrutiny of securities analysts. As a result of this preoccupation, boards of directors and managers from the president on down tend to be short-term optimizers. When asked how long he had been in his present position, the president of a medium-size, publicly held company promptly replied, "Fifteen quarters." To the extent that strategy implementation requires a commitment of resources that will not pay off in the short term—indeed may diminish short-term results—mechanisms must be devised to ensure a productive balance between the present and the future.

Is There a Consensus within the Company as to Strategy?

It is unlikely that a strategy will be implemented, except by happenstance, if it is not understood. A strategy audit can help top management determine the extent to which there is concurrence among key employees on:

- What the firm's strategy is
- How the strategy is to be implemented
- What the real priorities of the company are

The reason that a strategy appears to be faltering may have more to do with its not being understood than any inherent deficiencies in the strategy itself. The way a strategy tends to be internalized within a firm is a function of how well or poorly the strategy integrates with organizational arrangements, reward systems, and so forth, as discussed above.

In the American business culture, the role of consensus is often neglected. Japanese companies attribute their superior performance in such areas as productivity, quality control, and bringing new products to market in part to their ability to gain consensus and to focus the attention of all employees on strategic priorities.

PERSPECTIVE ON STRATEGY AUDITS

With this overview of the strategy audit behind us, we are now in a position to provide some perspective on the key question related to strategy audits: why do one at all?

The answer is straightforward. The success of a strategic planning effort derives from the analytical rigor and thoroughness applied during strategy formulation, and from appropriate leadership and coordination of all the elements involved in implementation. When a strategic plan—or, more often, part of one—does not lead to the desired results, the problem may lie anywhere within what we previously called the strategic system. The strategy audit is the best way to get at the wide number of complex and interdependent variables that need to be analyzed in order to reap the growth and profit benefits from all of the effort that went into strategic planning.

CONDUCTING A STRATEGY AUDIT

A strategy audit is conducted in three phases: diagnosis to identify how, where, and in what priority in-depth analyses need to be made; focused analysis; and generation and testing of recommendations. Objectivity and the ability to ask critical, probing questions are key requirements for conducting a strategy audit.

PHASE ONE: DIAGNOSIS

The diagnostic phase includes the following tasks.

- Review key documents such as:
  —Strategic plan.
  —Business or operational plans.
  —Organizational arrangements.
  —Major policies governing matters such as resource allocation and performance measurement.
- Review financial, market and operational performance against benchmarks and industry norms to identify key variances and emerging trends.
- Gain an understanding of:
  —Principal roles, responsibilities and reporting relationships.
  —Decision-making processes, and major decisions made.
  —Resources, including physical facilities, capital, management, technology.
  —Interrelationships among functional staffs and business or operating units.
- Identify strategic implications of strategy on organization structure, behavior patterns, systems, and processes.
  —Define interrelationships and linkages to strategy.
- Determine internal and external perspectives.
  —Survey the attitudes and perceptions of senior and middle managers and other key employees to assess the extent to which these are consistent with the strategic direction of the firm. One way to accomplish this task is through carefully focused interviews and/or questionnaires, wherein employees are asked to identify and make tradeoffs among the objectives and variables which *they* consider most important.

- —Interview a carefully selected sample of customers and prospective customers and other key external sources to gain an understanding of the way in which the company is viewed.

- Identify those aspects of the strategy that are working well. Formulate hypotheses regarding problems and opportunities for improvement based on the findings of the above steps. Define how and in what order each should be pursued.

PHASE TWO: FOCUSED ANALYSIS

- Test the hypotheses concerning problems and opportunities for improvement through analysis of specific issues.
  —Identify interrelationships and dependencies among components of the strategic system.
- Formulate conclusions as to weaknesses in strategy formulation, implementation deficiencies, or interactions between the two.

PHASE THREE: RECOMMENDATIONS

- Develop alternative solutions to problems and ways of capitalizing on opportunities.
  —Test in light of their resource requirements, risks, rewards, priorities, and other applicable measures.
- Develop specific recommendations.
  —Develop an integrated, measurable and time-phased action plan to improve strategic results.

Chapter 9
THE BENEFITS OF ENVIRONMENTAL ANALYSIS*

IAN WILSON†
Senior Management Consultant, International Development Center, SRI International

We shall not cease from exploration
And the end of all our exploring
Will be to arrive where we started
And know the place for the first time.
T. S. ELIOT

If we could first know where we are and whither we are tending, we could then better judge what to do and how to do it.
ABRAHAM LINCOLN

The business environment is likely to be, for the indefinite future, as changeful, as turbulent, as uncertain as the 1970s were. Since the late 1960s business has passed through a decade in which the critical success factors were increasingly external to the business, as Reginald H. Jones,

*This term is intended to be inclusive of all the activities covered by other similar terms such as environmental scanning, monitoring, tracking, or forecasting. In other words, it encompasses picking up "signals" from the business environment, analyzing their significance for the business, and forecasting their probable future development.

†With inputs from materials developed by Arnold Mitchell, Peter Schwartz, and James B. Smith, all of SRI International.

former General Electric chairman, pointed out. This has put a high premium on corporate sensitivity, flexibility, and responsiveness to change.

While successful corporations have, of course, always been those which were most flexible and adaptable, what is new in the current situation is the diversity, pace, and interconnectedness of change. No longer is it only the measured pace of consumer choice and technological change that demands a corporate response; changing social values, government regulations, and shifts in the energy and economic growth equations are now also important factors in managerial decision making. No longer does the relevant business environment end at the shores of a particular nation; competition has become globalized, and trade, geopolitical factors, and actions by multinational corporations have become integral parts of the national business scene. Worldwide communications and the ever-shortening "doubling time" for new knowledge ensure that social, economic, political, and technological change is accelerated, and its effects throughout a highly interconnected system are made more complex.

In such a situation it is not only the future that is unknowable; even the present becomes an enigma. Hence the two quotations at the opening of this chapter. It is still true, as Lincoln noted, that corporate strategy should be based on as accurate an assessment as possible of "where we are and whither we are tending." And, as Eliot's quotation poetically suggests, often one of the principal benefits of futures research is a better understanding of the *present.*

In any event, environmental analysis must treat the business environment as a space-time continuum. Although its principal aim is to contribute to a better understanding of the future (because strategic decisions are concerned with the future), it must build its speculation about future possibilities upon an analysis of the past and the present. Past, present, and future are all grist to the environmental analysis mill.

PRESENT AND FUTURE PERSPECTIVES

The "theory of the case" for a necessary linkage between the present and the future in environmental analysis is best illustrated by the schematic design in Figure 9-1.

The central focus of both strategic planning and environmental analysis, as practiced in most corporations, is a "window in time" looking three to five years beyond the present. What planning systems try to bring into the sharpest focus seems to be the situation as it may be some five years out and the implications for the business that can be drawn from such a situation assessment. This time frame certainly does not apply to all businesses; the planning horizons of consumer goods and energy companies clearly range from three to twenty and more years. Nor should this statement be taken to mean that exploratory thinking and planning do not, or should not, deal with more distant time frames.[1]

However, when strategic planning comes to assess the actionable implications of its environmental analysis, and to assess alternative strategic options for the corporation, most attention tends to be focused on a time horizon three to five years out.

Both conceptually and practically, then, there are two different approaches to this "window in time." On the one hand, it is possible by identifying and analyzing the macro sweep of long-term trends, to take a leap into the future by developing sets of alternative scenarios for the future ten to fifteen years hence.[2] Then, calculating backward by a process of deductive reasoning, one can develop hypotheses as to corporate

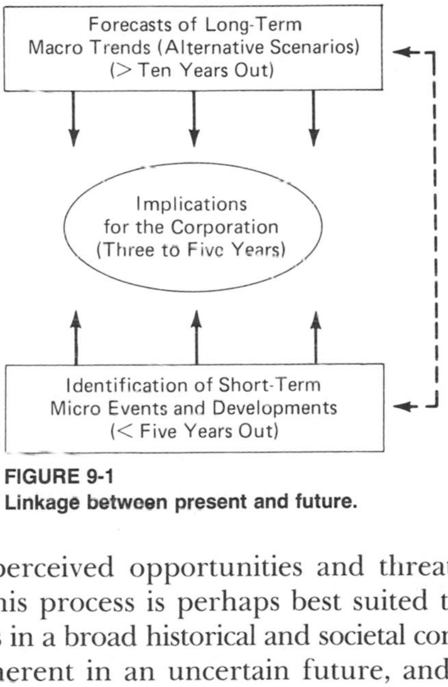

FIGURE 9-1
Linkage between present and future.

implications—the perceived opportunities and threats—for the intermediate period. This process is perhaps best suited to placing the environmental analysis in a broad historical and societal context, emphasizing the alternatives inherent in an uncertain future, and highlighting the key branching points that lead to one outcome or another (and that, therefore, deserve the most careful monitoring).

On the other hand, one can focus one's attention on the micro picture (the present), monitoring events as they occur, assembling the jigsaw of evidence into a coherent picture, and then projecting forward by a process of inductive reasoning to create a picture of the future five years from now. This process—which is somewhat analogous to intelligence gathering and analysis in an espionage network—appeals strongly to the empirical nature of most managers and planners, and has the great merit of developing a better understanding of the present as a basis for forecasting.

These two approaches, it should be noted, are not antithetical. They are more appropriately viewed as complementary than as alternatives. Environmental analysis can make its soundest contributions to planning when it provides perspectives from both macro (long-term) and micro (short-term) analyses. For one thing, the longer-term scenarios are, at best, hypotheses as to plausible futures. The trajectory of these scenarios must be constantly compared with the trajectory of actual events in order to confirm or correct one's assessment of each scenario's probability, and to determine what revisions to the forecast and planning assumptions may be required. For another, analysis and interpretation of the micro events of the present is usually easier and more complete when done in the context of the "big picture" of the future.

Scenarios, thus, provide a frame of reference and illumination for current environmental monitoring, while the latter supplies the needed cybernetic feedback for keeping scenarios up to date. The macro and the micro, the future and the present, are mutually reinforcing parts of the environmental analysis whole.

RELATIONSHIP TO STRATEGIC PLANNING

The role of environmental analysis in the planning system stems from the basic purpose of strategic planning. Viewed in the broadest terms, the *primary* purpose of strategic planning could be described as optimizing the "fit" between the business and its current and future environment,[3] to enable the business to operate with maximum congruence and minimum friction in the changing conditions of an uncertain world. In this context, *business environment* should be thought of as including:

- Markets and customers for goods and services
- Economic conditions (such as growth rate, inflation, energy)
- Capital markets (including the business's shareowners and creditors)
- Labor markets and the changing wants and expectations of the work force
- The state of technology
- Competition
- The political environment (legislative, regulatory, and judicial developments)
- The state of public opinion and expectations, at the national and community level (for example, interest groups' activities)

And increasingly, as already noted, this environment must be defined in international terms, particularly for competition, technology, and economic conditions, even for businesses that are not multinational themselves.

Viewed in this light, environmental analysis of the total business environment becomes an essential and integral part of the planning process (see Figure 9-2). It is one of the starting points (along with resource analysis and strategy concept, or "vision of the business"), and establishes the contextual framework for strategic planning. It also forces a change in the concept of an adequate strategy. A business strategy that meets the totality of these changing environmental conditions must be a strategy for the *total* business. That is, it can no longer remain, as many corporate strategies still are, merely a marketing strategy; it must also encompass a technology strategy, a human resources strategy, a financial strategy, a strategy for public affairs and government relations, and so on. In other words, a total business strategy can be likened to a cable made up of intertwined, mutually strengthening cords.

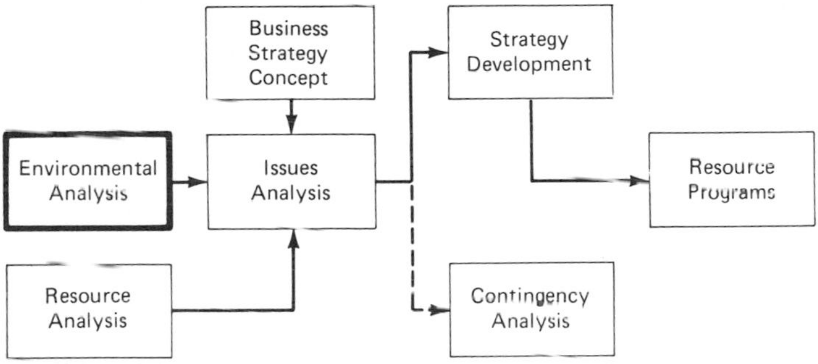

FIGURE 9-2
Positioning of environmental analysis in the strategic planning process.

A holistic approach to environmental analysis, that is, viewing the environment as a whole and as integral to planning, thus tends to generate and reinforce a holistic approach to strategy: planning for the business as a total system.

Environmental analysis also plays a vital role in these turbulent times as a corporation's sensing mechanism. The radar analogy immediately and appropriately comes to mind. If a boat (a business) is sailing on a "sea of uncertainty," there are two essential requirements for a successful voyage. One is a star to steer by (vision of the business); the other is a radar system (environmental analysis) to pick out the rocks, reefs, headlands, and clear water in the unchartered area ahead.

The radar analogy is singularly appropriate in at least three respects when contemplating the establishment of an environmental analysis system in strategic planning:

1. Radar covers all 360 degrees of the horizon, not merely a segment of it (though it can focus, if need be).

2. It engages in continuous, not intermittent, scanning.

3. It suggests, appropriately in this context, what has been termed a "cybernetic pulsing through the future."

ESSENTIAL CHARACTERISTICS OF ENVIRONMENTAL ANALYSIS

This analogy, in turn, suggests some of the essential characteristics that should be designed into any corporate environmental analysis system:

1. INTEGRATIVE. It is vitally important that the environmental analysis system should be an integral part of the planning and decision-making system of the corporation. Interpretation of the present and speculation about the future make no real contribution to corporate success if they result merely in interesting studies. To be synergistic, the linkage between the two systems must be tight and explicit.

Strategic planning must be designed with environmental analysis as its starting point and frame of reference. Organizationally, responsibility for the identification, analysis, and interpretation of environmental data should be located in the strategic planning component; or, at a minimum, this component should be the focal point of the system, even if other corporate and operating components act as specific monitoring posts in an environmental network.

2. RELEVANT. The relevance that environmental analyses should have to strategic planning can perhaps best be defined as (*a*) a focus on strategic issues,[4] and (*b*) assistance in making *today's* strategic decisions with greater environmental sensitivity and with a better sense of futurity. The first point is process-oriented; the second deals more with managerial psychology. To be issue-oriented in this sense, environmental analysis must be alert to both the social, economic, political, and technological trends impacting *current* strategic issues, and the emergence of *new* strategic issues. To raise the level of managerial sensitivity and "futures consciousness," it must constantly stress such factors as the past-present-future continuum, uncertainty, and the interconnectedness of all environmental trends.

3. HOLISTIC. If for no other reason than the simple fact that everything is related to everything else, environmental analysis should be holistic in its approach to the business environment, viewing trends as a piece, not piecemeal. The corporate radar must scan the whole circumference of its environment in order to minimize the chance of sur-

prises and maximize its utility as an early warning system. As a practical matter, there are two simple guidelines that can be followed to ensure the necessary comprehensiveness of the system:

a. Define the environment in terms of four interlocking or "nesting" segments:
   - Macro—the broad sweep of societal and, to the extent appropriate, international trends.
   - Industry—the structure, products, pricing, technology, government regulation, international position, and so on, of the industry (or industries) in which the company is engaged.
   - Competition—the history, strengths, weaknesses, goals, strategies of major competitors (increasingly, with technological diversification, these are *not* necessarily found within the neat classifications of discrete industries—or countries).
   - Company—changes in the performance, resource quality and availability, corporate culture, stakeholder values (including management, customers, employees, owners, suppliers, lenders), and competitive position of the company.

b. Remember the "SEPTember formula" (so termed by Lynne Hall, currently with Shell Canada, and myself)—a convenient mnemonic to underscore the importance of covering all social (demographics, values, lifestyles), economic (GNP segments, inflation, labor force, energy, mineral resources, and so on), political (party structure, legislation, regulation, litigation), and technological (R&D, new products and processes) trends. Figure 9-3 illustrates this point with the comprehensive list of trends used by Sears, Roebuck and Co. in its monitoring system.

4. ITERATIVE OR CONTINUOUS. Like the radar, an environmental analysis system must operate continuously in order to keep track of the rapid pace of developments. In these times it is nonsense to engage only in periodic operation of the system, to trust (implicitly) that the "blips" registered on the radar screen after a few sweeps of the horizon give a true and lasting picture of the situation. Only *continuous* operation of the system can sort out the true from the "ghost" images; define the nature, trajectory, and impact points of the incoming "missiles"; and pick up the inevitable new "blips" that will be constantly appearing on the screen.

It is worth noting on this point that, in the typology of environmental scanning and forecasting systems developed by Liam Fahey, William R. King, and Vadake K. Narayanan,[5] continuous systems are listed as the ideal (see Figure 9-4). *"These systems,"* the authors note, *"attempt to enhance the organization's capability to handle environmental uncertainty rather than to*

- DEMOGRAPHICS
  - POPULATION
    - Size and Characteristics
    - Size
    - Growth rate
    - Sex
    - Age
    - Marital status
      - Singles
      - Marriages and Divorces
      - Remarriages
    - Births
      - Birth Expectations
      - Birth Fertility Rate
    - Location and/or mobility
      - Regional
      - Metropolitan or nonmetropolitan
      - Farm
      - Central cities
      - Congressional districts
    - Households and families
      - Age of head
      - Average size
      - One person households
    - Minorities
      - Illegal aliens
      - Spanish Americans
  - EMPLOYMENT
    - Civilian labor force
      - Growth rate
      - Size and characteristics
        - Full time or part time
        - Sex
        - Working spouses
        - Occupation
    - Regional distribution
    - Labor union membership
    - Hours
    - Benefits
  - INCOME
    - Distribution by
      - Region
      - Age
      - Earners per family
      - Education
    - Median income
      - Household
      - Family
      - Individual
    - Personal income
      - Components
      - Disposable personal income (DPI)
  - SPENDING
    - Personal consumption expenditures (PCE)
    - Consumer price index
    - Consumer credit
  - HOUSING
    - Existing housing
      - Units
      - Type
      - Region
    - Housing costs and sales
    - Housing starts
    - Incomes of purchasers
- VALUES—LIFESTYLES
  - VALUES
    - Work and leisure
    - Entitlement
    - Consumption versus conservation
    - Consumer assertiveness
  - LIFESTYLES
    - Marriage and family structure
    - Homes and mobility
    - Shopping habits
    - Aging and retirement
    - Singles
- RESOURCES
  - ENERGY SUPPLY AND DEMAND
    - Coal
    - Electric power
      - Backlog of appropriations
    - Natural gas
    - Petroleum
  - MINERAL AND CHEMICAL SUPPLY
    - Imported versus domestic
    - Metals
  - AGRICULTURE
    - Food
    - Fertilizer
    - Agribusiness
  - WATER AVAILABILITY
    - Supply, surface and underground
    - Delivery problem areas
    - Drought areas
  - STRATEGIC DEPLETION
    - Shortage
      - Industrial capacity
  - LAND
- TECHNOLOGY
  - EXPENDITURES FOR R&D
    - Federal
      - Total R&D expenditures
      - Defense
      - HEW
  - ALTERNATE ENERGY SOURCES
    - Nuclear
    - Solar
    - Hydro, geothermal, photochemical and other
  - PLASTICS
  - ELECTRIC COMMUNICATIONS
    - Computers
      - Personal and small business
    - Network systems
    - Entertainment and games
    - Satellite communications
  - TRANSPORTATION
    - People
    - Materials
    - Automobile
      - Electric car
  - MANUFACTURING TECHNIQUES
    - Durables
    - Nondurables
  - PRODUCT DEVELOPMENT
- PUBLIC ATTITUDES
  - CONSUMER CONFIDENCE
    - Buying plans index

FIGURE 9-3
External trends followed by Sears, Roebuck and Co.

PUBLIC ATTITUDES TOWARD
- Government regulations
- Large companies
- Corporate social responsibility
- Industries and products
- Energy situation
- Environment

PUBLIC INTEREST GROUPS

CONSUMERISM

GOVERNMENT

OPERATIONS
- Government purchases
- Government expenditures
  - Social welfare
  - Social security cost
  - Veterans benefits
  - Employees
- Public debt
- National economic planning

GOVERNMENT REGULATIONS

AGENCIES
- Cost and criticism
- Reform
- Corporate crimes
- Business lobby

LEGISLATION
- Antitrust
- Consumerism

EMPLOYMENT
- Physical conditions
- Equal opportunity

GOVERNMENT REGULATIONS (*Cont.*)

Benefits and security

ECONOMIC CONTROLS
- Reporting and disclosure

ENVIRONMENT
- Land use
- Air, water, noise, and waste disposal

CONSUMER CREDIT

PHYSICAL DISTRIBUTION
- Transportation
- Warehousing

PRIVACY
- Consumer
- Employee

PRODUCTS
- Safety
- Quality
- Life cycle

COMMUNICATION WITH CUSTOMERS
- Advertising and selling practices
- Complaint procedures and redresses
- Warranties

SERVICE
- Repair quality
- Standards
- Licensing

POSTAL SERVICE

HEALTH CARE

TAXES
- Personal
- Corporate
- Social security

INTERNATIONAL

WORLD POPULATION

RESOURCES
- Food
- Energy
- Raw materials

TRADE
- Trade and payments balance
- Protectionism of exports and imports
- Tariffs
- Cartels

DEVELOPING NATIONS
- OPEC
- LDCs

TECHNOLOGY TRANSFER

ECONOMIC INDICATORS

ECONOMICS
- Gross national product
- Inflation rate
- Interest rate
- Unemployment rate
- Productivity
- AAA bond interest rate
- Capital investment requirements
- Wage levels
- Benefit cost levels
- Economic forecasts
- Corporate profits and cash flow
- Capital formation—needs

LONG-TERM TOPICS
- Weather modification

FIGURE 9-3 (Cont.)

reduce perceived uncertainty" (original emphasis)—surely an important and commendable statement of facing up to reality.

At this stage a distinction should be drawn between the scanning and monitoring aspects of the system. General scanning of the horizon (broad sweeps of the early warning radar) is essential to pick up new signals from the environment and to keep track of shifts in the overall pattern of developing trends. Monitoring, on the other hand, is designed to focus closely on the track of previously identified trends which have

	IRREGULAR	PERIODIC	CONTINUOUS
Impetus for scanning	Crisis-initiated	Problem-solving decision or issue-oriented	Opportunity finding and problem avoidance
Scope of scanning	Specific events	Selected events	Broad range of environmental systems
Temporal nature	Reactive	Proactive	Proactive
1. Time frame for data	Retrospective	Current and retrospective	Current and prospective
2. Time frame for decision impact	Current and near-term future	Near-term	Long-term
Types of forecasts	Budget-oriented	Economic- and sales-oriented	Marketing, social, legal, regulatory, culture, and so on
Media for scanning and forecasting	Ad hoc studies	Periodically updated studies	Structured data collection and processing systems
Organization structure	1. Ad hoc teams	Various staff agencies	Scanning unit, focus on enhancing uncertainty-handling capability
	2. Focus on reduction of perceived certainty		
Resource allocation to activity	Not specific (perhaps periodic as "fads" arise)	Specific and continuous but relatively low	Specific, continuous, and relatively substantial
Methodological sophistication	Simplistic data analyses and budgetary projections	Statistical forecasting oriented	Many "futuristic" forecasting methodologies
"Cultural" orientation	Not integrated into mainstream of activity	Partially integrated as a "stepchild"	Fully integrated as crucial for long-range growth

FIGURE 9-4
Typology of environmental scanning and forecasting systems.
(Fahey, King, and V. R. Narayanan, 1981.)

been analyzed and assessed as being of particular importance to the corporation. This is not merely a semantic distinction. There is substantive difference in the focus and content, and even in the talents required for the two operations. Monitoring requires meticulous aggregation and analysis of details, while scanning puts a high premium on intuition, "sixth sense," and pattern recognition. The two operations are equally important and, indeed, sufficiently different to merit separate attention, systems, and (maybe) staffing.

5. HEURISTIC, OR EXPLORATORY. While, admittedly, the monitoring

part of the system concerns itself with present developments, a large part of environmental analysis seeks, as Peter Schwartz and Arnold Mitchell put it, "to explore unknown and in a real sense unknowable terrain . . . the dimensions of possible futures—what could happen, not necessarily what will happen."[6] As far as the future dimension of environmental analysis is concerned, the emphasis must be on *alternative* futures. In an uncertain environment we can never truly know the future, no matter how much we may perfect our forecasting techniques. It is highly misleading, therefore, to claim that environmental forecasting can predict the future. What it can do—and do effectively—is to help clarify our assumptions about the future, speculate systematically about alternative outcomes, assess probabilities, and make more rational choices.

6. QUALITATIVE. A large part of environmental input to strategic planning consists of soft data, or "weak signals" as Igor Ansoff termed them. To quote Peter Schwartz and Arnold Mitchell again on the nature of exploratory planning methods:

> They do make use of quantitative inputs such as poll data or specific forecasts, but they are not bound by the limits of what can be quantified. The methods focus on the structure, process, and dynamics of a system. They take into account elements that we do not know how to quantify rigorously, such as values, aspirations, and culture. This does not mean that the methods are not systematic, however; quite to the contrary, a primary value of these techniques is that they systematize the process of looking at phenomena that are exceedingly "slippery" and elusive.[7]

REPRESENTATIVE METHODOLOGIES

Clearly, the first task in establishing an environmental analysis system is a clear definition of the relevant environment—relevant, that is, to the needs of the business and its strategic planning system. It is at this point that the two guidelines mentioned above come into play: defining the four environmental segments (macro, industry, competitive, and company), and identifying the appropriate social, economic, political, and technological trends, domestic and international. The question then becomes: what are the next steps, and what are some of the methodologies that can be used?

In general terms, the flow of environmental analysis passes through the following stages:

1. Definition of the environment
2. Scanning and monitoring
3. Issue identification and assessment
4. Input to strategic planning

What follows is a discussion of some of the methodologies involved in stages 2, 3, and 4 of this process, with particular emphasis on scanning and monitoring, which is a particularly crucial and difficult stage.

Scanning and Monitoring

"Important changes don't just occur spontaneously," states an SRI International introduction to its SCAN service. "Most start as ideas, and these ideas eventually are expressed publicly in the press, on radio or television, at conferences, in scientific journals, and in a wide range of other public arenas." One of the most straightforward and widely used methodologies is, not surprisingly, monitoring and analyzing media. Over the years a variety of approaches has been developed, some (such as the *Trend Report*, developed by John Naisbitt) depending on content analysis of publications, and others relying on efforts to pick up early hints of change.

Among the latter is the system developed by the Weiner, Edrich, Brown organization in New York City. Initially designed as the trend analysis program (TAP) for the insurance industry, trend evaluation and monitoring (TEAM) has been broadened and applied in a number of different organizations, including corporations, SRI, and the Congressional Clearinghouse on the Future. The system (Figure 9-5) depends upon the establishment of a network of scanners in the organization, and upon Weiner, Edrich, Brown's own scanning of a core list of fifty or so publications (as diverse as *The New York Times, The Wall Street Journal, Daedalus, Mother Jones, National Review,* and *Science*). Each scanner is assigned a single publication not on the core list, and he or she reads that publication, looking for articles that meet certain predetermined criteria which vary from organization to organization. Scanners abstract such articles, together with any abstracts from conferences, books, movies, and miscellaneous events, and submit them to a program administrator.

Abstracts are reviewed, preferably monthly, by an analysis committee made up of middle management and the program administrator. The function of this committee is, in fact, more nearly that of synthesis: The committee performs the critical role of relating each bit of information to all the others and developing implications for the future environment and the future of the organization. Summaries of the analysis committee meetings serve as monthly reports to the scanners and other personnel. In addition, these summaries are submitted to an oversight or steering committee composed of senior managers who oversee the operation of the program, determine the content and form of the program output, and decide on actions to be taken on implications for the organization.

Graham T. T. Molitor, president of Public Policy Forecasting in Washington, D.C., has developed a forecasting system based on a wider system of monitoring. He has argued that harbinger trends and developments can be identified, not only in literature and the media, but through leading events (Figure 9-6), leading authorities, leading organizations, and even leading political jurisdictions (Figure 9-7).[8] Figure 9-8 depicts Molitor's perception of the rhythm of emergence of these various indicators as change moves from the early stages to full maturity.

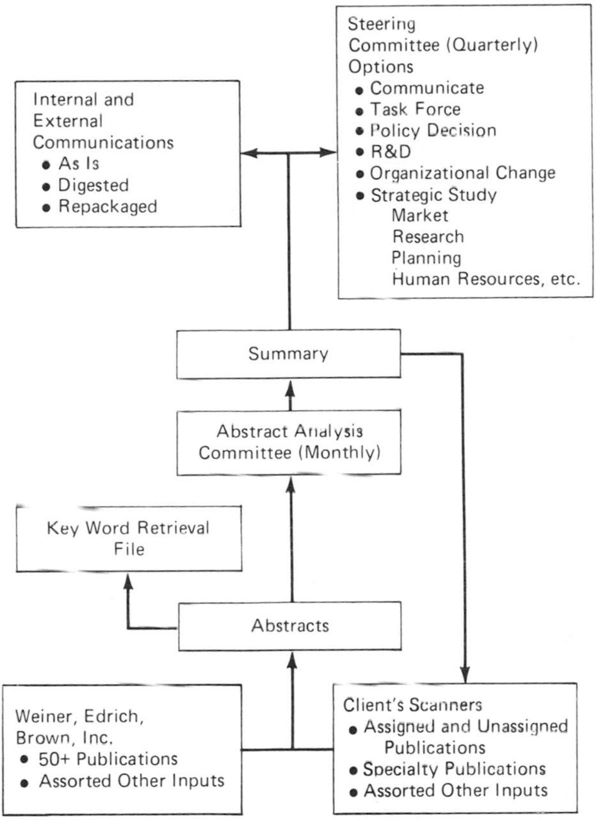

FIGURE 9-5
The trend evaluation and monitoring system (TEAM).
(Weiner, Edrich, Brown, Inc., New York, NY.)

Issue Identification and Assessment

If environmental analysis is a starting point for strategic planning, issues analysis is its central focus (see Figure 9-2). An essential function of environmental analysis is, therefore, to contribute to the identification and assessment of the strategic issues confronting the business. From a planning point of view, the essential question is: What are likely to be the positive or negative impacts of macroenvironmental forces on the microenvironment of the business? This suggests defining issues as opportunities or threats, and adopting a matrix approach to issue identification (see Figure 9-9).

The matrix can and should be viewed both horizontally—to identify, for each element of the microenvironment, what past SEPT forces have affected them—and vertically—to assess what changes in *other* macroenvironmental forces may affect the microenvironment in the future. This iteration between horizontal and vertical perspectives should lead to a

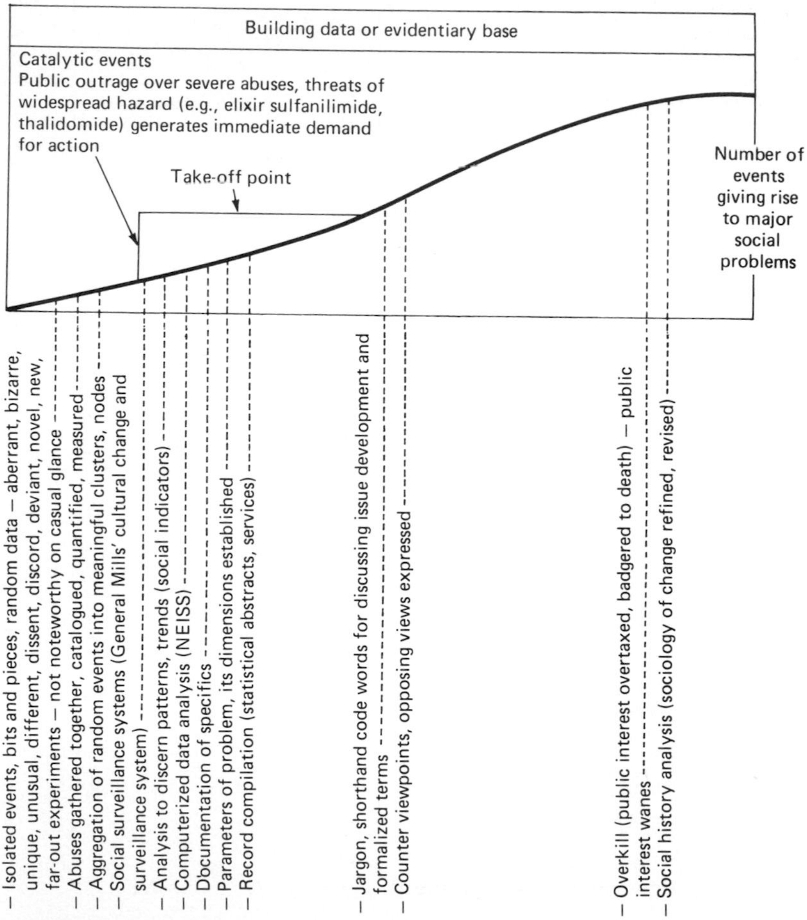

FIGURE 9-6
Leading events as a forecasting device. (*Graham Molitor.*)

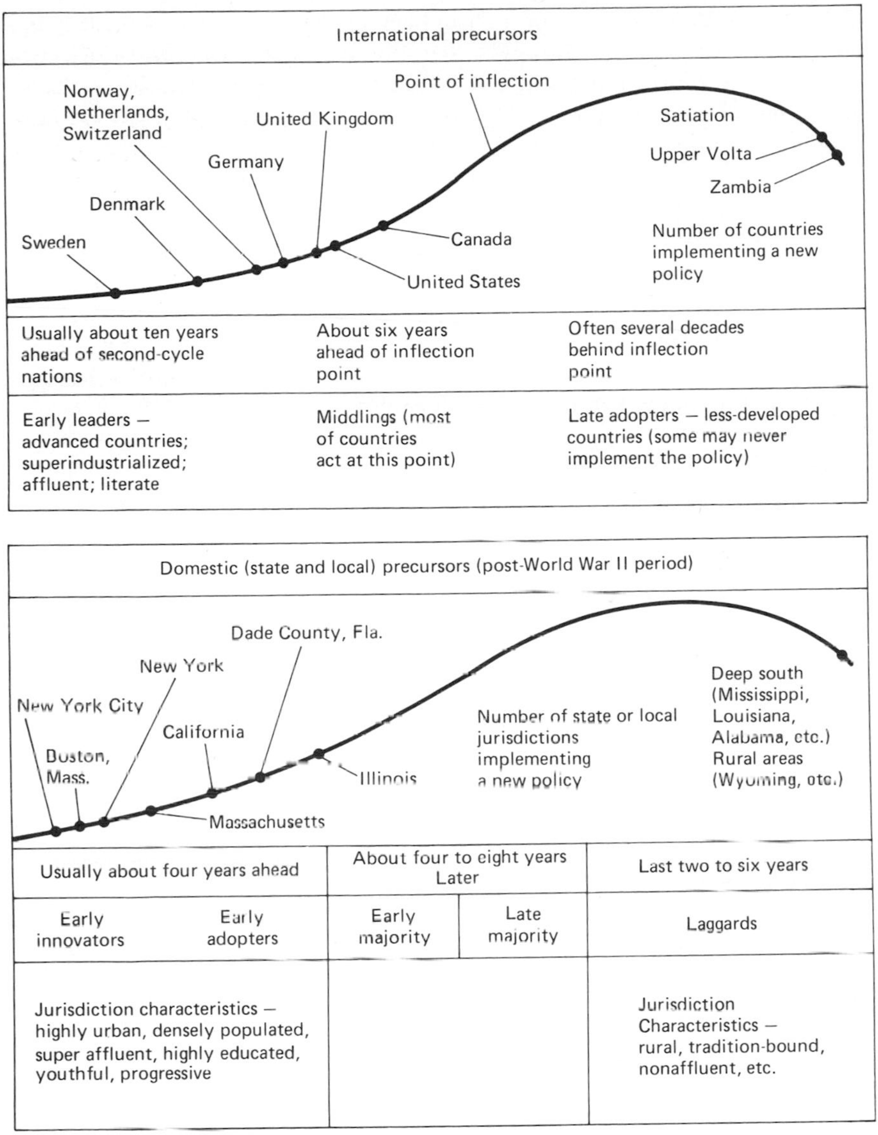

FIGURE 9-7
Leading political jurisdictions as a forecasting device. (*Graham Molitor.*)

clearer focus on the most significant macroenvironmental forces whose impacts should be assessed. These forces, in turn, then form the basis for the identification of issues (that is, impacts on the microenvironment) in various cells of the matrix.

As noted above, it is generally helpful to work toward the issues by thinking of the environmental impacts in terms of the potential opportunities and threats they pose for the business. Thus, the impact of a forecast rate of inflation might be seen as posing threats in the form of increased production costs, reduced discretionary spending by consumers, erosion of the motivational force of employee compensation, high interest rates, and so on. However, inflation can also present opportunities such as serving consumers' new financial needs or their demands for quality products, designing nonfinancial incentives for employees, taking public policy initiatives, as well as a strong push to rethinking old ways of doing things.

Because most managers and planners think of environmental change and uncertainty as threatening, it is particularly important to think through the potential opportunities. Threat statements come relatively easily; those pertaining to opportunities tend generally to require more disciplined and concerted thought. But the effort is worthwhile since, after all, a major purpose of environmental analysis is to provide early warn-

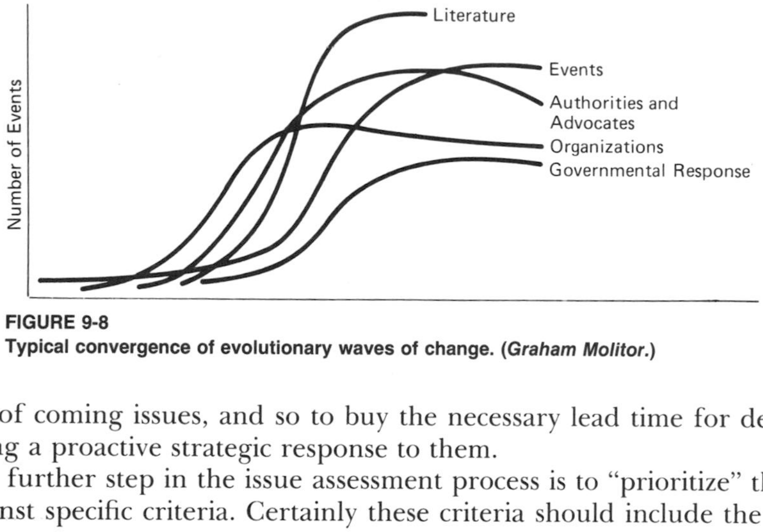

FIGURE 9-8
Typical convergence of evolutionary waves of change. (*Graham Molitor.*)

ing of coming issues, and so to buy the necessary lead time for developing a proactive strategic response to them.

A further step in the issue assessment process is to "prioritize" them against specific criteria. Certainly these criteria should include the following:

- What is the probability that this will develop into a major issue?
- How great will the eventual impact on the company be (that is, assuming that the issue *does* develop)?
- When is the issue likely to peak—Near-term? Medium-term? Long-term?

While the scoring system for this assessment of probability and impact can be complex or simple, a general categorizing of high, medium, or low is usually sufficient in the end. Issues can then be conveniently arrayed on a priorities matrix (see Figure 9-10), with a separate matrix being prepared for each of the three planning periods. The merits of using such a display system are that it provides a comprehensive, at-a-glance arraying of the issues; orders them in a manner that facilitates discussion and planning; and places them in time frames appropriate to the allocation of resources and management attention.

Input to Strategic Planning

The final product of environmental analysis is, when all is said and done, its contribution to strategic thinking and its input to the development of a strategic plan for the business. Merely interesting studies will not suffice. More relevant and specific contributions include the development of planning assumptions, the framing of issues for strategy development, and the pursuit of studies of strategic environmental issues.

	Trends, Events, Developments in the Macroenvironment			
Microenvironment	Social	Economic	Political	Technological
Markets Customers Employees Competitors Technology Materials and suppliers Production Finances, shareholders Public and government relations				

FIGURE 9-9
A matrix approach to issue identification.

When a set of coherent and comprehensive environmental assumptions is developed, it becomes the first and most obvious input to the strategic plan. This is one leg of the three-legged stool on which strategy development rests (the other two being resource analysis and strategy concept), so it is important that it should be sturdy. The environmental analysis chapter of the strategic plan should, at a minimum:

- Identify the key forces operating in the business environment (past, present and future)

- Make explicit the assumptions about their future course
- Analyze the strategic significance of these forces—the threats, opportunities and issues that they pose
- Highlight the major contingencies (and their trigger points) for which contingency plans should be developed

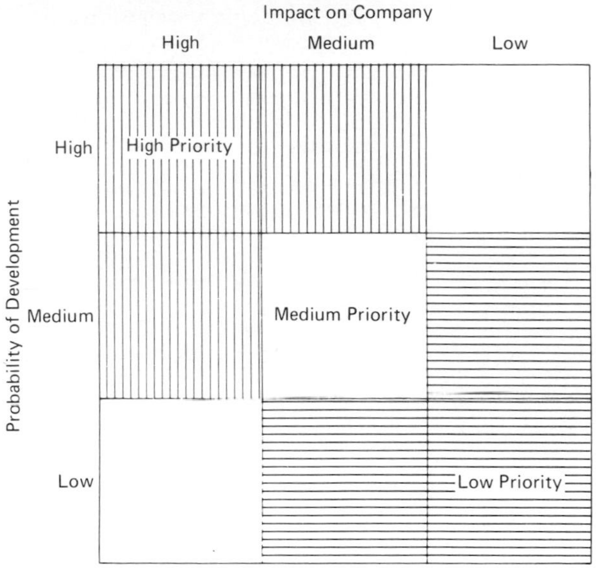

FIGURE 9-10
Issues priorities matrix.

Issues should be framed, in an orderly and disciplined manner, so that constructive strategies can be developed to respond to them. A suggested framework for this framing is the following eight-step sequence which organizes the necessary information to focus on the needed strategic responses:

1. Definition of the issue—a succinct (one-sentence) statement of the issue, from the point of view of business strategy
2. Strategic significance—identification of the threats and opportunities posed by the issue
3. Driving forces—the key environmental forces that converge (now and in the future) to make this an issue
4. Prospects—the potential outcomes and the development of the issue under alternative scenarios
5. Impact on industry
6. Impact on company

} sectors of the industry and/or aspects of the business most likely to be affected by the threats and opportunities

7. Planning challenges—a set of "need to . . ." statements setting out the overall actions required of the business to maximize the opportunities and minimize the threats

8. Strategic responses—a set of specific strategy alternatives to be considered as ways of implementing the "need to . . ." statements

Finally, environmental analysis should be the source of those in-depth studies of critical external trends and factors—inflation, energy prospects, global competition, new technology—which may require detailed and specific analysis because of their special significance for business strategy.

CONCLUSION

The new centrality of environmental analysis in the strategic planning process is no fad and no accident. It is a reflection of reality: the growing importance of external factors to business success. While we should strive to improve its methodologies and the discipline of our thinking, we should always have a clear and realistic expectation of what it can achieve. Environmental analysis is intended to help us cope with an uncertain world. It should not be expected to remove the uncertainty; but, by using this tool well, we can reasonably expect to make the inevitable uncertainty more manageable.

NOTES

[1]One of the strongest and most valid criticisms of U.S. managers (particularly as contrasted with the Japanese) is that they lack the long view and concentrate too much on short-term results. Futures research and environmental analysis at its best and most comprehensive are indeed designed to help remedy this defect.

[2]See Chapter 10, "Futures Scenarios and Their Uses in Corporate Strategy," by Thomas F. Mandel.

[3]Other purposes flow from this: establishing the corporation's mission, goals, objectives; identifying and analyzing key strategic issues (opportunities and threats); developing strategies to deal with the issues; and allocating resources for the implementation of strategies.

[4]For purposes of this discussion, a strategic issue can be defined, rather loosely and colloquially, as a major external or internal trend or development that critically affects future corporate success (that is, a "make-or-break" issue).

[5]Liam Fahey, William R. King, and Vadake K. Narayanan, "Environmental Scanning and Forecasting in Strategic Planning—The State of the Art," in *Long Range Planning,* April 1981.

[6]In "The Art of Exploratory Planning: Identifying the Corporate Long Range Course," *Business Intelligence Program Research Report No. 582,* SRI International, December 1976.

[7]Ibid.

[8]"The Hatching of Public Opinion," in R. J. Allio and M. W. Pennington (eds.), *Corporate Planning Techniques and Applications,* American Management Associations, New York, 1979.

Chapter **10**

FUTURES SCENARIOS AND THEIR USES IN CORPORATE STRATEGY

THOMAS F. MANDEL*

Senior Strategic Analyst,
Business Intelligence Program,
SRI International

BACKGROUND

Scenarios are one of a variety of methods strategic planners use to make sense out of a fluid, turbulent business environment and an uncertain future. In use ten years ago in only the largest, most sophisticated planning operations, scenarios play an integral role in long-range planning in many large companies today. And their use seems to be spreading, even to businesses with annual sales below $50 million. To their adherents in strategic planning, they constitute an effective device for sensing, interpreting, organizing, and bringing to bear diverse information about the future in planning and strategic decision making. Simple in concept—scenarios are essentially stories about the future—they are also often expensive to generate and hard to apply. Their detractors report them to be too fuzzy, too imprecise, and too different from conventional methods to apply to the "hard" decisions of business. In fact, however, scenario approaches represent both a significant departure from and an ideal complement to traditional forecasting and planning methods. Ideally, they closely link, for planners and decision makers, perceptions and analyses about external change and a company's specific strategic concerns.

*Richard Carlson, Willis Harman, Arnold Mitchell, James Ogilvy, Peter Schwartz, and Victor Walling contributed significantly to the scenario approach described here.

If they are so difficult to develop and use, why then have scenarios enjoyed their current renaissance? The answer lies in two places—in the nature of the business environment itself and in the evolution of strategic planning. Until the early 1970s, business planners enjoyed a relatively stable world, punctuated occasionally by cyclical recessions. Long-range planning, for the few companies that peered more than five years ahead, most often meant extrapolating past trends into the future. Typically, the only worrisome uncertainty was the rate of economic growth. A long era of relative stability and steady growth gave rise to a number of formal forecasting models, the most successful of which were econometric in nature. Some planners used scenarios but the assumptions underlying these were typically concerned with different rates of economic growth. Most companies had three scenarios, labeled *optimistic* (high growth), *most likely* (moderate growth), and *pessimistic* (recession or low growth). Their corporate plans assumed the most-likely path, and treated the other scenarios as simple contingencies.

A Changing Environment and Responses in Planning

By the mid-1970s, however, the macroenvironment was becoming increasingly turbulent, even chaotic, and planners were finding that conventional methods and most-likely projections weren't working as well as they'd hoped. For a lot of reasons, a good many rules of the game were changing. Almost overnight, the United States and other industrial nations had to cope with an energy crisis. Inflation, which had been rising gradually since the Vietnamese war, became an increasingly serious problem for businesses, government, and consumers. The rate of inflation, interest rates, and energy prices reached levels which a few years before most expert forecasts had regarded as impossible. The economy had become much more erratic. U.S. industry and technology no longer led in many areas, and U.S. businesses were facing increasingly stiff competition from abroad. Political reflections of public concerns about the quality of life had become the foundations of a complex and often contradictory regulatory environment. Consumer values and expectations were changing in unexpected ways and the mass markets of the 1950s and 1960s were fragmenting into more narrowly defined market segments. These and other developments undermined many of the old assumptions, highlighted the inadequacies of formal models built solely on past experience, and ushered a new era of admitted uncertainty (and sometimes anxiety) into corporate boardrooms.

Strategic planning evolved during this same period, partly in response to the close interplay between business activities and environmental forces. Uncertainty about the economy, the marketplace, government intervention, and the rising cost of capital began extending the time horizon within which basic strategies and capital investment had to be made. Where five- to ten-year plans were once sufficient, ten-, twenty-, and even thirty-year strategic plans have now become necessary. The changing perceptions, beliefs, and behavior of consumers, employees, shareholders, and special-interest groups have greatly increased the complexity of the array of forces that shape the strategic business environment. Analyses of changing values and lifestyles now frequently accompany projections of more traditional variables such as technology and the economy. Industries sharply affected by external forces—among them energy, basic resources and manufacturing, automobiles, and other foundations of the U.S. economy—began looking about for planning methods and systems which provided insights about the uncertainties they felt. With the rules of the game rapidly changing, unexpected risks came. Frequently, corporate strategy now addressed not so much how to play the game but rather what games were worth playing. Strategic management and planning, alternative scenarios, and a number of other methods came into vogue during the late 1970s and early 1980s in large part because of these uncertainties.

WHY SCENARIOS?

As rewarding as it would be to do so, no one and no method can predict the future. Certainly some factors that make a difference to business—basic demographics, for example—seem relatively easy to forecast. Most, however, remain part of the increasingly complex setting of interrelated political, social, economic, technological, international, and other factors called the external environment, or macroenvironment. The more we understand about the nature of such factors, about the "facts," the more genuinely complex and unpredictable the world appears. Feeling uncertain about the future is a natural symptom of an era of rapid change.

Modeling and other conventional quantitative approaches do help in sorting out general tendencies in and relationships among key forces shaping the business environment, but they also have built-in weaknesses. In an era of major structural change—from an industrial to an information economy, from an era of rapid, stable economic growth to one of slower, cyclical growth, from a superpower-dominated world to one better characterized as a collection of competing interests, from one Kondratieff wave to another—the very assumptions upon which the structures of such models rest become questionable. Economic forecasts untempered by insight and imagination tend to miss their mark wildly when a changing industrial structure and a vigorous "underground economy" remain outside their domain. Projections and even descriptions of general inflation have less value when the consumer index is based on a ten-year-old market basket and consumers are adjusting quickly to rising prices by changing their buying patterns. Formal statistical measurements systems tend to lag behind the real world anyway. When the environment is changing quickly and fundamentally, they fall faster and further out of date.

In such times, what are needed to complement traditional approaches are methods that focus planners' attentions on the critical assumptions that underlie a strategic business decision, on the very real complexities of the macroenvironment, and on different logics of change. For example, a company undertaking a major investment in synthetic fuels because of rising oil prices, long-term demand trends, and government support ought to be asking serious questions about the continuation of these and related trends over the lifetime of the investment. The scenario turns out to be one very useful device for analyzing both the logic and uncertainty of such strategic decisions.

SCENARIOS AND THEIR CHARACTERISTICS

Scenarios are descriptions of plausible alternative futures of the macroenvironment. Their principal purpose is to bound the range of uncertainty in the factors most critical to a particular decision or forecast. Scenarios should also serve as an explicit context for evaluating risks and for clarifying the assumptions and perceptions about the macroenvironment. They should contain sufficient information both to inform the strategic questions they address and to ensure their internal integrity and plausibility. As an important communication medium in strategic planning, they should be straightforward and easy to understand. Typical scenarios include qualitative and quantitative descriptions of key social, political, economic, demographic, and also other conditions bearing on their ultimate use. They also should describe basic trends, assumptions, conditions, and dynamics that lead from the present to the future period the scenarios cover. They are not, in themselves, forecasts or predictions, and they rarely have probability estimates associated with them or their particular elements. Thinking of them as carefully thought-out heuristics for exploring and evaluating different assumptions about future change in the macroenvironment helps to avoid the trap of probability. Participating to one degree or another in their creation is especially helpful for planners and decision makers who wish both to gain insight about factors influencing a decision and to improve their understanding of the dynamics of change in an uncertain macroenvironment.

The characteristics of scenarios are linked quite closely with the problems or issues they address:

Multiple Scenarios

Using a scenario approach always means working with multiple scenarios. Sometimes as few as two alternatives will do. Some issues require many scenarios, but the general rule of thumb is to work with as few as possible. Typically, between two and four scenarios are sufficient for most strategic plans. Generating and using scenarios means being explicit about basic uncertainties that will influence the success of particular strategies.

Comprehensiveness

Strategic scenarios should be holistic, integrated, and, as much as possible, internally consistent. This means that, insofar as possible, they should include analyses of societal forces that directly affect the strategic decision and other factors that indirectly shape the most significant forces. A scenario looking at petroleum demand parameters ought to consider not only future prices and economic growth but also such factors as consumer values, economic restructuring, international and domestic political conditions, and technological substitutes for transportation (among other things) that are both important and uncertain in the long run.

Testing Perspectives and Assumptions

Scenarios are an explicit framework for proposing and testing basic perceptions and assumptions about the important elements influencing strategy. Very often, each scenario reflects a different perspective, a different set of assumptions, and a different logic about the future. One scenario sometimes echoes the concerns and beliefs of the senior planner or chief executive officer (CEO); others ought to be based on different and often conflicting views.

Links to Strategic Decisions

Since they describe the macroenvironment, scenarios are the most general element in the corporate framework for strategic decision making. They must inform, either directly or indirectly, other elements of that framework. Some of the links are obvious: the economic element in a set of scenarios should tell the rest of the planning process about demand, prices, financial parameters and so on. Other connections are less obvious: changing social values (and lifestyles) may address, for example, such topics as employee concerns and relations, the activities of key stakeholder groups, and, although not immediately measurable, subtle indications of change in the marketplace.

Linking Strategic and Operational Planning

Scenarios can help to bridge the gap between strategic and operational planning concerns. Generating and, especially, reviewing scenarios work best when division executives, who will be affected by the outcomes of planning, have a real role in shaping and an understanding of the assumptions beneath the plans. For one thing, they often have a better understanding than staff planners of forces shaping their immediate businesses. For another, both scenarios and the planning process will generally be more realistic if their ultimate users have some input.

Context for Other Forecasts

Scenarios often provide the explicit context for other forecasting methods. A scenario should include estimates (consistent with that scenario) of the assumptions used for running quantitative forecasting models. More important, scenarios serve as a collection of insights for evaluating, adjusting, and ultimately making sense out of the results of more formal models. A good set of scenarios, for example, should inform their users about the plausibility and overall consistency of the results of econometric simulation models.

Environmental Monitoring Base

Finally, scenarios inform strategic environmental monitoring. By identifying critical uncertainties, they point to the political, social, economic, and other developments that planners need to watch and review on a regular or periodic basis. Insights gained from monitoring the environment are, of course, a good first step in updating or redefining a company's basic strategic scenarios.

For reasons that will be illustrated in a subsequent section of this chapter, the process of developing scenarios is nearly as important as the resulting scenarios. Creating and using them informs strategic planners and executives about both the real world and about themselves. The macroenvironment is fundamentally unpredictable and individuals who must look ahead will naturally be unsure about the future. *Scenarios don't reduce uncertainty, they clarify it.* The process of creating and applying them can help their users cope with their own unsureness and, at the same time, increase their knowledge and understanding of the macroenvironment.

SCENARIO DEVELOPMENT

There are many different ways to generate scenarios, but two parts of the process are especially critical. The first is that the entire process must be tied to—in fact, must start with—the strategic decisions it is intended to inform. Strategic scenarios for a toolmaker supplying the automotive industry should be quite different from scenarios mapping out long-range strategic considerations for a food processor. They may have common elements and data, and some other similarities, but they serve to address entirely different questions. The same point applies to scenarios developed by a particular company to address different strategic questions. Scenarios intended to help in identifying new business opportunities may be quite different from scenarios that inform a major capital investment in an existing business. It is not especially useful to start with general societal scenarios, developed by consultants or published by reputable futurists, and then to try to apply these to a particular company's strategic problems. This is not to say that considerable insight cannot be gained from incorporating elements and analyses of such scenarios into a company's specific analyses, only that issue-specific scenarios are always more useful.

The heart of the scenario process is selecting the basic logical underpinnings of each scenario. A scenario logic is the skeleton upon which hang the flesh and muscles and details of the scenario. Scenario logics come from formal theories of how societies change, the mental maps held by participants in the scenario process, and formal and informal arguments put forth by authorities or experts. Post-Keynesian economics, monetarism, and supply-side economics are simple examples of different economic logics. Whether the logics for a set of scenarios are economic, political, technological, some combination of all three, or something else, from them must flow the scenario details that will inform corporate strategy.

The Scenario Process

In concept, generating and elaborating scenarios is an elegantly simple process. In practice, it is messy and hard, and much more an art than a science. At SRI's Business Futures Program an eight-step process is used that seems to fit most situations:

1. Analyzing the decision(s)
2. Identifying key decision factors
3. Identifying key (societal) forces
4. Analyzing key forces separately
5. Selecting scenario logics
6. Elaborating scenarios
7. Identifying and analyzing implications in terms of key decision factors
8. Incorporating scenario insights into strategic decisions

The process both begins and ends with the decisions it informs. Figure 10-1 shows this process as a loop.

1. Strategic Decisions The first step is to identify the nature of decisions which are to be made. Examples include strategic opportunities and risks for current business areas, new areas of opportunity (diversification), expansion or contraction of specific business lines (allocation of capital), building new or expanding old manufacturing facilities (major capital investments), long-term advertising and public relations strategies, and the like. The more precisely these decisions or strategic concerns can be defined, the easier it is to construct scenarios and to apply them effectively. Scenarios can also be designed to address broader, longer-term concerns such as the overall strategic positioning and goals for the company over the next ten to twenty years, a consideration quite significant for some industries. Such scenarios are likely to be more generally exploratory than those focused on specific decisions, but the same initial step is crucial.

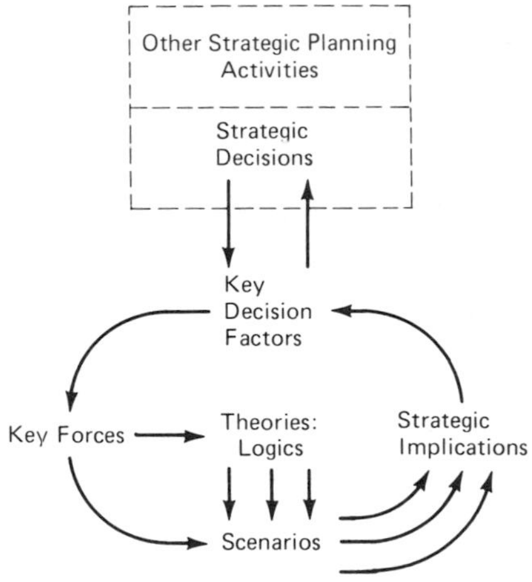

FIGURE 10-1
The scenario process.

The purposes of this process of definition are to focus and constrain subsequent steps in generating, refining, and applying the scenarios. Insufficient focus results in scenarios too global and too general to be useful. Inadequate definitions of strategic concerns often lead to too many scenarios, or to scenarios that roam too far afield from what is most relevant.

2. Key Decision Factors Once the decisions or areas of strategic concern have been defined, the next step is to specify what factors will most directly inform that decision or strategy. Typically, these include such things as market size, capital resources, human resources, regulation, technological availability and capacity, economic performance, profit margins, and the like. Which and how many key factors are relevant is of course determined by the nature of the decision or strategy. Important to specify here as well are "softer" and often "controllable" decision factors related to the corporate culture. Such things as the company's strengths and weaknesses, the organization and style of management, the long-range goals of key executives, and the like are all matters that directly influence a major decision or strategy.

The key decision factors are what the scenarios will ultimately inform. For example, if the strategic decision involves diversification into new areas of business, the scenarios should provide information that will lead to evaluating the sizes of markets of interest, new products or technologies that would serve such markets, the economics of prospective marketplaces, government regulation (if any) in that area, and so forth. But statements of corporate goals and of strengths and weaknesses, which are outside the scenarios themselves, serve to constrain further what the scenarios must address. A company experienced in distributing products for use in households may find that its capacity for entering manufacturing of high-technology consumer durables is extremely limited.

3. Key Societal Forces In this next step, the job is to identify the forces in the macroenvironment that will determine changes in the values of the key decision factors. This involves developing a qualitative model of the most significant forces. For example, if the decision has to do with a major expansion of a business segment for a media conglomerate, the forces might include:

- The growth and structure of the economy
- Communications technology
- Printing technology
- Educational systems
- Postal and communications regulation
- Lifestyles
- Reading habits

There are no hard-and-fast rules for identifying these forces. A good rule of thumb, however, is to draw on the expertise of staff planners and, if needed, outside consultants to review forces in the following general areas:

- Economic trends and conditions
- Demographic and migratory trends
- Technological forces
- Political and regulatory environment
- Social and lifestyle factors
- The physical environment
- Natural resources
- International conditions

Not all these areas are relevant to all scenario exercises, of course, and other topic areas may have to be addressed for particular topics.

4. Analysis of Key Forces Each of these topic areas should be analyzed in considerable detail in this step, indicating major trends and uncertainties, relationships with other key forces, and underlying *societal forces* that in turn bear on the eventual direction of these most significant elements.

The relationships among these most important forces or elements are especially important to analyze. Doing so helps to reduce further the number of plausible scenarios that will be developed in the next step. Analyses at this stage, for example, will point to forces that tend to move together, or to future conditions in key forces that are mutually inconsistent. Analysis might indicate, for example that the growth of video-based home information systems will be severely inhibited by emerging regulatory and political trends, in spite of the likely availability of the appropriate technology. Or, in another analysis, it might become clear that psychological and lifestyle factors will tend to inhibit the speed with which consumers will embrace new nonprint media.

There are a great many different ways the analyses here can be organized and carried out. The main guiding rules are:

- Relevance to the eventual uses of the scenarios
- Internal consistency among the forces that will ultimately shape the decisions
- Enough completeness to avoid risk-laden surprises
- Sufficient detail to flesh out the scenarios so that they are believable and plausible
- Identification of underlying societal forces that shape these aspects of the macroenvironment

5. Scenario Logics This step is the heart of the scenario process. It typically takes the least time to do, but it draws on years of experience and analysis and is the hardest part of the whole process. Its purpose is to identify as many different scenario logics (or themes), based in part on the preceding analyses and in part on the collective insight of the scenario team, that will encompass the trends and uncertainties affecting the decision.

Scenario logics derive from perceptual models—theories—of societal change. These may include the perceptions of members of the scenario team, those held by outside experts, or, more broadly, established theories of social, political, economic, and other societal change. In practice, many such theories come into play in defining scenario logics. The preceding analyses of key forces—of the "facts" and uncertainties—constrain the scenarios. The perceptual models point to what kinds of change are plausible, and how much.

Picking the appropriate scenario logics involves considering the decision itself, the analyses of factors, and the relevant perceptual models. If the preceding analyses have indicated that the key forces shaping the relevant macroenvironment are technological, regulatory, and related to consumer values and lifestyles, then three distinct scenario logics, each based on the evolution of one set of these forces as a driving factor, *might* be appropriate. One scenario logic could assume that the emergence and existence of particular technologies will most shape the significant macroenvironment; lifestyles and regulations would change to reflect the new technology. Another logic might assume that changing consumer aspirations and lifestyles were the principal force for change. A third would assume that regulation was the main driving factor. Were the economy a central factor for a particular scenario analysis, then alternative economic logics might be considered, with the other key forces responding to these economic forces.

The process of selecting the scenario logics is not, however, intended to cover all possible scenarios. The basic rule of thumb is to use as few as possible scenarios—too many confuse and unnecessarily complicate the decision process later on. The most difficult part of selecting scenario logics is to encompass the key forces in consistent ways without creating too many different logics.

The following are very abbreviated summaries of two integrated scenario logics from a scenario study that addressed long-term strategy for a major multinational resource company:

- One basic logic argued that there would be a continuing inability to reach a national consensus in the United States about appropriate economic and energy policies. The underlying theory was that no external or internal threats are sufficient to cause political or social consensus. Regional and political special interests would be constantly at odds with particular policy initiatives and would feel frustrated by the slow results accruing from policies that they felt were appropriate. Among the consequences, over the long term, would be persistent deterioration in the political and economic environment, incoherent and conflicting regulatory policies that changed with every new administration, diverse and constantly problematical interest group pressures, slow or negligible economic growth, and so on.

- A second logic argued that, in response to perceived economic and energy threats from abroad, the country gradually turns toward consensus and redirection. Here the theory was that external threats force a national consensus. This logic implied a slow return to stable economic growth; reduced interest group pressures; a general inclination to tolerate and accommodate different political, social, and regional interests; a more consistent regulatory environment over the long run; particular kinds of government investment incentives; and so on.

(These are only two of several scenario logics employed for this particular study.)

Following the selection of scenario logics, the scenario team specifies basic conditions and changes in the broad areas of the macroenvironment that were identified in the preceding steps as most important. Usually, this means making relatively simple statements about social, environmental, political or regulatory, technological, economic, and other conditions implied by each scenario logic. Together with the scenario logic, these constitute a set of skeletal scenarios which next must be elaborated to complete the scenarios.

Scenario logics can be determined by an individual working alone, but the process works much better with a larger group together in a workshop setting. In the group should be representatives of parts of the company that will ultimately be affected by the strategic decision, as well as a core scenario team.

6. Elaborating the Scenarios The purpose of this step is to combine the results of the preceding two steps. The scenario developers start with the skeletal scenarios, which are in effect alternative sets of assumptions. The future dynamics of each major force must then be determined using these different assumptions. At this point, introducing quantitative forecasting models is usually appropriate.

Depending on the needs and style of the management group the scenarios will serve, results at this stage can range from simple summaries of the major forces and logics to highly detailed analyses of each scenario and force. The organization of the final scenarios is also a matter of preference. A general outline that covers most of the critical areas follows, but each company must tailor the presentation of scenarios to fit its own needs.

- Summaries of the scenario logics and highlights of the key forces.
- Implications of the scenarios for the business strategic decisions (see the next step).
- Text descriptions of each scenario that weave together the logic and conditions that make up the scenario. Usually this is done in the form of a "future history."
- "Wild cards" and other surprises identified in the course of the preceding analyses but left outside the scope of the main scenarios. Often these are developments identified by the analyses as quite unlikely (not deserving of a scenario logic), but nevertheless plausible and with a large potential impact on the business decision.

Presentation of scenario information should include both qualitative and quantitative information, as is necessary for the next step.

Since most completed scenarios for strategic planning are both lengthy and proprietary, no fully elaborated examples have been included here. However, interested readers will find good presentations of contemporary scenarios in *Seven Tomorrows* by Paul Hawken, James Ogilvy, and Peter Schwartz (Bantam Books, New York, 1982) and in Paul Dickson's *The Future File* (Rawson and Associates, New York, 1977; also Avon Paperback).

7. Implications for Decision Factors Properly constructed and elaborated, each scenario implies particular directions or values for the decision factors identified in step 2. These values may be determined by qualitative analyses or by using formal models. Overall, the purpose of this step is to draw out of the scenario what they mean for the factors decision makers will take into account.

By no means will all the uncertainties be removed from the decision factors at this stage. The important thing is to determine the basic characteristics of decision factors consistent with each scenario. Implications can be approached from two complementary directions. In most scenario analyses, there will be a common set of conclusions across all scenarios, at least for some of the key decision factors. The value of other factors will, however, vary from one scenario to another, and should be presented accordingly.

Again, how the implications are presented should take into account the most effective way of communicating to the decision makers in a particular corporate setting. Usually, the detailed analyses of the scenarios serve only as background for such a presentation.

8. Decisions The last step is of course making the decision. Properly speaking, this is outside the scenario process itself and involves many other corporate concerns. The scenarios inform but do not prescribe what decisions are most appropriate. The scenarios may suggest that the original decision is appropriate, that part of the decision should be deferred, that further intelligence should be collected, or that substantially different choices are in order. The decision process itself likely involves other actors and considerations than may have been involved in creating the scenarios.

KEY PROBLEM AREAS

Several specific problem areas tend to complicate the process of developing scenarios:

The Scenario Team

Selecting members of a scenario team, supporting staff, and other participants in the overall process requires sensitivity to the particular skills needed to generate and refine scenarios, to personal styles of leadership and interaction, and to internal company politics. A core team of scenario analysts with a mix of analytical and intuitive skills, a scenario leader knowledgeable about and sensitive to the styles and needs of executives involved in strategic decision making, a support staff of planning professionals and outside consultants, and a large base of senior management from both corporate and division levels to review the work constitute an ideal arrangement. Often, this requires using outside consultants to aid the process.

Communicating the Scenarios

The scenario process and its products are not very useful unless they can be effectively communicated to both senior management and division executives who must ultimately implement strategy. There is no universal template for communicating scenarios. How to do it best depends on the nature of the strategic decision, on the parties involved, and on the overall style of the corporation. Attention to how this is done—and this differs greatly from one company to another—is crucial to the successful use of scenarios.

Length and Completeness

Two kinds of considerations tend to complicate the matter of how "complete" scenarios are to be. Their users, especially those with decision responsibilities, usually want them brief and to the point, with only enough supplementary material to support the plausibility or to answer questions about the sensitivity of the scenarios. Analysts and executives with broader strategic responsibilities tend to prefer much more detail. Again, a balance has to be found that is appropriate for each separate corporate setting. Using two different scenario presentations often works best.

The Probability of Scenarios

Some traditional forecasting methods rely heavily on estimates of probability, especially those approaches lumped together under the label of decision theory. There are good ways of linking scenario analyses with decision trees and probability estimates, but care should be taken not to impute probability to any particular scenario. A scenario is a holistic description of a future society or macroenvironment. Values are usually assigned to particular variables for both analytical and descriptive purposes. But the probability of any scenario happening just as described is obviously negligible. Where estimates of the relative likelihoods of a set of scenarios would be useful, this assessment can best be made by collective judgment. The opinions of the scenario team, the scenario users, and outside experts about the likelihood and impact of the scenarios are helpful for doing this.

Bias

Everyone involved in any forecasting activity has personal, professional, and cultural biases. Their biases are in fact often linked closely with the scenario logics or themes they propose, that is, with their own perceptual models of the macroenvironment. One of the purposes of a balanced scenario team is to smooth out the biases of participants and reviewers. Overall, however, participants should generally recognize and be explicit about their particular biases and the likely effects on the process and results. Explicitly attempting to stand outside one's own culture to explore the bias that comes, for example, from being immersed in a "consumer society" is particularly useful.

Updating and Revising Scenarios

One certainty about strategic scenarios is that they will be out of date long before the decision they serve to inform is completed or the future is reached. Used in ongoing strategic planning processes, scenarios deserve periodic reviews and revisions. In addressing particular decision areas, they point to significant uncertainties in the macroenvironment that should be monitored on an occasional or regular basis. Some companies will work with the same set of long-range strategic scenarios, revising them from time to time, but creating an entirely new set when societal conditions warrant doing so. When a set of planning scenarios no longer provides sufficient insight about the macroenvironment, it is time to reconsider them. Other companies will find it more effective to create specific sets of scenarios for particular projects, paying some attention to consistency across different scenario analyses. But scenarios in all cases do have a visible half-life, and should be revised as often as necessary.

OTHER SCENARIO APPROACHES

The process described above is our general scheme for creating and using scenarios. There are a number of distinctly different approaches used by companies that have developed them internally or constructed by other consulting organizations. What all approaches share in common—or should—is their focus on the strategic areas that they inform. Some of these other approaches may, in fact, fit better with particular company styles. Among the major approaches are scenarios developed by outside experts, scenarios created by morphological analyses, and scenarios based on quantitative cross-impact techniques.

1. Experts' Scenarios

Some companies prefer to externalize their scenario process by asking outside consultants to provide structured information about the future macroenvironment. In effect, this means inviting a number of knowledgeable people with their own perceptual maps of the future to provide input to the strategic decision. This sometimes proves awkward to manage, but of course depends on the skills of both the internal scenario staff and the capabilities and views of the outside experts. The key point to remember is that scenarios of this sort implicitly reflect scenario logics deemed likely and plausible by outsiders. Making sure these logics are made explicit will make the resulting scenarios more useful.

2. Morphological Approaches

Some strategic decision makers prefer a larger number of different scenarios to review before making their decision. One process for creating such scenarios is to identify different plausible future "states" for the key driving forces. For example, if the underlying societal forces shaping the macroenvironment for a strategic issue include the economy, the natural resource base, values and lifestyles, and the effectiveness of the national government, scenario analysts will look at different possible conditions for each of these forces.

Economic growth might be high (E_1), moderate (E_2), or low to negligible (E_3). Critical natural resources might be seen as available and inexpensive (R_1), available but expensive (R_2), or of restricted availability and expensive (R_3). Lifestyles might be traditional (L_1), oriented toward survival needs (L_2), or changing toward simpler, less consumptive attitudes (L_3). And the future effectiveness of the government might be viewed as highly effective (G_1), muddling through (G_2), or generally ineffective (G_3). The scenario analysts then array the different combinations of each of these factors together for future points in time, creating a tree of scenarios that grows outward into more and more branches. Branches that have internal inconsistencies—for example, unavailable and expensive natural resources and high economic growth—are removed. Other scenarios that lead to similar results and implications can also be deleted.

The remainder of the process proceeds as above—fleshing out the scenarios and analyzing them for implications. Our experience using such an approach is that it tends to consume too many resources and to result in too many scenarios. It does not seem to provide any greater insight than fewer scenarios couched in carefully constructed logics, but it does describe many more specific alternatives.

3. Cross-Impact Approaches

Cross-impact analysis involves identifying a large number of potential events and conditions that appear to influence not only the outcome of the decision but each other as well. These events, trends, and conditions typically have probabilities assigned to them, and a computer is used to sort through different combinations in terms of probabilities and cross-impacts. The advantage of such an approach is that it allows scenario analysts to work through a large number of variables and scenarios, and to be explicit about the interrelationships of particular events and conditions. The logics of scenarios arrived at in such a matter is built into the structure of the cross-impact model and the judgment of the experts who put in data and interpret results.

APPLICATIONS

Scenarios are by no means a magical device for helping make all kinds of decisions. There are many instances when the approach is not specifically useful and would, in all likelihood, make decision making overly complex. There are, however, four particular applications that seem generally useful.

1. In general, any long-range strategic decision—whether to build a new facility, enter new markets, or consider the broad direction of the company—deserves a consideration of forces and uncertainties in the macroenvironment. In today's environment *long-range* generally means five years and beyond. However, businesses working with shorter-term plans in a highly volatile business environment will also find scenario approaches useful.

2. Scenarios are very effective as a context for guiding and evaluating other long-range forecasts and analyses. In effect, they provide a background description of societal forces and conditions for considering the assumption, the interactions, and the outcomes of other kinds of projections. In this role, they are especially useful for identifying inconsistencies in other projections and areas of possible surprise.

3. A scenario framework is usually essential when long-range risk and vulnerability analyses are conducted. Formal vulnerability analyses done without explicit consideration of plausible changes in the macroenvironment will likely identify only those problems that will emerge were the future much like the present. Full-blown scenarios are not necessarily needed for such analyses, but at least skeletal scenarios, with their internal driving logic clearly stated, are.

4. A number of companies today pay close and continual attention to forces in the macroenvironment that will soon or eventually affect them. Scenarios focused on the broad strategic concerns of the company are an ideal mechanism for identifying crucial uncertainties for environmental monitoring. The process of monitoring the environment is itself an important step in revising scenarios and reviewing strategic plans.

In our experience, societal scenarios serve especially well in these particular kinds of strategic decisions:

- There are a number of businesses, among them natural resource companies, basic manufacturers, the automotive and related industries, and the like, which must plan over the long term. Twenty-five- to thirty-year strategic plans for international petroleum producers are not uncommon these days, for example, and some of these companies look even further ahead. Long-range scenarios, in our view, are absolutely essential if planning has a very long time horizon.
- Certain kinds of business decisions also have an inherently long time horizon no matter what industry they are in. An example would be a decision to construct a major new manufacturing facility that will have to operate at high rates for twenty to twenty-five years. Making such a decision involves asking questions about the very long range demand for the products such a facility would produce. Where there are uncertainties about technological substitution, the changing structure of the economy, international manufacturing trends in the same areas, or a marketplace influenced strongly by consumer values and lifestyles, a scenario approach is extremely helpful in sorting out the key decision.
- Some kinds of businesses are today facing significant changes in their markets or competitive environments. For example, with U.S. pop-

ulation growth slowing, long-range rates of growth in major consumer durable goods such as cars are likely to slow significantly from levels of even a decade ago. Where new kinds of structural change in markets appears ahead, that is, for industries facing maturation in their traditionally high growth markets, scenarios are a useful approach.

- Finally, not only businesses that must plan for the long terms will find scenarios helpful. Businesses that serve new markets or markets that are highly volatile in the short run would do well to consider scenario approaches for strategic decision making. Examples include businesses that are the focus of swings in regulatory attitude, that provide goods and services linked with national and regional fads and fashions, and that are influenced by international political and economic developments.

ORGANIZING TO USE SCENARIOS

Some companies produce scenarios internally with little or no outside assistance. Others rely almost wholly on consultants to develop and evaluate scenarios of the macroenvironment. Most, however, fall somewhere in between these two extremes. In all cases, there are organizational concerns that should be addressed to ensure the effective use of scenarios.

In the first place, scenarios divorced from ongoing strategic planning activities rarely make sense and are difficult to apply. The single exception is the development of scenarios to address a very specific decision, such as a new manufacturing facility, but even here information from other, regular planning processes must be reviewed and incorporated into the scenarios. In a formal strategic planning and management system, the role of scenarios is to provide information about the changing external environment.

In most companies that do strategic planning, there is usually a senior executive or office responsible for environmental monitoring and analysis. In many companies, this activity is distinct from more operationally and financially focused corporate planning. In some, corporate planning executives and staff perform both functions. Basically, two rules should guide answering the question of where scenario development should be located. The first is that scenario development should be close organizationally and in practice to the decision makers it will serve. The second is that it should be organized so that it can interact with other staff departments that can provide it with information, and that it should involve managers or analysts from operating divisions in one way or another.

Selecting the scenario team involves several considerations. Foremost is the management group the scenarios will serve. As indicated above, having a core scenario team of executives and senior staff analysts is the central component of a scenario activity. The leader of the team should be or have close access to the client for the scenarios. Members of the team ought to represent different analytical perspectives, different educational and professional backgrounds, and by proxy, different points of view in the company. They should also be able to work well in a group setting, without any one individual dominating the process. Scenario team members should be committed to the process. It helps to have on the team individuals who by position or preference pay a lot of attention to what is going on in the macroenvironment. There should be a balance between quantitative and qualitative analytical skills. Good intuition should balance out good analysis.

Most scenario-generation activities tend to make considerable use of outside consultants and research organizations. The roles these resources effectively play are as varied as the different organizations they serve. But the principal roles in the scenario process involve filling in gaps in the substantive expertise of internal staff and the scenario team, providing detailed analyses of specific topics raised by scenario analyses, aiding the process itself, and especially, bringing a fresh perspective to the job of creating scenarios. This latter role, providing a different perspective, is often one of being an intellectual gadfly. Most internal staff on the scenario team, their views and opinions shaped by the day-to-day business environment, often see the external environment from a relatively narrow perspective. Developing scenarios, however, requires broad, fresh, and often contrary perspectives in order to discover the most appropriate scenario logics.

As a part of strategic planning, scenarios deserve periodic attention. The issues that led to creating them in the first place and the societal conditions they describe will both change. Some companies use different sets of scenarios arranged in a hierarchical fashion. There will be a set of very long-range thematic scenarios that get reviewed every five years or so. Beneath these, and much more detailed, will be several medium-term scenarios that more directly address the company's business area. These are consistent with the long-range scenarios, but not dependent on them. Such medium-term scenarios may be revised every two years or so. Other companies annually update their basic strategic scenarios as part of the annual cycle of strategic planning. In no case should scenarios be considered the final word. Leaving them on the shelf for too long a time without a review is asking for problematic surprises in a changing world.

PITFALLS AND FINAL THOUGHTS

This chapter has been about futures scenarios for strategic planning—how to create them, how to use them, and how to organize them. But some warnings are also in order. Scenarios are expensive to create and hard to use. Creating them often requires staff and consultants with skills and sensitivities that are at the very least unusual in traditional business planning. Typical strategic scenarios are more qualitative than quantitative, more concerned with perceptions than with facts, more exploratory than extrapolative, and more a product of imagination than of scientific method. Planners and executives who are used to formal forecasting models, econometrics, and financial planning often find scenarios an uncomfortably alien approach. Decision makers expecting hard answers about the future will invariably come away disappointed. Contemplating using scenarios means being sensitive to these potential problems as well as to the specific needs of the company.

Scenarios—and especially the process of creating scenarios—nevertheless can bear special fruit for a company that takes the time and resources to develop and use them. They tend to sensitize their users to the very real indeterminacy of forces shaping the business environment. They force a company to make explicit its institutional assumptions and habits, good and bad. They provide strategic decision makers with a context for admitting and making the most out of what are normal feelings of uncertainty. They point to the kinds of changes outside the company to which attention should be paid. They can act as a focusing medium for top management, planners, and operating management alike. Above all, scenario processes help their users understand, plan, and manage better in an era of rapid, often surprising, and sometimes upsetting change.

Section Three

Strategic Planning for Major Business Functions

Chapter 11
MARKETING STRATEGY

THOMAS S. ROBERTSON
Professor and Chairperson, Department of Marketing, The Wharton School, University of Pennsylvania

YORAM WIND
Professor of Marketing and Director, Center for International Studies, The Wharton School, University of Pennsylvania

With some trepidation we suggest that there are three generic strategies for achieving success in the competitive marketplace. The first of these strategies is to gain *control over supply or distribution*. The second is to achieve significant *competitive cost advantage*. The third is to achieve *product differentiation* relative to competitors. These are by no means mutually exclusive, although most successful corporations dominantly pursue one strategy.

Marketing as a discipline is a critical component of all three strategies but has its greatest role in product differentiation strategy. The focus of marketing is on customer needs assessment and the positioning and differentiation of products and services for identifiable target market segments. Marketing performs a boundary role function in the firm's selection of an appropriate strategy; that is, marketing spans the customer interface and provides the assessment of needs which must ultimately guide all strategy development.

MARKETING AS A BOUNDARY ROLE FUNCTION

Marketing performs a boundary role function between the company and its markets. It guides the allocation of resources to product and service offerings designed to satisfy market needs while achieving corporate objectives. This boundary role function of marketing is critical to strategy development. Before marshaling a company's resources to acquire a new business, or to introduce a new product, or to reposition an existing product, management must use marketing research to cross the company-consumer boundary and to assess the likely market response.

The logic and value of consumer needs assessment are generally beyond dispute, yet frequently ignored. It is estimated, for example, that a majority of new products fail. Yet, there is most often nothing wrong with the product itself; that is, it works. The problem is simply that consumers do not want the product.

AT&T's Picturephone is a classic example of a technology-driven product which works; but people do not want to see each other on a telephone. It transforms a comfortable, low-involvement communication transaction into a demanding, high-involvement one. The benefit is not obvious to consumers. Of course, the benefit could become obvious if transportation costs continue to outpace communication costs, and if consumers could be "taught" the benefits of using a Picturephone.

Marketing's boundary role function is similarly important in maintaining a viable competitive positioning in the marketplace. The passing of Korvette from the American retail scene, for example, can be attributed to consumer confusion as to what Korvette represented—how it was positioned relative to competition (Hartley, 1981). Korvette's strength was as a discount chain—high turnover and low margin. This basic mission of the business was violated, however, as Korvette traded up in soft goods and fashion items and even opened a store on Manhattan's Fifth Avenue. The result was that Korvette became neither a discount store nor a department store and lost its previous customer base. Sears encountered a similar phenomenon as it opted for higher margins in the 1970s and lost its reputation for value in the marketplace. The penalty has been declining sales and profitability for its retail store operation, which it is now trying valiantly to arrest by reestablishing its "middle America" value orientation. Nevertheless, consumer research could have indicated the beginning of the problem long before the crisis in sales and profits occurred.

HIERARCHY OF STRATEGIES

Marketing is, of course, only one component in the strategic planning process. Marketing strategy operates in conjunction with financial, technological, production, and human resources strategies in the development of viable overall strategic plans. Each discipline provides propositions and approaches which apply to all levels of strategy development—the product or brand level, the product category level, the SBU level, and the corporate level. Indeed, we may think of a matrix approach to strategy development and evaluation as shown in Figure 11-1.

	Discipline Input				
Strategic Level	MARKETING	FINANCE	TECHNOLOGY	PRODUCTION	HUMAN RESOURCES
Product or brand					
Product category					
SBU					
Corporation					

FIGURE 11-1
Matrix approach to strategy development and evaluation.

In order to demonstrate the levels of strategy within the firm, let us develop two separate examples for General Foods Corporation and Tiger International Corporation. General Foods, with 1980 revenues of $6.6 billion, is a diversified manufacturer of food products and also participates in the restaurant business. Tiger International, with 1980 revenues of $1.6 billion, is a diversified transportation company operating in air freight (Flying Tiger), trucking, and railroad car leasing.

	General Foods Corporation	*Tiger International Corporation*
Product or brand strategy	Maxwell House Instant coffee brand	JFK-LAX air-freight product
Product category strategy	Instant versus ground versus decaffeinated coffees	Domestic versus European versus Asian air freight routes
SBU strategy	Maxwell House Division versus other General Foods' SBUs	Flying Tiger versus other Tiger International SBUs in trucking and railroad car leasing
Corporate strategy	Total portfolio of General Foods	Total portfolio of Tiger International

Product or Brand Strategy

The lowest level of strategy in the corporate hierarchy is at the individual product or brand level: strategy for the Maxwell House Instant coffee brand or for Flying Tiger's JFK-LAX (New York to Los Angeles) air-freight product. Frequently, brand strategy is heavily marketing-dominated; yet, explicit financial guidelines and resource allocation procedures are necessary to optimize the total corporate portfolio. Maxwell House Instant is interdependent with other Maxwell House Division brands, and cannibalization should be controlled. Flying Tiger's JFK-LAX product is interdependent with other routes; and its quality must meet minimum standards, or it will adversely affect other Flying Tiger products.

Product Category Strategy

Within the product category level, tradeoffs and resource allocation become more explicit. Maxwell House Instant is given more resources than Maxim because it is more profitable. Flying Tiger's higher-margin, long-haul routes are given greater resources than the lower-margin, short-haul routes. The several strategic components of the firm must all focus on this long-haul strategy—providing the marketing, financial, people, and operations resources to execute a high-quality, differentiated long-haul air-freight service.

SBU Strategy

At the SBU level further resource allocation is made. Maxwell House Division must decide which product categories should receive emphasis—perhaps decaffeinated because it is more profitable and has higher revenue growth. For Flying Tiger, perhaps the Asian division should receive priority over the United States and Europe, since it is more profitable and has better price stability.

Corporate Strategy

Here the concern is the overall company strategy for the General Foods or Tiger International portfolio. Should Maxwell House Division be treated as a "cash cow" or is it vulnerable to competition from Folgers and Nestlé and does it thus require ongoing investment? Should the General Foods portfolio be expanded beyond the low-growth food industry, and what criteria would be used for acquisitions? For Tiger International how much additional investment should be made in its Flying Tiger SBU, which is less profitable than its North American Car (railroad equipment leasing) SBU or its Hall's Motor Transit SBU? But which SBU has greatest long-run potential? Should its North American Car continue to be treated as a cash cow or is there the opportunity to aggressively expand profitably its share of the served market?

Obviously, a company should have a strong sense of corporate strategy if it is to avoid suboptimization at lower strategic levels. The Maxwell House Instant brand manager should not have market share gains as the dominant objective if General Foods wishes to treat the coffee SBU as a cash cow in order to fund new acquisitions.

THE ROLE OF MARKETING IN STRATEGIC PLANNING

The uniqueness of marketing strategy is in the *conceptual* and *methodological* bases which it brings to strategy development at all levels of the firm. In contrast, much of the strategy literature consists of normative frameworks and paradigms. The recommendations of these paradigms are, unfortunately, seldom testable or supportable by empirical research. Although some notable attempts (such as the PIMS project[1]) are under way to provide empirical generalizations, the field is still more intuitive than evidential, and could benefit greatly from the conceptual and methodological advances of the marketing discipline.

Conceptual Contributions

The marketing literature provides a guiding rationale for the firm's strategy selection in terms of matching *customer needs* with the firm's offerings and capabilities. Meeting customer needs is the only conceptually sound strategic direction. When consumer needs go unfulfilled, the market is unstable and susceptible to change. Consider, for example, the unfulfilled need for overnight delivery of small packages and the success which Federal Express had in entering this market. Similarly, consider the success of Southwest Airlines in meeting the need for high-frequency reliable commuter service in the Texas market which Braniff and Texas International had ignored.

The marketing discipline further contributes such concepts as market segmentation, product and competitive positioning, the marketing mix, life cycle management, and a marketing-guided approach to resource allocation. These concepts are by no means alien to strategic planning but are often not explicitly developed. For example, in the Boston Consulting Group growth-share matrix, the concept of the "market served" builds on market segmentation theory and the classification of business within the portfolio represents a form of competitive positioning and bears some relationship to life cycle theory. Some of the key (and often unanswered) questions underlying the growth-share and other product-portfolio analyses are:

---

[1]PIMS (Profit Impact of Market Strategy) is a shared data base which includes over 150 companies and close to 2000 businesses. It was originally developed by General Electric but is now administered by the Strategic Planning Institute, a nonprofit corporation. The objective is to develop overall generalizations as to what factors lead to strategic success and what the weights of these factors are. (For a further discussion of PIMS, see Chapter 23, "The PIMS Program"; see also D. F. Abell and J. Hammond, *Strategic Market Planning: Problems and Analytical Approaches,* Prentice-Hall, Englewood Cliffs, N.J., 1979.)

- What market segments should the firm serve and what is the logic of segment selection?
- How should the firm's products be positioned and differentiated from competition in order to achieve competitive advantage?
- What is the optimal mix of pricing, distribution, and promotional strategy for each of the product offerings of the firm? What often goes ignored is that different types and levels of marketing mixes can lead to entirely different results and levels of success. This raises the issue of how a firm should allocate resources as a function of the market response elasticity to different types and levels of marketing mix expenditures.
- What is the likely life cycle of the product, and how can it be managed to the firm's advantage?

These questions are all based on well-accepted and tested marketing concepts, which are briefly discussed below.

Methodological Contributions

The marketing field has accumulated an inventory of applied methods appropriate to research on the above concepts. These include methods for:

- *Assessment of consumer and organizational buyer needs* from projective techniques to psychometrics, econometrics, and computer simulations.
- *Market segmentation,* which encompasses most of the multivariate statistical methods.
- *Competitive and product positioning* based on market structure analysis and multidimensional scaling.
- *Generation and evaluation of marketing mix strategies* encompassing marketing research approaches to the design and evaluation of product features and positioning, price levels, advertising and promotion levels, and distribution channels. In addition, adaptive experimentation, response elasticity models, market-tracking systems and various optimization and simulation models have been widely used.
- *Product life cycle forecasts* based on a variety of time series, econometric, and subjective judgment methods.

This chapter will proceed now by examining a number of concepts and associated methods.

PRODUCT POSITIONING

Concept

Perhaps the most fundamental factor accounting for business success is the ability to offer differentiated products and services, that is, to position product offerings in a manner such that consumers perceive them to be distinct from competition.

Bruce Henderson (1979), the founder of the Boston Consulting Group, offers a persuasive analysis of Chrysler's repeated difficulties. His thesis is that survival depends upon competitive uniqueness, which Chrysler has traditionally lacked. Chrysler has made cars similar to those made by General Motors and Ford but has had roughly ten percent higher costs than General Motors. The obvious question is why has Chrysler chosen to confront the market leader without differentiated products and with a higher cost structure? Logic would suggest avoiding frontal competition and producing differentiated products for identifiable consumer groups, much as the German and Japanese imports have done, or as Chrysler started doing in 1982 with the first convertible made in the United States since 1976.

Product differentiation is not the only strategic direction to profitability, but its absence must be countered by lower costs or control over supply if profitability is to be achieved. The lack of differentiation generally means vigorous price competition, whereas differentiated positioning in a market generally allows a premium price. A firm may have the latitude, therefore, to combine differentiation with aggressive pricing or to seek a premium market price, as in such cases as Federal Express, IBM, and Perrier.

It must also be emphasized that differentiation is achieved only to the extent that it is perceived by the customer. Many superior products are never seen as such by consumers, and therefore the differentiation is without value. By contrast, in many product categories the differentiation may largely be perceptual rather than inherent in the product. IBM is perceived to have higher value than other computer manufacturers, even when a majority of its products are at technological parity with competitors. Much of the perceived differentiation is in terms of the augmented IBM system, which provides benefits beyond the hardware itself. For beer consumers Budweiser may have higher value despite the average beer drinker's inability to distinguish brands in blind taste tests.

Methods

Positioning involves two sets of decisions: (1) assessment of the brand's current position, and (2) determination of the most desired positioning. Analysis of a brand's perceived positioning may reveal that the brand is well positioned relative to its competitors and the consumer ideal, or that repositioning is necessary, or that new-product introduction is advisable. In determining the brand's current positioning, a variety of multidimensional scaling and clustering approaches have been employed (Pessemier, 1977; Urban and Hauser, 1980; Wind, 1982).

Multidimensional scaling (MDS) and clustering are two sets of techniques used to portray graphically consumer evaluation of objects (for example, brands). Developed by mathematical psychologists, MDS techniques take consumer judgments of perceptions and preferences and find geometric representations (maps) in which objects (brands) which are judged to be similar psychologically plot near each other in the geometric space. The map in Figure 11-2, for example, was derived in

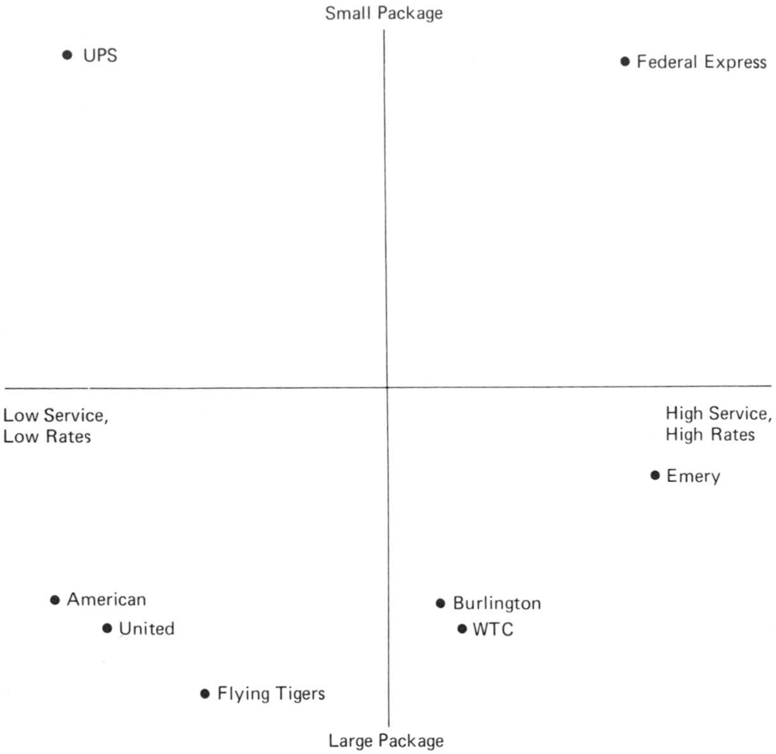

FIGURE 11-2
Multidimensional scaling example: competitive positioning of air freight and air express companies. (*Source: Flying Tiger Line Marketing Research. Used by permission.*)

a 1978 research project for Flying Tiger Line. Based on this map, Flying Tiger has implemented strategic initiatives to broaden its portfolio and to compete not only in the large package (freight) part of the market but in the small package part of the market as well.

More recently, designs based on conjoint analysis also have been utilized to establish a brand, product, or firm's positioning (ideally by market segment). Conjoint analysis is an approach developed by mathematical psychologists which is used heavily in marketing (a recent review suggested its use in more than 700 commercial marketing studies encompassing all areas of marketing from concept and product design to positioning and segmentation, price sensitivity, promotion, advertising, and distribution options).

The conjoint approach is concerned with measuring the joint effect of two or more independent variables (strategy components) on the ordering of a dependent variable (overall liking, intention to buy, preference, or some other evaluative measure). In making their judgments, respondents are typically confronted with trade-offs among various options and are required to give their evaluation of the relative attractiveness of the various combinations of offerings.

The output of a conjoint analysis study, as illustrated in Figure 11-3, offers a utility function for each factor studied (for example, price levels or specific product features). This allows the researcher to determine (1) the best possible offering (the combination of features with the highest utilities) for each respondent, (2) the relative importance of each factor, and (3) the answer to the question "what will happen if" by assessing the utility gain and loss associated with changes in any of the offerings. This latter stage is typically accompanied by a computer simulation which provides management with brand-switching matrices revealing the likely outcome of any new product introduction or modification in a product offering (change in features, positioning, and so on). In addition, the simulation allows management to assess the likely impact on share and profitability of any competitive actions or retaliation in response to the firm's own strategies.

MARKET SEGMENTATION

Concept

Related to the need for differentiation is the need to segment markets. For most products the target market is a small part of the total market. Even for products which are supposedly universally consumed, the 80:20 phenomenon frequently occurs, so that 80 percent of the sales are derived from 20 percent of the market. Thus, 88 percent of beer is drunk by 17 percent of the market, 85 percent of cake mixes are purchased by 37 percent of the market, and 87 percent of dog food is purchased by 17 percent of the market. Even water may sell to target segments, as witnessed by Perrier's ability to command as much as two dollars for a four-pack.

The selection of target market segments (the desired customer base)—whether at the corporate, SBU, product category, or brand level—is a key strategic decision. What parts of the market are we in business to

Attribute	Level	Utility Score	Relative Importance of Factor, %
Geographic Coverage	1. Top Twenty Metropolitan Markets	0.16	26
	2. Top Fifty Metropolitan Markets	0.28	
	3. Total U.S. Market Coverage	0.56	
Carrier Responsibility	1. Own Trucks and Planes; Responsible	0.32	14
	2. Own Trucks and Scheduled Airlines; Responsible	0.25	
	3. Own Trucks and Scheduled Airlines; Shared Responsibility	0.15	
	4. Local Truckers and Own Planes; Responsible	0.16	
	5. Local Truckers and Own Planes; Shared Responsibility	0.11	
Call Response Time	1. On Call within Two Hours	0.32	4
	2. On Call before the End of the Business Day	0.36	
	3. Regular Daily Pickup at Specified Time	0.30	
Pick-Up Availability	1. During Regular Business Hours	0.33	8
	2. During Regular Business Hours and Extended Business Hours	0.24	
	3. During Regular Business Hours and on Weekends	0.21	
Price	1. $50	0.70	40
	2. $65	0.22	
	3. $80	0.07	
Company Names	1. Company A	0.19	8
	2. Company B	0.31	
	3. Company C	0.26	
	4. Company D	0.23	

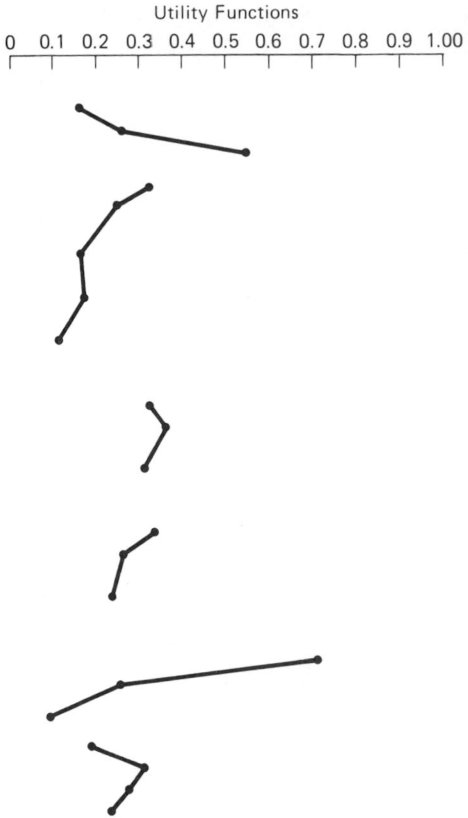

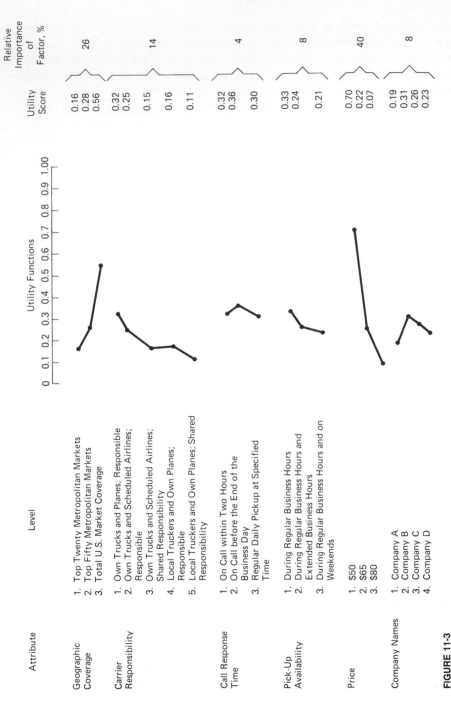

FIGURE 11-3
Conjoint analysis example: utility functions and relative importance of six factors for door-to-door air package service. (*Source: Flying Tiger Line Marketing Research. Used by permission.*)

serve and what parts of the market do we choose not to serve? An airline may decide to segment its market in such a way as to emphasize long-haul traffic and to abdicate short-haul traffic. A bank, such as Bankers Trust in New York, may make the deliberate decision not to serve the retail banking segment. A cosmetics company may define its market segment as the "department store" segment and choose not to compete at the "mass merchandise" segment level.

The rationale for segmenting a market is well-established conceptually. It is the operationalization of the marketing concept. Together with positioning, it offers guidelines for the design of the marketing program and, as such, increases the firm's chances of achieving its objectives.

There is no single best way of segmenting any market; a variety of bases for segmentation have been used by both consumer and industrial firms. Table 11-1 suggests some of the more common bases for segmentation.

Methods

Segmentation strategies should be based on empirical data. Typically, segmentation research focuses on two questions:

Table 11-1 Illustrative Bases for Segmentation

For general understanding of a market
Benefits sought (in industrial markets, the criterion used is purchase decision)
Product purchase and usage patterns
Needs
Brand loyalty and switching pattern
A hybrid of the variables above
For positioning studies
Product usage
Product preference
Benefits sought
A hybrid of the variables above
For new product concepts (and new product introduction)
Reaction to new concepts (intention to buy, preference over current brand, and so on)
Benefits sought
For pricing decisions
Price sensitivity
Deal proneness
Price sensitivity by purchase and usage patterns
For advertising decisions
Benefits sought
Media usage
Psychographic, life style
A hybrid (of the variables above and/or purchase and usage patterns)
For distribution decisions
Store loyalty and patronage
Benefits sought in store selection

1. What is the best way of segmenting the market? This question involves the identification of bases for segmentation—usage, demographics, benefits sought, psychographics—and may involve an a priori classification of consumers (for example, users versus nonusers) or a clustering-based segmentation (for example, benefit segments, such as those seeking taste versus those seeking cavity prevention in toothpaste). Conceptually, any market should be segmented in a way which identifies homogeneous segments with respect to their response to marketing strategy variables. No single basis is applicable to all situations and a number of bases should be investigated for every major marketing decision.

2. What are the characteristics of consumers in each segment? Once the market has been segmented and its size estimated, the characteristics of the various segments should be assessed. In this context, a variety of analytical techniques have been utilized, including discriminant analysis, regression, and other approaches. In fact, most of the multivariate statistical techniques have been utilized in some form or another in market segmentation studies. (For a discussion of the various segmentation research methods, see Wind, 1978.)

SEGMENTATION AND POSITIONING

Concept

Early marketing writings viewed market segmentation and product differentiation as *alternative* strategies (Smith, 1956). Yet the two are rather complementary. Four major strategies can be developed on the basis of the two extreme positions on each dimension—positioning as a specialty product versus positioning as a commodity, and market segmentation versus market aggregation. The four resulting prototypical strategies are presented in Table 11-2.

Cell 1 represents the ideal in meeting consumer needs (assuming market heterogeneity) by offering specialty products for specific market

Table 11-2 Four Key Market Segmentation and Product Positioning Strategies

	Market segmentation	Market aggregation
Specialty	CELL 1 Specialty products to specific segments	CELL 2 Specialty products to the mass market
Commodity	CELL 3 Commodity products to specific segments	CELL 4 Commodity products to the mass market

segments. This strategy should generally maximize sales to the served market (by meeting consumer needs more successfully) and usually allows the highest price. Even with the likelihood of higher costs—due to increased expenditures on product design, higher production costs for more limited runs, and higher vertical marketing costs—this strategy is likely to be profitable due to premium pricing. The opposite strategy (cell 4) suggests a commodity product sold to the mass market. This generally results in the lowest price being charged (since no consumer would pay premium prices for a commodity-type product). This strategy offers no long-term consumer franchise, because the product is likely to be bought on a price basis, and unless the firm has substantial experience curve advantages or large economies of scale, it is difficult to assure continuity of the lowest competitive cost and, therefore, profitability may be tenuous.

Cells 2 and 3 represent interesting alternatives. In cell 2 specialty products may be offered to the mass market if the ability to identify and reach unique segments is limited; yet there is a range of consumer needs. A company may offer multiple brands under a brand proliferation strategy without much segmentation because little segmentation is possible; that is, the users of one brand of the product may be much like the users of any other brand. If segmentation were feasible, it would be preferable to orient brands by segment (move to cell 1).

Cell 3 represents the marketing of a commodity product to unique segments, perhaps at different prices and offered with unique brand names. It is not uncommon for services, such as hotels and airlines, to differentially price a nearly identical product by market segment in line with price-sensitivity levels. Of course, it may be difficult to sustain price discrimination if the product is truly nondifferentiated. More commonly, the firm will seek to create differentiation (if only symbolic) and to move to cell 1. U.S. government regulations, for example, preclude actual product differences among vodkas made in the United States, yet Heublein has successfully created multiple brands and prices for this product—Smirnoff, Popov, and Relska—by creating symbolic differentiation.

Methods

Necessary input to the segmentation-positioning decision is information about the positioning of the given brand and its competitors as perceived by various market segments. The results of positioning studies are meaningful only if analyzed by segment, and most positioning studies do so.

Among the more recent developments in the determination of the most desired positioning-segmentation strategy are conjoint analysis-based simulations which allow management (1) to select a positioning and get as output the identity of the market segment most likely to respond favorably to this positioning or (2) alternatively to select a target segment and get as output the characteristics of the most desirable product positioning (and associated product features and price) for this segment.

The output of positioning-segmentation studies can also be incorporated in a number of formal models for marketing-strategy planning. The analytic hierarchy process (AHP) offers management formal ways of evaluating alternative strategies based on their judgment of the likely market-response functions under a variety of strategies and conditions (Wind and Saaty, 1980).

MARKETING PROGRAM DESIGN AND RESOURCE ALLOCATION

Concept

The core of the marketing literature involves the design of internally consistent marketing programs (product, price, promotion, channels) to achieve desired objectives, such as sales, market share, and profitability. Strategic success or failure depends on each element in this mix as well as their interdependencies. Failure may be due to a poor product or service (REA), too high a price (Corfam), the wrong advertising or sales program (one of Schlitz's problems), or inappropriate selection of distribution channels (Metrecal sales took off when it was deemphasized in drug stores and placed in supermarkets). Failure may also be due to an inconsistent mix, for example, if a poor movie were to violate the rules of mass showings and mass advertising on a concentrated one- or two-week basis and try to rely on reviews and word-of-mouth with limited advertising and limited showings.

The marketing program should be consistent with the selected segmentation-positioning decision. For example, if the overall strategy for a camera company is to serve an upscale market with a highly specialized product, a marketing program emphasizing high price, specialty channels (for example, camera stores), and limited advertising in upscale vertical (camera buff) magazines should be designed. By contrast, if the overall strategy is to reach the mass market with a relatively standardized product, the marketing program should be designed to emphasize lower price, mass distribution channels, and mass advertising in horizontal media that reach numerous market segments.

The design of a marketing program should explicitly take into account the interdependencies among the various options and include a resource allocation procedure to guide the firm's commitment of resources among products, market segments, and the associated marketing strategies designed to accomplish the firm's objectives. This allocation not only should be guided by the firm's objectives but also should be based on market response data (for example, the likely sales response to a change in the advertising budget or message).

Conceptually, allocation rules should be provided for apportionment of resources among the components of the firm's portfolio of businesses, products, and market segments (and, if the firm is involved in international operations, country and mode of entry should also be considered). In addition, specific allocation rules should be established for marketing decisions, including (1) the allocation of resources *within* each component of the marketing mix, such as the split in the advertising budget among media, creative, and research; and (2) the allocation of resources among the various marketing mix components—how much to allocate to promotion, advertising, distribution, and product design.

Methods

Three sets of methods can help management in the design of a marketing program—approaches to strategy generation, consumer studies to evaluate the generated strategies, and methods for management evaluation of the alternative strategies. (See Wind, 1982.)

Approaches to Strategy Generation Not unlike new product ideas, which can be generated by the use of a number of approaches (ranging from focus group interviews with consumers, to management brainstorming, structured consumer surveys, and a variety of morphological approaches), strategic options can benefit from the use of a number of idea-generation approaches. Approaches of special value include competitive and environmental analysis, the selection of analog models (for example, military strategies), and the use of analytical approaches which encourage the challenging of current strategies and their assumptions.

Consumer-Based Strategy Evaluation Important input to the final selection of any strategy is the likely consumer reaction to it. Concept-testing studies can be used to assess consumers' likely reactions to proposed strategies. Such studies can incorporate the proposed positioning, product features, price, distribution outlets (where the product will be available), and even alternative advertising copy. These studies can include specialized studies for the design and evaluation of each component of the marketing program (for example, advertising copy testing) or more comprehensive studies encompassing most or all of the proposed marketing strategy (for example, simulated test-market studies). Some of these studies can also be used as a way to help generate strategic options. Large-scale conjoint analysis studies, for example, allow for not only the evaluation of a selected strategy but also the evaluation of a large number of options.

The final evaluation of a marketing program has been, typically, via a test market. Yet, in recent years, a number of major alternatives to test markets have been developed. Most notable are simulated test market procedures which allow for the estimation of likely trial and repeat-purchase probabilities for a number of alternative strategies.

Most advanced among the various approaches to strategy evaluation are integrated analytical approaches such as the POSSE system and adaptive experimentation. The *POSSE system* (Green, Carroll, and Goldberg, 1981) combines consumer utilities for various offerings with an optimization procedure which allows management to select the best product-marketing offering for any selected market segment or select the market segment most appropriate for a given product-marketing offering. *Adaptive experimentation* offers management a tool for continuously evaluating a number of alternative strategies. It allows the development of empirical response functions and facilitates the selection of optimal strategies.

Management Evaluation of a Marketing Program The final evaluation of a marketing program cannot be based on consumer input only and should incorporate a complete economic evaluation of the likely return and risks of the various strategies. A number of evaluation models, typically along the lines of risk analysis simulations, can be employed. The decision calculus (Little, 1970 and 1979) philosophy of model building has guided the development and implementation of a series of models on various marketing strategy decisions, such as advertising and comprehensive marketing planning for a brand.

An important aspect of the overall program evaluation is the explicit allocation of resources among the program (marketing mix) component and various market segments over time. The complexity of the resource allocation decisions suggests that management should supplement the typical rules of thumb for allocation (for example, spend x percent of sales on advertising) with more explicit resource allocation models.

Resource Allocation Procedures Mathematical programming can and has been a valuable resource allocation tool. Other methods which explicitly incorporate management's subjective judgments such as the AHP can also be utilized to determine the best resource allocation among the various strategic options.

The AHP is a planning approach of particular value for a marketing-oriented planning process. It allows management to develop marketing-oriented mission statements and objectives (criteria for evaluation of courses of action), and to generate strategic options. This procedure offers a quantitative assessment of the relative importance of each criterion and expected contribution (across all criteria) of each course of action (such as different products in a portfolio or various marketing mixes).

An interesting and relatively simple procedure for determining the optimal allocation of resources is the use of a log regression in which the independent variables are the marketing strategy variables (among which the manager wants to allocate resources) and the dependent variable is some desired performance measure (sales or profitability). If one controls for multicolinearity among the independent variables, the regression coefficients will offer an approximation for an optimal resource allocation among them (Carroll, Green, and DeSarbo, 1979).

LIFE CYCLE MANAGEMENT

Concept

The introduction of new technologies and products to achieve corporate sales growth is a common strategic objective, as perusal of any annual report will verify. Marketing theory would suggest the development of differential strategies for the management of products at different stages of their life cycle—from introduction to growth to maturity to decline.

A "typical" product life cycle (PLC)[2] pattern is shown in the right panel of Figure 11-4. A key issue is the extent to which it can be modified by management actions. Management may generally prefer a more rapid acceleration of sales and may wish to avoid the decline phase—unless higher sales can be generated by a new generation of technology over which the company has control (migration strategy).

The logic of an expected logistic curve, such as that shown, is that sales growth is achieved gradually, especially when there are high market information needs. It may also take time to build cumulative effectiveness of the marketing program, particularly in advertising and distribution. The rapid acceleration in the growth phase may be partly accounted for by social effects—customers influencing one another—and partly by a carryover effect of advertising, personal selling, and distribution. Maturity inevitably occurs as the market becomes saturated or as substitutes become available. Finally, decline begins as the product becomes obsolete technologically, stylistically, or as consumer tastes change.

Management's ability to change this curve in order to achieve more

---

[2]It is important to note, however, that a number of empirical studies have found numerous other PLC patterns. For a review of them and some of the limitations of PLC prescription, its measurement problems, and values in forecasting, see Wind, 1982.

rapid growth and control over decline is a function of a number of factors:

- *The Market.* The degree to which the product meets consumer needs and the consumers' response to the associated marketing strategy of the firm and its competitors
- *The Firm.* The efficiency of the firm's operation—experience curve in production, marketing, distribution, and management—as well as the effectiveness of the firm's marketing strategy (with respect to positioning, price, promotion, advertising, and distribution)
- *The Competition.* The nature and effectiveness of the competition's activities and retaliatory actions in response to the firm's operation

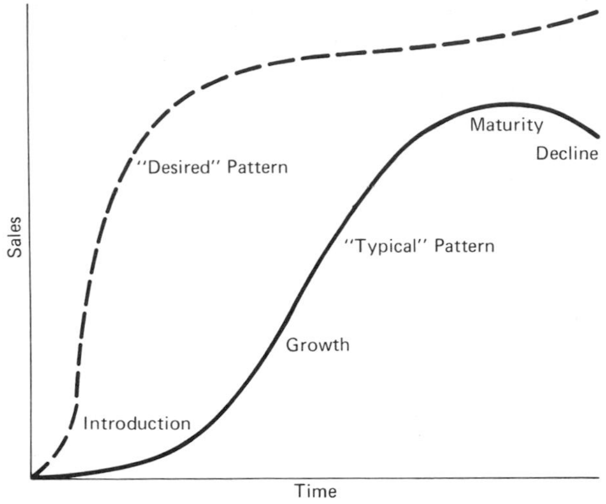

FIGURE 11-4
Product life cycle patterns.

- *The Marketing Environment.* In particular, the distribution system, its effectiveness, and its characteristics (traditional retail outlets vs. direct marketing and, more recently, electronic marketing via two-way cable TV and home computers)
- *The Environment.* The technological and legal factors which affect the market response to the product and its associated strategy (introduction of new technology which makes current products obsolete; deregulation which introduces new competitors into a market, and so on)

A product's stage in its life cycle has important strategy implications. Home computers and video discs face different strategic options at the *introduction* stage than do cable and video tape at the *growth* phase, color television at the *maturity* phase, or black-and-white television at the *de-*

cline stage. A company such as K Mart, which appears to have reached market saturation, would be well advised to harvest this retailing concept and invest in new growth retailing concepts. In the 1960s K Mart did just this by replacing S. S. Kresge stores. McDonald's may well be reaching saturation and may have difficulty finding growth in new outlets or achieving more sales per outlet. Again, it may be time to explore higher growth alternatives in line with the company's unique capabilities (or to exploit international market potential).

Methods

Forecasting of a product's life cycle has been one of the major focuses of marketing research during the last two decades. Numerous models have been proposed and implemented for the forecasting of the PLC of durables as well as for frequently purchased products. The reported experience with the various forecasting approaches has been very encouraging, and most of the PLC modeling effort has resulted in reasonable predictive accuracy. (For a discussion of product life cycle forecasting methods, see Urban and Hauser, 1980, Chapters 11 and 14.)

Forecasting of sales (as well as other dependent variables such as share or profitability) is a key component of most marketing research efforts. It is a part of the simulated test market models as well as most test market efforts.

In addition, recent efforts to forecast the PLC have incorporated a number of new dimensions—for example, the effects of the firm's marketing strategies, the effects of competitive strategies, and the effects of other forces which can influence the expected level of saturation and speed of response. (For a review of many of the major PLC forecasting models see Wind, Mahajan, and Cardozo, 1981.)

CONCLUSIONS

The ultimate test of the marketing strategy concepts and methods discussed is their value in building successful company strategies. We shall close this chapter with some examples of strategic success utilizing the concepts introduced.

If the basic premise of all corporate strategy is the satisfaction of consumer needs, then Federal Express is a model for strategic success. The start of Federal Express was predicated on fulfilling a gap in the marketplace for reliable overnight delivery of small packages. Competition simply was not meeting this particular need.

The positioning of products in the competitive marketplace is another key element of strategic success. Products such as Revlon's Charlie, Miller's Lite beer, Frito Lay's Tostitos, and Beacham's Aqua Fresh toothpaste are positioning masterpieces. None involves new technology, but all involve designing products of interest to consumers and positioning them with unique advantages in the competitive marketplace.

The ability to segment markets and to appeal to particular segments in line with unique needs is a further key to strategic success. Boeing's ability to segment the overall air travel market and to position aircraft accordingly earns it high marks. Coca Cola's ability to segment the wine market and to offer different segments multiple brands from Taylor to Sterling is another segmentation success.

Bringing technology to market and managing the product life cycle is critical in any technology-based industry. IBM's successes in commercializing technology earn praise, as does Intel's ability to design new technology.

Strategic success is a function of many factors, but these marketing-based concepts are prerequisites to effective and viable strategic plans. Ultimately, a firm must be responsive to consumers if financial, production, and organizational strategies are to be relevant.

BIBLIOGRAPHY

Carroll, J. D., P. E. Green, and W. S. DeSarbo: "Optimizing the Allocation of a Fixed Resource: A Simple Model and Its Experimental Test," *Journal of Marketing,* vol. 43, January 1979.

Green, P. E., J. D. Carroll, and S. Goldberg, "A General Approach to Product Design Optimization via Conjoint Analysis," *Journal of Marketing,* vol. 45, Summer 1981.

Hartley, R. F.: *Marketing Mistakes,* 2d ed., Grid Publishers, Inc., Columbus, Ohio, 1981.

Henderson, B. D.: "Lessons from Chrysler (1979)," Client Newsletter, The Boston Consulting Group, Boston, 1979.

Little, J.: "Models and Managers: The Concept of a Decision Calculus," *Management Science,* vol. 16, no. 8, April 1970.

———: "Decision Support Systems for Marketing Managers," *Journal of Marketing,* vol. 43, Summer 1979.

Pessemier, E. A.: *Product Management: Strategy and Organization,* John Wiley & Sons, Inc., Hamilton, New York, 1977.

Smith, W. R.: "Product Differentiation and Market Segmentation as Alternative Marketing Strategies," *Journal of Marketing,* vol. 21, July 1956.

Steiner, G. A.: *Strategic Planning,* The Free Press, New York, 1979.

Urban, G. L., and J. R. Hauser: *Design and Marketing of New Products,* Prentice-Hall, Inc., Englewood Cliffs, NJ, 1980.

Webster, F. E.: "Top Management Views of the Marketing Function," *Journal of Marketing,* vol. 45, Summer 1981.

Wind, Y.: "Issues and Advances in Segmentation Research," *Journal of Marketing Research,* vol. 15, August 1978.

———: *Product Policy: Concepts, Methods and Strategy,* Addison-Wesley, Reading, MA, 1982.

——— and V. Mahajan: "Diagnosing Product and Business Portfolios," *Harvard Business Review,* vol. 59, January–February 1981.

———, V. Mahajan, and R. Cardozo: *New Product Forecasting: Models and Applications,* Lexington Books, Lexington, MA, 1981.

——— and T. Saaty: "Marketing Applications of the Analytical Hierarchy Process," *Management Science,* vol. 26, July 1980.

Chapter 12

PRICING POLICY AND STRATEGY

ROBERT E. LIENHARD
Vice President, The Boston Consulting Group, Inc.

Pricing policy is an inseparable part of overall strategy. Many possible pricing tactics may be employed, but sound strategy development requires the articulation of a pricing policy which is carefully integrated with the other elements in strategy formulation. The appropriate pricing policy, like the overall strategy it supports, will vary with:

- Industry structure
- Stage in the life cycle
- Characteristics of targeted market segments
- Company strategy objectives

In some situations a company will have effectively little control over its pricing policies. This usually results from a weak competitive position in an industry or a situation of stalemated industry structure. In others, the range of pricing options may be quite wide. In some situations pricing policy may be the decisive strategy variable. In others, it will pay to relegate pricing to a subsidiary role. Pricing may be the key to capturing important volumes in critical market segments. For others, nonprice considerations will be far more important. In some situations the company may have established aggressive goals where the achievement of future position is paramount. On the other hand, there are situations in which strategies should be oriented to producing shorter-term results where the company is willing to forgo possible longer-term benefits.

Pricing policy must be orchestrated with all these factors carefully weighed and integrated into a whole. All too often these requirements suggest conflicing pricing policies which must be then traded off to provide a proper balance. Transparency in pricing policy is as undesirable as it is for overall strategy. The art in pricing policy is *not* to transmit clear signals to competitors which might provide them with the time to adopt appropriate adjustments to their own strategy. Even better is to be so misperceived that the attainment of overall strategy objectives is made easier. There is no better compliment than to be "that crazy company XYZ. They've cut price again—they obviously don't know their costs."

Pricing is often discussed in nonstrategic terms. For example, pricing policy is designed to produce a satisfactory margin over costs. Or prices are increased to offset the effects of inflation on the company. The dream of many managers is to price to capture the value in use of the product from each of the customer groups in the market. Each of these is an incomplete or erroneous basis on which to set price—precisely because it is not related to, or perhaps is even in conflict with, overall strategy objcctives.

The goal of overall strategy development is to develop competitive advantage—that is, cost or revenue generation superiority against specific competitors. High margins are the result of the development of imaginative and aggressive strategies which produce competitive advantage. Pricing policy does not produce superior margins. On the contrary, "high" prices—and therefore high margins—are the *result* of superior overall strategy.

INDUSTRY STRUCTURE

Industry structure can vary widely in its key characteristics. A corresponding shift in the role of pricing policy in different industry structures can be observed. Some industries are highly concentrated, with no more than three or four participants holding a very large combined share of the market. One of these is usually dominant, with a significant market share advantage over the remaining competitors. The second competitor usually also enjoys a market share advantage against the remainder of the industry participants. The wide differences in market shares usually signify correspondingly wide differentials in cost position with the leader often as much as 10 to 15 percent below the cost level of the second. This position almost surely has resulted from significant experience and scale effects in the industry.

If the leading competitor has 40 or 50 percent of the total market, is one and a half to two times as large as the next largest competitor, and enjoys a 10 to 15 percent advantage in total costs, it is clearly the leading competitor who holds most of the cards. If the leader is alert and well managed, the smaller and higher-cost competitors must defer to the pricing initiative of the industry leader. If the industry is moderate-to-low growth and not undergoing major structural change due to factor cost, technological or other influences, the determinants of industry pricing are fairly straightforward.

At all price levels, the industry leader earns the most money and has the highest margin on sales. Any given change in the price level, however, will increase or decrease the industry leader's profits by a far smaller percentage than it will those of the marginal competitor, to whom a 5 percent price change may turn a small profit into a loss—or vice versa. This creates a situation of considerable power for the leader, and corresponding vulnerability for the follower. If, as is often the case, the profit and cash flow of the leader are more than adequate to fund the reinvestment needed for continued growth in line with industry demand, what is at risk for the leader is the cash surplus from this business for dividends or other corporate purposes if the business is part of a larger portfolio.

For the marginal competitor, the opposite is usually true. The thin and highly fluctuating margins are a continued point of stress. Prices almost always appear to be too low. Moreover, the profits and cash flow are barely sufficient to permit necessary reinvestment in the business to keep pace with technological change and market growth. Pricing in this oligopolistic structure is the control to keep the marginal competitor from accumulating too many resources with which to challenge the volume and cost superiority of the leader.

In this case, the leader, although having enormous control over industry pricing, should carefully balance two major objectives. First, price levels should be sought that are high enough to allow the high-cost competitor to survive and grow with the industry. This produces very high returns for the leader. Also, however, the leader should hold prices low enough to dissuade entry by newcomers or too rapid a rate of cash accumulation by the marginal competitor. In this case a high degree of pricing control by the leader has been the *result,* rather than the cause, of the dominant position in the industry structure. The weak competitor may lead prices up in periods of cyclical improvement, but no price adjustment is ever complete until the industry leader has acquiesced.

In other industries lacking the dominant competitor with high market share and a superior cost position, pricing behavior is quite different. In industries such as this, in which cost differentials among competitors are low, pricing tends to be a barometer of the state of short-term industry health and acts to encourage the necessary entrance into or exit from the industry due to technological improvement and/or fluctuations in demand. Here the range of choices within which pricing policy can be exercised is far narrower. These tend to be industries in which scale in manufacturing is reached at a low proportion of overall product demand, in which technology is largely external to the industry, and in which products are largely undifferentiated by performance or quality differences.

The manufacture of synthetic ammonia provides a good illustration. Even the largest and most modern ammonia plant accounts for only a small fraction of industry demand. Most users understand the product and buy on price, credit, and delivery terms. Ammonia plants are designed and built by engineering contractors such as Kellogg who hold the key process technology.

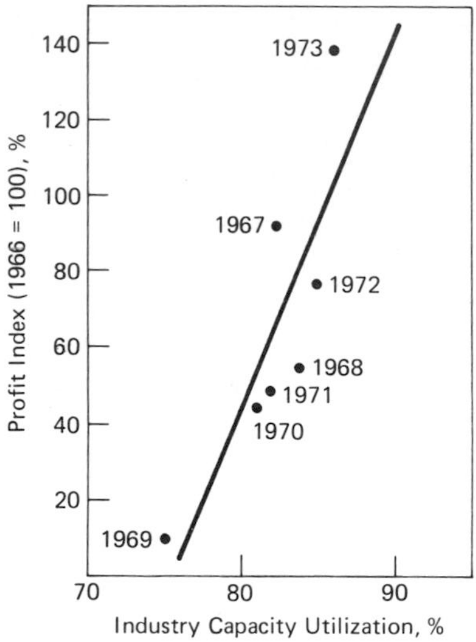

FIGURE 12-1
Ammonia manufacturer profitability versus industry capacity utilization.

Figure 12-1 shows the index of profitability for an ammonia producer in the United States between 1967 and 1973. The violent profit swings resulted from the rapid changes in industry supply-and-demand balance. In periods when overall operating rates were falling (1967–1969), the combination of rising unit costs and sharply falling prices produced the disastrous profit results. Conversely, in periods of rising operating rates (1969–1973), prices rose rapidly, with a corresponding effect on profitability. This producer may have *thought* that there was a pricing strategy during this six-year period, but the evidence suggests that price levels were really determined by aggregate industry capacity expansion and the effects of farm prices, weather, and other factors on the demand for chemical fertilizers. At the trough of the industry cycle virtually all producers were losing money, while at the peak all were profitable. In this environment it is hard to imagine the development of a pricing policy which would have much impact on competitive behavior. Here the real strategy question is whether the company wishes to commit resources to a stalemated industry in which pricing flexibility is so limited.

In situations only slightly different, however, pricing can have a considerable impact on the evolution of competitive position. In general, people invest when they have funds available and when they feel optimistic about the results to be expected from future investment. Cash flow, of course, peaks during periods of high profit. While the relationship is not so direct, it can be argued that optimism and willingness to invest also peak when prices and profits are high. The data on the pattern of capital expenditures in the U.S. steel industry between 1949 and 1975, portrayed in Figure 12-2, illustrates the point.

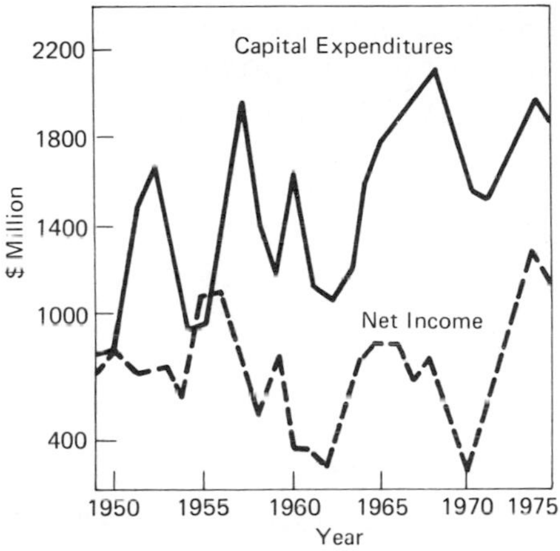

FIGURE 12-2
Reinvestment versus cash generation.

Virtually every peak in capital spending coincided with a peak in internal cash generation, that is, when prices and operating rates were high. Most "modern" managements use a discounted cash flow (DCF) method of investment evaluation. Anyone who has ever done such an analysis knows that the range of expected returns is sensitive to many assumptions—but the assumptions about future price levels are usually the most critical. Not surprisingly, DCF calculations in which future sales are heavily influenced by current price realizations tend to make capacity additions appear more attractive at cycle peaks than troughs.

When an industry follows such a pattern of behavior, countercyclical investment and pricing strategies can be considered. These are high risk and potentially dangerous because they rely on the misperceptions of competitors. Here investment is made *before* industry operating rates and prices peak. The significant hangover of excess capacity holds a lid on prices. A competitor who considers further investment in a large-scale facility will have to consider the effects of the investment to further depress industry capacity utilization and further weaken prices.

Such preemptive pricing and investment strategies have been observed to be particularly effective in markets with significant regional distribution cost barriers or in small but high-growth markets in developing countries. In each case the key is the relationship between the large capacity of a scale unit and the small market size which makes it all but impossible for a second competitor to rationally follow this strategy after a first has successfully implemented it.

Knowing industry structure and predicting how it will evolve are critical to the development of pricing strategy. Some structures permit the leader to exercise considerable price initiatives to preserve and enhance leadership position. Others do not. One should be especially wary of investment in the latter, unless preemption can be successfully implemented.

LIFE CYCLE

Growth changes the rules. In situations of very high growth, often found when products are early in their life cycle, pricing can be critical to strategy development. It is precisely under these conditions that *experience curve pricing* is most relevant and most powerful. The message from the experience curve is simple and clear: real costs, net of inflation, and decline in a predictable pattern imply a constant percentage with each doubling of cumulative production (or experience). Higher industry growth rates imply faster progress down the experience curve, hence more cost reduction per unit of time. A company operating in such a rapid-growth environment usually faces a clear choice—if it understands the issues. A more rapid rate of growth in output than the industry standard will permit a more rapid rate of cost improvement. Since profit margins will eventually be determined by cost differences between the company and the rest of the industry, a high rate of growth to ensure eventual cost superiority can be a very attractive "investment." In this case, pricing policy must be directed toward the achievement of the growth, volume, and cost differences implied by this model. This potential is, of course, available to all competitors; therefore, quite obviously, it is inappropriate to price and invest in such a fashion, unless one believes that others will not follow.

This is in direct contradiction to the pricing policies set by many companies in high-growth product areas. The high growth rate requires a rapid rate of fixed and current asset growth to hold position and a lot of "expense" investment in building sales capability, technical support, training, and the like. The question is who is to pay for these investments. If the business is to be held cash neutral during the high-growth phase—as the single business company is almost forced to do—then the current customers are the major source of financing. This is why margins tend to be high during the growth phase of the industry. In a sense, this is logical since the early customers are generally the ones to whom the product has a high value.

On the other hand, there is considerable competitive vulnerability to this pricing strategy. A high price level coupled with high market growth is a tempting invitation to further entry and a loss of market share. The one business company may have little choice but to run this risk—or sell out to a financially stronger partner—but there is little excuse for such a short-term orientation inside a diversified multibusiness company. Overall strategy for the leader in a high-growth business should be to hold position—the major financial rewards will be enjoyed later in the life cycle. Pricing policy should be consistent with this goal—even if the business, that is, the current customers—cannot or will not finance all the growth.

In general, experience curve pricing also provides the means to stimulate overall market development to obtain a rapid rate of market growth. It is important to shorten the period to recover the "investment" and also to increase the eventual size of the market in which the leading market share position can be created. In this case the need both to establish cost superiority and to expand the market pulls in the direction of lower prices—even if current margins are reduced. Pricing policy in this case must have a heavy future orientation and should become almost indistinguishable from the other elements in the overall investment.

High growth often occurs in situations in which significant product substitution is taking place. Figure 12-3 traces the pattern of substitution between the new generation of electronic desk calculators which was introduced in the late 1960s and the older generation of electromechanical calculators they replaced.

This substitution was driven by the rapidly decreasing prices of electronic calculators and moved with astonishing speed—from virtually no penetration in 1967 to almost complete substitution by 1973—a span of only six years! Little wonder that aggressive product pricing to stimulate market demand and establish competitive position is found in industries such as these.

Although there is a tendency to think of it as a modern phenomenon, examples of experience curve pricing can be found as early as the Model T Ford. See Figure 12-4.

Henry Ford experimented with several models until he settled on the design for the Model T in 1908. Confident that the Model T would open up a large market in a world in which the automobile was still a high-priced luxury, he made a commitment to a highly standardized design and geared up for volume production. The sharp price cuts on the Model T in 1908 opened up the era of mass automobile transportation. The considerable volume growth permitted the achievement of substantial cost and further price reductions. By the early 1920s the real price (net of inflation) had dropped by more than two-thirds and Ford was the undisputed industry leader with a 50 percent market share.

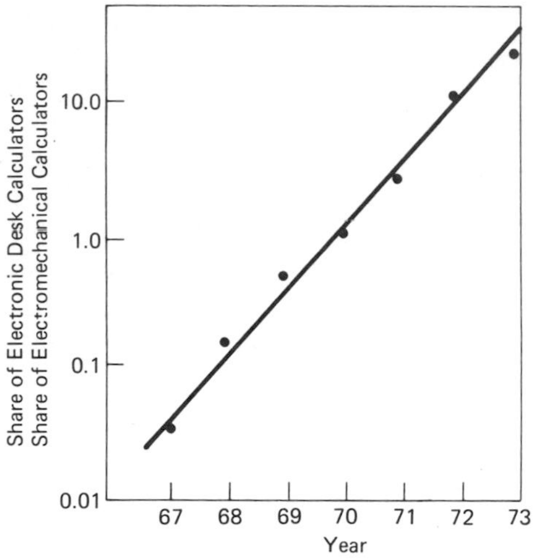

FIGURE 12-3
Substitution of electronic desk calculators for electromechanical calculators in the United States.

Not surprisingly, experience curve pricing has been quite common in industries in which the Japanese have achieved export competitiveness. In these cases the relatively sudden entry into foreign markets, often the U.S. market, at price levels well below current industry levels has provoked an emotional reaction. The charge is usually "dumping," that is, selling below full costs in the export market while "taxing" consumers in the protected home market who pay far more than full cost. Studies have generally found this to be an overly simplistic and not particularly enlightening description of Japanese pricing policy.

First, it must be remembered that all the industries in which Japan achieved export success were ones in which the Japanese domestic market grew very rapidly and became quite large. Thus the logic for aggressive market development, high volume, and cost-improvement pricing usually developed among several Japanese firms struggling early in the life cycle for *domestic* market share. In this sense the phenomenon is not really much different than that found in many high-growth areas (such as electronics) in the U.S. economy. The major difference is that Japan, on the average, has been a far higher growth economy.

Not surprisingly, the prospect of sustained high growth by entry into an even larger U.S. or world market logically leads to an extension of

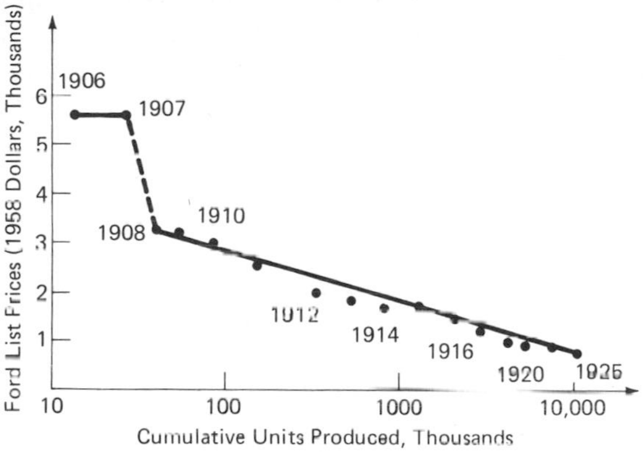

FIGURE 12-4
Ford Motor Company price experience curve (1906–1926).

the same philosophy. Won early, volume and market share gains permit further reduction in manufacturing cost—typically still in the Japanese export factory—but they also bring additional advantages in the export market, where volume growth helps reduce the unit costs of selling, inventory, logistics, service, and so on.

Thus the use of experience curve pricing in the export market is a logical extension of the competitive struggle between Japanese firms. Overall volume from all markets, that is, world market share, determines overall competitive cost differentials and hence profit potential among them. It is also important to remember that successful Japanese penetration has seldom been based entirely on price. The successful Japanese product inevitably provides a user advantage in quality (television sets) or in performance or economy in use (automobiles), or the inclusion of desirable features without price premium (machine tools). Price and performance characteristics must be viewed as a whole, and for the Japanese, too, pricing is only one element in an integrated strategy.

Curiously, most dumping investigations of Japanese competitors in the U.S. market have occurred much later in the life cycle, when overall volume growth has slowed and the relative sizes of the U.S. and Japanese markets have been largely determined. By this stage the Japanese competitor is typically selling at equal or higher prices in the U.S. market than in the Japanese. Margins on the export business are generally better than those obtained in the home market. Responding with trade restrictions such as were earlier invoked in steel and color television and, more recently, in automobiles forces an even more dramatic shift to high pricing in the U.S. market, since further market share gains are not achievable. Thus the American consumer pays to fund further investment in European or third world markets.

Pricing policy, like strategy overall, must be reviewed and adjusted at major transitions in the product life cycle. At these junctions, the relative importance of price and nonprice elements can change drastically. As was pointed out previously, Ford established a formidable volume and cost position as a result of his aggressive pricing of the Model T. What he failed to observe, however, was a shift on the part of many consumers to a far greater sensitivity to product variety and performance differentials. General Motors, which could not match Ford in terms of volume or unit cost, perceived the market shift and successively introduced the closed chassis, the electric start, and the automatic transmission. This was competition based on performance, not price, differentials. Thus, General Motors was able to capture enough market share that Ford actually lost volume and cost position and eventually had to shut down for a year to retool and revamp his product line.

At maturity, the world is different. Cost structures become embedded, and the pattern of competition has often been established. Often significant volume growth can be achieved only at the expense of competitors' volumes. Aggressive pricing to increase industry concentration by squeezing marginal competitors may so severely limit the returns of the low-cost competitor as to be unwise. The high-cost competitors at this stage usually have no choice but to price to provide cash contribution from the business—irrespective of reported profit or loss. This situation should signal that additional resource commitment—unless it revolutionizes the cost structure—is unnecessary and probably unwise. Strategically seen, the marginal competitor in such a situation should be trying to extract whatever cash flows are available from the business for redeployment elsewhere. Sale of the business is one obvious possibility. In many cases, however, a targeted policy of price increases—even in the face of possible volume declines—can produce better overall cash results.

Here, a conscious policy of "cream skimming" may produce surprising results. There may be some customer groups—defined in terms of geography, application, or other criteria—who will pay a bit more for supplier continuity. Since the value of a company's price, product, and service offering can vary according to different user groups, pricing policy is one way to sort customer groups along these dimensions. A conscious policy of price increases, coupled with a program to trim product line breadth, additional services, and other costs of complexity, can often result in a surprising improvement in overall profit and cash flow.

This pricing strategy need not be confined to exit strategies late in the life cycle. Knowing how customers value price and nonprice considerations is a critical element in the development of pricing policy.

MARKET SEGMENT CHARACTERISTICS

A fundamental starting point for any consideration of pricing policy must be the question of the integration of price with other competitive variables at the company's disposal. Price is always part of the marketing mix, but its importance relative to other variables can vary considerably—from business to business, and, as previously discussed, in the same business over time.

At this point I am reminded of a discussion in the early 1970s with the chief executive officer of a diversified manufacturer of equipment for the chemical, medical, and other industries. We at The Boston Consulting Group had only recently discovered the powerful relationships between market share and cost position and profitability and—its logical corollary—the value of aggressive pricing to improve market share. We were often called upon to explain, to a world which did not yet accept and understand these relationships, why they worked and how they could be used in the development of strategy.

The CEO at the equipment manufacturer would have none of it. Quite the contrary, he argued. He had found that his company had achieved superior results by forcing all the divisional operating heads to believe exactly the opposite. His instructions were to always price *above* the market and to never engage in price competition to gain market share. Since his instructions were clear and his authority unquestioned, the company's managers followed the edict. It should surprise no one that this had the effect of forcing the company out of many increasingly price-sensitive areas and into more specialty businesses in which competition was based more on design, delivery, and service support than price alone. What this CEO interestingly had done was to direct resources into businesses in which competitive advantage could be best obtained in nonprice variables. True, he was a bit dogmatic about it, and no doubt forced managers to pass up good business opportunities, but his instincts seemed to work for his businesses at that time.

Few situations can be more embarrassing or painful than the one in which the roles of price and nonprice variables become confused.

This is perhaps most clearly illustrated in the area of consumer goods, in which retail price points often become well established and price differences within product categories tend to signify perceived quality or status differentials. An offer of a Nikon camera for $100 may signify a great "buy," but to many could equally well connote a damaged or stolen item or a model being replaced in the product line by a new one with superior features. The following example may illustrate the point.

Product B (see Figure 12-5) was a weak brand with low share of shelf space and overall acceptance in comparison to A, which dominated sales in this product category at its price point. Brand strength had been established by significant advertising investment spread over many years. As a result, product A sold at a price premium; B decided to cut price to expand its share against A. The steady reduction in price of B relative to A did not lead to increased sales of B; rather, it led to the dramatic market share loss indicated. The product manager for B did not realize that the widening price difference was viewed not as superior value but, rather, as distress merchandise. In this case A's position may have been unassailable. If a competitive battle were to be joined, however, nonprice means such as increased advertising, trade promotion, or product quality would undoubtedly have represented superior weapons.

Another common pricing policy problem arises when two or more distinct customer groups purchase the same product but in different volumes and with differing service and other requirements in use. This poses a difficult pricing dilemma. The large-volume customers may understand the product attributes quite well and may hold stock and provide internal maintenance and other related services. Not surprisingly, these customer groups can be extremely price-sensitive—particularly if the purchased product becomes an important element in *their* cost structure. At the same time, smaller customers may purchase in smaller lot sizes, require delivery in more expensive form, and need and expect a variety of costly technical and other customer support. A price level high enough to cover the costs of serving the latter segment will leave the large customers vulnerable to attack by focused competitors. A price level low enough to hold the price-sensitive customers will not provide enough revenue to cover the costs of serving the smaller ones. Volumes sold to both customer groups, however, affect manufacturing costs and, therefore, the costs of serving both groups. The challenge of a pricing policy is to preserve volume in both segments.

Many companies are, unfortunately, unaware of this dilemma. Perhaps this has occurred because the emerging price sensitivity of the volume users is not recognized, or because the problem has been papered over by a system of cost accounting which understates or even

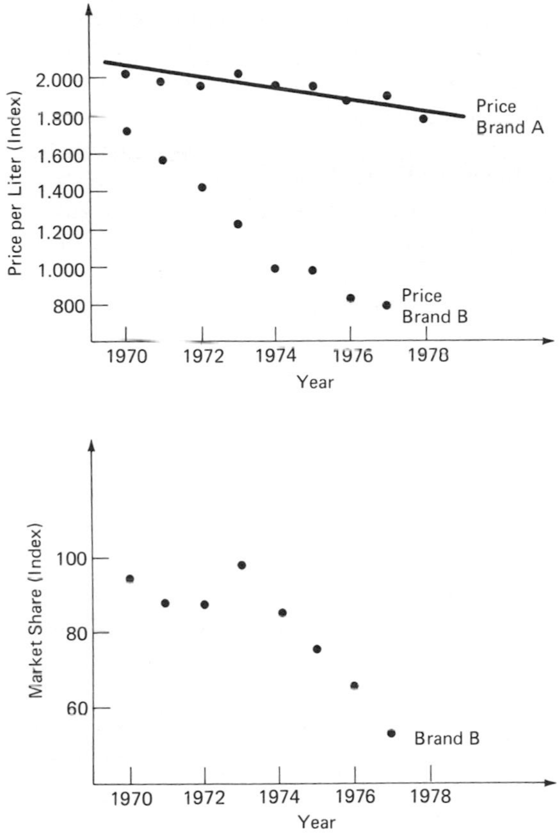

FIGURE 12-5
A consumer product.

totally obscures the cost-to-serve differences between the groups. Pricing policy in this situation then tends to compromises which may reflect average costs to serve. This is to some degree true in all companies since, in fact, no accounting system is able to distinguish accurately which cost elements are incurred in which proportion for all customer groups.

The average costing becomes competitively dangerous, however, when a focused competitor or new entrant chooses to target the "overcharged" high-volume core customer group. In the absence of cost allocation by customer segment, a pricing policy is difficult to formulate. Worse yet, if the loss of share among the high-volume customers occurs gradually across regions and over time, the volume losses will tend to raise the average costs of serving the remaining customers—first, through volume loss within the factory and second, because the costs to serve the second group do not disappear as the volume is lost among large customers. This can lead to the "doom loop" of segment retreat. Average costing leads to average pricing, which leads to loss of volume with high-volume customers, which raises average costs, which requires even higher average prices to maintain margins, and so on.

The solution here is obviously a much more selective pricing policy in closer coherence with the widely differing economics of serving each customer segment. No single price applied to both groups will resolve the dilemma. Equally, no system of differentiated pricing by perhaps providing volume discounts to the lower cost-to-serve core is possible without a highly discriminating understanding of segment costs. Here one must appreciate the strategic necessity to protect volume—with different pricing policies—in both segments.

CONCLUSION

Pricing must be addressed in a strategic context. Sustainable performance differentials among competitors result from competitive advantage which a leader has established against the rest of the industry. This will vary from business to business and over time in the same business. Pricing policy must be integrated with overall strategy considerations in the achievement and protection of the competitive advantage. If no significant competitive advantage can be established, pricing policy should be directed toward extracting resources, that is, cash flow, from business areas when assets are currently committed.

Pricing flexibility will be present to a greater extent in some industry structures than in others. Its importance will also vary over the life cycle. Finally, price and nonprice elements must be combined into a coherent whole as the complexity of the business segment structure grows.

Chapter 13
OPERATIONS STRATEGY

JOSEPH D. ROMANO
Vice President, A. T. Kearney, Inc.

The questions are the same—but the answers are different.

Operating management has always answered questions about inventory, productivity, quality, and cash flow, among others. Management has tackled these problems and issues by using traditional approaches and rules developed over years of experience. And it's worked.

But the future will look nothing like the past. Because of the technology, interdependence, and complexity that the future will bring, the old answers will no longer suffice. Yes, the questions will be the same. But management now needs new answers—new approaches and rules—for a new manufacturing environment.

CONCEPTS OF OPERATIONS STRATEGY

Operations encompasses activities which add utility to a product or good while it is being processed, converted, or moved. Although operations includes both the manufacturing and the physical distribution of a product, management has traditionally treated these activities independently, often without reference to the company's overall corporate strategy or its other major functions, such as finance, marketing, and human resources. Yet, because of escalating operating costs and intense competitive pressures, this segregated approach is dangerous to a company's health. It may, in fact, be fatal. Why? Because the operating environment is changing so dramatically that the consequence of a mistake leaves a much smaller margin of error.

Top management can no longer focus exclusively on corporate strategy or marketing strategy and allow operating policy to be determined "from the bottom up" by industrial engineers or technical specialists; nor can these operating managers "do things right" if they do not understand the higher-level corporate strategy defining "doing the right things." Harvard professor Wickham Skinner characterized this condition as follows:[1]

> Top management unknowingly delegates a surprisingly large portion of basic policy decisions to lower levels. . . . Generally, this abdication of responsibility comes about more through a lack of concern than by intention. And it is partly the reason that many policies and procedures developed at lower levels reflect assumptions about corporate strategy which are incorrect or misconstrued.

An operations strategy based only on measures such as profit center incentives, economies of scale, or overhead absorption is no longer appropriate. Rather, it must reflect a company's fundamental business objectives, considering competitive and marketplace characteristics. Operations strategy must be *a set of policies that guide operating actions so that they not only support the overall business strategy but also enable it to be achieved.*

The operations strategy should answer two basic questions:

- What role should operations play?
- How should this role be supported?

These questions encompass the following more detailed ones:

- *Scope of Activities* (What role should operations be playing?)
  - *Level of vertical integration.* What degree of make-versus-buy is most appropriate?
  - *Process technology selection.* What process is most appropriate for "make" parts?
- *Resource Deployment* (How should this role be supported?)
  - *Physical assets.* How should physical resources be allocated?
  - *Infrastructure.* How should the organization and information resources be managed and controlled?

Operating actions must, of course, be implemented before they can achieve results. And to be implemented, they require a focus, a framework found in a plan or strategy. The balance of this chapter will describe the development of such a strategy.

[1]In *Manufacturing in the Corporate Strategy,* Wiley, New York, 1978.

OPERATIONS STRATEGY ELEMENTS

Interrelated elements (Figure 13-1), which evolve from the business strategy, are fundamental to an improved operations strategy. Some industries, for example, capital goods made to order, center on manufacturing activities, while others, such as consumer goods made to stock, focus on product distribution activities. While the emphasis will vary, operating strategy must encompass three major analyses for all industries:

1. Operating policies begin with an understanding of the business strategy, the future objectives, and the market conditions for specific products and markets.
2. This strategy is then dissected and, subsequently, reconfigured to determine those actions critical to the successful achievement of goals.
3. Finally, manufacturing and distribution activities are planned to form a coherent, comprehensive, and appropriate operations response.

Business Strategy Definition

This first element of an operations strategy is typically a comfortable area for corporate planners but not for operation managers. Since a

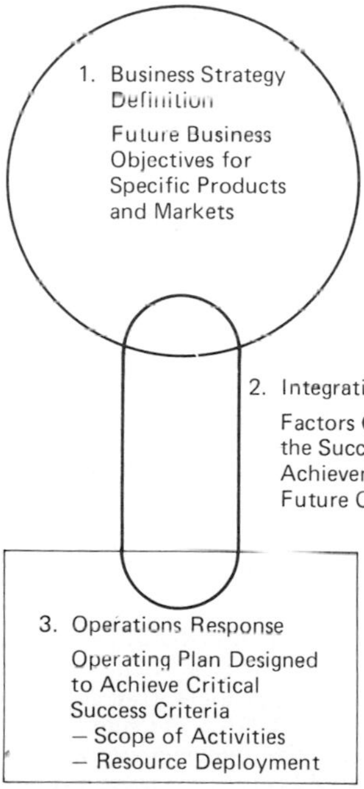

FIGURE 13-1
Operations strategy overview.

business strategy is the core of a company's self-definition, however, it must be fully comprehended by all organizational levels.

Segmenting products and markets is the starting point for understanding the differences both within and between current products. Coupled with business objectives, this segmentation then indicates market share changes, product mix changes, relative product profitability, and other factors relevant to the competitive environment. This first step offers a different perspective, a perspective not related to physical characteristics but to marketplace differences. It should define the key product and market characteristics which are fundamentally different among product segments. Different market conditions for specific products require different operating responses.

Fundamental characteristics may include, but are not necessarily limited to:

- *Product variety.* Breadth of product line
- *Unit volume.* Annual production volume
- *Product standardization.* Degree of commonality
- *Market growth.* Rate of change in demand
- *Pace of product design change.* Timing of future modifications
- *Design complexity.* Level of product sophistication
- *Demand variability.* Amount of customer order volatility
- *Response time.* Order-to-delivery time requirements
- *Cost sensitivity.* Manufacturing versus physical distribution cost emphasis

If a traditional product group does not have common characteristics such as those in this summary, it should be split into an expanded number of product segments, each of which is consistent in its key product and market characteristics and, therefore, its market condition.[2]

Integration or Linkage

How does management translate market conditions into operating policy? Given specific market conditions, management must determine the relative importance of alternative success criteria. These criteria, in turn, elicit specific operating responses. This second element, the integration

[2]One final thought before we leave this first element of operations strategy development: What if the business or marketing strategy is unclear or ill-defined? In a situation such as this, there is an implied or de facto business strategy. The operating response to this situation is, by definition, not integrated. An understanding of the relationships presented in this chapter, however, can provide management with an operations insight to address business strategy issues. Feedback in a reiterative process from the operations response to the business strategy will challenge the business assumptions. This, in turn, will force more attention on the business strategy issues.

of the business strategy and the operating response, reorients the key product and market differences to determine these criteria critical for success. The key question for this transition from a business strategy to an appropriate response is: From an operations sense, what are the different businesses in which the company participates?

The grouping of product segments into discrete categories for operations analysis depends on those characteristics which differ among segments. The importance of a factor such as unit volume (low, medium, high, or very high) will typically vary from one product to another. Other factors which often describe product and market variables include user orientation and growth projections. These often take the following form:

User Orientation	*Growth Projections*
Custom	Stable
Special	Growing
Standard	Volatile or unstable
	Uncertain
	Declining

While the "product life cycle" concept has its critics and is not appropriate in certain instances, it is helpful to visualize the behavior pattern of some similar product segments. Time, volume, and volatility relationships, shown in Figure 13-2, are frequently encountered.

These judgments should be integrated to form new groupings of products facing similar market conditions. Examples of potential groups include:

- Low-volume products with customized applications for many customers
- Medium-volume products with a technological advantage
- High-volume, mature commodity products

These groups, typically three to five or six, represent a company's fundamental businesses. Once these groupings have been made, management then must ask: Which criteria are critical to achieve competitive success for each group?

The operating criteria essential for success, depending on various market conditions, should be chosen from the following objectives. These encompass fundamental product and service traits which, in essence, drive the customer to purchase.

- *Cost.* Lowest landed product cost
- *Performance.* Product superiority
- *Adaptability.* Reaction to changing product requirements

- *Reliability.* Product dependability
- *Responsiveness.* Achievement of changing requirements for customer service time
- *Flexibility.* Reaction to changing levels of customer demand

Since an organization can accomplish only one or, at the most, two objectives extremely well, the identification of the critical success criteria is, of itself, a critical issue. In the same sense that "a person can serve only one master" and "a prize fighter can possess either speed or power, not both," an operating response for each product segment cannot focus primarily on all of these criteria. (Those criteria which are not selected are still important; they're just not as important as the one or two selected.) The choice is not, in fact, one that should be made independently, for the particular market condition for the product should be the prime determinant. The critical success criteria are determined by the

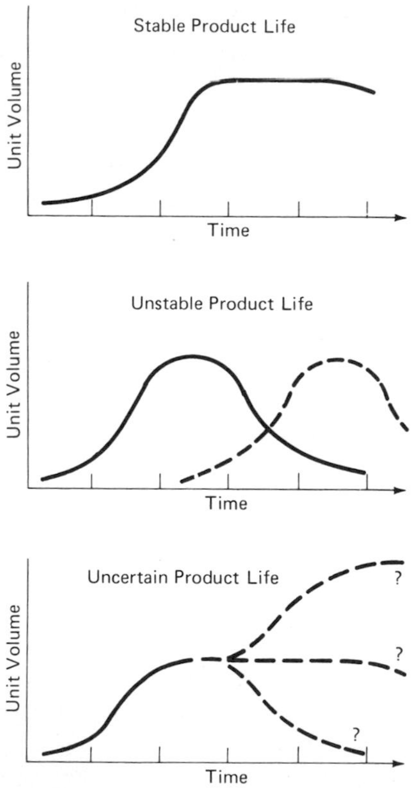

FIGURE 13-2
Product life cycle examples.

needs of the market and are indicative of the level of predictability of future market conditions.

Operations Response

The third and final element of operations strategy is the development of a plan responding to the critical success criteria. As previously noted, the operations plan encompasses the scope of activities (What role should operations be playing?) and resource deployment (How should this role be supported?).

The answers to these questions change radically according to which traits are critical for a product's success. In addition, the analysis for a particular product changes as the product is developed, grows, matures, and eventually declines. Without recognition of the importance of time, management can make three mistakes. Incompatibility, multiplicity, and inconsistency result from a mismatch between business objectives and operations response.

1. *Incompatibility* occurs when the criteria required for competitive success and the criteria targeted by operations do not match. Maintaining a flexible job shop which is geared to anticipate change, for example, is no longer appropriate after a product has matured and is now competing on a lowest delivered-unit cost basis. The reverse is also true. Pressures to reduce unit costs, arising from costly dedicated equipment, are incompatible with a competitive environment requiring flexibility and responsiveness to change.
2. *Multiplicity* results if two or more products with different success criteria are in one facility or organization. Adding a new product line to an established facility, for example, may introduce significant problems for both lines because of fundamentally different operating requirements. This happens when a growth product is integrated with a mature one, as well as when a made-to-order product is mixed with a made-to-stock one.
3. *Inconsistency* occurs when the operating responses vary; parts of operations strive for flexibility, for example, while others respond to performance and yet others are driven by cost. Inconsistency reflects the introduction of sophisticated information systems and/or integrated materials-handling systems into an environment which does not have the stability required of these systems.

The following operational responses are controllable by management. These responses must be made in a way that is *compatible* with market requirements, is internally *consistent,* and reduces *multiplicity* to a practical minimum.

- *Scope of Activities* (What role should operations be playing?) The primary decisions that management must make relative to the role of operations, to assure that the above desirable conditions are fulfilled, involve *vertical integration* and *process technology*. Management must ask:
  - What is the value-added structure which optimizes the company's ability to respond to market needs?
  - What components of each product should the company manufacture and which should it buy?
  - What levels of sophistication and integration of manufacturing process technology are appropriate?
- *Resource Deployment* (How should this role be supported?) After deciding on the role of operations, management must determine how this role will be supported by the company's *physical assets* and *operational infrastructure*. Management should ask:
  - Is the number of facilities compatible with the capacity plan?
  - Should operations be organized around a product or a manufacturing process?
  - How should the manufacturing and distribution network be configured?
  - What systems are required to provide planning and control consistent with the operational role?
  - How should operations be organized to carry out its role?
  - What philosophy and policies will guide the operational organization?

These four major elements—vertical integration, process technology, physical asset deployment, and infrastructure—describe the operating response appropriate for each selected success criteria. When this is visualized on a matrix, one axis lists each product segment with its one or two success criteria, and the other axis has the four operating response categories.

Strategy development requires that management match the business objectives for each product segment with an appropriate operating response. For ease of discussion, these responses can be classified from low to high, signifying the range from a totally variable and unpredictable condition to one that is totally predictable.

In the hypothetical situation shown in Figure 13-3, the three product segments have the following critical success criteria:

1. Flexibility and responsiveness
2. Performance and adaptability
3. Cost and reliability

Each product segment elicits a significantly different operating response. Product Segment 1 (flexibility and responsiveness), for example, requires operations which can change rapidly without knowledge of future market directions. Products in this segment have a significant market condition which can be "here today and gone tomorrow." This implies:

- A low level of vertical integration with work done by subcontractors rather than major capital investment for in-house manufacture.
- The selection of general-purpose processes for those items which (for product design or other reasons) are to be manufactured in-house. *General purpose* implies that the processes and equipment could be used elsewhere should they no longer be required for this product. This area is changing rapidly as new process technology is developed. This technology provides the required "general purpose" flexibility with sophisticated, programmable equipment. This new technology, computer-integrated manufacturing (CIM), provides much greater flexibility with only a minimal or no unit cost penalty. Companies adopting CIM will have many more strategic options in both their factories and markets.
- Flexible physical assets, such as leased manufacturing and distribution facilities or a series of smaller plants rather than one large one. Again, because the future is unpredictable, the appropriate response is

	1. Flexibility and Responsiveness	2. Performance and Adaptability	3. Cost and Reliability
Scope of activities			
Level of vertical integration	Low, ready to change	Medium, critical items	High, economies of scale
Process technology selection*	General purpose, flexible	Specialized, programmable	Automated, dedicated
Resource deployment			
Physical assets	Flexible, anticipate change	Selective, product and process improvements	Cost reduction, operations effectiveness, and productivity
Infrastructure	Job shop, generalized	Mixed, process-oriented	High volume, throughout

*Rapidly changing as new technologies are developed.

FIGURE 13-3
Simplified operations response.

to anticipate change and not be "locked into" assets which can restrict future options.

- A job shop organization with people and information systems conducive to change. A "job shop" mentality revels, rather than rebels, in a changing environment.

At the other extreme, Product Segment 3 (cost and reliability) must achieve the lowest delivered-unit cost in a stable market environment. Products in this segment tend to be mature, with aggressive price competition. This implies:

- A high level of vertical integration to maintain close control over all costs.
- The selection of automated equipment, often dedicated to a particular product or process, to achieve economies of scale. The process mode should be continuous rather than batch.
- Assets focused toward maximizing productivity through automated handling systems instead of indirect labor, and facility location in cheaper labor areas.
- An organization, designed for high volume, with people and information systems molded for that purpose. With predictable conditions, the organization can be more formal and systems more sophisticated to maximize throughput and minimize cost.

Products in Segment 2 (performance and adaptability) obviously require a mid-range response with selective, mixed reactions, depending on the specific product characteristics.

While hypothetical Product Segments 1 and 3 represent the extremes of unpredictability and predictability, they provide a sense of operating logic. A fixed or locked-in response is not appropriate in unpredictable conditions, and one with variable elements is equally inappropriate in predictable conditions.

OPERATIONS STRATEGY IMPLICATIONS

Most industries are facing competitive, economic, and managerial problems that are increasing at ever faster rates. Operations management has been slow to recognize and react to the forces of these pressures. In fact, many operations were managed during the 1970s and are being managed during the 1980s the same ways they were in the 1950s and 1960s. Management has not matched business objectives and operations response. Nor has management realized that strategies, the appropriate responses, must change over time as market conditions evolve.

Management must now shift its focus from the narrow elements of operations to the broader, strategic ones. Only in this way can industry reduce competitive vulnerability and meet the challenge of revitalization.

An operations strategy provides management with the framework with which to understand the implications of changing operating system characteristics. Some of these implications, shown in the accompanying table, are potentially profound as management rationalizes the past with the future.

Orientation of the Past	*Future Potential*
Standardized product design	More unique, customized products
Long product life cycles	Truncated product life cycles where maturity may be short-lived or never occur
Regional and national markets	World markets
Large factories	Disaggregated capacity; experience curve losing validity
Balanced production, smooth flows	Flexibility, volatility; surges in production
Moderate technological progress	New computerized process technologies, rapid process innovation
Inventory used as a buffer	Production tied to demand, "just-in-time" deliveries
"Cheap" transportation	True cost with deregulation

When considered in total, these changes exponentially increase operations' complexity and management's corresponding challenge. Fortunately, both mechanical tools and an analytical framework for improvement are available. If top management applies them properly while determining policy for manufacturing and distribution, operations will become the valuable asset it can be. Skinner has referred to operations as being the competitive weapon of the future. The use of this weapon will determine how well future business objectives are achieved.

Although the questions that operating management must answer in the future will be the same as those in the past, their old answers will no longer suffice. Management must now learn new rules—new answers—to achieve success in the coming years.

Chapter 14
DISTRIBUTION STRATEGY

THEODORE E. POLLOCK*
Manager, A. T. Kearney, Inc.

It must be remembered that there is nothing more difficult to plan, more uncertain of success, nor more dangerous to manage than the creation of a new order of things. For the initiator has the enmity of all who would profit by the preservation of the old institutions, and merely lukewarm defenders in those who would gain by the new ones.

NICCOLÒ MACHIAVELLI

What is the scope of distribution and its related strategic planning process? Where and why is distribution strategy planning being emphasized? Why is it becoming so vital a process? How does one address such a task? These questions form the framework for this chapter.

American Dream Fabricators, Inc. (the name is fictitious) is a company with an enviable record of sales and profitability growth spanning a half century. Later in this chapter, the ADF story will be used to illustrate the emergence of the distribution function as an important business force and to explore the issues and approaches inherent in distribution planning.

*The author is grateful to Dr. Richard Powers, president, Insight, Inc. and Mr. Wendell M. Stewart, vice president of logistics, A. T. Kearney, Inc. for their contributions to this chapter.

THE SCOPE OF DISTRIBUTION STRATEGY

A few definitions are in order to ensure a common understanding of the scope of this chapter.

1. *Corporate strategy* is the basic long-range plan for operating the company. It defines:
   a. The *businesses* in which the company chooses to participate (compete)
   b. The *objectives* (for example, sales volume, profit, investment, and return on assets) that management has established for each business
   c. The nature of the *processes* (marketing, production, logistics) that should be operated in conducting each business to obtain these objectives
   d. The nature and magnitude of the *resources* (labor, materials, technology, capital, and energy) that must be applied to the processes in each business
   e. The *policies* (freight policies, pricing, service, quality), to be followed in guiding implementation of the strategy established for each business

Strategic plans are long term (perhaps one to ten years). *Tactics* are the programs, methods, and procedures for operating each business month to month, week to week, and day to day, within the framework of the overall strategy. Strategy, then, points the corporate body in a particular direction while tactics make it move.

2. *Distribution* has been defined in numerous ways. The following are three viewpoints.
   a. From a *value-added* perspective, distribution provides time and place utility. The sale is completed when the product reaches the customer and payment is received by the supplier for the merchandise. An inability to deliver the product ordered consistently within the promised time frame will often result in lost sales and/or increased operating costs as expensive expediting becomes a rule rather than an exception. The distribution process provides the physical link between the assets of finished goods inventory and accounts receivable (see Figure 14-1). Increasingly, distribution and sales organizations are working more closely to speed up this conversion process and, thereby, to improve cash flow.
   b. From a *structural* viewpoint, distribution encompasses the system (network) of inventory stock points (plant, regional or local warehouses) and the flows through these points to customers.
   c. From a *managerial* viewpoint, distribution—within the framework of marketing, production, and financial plans, as well as external

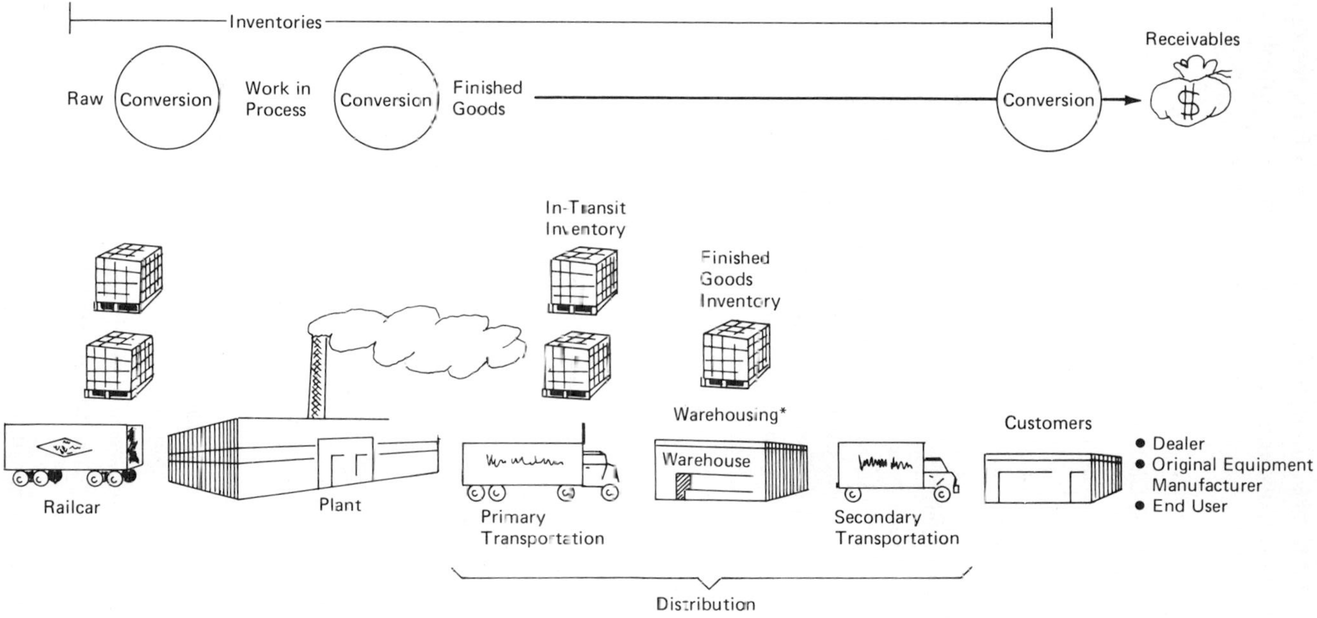

*May be More than One Echelon of Warehousing.

FIGURE 14-1
Distribution's role.

environmental forces—identifies the means to satisfy customer service through cost-effective inventory deployment and control, capacity management, warehousing, and transportation.

RELATIVE IMPORTANCE OF DISTRIBUTION

Is distribution important to all industries? Yes! Does distribution affect all companies' operating statements and balance sheets equally? No!

Made-to-order products, shipped F.O.B. factory with a three-month customer lead time, are at the opposite end of the distribution spectrum from those goods made-to-inventory, shipped from local (market-oriented) warehouses, freight prepaid with a seven-day lead time. High-quality custom furniture and packaged food products are representative of this spread in value added by distribution.

The concerns and attention of management toward distribution are (or certainly should be) different for different industries. Likewise, the placement of the distribution organization in the company hierarchy reflects its importance in attaining corporate objectives. This importance can manifest itself through the elevation of the top distribution position to a vice presidential level with involvement in corporate planning.

Distribution Strategy

Figure 14-2 illustrates schematically where distribution "fits" in the corporate strategic planning process. Distribution strategic planning is both a periodic and an ad hoc activity. The latter action is usually in response to top management requests for input to specific analyses. For example, a major food processor decided to assess the acquisition of a tobacco products company. Distribution's role in the study was to prepare a feasibility plan, which would identify:

1. The company's capacity to absorb the target company's volume
2. The synergy of such an acquisition from a distribution operating-cost point of view
3. The desirability of combining food and tobacco products in the warehousing and transportation operations, including the benefits of common shipments to similar distribution channel members

This information enabled corporate planners to develop a more rigorous cost-benefit analysis and top management to make a better-supported decision.

Distribution strategic planning on a periodic basis includes both the development of an annual plan and, typically less frequently, a study of the asset (inventory, facilities, equipment) deployment process.

The annual plan should be guided by the elements within, and the factors outside, the scope of distribution.

Figure 14-3 illustrates the elements of distribution planning and provides, through its flow, a glimpse of the distribution strategy planning process. This process includes converting customer service goals (guided by internal and external factors) into inventory, warehousing, and transportation strategies and tactics and then managing the resultant operations through effective systems and organizations.

While all distribution organizations prepare annual budgets, too few take the time to prepare a plan which considers both the elements *and* the flow of the planning process shown in Figure 14-3. The budget is

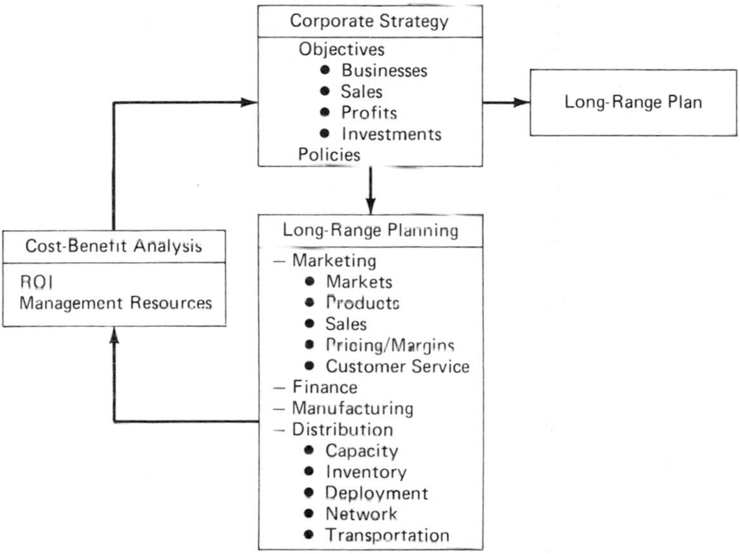

FIGURE 14-2
Distribution's role on the strategic planning process.

usually a combination of: (1) inflation-adjusted warehousing and transportation rates applied to estimated product flows; (2) estimated impact of cost reduction efforts; and (3) estimated cost of planned projects. As a result, top management often is not able to relate the plans of the distribution organization to other functional plans or to corporate goals. This produces a degree of discomfort for corporate executives as they wonder whether the distribution function operates in a proactive manner or simply reacts . . . whether distribution management develops creative strategies and tactics or simply carries on "business as usual." The lack of comprehensive planning often manifests itself in requests for unbudgeted capital for unplanned-for projects, as well as significant variances in operating expenses.

Factors Guiding Distribution Strategy

Given that distribution is a support function (Figure 14-4), what are the factors which guide and constrain the distribution strategic plan? There are internal factors caused by forces within the company and external factors based on the environment within which the company operates.

Internal Factors Internal factors should be embodied in plans from other corporate entities (upper left side of Figure 14-3). The depth and availability of these plans are dependent on the sophistication of the planning

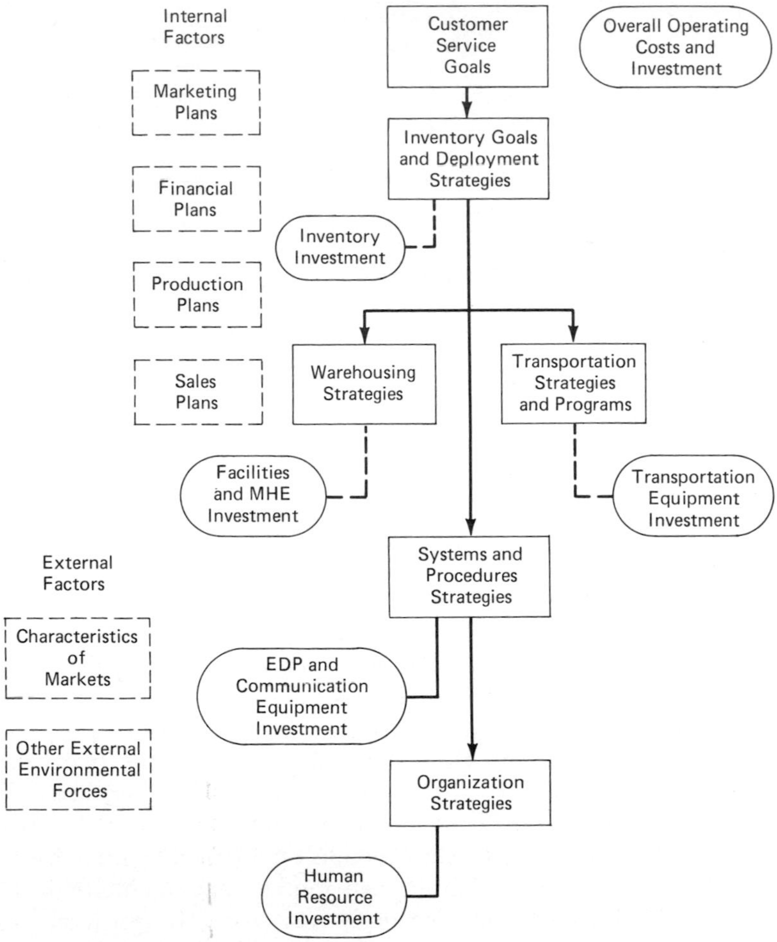

FIGURE 14-3
Distribution planning elements.

process of the company in general. Key inputs, nonetheless, include the following:

1. FROM MARKETING: Plans for new products, the discontinuance of specific current products, new target markets and promotions, a definition of the long-term marketing strategy, and service levels (order cycle time and item availability) by product or product group and by channel of trade.

2. FROM SALES: Sales volume by product group and specific geographic area, including variations in sales according to seasons or specific periods. In addition, it should identify customers by class, while detailing how the sales force will service them including the processing of orders and order cycle time.

3. FROM MANUFACTURING: Locations for the production of each product, including product volume, production cycle, and capacity for each product group. If products can be made at various sites, manufacturing should specify production trade-offs and the requirements for stock transfers between production locations.

4. FROM FINANCE: Costs associated with manufacturing (by product for each production site), selling (by channels of trade), and marketing (by individual product groups). In addition, finance should specify cost of capital and inventory turns goals.

While it cannot be disputed that distribution is a support function, this role should not be viewed as a subservient one—receiving and executing instructions. Indeed, the level of sophistication of the distribu-

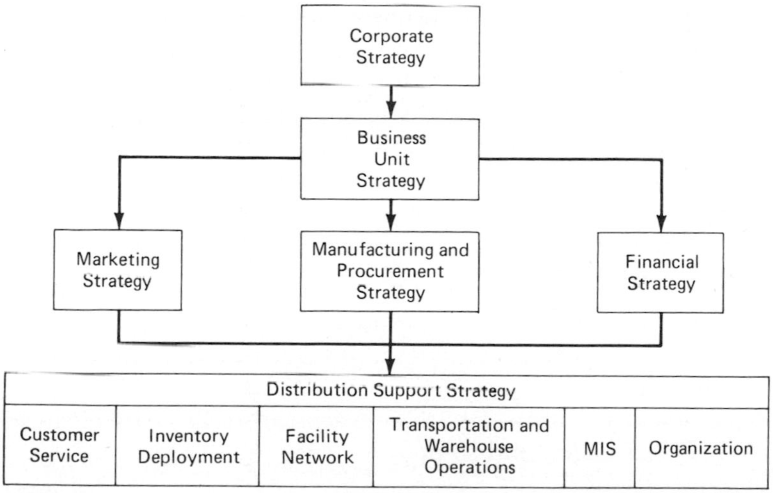

FIGURE 14-4
Distribution supports marketing, manufacturing, and financial strategies.

tion organization, the technical tools available to its planning personnel, and (in many companies) the close working relationships between sales and distribution personnel have fostered a significant degree of input from distribution to the plans of other corporate functions.

For example, a major pharmaceuticals manufacturer develops customer service goals through a joint marketing-distribution effort called "zero-based customer service" planning. The process involves looking at a number of factors which segment the product line (for example, is the product a critical or life-sustaining one?). By applying a weight to each factor and a value to each product, management can develop a weighted average "score" for each product. This score, in turn, enables the assignment of a service level to each product in terms of product fill rate. Not only is this a rational way to develop service levels, but it also further promotes routine dialogue between two functions which all too often do not communicate adequately.

Further contributions by distribution to aid marketing in establishing customer service goals is often provided by computer inventory simulations, whereby an inventory investment versus service-level curve is developed by product family (see Figure 14-5). This information enables the financial impact of service decisions to be assessed. In Figure 14-5, for example, the incremental investment in inventory accelerates significantly at service levels beyond a 92 percent unit fill. Typically, significant savings, coupled with a better balance of service (high where needed and lower elsewhere), are realized through this simulation approach.

External Factors Frequently "uncontrollable," external factors are elements which shape and constrain the strategic planning process.

They are alluded to in the two lower left boxes of Figure 14-3. The "Characteristics of Markets" refers to the specific requirements of the customer base. In the context of this chapter, the base of existing and target customers is given. Distribution's challenge is to provide a specific level of service at the lowest possible cost to those customers. The uncontrollable elements, then, are the location and the physical characteristics of the markets, for example:

- Available appropriate warehousing
- Available transportation modes and carriers within these modes
- Weather factors
- Profile of order sizes—less than truckload (LTL), truckload (TL), carload (CL), packages, and so on
- Volume of orders
- Transit times from existing and potential shipping points
- Product demand trends and forecasts (demographics)

Any project aimed at improving distribution cost effectiveness must consider these data as a minimum. The costs associated with warehousing, transportation, and holding inventory, in concert with the above data, form the information base for distribution strategic planning.

In addition to the characteristics of markets, however, strategists are faced with external *environmental* forces, farther beyond the enterprise's control than the markets in which it competes.

Subsequent to the mid-1970s, many of these factors or issues became pronounced and volatile, introducing a high degree of uncertainty and risk in planning.

These issues, the nature of the related changes and resultant impacts, are presented in Table 14-1. Each one has distribution implications and should be considered in developing the distribution strategic plan.

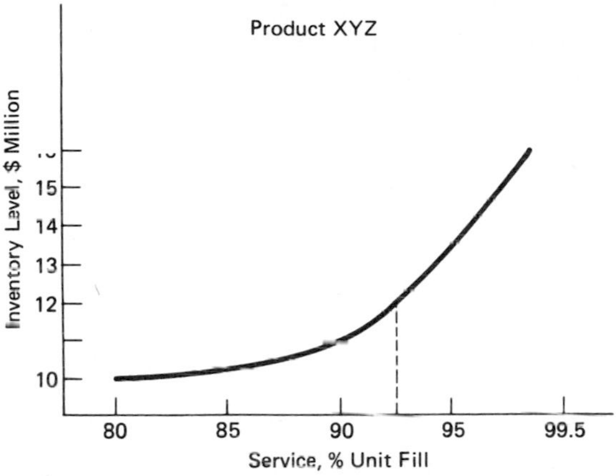

FIGURE 14-5
Inventory versus service curve.

THE EMERGENCE OF DISTRIBUTION: CASE STUDY

Before the steps in the strategic planning process are enumerated, it should be understood why this function has rapidly come of age. We'll use a case study to provide both this insight and the lead-in to the planning methodology.

Why has distribution emerged as a potent marketing tool, and grown into a large slice of the business expense pie? Why has the distribution manager changed from a traffic expediter to a key player on the top management team—a professional who now frequently challenges the objectives and strategies of other functions in an attempt to arrive at optimum overall approaches to satisfying the corporate mission?

The following case study will assist in answering these questions and

Table 14-1 External Forces

1. *Demographic Shifts*
    - Nature of changes
        - Population
        - Industrial base
    - Impacts
        - Misalignment of facilities and markets
        - Increased delivery costs
        - Longer lead times—greater variability
        - More warehouses
        - Increased inventories
2. *Cost and Supply of Capital*
    - Nature of change
        - Interest rate trends
        - Capital formation trends
        - Low profits
        - Low savings
    - Impacts
        - Higher inventory-carrying costs
        - Reduced long-term borrowing
        - Reduced investments in R&D
        - Deferred investment in plant and equipment
        - Expansion of manufacturing into plant warehousing space
        - Responsibility for carrying inventory being pushed back up the supply pipeline
        - Changing economies of "make or buy"
3. *Increasing Differentiation of Customer-Market Segments*
    - Nature of change
        - More market segments
        - Shifts in relative importance
        - New, specialized service requirements
        - More bypassing of industrial distribution going direct to original equipment manufacturers (OEMs)
        - Shifts in leverage between suppliers and customers
    - Impacts
        - Fragmented production focus
        - Wider range of profitability between segments
        - Proliferation of selective, tailor-made customer service programs
        - More widespread measurements of customer service—better management information systems (MIS)
        - Shifts in relative competitiveness—cost effectiveness
4. *New Supply Sources and Constraints*
    - Nature of changes
        - Diminishing supply of basic resources
        - Remaining supplies in hands of cartels and unfriendly governments
        - New sources farther away
    - Impacts
        - Higher material costs—increasing substitution in materials and sources
        - Loss of control—greater vulnerability
        - Higher costs
        - More material substitutions requiring new processes
        - More backward integration
        - Misalignment between plants and sources
5. *Energy Cost and Availability*
    - Nature of changes
        - Significant price increases
        - Increasing volatility (unreliability) in supply

Impacts
- Product redesign
- Demand shifts to less energy-intensive substitutes
- Increased transportation costs
- Increased manufacturing costs
- Disruptions in manufacturing and distribution operations
- Shortages of energy-intensive PD facilities (for example, frozen food warehousing)
- Reduced plant location options

6. *New Regulatory Freedoms*

Nature of changes
- Revised depreciation tax rules and other capital formation and investment tax incentives
- Deregulation (transportation, and so on)
- Government priorities (spending patterns)
- Trade policies
- Imposition of cost-effective criteria

Impacts
- More control over product design
- Increased incentive to invest in new, more cost effective technology and facilities
- Elimination of cost subsidies in transportation rates
- Strong trend toward more cost-based transportation rates
- New service-price packages and greater dependability
- Less investment required in nonproductive capital equipment

---

demonstrate modern approaches to dealing with the complexities of distribution planning implicit in Figure 14-3. Although ADF is a producer of consumer nondurable goods, we will discuss broad concepts and activities relevant to other manufacturing sectors. Furthermore, the term *integrated operations strategy* will be used to convey the need for considering the interaction between distribution and manufacturing to obtain an optimum strategy.

ADF started operations just before the Great Depression with a plant in the Northeast. At the beginning of the 1930s distribution was achieved by plant shipments direct to "local" customers (essentially retailers) and shipments to midwest customers from a Chicago warehouse, replenished by rail from the plant (see Figure 14-6). The company's line was limited, consisting of about six items or stockkeeping units (SKUs). Competition was negligible, and the reason for the Chicago warehouse was that it "came with the territory" when a partnership was developed with a Chicago distributor. While actual cost information from that time is not available, the relationships among distribution costs can be assumed (see Figure 14-7).

Dominant concerns of management for the decades of the 1930s and 1940s were production efficiency (long runs), production capacity expansion, and widening the market. Competition started to emerge during the 1940s; however, product innovation and quality and production efficiencies enabled ADF to maintain a major dominance in all markets.

During those years, energy was abundant and cheap, capital readily available at low borrowing rates, and transportation inexpensive and stable.

Distribution planning consisted of traffic studies exploring alternative rates by motor or rail carriers. The traffic function reported to plant managers. Warehouses were opened to keep freight costs down (the cost of the extra inventory was negligible). Plant locations were based on sources of labor, raw materials, and energy. Inventory management

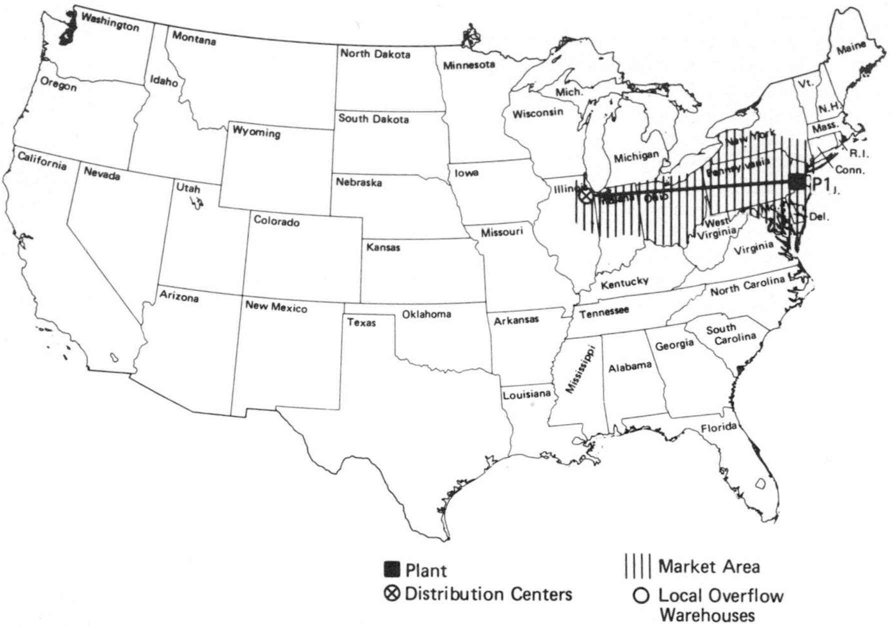

FIGURE 14-6
Historical situation: 1930.

was a marketing responsibility; control was exercised by perpetual inventory records. The prime rate was in the 4 to 6 percent range, and excess safety or buffer stocks were the rule to preclude stock-outs and costly back orders.

With large production runs, a relatively low level of product proliferation, a glut of inventory, market dominance and improving productivity, management's collective mind was uncluttered with operational problems, especially distribution.

During the 1940s, technology from World War II was employed in a new product line consisting of a half dozen product categories. A plant to produce the new product line had been constructed in Richmond, Virginia (near the source of key raw materials), and the Chicago plant was also expanded to produce the new line. By 1950 distribution centers had been added in Minneapolis and Boston, primarily to provide better service in New England and the upper Midwest (see Figure 14-8).

During the 1950s top management shifted its emphasis toward aggressive marketing. By 1960 market coverage had been expanded into the Southeast and the Southwest, and to the West Coast. To support these sales efforts in the new market areas and to provide a higher level of customer service in existing markets, the company acquired distribution centers in Los Angeles, San Francisco, Fort Worth, Atlanta, Columbus, and Memphis. The Cleveland distribution center had been closed when the Columbus one was opened (see Figure 14-9). Throughout the 1960s, a marketing orientation continued to dominate the company's policies. Demand grew significantly, and marketing became nationwide except for Wyoming, Montana, and Idaho. To deal with the increased demand and to employ some modernized production technology which emerged in the 1960s, the company built plants in Atlanta and Fort Worth. Distribution centers were added in Newark, Jacksonville, Houston, Detroit, and Portland. The distribution center in Columbus was closed.

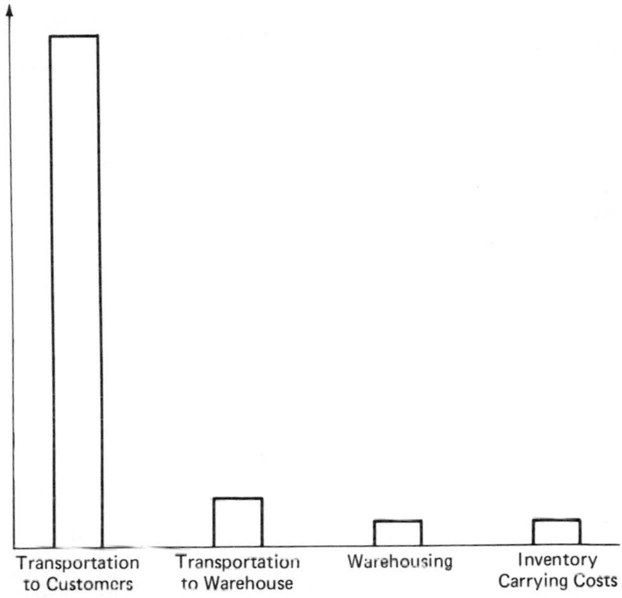

FIGURE 14-7
ADF distribution cost relationships.

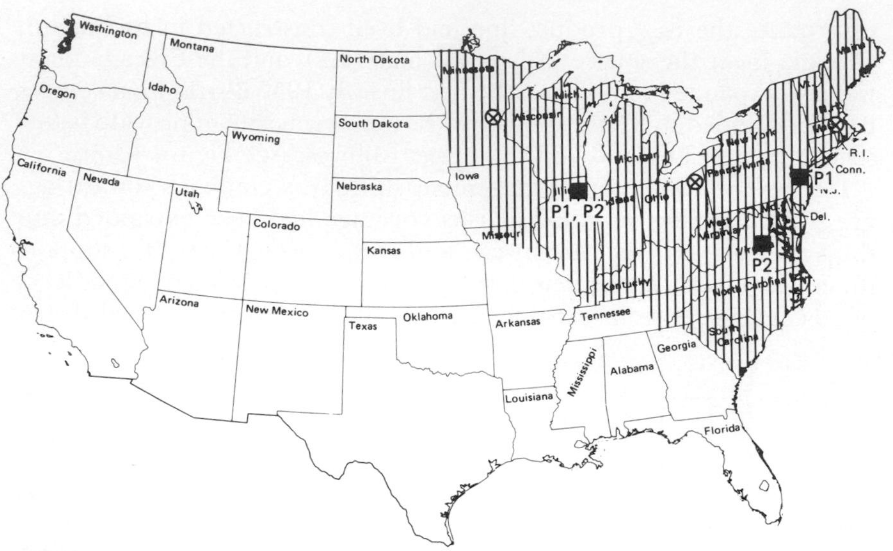

FIGURE 14-8
Historical situation: 1950.

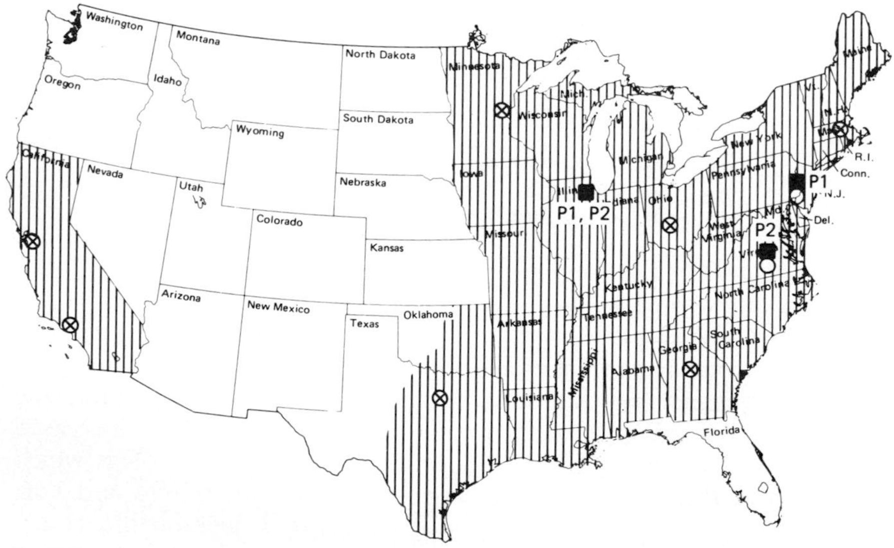

FIGURE 14-9
Historical situation: 1960.

By 1980 the heavy marketing thrusts of the 1960s and 1970s were paying dividends in record sales. To support its customer service objectives, the company had opened distribution centers in Kansas City, Buffalo, Phoenix, and Denver and reopened a distribution center in Columbus. In addition, major distribution facilities were built at the existing five plants—Newark, Richmond, Chicago, Atlanta, and Fort Worth. By this time, most of the major market areas were supported by nearby distribution centers. Because of this, resupply operations for those distribution centers were becoming very complex and expensive (see Figure 14-10).

Table 14-2 summarizes the environment in which ADF's growth flourished versus the new characteristics of the external environmental forces

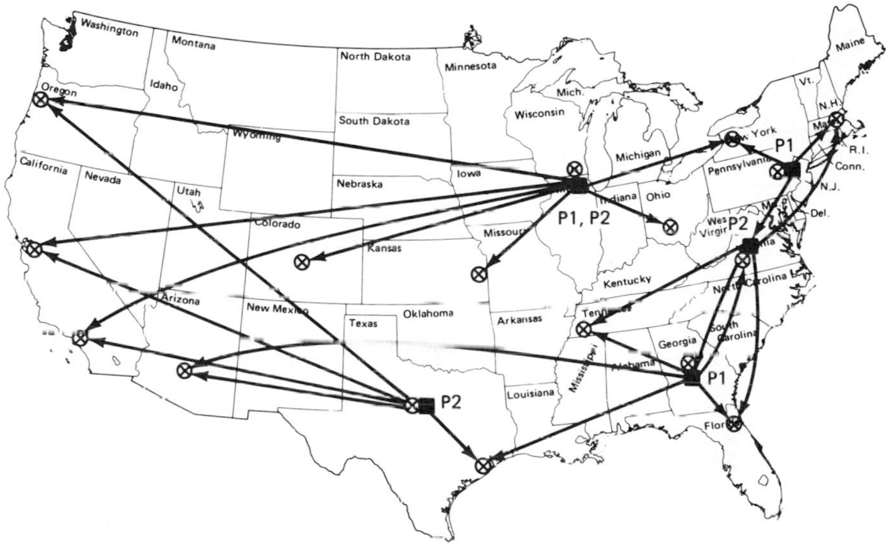

FIGURE 14-10
Present situation: 1980.

discussed earlier in this chapter. Through the early 1970s, the company operated in a supportive environment, in which a marketing orientation could thrive. Starting in the mid-1970s, the rapid growth opportunities gave way to a more constrained environment. Operations requirements began to emerge as the dominant concerns of top management.

The changes rendered prior distribution strategies obsolete. Further, simply maximizing production efficiencies through long runs of large batches had become dysfunctional. Finally, attempts to reconcile these problems resulted in deteriorating market support.

These impacts are clearly illustrated by the trend in physical distribution costs as a percentage of the cost of goods sold (Figure 14-11).

Table 14-2 Situation Analysis

Elements	Through early 1970s—Marketing driven in a predictable environment	Mid-1970s through 1980s—Operations driven in an uncertain environment
Markets	Growing	Maturing
Materials	Available	Scarce
Energy	Cheap, available	Expensive, scarce
Transportation costs	Low, predictable	High, unpredictable
Transportation service	Regulated	Deregulated
Capital	Cheap, available	Expensive, scarce

Between 1960 and 1980, that percentage had almost doubled, and the increase had accelerated during the preceding ten years.

Furthermore, looking at costs as a percentage of sales over the past ten years (Figure 14-12), it can be seen that distribution costs grew faster than sales revenues.

Attempts to react to marketing pressures with the existing manufacturing system and policies led to inventory buildups. Between 1970 and 1980, inventory turns decreased by 20 percent (Figure 14-13). Furthermore, those increased inventories were held at much higher cost in 1980 than in 1970.

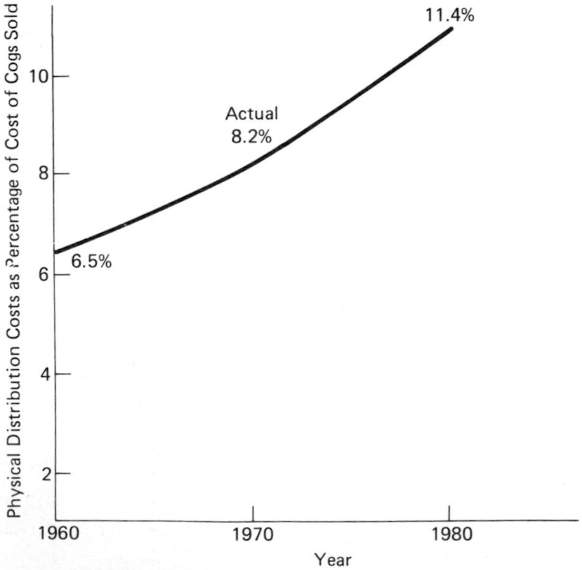

FIGURE 14-11
Physical distribution costs grow faster than manufacturing costs.

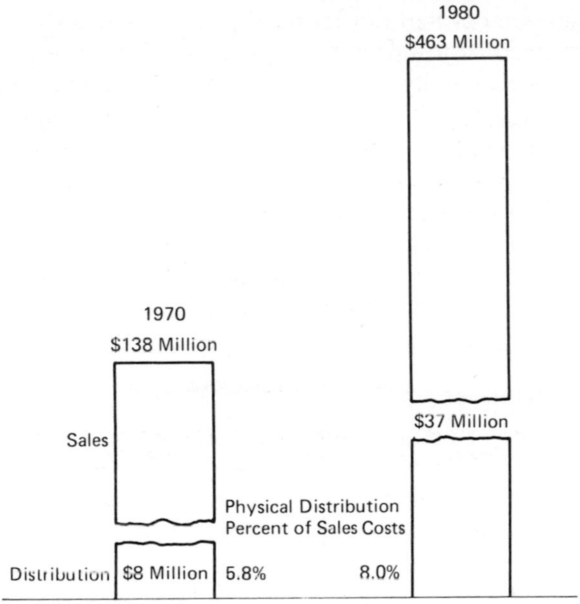

FIGURE 14-12
Physical distribution costs grow faster than sales.

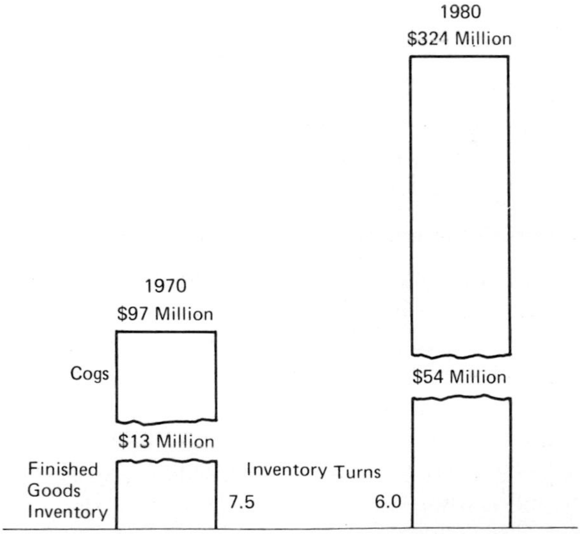

FIGURE 14-13
Inventory turnover declines.

ADF's management had not ignored problems as they arose or failed to act as perceived conditions changed. However, management reacted to pressures incrementally, often not recognizing the interdependencies of the system. Figure 14-14 illustrates four such actions and the resultant impacts. (1) As inventories and interest rates rose, for example, arbitrary inventory reductions were ordered. Because management still wanted to maintain service objectives, the inventory reductions caused higher manufacturing and transportation costs. (2) When it was perceived that competitive requirements dictated additional warehouse locations, customer service improved and freight costs to customers went down. However, these desirable results were achieved at significantly increased

	Impact on Functional Area				
Action Examples	Manufacturing Costs	Transportation Costs	Warehousing Costs	Inventory Costs	Customer Service and Sales
Arbitrary Inventory Cuts	↑	↑		↓	↓
Additional Warehouses		↓	↑	↑	↑
Mode Mix Changes		↓	↑	↑	↓
Plant Warehouse Space Usurped	↓	↑	↑	↑	

FIGURE 14-14
Attempts to cope have been incremental and unsuccessful.

warehousing and carrying costs. (3) To reduce replenishment transportation costs to the expanding West Coast market areas, management negotiated favorable rail rates. Rail shipments replaced truck shipments. As expected, freight costs to distribution centers did decrease; unfortunately, so did customer service since inventory safety stocks were not adjusted for the change in lead times. Eventually inventory levels rose to meet service objectives. (4) As manufacturing capacities became strained by increasing sales, what had been warehousing space was turned over to production. This saved manufacturing dollars but resulted in high overflow warehousing and local shuttle transportation costs. In addition, control of inventory became more difficult. Inventory costs went up.

In short, the incremental approach to solving management problems failed to recognize the interactions inherent in a complex production-distribution (operations) system. After much introspection, top management recognized the need to concentrate on and develop an operations strategy. The specific means it chose to develop such a strategy was the application of a *management support system.*

A management support system is created or exists for one reason only, to assist a manager in making better decisions by making better infor-

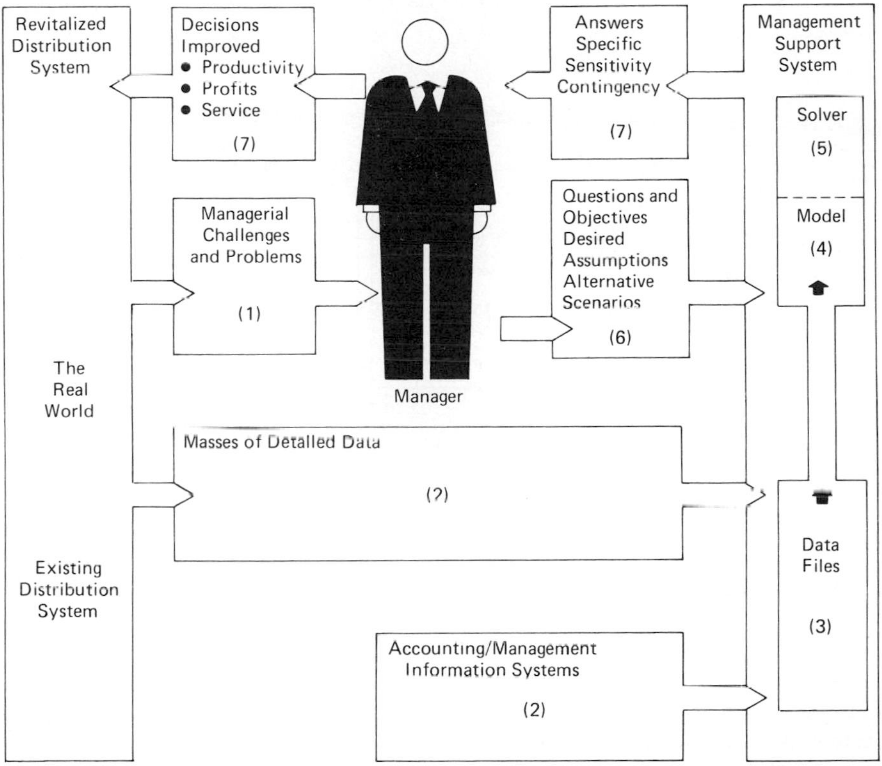

FIGURE 14-15
Management support system. (*Reprinted from Powers and Geoffrion, "Management Support Systems," The Wharton Magazine, Spring 1981.*)

mation available. The process is illustrated in Figure 14-15 (the following numbers in parentheses are keyed to the figure). Functioning in a real environment laden with challenges and problems (1), managers are often surrounded by masses of detailed, but meaningless data (2). A management support system brings together the masses of data (3) and organizes them in an orderly, rational way, using a model (4) of the real system in which the manager must function. With a solver (5), normally a computer program, and interface facilities, which enable the manager to communicate conveniently with the solver, the model can be used to evaluate many alternative scenarios (6) before resources are actually committed (7). It was just such a management support system which was brought to bear on the strategic questions of ADF.

The management support system was used to help top management develop an operations strategy for resource deployment. The fundamental question asked by management was, What production-distribution network will yield the greatest return on assets, given all the trade-offs inherent in the total system? The specific issues identified by top management were:

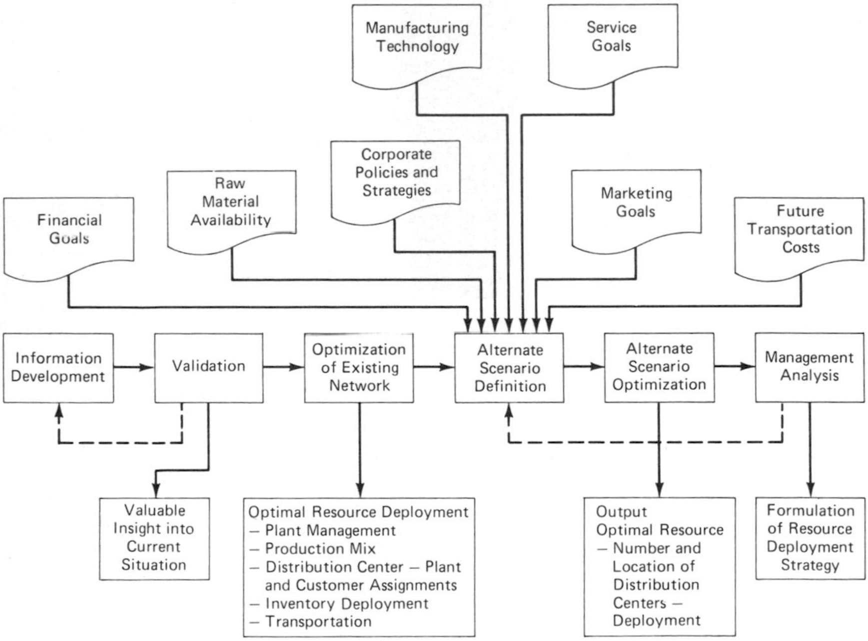

FIGURE 14-16
The network evaluation process.

- What were the appropriate customer service goals to pursue?
- How should inventory be stratified and positioned in the various echelons of the production-distribution system?
- How many distribution centers should there be, where should they be, and what service areas should be assigned to each?
- Should new plant locations be opened up and should the product mix among plants be changed?
- Which plants should provide which products to each warehouse and what mix of transportation modes should be used?

Each of these issues, complex in itself, had to be viewed in the context of all the issues because of their interactions. Returning briefly to the model of ADF's production-distribution system as it existed in 1980, we can understand more clearly now how that system emerged through incremental responses to market forces and other environmental factors. We can also understand why, given the trends in transportation economics and interest rates over the last several years, distribution costs were becoming a major concern to top management.

By completing the fully integrated analysis shown schematically in Figure 14-16, using a management support system, management was

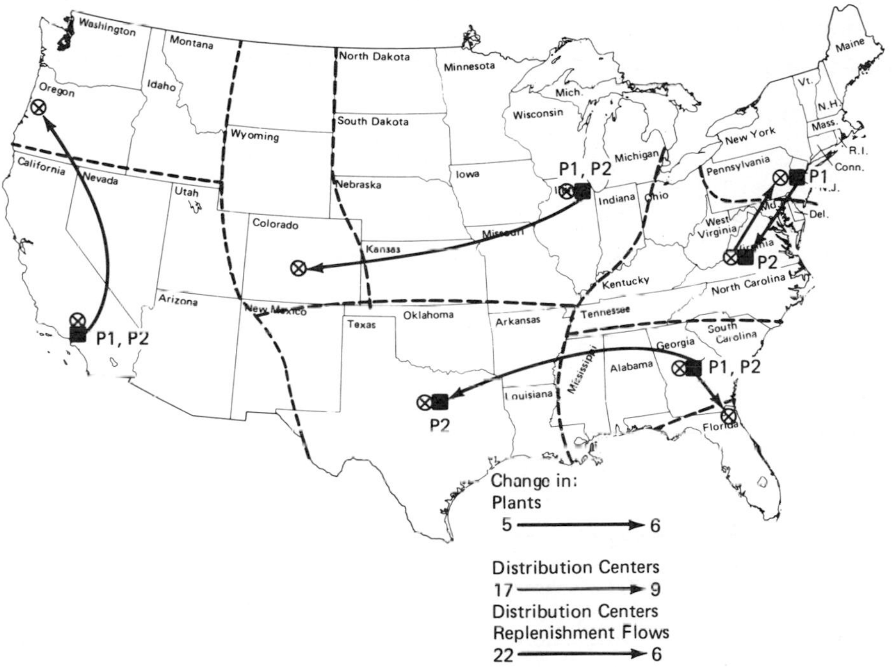

FIGURE 14-17
Revitalized system.

able to discover, among the millions of possible alternatives, the best way to deploy its production-distribution resources. It was able to come up with what can be termed a "revitalized" system. That revitalized system (Figure 14-17) entailed building a full-line plant in Los Angeles and adding product lines in Atlanta to permit that plant to be full line. It was found that eight distribution centers could be closed and that the service areas could be reconfigured to greatly reduce freight costs while maintaining service levels. It was recognized that some efficiencies in production would be lost by spreading production among more locations, but it was demonstrated that these "diseconomies" would be more than offset by the substantial savings in freight costs and inventory costs possible with the streamlined configuration.

In arriving at the revitalized system, management analyzed many economic trade-offs under different environmental conditions, such as the cost of capital and freight costs. The graph in Figure 14-18 illustrates one such analysis involving interest rates. If the cost of capital is low, the optimal number of distribution centers is greater than if the cost of capital is high, because the relative importance of transportation and warehousing costs would be greater when compared to inventory carrying costs. As the cost of capital increases, the optimal number of distribution centers shifts downward to cut inventories and the costs

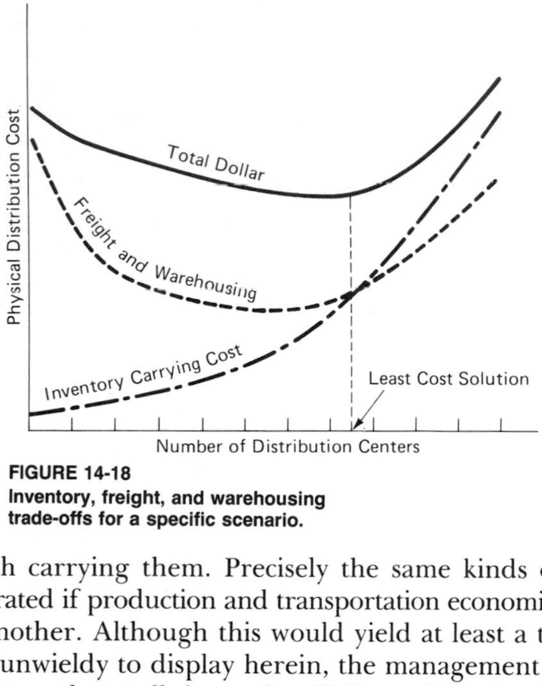

FIGURE 14-18
Inventory, freight, and warehousing trade-offs for a specific scenario.

associated with carrying them. Precisely the same kinds of trade-offs could be illustrated if production and transportation economics are traded against one another. Although this would yield at least a three-dimensional graph, unwieldy to display herein, the management support system was able to evaluate all the trade-off dimensions simultaneously.

Developing an integrated operations strategy through the management support system yielded varying outcomes (or costs) for each type of action indicated. If the company had done nothing more than optimize the flows in its existing production distribution network, about 25 percent of all the savings possible from a complete system revitalization would have been possible. These savings would all have been in freight costs. One further step, permitting the management support system to reconfigure the distribution network, resulted in closing several warehouses and, thereby, increasing the cost of freight to customers. However, those increased costs were more than offset by the savings in inventory and warehousing costs. The next step, evaluating new plant locations, revealed the largest increment of savings in the analysis. A location on the west coast would result in major savings in freight costs to distribution centers, even though some increases in manufacturing costs would occur and minor increases were likely in freight costs to customers. Savings were also found to be possible from expanding the product lines manufactured in one of the single-line plants. Again, the savings were mainly in freight costs to distribution centers, offset slightly by increased costs in manufacturing. Finally, it was found that additional savings could be realized by stratifying customer service goals by market segments, and determining inventory needs to support each segment. A conservative estimate of the net impact of the defined operations strategy was a significant increase of 8 percent in return on assets (from 12.5 to 13.5 percent).

While the above analyses showed significant benefits, of almost equal value was the capability for top management to ask "what if" questions across a wide range of issues (Figure 14-19). With its management support system now in place, management could evaluate the *sensitivity* of the revitalized system to various potential outcomes of governmental transportation policies, energy cost and availability, interest rates, marketing policies, and automation opportunities (external environmental forces).

To test the stability of the selected operational strategy, management evaluated many alternative scenarios. If truckload freight costs were to increase disproportionately because of fuel costs, for example, a West Coast plant would become even more advantageous. On the other hand, if unit production costs at the new plant turn out to be 10 percent or more above estimates, the logistics benefits of having the new plant would be marginal. With respect to customer service, if the order cycle time were relaxed, the company could get by with one fewer warehouse and thereby achieve some additional savings. Further, if product-oriented service levels (a stratified approach) were adopted, inventories could be decreased by an additional 9 percent.

In summary, the lessons learned from this case study in strategic planning were that:

- Incremental solutions don't work very well.
- State-of-the-art management support systems (data-model-solver) permit integrated operations strategies.
- Sensitivity analyses permit top management to conduct riskless experiments—to develop valuable insights before committing resources.

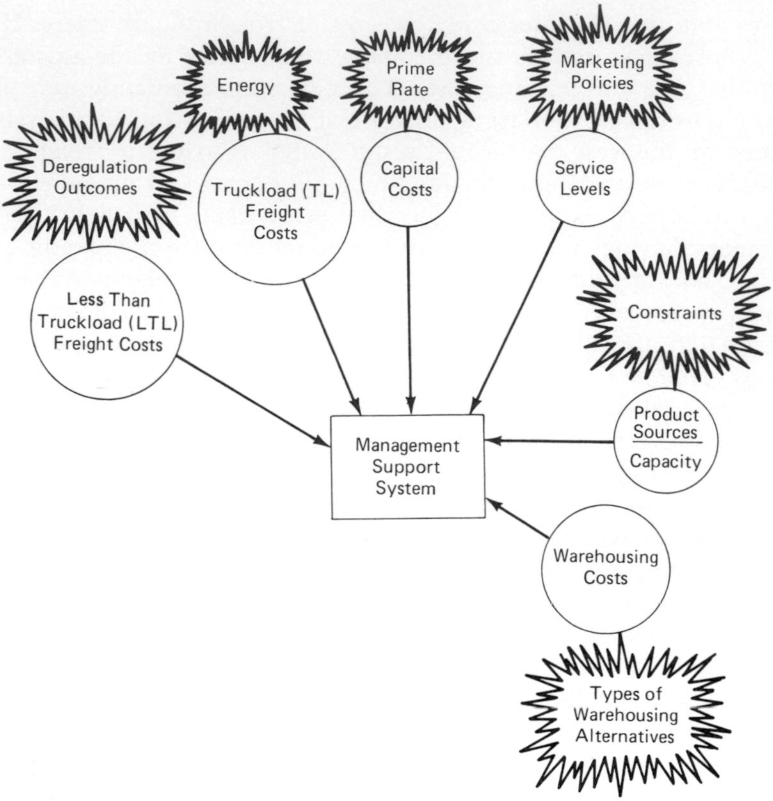

FIGURE 14-19
"What-if's" sensitivity analysis.

The preceding case study illustrated the power of comprehensive strategic planning. The next section explores the individual elements in routinely developing the strategy.

DEVELOPING A DISTRIBUTION STRATEGY

Key Elements of Distribution Strategy

There are five key elements that must be considered in any such strategy.

1. *Customer service goals* act as a magnetic force drawing inventories through the procurement, production, and distribution processes.

2. *Materials management* is the integrated planning and control of materials flowing through the distribution "pipeline."

3. *The physical distribution network and operating plan* consist of the sequential group of activities (warehousing, transportation, order process-

ing, and so on) that receive, store, order, pick, transport, and deliver goods to customers.

4. *Management information systems* are the millions of bits and pieces of information flowing through the business which act to animate the organization, to orchestrate the key processes—in effect, to make the business function. Relevant, pertinent information, available in suitable formats, with requisite timeliness and accuracy, is the key to management effectiveness.

5. *Organization* is the allocation of responsibilities, authority, and accountability for management of the distribution process (that is, the management structure).

Basic Issues to Be Resolved

There are six key issues that must be resolved in establishing any viable logistics strategy. These include:

1. *The levels of service* that the logistics process must provide. Such levels of service must be realistic and competitive and must meet the needs of each geographic area, market segment, and product group.

2. *The size and location of procurement, production, and distribution capacities.* Capacities must provide an economical means of meeting the necessary customer service criteria within acceptable investment limits.

3. *Staging of inventories* (raw materials, work in process, semifinished or finished goods) that define what volume of each product should be in each stage of inventory at any particular time or season.

4. *The geographic deployment of inventories* (echelon warehousing) that considers such factors as location of A versus B versus C items, and categorizes inventory based upon turnover and other considerations.

5. *Transportation mode mix* that considers all the various possibilities of both public and private transportation.

6. *Personnel staffing levels* that are required to operate the logistics strategy defined in items 1 to 5.

Approaches to Resolving the Basic Issues

There are five major factors to be considered in resolving the basic issues of distribution strategy:

1. To resolve the level of *customer service issue,* it is necessary to:

a. Conduct external research through interviews with customers and possible competitors to determine:

Customers' real service needs

Competitors' abilities to satisfy those needs and define what competitors can and cannot do

The impact of any changes (either up or down) in service levels on sales

A stepwise approach to determining customer service requirements is shown in Figure 14-20.

b. Determine internally:

Existing service levels

"Price tags" of higher or lower service levels

Realistic, economical, and competitive service goals

Cost-effective means of measuring actual results and performance[1]

2. To resolve *the issue of capacity configuration,* it is usually necessary to develop a model of the distribution system.[2] In determining the input to such a model, the following steps are typical:

a. Review marketing strategy and individual product-market segment objectives to determine:

Marketing strategy with respect to channels of distribution and product flow

Anticipated sales volumes of each product in each market segment during each time period at each stage of product life cycle

Marketing objectives (increased penetration, hold or harvest, and so on) in each product-market segment

Profit objectives in each product-market segment

b. Review manufacturing strategies to determine:

Basic manufacturing philosophy (that is, full line versus specialized plants; level production for seasonal inventory buildup versus variable manufacturing levels)

Present capacity and degree of utilization in each plant

Product unit cost at the end of the production line

Basic inbound material and sourcing strategy

c. Review financial strategy to determine objectives with respect to:

Physical distribution operating cost levels

Inventory level objectives

Total allowable investment in procurement, production, and distribution activities

Return-on-investment (ROI) objectives

d. Select a particular solution methodology. This could be a manual calculation or a computerized management support system. The latter is required for all but the most simplistic issues. The use of management support systems to aid in the decision-making process was shown schematically in Figure 14-15.

---

[1]See Lalonde and Zinszer, "Customer Service: Meaning and Measurement," *NCPDM,* 1976.

[2]See A. Geoffrion, "Better Distribution Planning with Computer Models," *Harvard Business Review,* July–August, 1976.

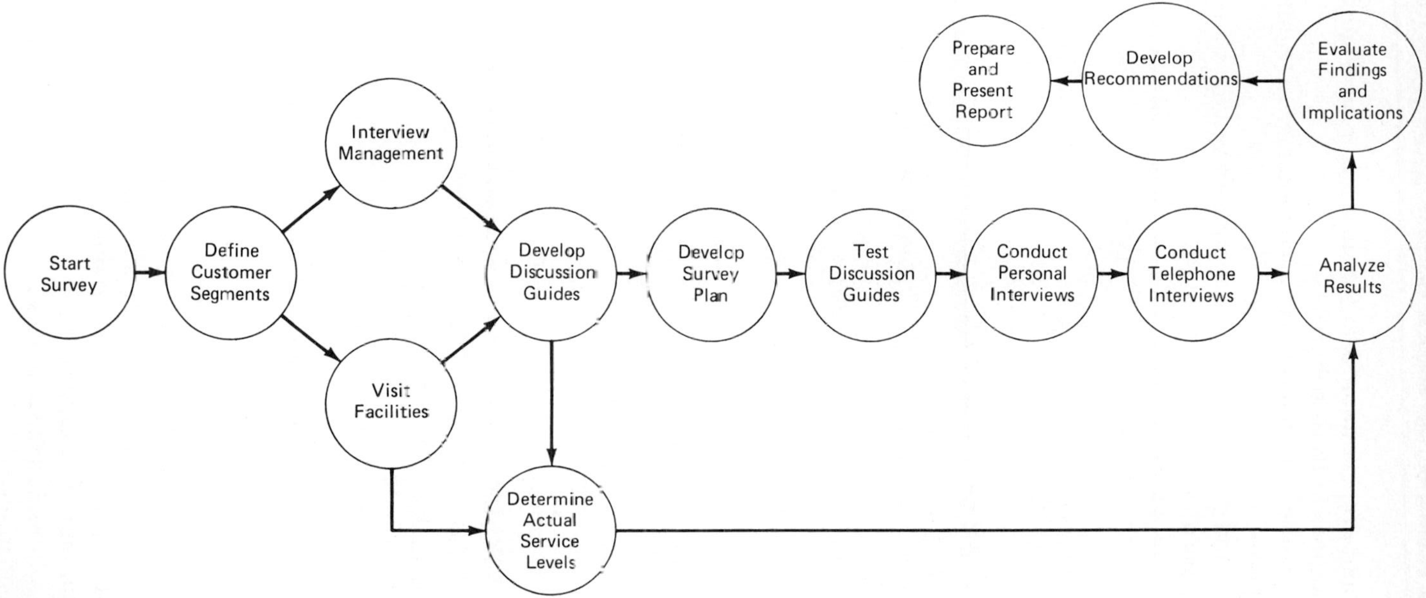

FIGURE 14-20
Survey of customers.

e. Identify and prepare input data for such factors as (Figure 14-21):
Commodities to be distributed
Demand for each commodity in each customer zone during each time period
Existing and potential plant locations and vendor sources
Plant capacities where definable

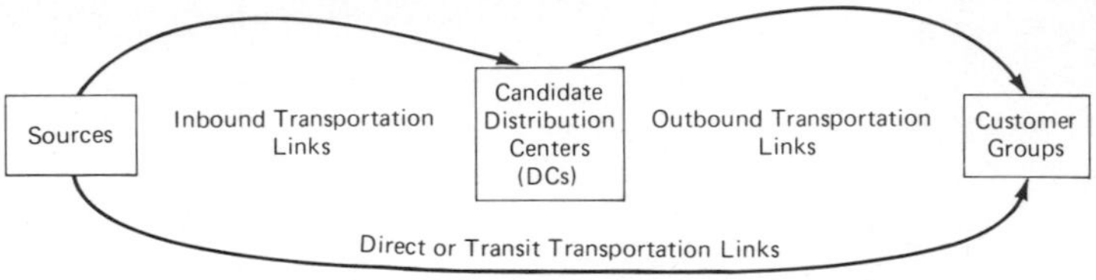

SUPPLY DATA
1. List of products
2. List of sources
3. Annual supply limits, cwt/yr (source × product)
4. Unit supply costs, $/cwt (source × product)

DISTRIBUTION CENTER DATA
5. List of candidate DCs and their missions
6. Minimum and maximum allowable annual throughput volume for each DC, cwt/yr
   a. Throughput volume can be weighted by product.
   b. Volume limit violations can be permitted at a given penalty cost rate.
7. Fixed cost for each DC, $/yr
8. Variable costs, $/cwt (DC × product)

CUSTOMER DATA
9. List of customer groups
10. Annual customer demands, cwt/yr (customer group × product)
11. Single-source product bundles (a customer group must receive all products in a given bundle from a single distribution center)
12. Net selling prices, $/cwt (customer group × product)

TRANSPORTATION DATA
13. List of permissible inbound links and freight rates, $/cwt (product × source × DC)
14. List of permissible outbound links and freight rates, $/cwt (product × DC × customer group)
15. List of permissible direct or transit links and freight rates, $/cwt (product × link)

NOTE: Some data may be optional.

FIGURE 14-21
Modeling framework and data elements.

Existing and potential distribution center locations
Fixed and variable distribution center costs at each location
Inventory stocking configurations at each distribution center
Transportation costs on each origin-destination link
Distribution center capacity limits

f. Develop solutions, analyze results, draw conclusions, and develop recommendations.

3. To resolve *the staging-of-inventory issue,* it is generally necessary to utilize a computerized simulation tool. The basic steps in this effort are to:

a. Rationalize the flow of inventory through the procurement, production, and distribution process by:

Minimizing individual SKU inventories using economic order quantities

Minimizing inventories within acceptable service limits

Looking for ways to delay inventory differentiation at every stage, but especially in finished goods

Separating finished goods inventory into A, B, or C classes based upon such factors as turnover, value, original equipment, replacement, emergency repair, legal requirements, and uniqueness

b. Determine service requirements of groups for each class of finished-goods inventory

c. Identify the specific number and locations at which to stock each class of product in order to satisfy service requirements and minimize inventory in the distribution pipeline

d. Determine safety stock levels and replenishment shipment frequency required to support acceptable in-stock performance

e. Calculate safety stock and replenishment cycle stock unit volumes for each inventory class-location combination

f. Develop inventory-unit volume curves representing inventory requirements as a function of throughput volume

g. Input inventory curve data to a network rationalization model

h. Run the model

i. Determine the optimum number of distribution centers based upon total freight and warehousing costs, service, *and* inventory investment considerations

4. To resolve *the transportation mode mix issue,* it is necessary to:

a. Identify every transportation lane in the procurement, production, and distribution network (using the 80:20 relationship whereby 80 percent of the costs can be found in 20 percent of the lanes; this means that at least the initial focus should be on this 20 percent)

b. Determine the characteristics of the traffic moving in these key lanes (volume, frequency, shipment size, service requirements, transit time, present costs)

c. Identify alternative transport modes, and the costs and service capabilities of those modes

d. Select the most appropriate mode for each tonnage segment in each traffic lane (for resupply lanes, inventory carrying costs should be included along with freight rates)

5. To resolve *the issue of personnel staffing levels,* it is necessary to:

a. Identify each work center (plant warehouse, field distribution center, order processing center, fleet driver domicile, and so on)

b. Determine the range and volume of work to be handled at each work center each day and the daily, weekly, monthly, or seasonal variation in work load

c. Define types of equipment best suited to each particular type of operation at each work center considering volume of work and service requirements

d. Establish personnel planning guides for each type of operation using the equipment selected at each location

e. Apply personnel planning guides to anticipated work loads to calculate direct labor staffing requirements

Integrating Logistics Strategy with Marketing, Manufacturing, and Financial Strategies

1. To *integrate distribution strategy with marketing strategy* it is necessary to review:

a. Marketing-sales strategies to identify points of interface (for example, customer service, inventory deployment, customer profitability)

b. Customer service programs and goals to assure synchronization with product-market segment sales and profit goals

c. Policies, programs, and standard operating procedures that interface with physical distribution

d. Terms of sales, price, and discount schedules

e. Sales coverage and call frequency patterns

f. Operation scheduling

g. Product price marking, packaging, and unitizing requirements

And resolve points of conflict!

2. To *integrate distribution strategy with manufacturing strategy* it is necessary to review:

a. Manufacturing strategy to identify points of interface with logistics

b. Incorporation of logistics considerations in the manufacturing guidelines (economic production quantities, production cycle schedules, and so on)

c. Manufacturing policies, programs, and operating procedures that interface with logistics

And resolve points of conflict!

3. To *integrate distribution strategy with financial strategy* a review must be made of:

a. Financial strategy to identify points of interface (for example, inventory, cost, budgeting, and ROI objectives)

b. Policies, programs, and financial report systems to ensure the inclusion of logistics considerations and realistic treatment thereof

c. Corporate profitability objectives to assure logistics support for the most profitable product, market, and customer segments

And resolve points of conflict!

TEN STEPS TO SUCCESSFUL STRATEGIC PLANNING

In summary, to develop a successful strategic plan for your company it is necessary to complete these ten steps:

1. Define the unique distribution support needs of key groups of customers.
2. Determine the unique distribution requirements of key product-market segments.
3. Develop a realistic set of time-phased distribution goals.
4. Select the most appropriate network analysis methodology.
5. Collect the right type and amount of data in a format suitable to the selected methodology (management support system).
6. Validate input and output data.
7. Communicate preliminary conclusions to other functional managers and discuss their implications.
8. Develop a working draft of the distribution strategy statement. Review this with top and functional management to be sure that they thoroughly understand and agree with it.
9. Develop a detailed, time-phased implementation program and responsibility assignment matrix.
10. Develop a set of criteria to control implementation.

Chapter 15
HUMAN RESOURCES STRATEGY

RUSSELL G. ROBERTS
Director, Hay Associates

MARTIN G. WOLF
Senior Principal, Hay Associates

There has been a dramatic shift in the nature of the economy in the United States during the last two decades, with an accelerated movement from a manufacturing-dominated economy to a service-dominated one. During this period, we have witnessed an increasing percentage of manufactured goods being imported from other nations that offer cheaper labor (textiles, shoes), more advanced technology (steel), or both (automobiles).

With the movement away from manufacturing has come an explosive growth in the service sector. Personnel costs have become an ever-increasing part of our gross national product as a result of this shift, because the service sector is relatively more labor-intensive than manufacturing, and because services, at least to date, are less susceptible to automation and other productivity-enhancing approaches.

Most informed observers call for a continuation of this trend. During the remaining two decades of this century, the United States' GNP is expected to include a relatively strong and growing services sector and a relatively weak and diminishing manufacturing sector. As this scenario continues to unfold, the success of American enterprise will become ever more dependent on the ability to select, train, develop, and manage human resources.

Further, as the "people factor" continues to grow in relative importance, the success of any one organization relative to its competitors will become more and more a function of its ability to plan and execute a human resources strategy that is more effective than that of its competitors. Since expenditures for personnel will represent an increasing percentage of total corporate expenses, it then follows that those organizations achieving the greatest productivity from their work force will enjoy a distinct competitive advantage. Additionally, in an increasingly service-dominated economy, ease of entry into new business ventures will likely become ever more dependent upon the availability of sufficient numbers of appropriately skilled human resources and relatively less dependent upon access to investment capital.

In a nutshell, as American industry's requirement for a highly skilled work force increases, an organization's need for a well-conceived strategic human resources plan will become ever more critical. During the remainder of this century, the performance of an organization's human resources is likely to have a much greater impact upon short-term attainment of profit and return on investment goals than has historically been true. Similarly, the quality of the organization's human resources will have a much larger impact on the attainability of corporate business strategies and objectives.

From this perspective, it is obvious that the development and formulation of an effective human resources strategy will be a key element of a total corporate strategy. The remainder of this chapter is devoted to a discussion of the processes of planning, developing, implementing, and controlling the human resources strategy. It is no accident that the words chosen to describe the sections of this chapter sound as if they came from a "Management 101" textbook. We believe that the human resources of an organization must be more effectively managed in the future than they have been in the past if the organization is to continue to prosper. As will be developed more fully in the following sections, we hold that increased effectiveness of the human resources management process depends on the same source as does an increase in the effectiveness of the other management processes of the organization—the formulation and implementation of an appropriate strategy.

HUMAN RESOURCES STRATEGY PLANNING

A human resources strategy is necessarily proactive; it is a program for ensuring that the organization's human resources will be capable of fulfilling the stated business mission. The human resources strategist must assess the shape and nature of the future organization and formulate and implement plans to achieve the necessary human resources to support that organization.

Derivation of the Human Resources Strategy

Previous chapters of this book have explained the need for an enterprise to articulate and communicate a vision of what that enterprise will be in future years, and how it will, according to plan, evolve to fulfill that vision. Once an organization has finalized its vision, or strategic business mission, it is ready to formulate the integrated marketing, financial, and operating plans which serve as the vehicle for translating the strategic vision into tactical plans that will make the vision a reality over time. This process, too, has been articulated in earlier sections of this handbook.

As was discussed in Chapter 7, the enterprise's tactical plans are translated into a series of integrated management steps or processes. These, in turn, imply the arrangement of the enterprise's resources into an organization structure designed to maximize the likelihood of the attainment of the enterprise's objectives. Thus, the structure of the organization follows from tactical plans, which in turn flow from the business strategy. The development of this organization structure includes mapping out the accountabilities and performance measures of key jobs. Since job design and performance measures are derived directly from the business strategy, the selection and/or development of the appropriate type and mix of personnel to populate this organization structure is mandatory if the enterprise is to fulfill its strategic mission. This is but another variant of the concept of interlocking, coordinated management decisions and processes introduced in previous chapters in the discussion of strategic management.

Like all other management processes within the enterprise, human resources management must be approached within the context of what needs to occur in order to facilitate achievement of the enterprise's strategy. Thus, human resources strategy takes its cue from the key plans, performance measures, and climate requirements of the enterprise. To ensure that this occurs, the chief human resources officer (CHRO) must be a strategic thinker who has full awareness of the business and success factors of the enterprise. The CHRO must be a key member of the strategic planning and strategic management effort. In this way, human resources strategy is driven by a top-down planning process in which all human resources decisions are made with an awareness of what does and what does not constitute support for the achievement of the enterprise's strategic vision and plan. A schematic illustration of how the business strategy drives human resources strategy and decision making is shown in Figure 15-1.

Although the top-down strategic management approach to human resources strategy may seem very logical—indeed, obvious—our observation as consultants to a large sample of major U.S. corporations is that most human resources functions are run in what can be called a "bottom-up" fashion. The bottom-up approach to human resources management is typically practiced by functional specialists in one or more human resources skill areas. Often such specialists have little or no appreciation of how the strategic direction chosen by the enterprise places distinct requirements on the plans and priorities of the human resources function, or how the strategic direction guides the development of the culture, climate, and people in the enterprise.

The Process of Human Resources Strategy Development and Implementation

While subsequent sections of this chapter are devoted to problems and issues in the development, implementation, and control of the human resources strategy, an overview of the steps and issues of human re-

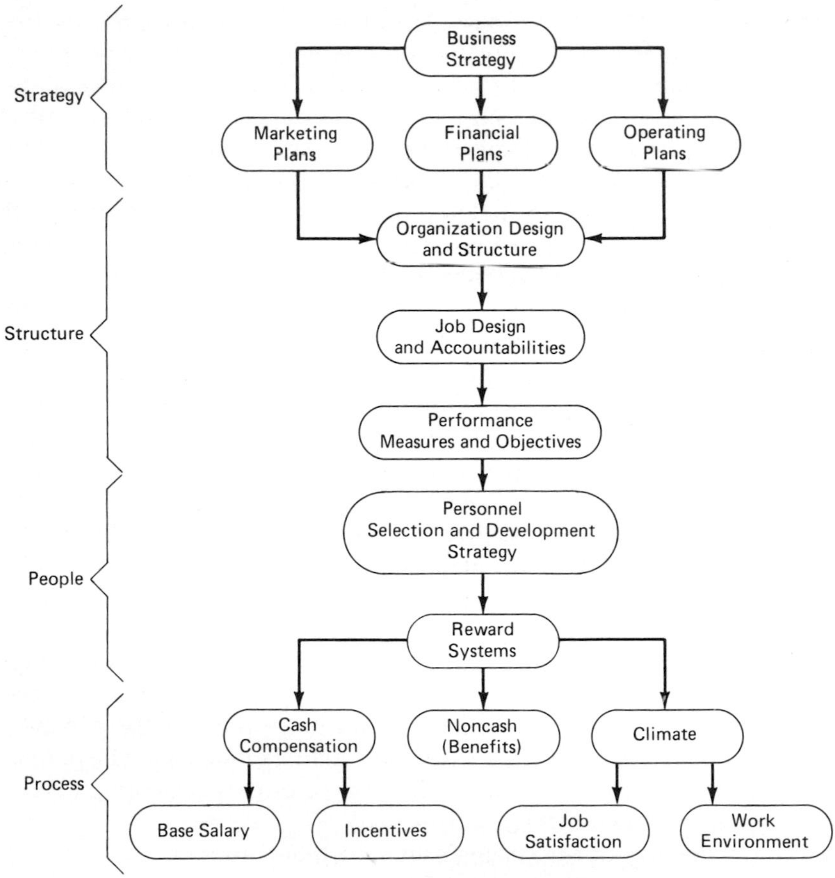

FIGURE 15-1
The flow from business strategy to human resources strategy.

sources strategy development and implementation is provided here (see Figure 15-2). The following three major sections of this chapter will present an in-depth discussion of the steps and issues outlined in Figure 15-2.

Although Figure 15-2 may suggest that the implementation of such a strategy has a discrete beginning and end, the actuality is that formulating and implementing the human resources strategy entails a continuing process of refinement, in concert with the evolving direction of the enterprise.

HUMAN RESOURCES STRATEGY DEVELOPMENT

As noted previously, human resources goals derive from an analysis of how key marketing and operating plans must be supported by people. For example, if an enterprise plans to start up a new operation, then the human resources strategy must include an analysis of what kinds of people will be required to staff the venture, when they must be hired and fully trained, and whether to "make or buy" (develop internally, which requires longer time frames—or recruit from the outside, which is costlier and entails greater risk).

Human Resources Strategy Goal Identification

As was described in previous chapters of this handbook, business strategies can be described generally as falling into one of three categories: invest to grow, earn and protect, and harvest and divest. Each of these strategies has major implications for the enterprise's human resources strategy. Figure 15-3 illustrates how different corporate strategies have unique ramifications for human resources strategy in areas such as organization structure, job design, organization climate, management style and selection, staffing, and reward systems. (We will develop this theme further in Figure 15-8. At that point we will look specifically at the implications that the position in the product life cycle has on the characteristics required of managers.)

Situational Diagnosis

After developing the implications of the organization's strategy for its human resources, it is necessary to evaluate the present human resources against these future human resources requirements. This is generally done by means of an audit of the current organization, its people, and its human resources programs. While the exact focus of the audit will depend on the key human resources goals, the approach to such a diagnosis usually includes the following:

Step	Key Issues
1. Human Resources Goal Identification	▪ What demands do the mission and strategic plans place upon the organization's climate and human resources? ▪ What kind of people, with what skills and performance capabilities, does the organization require? How many and how soon? ▪ What leadership styles and management skills will be needed for each relevant division, location, or business group?
2. Situation Diagnosis	▪ What are the present status and nature of the organization's culture, people, human resources systems, and personnel programs? ▪ What is the existing inventory of managerial and specialized skills? ▪ What are the prevailing leadership style and management profile?
3. Needs Assessment	▪ What gaps exist between the organization's future requirements for its human resources and working climate and the status quo? ▪ What are the key needs in terms of management abilities, technical skills, staff size and experience, management succession, problem-solving skills, organizational values and styles, performance levels, productivities, and so on?
4. Developmental Plans	▪ What developmental steps, or actions, need to be implemented in order to bring the organization's people and culture to the level and nature of strength required by the mission and strategic plans? ▪ What priorities, costs, resources, and probabilities of success are associated with meeting these developmental needs?
5. Plan Implementation	▪ How must the enterprise design, communicate, phase in, and gain individual commitment to the various pieces of its human resources development plan?
6. Implementation Control and Corrective Action	▪ How is progress toward human resources strategy goals to be measured? ▪ What level of actual performance shall constitute acceptable progress in each development plan area? ▪ What obstacles threaten fulfillment of the human resources strategy and how should they be addressed? ▪ What remedial actions are necessary? ▪ How must the basic strategy be modified through experience?

FIGURE 15-2
Steps and issues in human resources strategy development and implementation.

1. A survey of the corporate climate to assess perceptions of the organization's decision making, communications, performance orientation, human resources development, and goal clarity. This assessment will indicate whether the current climate is sufficient to support the desired human resources strategy.

2. A review of the current management succession plans to test their

	Phase in Life Cycle		
Process	Invest to Grow	Earn and Protect	Harvest and Divest
Resource allocation	Strategic investment	Protective investment	Minimized investment
Marketing strategy	Product differentiation	Selling-system differentiation	Individual selling and distribution
Organization structure	Flat Minimum organization	Highly supportive Complex	Centralized Hierarchical
Job design	High freedom to act Innovation encouraged	Interdependent Team-oriented	Highly controlled Task-oriented
Climate and culture	Highest urgency	Paced urgency	High loyalty Routine Security
Management style	Entrepreneurial Few formal processes	Sophisticated management processes	Sophisticated control processes
Staffing	Aggressive Risk oriented Top quality people predominate	Broad specialists Challenge-oriented Above average people predominate	Narrow specialists Security-oriented People of a broad range of abilities
Reward systems	High total compensation Modest base High incentive compensation Big risks—big rewards	High to average total compensation Average base Above average incentive compensation Moderate risk—moderate reward	Low to average total compensation Above average base Modest incentive compensation Low risk—low reward

FIGURE 15-3
SBU/strategic management implications for human resources strategy.

adequacy against the enterprise's human resources goals and needs for a specific quantity and mix of personnel.

3. An analysis of the performance management process to ascertain whether it is generating proactive performance counselling that works to improve employee performance.

4. A review of the management assessment process to ensure that strengths, talents, and development needs are being identified and addressed in a systematic and adequate fashion.

5. An investigation of the breadth and efficacy of management development programs to determine if the organization has the necessary complement of both specific training and broad development programs to prepare its human resources to fulfill corporate strategic plans.

6. An analysis of recruiting and selection procedures to ensure that newly selected employees have the talents, potential, and styles required to facilitate achievement of the business plan.

7. An audit of corporate compensation programs to ensure that their market competitiveness is appropriate.

8. A review of management incentive plans to ensure that they are of a size and design appropriate for the business strategy and that they direct behavior to those key elements required by the business plan.

Such an audit normally involves both review of appropriate program documents and informational input from managers and employees throughout the organization. The interview and/or questionnaire process should touch upon all of the audit areas listed above, with particular focus on how existing climate factors and human resources programs appear to be shaping, directing, and impacting the organization's human resources.

Needs Assessment

Once the human resources goals have been identified and the existing situation has been diagnosed relative to those goals, the human resources strategist can fairly readily identify the gaps between what needs to be and what is. In so doing, the strategist usually identifies quite a number of gaps. It is generally useful, therefore, to have some means of codifying, relating, and prioritizing human resources needs. It is also necessary to project the required time, dollars, and human resources which will be required to address those needs. Figure 15-4 presents a simple but useful summary format which can be used to highlight the key aspects of the enterprise's human resources needs, required developmental actions, and related issues.

Developmental Plans

It is an obvious, but often overlooked, truism that human behavior is not always logical, at least from the perspective of the observer. Thus, it is indeed true that "The best-laid schemes o' mice an' men gang aft a-gley." It is thus necessary to review regularly all development plans and periodically to reassess progress against the human resources plan.

Issue Area Illustrative	Goals	Current Situation	Development Needs	Development Steps Required	Total Work Days to Complete	Priority Level	Costs and/or Comments
Climate	1						
	2						
	3						
	4						
Job design	1						
	2						
	3						
Performance management	1						
	2						
Management continuity	1						
Management assessment							
Management development and training							
Recruiting and selection							

FIGURE 15-4
Human resources strategy planning matrix.

A detailed review of the various developmental approaches and their relative strengths and weaknesses is clearly beyond the scope of this chapter. Suffice it to say that the human resources strategist must move from the identification of specific needs to the proper action to fill those needs. Figure 15-5 represents one method of assessing the appropriateness of various types of development approaches for meeting particular needs. (The choice of needs dimensions in Figure 15-5 reflects a development approach based on an adaptation of the Hay job measurement dimensions to the assessment of the person-job fit. Readers can, of course, substitute dimensions appropriate to their needs assessment approaches.)

Development Methods	DEVELOPMENT NEED							
	Technical Know-How	Managerial Know-How	Human Relation Skills	Problem Solving Breadth and Disciplining	Thinking Skills	Accepting Freedom to Act	Magnitude	Type of Impact
Style of (Your) Management Coaching	▲	○	●	○	○	▲	●	▲
Job Exposure Part Time	▲			●		▲	●	▲
Job Exposure Full Time	○	▲	▲	▲	▲	○	○	○
Participation in Outside Organizations			▲	●		▲	▲	▲
Typical Classroom Programs	○	●	●	●	●			
Reading	○	●		●				
Outside Contacts	▲	▲	▲			▲		

○ Method Is Very Useful ▲ Method Can Facilitate Development ● Method Has Important but Limited Impact

FIGURE 15-5
Development guide relating to methods.

THE GORDON PHILLIPS AND ASSOCIATES, INC. CASE

The following case study focuses on a real company. It is essentially true to life. Minor alterations of history and fact have been made to conceal the identity of the organization.

Background

Gordon Phillips and Associates, Inc. (GPA) was founded in Boston in 1947 as a specialized management information and advisory service company. Through the 1950s the company grew steadily as it developed its unique product technology. The product technology continued to grow in depth, although in a fairly narrow functional area. The late 1960s and early 1970s saw increasing geographic expansion of GPA, both domestically and internationally. GPA became the leader in the marketplace, and revenues grew rapidly. Product diversification was limited to closely related professional services.

By the late 1970s GPA began to saturate the marketplace in its specialty. Further, the visibility that came with GPA's increased size and its obvious success attracted new entrants into the market. GPA management came to see the firm's market position as that of a relatively mature business which would generate a desirable cash flow but which would no longer grow at the rapid rate of the past.

Present Situation

The expected future for GPA's essentially single group of products clearly indicated a flattening of the growth curve. GPA management made the strategic decision to invest to maintain its traditional product line but to allocate some of the cash generated to fund the development of new service areas. GPA thus moved from geographic expansion into service expansion. Management sought to add new services which could be sold to existing clients. To offer the kind of long-term growth and profit potential that GPA managment desired, these new services were of necessity essentially unrelated to GPA's existing product area. Further, given the business climate of the late 1970s and the size and sophistication of GPA's clients, these services were already being offered by other firms to GPA's existing clients. Using the financial resources generated by GPA's traditional line of business, management moved quickly into several areas that appeared to offer high growth potential. They immediately ran into complications. The geographic expansion had been accomplished by sending out to the new offices a cadre of personnel from the existing units. This was not possible in the new areas of service since existing personnel lacked the requisite technical skills. It was decided, therefore, to head the new service areas with a GPA general manager and to staff them with appropriate technical specialists from outside. Despite the infusion of large amounts of cash and the absorption of considerable management time, a number of these ventures proved less than successful.

For example, one promising area involved offering specialized computerized information systems to the functional heads who had been GPA's primary customers. Relying on its reputation and excellent client relationships, and pricing the product competitively, GPA was able to obtain several large contracts. The technical specialists, in the full glory of their field, oversold the capabilities of the system to the clients and overbuilt the system. The GPA general manager, lacking the technical sophistication to identify what was happening, was caught up in the enthusiasm of the technical specialists for a "state of the art" product. The inevitable result was a large cost overrun and a slippage of schedules for delivery. After a few large losses of capital, and faced with the tarnishing of its reputation with important clients, GPA withdrew from this business.

A few years later, after several such abortive ventures, GPA management identified another endeavor which promised the kind of future revenue growth and profit potential which the company had experienced over the past thirty years. GPA perceived a clear niche that it could carve for itself in a competitive but lucrative marketplace. It was felt that the company's existing customer base and international network of offices could complement the new venture. After careful assessment, GPA management made the decision that this new line of endeavor would be the central focus around which the company would be organized in a few years' time. GPA developed a strategic plan for the new venture, which was named Services for Management (SM).

An analysis was made of the human resources strategy necessary to support SM as contrasted to GPA's current human resources strategy. The results of this are summarized in Figure 15-6. Based on this analysis, it was determined that SM should be separate and independent from the formality and control that had become part of GPA. Thus it was spun off as a separate company under the overall GPA umbrella. An invest-to-grow business strategy for SM was approved and funded by GPA.

The expectations for SM were revenue growth well in excess of GPA's traditional business and geographic expansion. The marketing, financial, and operating plans demanded a quintupling of the professional staff over a period of five years. Plans were developed for both the recruiting and internal development of a professional staff commensurate with the size that would be required in five years' time.

Implications

In retrospect, the management of GPA showed excellent insight in recognizing the need to spin off SM as a separate business even though the long-range strategy was to make SM the central core of GPA's business within a few years. Given the difference in the two human resources strategies evidenced in Figure 15-6, it is unlikely that SM would have had the freedom to manage its own destiny while functioning as a controlled division of GPA. While the human resources strategy implementation and control process is still ongoing at SM, the initial results are encouraging.

This case clearly is one where the presence or absence of the proper human resources determines the success or failure of the business strategy. The earlier failures at GPA were, in retrospect, clearly attributable to weaknesses in the human resources strategy and the associated systems of people management.

The apparent success of SM is attributable in no small measure to the human resources strategy. Particular credit must be given to the staffing parameters that evolved from the articulation of the human resources

Strategy Focus	Services for Management (Invest to Grow)	GPA (Invest to Maintain or Earn and Protect)
Style and profile		
Leadership skills	Entrepreneurial	Sophisticated manager
Professional style	Risk-accepting and innovative	Moderately conservative
	Effective more than efficient	Moderately venturesome
	Minimally controlling	Effective and efficient
		Moderately controlling
Array of skills		
Management skills	Generalist	Specialized-integrated
Human relations skills	High	High to moderate
Thinking skills	High	High to average
Freedom to act	High	Average
Organization and job design		
Organization structure	Flat	Moderately layered
Importance of the individual	Critical	Important
Job scope	Broad and deep	Narrow and very deep
Performance orientation	High goals	Moderate goals
	Direct accountability	Shared accountability
Staffing strategy		
Advancement ambition	High	Above average
Energy level	High	Above average
Technical education	Very high	Above average
Person versus system trade-off, %	Person: 75 System: 25	Person: 60 System: 40
Compensation strategy		
Total compensation	High	Above average
Cash incentive	High	Above average
Incentive complexity	Few objectives	Multiple objectives

FIGURE 15-6
Comparison of services for management and GPA human resources strategies.

strategy. The typical SM staffer is more educated but less experienced than the typical GPA staffer. There are clearly apparent differences in the value systems of the two groups of employees. Indeed, the differences are so broad that some good-natured (and some not so good-natured) rivalry has developed between employees in the traditional area of business and the SM staff. This rivalry in many cases accentuates the differences in management style and personal expectations of the two groups.

Figure 15-6 presents in detail some of the key differences in human resources strategy required by these two businesses because of their different positions in the product life cycle. In this regard, note the section Human Resources Strategy and the Product Life Cycle later in this chapter.

ISSUES IN IMPLEMENTING THE HUMAN RESOURCES STRATEGY

In the previous sections of this chapter, concepts regarding the process of translating the corporate strategy into a human resources strategy have been discussed. Once an organization has formulated its human resources strategy, it must then determine how and by whom this strategy is to be implemented. The focus in this section is on implementation.

Practicing consultants find that most members of management are relatively dissatisfied with the outcomes of their *past* human resources development efforts. While consultants may get a somewhat less than representative sample in this regard, since those fully satisfied with their human resources development programs may be less likely to employ consultants, we believe that our experience constitutes a fair assessment of today's situation. Similarly, there is a distinct concern among top management as to the efficacy of *current* human resources development efforts. When questioned, most top managers are less than confident that the human resources "in the pipeline" will be adequate to meet tomorrow's needs.

There are sound reasons for this concern. The problem is rooted in the fact that most current human resources efforts are *not* based on a well-formulated human resources strategy tied to the organization's overall business strategy. In order to understand this thesis, it is necessary to look at the hierarchy of strategy.

The Hierarchy of Strategy

Just as with all other elements of strategy, the human resources strategy arrays itself into three hierarchical levels: enterprise strategy, corporate strategy, and business unit/function strategy. As one moves from the enterprise strategy level to the corporate strategy level and, ultimately, to the business unit/function strategy level, the focus necessarily moves from the very broad to the highly specific. Figure 15-7 compares and contrasts the human resources strategy at the three hierarchical levels across a variety of strategy characteristics.

Characteristics	Level of Human Resources Strategy		
	Enterprise	Corporate	Business/Unit Function
Focus	Changing the pool of basic human resources and management climate to attune these to changes in corporate directions	Rationalizing the needs of the various business units and functions by managing the human resources development and allocation processes on a corporate basis	Finding an effective match between individual needs and talents, the needs of the business unit and function, and the needs of the enterprise, as developed in the corporate strategy
Individuals accountable	Board, CEO, and corporate human resources officer	CEO, corporate human resources officer, chief operating officer, group or division heads, group or division human resources officers	COO, group or division heads, group or division human resources officers, business unit–function manager, business unit–function human resources
Role	Vision and leadership	Direction and management	Administration and management
Purpose	Develop a unifying theme which integrates the enterprise's human resources directions with its business directions	Develop a human resources strategy for the existing business unit and function of the enterprise	Determine how to develop human resources effectively
Perspective	Total human resources needs of the longer-term future (5–10 yr)	Human resources needs of the present and the short term future (3–5 yr)	Human resources needs of the present (1–2 yr)
Directional emphasis	Fundamental change	Human resources allocations among existing business units	Development plans and recuitment
End result	Determination of what type of organizational structure will exist and what the organization climate will be	Determination of what types and numbers of talent to develop or recruit; make-or-buy decisions on human resources strategy	Determination of specific individual development plans Recruitment of individuals with needed skills and potential

FIGURE 15-7
Human resources strategy hierarchy.

At the *enterprise level,* the focus is on assuring the availability of the proper human resources and on the creation of the proper organizational climate to permit the effective utilization of these resources. At the *corporate level,* the focus shifts to assuring that the human resources are properly allocated among the competing groups based on total organizational need rather than present availability, or lack thereof. At the *business unit/function level,* the focus is on optimizing the development and utilization of human resources based on finding the best possible match between the needs of the individuals on the one hand and those of the business unit/function and the enterprise on the other.

Similarly, the responsible individuals' accountability for strategy development and implementation, the time perspective in which they operate, their directional emphasis, their role, indeed their very purpose, narrow and become more immediate as one moves down the strategy hierarchy. Thus the indicated differences in the end results of human resources strategy at the three levels, as shown in Figure 15-7.

The Current Focus in Human Resources Strategy

Most attention today is focused on the means leading to the end results associated with the business unit/function level of human resources strategy. That is, most journal articles, books, seminars, and consulting efforts are focused on determining and successfully implementing various individual development plans and/or assuring a continual inflow of the proper types of skills and abilities. Much less common is attention to the types and numbers of talents that will be required to meet the organization's needs of the future, or whether it is more effective to develop present personnel to meet these needs or to bring in the needed skills and abilities from outside the organization.

However, in recent years, there has been a growing focus on these issues of corporate-level human resources strategy. Today most large, sophisticated organizations have at least the beginnings of some focus on human resources strategy issues at the corporate level.

Why Most Current Human Resources Efforts Fail

We believe that most of the failures of human resources efforts in the past, and most of the anxiety about present programs and the human resources of the future, are reflective of the fact that enterprise-level human resources strategy has generally been neglected. Human resources development programs have been largely bottom-up, with relatively little top-down guidance and direction. As a result, even though most *individual* development efforts may succeed, the *overall* development effort appears to be less than successful since its output fails to meet the emerging organizational needs. Again, we believe that this failure is more often due to lack of proper focus of these development programs than it is to their poor execution.

It follows then that the greatest increase in effectiveness of human resources development expenditures can come from the effective articulation of enterprise-level human resources strategy to give focus and direction to these development efforts. Adding training staff, sending more managers to advanced management programs that are affiliated with business schools, increasing seminar attendance budgets, and so on, can result in large increases in expenditures on the organization's human resources without concomitant increases in the effectiveness of these expenditures in meeting the organization's true needs. The articulation of human resources strategy at the enterprise level enables the expenditures to be focused rather than diffused—rifle versus shotgun in nature.

Human Resources Strategy and the Product Life Cycle

Anyone who has read this far in this handbook is familiar with the concept of the product life cycle. The product life cycle is traditionally used to indicate likely investment needs, cash flows, product-market strategies, and so on. Similarly, the position of the business unit in its product life cycle has important implications for the requirements for management talent. The position of the business unit in the invest-to-grow, the earn-and-protect, or the harvest-and-divest modes carries with it some immediate and specific implications for the types of managers required. Figure 15-8 contrasts the human resources requirements on the various relevant dimensions for the three product life cycle phases. From inspection of Figure 15-8, it is readily obvious that today's selection decisions must be made in full knowledge of tomorrow's human resources requirements as indicated by the product life cycle.

Figure 15-8 also gives another perspective to the Peter principle and/or the issues of management obsolescence. It is not just that individuals are promoted into jobs beyond their level of competence or that jobs outgrow the level of competence of existing individuals. Equally as frequently, individuals who have characteristics that are related to success in an earlier phase of the product life cycle are unable to adapt effectively to the shifting requirements of a maturing business. Thus Figure 15-8 has implications not only for personnel selection but for present and future personnel allocation. The enterprise must put its human resources into situations in which the individuals will be playing to their

	Invest to Grow	Earn and Protect	Harvest and Divest
Technical skills	Original technological applications New knowledge	Problem solving Current knowledge of field	Repetitive Maintenance of existing technology
Management skills	Generalist	Specialized-integrative	Specialized-functional
Human relations skills	High Must integrate free spirits	Moderately high Must enthuse the team	Moderate Must maintain loyalty
Problem-solving skills	Broad Focused on the new and untried Intuitive	Complex Focused on adapting the existing Inductive	Compartmental Focused on interpolating from the past Deductive
Thinking skills	High abstraction Low detail and precision	Average abstraction Moderate detail and precision	Limited abstraction High detail and precision
Ability to accept freedom to act or the lack thereof	High on need for freedom Can refuse to play by the rules as they are nominal anyway	Average on need for freedom Helps to create the rules and must accept them as they develop	Below average on need for freedom Must prefer to live by detailed rules and enforce them
Size of area impacted	Very small to small	Large to very large	Medium to large
Type and timing of impact	Primary Effect is immediate	Primary and shared Effect is obvious in the short term	Shared and contributory Effect is measured in the longer term and not always obvious in the short term

FIGURE 15-8
Relationships of business unit position in the product life cycle to human resources requirements at management levels.

strengths and not their weaknesses, in which individual styles and values will be compatible with the needs of the business.[1]

The Role of the Chief Executive Officer (CEO)

In human resources strategy, as in other aspects of strategy, the CEO's role is critical. Unless the CEO sees the human resources strategy as a key factor in corporate success, the articulation of a human resources strategy and the development of implementation plans for this strategy are simply academic exercises.

Although the CEO's commitment to the importance of the human resources strategy is a necessary component of success, it is not by itself sufficient. As in all other areas of the enterprise, successful implementation requires an executive dedicated to the fulfillment of the strategy. However, because of the nature of human resources strategy and of the CEO's role in its successful implementation, the availability of a technically competent CHRO is not enough. There must be the right "chemistry" between the CEO and the CHRO. The CEO must have confidence in the CHRO not only from a technical standpoint but also from a business standpoint. That is, the CEO must believe that the CHRO not only understands the enterprise's strategy but is committed to assisting in achieving its business objectives; the CHRO must be viewed by the CEO as an integral part of the solution, not as part of the problem.

Organizing for Human Resources Strategy Implementation

Assuming that the CEO properly appreciates the importance of the human resources strategy, and assuming further that the CHRO enjoys his full confidence, the decision must be made as to how the human resources planning process will be organized. Figure 15-9 presents two alternative ways of structuring the human resources planning process. In alternative A, the accountability for human resources planning rests with the line executives, and the human resources officer serves as a classic staff resource. In alternative B, the line executives exercise their human resources planning responsibility through the medium of a human resources planning committee.

Figure 15-10 illustrates some of the key differences between these two alternatives. The specifics of organizational history and the need to follow—or break—the traditional organizational mores regarding the role of line and staff will determine which of these two alternatives is best suited for any individual organization.

---

[1]Readers interested in further discussion of this topic should refer to William Macomber's *Red, Yellow and Green Managers—Strategy and Style,* unpublished manuscript, Hay Associates, 229 South 18th Street, Philadelphia, 1979.

In those instances where alternative B is indicated, a human resources planning committee is created (see Figure 15-9). The nature of this committee is illustrated in Figure 15-11. In order to achieve its mission, the human resources planning committee requires the inputs and involvement of all relevant parties. The membership is chosen to achieve this.

The CHRO serves ex officio as chair, reflecting the role of this position in the attainment of the human resources strategy. The group or division heads are included to represent their human resources needs and potential. As the ones who have a direct financial stake in the outcome of the human resources strategy, their participation is essential. The group or division human resources officers are there as staff support for the line heads. They are the ones who will in large measure carry out the implementation process.

The chief planning officer is included on the committee to ensure that all of the human resources plans are tied to the corporate business plans. This linkage is essential. Without it, the human resources plans are niceties rather than necessities. As such, these plans would get little

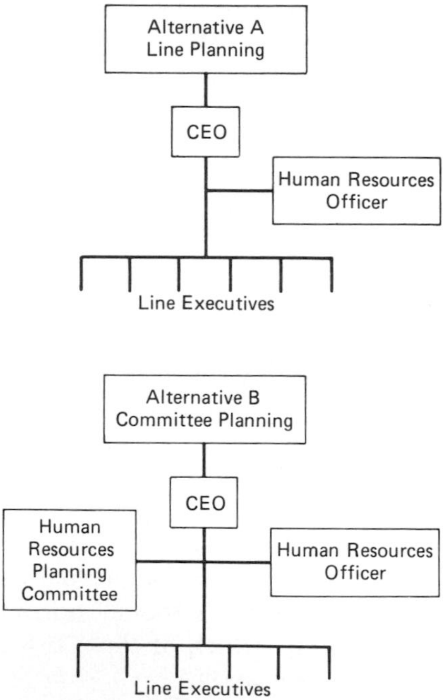

FIGURE 15-9
Organizing the human resources planning process: two structural alternatives.

Element	Alternative A: Line Planning	Alternative B: Committee Planning
Accountability focus	Line managers primary	Line managers shared
Role of human resources officer	Consultative	Policy making and strategy formulation
Major benefits	Increases line involvement in the process Accountabilities for planning and implementation are combined	Specializes the human resources planning function Provides a more global perspective to line managers
Potential risks	Lack of total perspective for line managers Operations requirements might supersede more strategic goals	Lack of real line involvement Possible bureaucratic dimension

FIGURE 15-10
Organizing the human resources planning process: comparison of two structural alternatives.

serious commitment from anyone and would be the first to suffer in times of budgetary reversals. Similarly, the heads of finance and of development and technology are there to insure that all relevant inputs as to the future nature and needs of the enterprise are considered in the development of the human resources plan.

ENSURING THE ACHIEVEMENT OF THE HUMAN RESOURCES STRATEGY

In the earlier sections of this chapter, issues in the formulation of human resources strategy were discussed. In the section immediately preceding this one, some of the "how-to" issues of implementation were discussed. As in any other management process, however, it is not enough simply to develop a plan and implement it. There must also be a mechanism for review and control.

We said earlier that the CEO is critical to the successful development and implementation of an effective human resources strategy. It is only through the CEO's continued emphasis on the importance of formulating and implementing an effective human resources strategy that such will occur. This means that the human resources area must be subject to the same type of periodic management reviews as are all other aspects of directing and operating the enterprise. While human resources development and implementation efforts can be monitored via special periodic reviews strictly for this purpose, we feel that this is not the most

MISSION	Provides the CEO with information, assistance, and advice in translating enterprise strategy into human resources strategy, in allocating near-term corporate human resources, and in monitoring the implementation of business unit/function human resources strategies
CHAIR	Chief human resources officer
MEMBERS	Group or division heads Group or division human resources officers Chief planning officer Head, Finance Head, Development/Technology

Figure 15-11
The human resource planning committee: a profile.

effective way to proceed. Rather, it is our belief that human resources strategy development and implementation must be monitored by integrating its review with the reviews of strategy formulation and operating results for each business unit.

If one adopts this view, then each business unit's presentation of its short- and long-term plans must include not only a statement of the financial implications of these plans but also a statement of the human resources implications of these plans. That is, business units will be looked at not only as suppliers or users of corporate financial resources but as suppliers or users of human resources. Further, longer-term strategies should be analyzed not only in terms of their impact on market position, profitability, facilities requirements, etc., but also in terms of their human resources implications. Similarly, operations reviews should evaluate performance against plan not only in the areas of sales, margins, market share, and so on, but also in terms of performance against plan in the human resources area.

As contrasted to separate reviews of human resources, this type of integration makes it clear that the human resources area is an integral part of running the enterprise. With this type of integration, human resources strategy formulation and implementation are not diversions from the critical tasks of management but necessary components thereof.

Section Four

Strategy Implementation

Chapter 16
IMPLEMENTING STRATEGIC CHANGE

ROBERT H. ROCK
Partner, Strategic Management Group, Hay Associates

MARV EISTHEN
President and Chief Executive Officer, OPI, Limited

Implementing changes in the strategy of any organization is ultimately the responsibility of the chief executive officer (CEO). A CEO's efforts in this area will focus on effectively managing: (1) personal leadership, (2) corporate culture, (3) organization, (4) executive people, (5) corporate communications, and (6) strategic rewards. The body of this chapter will discuss the relationships among these six levers for implementing strategic change (see Figure 16-1). Before we discuss how to implement strategy, however, some explanation of the different levels of strategy is necessary.

THE MOVEMENT TO AN ENTERPRISE STRATEGY

During the past twenty years, approaches to strategic change have themselves been changing. During the 1960s, general managers, corporate planners, business consultants, and academicians developed the discipline of business strategy. Business strategists segmented a market and then differentiated a product in order to compete effectively in the selected product-market segment.

During the 1970s, as industries matured, practitioners and theoreticians developed the discipline of corporate strategy—strategy directed to allocating resources among investment opportunities within the portfolio of a company's product-market segments, or as they are commonly referred to, strategic business units (SBUs). The goal here is to optimize cash flow.

Today, as CEOs in large organizations realize that resource allocation alone will no longer satisfy a corporation's need for growth, they are developing the discipline of enterprise strategy. Enterprise strategy seeks to create significant new wealth or value for the company's stakeholders through the identification and exploitation of *new* investment opportunities. Figure 16-2 illustrates the differences in purpose, perspective, and accountability between the three strategies.

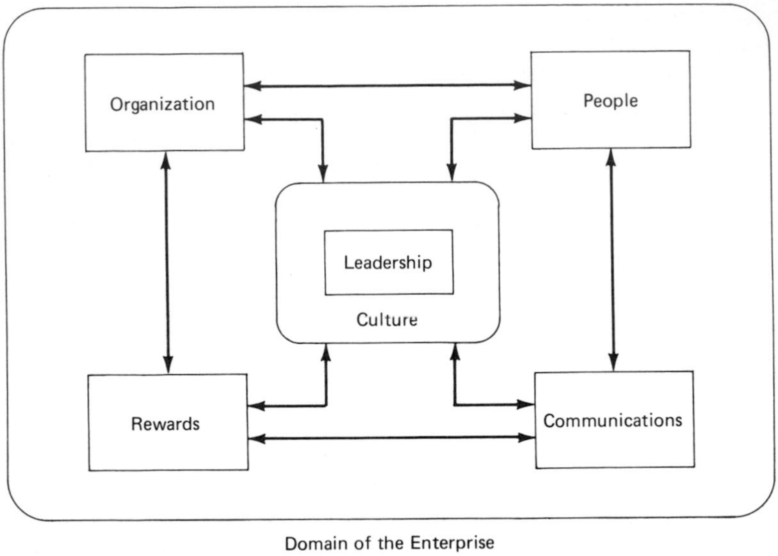

FIGURE 16-1
The levers for implementing strategic change.

Although 1970s-style corporate strategy is still very necessary, many are feeling its limitations. The elegant simplicity of corporate strategy may convince a general manager that the portfolio allocation approach provides a comprehensive technique for selecting business opportunities, but it does not. For although the portfolio approach offers a powerful tool for choosing from already existing business opportunities, it fails to generate *new* investment options. In fact, because the portfolio approach is built around a political advocacy process, it actually can hinder the identification and evaluation of new opportunities. By its very nature, corporate strategy dissuades business unit managers from taking the personal risk of advocating resources for an investment outside their familiar operating boundaries or beyond their near-term objectives. Without a strong advocate, a proposal for a new investment is rarely given a fair hearing; consequently, it cannot compete for resources, and often dies without a proper evaluation.

Given this political reality, more and more companies are finding that their business horizons are expanding only incrementally, an observation that is reflected in the accelerated maturity of U.S. business in general.

	Level		
Characteristics	Enterprise	Corporate	Business
Fundamental purpose	Creation of significant new value for stakeholders	Optimization of cash flow from portfolio	Accomplishment of product-market positioning
Primary goal	Positioning of the enterprise for change	Achievement of "all-weather" financial performance	Strengthening of competitive position
Objective	Acquisition of resources	Allocation of resources	Utilization of resources
Perspective	Technology and society	Industry sectors and economic environments	Markets/competitors
Accountability	Board and chief executive officer (CEO)	CEO, chief operating officer (COO), group executives	COO, group executives, business unit managers

FIGURE 16-2
The hierarchy of strategy.

THE CEO's ROLE IN ENTERPRISE STRATEGY

Most forward-looking CEOs realize that they need a range of alternatives that includes *new options.* These CEOs probably would echo the statement of one of their colleagues who laments that his "involvement in strategic planning has been reduced to little more than the broad allocation of resources among preselected alternatives." In the 1980s, however, CEOs will need to reassess their roles and contributions to their company's strategic planning processes. As businesses in their portfolio begin to reach their limits—or even begin to contract—they must begin to identify and evaluate opportunities that lie beyond the framework of present operations.

Enterprise strategy encourages the CEO to imaginatively consider fundamental changes in direction. At present there are a few planning tools that can substantially help the CEO generate these alternatives; there is no substitute for a CEO's creative, entrepreneurial thinking—a mode of thinking that contrasts markedly with that imposed by corporate strategy. Whereas corporate strategy is deductive and analytical, enterprise strategy is inductive and intuitive. Whereas corporate strategy adapts to past precedents, enterprise strategy searches for new trends. Figure 16-3 shows the difference between the skills and behaviors necessary for formulating and implementing enterprise strategy and those necessary for corporate strategy.

	Hierarchy of Strategy	
Skills and Behaviors	Enterprise	Corporate
Cognitive process	Intuitive and inductive	Analytical and deductive
Problem solving	Creative	Extrapolative
Thinking environment	Conceptual and nonlinear	Structured and linear
Posture toward conflict	Conflict generator	Conflict resolver
Influence	Charismatic	Persuasive
Political nature	Statesman	Power broker
Leadership style	Entrepreneur	Manager

FIGURE 16-3
Skills and behaviors necessary for enterprise strategy and corporate strategy.

A large diversified company usually has a chief operating officer (COO), group vice presidents, and division managers who generally are accountable for corporate strategy. In essence they are responsible for wringing more growth and/or higher profits from existing businesses. By taking this responsibility, these key subordinates allow the CEO the freedom to seek out new growth businesses. Rather than spending energy refining the resource allocation process for the corporate strategy, the CEO can focus efforts on generating new investment opportunities (see Figure 16-4).

LEADERSHIP

Because the very definition of enterprise strategy implies new corporate directions, implementing this strategy requires a leader who can drive an organization, energize its operations, and inspire its people. This kind of leader must personify the organization's purpose—through sheer personal magnetism, vitality, and force. There is no substitute for the pronounced personal style and strong interpersonal skills that most effective leaders possess. This style and skill reflect the quality of a leader's values, thinking, and character—all necessary to inspire commitment to the strategy and goals of the leader and to secure the allegiances required to make any bold purpose succeed.

Why is the successful implementation of strategy so dependent on an individual leader? Because strategy is a human manifestation. To work,

	Decision Level			
Hierarchy of Strategy	Board of Directors	CEO	Corporate Management	Division Management
Enterprise strategy				
Formulation	Primary			
Assessment		Primary		
Implementation		Primary	Contributory	
Monitoring	Primary			
Corporate strategy				
Formulation	Contributory	Primary		
Assessment	Primary			
Implementation			Primary	
Monitoring	Contributory	Primary		
Business strategy				
Formulation			Contributory	Primary
Assessment		Contributory	Primary	
Implementation				Primary
Monitoring			Primary	

FIGURE 16-4
Strategic decision-making accountability.

it must live and breathe, grow and change. But, at the same time, the leader must ensure that management's general conception of the corporate purpose is the same as his or her own, and that all members of management realize that they are working together to achieve it.

CULTURE

Organizations possess their own culture—a system of shared beliefs and values that the people within the corporation hold. The corporate culture creates and, in turn, is created by the quality of the internal environment; consequently, it conditions the extent of cooperation, the degree of dedication, and the depth of institutionalization of purpose within an organization. The CEO's principal challenge here is to set the tone, pace, and character of this culture—to see that it is conducive to the strategic changes that the CEO is charged with implementing.

To accomplish this, the CEO must recognize the prevailing philosophies, ideologies, and aspirations of the organization's collective membership, then understand how these forces affect any move to change, and finally, develop approaches to managing change within the corporate culture.

How does the CEO manage strategic change within the organization's culture? First, the CEO must constantly survey and evaluate the strong beliefs, policies, and ideologies in the organization, separating those that are beneficial to the creation and implementation of strategic change from those that are detrimental. Those elements that are beneficial can then be used to build for the future.

After analyzing the parts of the corporate value system that are negative, the CEO determines the extent of their effects and plans how they can be eradicated or confined. The net effect of the beneficial and detrimental segments of those value systems determines the organization's readiness and willingness to change.

But there is an important element that acts to drive the corporation's system of beliefs and values: *aspiration.* Whereas value systems determine the readiness and capacity for change, aspirations reflect the direction and potential for significant change. The individual and collective aspirations of an organization's members mirror their desire for the achievement of goals and objectives. Because aspirations determine culture, the CEO is constantly probing, sensing, and directing the people in the organization to help create comprehensive, coherent, and explicit statements of the aspirations of the enterprise. These statements include declarations of the mission, goals, goal priorities, and objectives for the firm. When these aspirations meld with a strong and positive set of values, they earn enthusiastic endorsement by the organization members. This endorsement becomes commitment, the single most important factor in effectively implementing strategic change. Figure 16-5 portrays the role of leadership in shaping and aligning the value systems and aspirations of the culture.

ORGANIZATION

The organization of a company is the instrument through which the aspirations of its members are achieved. Each company builds and commits to plans and then takes actions to fulfill the plans. This is its *strategy.*

In developing an effective organization, the CEO looks to both the aspirations to be achieved and the strategies to be executed.

Organization should be considered in two parts—its structures and its decision flow processes. Structure is the deployment of accountabilities that produces results which enable the entity to achieve its goals and objectives and ultimately its mission. Decision flow processes are the vehicles used to integrate results into coherent patterns for developing, implementing, and controlling decision making. The mission and goals

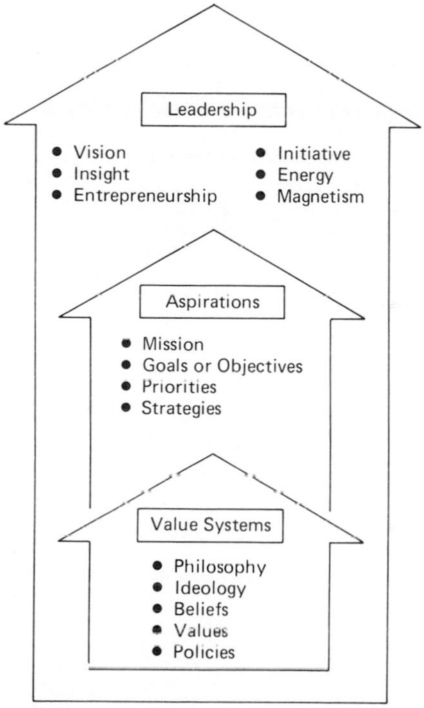

FIGURE 16-5
The role of leadership in shaping culture.

established for the enterprise are the general and specific accountabilities of the CEO. In effect, the creation of an explicit strategic frame of reference defines both the direction of the firm *and* the CEO's job. The goals are subdivided into objectives that are then delegated to the next level of executive management. This level further subdivides and delegates these objectives to their subordinates, and so on, as shown in Figure 16-6.

This technique creates an *integrated cascade of accountabilities* that defines the positions and the structure required to be organized effectively. Furthermore, this structure will produce the results that will enable both the CEO and the enterprise to achieve success in terms of their goals and aspirations.

Decisions are the sole output of management. In large, diverse or

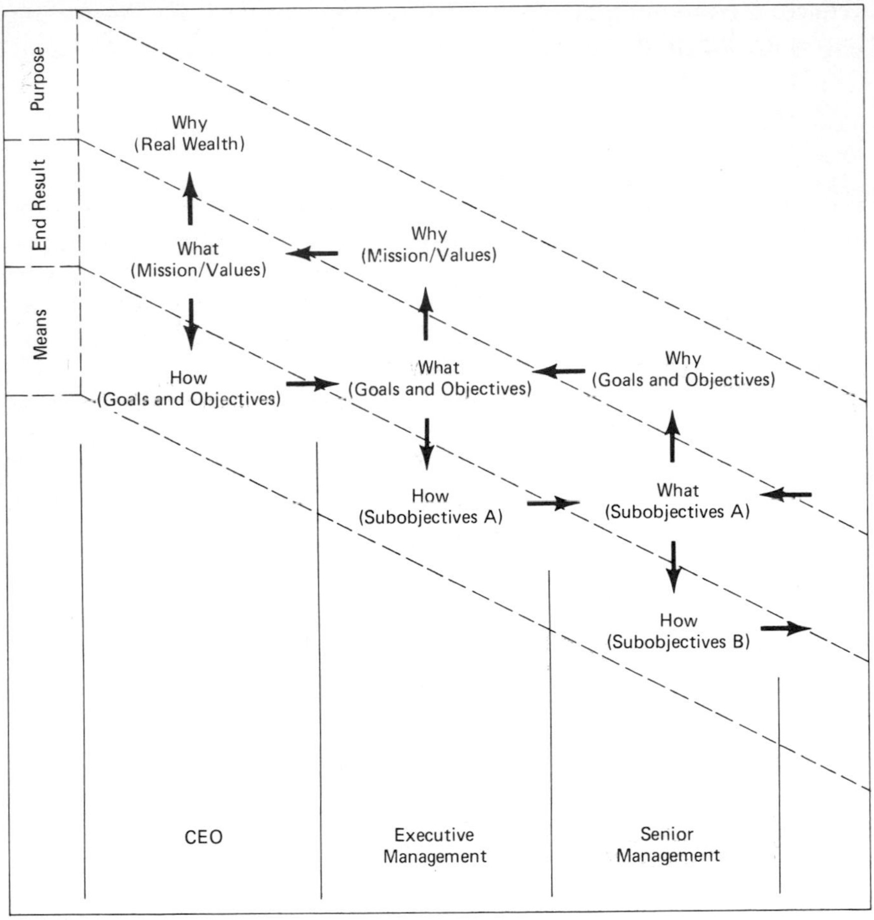

FIGURE 16-6
Organizing through deployment of goals and objectives.

complex organizations, these can rarely be made effectively without the support of others. Furthermore, myriads of decisions are required continually at every level. Decisions can, therefore, be viewed as a series of streams of inputs and outputs in a flow of sequences that overlap.

Systems and people provide the essential information used to make decisions. The delineation of goals, objectives, subobjectives, and so on, throughout the organization set a foundation to create the flow sequences for key decisions. The weighting or priorities set for various goals and objectives energize the decision processes; the deployment of accountabilities clarifies the role that a specific manager plays in the decision.

Once the structure and decision flow sequences are established, getting the right people to operate and enhance them is the next critical concern for the CEO.

PEOPLE

Implementing strategic change requires the confidence, cooperation, and competencies of the organization's technical and managerial people; consequently, the continual development of this resource is a very high priority for the CEO. The CEO is not only accountable for securing and developing the key people needed to implement strategy but also responsible for ensuring that they can help with its reformulation. When carrying out this function, the CEO should make certain that the strategy is consistent with corporate capabilities and resources. By aligning the personal values and aspirations of core management with corporate goals and objectives, the CEO develops the collective strength, focus, and dedication of the organization's people.

To implement strategy, the CEO manages the "live" management processes of measurement, evaluation, motivation, control, and development. These processes encourage and contain individual performance and personal development. Behavior is the outcome of these processes, and the CEO should determine, rather than leave to chance, their net effect upon people.

Specifically, the CEO uses person-job analyses to: (1) relate the capabilities of current people to current job requirements, thereby highlighting immediate needs for improvement; (2) relate the potential of people to projections of current jobs, thereby revealing development needs for a steady state; and (3) relate the potential of people to projections of pro forma jobs, thereby indicating both development and recruitment needs for implementing strategy. These processes help the CEO to use the right people in the right jobs.

COMMUNICATIONS

Through the communication process, the CEO interacts with the various internal and external stakeholders of the corporation—employees, shareholders, suppliers, customers, legislators, advocates, and the public at large. Moreover, the CEO uses communications to formulate, test, and disseminate his or her vision for the future of the enterprise.

In implementing strategic change, the CEO uses communication processes to shape a coherent productive culture, which in turn helps to marshal the commitments of the management and staff to the goals and objectives of the enterprise. Some conflict in organizations is inevitable—and actually desirable. By airing and then resolving issues and critical concerns, the CEO can secure not only this commitment but often dedication as well.

Communication can be formal, informal, or broad-based. Communication can range from one-on-one interpersonal contacts to small group, in-depth discussions to large audience broadcast transmissions. In every situation, the CEO—through actions, behaviors, language (verbal and nonverbal), and technique—communicates what the enterprise stands for. More important, however, by symbolizing and dramatizing the vision of the CEO, these communications help secure the enthusiastic commitment of people and contribute to the successful implementation of strategic change.

REWARDS

To help inspire the sense of shared purpose and achievement necessary to power strategic change, the CEO must manage a program of rewards that blends total remuneration with other, less tangible motivational factors. Even the most enthusiastic and dedicated members of an enterprise ultimately must see a link between the corporation's success and their personal gain.

The mix of remuneration should both reflect and support the direction of the enterprise. Where boldness and entrepreneurial action is called for, the CEO might install a program emphasizing rewards that reinforce the successful development of new business. Similarly, when the enterprise strategy demands an all-weather stabilizing approach to business, the CEO might create a reward package emphasizing return on invested capital.

Figure 16-7 shows how performance management, in particular total remuneration—salary, benefits, bonuses or incentives, perquisites, capital accumulation, and equity participation—is adjusted according to the enterprise's strategic needs. But the CEO and the recipient must also evaluate and judge total remuneration in relationship to the external market opportunities for similar work, the internal equity or fairness of the rewards, and the size of the rewards relative to the risk undertaken and success achieved.

PERFORMANCE MANAGEMENT	STRATEGY HIERARCHY: ENTERPRISE	CORPORATE	BUSINESS
Performance planning	Resource acquisition	Resource allocation	Resource utilization
Performance measurement	▪ ROE ▪ Stock price	▪ ROI ▪ Cash flow	▪ ROA ▪ Operating margins
Performance appraisal	Relative stock market performance	Relative industry performance	Relative product/ market performance
Performance reward	▪ Salary ▪ Bonus ▪ Equity participation	▪ Salary ▪ Bonus ▪ Capital accumulation	▪ Salary ▪ Bonus ▪ Perquisites

FIGURE 16-7
Strategy and reward mix.

Other, less concrete rewards can be just as useful—both as timely recognition for a job well done and as motivation to do even better. The prudent CEO cannot always retain top management merely by raising salaries or paying out bonuses. The CEO must realize that opportunities for personal challenge, growth, excitement, job advancement, and career development are very important to managers—particularly to the younger manager who may desire to exert more impact in the job, not just gather more dollars from it.

SUMMARY

The CEO develops the vision for a company and then—through leadership—shapes the corporate culture that energizes this vision. The culture, in turn, manifests itself in its organization, its people, its system of communications, and its program of rewards. The CEO who understands these relationships—and learns how to use them—will be best positioned to implement strategic change in a company.

Chapter 17
MOTIVATING THE ORGANIZATION TO IMPLEMENT STRATEGY

EDWARD W. MORSE
Director, Hay Associates

KENNETH G. MARTIN
Director, Hay Associates

Achieving a corporate goal requires managers who have the correct blend of ability and motivation. It is not sufficient merely to have people who *can do* the job; it is necessary to have people who *want to do* the job—the way you need it done. Motivating managers, especially those who are expected to implement an organization's complex strategy, must be an ongoing corporate activity. Traditional approaches—while still popular, pervasive, and effective—must be supplemented with newer, more relevant motivational methods.

TRADITIONAL MOTIVATIONAL APPROACHES

The great majority of today's business organizations motivate employees through a traditional system of promised rewards and implied punishments. Both behavioral theory and common sense dictate that managers typically work hardest to achieve cash bonuses and to avoid termination or demotion. The arsenal of traditional motivational techniques that are based upon this familiar concept involve salary programs, performance appraisals, and performance-based incentive programs. Each of these approaches, along with traditional management by objectives (MBO) programs, suggests that specific results are best achieved by clearly outlining realistic goals, and then suitably rewarding those managers who achieve them. The relationship between strategy and implementation, as perceived by many managers, is a direct cause-and-effect relationship. (See Figure 17-1.)

Despite reports of dissatisfaction from some quarters, the utility and effectiveness of these traditional programs should not be underestimated. When properly designed and well implemented, these performance-oriented approaches can motivate managers, especially if the MBO or performance appraisal program involves mutual goal-setting between manager and subordinate. This ensures that objectives are not arbitrary and unrealistic.

It is also important for the managers to feel that their actions will significantly help achieve the agreed-upon goals. For example, an ex-

FIGURE 17-1
The perceived relationship between strategy, organizational motivation, and performance.

ecutive in the housing industry can be expected to respond more energetically when his or her performance is measured against personal goals that are compared to industry performance. When personal performance is measured against goals that are tied to absolute performance—performance that is driven by the cyclicality of the entire industry—the executive is often less responsive.

Another ingredient of traditional motivational programs is the clear, direct, and timely feedback of results. When the scorecard is clearly reviewed at regular intervals, a participant in such a program will be better able to attain or maintain a high level of performance. Of course, the reward itself must be a major motivational factor. To some extent, the desire for the raise, or the promotion, or the bonus will dictate the level of effort put forth. Establishing rewards that motivate appropriately is a complex undertaking—one that must consider such factors as job content, company performance, and industry segment. Although these factors cannot be fully addressed here, it is important to note that, as these rewards increase, they eventually reach a point of diminishing returns. Consequently policy makers must recognize the limitations of such monetary motivational methods; reward levels must be carefully constructed and managed.

These traditional motivation programs are advantageous because they are systematic, consistent, and relatively easily administered. Once developed, they can be applied and adapted to large groups of managers. This consistency suggests an evenhandedness and sense of fair play that is often encouraging to the participants. Further, such programs strive to emphasize objective, quantifiable targets. These targets are clearly achieved or missed, leaving little room for argument or misinterpretation. Results are then matched to varying levels of base or incentive compensation: achieving only partial profit objectives produces only partial payout.

The logic of a well-designed performance-based motivational program is compelling. The rational, quantitative orientation is supported and subscribed to by most senior executives, particularly those who have advanced through the financial, legal, and engineering disciplines. It is consistent with the return on investment (ROI) strategy of emphasizing short-term results. The criteria for success and failure are soon clear, with minimal subjectivity influencing the process.

STRATEGICALLY MANAGED METHODS OF MOTIVATION

Although these traditional motivational programs will probably endure into the foreseeable future, they provide only one aspect of overall organizational motivation. Within an increasingly complex and volatile business environment, these approaches frequently assume that the most important managerial objectives can be specified well in advance. This view encourages a narrow, short-term perspective in those very managers who are expected to contribute most creatively to a firm's future. Furthermore, these traditional programs often are overly reliant on money as the primary motivator, while overlooking other factors that might be truly motivating to many managers.

Finally, these traditional approaches usually do not consider the organization's current culture and climate. Without fully understanding the values and assumptions present in the working environment, it is difficult to motivate an individual or a group.

Figure 17-2 shows that the relationship between strategy and specific motivators goes beyond simple cause and effect, as illustrated in Figure 17-1. First and foremost, a firm's long-standing culture—that combination of attitudes, beliefs, and philosophies that characterizes an organization—influences the implementation of strategy. A further influence is the short-term motivational environment—an environment that is linked to the culture, but related to the temporary swings in the organizational "mood." The short-term motivational environment changes more quickly than the entrenched culture.

Other motivational techniques, such as MBO, or incentive systems, or performance appraisals—all elements of a company's "performance

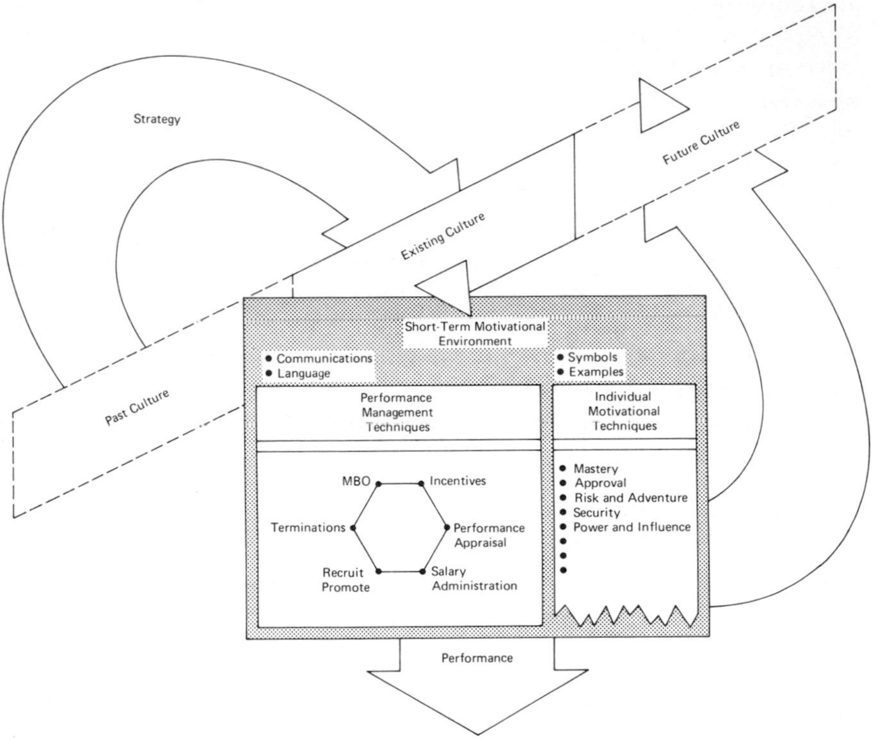

FIGURE 17-2
The complex relationship between strategy and implementation.

management" program—then act to affect strategy implementation. In today's business and social environment understanding how to use these techniques to meet the unique motivational needs of critical individual managers is essential to getting actual performance to meet expectations.

Figure 17-2 also illustrates the impact which strategy, short-term environment, performance management processes, and individual motivational techniques have upon the company's future culture and, eventually, upon the development of future strategies. The remainder of this chapter explores each of these areas.

CULTURE AND MOTIVATION

Savvy managers have long acknowledged that what is called a company's "culture" actually does exist, and they have learned to use it to their advantage. The culture of a company is that set of traditions, those ways of behaving, those shared attitudes and expectations that make each company unique. Culture extends from the more mundane issues—such as office decor, dress, and socializing after hours—to much more significant issues—such as taking or avoiding risks, encouraging or discouraging constructive conflict, resolving issues, debating them to death, or having all decisions made by groups. Among their many effects, these latter aspects of culture influence the boldness of a company's strategy, help determine its ability to respond quickly to opportunities, and affect the caliber of the people it attracts and retains.

Corporate cultures are varied, pervasive, and entrenched. For instance, recently the chairman and chief executive officer (CEO) of a major corporation noted that the corporation's products were becoming commodity-like, and the competition was coming increasingly from firms strong in marketing, not production. Therefore, his previous emphasis on low-cost production and technological innovation would not continue serving his company well. Because the firm had consistently promoted people who had solid track records of cutting costs, improving operating efficiencies, and running a tighter, better-planned, and more controlled organization, the CEO found that he now had no inside candidates to succeed him who would steer the new course. Accordingly, he went outside to find such an executive in a company renowned for its strength in marketing. Less than a year later the outsider resigned, citing stonewalling by those within the company who had been passed over and decrying a "culture that makes the necessary changes impossible to implement."

Beyond the stonewalling, what this executive faced was clearly a clash between cultures: that of his new company and that of the market-driven environment he was used to. His new culture prided itself in running like clockwork (including viewing people as gears and not wanting anyone to disrupt things unduly); its people valued planning things long in advance (a necessity, given the huge investments required by some of their world-scale production facilities) and sticking to these plans. This company's heritage emphasized consistency, continuity, incremental changes adopted only after they were proved to be free of risk, decisions based upon empirically derived quantitative analysis, and a perpetual search for ways of cutting costs. The new executive enters and tries to create a more appropriate culture—one that is more responsive to the marketplace, that values the sudden inspiration which can create or revitalize market segments, that values change-inducing conflict, that encourages risk taking based upon qualitative information as well as quantitative data, that is willing to spend money to build market share rather than continuing to cut costs. Without any motivation to implement a new strategy—except orders from above—the culture reacted to him predictably, with the xenophobia with which any group would treat someone from the outside. The result was his exclusion, his isolation, and eventually his resignation.

SHORT-TERM MOTIVATIONAL ENVIRONMENT

Whereas a company's culture affects strategy implementation over the long haul, the "short-term motivational environment" affects strategy implementation today. The short-term environment reflects the immediate mood of the company's employees and contributes to the way they approach immediate problems—in contrast to the way culture affects the employees' approach to all problems. This short-term environment sometimes can be quite different from the culture, as when a usually slow-moving company gets hit by a crisis and begins making and implementing decisions quickly. In situations like these, after the crisis is past, the short-term environment usually returns to mirror the company culture, just as an elastic band snaps back into position once the force pulling on it eases up. However, unlike the elastic band which always snaps back, the culture—through skillful management of this process—can ultimately be changed into something new by "freezing" the short-term environment. Thus, the short-term environment plays two critical roles in implementing strategy: (1) it affects implementation and performance in the short term and (2) it can help mold and reshape the future culture of the company.

Building this environment involves actions very similar to public relations activities—communications programs, morale-building conferences, visibility of charismatic leaders, use of awards, language, symbols, gestures, and the like. Clearly, such actions alone will not have a lasting impact upon the organization. However, they can *begin* to motivate an entire organization, and this will set the stage for acceptance of subsequent substantive changes in other organizational processes, in structures, or in people. Many worthwhile organizational improvements have foundered for lack of proper cultivation of the short-term environment.

PERFORMANCE MANAGEMENT

As noted earlier, the techniques described as traditional motivators (MBO, performance appraisal, and so on) are widely used by management—frequently with success. Companies benefiting from them fully, however, have taken an additional step to assure that all these motivators are logically, clearly, and firmly linked into what is called an integrated performance management process. These programs ensure that operating budgets do indeed reflect the strategic goals of the company. Similarly, they ensure that all key individuals know exactly what piece of the organization structure they are accountable for and what goals and objectives they must attain this year to stay on plan. The processes for communicating these objectives can be either formal (MBO or performance contracting, for instance) or informal.

Performance management ensures that rewards, such as salary increases and incentive payouts, and sanctions, such as termination, result from measures of good or poor performance. Performance management also links human resources planning into the firm's strategy formulation and performance appraisal processes in order to guide the firm's management development and recruiting efforts.

Taken individually, these are the critical components of a sound, traditional motivational program—one that every company needs to attract, retain, and motivate its managers.

The reality, however, is that these individual components rarely link and mutually reinforce to attain a common set of strategic goals. Budgets often are poorly tied into strategies; or the communication of performance direction and expectations to individuals is inadequate, is not linked to the budget, or is missing altogether; or the performance appraisal process is held in low esteem and, thus, not really used. Such weaknesses detract from the potential motivational impact that these otherwise excellent tools can deliver and, therefore, limit management's ability to successfully implement its plans.

INDIVIDUAL MOTIVATORS

As part of the reward-punishment methodology, traditional motivational approaches assume the existence of similarities among managers, and reinforce those similarities. This orientation continues to serve many organizations well, but it overlooks important ways in which business environments are evolving. One step needed in developing more effective motivational programs is for organizations to recognize the differences among managers.

Abraham Maslow's hierarchy of needs provides a framework for understanding how an individual's motivations may vary at different points along the career path. Maslow suggests that a person's most basic needs are physical; not until they are satisfied will that person be motivated by the next level of needs: security. Once security needs have been fulfilled, the higher-order needs of social acceptance, respect, and personal fulfillment (or self-actualization) will be the most powerful motivators. These need levels are never permanently satisfied; in the face of prolonged stress or a personal crisis an individual may require reinforcement of lower-order needs. An accomplished senior executive, realizing this, may find, for example, that after a dramatic change of corporate philosophy and direction, certain managers require having lower-order needs met (such as security), before they can operate at their full level of self-confidence and drive.

Another valid approach to understanding the differences among managers is to assume that different personality types require varying forms of motivators. While the logic of this is difficult to dispute, there are relatively few managers who are able to make use of this information. There are many formal and informal methods of typing personalities. Informal methods, in the widest practice, are used by those managers who choose to categorize their personnel into two or three discrete groups which may or may not validly correspond to their true motivational needs.

Among the formal methods, David C. McClelland's personality typings are most closely tied to implications for motivation. He describes the need-for-achievement personality, the need-for-affiliation personality, and the need-for-power personality. Clearly, to effectively motivate subordinates, the sophisticated manager will provide different motivators for each of these three personalities.

The most effective managers today are able to recognize and respond to the significant differences among their subordinates, and further recognize that individual needs and motivations can change dramatically during the course of a career. Overreliance on bonuses and incentives of the type typically seen in industry may not fully motivate individual managers in today's world. Although consistency is gained through the traditional approaches, so is a short-term, mechanistic orientation toward attaining results. While this may be motivating to some managers, it frequently demotivates the younger, more creative white collar and professional members of our work force. The challenge, then, for today's manager is to recognize and act on the individual motivational needs of subordinates. It suggests that a flexible understanding of others is most effective in implementing the firm's strategies—one which assumes the *differences* rather than the *similarities* among people. One difficulty with such an approach is that the very rational, quantitative orientation which has contributed to the success of so many senior managers makes this flexibility and sensitivity difficult to develop. This is illustrated by a senior vice president in a major bank who confessed to always feeling surprised when subordinates did not behave in a logical, predictable fashion or respond in the same way despite the vice president's efforts to treat them all consistently.

The irony here is that, while many executives feel comfortable adapting to each customer's needs, these same executives respond rigidly to employees in the belief that consistency aids motivation.

Because managers and their associated motivational needs are complex and ever-changing, static labeling of individual motivators can be dangerous. But even so, there are common motivators that frequently are present in various combinations. The following are examples that illustrate some of the different motivational factors.

Mastery A primary motivator for many successful managers is mastery. Certain individuals are most effective when they are given the opportunity to attain a new skill or to gain control over a new, complex challenge. It is the act of mastering which is most motivating, and the enthusiasm quickly wanes when the goal has been accomplished. Hierarchical advancement and external rewards are secondary to the individual who truly enjoys the challenge of accomplishing a difficult goal.

Approval A different sort of manager thrives and is most effective when motivated through approval. This manager may have much to offer, but requires the support, approval, and affirmation of an authority figure. The risk is that any lack of approval can hamper and constrict the performance of such an individual. An associated motivator is *affiliation*, in which case the employee requires the approval from a peer group.

Risk and Adventure There are those managers who perform optimally when they have the opportunity for risk and adventure. Within an organization this may mean high-visibility positions or running high-risk–high-reward projects. These managers are entrepreneurial and most effective in the start-up phase of projects.

Security This factor continues to play an important role in the motivation of many corporate managers. In order to perform more efficiently, they need to feel that there is little at risk with respect to their careers. More than rapid advancement or rewards, they respond to the implicit assurances of the permanence of their role in the organization.

Power and Influence Another major motivator among the most successful managers is power and influence. Because these managers see salary and bonuses only as a scorecard, they gravitate to positions that allow them to exert control over others. While such individuals are capable of intimidating superiors, a savvy superior will channel their drive for constructive purposes.

Altruism A strong interest in helping others can be a strong motivator for certain managers. More typically seen in those who are further along in their careers, altruism manifests itself in a manager's interest in developing and guiding subordinates. The opportunity to provide a mentor relationship to others not only can be highly motivating to the manager but also can contribute significantly to the well-being of the organization.

The executive who wishes to understand the motivational needs of subordinates through these factors is warned on two fronts. First, almost everyone is motivated in varying degrees by all these factors. There is always some danger in assuming that the primary motivator is the sole motivator. Second, there is compelling evidence that we tend to see others as *we* are, not as *they* are. Managers who understand their own motivators decrease the risk of misunderstanding those of their subordinates. An example is the power-and-influence manager who pushed a technically proficient mastery-and-altruism subordinate to increase her own sphere of influence. The subordinate transferred to another department, saying of his former boss, "She never understood that I'm very happy being an Indian, doing my job very well, and helping others learn about my field."

SHAPING THE FUTURE CULTURE

Ultimately, as Figure 17-2 shows, the interaction of the existing culture, the short-term motivational environment, and various performance management and individual motivational techniques will affect the future culture—and its ability to motivate its members.

The first steps in developing a culture that motivates people are fairly straightforward: acknowledge that culture exists, that it is important, and that by thoughtful actions over sufficiently long periods it can be managed. The first two points have been adequately addressed. The last point, which still might be an open question to some readers, is addressed in the rest of this section on managing cultural change. But those managers who expect to change an entrenched culture must be forewarned: making any significant change in a company's culture requires between three and four years (the amount of time it takes the average American company to turn over 50 percent or more of its managerial population). Changing a culture is major corrective surgery and takes a long time.

As with any surgical procedure, the manager must begin with a diagnosis—in this case an assessment of what type of culture currently exists within the organization. The three most common methods of doing this—in ascending order of accuracy, depth, involvement, time, and of course, cost—are self-assessment, group assessment, and anonymous survey assessment.

Self-Assessment Using some of the tools that will be discussed later in this section to focus the diagnosis, a broad-minded, candid, and involved executive can do a reasonable job assessing his or her own organization's culture. The risk of this approach is that this solo assessment will reflect the individual's limited depth and breadth of contact with the organization. In addition, this type of assessment unavoidably reflects personal biases. While the executive's assessment of the culture at the organization's top might be accurate, it usually is not valid for the rest of the company.

Group Assessment By enlisting the support of others from the outset, group assessment can overcome some of these problems. Having a group of key managers undertake the diagnosis serves to broaden awareness of what the culture is like at multiple levels of the organization, and also broadens the range of alternative solutions available for changing the culture. However, the biggest advantage of group assessment is that the process predisposes those who participate to become advocates of the needed changes rather than following the more normal path of either overtly or covertly fighting changes.

The biggest disadvantage of group assessment is that it still rests upon a perception of the organization that is developed near the very top. Those few people likely to participate in the assessment probably do not understand the company's culture deep within the organization or in its various divisions, geographic locations, and so on. Furthermore, controlling a group assessment can be tricky. Not only must the leader of the session avoid taking sides but he or she also must be careful to ensure that everybody is using words the same way. To one person, having a "conservative" culture connotes something desirable (judicial, weighing the facts before moving, not inclined to follow fads recklessly, and so on), whereas to another it connotes something outmoded (stodgy, old-fashioned, risk-averse).

Anonymous Surveys We have found that anonymous surveys overcome most of these problems, albeit at some cost to the organization and some raised expectations among employees. (The adage "Don't ask for advice unless you're prepared to take it" holds true here.) A broad-based survey penetrates into all levels of the organization and can allow management to identify the culture in every part of the company, thus providing insights impossible to obtain from the pyramid's peak. In addition, a survey usually provides a common language and a common framework for tackling the issues it turns up.

Another advantage is that the analysis of results from such a survey ensures that management commits sufficient time to come to grips with the existing culture and the problems that it poses for implementing tomorrow's strategy. Finally, such surveys are replicable, thus giving management the means to measure progress in changing the company's culture.

Critical Dimensions of Culture

The survey we are most familiar with is semicustomized to each company and measures nine or ten critical dimensions of the company's culture. The survey results indicate where the organization in question falls on these dimensions relative to several hundred other companies covered by the same survey. This survey examines:

- *Clarity of Direction.* How well the company's goals and plans for achieving them are known, understood, and found to be motivating throughout the organization.
- *Decision-Making Structure and Processes.* Whether the culture is decision-oriented or decision-avoidant and whether decisions are made on the basis of sound information or "seat of the pants" intuition.
- *Management Style.* Whether too little or too much participation in making decisions exists at each level of the company.
- *Integration of Effort.* Whether teamwork, sharing, and smooth meshing of activity—or the opposite—accurately describe the culture.
- *Performance Orientation.* Whether people feel accountable for end results and whether rewards are related to performance or not.
- *Compensation.* Whether it is equitable, fairly administered, and motivational, or not.
- *Human Resources Development.* How much this characterizes the culture.
- *Organizational Vitality.* That drive to perform—that sense of urgency and desire to be a winner—which some organizations have and others do not.
- *Risk Taking.* Whether it is encouraged or punished; whether employees are socialized by their company's culture to *not make* any mistakes (as many banks do) or to *learn from* their mistakes. (As one manager put

it, "With me you'll never get into trouble over anything you try, even if it fails, provided you learn from your failure. It's when you *don't* try, when you *don't* take action that you and I will have problems.")

- *Competitive Image.* Whether the company views itself as faster, sharper, and better than the competition, or vice versa. What culture helps make the leader in the industry the leader? What cultural attributes hinder us?

Determining the Desired Culture

The next step in the process is to determine what kind of culture and what kinds of subcultures will best support the company's strategy. The language used to assess the current culture should be the same as that used to describe the desired culture. The temptation is to develop a desired culture which is so close to a business school archetype that it is untenable. The difficult part, at this point, is to be realistic and tough-minded. Should all parts of the company be run in a participatory manner? Should high vitality characterize all business units—or just some? Should pay and performance be linked in the same manner for all groups in the company? In most organizations today, determining the desired culture is best accomplished by the senior executive group. We suspect that, in the future, this will become an area of involvement for strategic planners who are concerned with getting their plans implemented.

Changing the Culture

Once the desired culture is determined, the executive group and all relevant line and staff managers can meet to work out what changes in the organization are required to implement and support it. Using all the motivational tools presented previously is essential to building the new culture: recruiting and terminations, strategic planning, rewards, internal public relations, and so on. It is here, in the shaping of the long-term culture, that the techniques used to develop the short-term motivational environment can be used to reposition attitudes, self-perceptions, and morale permanently.

To make sure that the change which occurs in the company's culture is permanent, management must keep up continual pressure to change—usually over three to four years. During this time it is easy to lose track of where things stand or to lose faith in the effort. In our experience, combating both is best done through periodic *culture review* sessions (semiannually is preferred) devoted entirely to the issues, progress, and initiatives needed to keep the culture change on track.

One last point: firms that have embarked on this process, once the initial effort is over (and the initial effort can be significant), discover that the process is never-ending. The need to constantly monitor the culture, to understand how it facilitates or inhibits implementation of strategies, and to fine-tune it never stops entirely. For most companies the semiannual culture review sessions become regular events that closely follow the strategic planning process. In fact, they frequently become more broadly based than just a culture review and end up more as strategic organizational planning sessions than as anything else. The end result of this is a culture which will actively support implementing management's strategies, not impede it. Motivating the organization to implement strategy requires not only this supportive culture but also the alignment of the other motivational processes discussed here—the short-term environment, the linkage of traditional motivational techniques into a performance management process, and a focus on the unique motivational needs of key individuals within the organization. This alignment of individual motivational techniques through cultural motivational systems allows executives to turn from an era strong in generating strategic plans toward the 1980s, an era strong, it is hoped, in the strategic management of the entire enterprise.

Chapter 18
ACQUISITION STRATEGY

EDWARD H. SCHWALLIE
Senior Vice President, Booz • Allen & Hamilton, Inc.;
President, Booz • Allen's Acquisition Services

ALEXANDER R. OLIVER
Vice President, Booz • Allen & Hamilton, Inc.

MICHAEL G. ALLEN
President, Michael G. Allen Company

STRATEGIC ACQUISITION: A PHENOMENON IN OUR TIME

The purchase of a business tends to be unlike any other purchase in the economy. The cost to purchasers is almost always substantially higher than the list or market price of the stock. Purchasers are willing to pay this premium because they have reason to believe that they are really getting a bargain in terms of what they hope to do with the newly purchased business in the context of their existing businesses.

In more formal terms, the purchaser—usually a corporation substantial enough to buy an operating business or even the entire company from another corporation—becomes an acquirer.

The mere intention to purchase another business, rumored or real, tends to raise the market price of the target company. But it also tends to raise the pitch of activity in both companies, as management and other personnel strive to adjust the potential purchase to their own careers, and as suppliers, customers, and affected communities argue the pros and cons of the presumed acquisition.

When the intended purchase is resisted—the so-called hostile tender offer—ranks of lawyers, public relations people, chambers of commerce, and assorted interest groups enter the fray. But even a so-called friendly tender offer, the usual case, incites competition to join in, sometimes invited by the potential acquiree, sometimes self-invited.

Mergers and acquisitions thus become a kind of industry in its own right, a substantial realm of management attention, corporate expense, and socioeconomic considerations affecting entire geographic areas.

Questions of antitrust are often raised. In the case of an unfriendly tender offer, the target company may strive to acquire new businesses of its own, to make the potential acquirer a likely candidate for government antitrust action—a condition often motivating the Securities and Exchange Commission to veto the proposed acquisition.

Other substantial acquisition factors include the rights of shareholders of both the acquiring and the acquired companies, the role of the board of directors of both companies, and larger considerations that tend to range from the state of the physical environment to the working environment of the now bigger company: competition, innovation, productivity, and government regulation, among others.

These questions tend to roughen the road to acquisition and may well carry over once the new purchase is within the corporate fold.

The arguments for and against a given acquisition—and sometimes against acquisition per se—raise the cosmic question of the true nature of enterprise. Even if it is "cheaper to buy than to build," can a society—apart from its economy—continue to gain real benefits from the growing merger-and-acquisition phenomenon? Is there a tendency to deal more and more in paperwork entrepreneurialism than in the bricks and mortar to which the nation owes its industrial might?

Other observers see the acquisition path as adding to the survivability and strength of worthwhile enterprises, nourishing them with both resources and wisdom, creating synergistic activities of all kinds to the benefit of all concerned—those who sell as well as those who buy.

The merger and acquisition boom of our times must also be viewed from the point of view of the selling company—the acquiree, an entire company, or a part of it:

- High interest rates have so inflated the cost of carrying inventories as well as other debt that the ultimate returns are no longer perceived as being worthwhile, for example, Borden's sell-off of twelve operations, including Mystik Tape, Sacramento Tomato Juice, phosphates, sugar, and housewares.

- Desirable businesses are for sale because the parent company can no longer fund their growth (one estimate terms 70 percent of all acquired businesses successful, even prospering), for example, Esmark's sale of Vickers Energy to Mobil and others.
- Some companies say that they are selling businesses because Wall Street, not knowing how to analyze conglomerates, no longer favors them. This was Cooper Industries' stated reason for selling its Airmotive Division.

Whatever the stated reasons, the selling company utilizes the resulting cash—generally preferred to stocks, notes, and other paper—to fund the principal, higher-yielding businesses it retains, hoping that the divestiture will also give it the proverbial "leaner, cleaner, meaner" image on Wall Street.

THE STRATEGIC ENVIRONMENT: THE FERVOR TO ACQUIRE

For all the foregoing, the purport of this chapter is to assume that management has weighed and indeed confronted those of the above factors that may be relevant, that it has an acquisition in mind and, presumably, a good idea how it intends to use this new property for the greater good of management's own employer, the acquiring company that management serves.

Without question, a sizable percentage of American management has reached precisely that conclusion. Acquisition activity is more intense in the United States than at any time since the merger boom of the 1960s. The number of completed acquisitions purchased for more than $750,000 (or 5 percent of the acquired firm) has increased from fewer than 1000 in the mid-1970s to more than 1400 in 1979.

The pace has accelerated even faster in the first eighteen months of the 1980s. In 1980 about 100 acquisition proposals, each exceeding $100 million, were put forth; in the first quarter of 1981 the total value of forty recent bids—each exceeding $100 million—amounted to $19.5 billion, a sum larger than all publicly announced merger and acquisition transactions completed in 1975.

Another relatively new phenomenon is the trend toward larger acquisitions. Since the mid-1970s the number of transactions over $200 million has climbed steadily—from about five in 1976 to thirty-four in 1980 (see Figure 18-1).

Furthermore, the average real size of all mergers and acquisitions has more than tripled in the 1970s, from $15 million to almost $47 million.

The nature of the company combinations has also changed. Always commonplace have been mergers and acquisitions in such fragmented industries as financial services, retailing, and general services. But these have been joined for the first time by such new types of industries as natural resources, large technology-based companies, and foreign-based multinationals.

Oil companies have been particularly large acquirers of natural resource and technology companies, among others. Exxon's Exxon Enterprises, in fact, amounts to a huge venture capital business in its own right. Mobil is now trying to make a reborn winner out of Montgomery Ward. Atlantic Richfield bought Anaconda Copper, and other large oil companies have bought smaller oil companies.

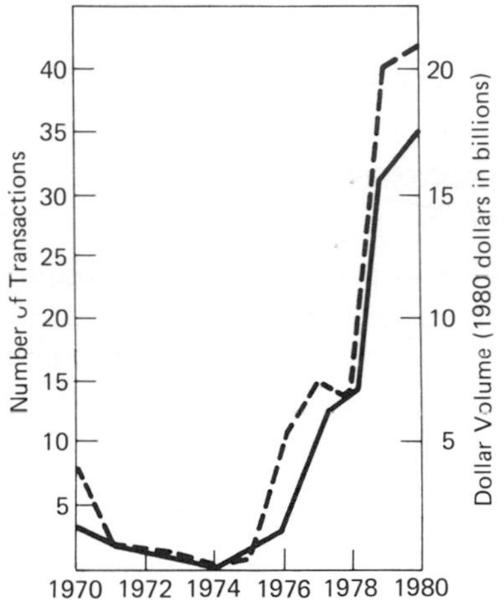

FIGURE 18-1
Mergers and acquisitions over $200 million, completed transactions. (*Mergers and Acquisitions: The Journal of Corporate Venture, 1970–1979.*)

But the biggest acquisition of all time—a record that may not last, given the merger and acquisition fervor of the age—is DuPont's 1981 acquisition of Conoco for $7.5 billion. Previously such large companies had been considered immune from takeover, friendly or otherwise, because of the money required to buy them. The resulting perception: all companies except the fifteen or so largest companies are susceptible to acquisition; Conoco, well within that group and in fact slightly larger than DuPont in terms of revenues, is presumably the exception that proves the rule.

Acquired companies represent such industries as electronics, computer services, cable television, and medical diagnosis. And, as noted above, foreign-based multinationals have increased their rate of acquisition in the United States, among them NV Phillips Gloeilampenfabrieken, Siemens AG, Royal Dutch/Shell Group of Companies, Brascan Ltd., British American Tobacco Company, and Ciba-Geigy AG.

Economic conditions have affected the activity in different ways at different times. In the late 1960s and early 1970s low inflation and interest rates, nourished by strong economic growth, encouraged new highs in mergers and acquisitions for the time.

But today's record-setting level is fueled by opposite economic conditions. High inflation and high interest rates (see Figure 18-2) have increased the willingness to sell—therefore the opportunity to buy—an environment further fueled by cash-rich companies confronting cash-hungry companies eager to grow leaner but richer, as noted.

ACCENT ON CASH

In 1969 about 57 percent of acquisitions were paid for in stock, 32 percent in cash, and the remainder in a combination of the two.

But in 1979 the situation had reversed itself: about 54 percent of acquisitions were paid for in cash, 26 percent in stock, and 20 percent in combined stock and cash.

The shift to cash bids is likely to remain the dominant approach throughout the 1980s. High inflation and interest rates are fueling the trend. These have compressed price/earnings (P/E) ratios, making stock a less attractive payment vehicle. At the same time, high inflation, eroding the purchase power of cash and liquid assets, encourages cash-heavy companies to divest themselves of these deteriorating assets in favor of something "real," namely, an operating business with tangible assets, often undervalued by the stock market.

Yet another cash purchase incentive is the frequent requirement for foreign firms to use the cash approach in acquiring U.S. assets.

The overall perception of cash-holding potential acquirers is that cash has *more* value today than it *will* have tomorrow, but what cash will buy has *less* value today than it *can* have tomorrow. Equally to the point is the idea that someone else's business may well be the biggest bargain the economy can offer, depending on the strategic planning that motivates both the purchase and its utilization.

The rising use of cash to acquire businesses has sparked yet another trend: the rising premium the buyer must pay over actual stock market value, here defined as the dollar amount higher than the stock value five days prior to the announcement of the acquisition.

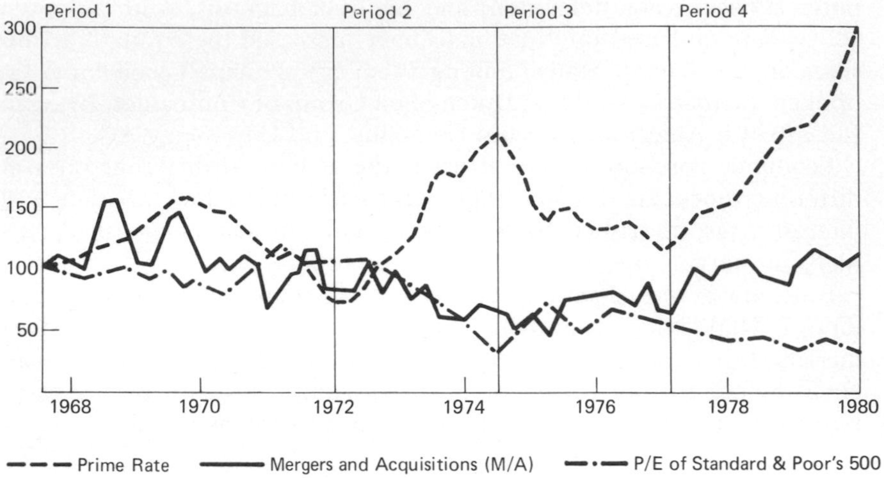

Period 1
1967–1972

Economic Scenario
- High Economic Growth
- Low Inflation
- Low Interest Rates
- P/E and P/E Spreads Are High
- Corporate Solvency Declining

Resulting M/A Activity
- M/A at Record Levels
- Mergers/Acquisitions Use P/E Leverage of Stock
- Acquisition Emphasis Is on Diversification and Growth Companies

Period 2
1972–1974

Economic Scenario
- Economic Crisis
- Inflation Surge
- High Interest Rates
- P/E and P/E Spreads Collapse
- Corporate Solvency Crisis

Resulting M/A Activity
- Collapse of M/A Boom
- Decline in Using Stock Acquisitions
- Reevaluation of Past M/A Strategies and Targets
- Disposition Activity Increases

Period 3
1974–1977

Economic Scenario
- Economic Recovery
- Continued High Inflation
- Continued High Interest Rates
- P/E and P/E Spreads Stay Depressed
- Corporate Solvency Recovery
- U.S. Dollar Declines

Resulting M/A Activity
- M/A Activity Recovers
- Cash Is Major Method of Payment
- Oil Companies and Large Companies Initiate Giant M/A Era
- Foreign M/As in the United States Surge

Period 4
1977–1980

Economic Scenario
- Economic Cycle Matures
- Inflation Surge
- Interest Rates Peak
- P/E and P/E Spreads Decline
- Corporate Solvency
- Crisis for Some
- Solvency Spread Increases

Resulting M/A Activity
- M/A Activity Approaches Record Levels
- Cash Remains Major Method of Payment
- Acquisition of Real, Inflation-Protected and Undervalued Assets Emphasis
- New Target Industries
- Foreign M/As in the United States Continue to Increase

FIGURE 18-2
Four distinct acquisitions periods.

But even rumors of the acquisition—days, weeks, and months before the announcement—tend to raise the market price of the stock of the prospective acquisition.

Apart from the seller's desire for cash, the seller's tax penalty for a cash sale is more immediate than for a stock transaction. An interest in compensating for the tax expense also tends to raise the premium.

Overall, the premiums paid for acquired businesses have risen from an average 33 percent in the early 1970s to 50 percent in 1974, dipping to about 40 percent in 1976, and then rising to slightly more than 50 percent at the end of the decade. Figure 18-3 shows the trend for publicly announced transactions of more than 10 percent of an acquired company.

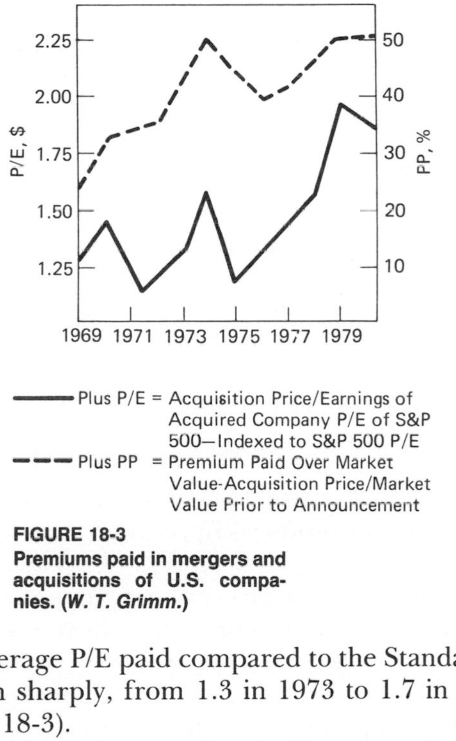

FIGURE 18-3
Premiums paid in mergers and acquisitions of U.S. companies. (*W. T. Grimm.*)

The ratio of average P/E paid compared to the Standard & Poor's 500 P/E has also risen sharply, from 1.3 in 1973 to 1.7 in 1978 and 1.9 in 1980 (see Figure 18-3).

For giant acquisitions, the premium paid over market value has often been extremely high offers difficult for management and/or stockholders to refuse even in the face of any inclination to do so.

Among high-premium acquisitions are DuPont's acquisition of Conoco, Raytheon's of Beech Aircraft, McGraw-Edison's of Studebaker-Worthington, and Cooper Industries' of Gardner-Denver.

Potential acquirers often compete vigorously for desirable acquisitions—most notably during the frantic three-way race among Seagram, Mobil, and DuPont for Conoco—another factor tending to bid up the premium price. Such contested bids undoubtedly pushed up the price of Fairchild Industries, Babcock & Wilcox, Crouse-Hinds, Bodcaw, General Crude Oil, and Pullman, among others.

In addition to the actual premiums paid, both the acquirer and the acquiree often sustain huge outlays for legal and other fees over the period leading up to the acquisition, even if the bid actually fails or loses to another.

One survey of 1148 interfirm tender offers during the 1956–1979 period shows some 80 percent to have been partly or entirely successful. But the figure mounts to 90 percent if only cash tender offers are considered. The survey was published in the summer 1980 issue of *Mergers & Acquisitions*.

Thus the race to convert depreciating cash reserves and borrowing capacity into healthy business assets and strong U.S. business positions has led to intense acquisition activity despite ever higher cash premiums.

JUSTIFYING ACQUISITIONS

All acquisition-oriented strategic planning must focus on and lead to justification of the acquisition—especially in terms of the 50 to 100 percent premium over market value. This immediately presents the challenge to achieve a "performance premium" that will exceed the market's own expectations as reflected in the market price of the stock.

Stock market analysts and indeed many stock purchasers, institutional and individual, tend to have superb access to company information in the context of up-to-date economic information. Many have correctly foretold the intentions of acquiring management, before and after the fact—and their consensus produces the market value of the stock at any given moment.

But they cannot know or foresee everything in the management mind, nor can they foresee the degree of management success in matching acquisition strategy to acquisition performance—as part of total company performance.

The management imperative, in fact, is to outperform the market-expectation consensus. Otherwise the acquisition will be perceived to have been unjustified—an error in judgment that will itself depress the market value of the acquiring company.

The justification pressure thus becomes considerable, especially from the American perspective, which looks for faster results than do investors in other major nations, notably Japan.

Here management's strategic planning comes into play: to improve the acquired company's performance, probably through changes in its operation that Wall Street may not have foreseen and thus accounted for in the preacquisition stock price of the acquired company.

Improved strategic planning is the one overall way to upgrade the performance of the acquisition. Such improved strategy can lower the risk of achieving this superior performance, at the same time creating a more favorable risk-return balance by avoiding deterioration in earnings quality and stock market valuation.

Corporate management can accomplish all this risk moderation only by designing its acquisition strategy with great care and precision. Of all great corporate decisions, the acquisition decision must be based on thoroughgoing analysis, preparation, discussion, and—above all—appreciation of the numerous factors governing the choice, as partly noted earlier. This is no place for impulsive buying, whatever the dominant corporate or management style.

CHOICE OF ACQUISITION STRATEGIES

No generalization can precisely fit the unique situation of the acquiring company in its own specific industry and competitive situation. Nevertheless, eight generic options or "plays" tend to span the spectrum of acquisition strategies that can improve overall corporate performance by means of the acquisition—even though the acquired business per se may or may not be performing better than it did in preacquisition times. This must depend upon how much the acquisition strategy is business-based and/or corporate-based, that is, how well management can improve its actual operating performance and/or how well management can help it improve overall corporate performance, through financial performance as well as operating performance.

Figure 18-4 shows how the eight generic options are applied to change the performance of the acquisition candidate in order to improve overall corporate performance.

Business Strategy-Based Approaches

These involve acquiring a single, fairly homogeneous business and enhancing its performance through a change in business strategy. They are traditional acquisition approaches and require little explanation. Nonetheless, they are not always executed effectively. Often the degree of synergy, or world-scale advantage, is overestimated in the first two. In the third, incorrectly assessed market forces can result in overvaluing an emerging growth market or technology. In the fourth case, the acquisitor may not understand the prospects of companies enough to jus-

Acquisition "Play"	Strategy to Achieve Performance Premium
Business-strategy based	
1. Acquire synergistic product-market niche position	Achieve scale economies of distribution, production, or technology.
2. Acquire position in key international markets	Achieve scale economies for global production and technology investments.
3. Acquire a "beachhead" in an emerging high-growth market	Anticipate high-leverage business growth equations by identifying market forcing functions.
4. Acquire a portfolio of minority investments	Apply pressure for improved short-term earnings and sell stock. Gain improved information on future potential.
Corporate-strategy based	
5. Acquire a company with underutilized financial strength	Use borrowing capacity or other financial strengths, e.g., underutilized tax loss carry-forwards or foreign tax credits to achieve an immediate performance premium.
6. Acquire an underskilled company in a related industry	Apply superior marketing, technology, or production expertise to enhance the competitive position and performance of the acquisition candidate.
7. Acquire an underexploited physical asset	Anticipate shortages and price increases in the physical asset's value. Invest to exploit the resource using distribution capacity.
8. Acquire an undervalued corporate portfolio	Apply more aggressive portfolio management to restructure resource allocation and upgrade results.

FIGURE 18-4
Strategic approaches to acquisition.

tify investing in either a minority or a majority basis. Thus premiums paid may turn out to be too high to justify.

- *Acquire a synergistic product-market niche position.* The acquired company benefits from newly gained access to the acquisitor's technology, production capacity, and distribution channels. Such direct economies of scale result in an immediate performance premium in costs, sales volume, market share—depending on accurate product-market segmentation to pinpoint real versus illusory synergy.
- *Acquire a position in a key international market.* A variation of the first approach, this can produce economies of scale in businesses with high fixed costs, for example, production investment applicable and amortizable on a global scale to a degree that overcomes increased marketing-distribution overhead (which can negate the economy-of-scale gains). Many multinational companies have encountered this problem. Postac-

quisition increases in overhead and management complexity can well outweigh any benefits of market scale.

- *Acquire a "beachhead" in an emerging high-growth market or technology.* This quintessential venture capital approach demands superior anticipation of high-leverage business growth and/or emerging technology opportunities. Satellite networking, for example, is a rapid-growth business because it provides an increasing portion of cable television programming, which in itself is a new kind of household service, an area in which consumers are spending a rising percentage of disposable income. Superior market research and analysis beyond that publicly available is an essential sine qua non of this acquisition strategy.
- *Acquire a portfolio of minority investments.* In recent years cash-rich companies—among them Teledyne, Siemens, American Financial Corporation, and Gulf & Western—have utilized this approach effectively, buying share positions of 20 to 30 percent in companies at attractive prices relative to book value. These and other companies have frequently liquidated such positions at a profit or increased them to majority ownership without incurring excessive premiums.
- *Corporate strategy-based approach.* Large acquisitions, the magnitude of those of the 1980s, tend to involve companies with a mix of businesses, often quite dissimilar from those of the acquisitor. This makes product-market synergy difficult to justify. In these instances, acquisitor management must seek a performance premium through approaches based on corporate- and finance-based strategy.

Approximately 75 percent of the giant acquisitions of 1981 were based on one of the four corporate strategy-based approaches—predominantly acquisitions of companies with underexploited physical assets or undervalued corporate portfolios.

- *Acquire a company with underutilized financial strength.* Financial synergy emerges from combining companies with complementary financial characteristics that can yield a strong performance premium and thus justify a part of the price premium paid for an acquisition. But management must consider financial synergy in the context of strategic potential, too, because weakness in this factor can undermine the financial synergy as well. Many acquisitions of the late 1960s resulted in costly divestitures in the 1970s through poor assessment of the basic business acquired, apart from their financial "plays."

Financial synergy opportunities include:

a. The acquisitor has substantial foreign tax credits and a very low domestic tax base to leverage the performance of a profitable domestic acquisition.

b. The acquisitor has a large domestic tax liability it can reduce by purchasing a business with substantial credits, such as RCA achieved through its purchase of CIT Financial Corporation, an equipment-leasing business.

c. The acquisitor is cash-rich, buys a cash-hungry growth company, and redeploys shareowners' funds without immediate taxation effects—a benefit anticipated in Westinghouse Electric Corporation's purchase of Teleprompter Corporation.

▪ *Acquire an underskilled company in a related industry.* The acquisitor has skills it can put to use in the acquired company in a field closely related or attuned to that of the acquisitor. A dramatic recent example of this approach is Philip Morris's acquisition of the Miller Brewing Company. Philip Morris revamped the brewing company's strategy by investing heavily in consumer marketing—as if the beer were a packaged good as well as a beer—and amazed the brewing industry with Miller's rise to a number 2 position. Philip Morris also distributed Miller's production capacity to new locations to exploit the increased market share.

▪ *Acquire a company with underexploited physical assets.* Inflation has multiplied the hidden value of North American energy reserves and metals. Such unexploited assets have often been ignored or undervalued by the stock market, but they have become major attractions to acquiring corporations—most notably DuPont's purchase of Conoco and its substantial energy reserves. Other physical asset-based acquisitions include the purchase by Sun Company, Mobil Corporation, and Freeport Minerals of oil and gas properties of Seagram, Esmark, and McMoRan, respectively. Acquisition proposals by four oil companies totaled more than $8 billion in March 1981 alone: Socal to Amax, Seagram to St. Joe Minerals (acquired by Fluor), Sohio to Kennecott, and Gulf Oil to Kemmerer.

▪ *Acquire an undervalued corporate portfolio.* The undervalued portfolio represents one of the newer, more sophisticated approaches to achieving a corporate performance premium justifying the acquisition of the portfolio. The popularity of this approach is a factor of high interest rates and investor emphasis on the quality of earnings. In the current investment climate, the market valuation of multibusiness companies is perhaps inordinately depressed, both by the weaker parts of their corporate portfolios and by stock analysts' sometimes confessed inability to understand the workings of such complex enterprises—where each individual business has its own dynamics and economics but where the operating and financial data are generally subsumed in the parent company's overall information and reports. The corporate challenge in acquiring an undervalued corporate portfolio resides in identifying the portfolio in the first place, and then identifying the reasons for the undervaluation. These tend to be due to poor performance of specific business units and/or the inability of the market to appreciate the real value of the portfolio components.

The acquisitor can realize the desired performance premium by a combination of aggressive portfolio management and the reallocation of resources after acquisition.

THE UNDERVALUED CORPORATE PORTFOLIO APPROACH

Many U.S. companies with multiple businesses fail to eliminate or withdraw from losers and redeploy their resources aggressively to their stronger businesses, those with greater economic potential. This corporate indecisiveness tends to preserve weak businesses that dilute overall company performance, drain managerial energy, and divert valuable resources from potential winners to these perennial losers. The resulting watered-down corporate performance leads to a lower stock market valuation because investors pay greater attention to downside risks than to upside potential, especially in the current economic environment, in which low-risk investment vehicles—such as money funds, U.S. Treasury bills, and commercial paper—offer highly attractive returns.

This situation represents a major acquisition opportunity to identify an "undermanaged" corporate portfolio, acquire it, and apply sound strategic analysis and managerial expertise to restructure the portfolio.

These opportunities, according to Booz • Allen & Hamilton, Inc., the management consulting firm, are more numerous than many may realize. The firm cites five recent examples of acquisitors seizing the initiative to announce or launch major restructuring efforts:

- Esmark, Inc. is pursuing a dramatic restructuring strategy by selling its oil and gas businesses, spinning-off or liquidating its Swift operations, and concentrating the recaptured resources on its consumer products businesses. Result: a rapid surge in Esmark's market value.
- SCM Corporation, the recent target of a proxy fight by dissident shareholders proposing to restructure the company's portfolio of business to increase shareholder returns, managed to reach an agreement resolving the issue.
- Gould, Inc., is pursuing a major restructuring of its entire portfolio.
- Richardson-Merrell has initiated a major design of its portfolio by selling its ethical pharmaceutical business to Dow Chemical. The goal: to redeploy the funds from that sale into more attractive areas.
- GAF Corporation announced that it will jettison nearly half its business operations, including copiers, films used in printing, graphic arts equipment, paper and millboard, vinyl siding, and electronic games.

Other restructuring strategies—by Borden, RCA Corporation, Allegheny Ludlum Industries, and Zale Corporation—demonstrate the dramatic impact such actions can exert on corporate performance.

One approach developed by Booz • Allen & Hamilton to test and identify undervalued corporate portfolios involves grouping the target company's business into four categories (see Figure 18-5). The following are some aspects of this approach.

Core Businesses

These tend to represent 25 to 60 percent of assets in a diversified enterprise. If these components are strong, profitability will be high and generally represent a higher fraction of the company's total earnings. Strategically, this business core is the heart of the company. It has excellent functional strengths on which to build: brand franchises, distribution reach, raw materials sources, and so on. Market demand and competitive position, however, may vary from stable to threatened, depending on the industry. The cash generated by a successful business core is often used in diversification efforts—both successfully and unsuccessfully.

Successful Diversifications

These are typically the stars of the company's portfolio. Competitive positions are strong in attractive, inflation-protected growth markets. While continuing to grow, they represent a significant proportion of sales at attractive levels of profitability.

Business profile	Assets, %	Earnings, %	Strategic profile
Core business	30	50	Stable demand; strong profitability and cash flow Excellent functional strengths
Successful diversifications	30	40	Strong growth; competitive leadership; inflation-protected
Unsuccessful diversifications	40	−10	Weak competitive position in good markets
Nonoperating investments		20	Carried below replacement costs
Total	100	100	

FIGURE 18-5
Analyzing an undervalued portfolio: Desirable case.

BUSINESS	A	B	C	D	E	F	G	H	I	AVERAGE
	Candidate Earnings Profiles									
Core business										
Percent of assets	37	34	27	23	16	32	38	30	9	27
Percent of income	37	36	33	21	18	44	56	30	28	34
Successful diversifications										
Percent of assets	30	33	31	50	23	27	37	25	49	34
Percent of income	39	40	38	66	35	31	41	24	52	41
Unsuccessful diversifications										
Percent of assets	33	23	42	27	61	41	21	47	42	39
Percent of income	24	14	28	NA	46	26	2	47	22	26
Book value ($ millions)	395	280	622	749	249	114	415	523	414	451
Market value/ book value ratio	1.01	0.99	0.90	0.87	0.70	0.53	0.91	0.82	0.72	0.83
Price/earnings ratio	8.3	4.0	6.0	7.0	3.9	4.1	8.2	5.9	6.3	6.0

FIGURE 18-6
Selected company profiles.

Unsuccessful Diversifications

The company with an undervalued corporate portfolio typically records a sizable proportion of its assets in its unsuccessful diversifications. Profitability is low, declining, or negative—a result of weak competitive positions in markets in which potential has probably been overestimated. These businesses, of course, dilute overall profitability.

Nonoperating Investments

These may be valuable stock investments or physical assets that have been carried below realizable market value and represent a significant proportion of potential earnings.

A corporation with such a business profile may tend to carry a stock market valuation well below the sum of its parts because investors are fearful of the risks associated with its weaker businesses in the current investment climate.

Nonetheless, the company may be likely to have a value well in excess of this valuation, given its core business, successful diversifications, and nonoperating investments. This would make it an attractive acquisition opportunity.

The acquisitor's incoming management could well achieve the performance premium needed to justify the acquisition through portfolio restructuring—liquidating, harvesting, or divesting unsuccessful diversifications and redeploying the resources thus produced to rejuvenate the company's core business and successful diversification.

Applying this analyzing and screening technique to acquisition candidates eliminates those that do not appear to have undervalued corporate portfolios. Unlike conventional acquisition-screening approaches, this one emphasizes market valuation and portfolio analysis rather than overall financial results. Greater emphasis is placed on the company's diversity and on an analysis of the business profile. Publicly available data tend to be insufficiently detailed; special research is typically required to unearth this needed detail.

The results of one such screen to identify undervalued portfolios are shown in Figure 18-6, in which nine acquisition candidates with varying restructuring potential are identified.

The effectiveness of this approach was verified within six months of the analysis. Restructuring or acquisition announcements were made for five of the nine candidates.

It would appear to be clear from the foregoing that acquiring an undervalued corporate portfolio is potentially the most highly rewarding strategy a company can pursue in today's feverish acquisition environment.

Success, however, must depend on the acquisitor's careful portfolio analysis to determine whether or not the contemplated restructuring will in fact produce the performance premium management needs to justify acquisition.

Without such premium performance, justification is impossible. Acquisition strategy is an endeavor that is also an adventure—worthy of the best management strategists, aided in all possible ways by the best minds available, both internal and external to the corporation.

Chapter 19
DIVESTITURE STRATEGY

JOHN E. ROBSON
Executive Vice President, G. D. Searle & Co.

As discussed in this chapter, divestiture is the process of shedding a business activity to redeploy its resources for some other purpose. Divestiture should function as an integral part of corporate growth strategy. A continuous process of renewal, divestiture represents one of the most important elements of creating and executing a strategic plan.

The divestiture decision can be made for several reasons including streamlining the corporation, eliminating a losing or low-return business, lack of "fit," or the avoidance of exposure of assets to political risk. Divestiture can take a variety of forms, including sale, merger, liquidation, and spinoff. The purpose of this article is to present the strategic role of divestiture rather than to discuss the mechanics.

We live in a volatile world where corporate success depends just as fundamentally on management's ability to make timely divestment as well as investment. The continuation of a business activity, whether by design or neglect, is a decision to invest assets and management resources in that business. Careful consideration and appraisal of an investment opportunity normally precede the decision to commit resources. Yet many companies fail to appraise existing investments or consider withdrawing from operations which do not meet strategic needs or offer financial benefits which are incompatible with the company's ambitions.

Divestiture is widely misperceived as a funereal activity, a confession of management's past mistakes. Yet a company can quite properly divest a profitable business with attractive growth prospects because it no longer fits the corporation's strategic objectives. Examples include decisions recently made by Esmark and Bendix to divest highly profitable energy businesses. Another reason for divesting a highly profitable business might be to avoid political risk. Several companies based in the West took actions to spin off their businesses in the Middle East to reduce their exposure.

Many companies which only a few years ago were actively diversifying through acquisitions are now trying to sell those same businesses. Many companies from various industries are restructuring assets to improve earnings. Examples include ITT, GAF, and American Can. One reason may be to restore a corporate "personality." Investors and analysts can become confused by a firm that appears to be a museum of disparate businesses. It is difficult to analyze a company when it is engaged in a multitude of businesses that are affected by different external factors and require widely divergent strategies. These complexities can become so burdensome to the investing community that the company becomes a victim of benign neglect. Divestiture, then, becomes a means for a company to return to the basics and concentrate in a few selected areas in which it can excel and achieve leadership. "Cleaning house" often exposes value that is quickly recognized by the market. The result is that G. D. Searle & Co., Esmark, Bendix, and many others have divested both profitable and unprofitable businesses in order to concentrate their financial and management resources and meet an overall strategic design.

Acquisitions are not the only means to increase shareholder wealth. Companies that divest businesses can receive as much attention as those making acquisitions. The effect of divestiture on improving the market value of a company can be significant. The rising number of divestitures betrays the notion in American business that bigger is better.

Many strategic planning specialists believe the divestiture trend will continue during the eighties. The 1980 Finance Act in Great Britain talks of "demerger of a company under the new taxation treatment." Demerger emerged as a way of splitting large, unwieldy companies so that profitable subsidiaries, smothering under the weight of the parent, could achieve their full growth potential. The predicted economic and political volatility in the eighties suggests that companies will regard divestiture analysis as a regular, routine aspect of strategic planning.

Yet with all the potential benefits offered by divestiture, the process of "agonizing reappraisal" required to reach a determination to divest can become a psychological torture chamber for management.

It is human nature to value highly those activities in which one is engaged. And it is corporate management's nature to perpetuate current business operations. Companies, like people, find it difficult to change.

Thus, one of the most difficult barriers to divestiture is the powerful tendency to keep doing what has been done and to ignore the questions: "Why am I involved in this business?" "What is it contributing to my strategic and financial objectives?" An established investment in people, plant, and markets can blur management's analytical capacities and its resolve to "bite the bullet" on a divestiture decision. Of the fifty largest U.S. corporations listed by *Fortune* magazine in 1960, only seventeen were among the top fifty in 1980. Business cannot stand still.

Senior managers should establish a strategic regimen that includes divestiture to deal with the climate of change in the eighties. A persistent, hard-nosed measuring of the corporate portfolio against financial and strategic objectives is essential to improve earnings and achieve growth.

SOME ILLUSTRATIONS

In this section, the divestiture activities of G. D. Searle & Co., Esmark, and Bendix are discussed. Each of these companies has employed divestiture as an integral part of improving earnings. Although there are substantial differences among the three companies in terms of industry and product representation, financial composition, and management style, their divestiture strategies suggest similarity in divestiture philosophy.

G. D. Searle & Co.

Since 1977 Searle has divested more than thirty-five businesses with sales in excess of $400 million. Today, G. D. Searle & Co. is a research-based health care company which develops, manufactures, and markets throughout the world prescription and consumer pharmaceuticals, prescription optical products, and specialty gases. Contributions by business segments in 1979 and 1981 are summarized below:

	Performance in 1979		Performance in 1981	
	Sales, %	Operating earnings, %	Sales, %	Operating earnings, %
Pharmaceutical group	54	87	68	83
Medical products group	25	(2)	0	0
Optical group	14	10	24	12
Other businesses	7	5	8	5

The foundation of Searle's approach is the conviction that divestiture is really an investment decision. It is a decision *not to* invest in a particular activity, just as an acquisition or the continuation of a business is a decision *to* invest. Divestiture is treated by senior management at Searle like any other resource allocation decision. These decisions were not made in a vacuum but against a backdrop of the company's strategic and financial objectives. Indeed, one of the benefits of the disciplined divestiture analysis program at Searle has been the refinement of corporate goals and objectives.

The penalty for conducting divestiture analysis on an ad hoc basis may be to delay the ultimate decision beyond the point where strategic or tactical options are available.

At Searle divestiture analysis is a regular part of the annual strategic planning cycle, not an ad hoc activity resorted to only when some business is found to be in trouble. It applies equally to healthy units. Managers become more accustomed to participating in divestiture analysis and the process can be conducted with considerably less anxiety and greater objectivity than is often the case.

Anticipatory divestiture planning and prompt execution of divestiture decisions have yielded benefits for the company as recognized by investors. The financial community seems favorably disposed to the idea that Searle management is continually scrutinizing what it is doing—asking the hard question whether, in the long run, its various businesses will contribute to the corporation's financial and strategic goals.

Searle has been open about its divestiture philosophy, not only in the internal strategic process but in published corporate documents. As an example, the 1979 Searle Annual Report states:

> We regularly evaluate businesses to assess their contribution to Searle's financial strength and strategic goals. When the prospect for positive contribution appears limited, divestiture is considered.

Searle also stresses the need to remain flexible, as stated in the 1978 Searle Annual Report:

> Most important, the attainment of bottom line goals in a rapidly changing world requires flexible strategies and the courage to change course or withdraw from an existing activity which no longer offers opportunities consistent with growth and profit.

The logic behind the frankness of the policy is that divestiture analysis becomes considerably more traumatic when it is conducted on a clandestine basis rather than as a regular part of the annual corporate strategic analysis.

Perhaps the most important divestiture criterion is the willingness of a corporation to recognize that no institution can do everything well, a concept which might be characterized as "corporate humility." The key is to concentrate on activities that the company can do well.

The challenge is to determine which units currently contribute to the goals of the company or have a reasonably high potential to contribute significantly in the future. One problem in this area is that the financial performance or strategic problems of individual businesses can be masked if included within a larger unit. It is essential to segregate activities that are routinely reported together.

Esmark, Inc.

Since late 1979 Esmark has proceeded with a restructuring and divestiture plan that included the sale of Vickers Energy and the fresh meat operations of Swift. In 1980 Esmark sold Vickers Energy and Trans Ocean Oil and wrote down its interest in the U.S. fresh meat operation in preparation for its eventual sale. Esmark's future operations will concentrate on branded consumer products and chemicals. Gains from the sale of energy operations are projected to outweigh losses on the divestiture of fresh meat operations.

A diversified holding company, Esmark was involved in five major business segments prior to its streamlining program. Sales and operating earnings by segment for 1979 are listed below:

	Performance in 1979	
	Sales, %	Operating earnings, %
Foods	66	11
Chemicals and industrial	8	15
Energy	14	41
Personal	8	23
Automotive and electrical	4	10

The parent company, Esmark, was created in 1972 to provide a means for diversifying the firm's operations and reducing its vulnerability to cyclical changes in the industries in which the company is involved, especially the food business. Prior to the divestment program, Esmark's businesses stretched over a wide scope, including fresh and processed meats, dairy and poultry products, edible oil products, peanut butter and pet foods; phosphate rock, fertilizers, adhesives and specialty chemicals; dental equipment; refining and marketing petroleum products and oil and gas production; women's foundation garments, hosiery and family products; and automotive aftermarket products for the consumer and electrical products.

Because Esmark decided to concentrate on consumer products and specialty chemicals, it became a strategic objective to divest the fresh meat and energy businesses. These businesses require large capital investments and commitments to fixed assets. Because of commodity trades, both the meat and the energy businesses of Esmark experienced wide fluctuations in profit margins. Energy was a significant generator of earnings compared to fresh meat, which absorbed millions in investments in the late seventies in an effort to turn the business around. One Esmark executive even went so far as to characterize the fresh meat business as the company's "Vietnam." Swift was Esmark's first business, dating back over 125 years. At one time in history, the business was the largest meat packer in the United States. While it remains an important competitive element in the market, Swift has lost leadership and market share to more efficient modern packers.

Bendix Corporation

Bendix is a large manufacturer with major interests in the automotive, aerospace, and industrial energy markets. In 1979 contributions by industry segment were distributed as follows:

	Performance in 1979	
	Sales, %	Operating earnings, %
Automotive	51	46
Aerospace-electronics	28	32
Forest products	12	9
Industrial energy	8	9
Other operations	—	(2)
Equity in ASARCO	—	7

Major Bendix products are automotive, including worldwide automotive systems and components, steering systems, electronic and engine controls, FRAM filters, fans, air cleaners, spark plugs, shock absorbers, brake fluid, clutch facings, and carburetors. Sales from aerospace-electronics consist primarily of flight, electronic, mechanical, and hydraulic systems for aircraft and missiles. A substantial portion of forest products was devoted to uses in residential construction. Industrial-energy operations include machine tools, oil machinery, and geophysical exploration services.

Bendix sold a shelter home subsidiary that marked the beginning of the major divestiture plan. That was followed by the partial divestiture of a French subsidiary that manufactures automotive electrical and mechanical parts. In 1980 two major decisions were made: the company would sell its forest products division and its 20 percent equity in ASARCO. These two sales made available as much as $400 million in cash for acquisitions. The strategic plan for Bendix now envisions a transformation to a high-technology company.

Investment analysts seemed as confused by Bendix's declaration of intent to sell the 20 percent share in ASARCO in 1980 as they were when Bendix acquired the interest for $120 million in 1978. The initial purchase was described by management as a desire to participate in natural resource fields rather than an investment opportunity. The ASARCO stock price doubled after Bendix made the purchase so the transaction benefited the stockholder in any case.

In 1980 Bendix acquired Warner and Swasey, a machine tool manufacturer. The $300 million purchase included nearly $65 million in liquid assets and a block of stock in Wang Laboratories, the word processor company. Bendix sold the Wang stock for $40 million in mid-1980. With the acquisition, Bendix became the second leading builder of machine tools in the United States.

One of the strategic questions which management continues to address is the degree of dependence on the auto industry that Bendix should maintain. Historically, sales of automotive products formed the backbone of the company. Efforts currently underway to redeploy assets away from the automotive concentration suggest the Bendix strategic direction toward less dependence on the automotive product lines. Bendix maintains a strategic planning process that includes divestiture assessment.

OTHER ISSUES OF DIVESTITURES

Several technical points related to divestiture planning and analysis are discussed below.

One frequently debated issue is whether to involve operating unit management in a divestiture decision. The decision not to involve unit management is founded on the belief that it is simply too unsettling to operating managers. However, when divestiture analysis is a regular part of managerial routine, unit managers become accustomed to the process. Involving senior unit management in divestiture analysis can be vital to an informed decision by top management. That is not to say that it is necessary or appropriate to involve unit management in the ultimate decision. If divestment does proceed, unit management feels more comfortable having participated, even if their views are not accepted by top corporate management. It is also important to involve directors at an early stage in divestiture planning. While every divestiture does not require board action, keeping directors informed as the analysis proceeds helps elicit their views at an early stage. By the time for final decision, the directors are familiar with the issues and have a good sense where management is heading. The result is usually speedy, informed action by the board.

No general rule exists for establishing a divestiture reserve. But there is no doubt that a good deal of judgment enters into the decision. Elements of the process include some mathematical calculations, a little bit of Kentucky windage, and a dose of Murphy's law (which advises you that if something can go wrong it probably will). All play a part in the establishment of a reserve. One pitfall to avoid is establishing an inadequate reserve. If the reserve must be adjusted upward, it does not reflect well on management.

Perhaps the most important point in the execution of a divestiture is to segregate it from ongoing activities. Basic responsibility for divestiture negotiations and for key decisions associated with it should be assumed by management personnel who will continue with the company. It is important that people who are fundamentally responsible for a divestiture are present for both the takeoff and the landing. Generally, employees who are expected to leave with the divested business do not participate in divestiture negotiations. In negotiations with a prospective buyer, the perceptions and loyalties of the people in the business being divested are ambivalent.

In some cases a company cannot announce its decision to divest before it has found a buyer and made an agreement in principle—because the business is fragile or the employee circumstances are too sensitive. However, the risk of unwanted "leaks" is high and there may be a variety of insider security-trading exposures in these situations.

If a company has a choice, there are advantages to "going public" with the decision to divest. Not only can it serve as advertising to attract potential buyers, but it permits open dealing with the employees, customers, and suppliers of the divested business. Frequently, companies offer special incentives to senior management in businesses under divestment to stay with the deal to the conclusion. Incentives of this kind can be extremely useful to the seller and the buyer.

One of the frequently neglected elements of divestiture execution is the postdivestiture responsibility. It is rare for a divestiture to occur that is absolutely sanitary in terms of the seller's further responsibility with the divested business. More likely, the sales contract requires activity that continues for six months or even years following the divestiture. Frequently, these activities have a financial impact on one of the parties to the transaction. For this reason, it is important to fix clearly the management responsibilities for these continuing activities.

A final aspect of executing a divestiture concerns the employees of the divested unit. Employees may feel a high sense of rejection at being "kicked out of the house." Yet in many cases they can improve their circumstances. Employees of a divested business may be far better off in the hands of a buyer that provides them a priority in management effort and financial resources than in the ownership of a firm whose financial and strategic objectives the business no longer serves. Communicating that idea can be a useful way to sustain morale in the divesting business prior to sale.

CONCLUSION

In summary, it is important that divestiture analysis, planning, and implementation are viewed as positive activities. They should be an integral part of a company's growth strategy. Divestiture should also be an integral part of the regular planning process, not an ad hoc exercise in crisis management directed only to critically ill businesses.

Three major benefits from an effective divestiture analysis and implementation program are:

- It helps to sharpen corporate strategies and objectives because management must measure the activity of each of its businesses against specific contributions to corporate goals and objectives.
- It gives line managers a keener sense that what they do in their unit must contribute to some higher goal. It helps them look upon themselves as part of a larger strategy and ask: "Am I doing something today that will contribute to the goals of the operating group and the corporation?"
- Finally, a sound divestiture program builds respect within the company and the financial community.

Chapter 20

CORPORATE TURNAROUND STRATEGY*

JOHN M. HARRIS

Senior Vice President, Booz • Allen & Hamilton, Inc.

Recent years have found some of the nation's most prominent institutions suddenly skirting bankruptcy. Whether the result was surrender of autonomy to the banks or the federal government (Lockheed, New York City, Pan Am, TWA), forced merger (Penn Central), or outright bankruptcy (Investors Overseas Services, Franklin National Bank, REA Express, W. T. Grant), the demise of these institutions invariably came as a shock. Had there been no warning signals? How could management have been so unobservant? What could have been done to turn these institutions around?

Recognizing when one's company may be in trouble is perhaps the most difficult task facing any chief executive. Not only is it difficult to accept emotionally; it can be difficult to detect because of the myriad of performance measures and the inherent tendencies of an organization to put the best possible face on the facts (that is, tell the boss good news whenever possible).

Every business in our competitive economy risks short-term and long-term fluctuations. But such fluctuations do not give management any excuse to ignore performance trends that could have ominous impli-

*This chapter originally appeared as "The Corporate Turnaround Situation—How to Manage It," in the *Handbook of Business Problem Solving,* Kenneth J. Albert, editor in chief (McGraw-Hill, New York, 1980).

cations. Almost all companies that go bankrupt, or even are exposed to a financial crisis, do so for reasons which had been building up over time. The challenge for management is to spot the danger signals, resolve to act, and develop and effect a turnaround plan before it is too late.

THE DANGER SIGNALS

Companies and industries vary widely, but experience has shown that the danger signals of impending trouble tend to be remarkably similar. Companies which are turnaround situations will probably exhibit one or more of the following characteristics:

1. DECREASING MARKET SHARE. This is perhaps the most telling signal of a major problem—a company losing ground to competition. Regular analysis of market share for major product lines forces a company to compare its performance with that of its competitors. Such analysis keeps a management from deriving a false sense of security from a long-term sales increase that may have stemmed from inflation or from a growth trend characteristic of the entire industry. Market share analysis frequently requires some knowledge of the business; statistics may mislead the unsophisticated. For example, a leading manufacturer of automotive aftermarket products was able to show an increase in market share year after year because it added new lines of purchased parts. While overall market share, which was closely watched by management, looked very healthy, the company's share of the assemblies it manufactured was steadily dropping and it suddenly found itself with an outdated plan, weak customer relations, and a financial crisis.

2. DECREASING CONSTANT DOLLAR SALES. Analysis of sales trends is more meaningful after adjusting for inflation. In addition, sales figures should be presented in whatever terminology best measures the accepted criteria of one's industry. Retailers, for example, watch the figures for sales per square foot of selling space. The now defunct W. T. Grant chain persisted in recording sales per linear foot of counter space. Use of this unusual statistic prevented comparison with other retailers and masked the fact that its sales per square foot had been only half the industry average for many years before its demise.

3. DECREASING PROFITABILITY. This can show up as lower profits in absolute terms, as lower profit per dollar of sales, or as a declining rate of return on investment. These numbers must be interpreted with care to avoid dangerous misjudgments, since a company can be in serious trouble even though it continues to report what appears to be a healthy profit. The U.S. steel industry, for instance, saw its profits in-

crease from $14.2 billion in 1967 to $20.3 billion in 1975 as sales more than doubled over the period; profit margins, however, declined from 14.8 percent to 10.3 percent; return on investment dropped steadily, and the average price/earnings ratio of steel companies' common stocks halved over the decade.

4. INCREASING RELIANCE ON DEBT. A substantial rise in the amount of debt, a lopsided debt-to-equity ratio, and a lowered corporate credit rating may cause banks and other lenders to apply restrictions. They shorten loan maturities, tie their loans to asset values rather than to the general earning power of the company, and become reluctant to provide funds. Once this happens other sources of funds become increasingly reluctant to lend; security analysts and investors downgrade the company's stock, hindering the sale of equity; and final alternatives such as equipment leases and sale-leaseback of major facilities soon become exhausted.

5. RESTRICTED DIVIDEND POLICIES. Dividends frequently must be restricted or eliminated to conserve cash or satisfy debt covenants. This danger signal generally indicates an advanced deterioration and a pressing need for a turnaround plan. Interestingly enough, many companies which cut dividends previously paid out substantially higher proportions of earnings in dividends than their competitors—when they should have been reinvesting in the business. This is particularly true of companies where major shareholder interests desire high current income from the business.

6. INADEQUATE REINVESTMENT IN THE BUSINESS. Adequate reinvestment in plant, equipment, and maintenance is necessary for a company to stay competitive. Deferring these expenditures is tantamount to unplanned borrowing from the future for which there has to be a day of reckoning. The now defunct Pennsylvania Railroad began a program of deferred maintenance in the 1940s which allowed it to continue to report higher profits—and mask the true maintenance requirements of its operations—for a number of years before the day of reckoning finally arrived. When a business is growing, the combination of new investment and reinvestment frequently requires borrowing. Until the 1970s, some companies—Montgomery Ward, Du Pont, and A&P, for example—refused to borrow for expansion and tried to finance growth through earnings. Competitors who took a more aggressive view of the future—Sears Roebuck, Dow, and Safeway, for example—have had a substantially better record over the last decade. Quality of management, of course, is the most important variable. As the director of a company in the midst of a turnaround remarked, "It's a good thing they [former management] didn't borrow any money; they would have wasted that too."

7. PROLIFERATION OF NEW VENTURES AT THE EXPENSE OF THE PRIMARY BUSINESS. A common tendency of management in troubled companies is to ignore the basic business and rely on new, "easier" tasks like new ventures. This is not to say that companies should not attempt to diversify, but rather that they should do so only as a supplement, not as a substitute. Frantic expansion and acquisition may be a coverup for management's reluctance to face up to its primary responsibilities in the core business.

8. LACK OF PLANNING. Formal planning is now a widely accepted tool for helping companies develop and implement strategy. Yet many companies, particularly those built up and controlled by a strong entrepreneur, do not have planning programs. The result can often be devastating. The W. T. Grant bankruptcy can be traced to a lack of planning, among other things. The company was a very successful variety chain which decided to compete with major discount chains. This required large stores, which required larger assortments of merchandise including big ticket items like major appliances and furniture, which in turn required consumer installment credit. A venture on the scale attempted by Grant required the most careful planning, operational as well as financial. The company soon found itself saddled with a half-billion dollars of bank debts to finance its consumer credit receivables. Bankruptcy soon followed.

9. CHIEF EXECUTIVE OFFICERS (CEOs) WHO RESIST NEW IDEAS OTHER THAN THEIR OWN. Either they lack new ideas or they fail to accept proposals from subordinates. Even if they recognize danger signals, they may think that they are doing everything possible to remedy a deteriorating situation and that no one else knows the situation better than they. To the extent that they recognize their own responsibility in causing things to go bad, they may be all the more resentful of other people's suggestions for improvement.

10. MANAGEMENT SUCCESSION PROBLEMS. When nearly all the managers reporting to the chief executive officer are in their mid-fifties, there may be too few promising young managers being developed. A growing number of good people may be resigning out of frustration over what they perceive to be diminishing opportunities for promotion. Their departure further weakens the company if, as often happens, they go to work for competitors.

11. A PASSIVE, UNQUESTIONING BOARD OF DIRECTORS. Directors who have strong family, social, or business ties to the chief executive are sometimes not as objective as they should be. This is especially true if—like the chief executive—they have served on the board during the years of decline and hence feel a personal responsibility for the current sit-

uation. Not only does the board become uncritical, but the chief executive becomes all-powerful.

12. A MANAGEMENT TEAM THAT FEELS NOTHING CAN BE LEARNED FROM ITS COMPETITORS. Companies which promote almost exclusively from within are likely to be highly insular and uncreative; they discourage their people from participating in trade association activities, and instead of trying to learn from the competition, they belittle it. The most successful companies regularly study the competition to see what they can learn, even if they then continue to operate their own way. Leading companies in the copier-duplicator business, for example, have continuously analyzed competitive technologies and products.

The first three danger signals—decreasing market share, decreasing constant dollar sales, and decreasing profitability—are at the top of my list because they are so important to company viability. They are also easy to determine, an attribute which allows management to establish procedures for making periodic comparisons with a target group of companies of similar size in the same industry or even with selected companies in other industries.

Managers frequently give all sorts of reasons why they cannot compare their figures with those of another company, inside or outside their own industry. "Accounting methods are different"; "We lease equipment, they buy"; and so forth. It's true that comparisons can't be perfect, but they can be useful even if they just indicate general directions. There is always an abundance of information available on the performance of competing companies, public and private, which can be obtained from the business press, trade association publications, and financial institutions.

Top management should insist on regular presentations of their company's results, or results of their major divisions or product lines, in comparison with a target group of competitors. If this kind of information on the state of the business is not regularly available at the board level, outside directors should press management to institute these comparisons.

THE DECISION TO ACT

Danger signals are valuable only if they are recognized and acted upon. Unfortunately, companies that let themselves decline to the point where drastic action is necessary are just those companies most likely to forgo whatever opportunity they still have left. Someone or some organization has to intervene and take charge.

A number of candidates emerge for this difficult role:

- The parent company (in the case of an ailing division or subsidiary)
- A member or group of the board of directors (most likely an outsider or group of outsiders)
- Major stockholders
- Banks

Management itself should not be overlooked. At one large consumer products company, for example, three group vice presidents recently got together with the outside directors and forced the chief executive to do what was necessary to develop a turnaround plan.

The agent for change can also be an external event. In one instance a company knowingly put up with declining performance of an acquisition for ten years until a brokerage house research report recommended selling stock of the parent because of problems with the acquisition.

It is critical that management, the board, the owners, the bankers, or whoever agree among themselves that the company is indeed in desperate straits. Only then will a turnaround action be seriously considered.

At least three months is usually necessary for such a consensus to develop for several reasons. First, the situation probably developed over a number of years and many of the directors served during the period of decline. Second, interests of the various parties are different—banks want money out, owners want ongoing operations and maybe growth, suppliers want prepayments, etc. Third, time is required to assemble all the required facts and logically develop and present a plan. Finally, the psychological processes at work require a period of time to develop; that is, people have to work out their roles, everybody has to be heard, a leading individual or group needs to emerge, and so forth, as in any crisis situation.

Once consensus has been achieved among the parties who must act, the turnaround situation can and should develop a momentum of its own as each party develops a loyalty to the plan.

THE TURNAROUND PLAN

Finally persuaded of the gravity of the problem, the directors of a business decide upon and implement a plan of action. In deciding what to do, the directors may depend on the company's internal resources or may reach for outsiders. At Federated Department Stores, for example, a corporate staff has been effective in analyzing performance and suggesting turnaround remedies for several operating companies.

Outsiders can bring fresh perspective to the turnaround task at a time when internal passions are high and objectivity imperative. Outsiders generally are most effective in a turnaround when they are responsible to the board but are working with management to develop and implement the turnaround plan. In many cases a large amount of the fact-finding and analysis required can be done by company staff under the direction of the outside team. In some cases, outsiders may be part of the problem—if they have worked closely with management for several years, for example—and cannot be objective in developing the turnaround plan.

Management changes are frequently an essential element of an overall turnaround plan. However, a blend of old and new management is often most effective. The turnaround at J. L. Hudson Company in Detroit, which is now leading the Dayton-Hudson Corporation to record profits, was accomplished by the chief executive and two new senior executives forming a three-person team. On the other hand, a number of turnarounds have been achieved by a new CEO who leaves other management virtually intact.

A Case History

A few years ago a large retail chain exhibited a number of the danger signals calling for a turnaround. Throughout the 1960s this company had lost market share to more aggressive competitors, and between 1968 and 1973 its market share declined in 90 percent of the metropolitan markets it served.

In the same period, when industry leaders were increasing capital reinvestment by 150 percent and more, this chain curtailed such expenditures. Because it was opening relatively few new stores and its existing stores were located in increasingly urban and low income areas, it was not able to exploit the growth opportunities in suburban shopping centers.

In addition, the chain's extensive manufacturing facilities were underutilized, and profits from its private labels had fallen off sharply in recent years. Severe cash management problems aggravated the situation.

The company's investments in people were also inadequate. Training programs were generally poor. Management was inbred; most of the top executives had started with the company as clerks and were emotionally involved with the status quo.

Management responsibilities and lines of authority were confused. For example, division managers had considerable discretion in major operating areas, but in many cases did not have the authority to go with their decentralized responsibilities.

Faced with this whole gamut of business difficulties, the company lost over $100 million in a few years. It was estimated that continuation of its current policies would mean annual losses which the company could not survive.

The cure—developed in part by outside consultants—was not easy. New management had to come in to meet the exceptional demands of managing a turnaround situation. A number of executives at the level of senior vice president and above were replaced, as were many vice presidents. Significant numbers of outsiders joined the company at the middle management level, and new emphasis was placed on training at all levels.

Under the leadership of new executives committed to change, the chain closed more than 40 percent of its retail outlets over a three-year period. Some of the existing stores were enlarged or remodeled, and new stores were opened or acquired. The objective was a reinvigorated profile of stores—larger, more modern, located in more profitable markets.

Reevaluation of private label and manufacturing operations led to the elimination of superfluous items and sizes from the private label line. There was consequently more room in the stores to display name brand products.

Large write-offs resulting from consolidation and asset redeployment programs affected not only stores and manufacturing facilities, but also warehouses and division offices. Major borrowings were required to support an accelerated store construction program.

Rapid change required two major reorganizations. The first reorganization strategy was to put two layers of management in the field so that lower and middle management could exercise more responsibility and authority. But it turned out that the division-region-headquarters structure was not well suited to a streamlined company with 40 percent fewer stores. The duplication of support services was especially costly. Accordingly, the second reorganization did away with the regional level and installed group executive vice presidents to oversee the divisions. The aim was not to reject decentralization, but to carry it one step further: the group vice presidents now serve mainly as counsel for the divisions, which are highly independent.

Along with new management and new organization came new management techniques. To tackle its critical cash management problems, the company developed new systems for inventory control and real estate management. It also adopted cost reduction programs in clerical and data processing activities and telecommunications.

Full implementation of the turnaround campaign will take over five years. Yet the chain made impressive progress in just two years: average weekly sales per store almost doubled, and sales per square foot of selling area increased by more than two-thirds.

What was the most important factor contributing to this company's success? While the brief summary here may make its turnaround efforts seem wide-ranging and even diffuse, the campaign never would have gotten off the ground if management had not first focused on two critical actions: a crash program to consolidate facilities and redeploy assets into more attractive markets, and a revitalization of the organization.

Commitment and Focus

Regardless of how the matter is resolved, the turnaround management team needs a commitment from the board and others representing the ownership to let it have a free hand in taking the remedial actions necessary. Equally important, there should be complete understanding of the time frame required for results to be measurable. It is usually a matter of two or three years, or more, before a decline that has been in the making for many years can be arrested and reversed to the point where operating and financial performance improve.

With this support guaranteed, the turnaround team needs to select and focus on the one or two activities offering the greatest opportunity to affect company performance. In fact, of all the qualities needed in a turnaround team, singleness of purpose is probably the most crucial. So important is this quality that turnaround management should make it standard practice to list one or two critical actions and then check progress on these items at least once a week. This helps them retain their focus in what can be very confusing and wild business circumstances.

Lack of this focus is a major reason why many turnarounds fail. Plans, remedies, and proposed emergency measures abound. Without a clear focus it becomes easy for management to become bogged down in all the pressing concerns of the moment. One prominent retail chain, in its death throes and losing $1 million a day, concerned itself with employees, computers, changes in merchandising, recruiting policy, and the like. Even though it was evident that the critical issue was cash conservation, many executives worried about the lack of adequate information systems, lack of training, and lack of an efficient distribution fleet. More than 100 people were sent out to count the inventory in all their stores at a time when it was inevitable that at least half these stores would be closed.

This curious obsession with order, structure, and business as usual in a crisis is one of those human traits that must be dealt with in a turnaround situation. It is mentioned here not because people's behavior can be changed but because this behavior needs to be recognized for what it is by the turnaround team. The turnaround leader who is going to be successful is the one who succeeds in getting the influential individuals in a company to focus on the central problem and then follow through on the leader's plan of action.

In the effort to identify those activities offering the greatest leverage, the leader may consider a dozen or so recommendations for action. Yet most of the desired short-term results can usually be accomplished by concentrating on the two or three courses of action that are likely to be the most immediately productive.

The best opportunity may often be in raising prices sharply to increase sales and gross margins without adding capital or personnel. A well-known manufacturer of writing instruments has recently been turned around largely on the basis of a single action: a successful price increase on its major product. Increasing sales dollars can yield results faster than the more traditional approach, which is to focus exclusively on cost cutting and consolidation. Ideally, one could work to increase sales and cut costs at the same time, but this is hard to do. A company should start out either in one mode or the other.

Often consolidation of organizations and physical plant is the only course that will achieve a turnaround. This can mean combining divisions, districts, plants, or warehouses. Cost reduction is more effective and rapid when an entire organization or facility can be eliminated, especially if this improves utilization of the remaining facilities. Management at A&P, for example, which reported sales increases in excess of 20 percent in stores which remained open after the consolidation of one-third of its stores in 1975, attributed much of this volume to customers from the closed stores.

When consolidation is indicated, management must be prepared to move as drastically as necessary the first time. Halfway measures don't work. Phasing out operations over too long a time prolongs the morale-shattering period of uncertainty for the people affected and thereby undermines the effectiveness of the move.

Consolidation of a money-losing operation not only stops the bleeding, it can also generate cash if the assets in question can be liquidated. These funds can be put to more profitable use elsewhere. This is particularly true in retailing turnarounds because ready cash can be received for inventory and redeployed to restructure financing or to build up other locations where there is a better chance of making money.

A consolidation frequently requires the board to face up to the need for a major write-off. While this is always a difficult decision, facilities should nearly always be written off if they prove unproductive. Public accounting firms should require management to write off unproductive facilities as a matter of standard business practice. However, often the accountants either don't understand the business well enough or don't press management hard enough. Frequently, by the time a situation deteriorates to the point where assets are clearly unproductive, the company is in deep trouble and a write-off is resisted strongly by management.

In a major consolidation situation, there are emotional as well as business considerations to contend with. Indecision and inertia must be overcome. Typically, the veteran company executive questions whether action called for by the turnaround plan will work; the executive would prefer to wait and see. Turnaround management must counter with, "Okay, if you don't think what we've recommended is going to work, what do you think *will* work?" The executive must be persuaded that sitting still is not the answer, and that business as usual is no solution. Much of this indecision comes from management's genuine concern for its employees. Management may feel obligated to employees of long service and, especially in company-town environments, may feel community pressure. However, the simple truth is that management's obligation to the employees means that the company has to survive for any jobs to exist.

In a company losing money, the turnaround executive needs a short-term plan of action to achieve a net positive cash flow as soon as possible. This is the kind of action generally sought by the outside lenders. Actions normally desirable from a longer-term standpoint should be put on the back burner until the success of the short-term plan is assured. A long-range plan means nothing until the business has been restored to profitability.

After the major decisions of the turnaround have been made and agreed to, management should use plain-talking, incisive communications to set the record straight. The grapevine has usually been working overtime and things may not even be as black as they seem.

The CEO should, as the turnaround scenario unfolds, let people know where they stand in the reorganization and spell out their responsibilities in the drive toward renewed profitability. Progress reports should be issued and problem areas spotlighted. The CEO's communications can also espouse the adoption of a company-wide viewpoint to minimize long-standing functional or geographical parochialism that may have contributed to the company's decline.

Finally, in the midst of a turnaround program, the CEO is entitled to maximum mileage from the board of directors; those who are not supportive and who don't have the time or inclination for the task should not stand for reelection. The CEO can help this process along by demanding a lot from the board. The CEO can establish a committee of the board to recruit new directors with criteria that make it plain to incumbents that the company needs all the strength it can get at the board level. Finally, improving the overall reputation and quality of the board can be very helpful in maintaining credibility with the financial community.

Nothing in this chapter should obscure the fact that the best turnaround is the one that does not have to happen. When an enterprise has declined to the point where a turnaround is indicated, it is bad news for all affected interests: management, rank-and-file employees, stockholders, bondholders, banks, suppliers, distributors, customers, and government jurisdictions. But since a possibly disastrous sellout or bankruptcy are the only alternatives, these interests have little choice but to accept and even welcome the strong medicine implicit in a turnaround.

It has not been unusual to find instances when draconian measures taken in a turnaround situation have been so long overdue that a company emerges from the ordeal in the best competitive trim ever. Still, a turnaround is the hard way for a company to shape up. In business management, as in other human endeavors, prevention is a lot easier to take than cure.

Section Five

Key Issues and Resources

Chapter **21**

THE POLITICS OF STRATEGIC DECISION MAKING

LIAM FAHEY
Assistant Professor of Policy and Environment, J. L. Kellogg Graduate School of Management, Northwestern University

V. K. NARAYANAN
Assistant Professor of Organization and Management, School of Business, University of Kansas

As with many management terms, no consensus exists as to a precise specification of the managerial phenomena, processes, and activities subsumed within the rubric of strategic management. However, most would agree that strategic management entails at a minimum the *processes* by which firms' product markets and modes of competing within them are chosen (that is, strategy formulation) and by which these choices are implemented (strategy implementation). The business strategy and policy literature has predominantly treated these processes from an analytical perspective. These same processes of strategy formulation and implementation can also be viewed from a political perspective, an approach which the business strategy and policy literature has largely neglected. The intent of this chapter is to develop and illustrate a political conception of strategic decision making. The specific focus is upon the impact of organizational politics internal to the firm on various phases of strategic decision making.

It should be noted that the concern here is with the making and implementation of strategic decisions. Such decisions may be broadly defined as those which are important to an organization in determining what its objectives should be and how it will achieve its objectives. In strategic management parlance, such decisions typically revolve around the choice of product markets and preferred competitive tactics within product markets. These types of decisions generally are "important in terms of the actions taken, the resources committed, or the precedents set" (Mintzberg, Raisinghani, and Theoret, 1976, p. 246). Furthermore, they frequently affect many organizational subunits, take considerable periods of time to formulate and implement, and involve many different types of uncertainties (customer, competitive, technological, legal, governmental, financial, and so on).

For discussion purposes, this chapter is organized around the often noted phases of strategy making: strategic issue (decision) identification and diagnosis, development of strategic alternatives, evaluation of alternatives and choice, implementation and evaluation of results. More specifically, the discussion begins by delineating the more prevalent rational or analytical model of strategy making, noting in particular its content and assumptions. Flowing from a different set of assumptions, a political conception of organizations is then developed. We next illustrate how political forces affect each decision-making phase. The intent is not to provide an exhaustive listing of such forces and their effects but merely to highlight some of the most prevalent means by which organizational politics impacts strategic decision making. In the concluding section, a number of implications of a political approach to strategic decision making are noted; particular emphasis is placed upon the integration of the rational and political perspectives.

THE RATIONAL PERSPECTIVE

At the core of the current theory of strategic decision making lie the classical models of rational decision making and choice. Rational decision-making models were originally developed in economics and statistical decision theory to describe and explain how individuals make decisions. These models conceive of decisions as the *purposive* acts of *consistent* actors. Decisions are not accidental, random, or rationalized after the fact; rather, purpose is presumed to preexist and decisions are guided by that purpose. Thus, all rational decision-making models start with the assumption that *a goal* or *consistent goal* has been set.

Rational models typically visualize decision making at the individual level as a sequential and logical process. Thus, given a consistent set of goals, the next step in rational decision making is to develop a set of alternatives. These alternatives are presumed to be differentiable, one from the other, such that each is uniquely identifiable. Once the alternatives are identified, decision making involves assessment of the likely outcomes or consequences of the possible lines of action. At this stage, the models assume that *sufficient information* about alternatives and their consequences is available or obtainable and that *cause-and-effect relationships* can be derived by the individual actor. Thus, it is assumed that the consequences can be fully and completely anticipated; where there is risk or uncertainty, probability estimates are often utilized in making assessments of consequences. In other words, everything that can possibly occur as a result of the decision process is presumably specified, although which of the various possibilities will actually occur may be subject to chance.

The final step in the model involves selecting the course of action, or that alternative which optimizes the actor's goal or goals. Once the alternatives are developed and their consequences known, the rational model advocates *consistent* application of the goals to these alternatives.

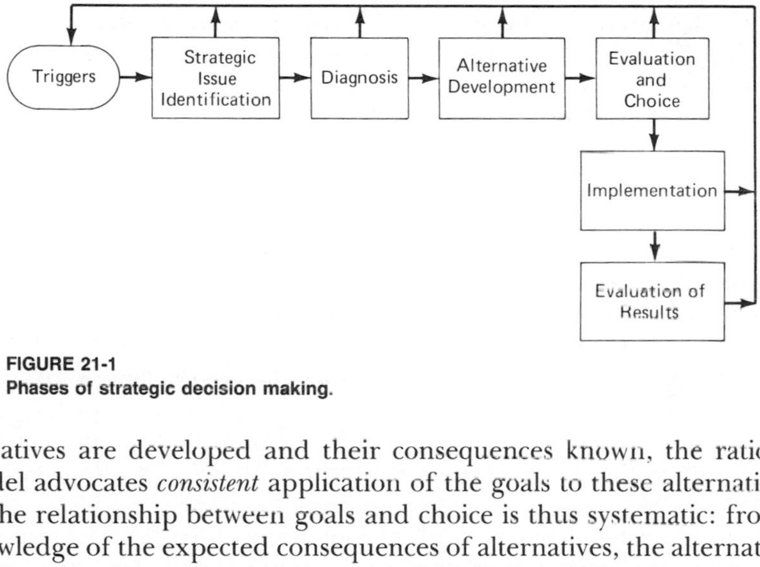

FIGURE 21-1
Phases of strategic decision making.

The relationship between goals and choice is thus systematic: from a knowledge of the expected consequences of alternatives, the alternatives can be ranked based on the extent to which they optimize the goals, and choice involves picking the most favorable alternative.

Currently, the predominant formulations of strategic decision making draw heavily upon the classical rational choice models in terms of prescribing how strategic decisions should be made in organizations. Though various models differ in terms of complexity, specificity, and sophistication, most typically postulate a sequence of steps for arriving at strategic decisions. These steps are portrayed in Figure 21-1 and are briefly discussed below.

1. ISSUE IDENTIFICATION AND DIAGNOSIS: Under the rational models,

strategic issues are identified as a consequence of analysis. Diagnosis involves environmental analysis and an assessment of the current performance of the firm: this leads to the detection of strategic problems and opportunities as well as to a comprehensive and integrated mapping of cause-effect relationships.

2. STRATEGIC ALTERNATIVE DEVELOPMENT: Development of alternatives within the rational model is tightly coupled to diagnosis: a systematic and comprehensive diagnosis results in the postulation of a broad set of well-developed alternatives. Objective and rigorous analysis—environmental trends, distinctive competence, financial resources, and so on—enables specification of feasible options.

3. EVALUATION OF ALTERNATIVES AND CHOICE: Once alternatives are developed, the rational model suggests that consequences of alternatives are evaluated in terms of the goals and choice is based on the assessment of consequences. The most often espoused goals are sales growth, profits, return on stockholder's equity, and the like.

4. IMPLEMENTATION: Implementation of a chosen strategic alternative logically follows choice in the rational framework. Organizational structures are redesigned, resources are allocated, reward and incentive systems are designed to motivate desired behaviors and control and evaluation systems are established to assess performance. Any given strategic decision leads to a variety and sequencing of operating decisions.

5. EVALUATION OF RESULTS: In the rational model, the control systems installed during the implementation stage enable continuous monitoring and evaluation of the results of the strategic decision as it is implemented. These results are assessed against established goals; thus evaluation is tightly coupled to previous stages. Deviations from expected results serve two functions: to focus on operating problems so that any deviations occurring during the implementation stage may be rooted out, and to trigger issues for strategic analysis at a future date.

As noted earlier, the current representations of strategy formulation draw upon the rational models of decision making. Thus, many of the assumptions underlying the rational models are implicit in the prevailing models of strategic decision making. It is worth repeating the more crucial of these assumptions. First, the rational models assume a consistent set of goals. In the case of strategic decisions, organizations are viewed as *consensual* entities with wide agreement among various actors with respect to the goals of the organization. This enables an individual actor model to be used as a shorthand for organizational decision making involving multiple actors. Second, these models assume an *inherently consistent logic* in the process of choice which emerges from purposeful analysis of alternatives and preferences. Choices are, therefore, assumed to be systematically and consistently related to consensual goals. Third, *objective information* is available to tackle most strategic issues. Finally, individual managers can fit individual strategic decisions into a *coherent and integrated whole,* that is, the manager can put the strategy jigsaw puzzle together.

A POLITICAL CONCEPTION OF ORGANIZATIONS

Each one of the assumptions underlying the rational model of strategic decisions can be questioned as to their representativeness of organizational realities. We suggest, and most social scientists agree, that except in very small organizations, the inherent characteristics of organizations bear little resemblance to those implied by the assumptions stated above, thus detracting from the utility of the rational model as a valid descriptor of strategic decision making. These organizational characteristics can be contrasted against the assumptions of the rational model as shown in Table 21-1. (Compare Pfeffer, 1981.)

Typically, business firms are organized into hierarchies and subunits. In social science jargon, they exhibit vertical and horizontal differentiation. Vertical differentiation refers to the existence of a hierarchy of levels within the organization: this represents a system of superior-subordinate relationships with its attendant characteristics of chain and unity of command, reporting relationships, delineations of authority and responsibility, and so on, as suggested in organization theory (Mintzberg, 1980). Horizontal differentiation refers to the existence of subunits, functional or divisional.

For example, in a functionally organized firm, subunits perform different functions such as R&D, production, marketing, and finance. In a divisionally organized firm, subunits typically cater to different product markets. It is widely acknowledged that differentiation (either horizontal or vertical) brings in its wake differences in goals held by subunits or individuals (Lawrence and Lorsch, 1967). Differences in goals would not be a serious issue if subunits were able to function independently of each other. However, this is often not the case. Differentiation brings with it interdependence among subunits: the subunits are dependent on each other to accomplish their tasks. For example, the marketing department is dependent on the production department for existing products and both of these may be dependent on R&D for new products. Interdependence creates a context in which a subunit can pursue its goals only by creating demands on other subunits, who have their own goals to satisfy. The context is, therefore, characterized by conflict rather than consensus as assumed in rational models. Indeed, political models suggest that beyond some very general organizational goals such

Table 21-1 Assumptions of the Rational and Political Perspectives

Assumptions of rational model	Organizational characteristics	Assumptions of political model
1. Goals are consistent and consensually shared	1. Differentiation *a.* vertical *b.* horizontal	1. Goals are inconsistent across social entities and therefore not consensually shared
2. The decision process is orderly and substantially rational	2. Interdependence of subunits and levels	2. The decision process is disorderly, characterized by push and pull of interests
3. The norm of optimization	3. Environment *a.* places constraints on resources *b.* creates ambiguities in information	3. The norm of frequent play of "market forces"; conflict is legitimate and expected
4. Extensive and systematic information search		4. Information search and usage triggered by political reasons leads to distortions
5. Cause-and-effect relationships are known at least probabilistically		5. Disagreement in cause-and-effect relationships
6. Decisions flow from value maximizing choice		6. Decisions are the result of bargaining and free flow of political forces
7. Underlying ideological, theme of efficiency and effectiveness		7. Ideologically, notions of struggle, conflict, "winners" and "losers" prevail

as survival and growth, goal consensus among organizational subunits is extremely difficult to achieve and/or sustain.

The conflict among subunits is exacerbated by the fact that organizations are open systems, interacting with the environment. Two aspects of the interactions between organizations and their environments need to be emphasized. First, most organizations are dependent on environments for critical resources. Typically, critical resources are scarce; thus, organizations are *resource constrained.* In the face of scarcity, various subunits must compete for resources and thus make demands on other subunits. For example, in a multidivisional firm, various divisions must compete with each other for financial and human resources. Second, except in a small number of cases, *environments are dynamic and uncertain.* Information about the environment is rarely if ever sufficient. Signals are weak and conflicting; often all the consequences of an action cannot be anticipated in advance under changing circumstances. Thus, the derivation of cause-and-effect relationships is problematic. To the extent that different individuals and subunits invoke different theories or explanatory models, different cause-and-effect relationships can be established even in the face of a similar set of data. Thus, in a differentiated organization, conflict is felt not merely at the level of goals but at the level of cause-and-effect relationships. Stated differentially, subunits must not only compete for resources but also for getting their world view (cause-and-effect relationships) accepted and legitimized.

These structural characteristics promote intraorganizational behaviors and processes which are heavily laden with political overtones. Such behaviors and processes in the context of strategic decision making are dynamic and fluid. The importance attached to any specific decision varies according to the individuals and subunits. Organizational boundaries in the form of personnel and task assignments change over time; communication systems and decision-making procedures change, sometimes quickly; participation in decisions varies and frequently varies for the same decision over time; and, not insignificantly, demands on managers' time and external pressures "to get things done" reinforce the above inconsistency and specifically lead to differential attention processes—different managers pay attention to different things. This dynamic character of organizations results in *changing goals.* This renders the assumption of consistent application of goals to alternatives as problematic. Rather, goals are likely to be loosely coupled to alternatives.

Under the above conditions—differentiation, interdependence, environmental uncertainty, insufficient information, and changing goals—organizations can be viewed as *loose structures of interests and demands,* competing for organizational attention and resources and resulting in conflicts which are never completely resolved. This is typically a political conception of organizations. From a political perspective, goals are not consensual but evolve as a result of negotiation and bargaining among political actors. Strategic alternatives are loosely coupled to goals; often goals evolve to justify the alternatives. The process is characterized by power and influence attempts by various actors. In the context of strategic decisions, we define organizational politics as those activities and behaviors engaged in by actors to acquire, sustain, and exercise power and influence over others in order to have their preferred goals, options or choices enacted. In a political arena, resources, information, expertise, social networks, and access to power centers assume importance as bases of power and influence. Revealing one's goals, parting with information, or promoting a specified alternative are intentional acts aimed at influencing others.

One further point central to the political perspective merits emphasis. The rational perspective emphasizes strategy content and analysis; it largely neglects the organizational processes or procedures (interactions among individuals and organizational subunits) necessarily involved in strategic decision making. The political perspective brings the dynamics inherent in these processes into sharp focus. Strategy content or individual decisions are viewed as an outcome of transactions of power and influence. A major implication here is that only by investigating the organizational processes out of which strategies emerge, can we understand and explain why they come to be.

IMPACT OF POLITICS ON PHASES OF STRATEGIC DECISION MAKING

The phases of strategic decision making suggested by the rational model provide a useful starting point to discuss the impact of power and influence on strategic decisions:

Issue Identification and Diagnosis

Strategic issues do not emerge in full bloom and present themselves ready for diagnosis and resolution. Information needs to be interpreted, attention must be directed, perceptions need to be shaped; these are acts of individuals rather than outcomes generated by the routine application of organizational and analytical procedures. The major questions here become: How do organizations become aware of strategic issues? What behaviors do organizational members engage in to unfold the nature of these issues?

The political perspective suggests that strategic issues emerge in organizations and assume importance only to the extent that they are sponsored by powerful individuals within the organization. Of critical import here are the roles of the individual's and/or the subunit's self-interest and their power and influence to bring the issue to a resolution. Individuals or subunits sponsor issues to the extent that such issues are perceived to be compatible with their own interests. Further, issues are likely to be sponsored only to the extent that participants consider they possess the power and influence to obtain a resolution.

Perhaps of more critical importance than the politics of issue identification is the politics of diagnosis. Diagnosis becomes politically charged as participants realize the importance of having their individual or coalitional interests represented in an early stage of strategic decision making. Information constraints always prevent a rigorous and unambiguous explanatory model of the issue from being developed; further, there are high stakes attached to having a particular diagnosis accepted. Individuals engage in various influence attempts in order to have their preferred diagnosis accepted. The process of diagnosis is thus adaptive and incremental.

It is to be noted that political conflict or differences do not automatically result in a broadening of the scope of diagnosis. Efforts to comprehend a strategic issue are again predominantly dependent upon the perceived self-interests of influential individuals and coalitions. Premature diagnosis could emerge when such diagnoses are compatible with the interests of affected individuals.

Consider the following example of diagnosis observed by one of the authors. The organization was a multidivisional organization with the divisions being further organized into product groups. The example concerns a single product group which we shall refer to as PG-X. At the time of observation PG-X had been in existence for about five years. Despite the rapidly growing market facing the product group, PG-X had never registered profits during its existence; this was widely known within the corporation. Given the product line's small market share and the stiff competition facing it, PG-X managers had serious doubts as to the viability of the product line almost from its inception. However, the PG-X management group had a successful track record in turnaround situations; therefore, this group had a clear self-interest in turning this loser into a winner. This was the diagnosis. As a result, these managers successfully staved off inquiries and criticisms from the division and corporate management. They relied on such arguments as the product line's market potential, its contribution to the company's technology development program, and its synergy or compatibility with other products of the division.

A couple of events occurred which tended to change the context within which the PG-X managers operated. First, corporate management began to emphasize attainment of divisional performance objectives. This led division management to establish specific targets for individual product groups. Second, corporate management announced that product groups which had to be divested should be identified. This in turn led to a milieu in which the management of divestment was highly regarded and managers accomplishing this successfully were given high visibility. The PG-X managers diagnosed that their product group be divested on the basis of product line's low market share position and future prospects—a diagnosis which they hoped would enable them to gain enhanced reputation and position in the eyes of division corporate management.

One other point needs to be mentioned with respect to the example of PG-X. Even when the decision to divest PG-X was being made, there were advocates of the retention of this product group in various other divisions, primarily because these advocates had been deriving some benefits from the existence of PG-X. However, this difference in self-interest did not result in any extensive broadening of the analysis, probably because of these managers' recognition that they were flowing against the tide and/or their assessment that, if they pushed their interests, the potential losses in reputation might not be worth the prospective gains.

Thus, a political perspective suggests that issue identification and diagnosis are not purely analytical activities. Resolution of strategic issues is likely to redistribute power and influence, and therefore, political forces come into play quite early in the decision-making process, either to thwart or to sponsor an issue.

Strategic Alternative Development

The rational model pays insufficient attention to the search processes involved in the development of strategic alternatives. These alternatives do not drop like manna from heaven; rather, they are the output of a search process which is "dynamic, operating in an open system where it is subjected to interferences, feedback loops, deadends and other factors" (Mintzberg, Raisinghani, and Theoret, p. 263). Search involves commitment of resources such as people and managerial time. The political perspective suggests the need to *manage* the analytical activities involved in alternative development. People must be motivated, time must be committed, and resources must be allocated in order to develop alternatives.

Organizational characteristics such as resource scarcity and interdependence infuse the process of alternative development with political overtones. In such a milieu, organizational members become sensitized to how suggested or potential options impact on their resource base and the degree of their dependence on other subunits. Subunits will support (oppose) the emergence and development of options which are perceived as lessening (enhancing) their dependence on other intraorganizational or external entities and those which broaden (narrow) their resource bases.

Political activity may be stimulated not merely by structural conditions but also by the concerns of individual members with regard to careers, rewards, visibility, and status. Alternatives which could potentially augment an individual's remuneration, enhance visibility, and contribute to the improved status and importance of one's position are obviously more appealing than alternatives with no potential. Personal interests often underlie many different forms of alternative advocacy—a pervasive form of political activity.

Within this context of ongoing, circuitous, multilevel, and protracted strategic analysis, managers individually or collectively may wield power or exercise influence through a variety of processes and activities to manage the evolution of strategic alternatives and the nature of the alternatives which do emerge. Managers can utilize their access to many different types of resources to affect emergent alternatives. Information may be disregarded; decision-making procedures such as task forces, committees, and ongoing planning processes may be stalled, side-tracked, speeded up, ignored, or used as a launching pad or mechanism to buttress preferred alternatives; external experts or consultants or members of external entities such as customers, suppliers, and governmental agencies (or arguments publicly stated by these) can be utilized to muster analytic support for or opposition to alternatives; and, finally, discretionary finance and available subordinates can be directed toward marshaling an analysis to enhance or discredit specific options.

Examples of these phenomena were observed in the context of energy conservation decisions reported by Fahey (1981). Entire conservation projects or alternatives within a given project often never reached the corporate-wide committee charged with exercising choice in such decisions. In many cases, as described by the managers themselves, the rejection or suppression of these options was due to political considerations. Managers at the division level were careful not to present options to the corporate-wide committee unless they estimated a high probability of acceptance. Acceptance was deemed to reflect favorably on division personnel, whereas rejection was seen as indicative of lack of preparation and inability to solve problems. Some projects were not presented for appraisal because of anticipated negative reaction by other personnel at the division level. Unless a project was seen as clearly compatible with the role and interests of line management, the engineering function was highly unlikely to commit the necessary resources to its development. Of particular note in this study was that above some cutoff return on investment criterion, the alternatives within a project that were promoted and accepted were largely determined by the types of political factors noted above.

Implicit in these activities is a critical and explicitly political behavior—mobilizing others around one's preferred alternative(s). Mobilization involves the use of formal (committee meetings, planning cycle procedures, and so on) and informal (chance encounters, telephone conversations, and so on) forums to channel information to those who might constitute potential allies. These same channels serve as sounding boards for the potential composition of alternatives and as a medium for detecting others' positions, biases, and preferences. The focus of mobilization is to discover those areas of common interest and agreement so that informal alliances or coalitions (Narayanan and Fahey) can be forged. The expectation here is that such alliances stand a much better chance to have their demands met or their interests protected.

Evaluation and Choice

A political conception of organizations places heavy emphasis upon the evolution of goals as a part of ongoing decision processes. Organizational goals or goals at any given organization level are a result of processes of negotiation and bargaining that take place over time—processes fueled by the representation of interests and the imposition of demands.

The rational conception of decision making presumes that goals are explicitly stated, known to organizational participants, and agreed to by them. Yet the reflections of many managers and a growing volume of research suggest that such a picture is not indicative of organizational realities especially when one gets beyond very general goals such as increased sales, more profits, and better products (Quinn, 1980). Indeed, efforts to establish precise goals or even the publication of intent to do so are what induce many of the political behaviors discussed in this chapter.

Thus, from a political perspective, analysis and evaluation of alternatives are inherently concerned with the advocacy and rejection of goals and decision criteria. For instance, an analysis of potential merger or acquisition candidates is very likely to center around how each would best "fit" with the present firm. Thus, financial, marketing, technology, personnel, and other decision criteria tend to be advocated and engulfed with supporting data by various actors within the firm. Even if the analysis is restricted to one domain, such conflicts may arise owing to different emphasis; for example, in the financial domain such conflicts may revolve around short-run versus long-run considerations.

Of particular importance here is the consideration that these activities are most likely to be undertaken in a rational or analytic guise. In other words, managers will project themselves as being rational—as being interested in collecting information, evaluating it, comparing and contrasting alternatives, and so on. Many have noted that rationality and efficiency are dominant social values upheld in organizations. Typically, the rationality gets defined in terms of organizational and societal goals. Thus, a political actor in pursuit of his or her own interest is often compelled to espouse rationality in organizational terms. *Appearance of rationality rather than rationality per se is important in a political milieu.*

Consider the Reagan administration tax policy as related in *Newsweek* (March 2, 1981, p. 29). The tax policies were based on the White House forecast of rapid economic growth, a plunging inflation rate, and a balanced budget. That forecast was the product of an internal debate reflecting conflicting economic views.

> Supply-siders, led by David Stockman, insisted that the tax-cut program would provide powerful new incentives for work and investment, and consultant John Rutledge maintained that Reagan's unorthodox policies would

> revolutionize public expectations and allow inflation to fall far faster than conventional analysis would indicate. Treasury Under-secretary Beryl Sprinkel, a monetarist, warned that a stimulative fiscal policy risked a recessionary collision with the tight monetary policies of the Federal Reserve, but he was appeased with assurances that the Fed would be supported regardless of the economic cost.
>
> Meanwhile, Murray Weidenbaum, the chairman of the Council of Economic Advisers, attempted to keep the forecast within limits that conventional economists might accept. "You must understand," says one insider "that the final bargain on the forecast was struck by Stockman, who had to produce a balanced budget in some way by 1984, and Weidenbaum, who had to defend the forecast whatever it was." The final compromise amounted to a curious exercise in circular economics: *aides simply assumed that the President's program would work as intended, then came up with the theoretical underpinning to prove they were right.* [emphasis ours]

As illustrated in the above example, the exercise of choice is not restricted to one time period or occasion when a listing of fully developed alternatives is available. Evaluation of alternatives is continually taking place as soon as they begin to take shape in the alternative development phase. Preliminary evaluations at one extreme may lead to the rejection of alternatives such that they receive minimal if any further organizational consideration or, at the other extreme, may lead to the intense advocacy of particular alternatives. These early evaluations or choices, which quite obviously critically affect the range and detail of the options available for evaluation and choice at later stages of decision making, may be particularly susceptible to political influences.

In many strategic decisions, as illustrated above in the context of President Reagan's tax policy, goals or decision criteria emerge to fit the alternatives which evolve. This is a consequence of the plethora of uncertainties which enmesh the choice of organizational strategy. Even for an individual strategic decision, the contours of the alternatives and the relevance of choice criteria evolve over time. Some choice criteria depreciate in relevance, others appreciate, and new ones may even appear.

Implementation

The rational model typically separates strategy formulation and implementation into two distinct and sequential phases. From a political perspective, however, this distinction is blurred and often misleading. Consider the context of strategic decisions as seen from a political vantage point. The context is conflict-filled; disagreements, quasi resolutions of conflict, ambiguities, and distortions of information are the typical characteristics of the organization. Under these conditions, the formulation of strategy does not end with the choice phase. The choice must be translated into action. This process of translation which takes place within the implementation phase is not smooth but chaotic. Mintzberg (1978) makes this observation when he distinguishes "emergent" strategy from "intended" strategy. The implication here is that the intended strategy, the output of the choice phase, is never fully realized. As new events unfold during the process of implementation, the choice is modified and transformed, leading to emergent strategy.

Why does this happen? First, we have observed that from a political perspective, commitment to strategic decisions begins to evolve during the early phases of decision making. These commitments most likely will have associated with them "winners" and "losers" after the choice phase. In other words, the antagonists of the strategic decision are often committed to choices other than the ones adopted by the organization.

Such commitments are often intense; it is, therefore, unrealistic to expect that these individuals are so flexible as to transfer their commitment to the choice adopted by the organization. Losers are likely to trigger further strategic issues with the intent to modify the strategy as it is being implemented. The winners are perceived as selling their choice or abating resistance, whereas the losers are perceived (by the winners) as not cooperating, not motivated, or sometimes not even competent. Such portrayals and perceptions during the implementation phase lead to a dynamic in which exercise of power and influence becomes inevitable in order to commit resources, to allocate tasks and responsibilities, and/or to monitor results. Thus, implementation, which is often described as an orderly process in the rational model, becomes prolonged, and as a result, it provides many opportunities for organizational politics.

Consider the case of a corporate divestment in a medium-sized pharmaceutical company observed by one of the authors. The company had three divisions: pharmaceutical products, agricultural products, and a small division which dealt with surgical instruments. The corporate management had allowed the subsidiary to be run autonomously. At the time the decision was being observed, the corporate management was involved in assessing the "degree of fit" of the various subsidiaries with their main line products, pharmaceuticals. As a result of an intense soul-searching process, the board of directors approved a proposal by the corporate management to divest both the surgical instruments and the agricultural divisions. Despite the rationale behind the decision, the corporate management ran into problems during the process of implementation. A number of reasons could be cited to explain this phenomenon. First, the corporate management had very little knowledge of either the surgical instruments or the agricultural divisions; they did not know prospective buyers, and they were ignorant as to how to "fix a price" for these divestments. Because the subsidiaries had been run autonomously, most of this information resided with division management. Second, division management was not committed to the divestment decision; they viewed themselves as losers despite their excellent performance in terms of profits and return on investment. As a result, they had very little incentive to carry out the implementation process. It has been noted that, in general, losers try to reverse the choice or more likely make it palatable to their own interests.

Typically, implementation involves sequencing of activities over time. Choices or decisions proceed from the general to the specific (commitments, allocations, and assignments). As these choices are made, a clearer formulation of strategy emerges. It may be observed that as the degree of specificity increases, so does the likelihood of resistance, since the actors now have targets to focus upon and mobilize around. This suggests that intended (formulated) strategy is the output of a process which invokes a rational frame of reference; the emergent (implemented) strategy is an output of political processes.

Evaluation of Results

The evaluation of ongoing operations of the company provides a critical input into the formulation of future strategies. As such, in the rational model this plays a fairly significant role in terms of triggering strategic issues. Yet it is a common observation that most managers resist evaluation of their own performance or the performance of their organizational subunit. We suggest that the resistance arises out of the inherently political nature of evaluation. Evaluation of results, especially when the results are less than admirable, has implications for the visibility, survival, and retention of the entities (individuals and/or subunits) being evaluated. In the strategic arena, the results of strategic choices cannot often be foreseen, not even by their protagonists. Many of the factors which control the results are environmentally determined and thus outside the control of the implementing subunit or individual. Yet, during the process of evaluation, the distinction between controllable and uncontrollable factors tends to be forgotten; there is a tendency to attribute the cause of failure to the individuals or subunits involved. Under such circumstances, the evaluation process provides an arena in which power and influence are exercised in order to deprecate an individual or subunit. We suspect that most managers are sensitive to the evaluation process because they are aware of its political implications; that is, they know how it can affect their own interests.

In the foregoing paragraphs we have discussed how the analytical and rational processes suggested by the classical models of strategic decision making are hampered or distorted by the inherently political characteristics of organizations. The suggestion here is that such analytical processes are played out against a background of a unique distribution of power and influence and have implications for the survival and resource base of the individuals and subunits involved. The rationality of the process therefore becomes a disguise to hide one's self-interest, power motivations, and ambitions.

IMPLICATIONS

The preceding discussion of a selected set of the manifestations of political forces at each stage of strategic decision making suggests that a much richer understanding of strategy making ensues when the rational and political perspectives are integrated. Each complements the other in explaining how and why some strategies are chosen and others are not. Either alone is insufficient for this task. Therefore, we suggest that in order to be effective, those entrusted with strategy formulation should pay attention not only to the rational aspects of management but also to the political aspects. In this section, some implications of the political side of enterprise are presented, from the vantage point of those charged with strategy formulation.

An immediate implication is that organizational politics cannot simply be denoted as "bad" or undesirable; it is, rather, inevitable. Indeed, one may argue that politics constitutes a key component of the glue that holds an organization together. Politics, in the sense of individuals and subunits, formally and informally negotiating and bargaining with each other, provides an indispensable mechanism for organizational coordination.

Further, the *content* of strategic decisions and the *processes* of arriving at such decisions are intertwined; analysis always takes place within a political milieu. This implies that the context or organizational processes of strategic decision making must be managed just as much as the content side. Each phase of strategic decision making involves the management of individuals, subunits, committees, task forces, project teams, and their interrelationships. If such processes are not carefully managed, opportunities exist for the various actors to skew the content of strategic decisions in the direction of their own interests. For example, the processes involved in information collection and appraisal—central analytical components in issue diagnosis and alternative development—must be managed, for these processes may be particularly amenable to political influence. Many channels or sources of information should be utilized, and different individuals or groups employed to interpret and evaluate information, so as to avoid the potential biases and political underpinnings of information from any one source.

The political perspective undermines the picture of strategic decision making as an orderly progression through a sequence of decision phases which the rational perspective suggests; rather, it shows how decision making is more likely to be *incremental* in nature. Actors will endeavor to protract the decision process if they suspect that it is not congruent with their own interests. They will negotiate and bargain to have their preferred alternatives considered and accepted, and they will fight to protect their preferred choices, once those choices have been enacted, or to defend themselves against the choices of others. The point here is that interruptions, delays, and demands for further analysis, while they may be couched in "rational" terms, may really be a reflection of political underpinnings. Such occurrences should alert strategic decision makers to the existence of *potential pockets of resistance* and to the need to reexamine and alter the organizational processes operating in the context.

Political motivations manifest themselves in many influence tactics, some of which are more relevant than others at particular decision phases. Tactics indicative of such political motivation are: (1) control of the emergence of issues and agendas at the diagnosis phase; (2) control of resources (capital, personnel, information) and mobilization of others at the alternative development phase; (3) control of choice criteria or goals at the evaluation and choice phase; and (4) promotion of choice criteria, commitments and results at the implementation and results evaluation phases. Table 21-2 presents a selected list of these activities. We suggest that politically astute actors may utilize similar or different types of influence tactics for different purposes at each decision phase—all of which may be clothed in apparently rational or analytical garb.

Implicit throughout this chapter and especially in the discussion of influence tactics are questions of *timing:* when should actors be expected to engage in such influence tactics? It will generally be necessary to create a receptive climate before many issues can be given broad public visibility within the organization, before some issues can be raised at all, or before one can be seen to be committed to a particular strategic alternative. Endless examples could be cited in which intense organizational conflict occurred when chief executive officers or others announced that major strategic changes were at an advanced stage of consideration or in which individuals became too quickly identified with strategic alternatives later deemed inappropriate. More specifically, information collection, withholding, and dissemination inherently are matters of timing: actors collect, withhold, or disseminate data when they assess that it is in their interests to do so.

When the rational and political perspectives are linked, the resultant sensitivity to the underlying political dynamics helps to ensure that feasible and desirable options are not unduly disregarded or expediently supported. If parochial priorities come into play, strategic choices that are not in the best interests of the total organization may be the result. A politically powerful R&D or marketing group with established access to the president and/or the board of directors can be surprisingly successful in suppressing options which might result in a lessening of their role, status, and power within the organization. Political dynamics of this nature assumes added significance when it is noted that many strategic changes or investments are initiated and developed at middle to lower levels of the organizational hierarchy and are most certainly implemented at these levels. However, the path from these lower levels to those who must ultimately evaluate and authorize such proposed alternatives is paved with opportunities for political interference in the form of support or opposition.

Table 21-2 Political Activities across Phases of Strategic Decision Making

Phases of strategic decision making	Focus of political action	Examples of political activity
Issue identification and diagnosis	Control of: *a.* issues *b.* cause-and-effect relationships	Control of agenda Interpretation of past events and future trends
Alternative development	Control of alternatives	Mobilization Coalition formation Resource commitment for information search
Choice and evaluation	Control of choice	Selective advocacy of criteria Search and representation of information to justify choice
Implementation	Interaction between winners and losers	Winners attempt to "sell" or co-opt losers Losers attempt to thwart decisions and trigger fresh strategic issues
Evaluation of results	Representing oneself as successful	Selective advocacy of criteria

Furthermore, when choices are made and resources committed, differences in viewpoint are never completely resolved. Quasi resolution of conflict is the norm. Additionally, attributions of "winners" and "losers" may arise. Such attributions may prove highly detrimental to organizations since structural characteristics make cooperation and joint commitments unavoidable if strategies are to be successfully implemented. A major implication here is that the politics of implementation is just as critical as the politics of formulation. Just as managers must be sensitive to timing considerations in raising issues, making choices, and so on, so must they also be sensitive to the political consequences of their choices (decisions) and thereby avoid the trap of believing that once choices are made, organizational commitment will follow.

Notions of winners and losers, quasi resolution of conflict, attention to timing, and the incremental nature of decision making suggest that new political issues or arenas are continually arising in strategic decision making. For instance, mobilization at the alternative development phase leads to the development of alliances. Once a choice is made, new alliances may emerge to oppose the choice or at least render its consequences as unharmful as possible to their interests. As implementation progresses and results become available, affected actors may redefine the decision criteria and mobilize to achieve new goals.

A number of implications for the management of strategic change flow from a political conception of organizations. At any given time, actors have vested interests in their own position and status, their past contributions to the organization, and what the organization is currently doing. Those who have introduced new products, consummated mergers or acquisitions, created new advertising themes, or affected improvements in distribution systems will be devoted to their implementation and success. When the rigors and demands of day-to-day activities are added to these commitments, it is little wonder that individual managers and organizations are frequently depicted as enmeshed in inertia in the face of major change. Yet new strategic directions are major changes, and are often inevitable if the organization is to survive and grow. Incrementalism and timing considerations as previously discussed indicate that such strategic changes should not be foisted upon those who will be charged with their implementation. Rather, such changes and the nature of their implementation should emerge out of deliberations with affected actors since, as we have noted, commitment begins to evolve at the alternative development phase. Actors should be afforded the opportunity to evaluate the proposed strategic changes in light of their own positions and interests. Also, formulation and implementation of new strategies take time. Consequently, the processes of strategy making should move from the general to the specific level. Strategic decision makers should have a fund of patience and must be able to deal with ambiguities with a certain degree of ease.

BIBLIOGRAPHY

Fahey, Liam: "On Strategic Management Decision Processes," *Strategic Management Journal,* Spring 1981, vol. 2, pp. 43–60.

Lawrence, Paul R. and Jay W. Lorsch: *Organization and Environment,* Harvard University Press, Cambridge, Mass., 1967.

Mintzberg, Henry: "Strategy Formulation as a Historical Process," *International Studies of Management and Organization,* vol. 7, 1977, pp. 28–40.

Mintzberg, Henry: *The Structuring of Organizations,* Prentice-Hall, Englewood Cliffs, N.J., 1980.

Mintzberg, Henry, Duru Raisinghani, and Andre T. Theoret: "The Structure of Unstructured Decision Processes," *Administrative Science Quarterly,* vol. 21, 1976, pp. 246–276.

Narayanan, V. K. and Liam Fahey: "The Micro-Politics of Strategy Formulation," *Academy of Management Review,* June 1982, vol. 17, no. 1, pp. 25–34.

Pfeffer, Jeffrey: *Power in Organizations,* Pitman, Marshfield, Mass., 1981.

Quinn, James Brian: *Strategies for Change: Logical Incrementalism,* Irwin, Homewood, Ill., 1980.

"Sizing Up the Program," *Newsweek,* March 2, 1981, pp. 25–29.

Chapter 22

PLANNING FOR UNCERTAINTY—THE SCENARIO-STRATEGY MATRIX

MICHAEL E. NAYLOR
Strategic Planning, General Motors Corporation

Strategic planning is receiving substantially more emphasis nowadays as more and more organizations begin to feel the effects of changes in their traditional business spheres. However, one thing that is equally apparent is that strategic planning means different things to different people.

One definition of strategic planning is the identification of needed changes in the structure of the business and its position in the external business environment.

Strategic planning aims to anticipate the unexpected—both the good and the bad—that could change the nature, or the needed positioning, of business in the future. Put another way, strategic planning is the action of developing plans to make the most of future opportunities and counteract the possible adverse effects of future changes in the business environment.

Peter Drucker draws a clear distinction between planning and strategy. He says, "Planning tries to optimize tomorrow the trends of today" whereas "Strategy aims to exploit the new and different opportunities of tomorrow."

The first important variable to determine is the time horizon for strat-

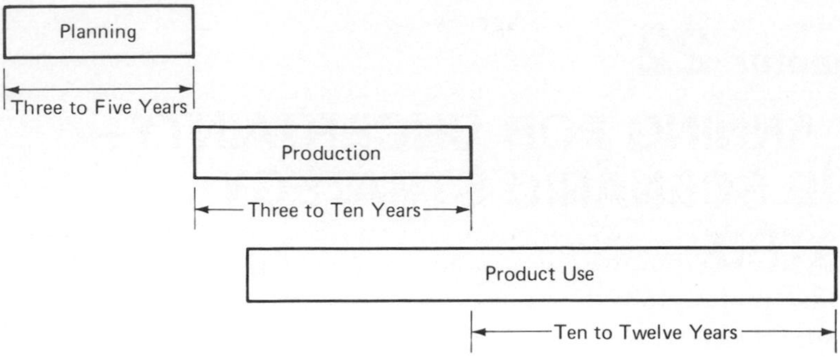

FIGURE 22-1
Traditional product cycle for automobile business.

egy evaluation. How far ahead one must look is a direct function of the specific nature of each individual business.

Most businesses have a reasonably defined product—and that product in turn has a distinct product cycle with three stages. Stage 1 is product planning, stage 2 is production, and stage 3 is product use.

The product planning stage starts with the go-ahead decision for a product and extends through the design and development, certification and plant changeover, and for most industrial enterprises also includes the tooling and supplier lead times.

The production stage is the actual operation of the manufacturing facility or assembly line, and the product use stage is that time period when the finished product is being used by the customer. Combining

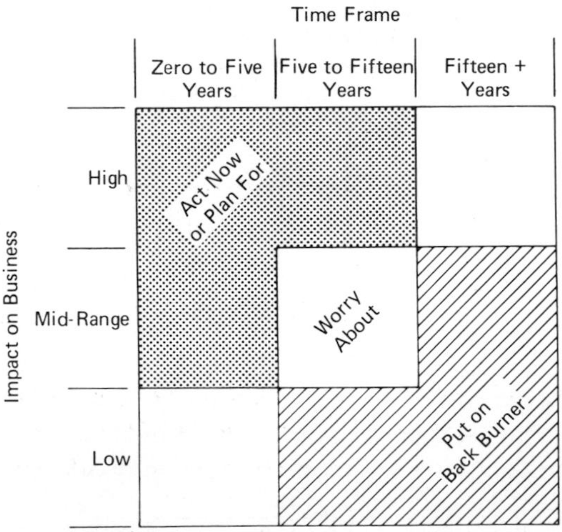

FIGURE 22-2
Classification matrix for external events.

the time frames for these stages will help define the time horizon over which you should be looking to evaluate your particular strategies.

Traditional product cycle times for the automobile business are three to five years for planning, three to ten years for production, and ten to twelve years for product life (see Figure 22-1). Taken in combination, these values lead to a time horizon in excess of fifteen years. One of the initial tasks of strategic planning is to evaluate the external events that could occur within this time frame to identify those that might have a significant impact on the business environment.

Again, to keep our definitions clear, external events are those things that are outside the direct control of the management team. Some examples of external events are:

- Economic cycles or downturns
- Availability of personnel resources
- Embargoes or supply disruptions of critical materials

Typically, external events have been classified according to the expected impact on the business. The matrix shown in Figure 22-2 is representative of many that have been experimented with over the past few years in an attempt to develop some type of classification system to handle external events. The scenario-strategy matrix provides a different approach to this problem. First, however, it is necessary to develop the planning definition a stage further.

Planning stages are taking longer. Because of the nature of the current and expected business environment, it is necessary to spend more time and effort in the planning stage in just about all businesses. There are environmental impact statements to be prepared and approved, there are many additional certification procedures required for many products and, in many cases, there are new facilities and tools to be designed, ordered, or built. The production stage is also being extended for many of the same reasons (see Figure 22-3).

These stretch-outs in the planning and production stages are coming

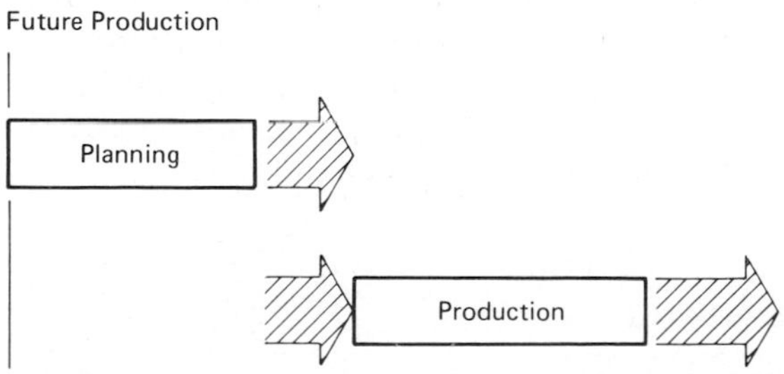

FIGURE 22-3
Trend in planning and production stages.

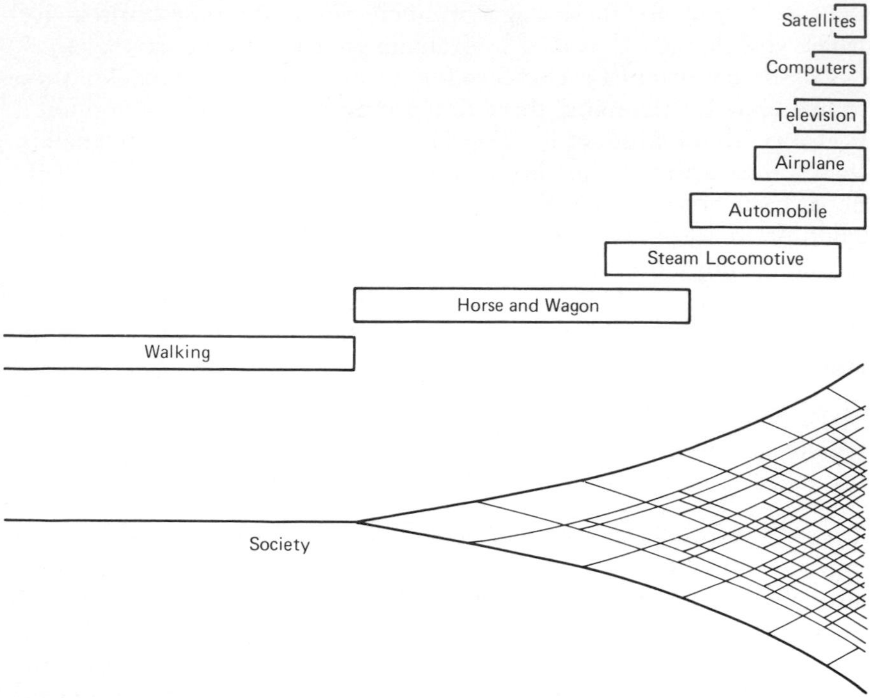

FIGURE 22-4
Trends in change and social complexity.

at a time when change and social complexity are increasing. It might be argued that the rate of change is no greater but the magnitude of the increments is substantially higher. Big improvements in the capability and cost of transportation, for example, have allowed the evolution of a wider degree of interrelationships within and between the various geographic and social constituents of society (see Figure 22-4).

Human beings are innovators. There has been a steady stream of inventions throughout history, and each invention, or discovery, has brought change. What is new is that today's changes are occurring faster, and are often unpredictable by conventional wisdom.

Simply stated, the future trend in business is that business cycles are tending to get longer at the same time that business environments are changing faster and becoming more complex.

STRATEGIC PLANNING

The job of strategic planning is to analyze the future business environment, develop alternative plans or strategies to address the possibilities,

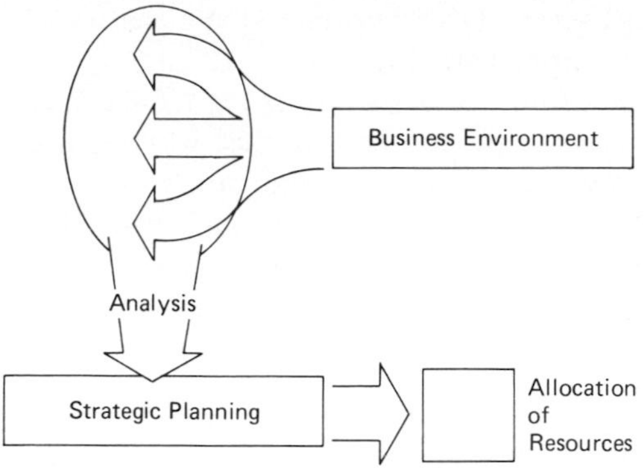

FIGURE 22-5
The job of strategic planning.

be a guide in the allocation of resources, and improve the competitive edge. See Figure 22-5.

Strategic planning faces one big problem: there are no facts about the future, only opinions. All the various predictions and trend extrapolations are at best just educated guesses based on previous experiences. What happens when new events occur that do not follow the prevailing trends? How good are forecasts?

Forecasting, at best, can really be credible only for the short range—approximately five years into the future—because many of the factors that will influence trends over this time frame are already in place. Beyond five years these major factors can change significantly, making the future unpredictable. (See Figure 22-6.)

Even in the short range, forecasts can have problems. When forecast quarterly changes in GNP are compared with the actual changes, as in Figure 22-7, it is clear that the batting average is not very good. It is very difficult to make accurate forecasts even as short as a year ahead

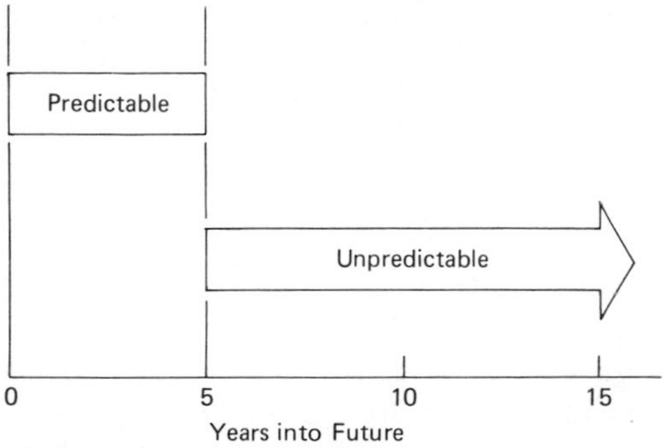

FIGURE 22-6
Forecasting time frame.

on something as basic as GNP because of the nature of change and the resultant state of unpredictability.

Another simple example, as shown in Figure 22-8, is the forecasts for the size of the 1976 U.S. population that were made in 1965 and in 1970. The estimates were lowered significantly between 1965 and 1970, but when compared with the actual population for 1976, it is apparent that the forecasts were again wide of the mark.

As can be seen from these examples, strategic planning appears to be facing a dilemma:

- There are no facts, only opinions.
- Forecasts are often unreliable.
- Trend extrapolations can be misleading.
- Turbulence is becoming the norm.

Faced with this situation, how can planners plan?

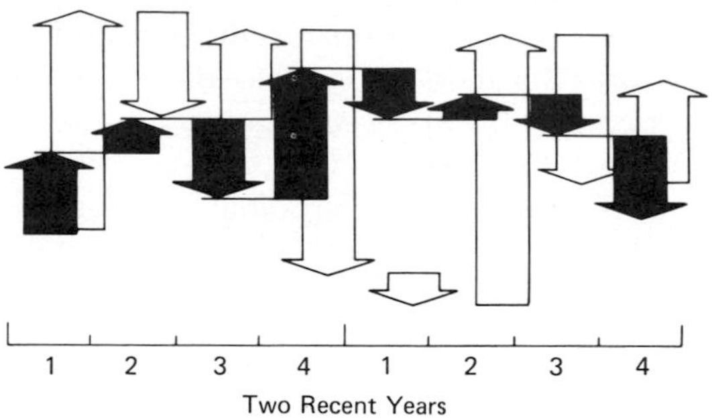

FIGURE 22-7
GNP forecast versus actual.

THE SCENARIO-STRATEGY MATRIX

One possible way out of this dilemma is the scenario-strategy matrix. It is a way to recognize uncertainty. There are seven specific steps in the process of producing a scenario-strategy matrix.

Step 1

Step 1 is to develop a "pair" of scenarios—optimistic and pessimistic. An important point to be made here is that it is advantageous to develop scenarios in pairs. A business should never have an odd number of scenarios spanning the range from good to bad because the middle scenario becomes compellingly attractive. The selection or development of scenarios in pairs forces the consideration of both alternatives. This is particularly important for those who believe that the future is essentially unpredictable.

It is also very valuable to examine possible events based on a comparison of optimistic versus pessimistic possible results. What is the best outcome of a given event? How does this contrast with the worst outcome?

The important elements of a scenario are the *key determinants* and the *principal impact factors.* Key determinants are those items, events, or situations that lead to or result in the realization of the specific scenario. In developing a scenario, one distinction to bear in mind is that those events or decisions that you cannot control are scenarios, while those events or decisions that you can control are strategy options. Principal impact factors are the resultant elements that affect your particular business.

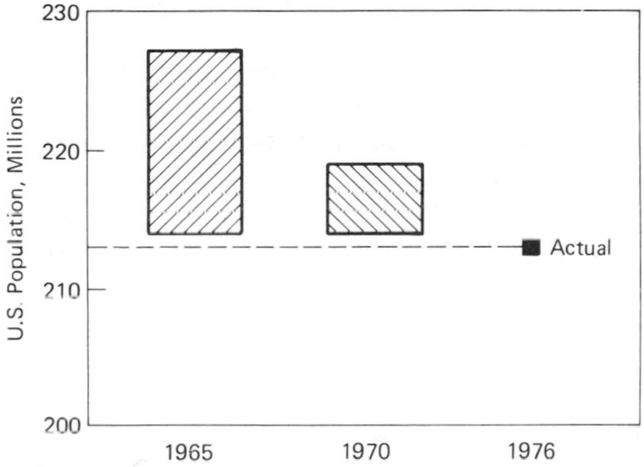

FIGURE 22-8
Actual versus forecast population.

For an example of a pair of scenarios, consider the future adequacy of electric-generating capacity in North America. The National Electric Reliability Council has published warnings for the past few years that we are running very close to the margins on capacity to generate electric power. The optimistic scenario would admit no problems. The pessimistic scenario would be that there is insufficient capacity to meet demand. These scenarios are shown in Table 22-1. The key determinants of this pair of scenarios include the state of energy regulations, the state of environmental regulations, and the growth in power demand. The principal impact factors for most businesses are power supply and cost. Both sets must be worked out in sufficient detail to allow the allocation of "ball park" estimates of quantities or magnitudes for each element.

Table 22-1 Sample Scenario Pairs

	Optimistic: No problems	Pessimistic: Insufficient capacity
Key determinants		
Energy regulation	Nuclear power encouraged Coal supplies growing	Nuclear power constrained Coal supply shortfall
Environmental regulation	Some relief from present standards	New, more severe standards
Demand growth	Slower than trend Lower peak-to-valley variation	Faster than trend Greater peak-to-valley variation
Principal impact factors		
Power supply	Adequate	Blackouts or curtailments
Cost	Higher than trend	On trend

Step 2

Once a pair of scenarios is developed, step 2 can take place: write down the basic strategy options that can be pursued. Possible strategies are going to be highly individualized for specific businesses. However, most strategies fall into one of these categories:

- Business as usual—make no changes in present programs, organization, personnel
- Reorganize the present business—regroup into different SBUs, shift personnel, relocate offices or plants, and so on
- Adjust the degree of integration—more or less vertical and/or horizontal integration of existing business areas
- Diversify into new businesses

Step 3

The third step is to evaluate the various strategies under the optimistic scenario. For the first pass, take each strategy in turn and rank it relative to the other strategy options assuming that the optimistic scenario will happen.

To rank the various strategies it will be necessary first to establish the various success factors for your business, that is, what the key elements

Optimistic Scenario	+ +	+	+ +	—	+
	Business as Usual	Reorganize	More Integration	Less Integration	Diversify

FIGURE 22-9
Strategies evaluated against optimistic scenario.

Pessimistic Scenario	− −	+	−	+	+ +
	Business as Usual	Reorganize	More Integration	Less Integration	Diversify

FIGURE 22-10
Strategies evaluated against pessimistic scenario.

are that your business uses to judge success. Representative examples might include:

- Use or development of existing strengths
- Growth potential
- Stakeholder benefits such as stockholders, customers, employees
- Return on investment
- Capital generation and cash flow requirements

A typical initial ranking is shown in Figure 22-9. In this case five strategies are being considered: business as usual, reorganizing, more integration, less integration, and diversifying. The relative rankings are shown by the plus and minus symbols: double plus is the best; double minus is the worst. Notice in this case that there are two double pluses, two pluses, one single minus, and no double minuses. Many times it is found (as it is here) that more than one strategy will satisfy the specific success factors under a single scenario.

Step 4

In step 4 the same procedure is followed for the pessimistic scenario, using the same success factors and ranking the strategy options in the same manner.

Under the pessimistic scenario the strategies might have rankings as shown in Figure 22-10. Notice this time that there is one double minus and one double plus, with the others falling between them.

Step 5

In step 5 these sets of strategy evaluations are combined into a scenario-strategy matrix as shown in Figure 22-11.

Optimistic Scenario	+ +	+	+ +	−	+
Pessimistic Scenario	− −	+	−	+	+ +
	Business as Usual	Reorganize	More Integration	Less Integration	Diversify

FIGURE 22-11
Complete scenario-strategy matrix.

In this example, the business-as-usual strategy has the highest spread and would thus constitute the highest risk strategy if it is believed that the pessimistic scenario is at all probable. The strategies required to change the level of integration are both somewhat similar in that each is a win-lose proposition dependent on the actual business environment that occurs. The reorganization and the diversification strategies are the only strategies that look good under either scenario.

These strategies, to reorganize or diversify (see Figure 22-12), are robust strategies because they will be able to satisfy the success factors under both optimistic and pessimistic scenarios. Since we are unable to predict with certainty which of the scenarios will actually occur, the robust strategies offer the best options to handle uncertainty.

Step 6

These same strategies are evaluated against other pairs of scenarios in step 6.

	Business as Usual	Reorganize	More Integration	Less Integration	Diversify
Optimistic Scenario	+ +	+	+ +	—	+
Pessimistic Scenario	— —	+	—	+	+ +

FIGURE 22-12
Robust strategy options.

In general, scenario pairs should be developed for each key area or specific underpinning of your business. SRI International has identified twelve basic classes of underpinnings that should be evaluated for each specific business. These are:

- Needs and wants served
- Resources and assets
- Stability of costs relative to competition
- Technologies
- Special abilities
- Strong corporate identity symbols
- Institutional barriers (or barriers erected by people) to competition
- Social values
- Sanctions, supports, and incentives
- Trust relating to products and organization
- Availability of complementary products or services
- Small customer base

Not all these classes of underpinnings will be relevant to each specific business, but they are shown here as examples of the types of scenarios that might have to be developed. In some areas, like the availability of complementary products or services, several sets of scenarios may have to be developed—one pair may not be sufficient.

Step 7

The last step in this process is to redefine the strategies by combining, modifying, and deleting, and then to reiterate the evaluations against the various sets of scenario pairs. As the choice of strategies narrows, it will be necessary to become more specific in evaluating the impacts on the success factors, but for the initial pass-through it is usually sufficient to remain relatively qualitative in the assessments.

In summary, the scenario-strategy matrix is a useful tool for strategic planning. It avoids dependence on forecasts, it encourages the consideration of alternatives, and it tends to produce more emphasis on flexibility.

It also allows a quick appraisal of a large number of strategy options against a wide range of scenarios and can lead to the identification of robust strategies needed to cope with the expected turbulence in the business environment of the 1980s.

One final observation: planning is but one part of the organization team, and strategic planning is but one part of the overall planning activity. Success requires real strength and competence in all areas of the business. Good plans are of little value without a strong and competent operational organization to use them; good strategic directions are of little value without equally sound short- and medium-term business plans and programs.

The organizations that will succeed in the future are those that have developed real depth in all areas of the business. Strategic planning has its part to play, but planners must always remember that they are part of a team.

Chapter 23

THE PIMS PROGRAM

SIDNEY SCHOEFFLER

Managing Director, The Strategic Planning Institute

The Profit Impact of Market Strategy (PIMS) program, operated by The Strategic Planning Institute, is a multicompany activity designed to provide each participating company with reliable data on the consequences of strategic actions.

PIMS operates by pooling information on the business-strategy experiences of the member companies.

Each member company contributes information about its experiences in several different strategic business units. The PIMS staff analyzes this experience to discover the general "laws" that determine what business strategy, in what kind of competitive environment, produces what profit results. The findings are made available to member companies in a form useful to their business planning.

The intent of the program is to provide business managers and planners with tools and data for answering questions like these:

1. What profit rate is *normal* for a given business, considering its particular market, competitive position, technology, cost structure, and so on?
2. If the business continues on its *current track,* what will its future operating results be?
3. What *strategic changes* in the business have promise of improving these results?
4. Given a *specific* contemplated future strategy for the business, how will profitability or cash flow change, short-term and long-term?

5. What strategic changes would optimize the *value of the business?*

In each case, the answers are derived from an analysis of the experiences of other businesses operating under strategically similar conditions.

More specifically, the objectives of the program are the following:

1. To assemble a *data base* reflecting the business strategy experiences of a group of participating companies
2. To conduct a *research program* on that data base in order to discover the "laws of the marketplace" that govern (*a*) profit levels, (*b*) other outcomes of strategic actions, and (*c*) outcomes of change in the business environment
3. To conduct an *applications program* to make the findings of the research available to participating companies in a form and manner they can effectively use

The confidential information entrusted to the Institute by its member companies concerning their businesses is held under stringent conditions of data security and confidentiality to minimize the possibility of leakage of such information among member companies or to outsiders.

The Strategic Planning Institute is a nonprofit corporation, governed by its member companies.

At present over 200 companies participate in PIMS, including:

- About 125 large U.S. corporations, drawn mostly from the top 500 companies on the Fortune list
- Many medium-sized companies in manufacturing and service businesses
- A growing group of large European companies

The unit of observation in PIMS is a strategic business unit (SBU), that is, a division, product line, or other profit center within its parent company selling a distinct set of products and/or services to an identifiable group of customers. An SBU is in competition with a well-defined set of competitors, and for which meaningful separation can be made of revenues, operating costs, investments and strategic plans.

Currently, the data base consists of information on the strategic experiences of more than 2000 businesses, covering a four- to eight-year period. The information on each business consists of about 100 items, descriptive of the characteristics of the *market environment,* the state of *competition,* the *strategy* pursued by the business, and the *operating results* obtained. Each data item has been pretested for significance and relevance to profitability. Table 23-1 contains an illustrative list of the items of information in the data base.

The PIMS staff has devised a set of *standardized forms* to be filled out by the participant company for the contribution of its experience records to the computer data bank. The forms are designed to break the required data items into simple elements that can readily be assembled from financial or marketing records, or that can be estimated by someone familiar with the specific business.

Table 23-1 Information on Each Business in the PIMS Data Base

Characteristics of the business environment
- Long-run growth rate of the market
- Short-run growth rate of the market
- Rate of inflation of selling price levels
- Number and size of customers
- Purchase frequency and magnitude

Competitive position of the business
- Share of the served market
- Share relative to largest competitors
- Product quality relative to competitors
- Prices relative to competitors
- Pay scales relative to competitors
- Marketing efforts relative to competitors
- Pattern of market segmentation
- Rate of new product introductions

Structure of the production process
- Capital intensity (degree of automation, and so on)
- Degree of vertical integration
- Capacity utilization
- Productivity of capital equipment
- Productivity of people
- Inventory levels

Discretionary budget allocations
- R&D budgets
- Advertising and promotion budgets
- Sales force expenditures

Strategic moves
- Patterns of change in the controllable elements above

Operating results
- Profitability results
- Cash flow results
- Growth results

SOME KEY FINDINGS

The study of the 2000-plus businesses in the PIMS data bank clearly establishes the following nine propositions:

Finding 1: Business Situations Generally Behave in a Regular and Predictable Manner

The operating results achieved by a particular business—its profit, cash flow, growth, and so on—are determined in a rather regular and predictable fashion by the "laws of nature" that operate in business situations. This does not mean that we can foretell the exact results of *every* business in any given short period. It means that we can estimate the approximate results—within three to five points of aftertax return on investment (ROI)—of most businesses (close to 90 percent) over a moderately long period (three to five years), on the basis of observable characteristics of the market and of the strategies employed by the business itself and its competitors.

Business situations can be understood by an empirical scientific approach, and therefore the process of formulating business strategy is becoming an applied science.

Finding 2: All Business Situations Are Basically Alike in Obeying the Same Laws of the Marketplace

In the same way that all human beings, despite their many differences in appearance, personality, religion, behavior, and state of health, obey the same laws of physiology, all businesses, despite their many differences in product, company personality, and state of profit health, obey the same laws of the marketplace. The first fact makes possible the applied science of medicine, in which a trained physician can usefully treat any human being. The second makes possible the applied science of business strategy, in which a trained strategist can usefully function in any business. Of course, many physicians and many strategists elect to specialize, but that merely implements a division of labor; it does not argue against the principle.

Finding 3: The Laws of the Marketplace Determine about 80 Percent of the Observed Variance in Operating Results across Different Businesses

Some businesses are very profitable or have favorable cash flows; others are very unprofitable or have unfavorable cash flows. When we try to understand the variance between them, the laws of the marketplace account for up to 80 percent of that variance.

This means that the characteristics of the served market, of the business itself, and of its competitors constitute about 80 percent of the reasons for success or failure, and the operating skill or luck of the management constitutes about 20 percent.

Another way of stating Finding 3 is to say that doing the right thing is much more important than doing it well. Being in the right business in the right way is 80 percent of the story; operating that business in a skillful or lucky way is 20 percent of the story.

Finding 4: There Are Nine Major Strategic Influences on Profitability and Net Cash Flow

These nine influences constitute most of the 80 percent of the determination of business success or failure. In approximate order of importance, they are the following:

a. INVESTMENT INTENSITY. Technology and the chosen way of doing business govern how much fixed capital and working capital are required to produce a dollar of sales or a dollar of value added in the business. Investment intensity generally produces a negative impact on percentage measures of profitability or net cash flow; that is, businesses that are mechanized or automated or inventory-intensive generally show lower returns on investment and sales than businesses that are not.

b. PRODUCTIVITY. Businesses producing high value added per employee are more profitable than those with low value added per employee. (*Value added* is defined as the amount by which the business increases the market value of the raw materials and components it buys.) Productivity is especially profitable to the extent that it does not require additional investment.

c. MARKET POSITION. A business's share of its served market (both absolute and relative to its three largest competitors) has a positive impact on its profit and net cash flow. (The *served market* is the specific segment of the total potential market—defined in terms of products, customers or areas—in which the business actually competes.)

d. GROWTH OF THE SERVED MARKET. Growth is generally favorable to dollar measures of profit, indifferent to percent measures of profit, and negative to all measures of net cash flow.

e. QUALITY OF THE PRODUCTS AND/OR SERVICES OFFERED. Quality, defined as the customers' evaluation of the business, product, and/or service package as compared to that of competitors, has a generally favorable impact on all measures of financial performance.

f. INNOVATION AND/OR DIFFERENTIATION. Extensive actions taken by a business in such areas as new product introduction, R&D, or marketing effort generally produce a positive effect on its performance *if* that business has strong market position to begin with. Otherwise, it usually does not.

g. VERTICAL INTEGRATION. For businesses located in mature and stable markets, vertical integration (that is, make rather than buy) generally impacts favorably on performance. In markets that are rapidly growing, declining, or otherwise changing, the opposite is true.

h. COST PUSH. The rates of increase of wages, salaries, and raw material prices, and the presence of a labor union, have complex impacts on profit and cash flow, depending on how the business is positioned to pass along the increase to its customers, and/or to absorb the higher costs internally.

i. CURRENT STRATEGIC EFFORT. The current direction of change of any of the above factors has effects on profit and cash flow that are frequently opposite to that of the factor itself. For example, having strong market share tends to increase net cash flow, but getting share drains cash while the business is making that effort.

There is such a thing as being a good or a poor "operator." A good operator can improve the profitability of a strong strategic position or minimize the damage of a weak one; a poor operator does the opposite. The presence of a management team that functions as a good operator is therefore a favorable element of a business, and produces a financial result greater than one would expect from the strategic position of the business alone.

Finding 5: The Operation of the Nine Major Strategic Influences Is Complex

Sometimes these strategic influences tend to offset each other. For example, greater investment intensity (which tends to reduce earnings) often goes along with greater productivity (which tends to increase earnings). In that case, the net effect (which, in the present instance, is negative) is what matters.

Sometimes they reinforce each other. For example, strong market position (which by itself acts favorably on earnings) and high quality (which also acts that way) usually go together. In that case, a cumulative effect occurs.

Frequently the effect of a strategic factor reverses, depending on other factors. For example, a high level of R&D effort tends to increase earnings if done by a business with strong market position, and to decrease earnings if done by a business with weak position.

Therefore, when business strategy is formulated, it is dangerous to use a simplistic logic.

Finding 6: Product Characteristics Do Not Matter

In making a strategic assessment of a business, it does not matter whether the product is chemical or electrical, edible or toxic, large or small, purple or yellow. What matters are the *characteristics* of the business, such as the nine cited before. Two businesses making entirely different products, but having similar investment intensity, productivity, market position, and so on, will usually show similar operating results. And two businesses making the same products but differing in their investment intensity and other business characteristics will generally show different operating results. (Characteristics of the product may, however, affect the speed at which strategic events occur.)

Finding 7: The Expected Impacts of Strategic Business Characteristics Tend to Assert Themselves Over Time

This means basically two things. First, when the fundamentals of a business change over time (for example, its quality level increases or its vertical integration goes down, whether by inadvertence or as a result of deliberate strategy) its profitability and net cash flow move in the direction of the norm for the new position. Second, if the actually realized performance of a business deviates from the expected norm (expected on the basis of the laws of the marketplace), it will tend to move back toward that norm.

Finding 8: Business Strategies Are Successful If Their "Fundamentals" Are Good, Unsuccessful If They Are Unsound

A good strategy is one that can confidently be expected to have good consequences; a poor strategy is one that can confidently be expected to have poor consequences. The laws of the marketplace are a reliable source of confidence in estimating both the cost of making a given strategic move and the benefit of having made it.

The fundamentals do not always operate in a simplistic way, as noted before. Thus, it is not always a good idea to expand a strong, well-situated business, or to harvest or divest a weak one. The former business may well be on the verge of trouble, and the latter may be in a situation in which a minor effort can produce a major improvement.

A model firmly based in the empirical laws of the marketplace is therefore a very helpful tool of strategy analysis.

Finding 9: Most Clear Strategy Signals Are Robust

When a particular strategic move for a business is clearly indicated to be a good idea (that is, when the cost-benefit projections look clearly favorable), that signal is usually quite robust. This means that moderate-sized errors in the analysis—such as wrong assessments of current product quality or wrong estimates of future market growth—do not usually render the signal invalid; and moderate-sized changes in the position of the business—such as its vertical integration or operating skill—do not either.

REPORTS ON INDIVIDUAL BUSINESSES

The research findings on business position and strategy are incorporated in a series of models; these models, in turn, are used to generate diagnostic reports on the individual businesses operated by the member companies. The major specific reports are:

The "Par" Report The par report specifies the ROI that is normal (or par) for the business, given the characteristics of its market, competition, position, technology, and cost structure. It reports whether this business is the kind that normally earns, say, 3 percent on investment or 30 percent, judging by the experiences of other businesses with similar characteristics. Also, it identifies the major strengths and weaknesses of the business that account for the high or low par.

The Strategy Analysis Report This is a computational pretest of several possible strategic moves in the business. It indicates the normal short- and long-term consequences of each such move, judging by the experience of other businesses making a similar move from a similar starting point in a similar business environment. It specifies the profit (or loss) likely to be achieved by such projected changes, along with the associated investment and cash flow. This report is used by (1) upper-level managers and planners, for evidence on potential effects of broad moves in market share, margin, capital intensity, and vertical integration; and (2) middle-level people, for evidence of the potential effects of *specific* action in such areas as programs to improve relative product quality, increases in the ratio of marketing expense to sales, improvements in capacity utilization or employee productivity, or changes in R&D outlays.

The Optimum Strategy Report The optimum strategy report nominates that combination of several strategic moves that promises to give optimal results for the business, also judging by the experiences of other businesses under similar circumstances.

This report offers such an opinion for any of several different measures of profit performance, for example:

- Discounted cash flow over ten years
- Return on investment for the next five years
- Short-term earnings dollars

Report on "Look-Alikes" (ROLA) ROLA provides managers with a way to discover effective tactics for accomplishing their strategic objectives (for example, increasing profitability or cash flow, gaining market share, improving productivity or product quality). ROLA retrieves from the data-base businesses that are strategically similar to the business being analyzed (its "look-alikes") and reports a large number of the strategic and operating characteristics that helped them to attain the specified objective.

Strategic Look-Alikes A closer look at the analysis of strategic look-alikes will illustrate how the relevant lessons recorded in the data base are being brought to bear upon the strategy and tactics of particular businesses.

The major tool of the analysis is a software package that carries out the following steps:

1. It focuses on the major strategic characteristics of the specific business under consideration.
2. Next, it searches the entire PIMS data base for the other businesses that are strategic look-alikes to the specific business, that is, that had a similar strategic position, in a similar market environment, facing a similar competitive situation, and employing a similar technology.
3. It subdivides the look-alikes into two categories: the look-alikes that turned out to be "winners" and the look-alikes that turned out to be "losers." (The program can accept a variety of definitions of winning or losing. For example, "winning" can mean high ROI, or positive net cash flow, or gains in market position, or increases in the market value of the business.)
4. It then examines about 100 behavior characteristics—pricing, marketing, R&D, inventory, personnel, and so on—of both the winners and the losers to find out whether they were different, and whether the differences were statistically significant.
5. Finally, it reports out the significantly different behavior elements that separate the winners from the losers. These are the high-leverage, high-reliability action elements to which the strategy of the business should be addressed. The analysis usually uncovers about five to ten such factors, from among the hundred being examined, that are especially promising for the business being studied.

CONCLUSION

The facts that (1) more than 200 major companies have decided to participate in this program, and (2) the research findings are highly valid and actionable, indicate rather strongly that strategic planning as a management activity is coming out of the dark ages. Business leaders have always had to make strategic decisions, and have always had a structure and process for making and implementing such decisions. Sometimes the structure and process were formal, other times informal;

sometimes they were energetic, other times low-key. The weakness was always in the informational and analytic input. The process worked well for executives with good intuition and/or good luck. It worked poorly for the others.

When we add elements of science—that is, relevant cross-sectional data plus rigorous analysis—to the process, strategic planning becomes a more *dependably* productive activity. More and more companies are recognizing this and are taking the requisite steps.

Chapter **24**

AVOIDING PLANNING BACKLASH

W. WALKER LEWIS
President, Strategic Planning Associates, Inc.

The original Henry Ford did not believe in formal planning. He announced, "The Ford factories and enterprises have no organization, no specific duties attached to any position, no line of succession or of authority, very few titles, and no conferences." Given the level of paper glut and bureaucracy of many planning systems in place in our companies today, some chief executives may look back longingly to Ford's way of thinking. We call this reaction "planning backlash."

Planning backlash occurs whenever a firm feels that the value of the planning process is not sufficient to justify the outlay of time and money. Planning backlash, in the most serious of cases, can result in the total dismantling of a firm's planning effort. See Figure 24-1.

Rather than accept Mr. Ford's solution of eliminating planning altogether, firms which are suffering from planning backlash should examine the underlying problems of the planning process and restructure the system so that it can be effective. We begin with a basic assumption: shareholder value can be created by employing a systematic planning system. While no planning system can *assure* the success of a business venture, the odds of winning can be improved by using strategic concepts.

If planning can create shareholder value, why are many firms failing to increase or even attempting to reduce the level of commitment to their planning systems? The answer is that most planning systems don't work or don't work well enough.

We believe that there are six generic reasons for planning disappointment. The beginning of effective planning lies in their recognition. They are:

- Installation of a boilerplate planning system
- Emphasis on process at the expense of content
- Unclear role definition for strategy "players"
- Lack of strategic understanding on the part of the corporate strategy developers
- Lack of communication between planning units
- Lack of appropriate planning automation

Each of these six reasons will be addressed in turn:

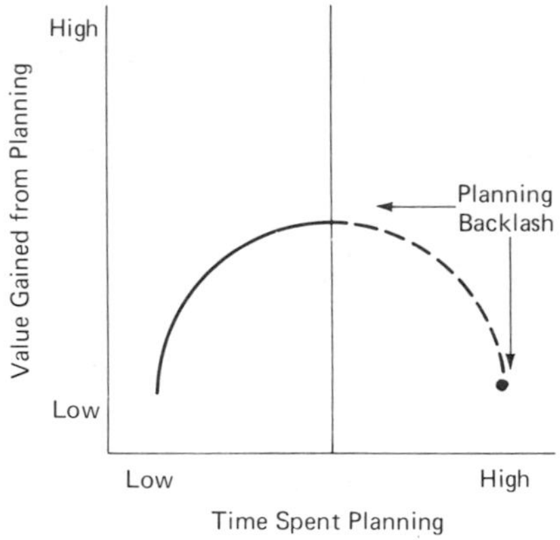

FIGURE 24-1
Planning backlash.

INSTALLATION OF A BOILERPLATE SYSTEM

One major planning problem is that many firms have blindly installed a planning system advocated in a book or journal. The truth is that every firm is different and the success of a planning system is not determined by the flow of paper but, rather, the matching of a firm's culture with its strategy requirements.

Much of the scholarly literature in planning journals discusses the differences between top-down systems (ones in which corporate develops goals for the business units which must be incorporated in the business plans) and bottom-up plans (in which the businesses feed plans to corporate which analyzes and aggregates them), focusing on their respective merits. In my view, both are needed, but on a far more streamlined basis than is frequently the case.

To analyze what a planning system should do, one must start with the needs of the chief executive officer (CEO). It is vital to review how the CEO views formal strategy and what the CEO hopes to get from a formal planning system. Planning systems that do not have the support of the CEO and the top managers of the firm are, by definition, marginal.

Many CEOs are their firm's top planners. For such planning-oriented CEOs, a planner must ensure that the quality of the input data and the value of insights are high. Planners who present to such CEOs without insightful analysis will often be greeted with the withering phrase "So what?"

Other CEOs have an aversion to theoretical frameworks, buzzwords, and anything which sounds like scientific management. These CEOs are looking for facts and insights and want them expressed in specific terms. Models and concepts without a specific applicability to their particular situation bore them.

For some CEOs the key to a good planning system is the amount of data they receive. These CEOs enjoy manipulating raw data to come up with their own answers and insights. A planning system designed for such a CEO must focus on the gathering, sorting, and easy display of key data as accurately as possible. Strategies must be accompanied by well-packaged numerical data and financial analyses for the plan to be considered valid. In other firms, however, numbers are taken to be a sign of lack of creativity, and plans which are mostly numerical are viewed dimly.

Some CEOs will not really be happy to accept the results of any planning system because they interfere with intuitive decision making. As the planner becomes an implicit participant in the decision-making process, some CEOs will begin to subvert the system themselves in order to maintain their total command of the decision making in the firm. Planners in this type of firm must be presenters of data while leaving the generation of conclusions to the CEO.

In some firms, the commitment to formalized planning is high, and the top management does not mind having line operating officers spending a great deal of time generating and communicating strategies. In others, the top management tolerates planning but is not really going to support the system when the operating management complains that the planning time is taking away from the "money-making" time. Any company in which planning is not seen as a money-making activity will eventually withdraw its support.

There are many other aspects of the firm culture which will determine the type of planning system to be installed. Equally important, the basic characteristics of the firm (asset intensity, type of business, geographical dispersion, size of customer segments, numbers of business segments) will have a great deal to do with the design of a successful planning process. The point should be clear: no one planning system is going to work for all firms. The situation, the culture, and the personality of the firm, which often derive from the personality of the CEO, should be a major determinant in the way the process is structured.

PROCESS WITHOUT CONTENT

It is an obvious but often ignored fact that the success of a planning system primarily depends on the quality of the plans it monitors. Process without content is doomed to failure in all but the most bureaucratic firms.

The emphasis on process at the expense of content also manifests itself in the "planning-by-the-pound" syndrome. In many firms the biggest plan is considered the best plan because so much data were unearthed and so much analysis performed. Unfortunately, it is not the quantity of data or the amount of analysis but, rather, the quality of insight which distinguishes a superior plan. But with the mountains of data provided by the various divisions, it is often hard to tell (or hard for the corporate planners to have the time to evaluate) which plans do or do not make sense.

If the lack of content is certain to cause planning backlash, then the development of an explicit strategy framework for strategy development becomes the initial task in setting up a planning system. The strategy framework must address the difference between corporate and business strategy and include the vital questions which must be addressed by both sides of the corporation. While the definition of an explicit framework is material enough for an additional chapter, if not a book, it is important in the context of this discussion of planning systems to give a brief outline of a workable framework. See Figure 24-2.

A Strategic Framework

The objective of a corporation is to create lasting value for its shareholders. Three specific aspects of this premise provide the foundation for all strategic analysis: (1) long-term cash flow is the basis of shareholder value; (2) corporate growth is valuable *only* if it is attached to sufficient profitability to meet the shareholders' cash flow requirements—otherwise, growth does not create value for a company's shareholders; (3) individual business segments within a corporation can add to or detract from a corporation's value, depending on their ability to generate cash flow.

These three rules provide a context for corporate strategy. They force companies to address the shareholders' required return, to select businesses (existing businesses, acquisitions, or new ventures) on the basis of that return, and to allocate resources accordingly.

In order to evaluate the allocation of capital, the firm must be seg-

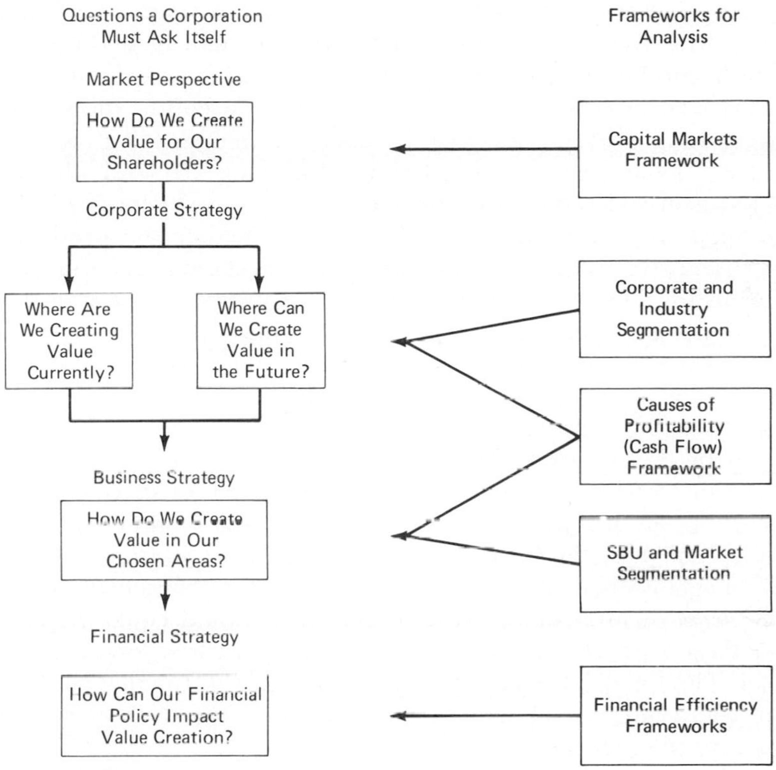

FIGURE 24-2
Strategy framework.

mented into its different strategic units; of course, the corporation will attempt to maximize the synergies between those units. A corporate strategy should address each of these issues, including suggestions regarding the way the firm can improve the cross-linkages between segments. Corporate strategy is more than a summation of the business strategies, more than a simple cash flow forecast derived from the business plans; it is an explicit description of the way the corporation works to create value for the shareholder by making the whole worth more than the sum of the pieces.

If each business can create or destroy value for the shareholder, then it is the job of business strategists to determine whether their business units do create value and what the prospects are for the future. The fundamental question which business strategy analysis must answer is: will the business ever return the cash flow necessary to satisfy the investors? If not, then restructuring, harvesting, or divesting the business is called for. To assess the potential of any business requires an analysis of the attractiveness of the industry structure in which the business operates, and how that structure will change. The leverage points of the industry, the factors which create competitive strength, should be revealed through industry analysis. Competitive analysis will indicate what the strengths and weaknesses of the competition are, and what room that leaves in which one's own business can operate or innovate.

Strategic marketing analysis will indicate whether the product is a price-insensitive specialty or a cost-dominated commodity and the implications for a business's ability to operate profitably in the industry. If the product is a specialty, it is possible to achieve levels of profitability without scale if the business is making the right product for a given market. If it is a commodity, the business must achieve low cost. This choice between a low-cost or a specialty strategy must come from an analysis of the industry. The business strategy should be, therefore, more than a review of the environment and a market share target with some financials attached. It is a discussion of what it takes to win in the industry and how the business plans to exploit its strengths while defending against its weaknesses in order to generate long-term cash flow.

The level of investment made by the firm should equal the sum of the outlays supported by the businesses that return at least the cost of capital. The financial requirements of the firm and the dividend policy are a fallout of this analysis—they do not serve as goals to be met upon going into the process.

Clearly, this is a cursory discussion of a fairly complicated framework which, if rigorously applied, gives each planning function an explicit charter and indicates the data that need to be collected and evaluated at each step of the planning process.

UNCLEAR ROLE DEFINITION FOR PLANNERS

Owing to the lack of a strategic framework, many planning systems suffer from an unclear definition of what the planners are intended to do. Are they support staff for the CEO? Are they part of the decision-making process or simply data collectors? In some firms the planner is meant to be a high-level public relations expert who makes speeches about the future of the firm to customers, analysts, and suppliers. In others the planner is a troubleshooter who studies particular issues of interest.

Without a clear charter, planners are in deep trouble—they have no idea what power they have to implement a system and, in fact, why a system is there in the first place.

The role of the planner will, of course, differ by firm. One extreme is provided by the role of chief strategic officer held by William Wommack of the Mead Corporation in the 1970s. Wommack was given overall responsibility for the firm's strategic direction and had responsibility for capital allocation and business divestitures. He developed a planning system which allowed him to understand which of Mead's businesses were going to be the ones that led the firm into the 1980s and which were not creating value for the shareholder.

Wommack's role was clearly more central to the firm's decision-making process than is acceptable to many firms. In many firms, the planner is more of an administrator—making sure that the process works without spending a great deal of time making substantive decisions.

The planner must understand his or her role—otherwise, by overstepping or understepping the boundaries, the planner may set planning backlash into effect. As with the design of the system, it lies with the top management of the firm to determine what the role of the planner is to be.

LACK OF STRATEGIC UNDERSTANDING

A clear understanding of the strategic framework on the part of the corporate planners is not enough to ensure that business plans are satisfactory. Many operating managers have intuitive ideas about what strategy is but find it difficult to formulate, communicate, and implement. Those who are familiar with strategic concepts may have been exposed to the simplistic matrix displays of the early 1970s and may need updating. This lack of understanding is a key reason for planning problems; the plans that are developed by business managers are often not founded on a solid set of assumptions, and are very often unrealistic.

There are several patterns of unrealistic, or hockey stick, plans. See Figure 24-3. The basic hockey stick is a plan which says that a business with falling sales or profitability will turn around immediately. Hockey stick plans are often submitted because divisional management believes that the CEO wishes to see them. Indeed, there are firms in which business is expected to grow at 15 percent per year, and whether it makes strategic sense or not, the business plan had better show annual

15 percent growth over the planning period. Another common plan pattern has been named the *mañana* syndrome because it assumes that a downward trend will continue for a year or so and then will dramatically reverse itself. This pattern is motivated by compensation systems which are based on short-term projections and by capital allocations which are based on longer-term results.

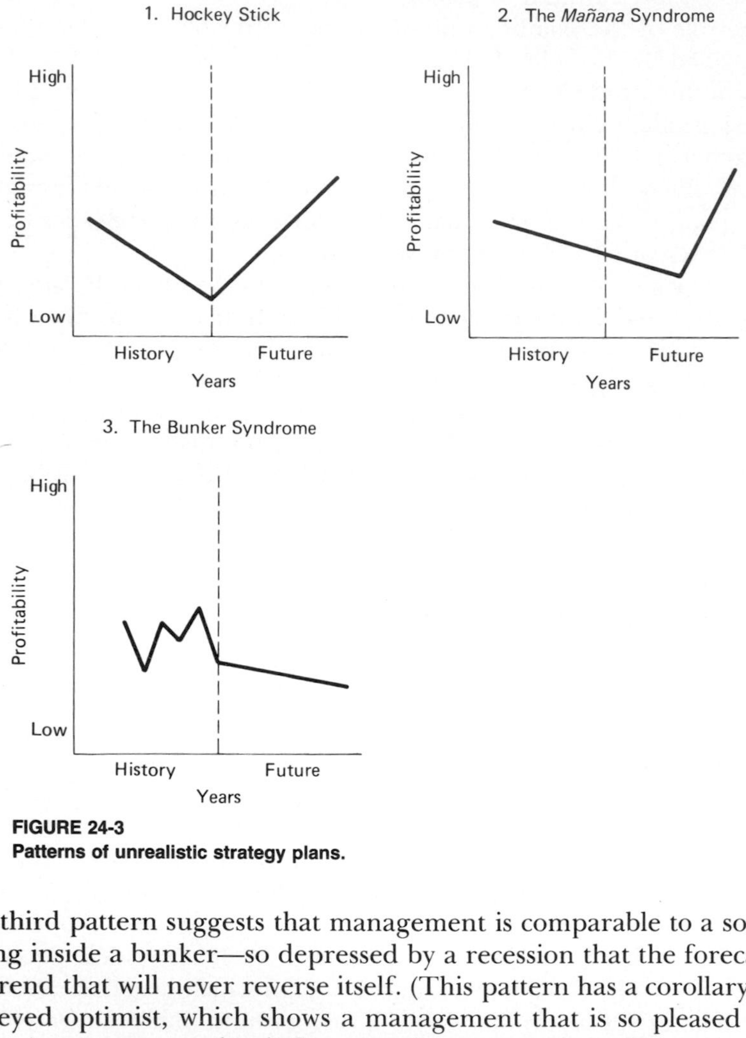

FIGURE 24-3
Patterns of unrealistic strategy plans.

A third pattern suggests that management is comparable to a soldier hiding inside a bunker—so depressed by a recession that the forecast is for trend that will never reverse itself. (This pattern has a corollary, the cockeyed optimist, which shows a management that is so pleased with recent improvements that it forecasts them to continue forever.)

The real problem with unrealistic plans is that the corporate strategy cannot be strong if the business plans that feed it do not present an accurate picture of what can be expected from each business. When hockey stick plans are submitted, the conspiracy begins. If you cannot believe the plans, you cannot believe the cash flow forecasts or the portfolio characterizations, and planning backlash rears its ugly head.

Even when strategies are developed by outside experts, be they consultants, corporate planners, or divisional planners, the real payoff from strategy comes in the implementation of the strategy—and staff personnel and hired consultants are *not* the implementers. The line managers must understand and believe in the underpinnings of a strategy they are responsible for so that they can implement the strategy. If they do not understand the basic model, they will not be able to implement the new strategy as environmental conditions change.

In too many firms the business managers are left with a large planning book to complete, and certain analyses to perform, but no real comprehension of the way the analyses fit into the framework and no real understanding of the implications of the analyses for their business. It is no wonder that most businesses submit hockey stick plans. What is needed is a comprehensive education program to explain to managers what a plan is, how to develop it, and what basic strategic principles are.

By encouraging executives to think strategically, and by fostering the understanding necessary to implement strategic plans, a relevant, well-designed program can upgrade the quality of a firm's strategy development. Education in strategy should, in fact, be considered an initial step in a firm's planning effort.

The program should be tailored to the different roles and responsibilities of line managers and staff personnel. Line managers, for example, are responsible for evaluating their business's strategic potential and for devising strategies to achieve that potential. In order to implement effective strategies, line managers should understand the concepts underlying strategies at the business level, and have at hand an efficient method for their development. Line managers, therefore, should analyze crucial issues that affect business performance, such as the structure of the industry, the capabilities of the competition, and the ability to achieve cost or price leadership.

Their staff planners must have in-depth knowledge of essential strategy techniques in addition to expertise in strategic theory, including productivity measurement, competitive assessment, and industry evaluation.

In their roles as business strategy evaluators and resource allocators, senior corporate officers are responsible for understanding key business strategy concepts. In addition, however, they require an understanding of corporate issues: capital markets evaluation, debt and dividend levels, acquisitions policy, and corporate strategy development. Programs designed for these officers must review the complete framework for corporate and business strategy development.

Corporate planners must comprehend the analytical techniques which support the development of a corporate strategy. Acquisitions, debt capacity, and field and capital markets analyses, in addition to the traditional business strategy topics, must be among the subjects included in a seminar for corporate planners.

Despite their necessarily different emphases, education and training programs should seek to establish a common language for corporate and business personnel. This shared foundation enables participants to leave the sessions having learned and agreed upon critical assumptions and premises, and having come to an understanding of strategic planning terminology and theory, and of the methodology for achieving strategic goals.

LACK OF COMMUNICATION

A major reason given for implementing formal planning systems is that communication between different functional groups and organizational units is facilitated by such a process. Ironically, a major reason for the failure of many planning systems is the lack of sufficient communication to make the system work.

At the business unit level, the required interaction between the different functional units is often missing. While a particular functional area might be of major importance for a given business, a complete business plan includes an integrated approach to such elements as marketing, manufacturing, R&D, and personnel management. It is impossible to build a cohesive strategic plan if the marketing people are solely responsible for the pricing and product information, the manufacturing people for costs, the R&D people for process and new product information, and so on. The marketing strategies will have clear impact on the manufacturing costs, and vice versa. In fact, low cost might not be the strategic motivation for a manufacturing policy at all. Perhaps the overall business strategy would lead to a desire for flexible, high-quality manufacturing rather than low cost. A business plan must be a coordinated set of functional plans which support an overall set of objectives.

Similarly, it is important for there to be interbusiness communication when the different business units share manufacturing, distribution, purchasing, or other synergies. Corporations which build synergies and scale economies between businesses are creating value. Unfortunately while such synergies are to be encouraged, they make formal planning more difficult. For formal planning to be effective, the different businesses sharing value-added steps must communicate how their respective functional strategies will impact each other.

Finally, the businesses must communicate with the corporate planning group, and vice versa. In many firms, planning dies because the business units believe that after having spent many valuable hours to develop a business plan, they never hear a response from the corporation as to whether the plan was acceptable, how the strategy was viewed, and what the corporation will do with the plan. This feeling of speaking into a dead phone is a major instigator of planning backlash, particularly when the operating manager does not believe in the inherent importance of strategic planning.

While a company's first priority is the development of a strategy, the communication of that strategy to all levels of the corporation and to its investors is imperative. For example, when approving capital expenditures, members of the board of directors often have no real basis for their decisions because they do not comprehend the corporate strategy which is driving the outlays. Division managers often believe that they are operating in a vacuum because they do not have a clear picture of the corporate strategy.

Just as the millions of financial facts generated by corporations are displayed in logical formats and subject to financial audits, so should corporate strategies be subjected to their own form of auditing. An integrated view of stock market expectations, corporate segmentation, business strategies, and cash flow results provides management with a powerful communications tool to be used with Wall Street, the board of directors, and business management.

LACK OF APPROPRIATE COMPUTER SUPPORT

Planners, like their operating counterparts, are being called on to improve their productivity each year. While the computer can be a valuable tool in support of planning productivity, in many firms automation of the planning system leads to planning backlash. While there is much the computer can do, it cannot replace the conceptual analysis, negotiating, and selling that constitute the real job of the planner; when the planner becomes the slave of the software and the entire planning process has to be manipulated to fit "what the computer needs," planning backlash is sure to follow.

Most firms have not really used the computer to its fullest potential as a planning system support tool. Most firms still use the computer as a data storage device or, at best, as an aid in simple analysis. Very few, though, have made the computer an integral part of an integrated planning system. That is because most firms have yet to explicitly accept a planning framework for themselves.

The computer can serve many functions in the planning system. It allows the planner the luxury of testing the implications of different scenarios of growth, profitability, and capital intensity. It can be a central element of a plan evaluation process. Hockey stick plans can be easily uncovered with the use of planning software: the planner can test the effects of "de-hockey-sticking" the plan and report the results to the line managers who are responsible. This ability to analyze by exception is the essence of planning productivity.

The computer can be a major communications tool in support of intra- and interbusiness communication as well as between corporate

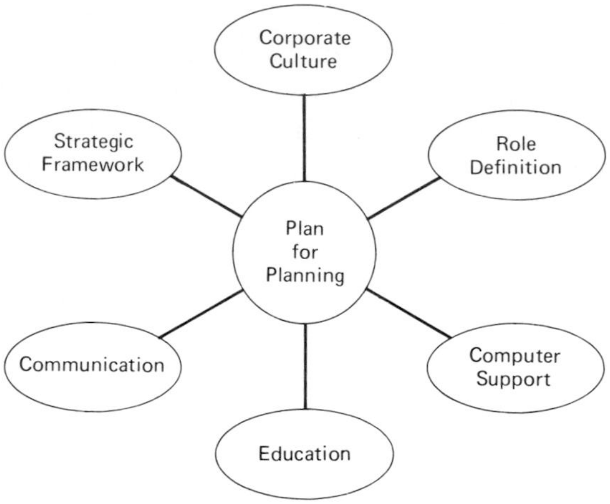

FIGURE 24-4
A plan for planning.

and business levels. In addition, the computer can build credibility for the planners by allowing them to perform timely analyses which link operations and finance; this would be impossible by hand.

But, most important, the computer frees the planner to do the things that no machine can do. Planners who spend all their time adding numbers and performing routine analysis will never have the time to develop the insights—the content which justifies the entire planning effort.

AVOIDING PLANNING BACKLASH: A PLAN FOR PLANNING

As the resources devoted to strategic planning increase, the costs of planning backlash increase as well. What is called for is a consistently executed *plan for planning*—a systematic attempt to integrate the culture of the firm with the requirements of the planning process. See Figure 24-4.

A plan for planning:

- Explicitly describes the requirements of the corporate culture
- Specifies a strategic framework
- Outlines an educational program for line and staff personnel
- Clearly defines the roles of the planners in the organization
- Denotes the communications links between business, corporate, and extracorporate entities
- Indicates the appropriate level of computer support given the placement of the firm on the planning life cycle

A plan for planning also describes the timing of the implementation of the planning system. While most firms want to start planning immediately, it is impossible to implement a system without laying the proper groundwork. Review of the corporate culture and planning framework must come first. Strategy education should precede strategy development. Computer support should be phased in; overautomation can be a major cause of backlash.

The quality of a planning process is measured by the insights it generates, as well as the smoothness of its operation. The goal of a plan for planning is to ensure that the system facilitates a maximum amount of strategic thinking and communication. Firms which carefully plan their planning activities will improve the odds of avoiding planning backlash.

Chapter **25**

THE ROLE OF OUTSIDE CONSULTANTS

WLADIMIR M. SACHS
Managing Director, The Philadelphia Consulting Group

GEORGE CALHOUN
Managing Director, The Philadelphia Consulting Group

CONSULTANT, noun. *An expert, a professional kibitzer, and a know-it-all; known to traffic in snake oil on occasion; the sort of person who borrows your watch to tell you what time it is—and keeps the watch!*

Peter Drucker has called attention to the "management boom" which took place in the early twentieth century, when owner-entrepreneurs began to be replaced by professional managers as the chief architects of business strategy. Today we are witnessing a "consulting boom." Because of the increasing complexity of the business environment, managers are coming to rely more and more upon outside talent to extend and enhance their capabilities, especially in the area of general management consulting: troubleshooting, problem diagnosis, and strategy development. The vice president for corporate planning at one $4 billion-a-year company estimated recently that at any given time there are about fifty consultants at work for that organization on various problems. Many of these consultants are involved in limited technical assignments, but increasingly the company is seeking outside help in the development of fundamental long-term goals and strategies. The company is developing long-term consulting relationships and, although fully appreciative of the growing need for outside assistance in developing business strategies, the vice president is concerned about the difficulty of managing outside resources properly and about the tendency of some managers to abdicate their own responsibilities to external consultants.

Jokes about consultants abound, and many of them have their point. But the "consulting boom" is no joke. It is a major challenge to the manager's traditional role, and it is by no means evident that the bulk of today's top- and middle-level managers are ready for it. Most managers know how to manage in-house personnel, but few (in our experience) have learned to handle consultants effectively. Consultants have different work incentives and pay scales, and their role in the corporate decision-making process is very different from that of an employee. When a firm hires an employee, it implicitly buys the employee's loyalty, as well as talent, and it implicitly offers in return a guarantee of continuing employment (assuming that the individual's and the company's performance are adequate). When a firm contracts with an outside consultant, it acquires those services for a limited period of time only. The promise of job security—a successful motivator for hired employees—cannot be used as a lever to obtain good performance. Moreover, while the firm has a right to expect discretion, it cannot expect to obtain the consultant's undying loyalty. The consultant retains, or should retain, a measure of professional independence. This "objectivity" is both an asset and a challenge to the manager who contracts with a consultant.

It is becoming an essential part of a manager's job to know how to hire, manage, and evaluate the work of outside consultants. This chapter addresses some of the reasons for which consultants should, or should not, be hired, the useful roles they can play in the formulation of business strategy, and the role of the manager in directing their activities and assessing the results. These issues have not been incorporated into the business school curriculum, and they have not received much attention in the management science literature. Therefore, this exposition is based mostly on our clinical observations as providers, and occasionally as consumers, of consulting services.

THE GENERAL ROLE OF THE OUTSIDE CONSULTANT

From a macroeconomic perspective, the "consulting boom" represents an increase in efficiency of allocating particular human resources to particular tasks. Highly trained, sometimes highly specialized, and often highly priced talent is most efficiently utilized through arrangements that allow a number of companies to share their cost. Consulting is one of the vehicles for this cost sharing (along with law firms, accounting firms, and other organized professions). It cuts down on the duplication of specialized personnel and allows consultants to maintain their particular skills even though no single client may require them on an ongoing basis.

From the standpoint of an individual firm, the availability of outside consultants allows the manager to match high-quality human resources more closely to particular tasks, instead of matching tasks to a fixed pool of human resources (as is the case in managing permanent employees). Potentially, the use of consultants can give the manager a greater flexibility in staffing and cost control; it allows the manager to treat some costs as variable or discretionary which would otherwise be relatively fixed and nondiscretionary. The manager need not be concerned with the possibility of expensive retraining or reassignment of administrative and technical personnel if the market goes into a downturn or a particular phase of a project is not completed.

However, not all companies look at consulting this way. The decision to hire a consultant is often made in response to a crisis: it is the corporate equivalent to throwing one's hands up in despair and summoning the plumber to fix the leaky faucet after one's own efforts have failed. Many consulting assignments are trouble-oriented, concerned with bailing a company out of a mess, recommending and sometimes performing radical surgery, and generally sanctioning the dirty and unpleasant decisions forced upon the organization by bad luck or mismanagement.

This accounts in part for the bad reputation of consultants among many companies, especially those that use consultants infrequently. Many managers believe that there is no reason to bring in consultants when the business is going well. But this is like saying that the only time a company should consider leasing equipment is when it cannot afford to buy it.

More sophisticated managers realize that outside consultants can play a useful role in the formulation of business strategy, and that there are good reasons for using consultants other than as a "quick fix" for a crisis. First, there is the economic advantage of shifting manpower expenses from fixed to variable cost categories, that is, reducing nondiscretionary overhead. There are three other important reasons:

1. OBJECTIVITY. Strategy formulation often benefits from the involvement of individuals who are not committed to justifying and defending current company policies and who are therefore capable of taking a fresh look at business opportunities.

2. EXPERTISE. A company may need outside expertise when (*a*) such expertise cannot be obtained in any other way; (*b*) it needs that expertise only for a limited period of time; and/or (*c*) the expertise required is such that it can best be developed by someone who is exposed to a variety of companies, problems, and information sources. For example, the design of a computer-based planning model is often best assigned to someone who has built several such models before. It is likely that only an independent consultant will have had this sort of experience.

3. CREATIVITY. Unfortunately, many large companies tend to be-

come bureaucratic, and few are really successful at fostering creativity. Even those which have done well at technical research and development still find it hard to generate creative ideas in the area of business strategy. Consultants are not necessarily more creative people. But with their broad experience and independent perspective, they can—if properly managed—stimulate creative thinking within the internal management team, especially if they are skilled at handling group "brainstorming" processes.

Overall, a company may hire a consultant to help counterbalance the negative aspects of its own organizational character: intellectual and technical inbreeding, the tendency to replicate and justify the status quo, the filtering out of dissenting (and potentially creative) alternatives before they reach the top, the narrow focus of many managers based on intensive experience with a limited aspect of a single business, and the timidity of other managers for whom concern about job security has become an obstacle to creative thinking. All these tendencies are present to some degree in every large organization we have seen, and in many small firms as well.

Unfortunately, many managers do not really know how to use outsiders to compensate for these "bad habits." Instead they try (often unconsciously) to co-opt the consultant, to get the consultant to reinforce their perceptions instead of allowing the consultant to challenge their perceptions. It is all too typical, in our experience, that a firm will hire a consultant to accomplish a particular task, and then spend considerable time and energy trying to prevent that task from being achieved. It is an organizational parallel to the psychiatric phenomenon of "resistance," in which a patient invites the therapist to "cure" some problem the patient has, agrees to pay for it, and then fights the therapist every inch of the way with great resourcefulness and cunning. The fact that this resistance is unconscious does not make it any less difficult to overcome.

For example, we were once commissioned to assist in the development of a marketing strategy for a company with a rather lackluster product line. A working group was formed internally to coordinate with us. Part of the effort involved the construction of a sales model, which required certain historical information. The working group delayed in providing us with hard data; the head of the group offered many helpful hints and observations but would not back them up with data. Often the pretext was mechanical ("Our departmental copier cannot handle the volume of copying involved; we'll send the job out and mail it to you in a couple of days." The information was never mailed.). When we became more forceful in our requests, the company responded by dumping on us a massive amount of disorganized data which we could not hope to analyze efficiently with the time and resources available to us. To make matters worse, the working group changed its composition from one meeting to the next, making it necessary to start from square one every time we got together. We later discovered that the company was genuinely dissatisfied with its current market position and plans but wanted to convince itself that the current situation, however bad, was the best it could hope for. The management group had a strong fear of the uncertainty involved in doing anything new.

This story illustrates another point about the inefficiency with which many companies manage outside consultants, even when they do want the project to succeed. In our experience, the information provided by clients tends often to be poorly organized, poorly analyzed, and far too voluminous. To make proper use of such information requires time and money to be spent on what is often simply a duplication of work that the company has already done internally (often in some other department).

THE USE AND MISUSE OF CONSULTANTS IN DEVELOPING BUSINESS STRATEGY

Managers hire outside consultants to assist in strategy development for a number of good and some not-so-good reasons:

- *As Technicians.* A consultant may be asked to apply certain technical skills to help formulate strategic plans.
- *To Confer Prestige and Legitimacy.* A company may hire a well-known consulting firm to place a stamp of approval on decisions it has already made—to impress a potential lender or investor, for example. (Although reputable consulting firms do not consciously engage in this, the agenda of the client is not always obvious, and this has happened many times.)
- *To Justify Inaction.* When managers wish to avoid taking some action, but feel compelled to demonstrate their intention to act, they can easily accomplish both objectives by commissioning a "study" from a consultant who is willing to cooperate by extending the investigations as long as possible. Major decisions have been known to be delayed for several years in this manner.
- *To Evade Responsibility.* Hiring a consultant is often a part of the corporate buck-passing ritual. It is a way for managers to shift responsibility for potentially risky decisions off their own shoulders. Again, the idea is to find a consultant who will validate the manager's own views. If the recommended course of action succeeds, the manager can claim the credit. If it fails, the manager can blame the consultant and com-

miserate with superiors ("I always had some problems with that idea, but the Ace Consulting Firm has such a good reputation . . . ").

- *To Achieve Psychological Catharsis.* Managers will sometimes "bare their souls" to outside consultants, confiding their "true feelings" about the job, the boss, the company, its policies, and so on. Such confessions often occupy a prominent place in strategy-oriented projects. While catharsis is an important function of the outside consultant, and while such sessions can be extremely useful and informative, there is a tendency for these sessions to lead nowhere. They make a manager feel better, perhaps, but they do not necessarily signal a willingness to act in order to bring about change.
- *For Stimulation and Entertainment.* Top corporate executives often maintain a network of contacts with individually brilliant "superstars" of the consulting world, whom they occasionally employ to highlight a "strategy session" at the annual corporate meeting, or as someone to bounce a few ideas off. Some of the very best consultants in the business never really get involved in "projects" as such, but make their living giving inspirational talks to groups of managers.
- *For Headhunting Purposes.* Frequently consultants wind up as employees of their clients. We are not certain of the extent to which this is the result of a conscious strategy on the part of companies. Yet it is often a superior method of personnel recruitment (as compared to traditional headhunting, in which the company relies upon recommendations and a necessarily limited appraisal of an individual's track record rather than actual collaborative working experience).

In our view, these are the wrong reasons, or at least the insufficient reasons, to bring a consultant into the strategy development process. For example, a strategy consultant may bring certain technical skills, but should not be hired as a technician. Business strategy rarely depends upon technical expertise per se, and a technically qualified consultant who is inexperienced in the realm of business strategy may be ineffective in strategy formulation.

This was illustrated in a case involving the construction of a computer-based planning model for a large foreign manufacturer of consumer food products. It was necessary to formulate sales, production, and financial strategy for the next five to ten years. There were two teams working on the project, one staffed by outside consultants and the other by personnel from the planning department. In the course of the work, it became necessary to specify the effects of a local tax on production in the company's home market. This involved a complex formula, in part because the law had recently mandated a changeover from a tax based on weight (kilograms) to one based on selling price. Some members of the internal planning department team, who generally approached their tasks as technicians rather than as strategists, became deeply immersed in trying to formulate precisely the legal and accounting implications of the changeover. The complexity of the issue threatened to delay the development of the model as a planning tool. Meanwhile, the outside consultants focused on the strategic implications and realized that what mattered most was that a switch in the basis of the tax would allow for a far more effective market segmentation based on price differences between brands. Indeed, the physical unit-based tax had a price-equalizing effect: a kilogram of a low-priced brand was taxed the same as a kilogram of a higher-quality, high-priced brand of the same product. In the country and product category in question, small changes in relative prices produce large swings in sales volume. Thus the tax reform constituted a major opportunity for the marketing arm of the company.

The point is that the precise tax formula was far less important than the representation in the planning model of this sort of strategic implication. Yet it was only because the consultants were skilled in business strategy as well as in the technical aspects of computer modeling that the deadlines for implementing the model as a planning tool were met. In general, experience has shown that the long delays in getting so many computer-based planning systems up and running have to do with the lack of strategic experience and understanding of strategy issues on the part of the often very skilled technical staff and consultants who are assigned the task of designing them.

Similar comments could be made about the other uses of consultants mentioned above. Catharsis may be useful, but a consultant should not be used as a psychotherapist. Recruiting new people from a consultant's staff may be a good way of seizing an opportunity, but it should not be the primary reason for involving an outside consulting group. Nor is there any law against a consultant being entertaining, but too often clients buy the show instead of the substance.

In our opinion, there are *five* useful roles, discussed below, which the outside consultant can play in the strategy development process. These are areas in which an outsider can often perform functions which cannot be satisfactorily duplicated by in-house personnel.

Design of the Planning Process

The outside consultant can serve as a *process designer* during the initial period when the company is structuring a systematic procedure for the review and development of business strategies.

Designing an effective planning process is no easy job. It must go beyond the budgeting cycle or the establishment of annual sales targets.

Strategic corporate planning requires the creation of a setting within which the most fundamental and "obvious" precepts of the business can be called into question, where even top management's concept of "the business we are in" can be challenged. Genuinely new ideas must be generated. Yet in many corporate cultures this is very difficult because people feel the need to justify and rationalize existing policies, rather than subjecting them to critical scrutiny (which can be threatening). Moreover, managers who spend ten to fourteen hours a day thinking about operational details must be allowed and encouraged to step back from these concerns, and to realize that those details, crucial as they may be, constitute only a part of the corporate picture.

Strategy development must be deritualized. Goals and objectives should be reformulated afresh, not merely transcribed from last year's agenda. New alternatives should be generated; choices should not be constrained to the consideration of traditional businesses and methods. Above all, planning should be subject to a system of formal *control.* Lessons should be learned from past experience, and new goals should be formulated in such a way that it is clear who will be responsible for achieving them. It should be determined how and when a deviation from expected results will be called to the attention of the planning group. This implies the need for a recording and monitoring system, and for a continuous planning cycle, not merely an annual convocation. It is surprising how few corporations plan in a controlled fashion.

Finally, the designer of a strategic planning process must struggle against the almost tribal character of corporate cultures. In many corporations, as in the "traditional societies" described by anthropologists, people find it difficult if not impossible to conceive of things as ever being very different from the way they are now. The culture is a closed system in which many people tell one another that the current situation is the best of all possible worlds, or at least the only feasible one, the least dangerous one; and they construct elaborate myths to explain and justify the status quo.

Insiders often underestimate these hurdles. The corporate culture may explain the behavior of internal "change agents" in terms of ulterior motives; by trying to upset the current situation, the insider is seen as merely making a grab for power.

An outside consultant is likely to be freer of such suspicions. The consultant wears the badge of objectivity and can therefore act as a credible stimulator of a creative strategy development process. Relying upon past experience with other companies, the consultant can be helpful in anticipating the problems mentioned above and is more likely to know how to handle them.

A case involving the nationwide marketing structure of a consumer products company illustrates the role of the outside consultant in launching and organizing a planning process. In response to poor morale among its marketing field force, the company decided to create a "round table" composed of representatives of district sales managers to propose a reorganization of the decision-making and information-gathering processes in the marketing area. Strategy consultants were commissioned to assist the round table and to interface with top management. The first meeting of the round table was little more than a forum for the participants to air their personal gripes and squabbles, often with bitter emotion. No actionable proposals emerged from this catharsis, and management was understandably disturbed at the lack of progress. The participants did not know how to act as representatives of their peers instead of as advocates for their own complaints, and they had difficulty identifying policy issues amid the chaos of individual anecdotes.

However, the consultants were able to convince the round table participants that their particular problems were the result of more general organizational dysfunctions, and that they should focus on coming up with positive suggestions for change instead of simply cataloging their bad experiences. Over several meetings, the character of the round table began to change. A host of policy issues were identified, and well-structured proposals for change were developed. Most of them were eagerly adopted by management since they represented small modifications of current policy. Over time, even more fundamental issues were addressed by the group, and management gave their proposals fair consideration (even when they were quite radical) because the group had established credibility for itself. The round table was transformed into a permanent consultative body, and the whole exercise was considered a success and a model for change in other parts of the company.

With this experience in mind, top management decided to repeat the process at a higher level in the sales organization, for divisional sales managers. This time around, outside consultants were not invited to participate, since the company considered that it had acquired the experience necessary to run this sort of exercise. Yet this second round table never evolved beyond the stage of individual catharsis and interdivisional bickering. It did not produce any significant policy proposals, and was eventually dissolved. The company's management has recently decided to revive this effort, this time using outside consultants to help set up the process.

Staff Support to a Management Strategy Team

Setting up a planning process places new demands on the support staff of the organization. Issues must be researched, and complex evaluations of new opportunities may have to be performed. The staff may be requested to develop and operate computer-based models to forecast sales, capacity requirements, financing needs, and the like. Alternative positions need to be documented. All this may require learning how to deal with new sources of information and new methods of analysis and presentation.

It may be hard for existing support staff to "gear up" to meet these new demands. An outside team can bridge the gap, providing effective staff support to get the process under way. Meanwhile, they can help train in-house personnel to assume this role for future planning sessions.

This is the one area in which companies often fail to manage consultants well. We find that the process of accustoming company staff people to new ways of doing things is the most important, and the most rewarding, part of our job as strategic consultants. The manager should make sure that there is a transfer of knowledge from the outsider to the insider. There is an old saying: "Give a man a fish, and you feed him for a day; teach him how to fish, and you feed him for a lifetime." Unfortunately, too many consultants rewrite the proverb: "Teach a man to fish, and you lose a paying client!"

Two contrasting cases involving similar projects illustrate this point. In both cases, the consultants interacted directly with the chief executive officer (CEO) and a few senior vice presidents in developing a computerized model to simulate the future effects of strategic decisions. In the first case, internal staff was involved only in supplying the information needed to build the model. Once it was fully operational, an attempt to transfer it to the company failed, because nobody in the corporate staff units really understood how to use it. The top management group continued therefore to use the outside consultants. After some time, this failed too, because key decision makers ultimately lacked trust in the "alien" model when its results were inconsistent with other, internally generated recommendations.

In the second case, the outside consultants organized themselves into a multilevel team so that a working relationship was established immediately with both top management and key staff units. This approach allowed for the painless transfer of the computerized tool to the company at an early stage of the process. Within a year and a half from the initiation of the project, the strategic planning model had become an integral part of the company's decision-making processes and its culture.

Challengers of Key Assumptions

As mentioned previously, strategic planning involves rendering explicit the key assumptions which underlie each manager's perception of the problems and opportunities facing the company. These assumptions must be laid on the table, examined, analyzed, criticized, and—insofar as it is possible—subjected to factual verification. This is more easily said than done.

Indeed, the social psychology of groups pushes them to develop ways of submerging disagreements about fundamental beliefs: many individuals strive to achieve consensus, to avoid or minimize conflict, and to establish a relative degree of certainty (even if artificial) about the goals and directions of the group. Because fundamental assumptions are rarely discussed openly, strategic choices come to be decided on the basis of personal persuasiveness or political clout rather than on rational analysis and a truly shared understanding of the alternatives.

An outsider can often break up these psychological logjams. The consultant can be a critic, a challenger of pet theories and cherished beliefs, in situations in which many insiders are afraid to speak out. Yet once the consultant has set the tone for the strategy session, it often becomes easier for others in the management group to speak up. In our experience, it rarely suffices for the top executive to announce a willingness to accept criticism of his or her beliefs. The people must be shown that the boss is willing to take a challenge and respond constructively to it. This is a job for which an outside consultant is well suited.

Integrating Nonfinancial Factors in Strategic Analyses

Many large organizations institute a process of collective self-censorship. Managers filter their own ideas and those submitted to them from below in light of what they believe their bosses want to hear or are likely to accept. This is quite natural, and all of us do it from time to time. The problem is that most managers are too conservative in their assessments of what their bosses will be willing to listen to. The result is a reduction of information flowing upward. The top levels are often the least well informed of all about what is really happening in the company.

This explains in part the overreliance of many top-level managers on financial information for making strategic decisions. Financial information is the type of information that is least likely to be filtered out, distorted, or subjected to personal interpretations. It is the best suited to aggregation, concise presentation, and abstraction.

Consequently, when it comes to business strategy, top-level managers often cannot rely upon the line organization to provide rich, meaningful information or to help them analyze business opportunities. This creates numerous problems, of course. The lower-level line people resent the fact that they are "not being heard"—although they generally fail to realize that they censor themselves often more severely than anyone else would. Policies that come down from the top are often developed on the basis of abstract financial analyses, and are often at odds with the street-wise perceptions of managers closer to the action. Such policies are often resisted, consciously or unconsciously, by the people who are expected to carry them out.

One of the steps which should be taken to combat this tendency is to broaden the staff work performed for the planning group to include more than merely financial analyses of business opportunities. No business problem has purely financial consequences. Yet in desperation at the lack of nonfinancial information, many companies resort to strategies based mainly on financial comparison of alternative investments. In our opinion, this is the Achilles' heel of many companies' growth and diversification strategies. Two examples will suffice.

A diversified foreign conglomerate acquired a very profitable company supplying apparel manufacturers with finishing items such as buttons. The acquisition was decided upon on the basis of pure return on investment (ROI) criteria, despite a strategy consultant's warnings that the company was operating in an industry in which the conglomerate lacked managerial experience. The conglomerate replaced the management of the company after the acquisition, and within a year experienced a dramatic loss of market share. Upon closer analysis, a peculiarity of the business came to light: in the country in question, most apparel manufacturers were small, family-based companies. They had no means with which to keep up with changes in international fashions. The button manufacturer had filled this role. Its economies of scale permitted it to send people to Paris and New York several times a year, which gave them an early insight into changing trends. This allowed them to change their own product lines and, in effect, to offer a fashion consulting service as part of their sales package. The small apparel manufacturers had developed a strong loyalty based on this added "service." Needless to say, the "financial wizards" from the conglomerate did not anticipate and had no idea how to factor this situation into their ROI analyses.

In another case, a cash-rich pharmaceutical company decided to evaluate its opportunities for diversification by means of the latest academic invention: an elaborate "quantitative" technique which combined sophisticated internal rate-of-return calculations with subjective preference weightings and equally subjective assessments of the company's strengths and weaknesses supplied by the top management group. The exercise was coordinated by a team from the planning department, headed by the vice president. The highest-ranked alternative was the acquisition of a chain of hotels. Somewhat surprised, an outside consultant pointed out that this line of business was totally outside the competence of the company's management. Yet the vice president of planning justified the choice in terms of the "validity" of the technique employed. Later, in a more informal setting, she let it slip that the CEO had been gratified by the outcome of the exercise since he was personally frustrated by experiences with poor service at hotels when traveling and had frequently stated that he "would love to run his own hotel chain." The "objective" ranking was easily (and probably unconsciously) manipulated to produce the desired alternative.

This suggests another useful role for the outside consultant. Most large companies maintain an in-house capability to perform financial analyses of business opportunities. The methodology of finance is well-developed, abstract, and easily learned. However, very few can afford to house the talent needed to flesh out the analysis with crucial nonfinancial considerations. Experience shows that diversification planning efforts can usually benefit by the involvement of outsiders capable of supplying knowledge about what it takes to be successful in a new business area that cannot be learned from combing publicly available financial statements.

Confidentiality and Objectivity

Finally, there are some tasks that require a special confidentiality or objective outlook which cannot be provided by anyone on the inside. For example, a single-product-line company faced the need to reorganize into a divisional structure as a prerequisite for diversification. Discussions between the CEO and outside consultants revealed that there was little possibility of entrusting top members of the current management team with divisional responsibilities, because in the past the company had promoted people "through the ranks" and none of the managers therefore had any experience outside the single product line. By the same token, as soon as it became known that a major reorganization was being considered, there was an epidemic of anxiety in the management ranks. It was clear that open discussions of organizational possibilities would have paralyzed the company. The outside consultants were able to work confidentially to help the CEO obtain the information needed to make decisions so that they could be announced in a way that minimized negative reactions.

In general, situations may arise in which the top executive in an organization (or in a department or division within an organization) believes that it is not possible to consult his or her subordinates about a key decision. Making important decisions in isolation can be both uncomfortable (we all like to share our thoughts and plans) and dangerous (there are fewer checks and balances to prevent an erroneous choice). Hiring an outside consultant can be a handy solution in such circumstances.

CHOOSING A STRATEGY CONSULTANT

Contracting for consulting services can sometimes seem like buying a suit of clothes: the customer is faced with the not altogether satisfactory choice between buying something "off the rack" that is cheap but doesn't fit very well, and commissioning a custom-tailored job, which involves much more time and money and still carries no guarantee that the result will be pleasing. Fortunately, in consulting there are alternatives, but to develop them the company must become an educated consumer. This means avoiding a number of pitfalls.

- *The First Error.* Most companies start by looking for a "quick fix," something they can plug in and run immediately, like a copying machine. The strategy development process does not work that way; it usually means redesigning the organization and its decision-making procedures, or at least reformulating the way in which problems and opportunities are analyzed. This has to involve *learning* by, and changes in the behavior of, top management.
- *The Second Error.* Most companies evaluate a consultant by tangible output. In the field of strategy, you should evaluate a consultant in terms of *your* tangible output. The consultant's role is to enable you to plan, not to do the planning for you. Unfortunately, some consultants (encouraged by their clients) have developed "study-itis": they have become skilled at writing impressive reports and making well-produced presentations. The financial temptation for the consultant is strong: once a consultant becomes proficient at the business, it takes far less time than the client imagines to turn out reports and presentations, especially when bits and pieces can be adapted from work done for previous clients. The client is also tempted to require a report or a formal presentation, since this provides a tangible "justification" for the money spent.

Elaborate reports usually bear scant relevance to the client's strategic planning process. They often contain generalizations that are only superficially suited to the client's needs. Such an approach casts the client in a passive role. A good strategic consultant will help the client (and even force the client, if need be) to assume an active, creative role. In general, it is a good idea to examine any report given to you by a consultant and ask how many words or phrases would have to be changed for the report to be applicable to some other company. If the answer is "not many," it is probably time to reassess your relationship with that consultant.

- *The Third Error.* Many companies hire a consultant to help them solve a particular problem, often quite narrowly defined. This may allow the manager to evaluate the consultant's skills before making a larger commitment, but the manager should recognize that an effective strategic consultant should be given a broader mandate. In strategic planning, the role of the consultant should be to improve the client's *planning capabilities,* to help the company learn how to gather information more efficiently, to analyze it more accurately, to formulate objectives meaningfully, to make decisions rationally, and to implement decisions in a controlled fashion that will allow the company to learn from its mistakes, instead of burying them.

Solving one problem usually brings others to light. Installing an improved management information system may highlight faulty decision-making procedures. Solving a production scheduling problem may expose a weakness in the product portfolio. A good consultant should be able to anticipate the "second round" of problems. Many clients complain that when they hire a consultant for one job, the consultant immediately begins to try to sell them a basketful of other services. Sometimes such complaints are justified, but often it is the consultant's job to diagnose an incorrect problem formulation and to anticipate ancillary issues that may arise. As a smart consumer of consulting services, a business should expect a good consultant to challenge its concept of the problem. That is part of the reason the consultant is hired.

- *The Fourth Error.* Many companies hire a strategy consultant for the consultant's analytical skills. In fact, with the exception of purely financial decisions (of which there are quite few), all strategic decisions depend upon motivating a considerable number of people to accept and work with them. The larger the company, the longer it takes to change strategic direction. The decision still requires the same amount of analysis in principle, but the process of implementation is attenuated. A strategy consultant can often be most useful not as an analyst, but by exercising human relations skills (often called "process skills") to help unlock creativity, avoid unproductive conflicts and encourage productive ones, and design a process that will produce an *understanding* of the plan among those whose job it will be to carry it out.
- *The Final Error.* When many managers look at a strategic problem, they think that they are looking for an "optimal solution." Probably the hardest lesson of all to learn is that there is no such thing. *Optimality* implies a static business and an unchanging environment. In times of turbulent change, what seems optimum today will be in need of overhaul tomorrow. Therefore, what matters is not so much "getting it perfect" (which is often very costly and time-consuming to even attempt) as "getting it going" and keeping it flexible. We know of one company that spent ten years and used thousands of hours of consultants' time to design and implement a computerized production-cost control system. It took them that long largely because they were pursuing the ideal of an optimum design. Yet the scope of the project was so large, and in-

formation processing technology has been changing so rapidly, that each new approximate optimum became obsolete before it could be fully implemented; the designers were always trying to catch up. When the system was finally set up, it was discovered that although the central processing system was close to the "state of the art," the peripheral data-entry systems were nearly ten years out of date. Thus, even the "optimal system" turned out to be considerably less than perfect.

Managers must learn to be comfortable in a world in which there is no one best answer to their problems. Again, this is an area in which the proper choice of a strategy consultant can help tremendously. The consultant can help the management team set up a planning process that has the capability to respond adaptively to each new change in the environment and to formulate objectives that are both guides for the long run *and* translatable into short-run programs. Managers should generally be wary of consultants who promise optimality instead of adaptability.

APPENDIX

THE GROWTH-SHARE MATRIX IN CORPORATE GROWTH STRATEGY*

BRUCE D. HENDERSON
Chairman of the Board, The Boston Consulting Group, Inc.

ALAN J. ZAKON
Chief Executive Officer, The Boston Consulting Group, Inc.

THE PROBLEM

"In what direction should I take my company?"

Simply stated, this question expresses the essence of corporate strategy. The chief executive officer (CEO) has a myriad of concerns and, at any given time, immediate problem solving or decision making may be paramount. Fundamentally, however, the CEO's mark on a company will be set by the direction chosen for the company, the strategies developed to get there, and the success in reaching stated goals.

In many ways, the problem is enormously complicated by its broadness of scope, the intimacy of the decision, and the magnitude of the investment to be made. Let us touch briefly on each of these now, and return to them later in a more specific context.

**Editor's note*: This appendix was originally published as a chapter in the *Handbook of Business Problem Solving* (McGraw-Hill, New York, 1980), an earlier book I edited. It is an excellent presentation of one of the most important developments in strategic management methodology.

Mr. Bruce Henderson, who coauthored this material, is also the author of the first chapter in this book, "The Concept of Strategy."

Broadness of Scope

A one-product company may express its goal in terms of doing better than the competition. Defining the competitive arena, the existing and potential competitors, and the economics of the business is fairly easy. The problem statement, method of analysis, and strategy development, though perhaps difficult in execution, are straightforward in concept. This task is appropriate for a *product* but not at all proper for a *company*—even a single-product company.

If the company is successful, it will eventually face slowing growth, that is, cash generated from the business will exceed reinvestment needs. Should that cash go back into the business? Should it be used to diversify and seek growth in new areas? If so, where? Should the cash be paid to shareholders as dividends rather than used to pursue new growth? If the company is not successful, the issues remain: where and how to deploy cash assets to build a new position.

In the most fundamental sense, the focus of corporate strategy includes not only the businesses a company now pursues but a range of areas new to the company. The straightforward goal initially expressed relative to the single-product company—outperforming the competition in that business—is a proper statement in terms of one business, but it begs the question of performance in terms of alternative uses of the shareholders' investment. Earning 7 percent on the assets of a steel company is good performance for steel but poor performance relative to the average for all companies. It is the responsibility of the CEO to redeploy assets toward returns in competition with *all* companies, not merely with existing competitors.

The multibusiness company is no different in concept. Here the first issue is developing appropriate strategies for each business independently, then looking at the corporate menu.

- What is the corporate resultant if each business pursues an optimal strategy?
  - Will overall returns be adequate?
  - Will cash generated balance cash required?
  - If not, what are the options to acquire additional cash or additional places to invest surplus cash?
    - If cash is needed:
      - Assume or increase external debt or sell equity
      - Decrease dividend
      - Sell or liquidate some businesses
      - Acquire cash-generating businesses
      - Manage some businesses for greater cash generation
      - Combine many of the alternatives listed
    - If cash is surplus:
      - Pursue some businesses more aggressively

- Repay debt or repurchase equity
- Increase dividends
- Acquire growth businesses in need of cash funding
- Combine many of the alternatives listed

In short, the strategy problem may be seen as the continual redeployment of assets to achieve a balanced corporate portfolio of high returns in which cash generation parallels cash reinvestment. Clearly, the scope of corporate strategy development far exceeds that of any other issue on the CEO's mind. The job of the strategy consultant is to delineate that scope and reduce the problem to a definable, analytical approach.

Intimacy of the Decision

The choices open to a CEO are broad. If the issue is diversification, it is often difficult to generate a hard logic, beyond financial parameters, for choosing some businesses over others. The choice will depend heavily on what the company is comfortable with; after having exhaustive analysis, the final choice will be a personal one.

Some companies (like Caterpillar Tractor) have chosen to pursue essentially one business as aggressively as possible. Others (like John Deere) have broadened their corporate scope, while staying within familiar manufacturing processes. Still others have chosen to be "multiform" with a wide range of unrelated businesses. While in some cases these directions were dictated by the apparent opportunity, each relates finally to the "level of comfort."

New businesses mean new risks, both operating and financial. Extension of existing businesses into new areas also means new risks. This is the personal province of the CEO. The consultant must provide the analytical framework and assist the CEO toward a personal decision. Development of strong trust and rapport between the CEO and the strategy consultant is essential.

Divestment, the other side of diversification, is the liquidation or sale of existing businesses (sometimes combined with the management of others for cash generation rather than growth). Divestment, too, has a strong personal dimension. It is no accident that most companies have difficulty in facing divestment except in a real emergency. This decision has major people and organizational concerns which the chief executive must foresee and handle.

Magnitude of the Decision

A major change in corporate strategy requires total commitment of the CEO and the organization. Our experience is that a major change in strategy will rarely be developed, implemented, and successful in less than five years. Further, it requires a massive redeployment of assets, change in organization and systems, and continued commitment to the new direction to achieve success.

For the single-product company, it is often a "bet your company" decision. For the complex multidivisional company, it is likely that only one major change can be effected within senior management's tenure. Often, the corporation must devote its full complement of debt capacity and investable funds. Failure to make and execute the investment properly means that options for growth will be virtually eliminated.

The consultant's great responsibility ranges from the proper execution of analytical work to involvement in the implementation of the total strategy in all of its dimensions of honesty in laying out, initially, the proper scope of the involvement. The consultant fees will be large in comparison with a straightforward problem, but negligible in terms of the corporate exposure in effecting strategic change. The prime, up-front responsibility of the consultant is to be sure that both the proposal and the effort expended are adequate for the assignment and that the client understands fully the exposure in terms of both consulting expense and the real job of executing a new direction.

THE APPROACH

Discussing the initial approach to a strategy connsulting assignment is difficult, partly because the client is rarely looking at a well-defined problem to "fix" or seek expertise in solving. More important, the very awareness of the nature of the issue—its diffuseness, intimacy, and importance—suggests that the client will not approach the central issue with a consultant in a direct fashion. Rather, the consultant may be asked to look at a piece of the issue that can be readily defined as a problem, which provides an easy basis for discussion and allows client and consultant to get to know one another.

Of key importance is the consultant's ability to set the problem in its proper strategic context and to pursue pieces of the problem only within this context first and then in the proper order. The Boston Consulting Group will not accept an organization study in advance of an overall strategy assignment because of our conviction that once the strategy is set, it is quite straightforward to develop organizational changes that reflect and enhance the strategy implementation. The other side of the coin is that a structure suited to one strategy will make a different strategy all but impossible to develop.

It becomes clear that no "cookbook" approach to corporate strategy development is possible. From the consultant's point of view, a proposal must convey, fundamentally, the depth of the consultant's experience in working with major strategic issues, sufficient knowledge of the client so that a proper budget can be allotted, an analytical framework within which to work, and the creativity to go beyond a pedestrian approach in handling the assignment.

From the client's point of view, it is almost impossible to evaluate a proposal in terms of the specificity of the work plan and budget. As a result, our usual approach to the corporate strategy issue is through an "entry" study that can be defined both by itself and in terms of its relationship to overall corporate strategy.

THE APPLICATION: WHERECO (A CAPITAL-INTENSIVE COMPANY)

Whereco, a major case experience, illustrates the nature of the strategy problem and highlights our approach to it. This fairly long (and early) involvement provides a feel for our own evolution in approaching corporate strategy.

The CEO of Whereco approached us to assist in developing an acquisition strategy. Whereco, a multidivisional, capital-intensive company whose prime businesses were modest growth at best, wanted to grow at a much more rapid rate in the future. The assignment was structured in terms of developing a set of acquisition criteria and screening potential acquisition candidates.

Our approach was to look at the existing businesses to understand their characteristics. It quickly became apparent that the existing businesses served relatively low-growth markets and, surprisingly, that their required reinvestment used all the cash that Whereco could generated on an operating basis.

Whereco: Phase 1

Termed a "strategy audit" and intended to broad-brush the major businesses but *not* to delve into intensive strategy development for each business, phase 1 took about two months and produced several overall conclusions:

- The basic markets served by all but a few businesses were low growth.
- The more rapid-growth businesses were not large enough to meaningfully lever Whereco's growth rate.
- The mature businesses were faced with the problem of continually building new capacity to maintain "world scale."
  - New, large plants were significantly more cost effective than older, smaller plants.
  - Although the mature businesses reported earnings, the required reinvestment in new plants exceeded, on trend, the sum of earn-

ings and depreciation. On trend, these businesses showed negative cash flow.

- If Whereco continued supporting the mature businesses, it would have *no* cash flow to finance an acquisition with growth characteristics.
  - The price paid for an acquisition is merely the entry fee.
  - A high-growth acquisition will almost certainly require *annual* cash investment over and above the cost of acquisition.
- Alternatively, the earnings and depreciation flow represented very large sums for redeployment into new businesses.
- Finally, Whereco could grow by investing more funds in the existing businesses and gaining market share, even though the market had only modest growth.

The net result of these observations: Whereco was not ready to look at the question of acquisition strategy. That is, Whereco had three dis-

Table A-1 Existing Options to Determine Acquisition Strategy

Existing business option	Cash implications	Acquisition options
▪ Maintain market share Invest with industry to hold relative cost position	▪ Use all cash	▪ Not a growth acquisition which would need cash funding
▪ Lose market share Close small plants Not reinvest in new	▪ Manage for cash Generate cash for redeployment	▪ Seek an acquisition to fund growth Must take up slack of gradual liquidation of base business
▪ Gain market share Invest in plants ahead of industry Improve relative cost position	▪ Manage for growth Cash needs exceed corporate cash flow and outside financing capability	▪ A mature acquisition To generate cash to redeploy to existing business

tinct options with its existing businesses that had to be addressed before it knew what kind of an acquisition to seek (Table A-1). Clearly, acquisitions would hold a major position in Whereco's strategy development. Equally clearly, Whereco's first task was to determine its strategy relative to its existing businesses.

Continuing to work with these observations, we developed a conceptual framework to allow Whereco to put its options into perspective. This framework came partly from our work with Whereco and partly from work with another client on a product strategy problem. That latter case provided strong evidence that relative market position and profitability went hand in hand. That is, if a company had the leading market share in a business and was significantly larger than the number two competitor, it would usually have better costs and hence better margins than its competitor. Alternatively, if a company was substantially smaller than the leading company in its field, its costs would be higher than those of the leader, and the margins would be corresponding lower.

This was a major strategic insight for Whereco. It explained why Whereco's major businesses chronically had modest returns. While the industry leader earned an average of 12 percent on its assets, Whereco earned about 7 percent, and competitors smaller than Whereco earned 3 to 5 percent. Since the ability of a business to generate cash is wholly a function of its return on assets, Whereco consistently generated less cash than its larger competitors. We could then array Whereco's businesses along the dimensions shown in Figure A-1.

From a purely financial viewpoint, it is clear that a business must invest at a more rapid rate to grow rapidly than to grow slowly. If a business grows at 20 percent per year, on trend, it must add to its assets at 20 percent per year, on trend. This means that if assets are to grow at 20

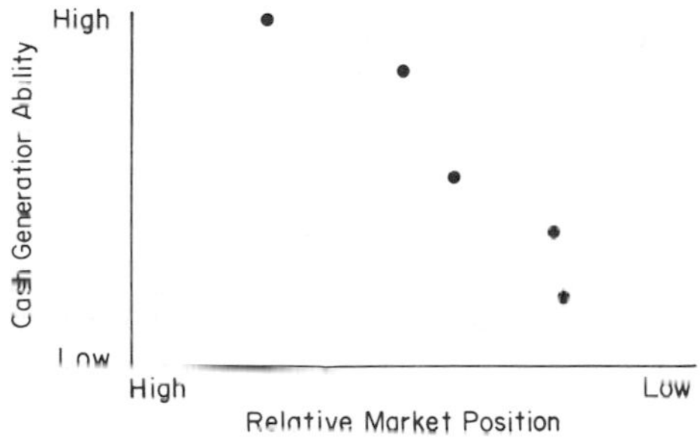

FIGURE A-1

percent per year, the pattern in Table A-2 must obtain. If a business grew 5 percent per year, it would require a 5 percent return on assets to be self-financing; a 40 percent annual growth would require a 40 percent return to be self-financing. Whereco's businesses could thus be arrayed along the financial dimensions in Figure A-2.

By applying these concepts to Whereco's businesses, we could make further observations:

- Whereco's low-growth businesses were also chronically low return as long as Whereco's market share relative to the leader stayed constant.
  - Specifically, the businesses grew at 7 percent per year, including inflation, and earned 7 percent per year, on trend.
    - This business growth and earnings rate means that *cash generation* (assuming constant depreciation reinvestment) was 7 percent of assets.

Table A-2 Growth Rate Pattern

Assets, $	Funds needed, $	Return on assets, %*
100	20	20
120	24	20
144	29	20
173	—	

*This relationship, including the impact of debt, dividends, and corporate charges, is explored in Alan J. Zakon, "Capital Structure Optimization," in J. Fred Weston and Maurice B. Goudzwaard (eds), *The Treasurer's Handbook,* Dow Jones-Irwin, Homewood, Ill., 1976, pp. 641–668.

    - The growth rate means that *cash use* was also 7 percent of assets.
    - With this growth and earnings rate, *net cash flow* would remain zero, on trend.
  - A business with no net cash flow and no promise of a future net cash flow has no value and is a *cash trap.*

- Whereco had to make a strategy decision on the basic business. The alternative of holding market position was not viable.
  - To grow at zero would entail a continual loss of market share.
    - It would, however, generate 7 percent of assets in *net cash flow for redeployment.*
    - It would generate more if depreciation were not fully reinvested.
    - In a cyclical upswing, return on assets would typically climb to the 10 to 12 percent level, providing more cash flow.
    - Since assets in a capital-intensive business take several years to add, Whereco would not lose relative market (and cost) position for five to seven years.
    - A combination of closing smaller plants and pruning lower-margin business as the market grew relative to Whereco's capacity would preserve basic profitability over a much longer period.

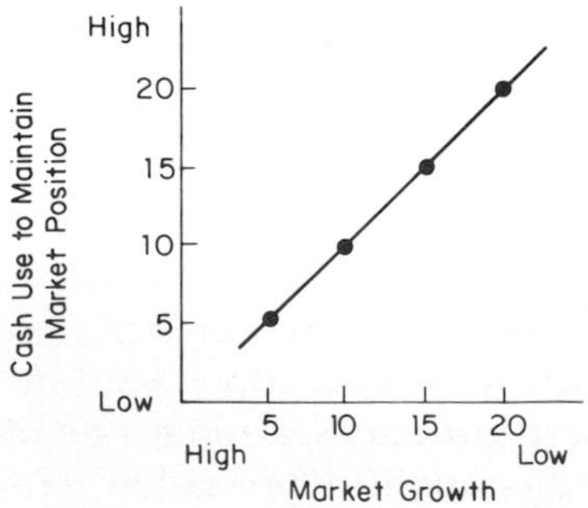

FIGURE A-2

- Cashing out was thus a viable alternative, subject to finding new businesses to accept the cash generated from the base businesses, which would be managed for cash generation.
- The alternative of gaining relative market share and, hence, cost position, profitability, and relative cash flow was probably a higher risk investment and required more funds than Whereco could afford.
  - Gaining share in a low-growth business is very expensive, especially in a capital-intensive business.
  - Whereco's business portfolio and options, when the industry leader has a profitable position to protect and the cash to do so, could be summarized as in Figure A-3.

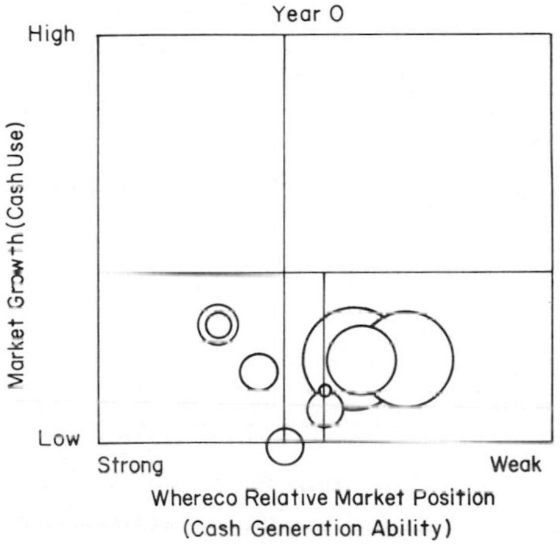

FIGURE A-3

Each circle represents a major business and the circle size corresponds to the sales volume of each business. It is now clear that Whereco has only two growth businesses and that they are too small to lever the corporate growth rate. Further, the predominance of Whereco's sales is in the low-growth, weak-market-position area where net cash flow is low. Whereco has no positions in the high-growth, strong-market-position quadrant or the high-growth, weak-market-position quadrant.

The Business Portfolio: Growth-Share Matrix Conceptually, exploration of the characteristics of the growth-share matrix provides a shortcut to understanding Whereco's existing position, options, and alternatives. This can best be seen by examining the characteristics of each quadrant (Figure A-4).

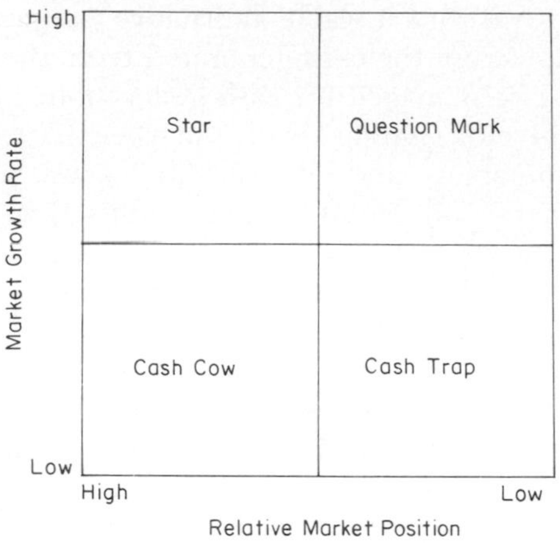

FIGURE A-4

Cash Trap The cash trap (Figure A-5) has little growth, so it does not represent an opportunity to invest funds for growth other than trying to take share from the leader. In a slow-growth market, the leader, who is unlikely to give up share willingly and probably has better costs than Whereco's cash trap, can defend the lead position at much lower cost than Whereco can take share. That is, the leader has far more margin to work with. Further, unless Whereco voluntarily gives up share in the cash trap, it will chronically use as much cash as it generates.

The cash trap, then, makes no real corporate contribution, supplying neither growth nor cash. Put another way, it will neither accept cash investment profitably nor generate cash for redeployment to other busi-

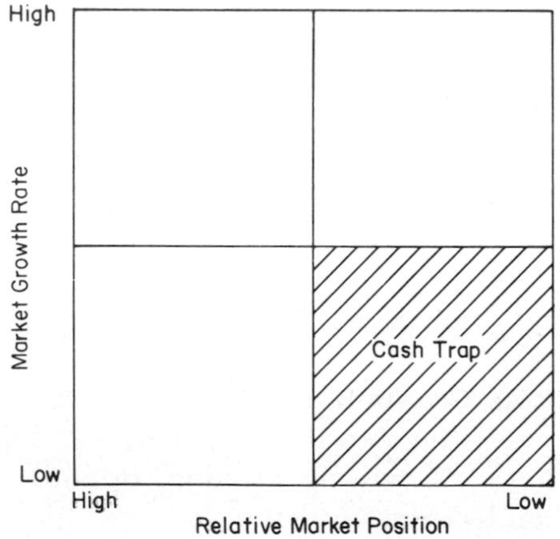

FIGURE A-5

nesses that can profitably use funds. The indicated alternative is *to manage this quadrant for cash.*

The automobile industry shows a vivid parallel. General Motors, Ford, Chrysler, and American Motors may be arrayed in terms of both decreasing relative market share and profitability. Ford earns less, traditionally, than General Motors and must reinvest a higher percentage of earnings to hold position. Chrysler and American Motors, with far weaker positions, have been chronic cash traps. While each may have an occasional year or years of relative profitability, they are constantly required to invest more in the business than they earn.

Question Mark The growth rate is high in the question mark quadrant (Figure A-6), so the cash use to hold market share will be high. Since

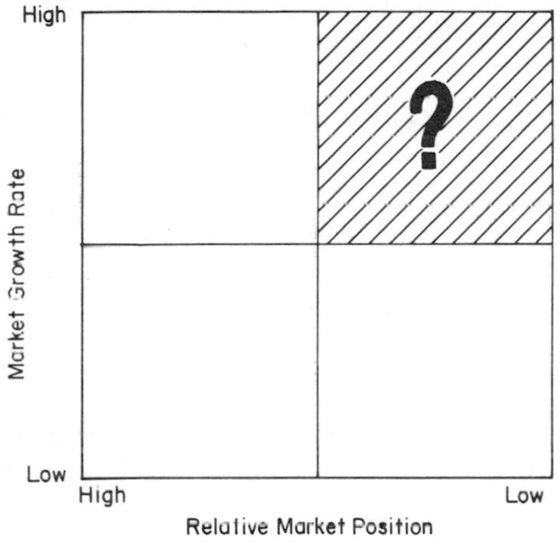

FIGURE A-6

the market position is relatively weak, cash generation relative to the leader will be weak. On balance, the question mark will almost surely have a negative net cash flow as long as relative market share is constant. The alternatives are interesting and very relevant to Whereco's acquisition strategy.

We can trace the alternatives open to a question mark business. Option 1 (Figure A-7) is to hold relative market share as the market growth slows—as all growth inevitably does. However, this means that the business will be a chronic cash trap over its growth and maturity cycle. In all probability it will remain a negative cash flow business and never provide a return on its investment. Each generation has its growth favorites—agricultural equipment in the 1920s, television in the 1950s, electronics in the 1960s, and mobile homes in the 1970s—and we may

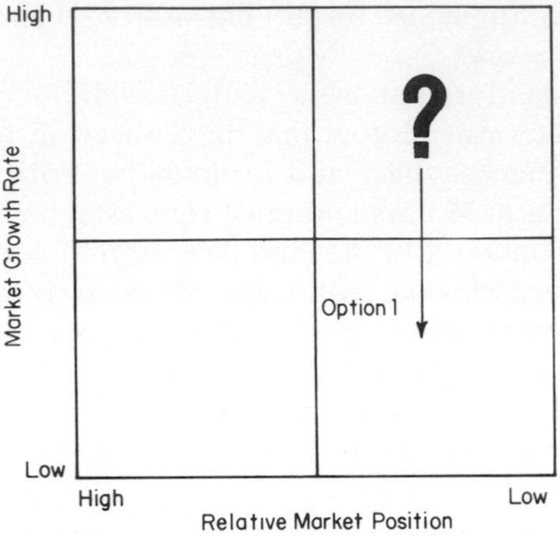

FIGURE A-7

observe that the chronically low-share competitors in each industry have either gone out of business as the industry matures or are now marginally profitable. *Option 1, then, is a cash trap.*

Option 2 (Figure A-8) is to gain market share relative to the leader and to achieve market leadership before the growth slows. The goal is to achieve leadership and, hence, net cash flow when the business becomes mature. The strategy issue is whether the company has the financial and emotional ability to keep investing in a business to gain market share relative to the leader, with the payoff dependent on ultimately displacing the leader. The costs are high:

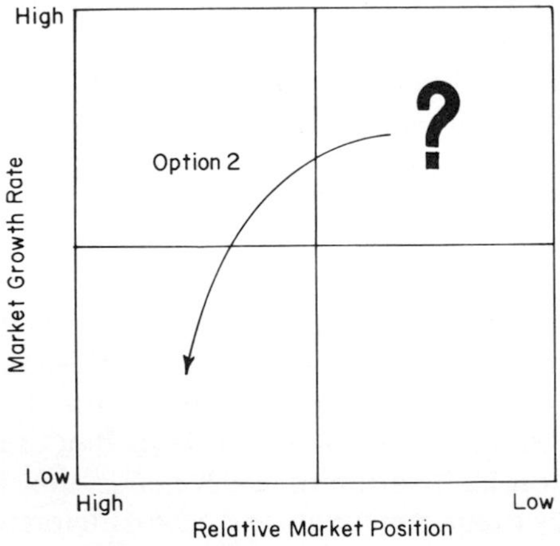

FIGURE A-8

- Enough cash would be needed at least to keep up with the growth rate of the market.

Plus

- Cash would be required so the company can add capacity faster than the market *and* the leader.

Plus

- Competitive tactics that reduce the profit margin in order to gain relative share would have to be deployed, such as:
  - Adding capacity well ahead of demand
  - Cutting price to fill capacity
  - Advertising or other nonprice competition
  - R&D

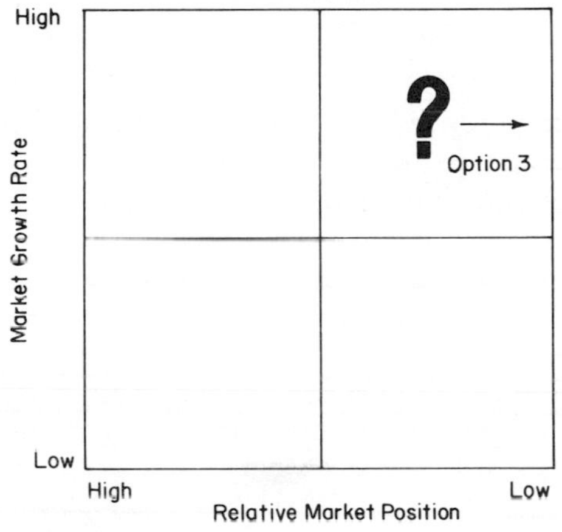

FIGURE A-9

Option 3 (Figure A-9) is to liquidate the business by sale or gradual share loss. Either will generate cash, and a high-growth business is usually very stable.

Option 4 is to redefine the business away from the leader and to become, in effect, a leader through segmentation. Digital Equipment has become a large and profitable computer company by focusing away from the leader (IBM) while such giants as RCA and General Electric were forced to accept option 3 by competing directly with IBM.

The Star The star business (Figure A-10) is both high growth and high relative share. Whether its net cash flow is positive, negative, or neutral depends upon how strong it is relative to the followers and how high the growth is. IBM and Xerox represent classic star businesses in computers and plain paper copiers, respectively. Ultimately the growth rate of these markets will slow and these businesses will fall into the cash cow

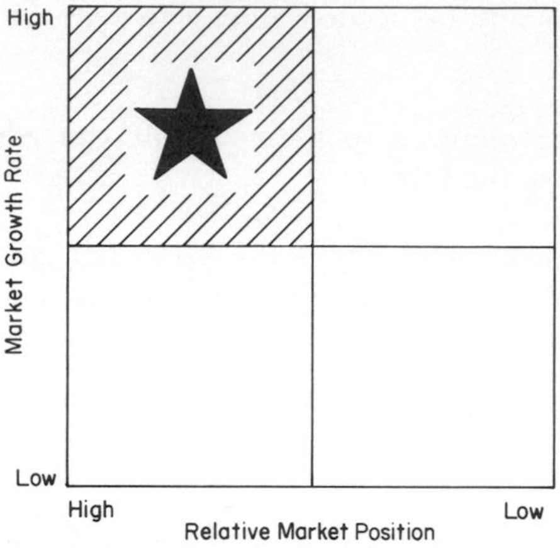

FIGURE A-10

quadrant (assuming they hold their share of the market and successfully fend off other companies' question marks).

The Cash Cow As indicated earlier, the cash cow business (Figure A-11) represents competitive success. General Motors, for example, typically earns 15 to 17 percent on its assets in a market growing at 6 percent. This means that General Motors is a major cash generator. In fact, if cash generation is 16 percent of assets, and cash use is 6 percent of assets, General Motors will have cash available for redeployment or dividends equal to 1 − 6/16, or 62.5 percent of earnings. That is, the

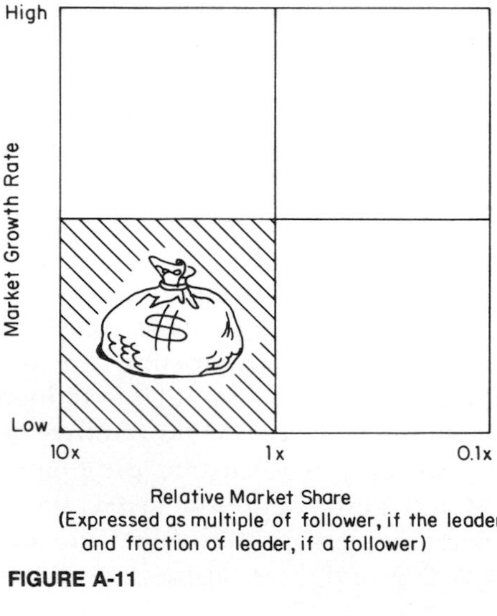

FIGURE A-11

percent of earnings that must be reinvested in a business, on trend, is equal to

$$\text{Percent reinvestment} = \frac{\text{growth rate}}{\text{return on assets}}$$

For General Motors

$$\frac{6\%}{16\%} = 37.5\%$$

Thus General Motors has the highest dividend payout among the automobile companies. The matrix can then be illustrated as in Figure A-12.

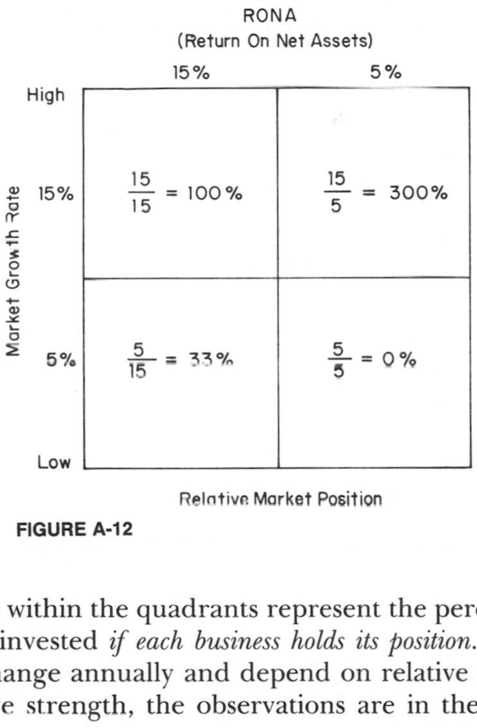

FIGURE A-12

The numbers within the quadrants represent the percent of earnings that must be reinvested *if each business holds its position.* While the true numbers will change annually and depend on relative growth and relative competitive strength, the observations are in the right direction (Figure A-13).

Further, changing cash behavior can be expected from changing growth rates of either the market or the business. That is, if the star is in a 15 percent growth market and has a 15 percent return on net assets (RONA), its cash characteristics are

$$\text{Reinvestment} = \frac{\text{growth}}{\text{RONA}} = \frac{15\%}{15\%} = 100\%$$

If the market growth slows or if the star loses share by growing less rapidly than the market, then

$$\text{Reinvestment} = \frac{10\%}{15\%} = 67\%$$

If the star spends less of its profit margin to protect its position, its RONA will probably increase, and

$$\text{Reinvestment} = \frac{10\%}{20\%} = 50\%$$

Reinvestment in a business depends on the market growth, the individual business growth, the aggressiveness employed to gain relative share, the returns from selling share, and the relative competitive position, schematically presented in Figure A-14.

Whereco Acquisition Strategy To recapitulate, the key initial step was a "strategy audit," followed by developing a portfolio concept to assist

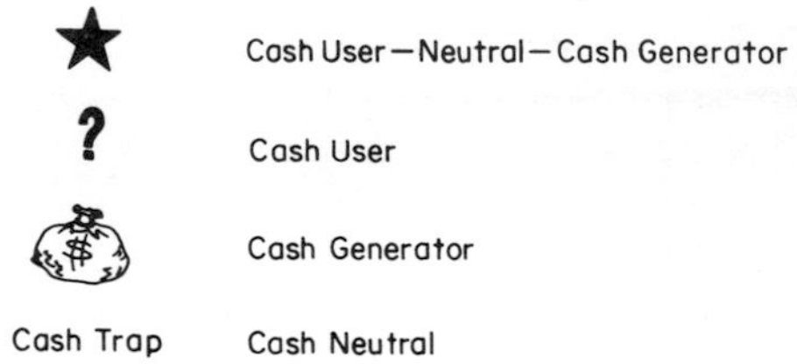

FIGURE A-13

Whereco in assessing first its basic position and second its acquisition criteria. This analysis suggested several procedures:

- Evaluate the capital-intensive businesses in a detailed manner to determine:
  - True competitive position
  - Base-level investment required
  - Opportunities to find business segments where relative market position is—or could be—strong
- Get a firm fix on cash available for redeployment based on that evaluation.
- Evaluate acquisition opportunities against existing business financial (cash for redeployment) guidelines.

Acquisition parameters could be expressed simply. If Whereco itself was not to be a cash generator, an acquisition that provided cash for redeployment and debt capacity would open Whereco's options. That

Percent Reinvestment

Relative Market Position (RONA: High → Low); Company Growth (High → Low)

Company Growth \ RONA	20	16	12	8	4	0
20	100%	125%	167%	250%	500%	∞
16	80%	100%	133%	200%	400%	∞
12	60%	75%	100%	150%	300%	∞
8	40%	50%	67%	100%	200%	∞
4	20%	25%	33%	50%	100%	∞
0	0%	0%	0%	0%	0%	100%

DOG

FIGURE A-14

means, in a growth-share context, an acquisition of leadership position with a relatively low growth rate.

Once financial options opened up, either through internal decisions to give up share or through a "cash for redeployment" acquisition, or ideally through both, a "question mark" acquisition could be explored. To understand the logic, it is necessary to return to the growth-share matrix and trace cash flows among businesses as well as business "trajectories" (Figure A-15).

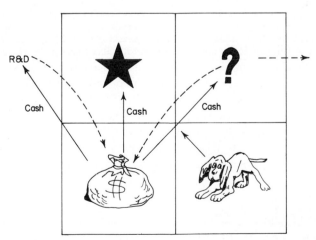

Cash should flow from businesses with a cash surplus to businesses that can profitably use the cash. In the simplest sense, this provides a way to fund growth. In a more sophisticated sense, it allows a growth business to *uncouple the profit margin from the growth rate.* That is, a cash-

FIGURE A-15

rich company—in an ongoing cash redeployment sense—can find a question mark for growth without forcing the question mark to generate its own growth funds. A one-product company must earn enough to finance its own growth and tap the debt and equity markets. A high-growth division of a "cash for redeployment" company, however, can fund a growth business without requiring that business to earn a profit. That means the growth business can invest as is needed to gain relative market share.

Whereco: End of Phase 1

The insights developed through the growth-share matrix and the above acquisition criteria left several major tasks:

- Each business had to be categorized properly in the matrix and an agreed upon mission established.
  - How much growth relative to competition?
  - How much cash for redeployment?
- A control system had to be established that mirrored the business plan.
  - Not earnings but growth in relative market share if it was a question mark business.
  - Not growth but cash for redeployment if it was a cash cow.
  - *Not decentralized profit center management.*
- An incentive system had to be established to motivate and reinforce an essentially new form of management.
- An educational program had to be developed and implemented to teach this approach to strategy and demonstrate management's commitment.
- An analytical strategy study had to be performed for each major business to determine *true,* not broad-brush strategy audit, options.

Whereco, a billion-dollar corporation with excellent internal staff, took prime responsibility for the organizational, planning and control, management information, and educational programs. Our role was limited to counseling and acting as a sounding board in these areas, which both client and consultant viewed as proper in terms of cost and effectiveness.

Following the initial six months of overall strategy development by our firm, this program took about two years to develop and implement. We maintained close relations with Whereco throughout.

Whereco: Phase 2

At the end of phase 1, Whereco management and the consultants felt that it was time for an intensive look at the individual businesses. Prior to starting this analysis, Whereco had disaggregated its major businesses into more precisely defined accountability centers. This "exploded" the portfolio from several major business areas to almost 100 discrete strategic business units. The problem of the consultants was to develop a proposal and work plan that met the company's needs, yet stopped short of being a life's work.

The consultants, based on their knowledge of Whereco and about five days of interviewing senior corporate executives, group executives, and divisional presidents, developed a work plan calling for a twelve-month effort for a four-or-five person case team. Since our professionals work on more than one assignment concurrently, this converted to about two worker-years of effort.

The work plan provided for several "screens" to limit the scope to manageable proportions. First, major businesses with significant impact on the corporation were agreed upon. These businesses were then divided into two groupings, deserving either a detailed strategy study or a moderate depth analysis.

- Detailed strategy study
  - Market growth and segmentation
  - Competitive economics
  - Competitive analysis
  - Strategy alternatives
  - Evaluation of alternatives
- Moderate depth analysis
  - Market growth
  - Rough cut at segmentation
  - Competitive analysis
  - Careful delineation of strategy issues
  - Comparison between stated strategy, five-year plan program, five-year-plan financial expectations, past performance

Each major business was then isolated as a separate assignment, with its own budget, timing, and detailed proposal. The remaining businesses were broad-brushed in terms of consistency:

- Did the business have a stated strategy that made sense?
- Was the strategy consistent with the five-year plan?
- Were expected results—relative market share, cash, RONA—consistent with the strategy?
- Could changes between past performance and expected performance be explained?

These efforts led to a number of developments and actions.

- For the major businesses with in-depth analysis:
  - Development of strategies for each business

  - Cranking these strategies into the overall corporate portfolio
  - Determining the competitive position and financial characteristics both at present and five years hence
- For the businesses with moderate analysis:
  - Statement of strategy issues
  - Hypotheses
  - Decision about whether businesses needed in-depth study or were pursuing appropriate strategies
  - Cranking these strategies into corporate portfolio
  - Determining the competitive position and financial characteristics both at present and five years hence
- For the broad-brush businesses:
  - Statement of strategy issues in terms of consistency between strategy, plan, past and future results
  - The consultants' judgment as to attainability of goals
  - Cranking these strategies into corporate portfolio
  - Determining the competitive position and financial characteristics both at present and five years hence

While the study left many issues unresolved and several businesses needing further analysis, the overall picture became clear enough for the corporation to take major action. The conclusions may be summarized as follows:

- The company overall should be a major cash generator.
- Internal growth options were limited.
- Businesses making no corporate contribution in terms of growth or cash constituted too large a proportion of the company.
  - Move into the "manage for cash" quadrant.
  - Target about 25 percent of corporate assets for divestment. (Whereco concurred and accomplished a major divestment program over a two-year period.)
- Two major businesses in the low-growth, low-share quadrant remained.
  - One was directed to pursue a stringent "manage for cash" policy.
  - The other had some growth prospects through distribution and product segmentation strategies, and this business was identified as needing further work. It was recognized that an apparent "dog" might be participating in growth segments, and redefining its competitive arena might turn it around.
- Several businesses with good growth potential were pursuing proper strategies. A strong corporate commitment was made to fund these as appropriate.

▪ Two significant businesses with good competitive positions were not achieving the proper financial results and were losing market share. These required major in-depth analysis.

At the end of this one-year effort, then, a fair amount of work remained to be done by both Whereco and the consultants. The major work—the corporate strategy—was complete to the point of being ready for action. Key to the realization that a major strategic redeployment of actions was necessary was the following analysis:

▪ Whereco's portfolio of businesses was weak in relative competitive position.
▪ The portfolio five years hence would be about the same.
▪ Net cash flows after dividends would be about zero during that period.

Thus, Whereco, if it continued on its old course, was faced with spending five years and large sums of money to end up in a position no better than where it started.

Whereco: Phase 3

Phase 3 took two years, during which we pursued several individual business strategy studies and Whereco implemented both the divestment program and the agreed-upon business missions. The net result of this work was a major restructuring of the corporate portfolio through pruning, pursuing growth, and developing discipline in adhering to business missions.

The divestment program was explained in Whereco's annual report as follows:

> We made a searching classification of all our businesses. . . . Then we projected ahead and took a look at where they—and the corporation as a whole—would be. That indicated clearly which businesses we should cultivate and which we should move out of to give us the soundest portfolio for the long haul.
>
> To put it simply, we expect to fund businesses with strong growth potential aggressively and to withdraw from those that offer neither growth nor cash.

Progress of the program was described in the following year's annual report as:

> The fact that earnings outpaced the 18 percent increase in sales was due in a good measure to the elimination of less promising enterprises and concentrating our energies on specific growth markets.

Among the programmed changes completed were the sale or closing of businesses that failed to meet the stringent standards that guide Whereco's capital investments:

- Standards of leadership in particular industry segments
- Market growth rates
- Ability to generate cash

Whereco: Phase 4

At this point Whereco can look back at major accomplishments:

- A strong and vastly improved overall competitive position
- Strong cash generation with internal programs and discipline to continue on an ongoing basis

Whereco Portfolio

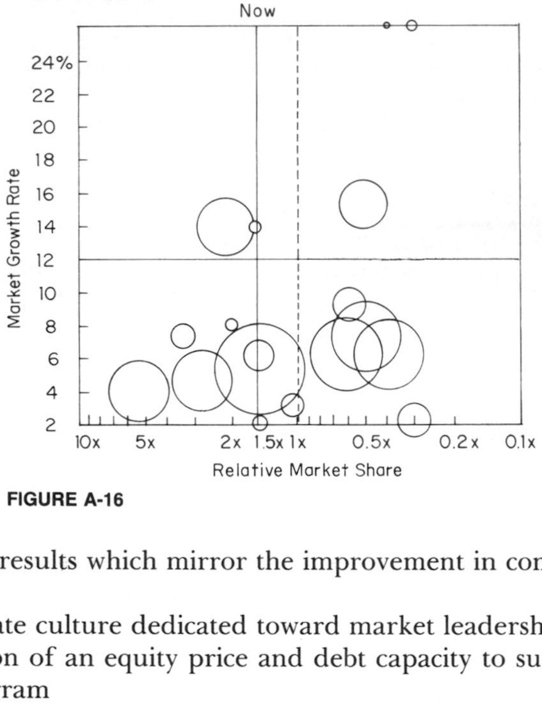

FIGURE A-16

- Financial results which mirror the improvement in competitive position
- A corporate culture dedicated toward market leadership
- Restoration of an equity price and debt capacity to support an acquisition program

After about five and a half years, Whereco is in a superb position to answer the original question: In what new areas should Whereco seek growth?

Whereco's current business portfolio is portrayed in Figure A-16. It is interesting to compare it with the portfolio of five years earlier (Figure A-3). Note that the ten-year financials, showing performance five years

Table A-3 Whereco Financial Data Five Years prior to Strategy Program

	−5	−4	−3	−2	−1	Beginning year
Sales	633	633	898	1032	1038	1056
ROE, %	9.8	7.0	7.5	8.0	4.5	5.2
EPS	1.39	1.02	1.10	1.15	0.47	0.61
D/E	0.33	0.39	0.42	0.42	0.52	0.56
Dividend	0.58	6.63	6.63	0.46	0.67	0.67

prior to the strategy program (Table A-3) and five years after its initiation (Table A-4), mirror the change in Whereco's portfolio.

ROLE OF THE CONSULTANT

The Whereco example provides, we hope, a fair picture to flesh out the initial comments made early in this chapter. We have tried to delineate those actions and studies performed by the client and those appropriate to the consultants. We have shown the phases during which the consultants are very active and those when involvement is tangential, primarily when the client company is catching its breath.

We have tried to explain the myriad of actions that must take place within a company to effect change. These actions must all be delineated and must support the strategy. It takes time for the CEO to develop a personal commitment first to *any* change and second to the *direction* of change. It then takes time and effort to educate the organization both to the change and to management's commitment to the change.

Finally, it is, we hope, clear that the consultants must navigate between having a conceptual framework and retaining flexibility and creativity in implementing this framework. The growth-share matrix is a powerful tool when business definitions are properly made and when the real facts and consequences of growth and competitive position are understood.

Table A-4 Whereco Financial Data Five Years following Strategy Program

	Beginning year	1	2	3	Now
Sales	1056	1129	1299	1526	1590
ROE, %	5.2	5.9	10.8	16.1	15
EPS	0.61	0.72	1.77	3.27	3.70
D/E	0.56	0.54	0.62	0.55	0.89
Dividend	0.67	0.40	0.43	0.60	0.55
Net Assets	745	728	796	848	912
Pretax RONA, %	7.1	7.4	14	21	25

It must be realized that not all high-market-share businesses are competitively strong and not all low-share businesses are competitively weak. The consultants' responsibility is to understand the true competitive economics to properly determine what causes competitive strength and weakness. It is the consultants' further responsibility to develop independent, outside confirmation of such key data as competitors' actions, market and segment growth rates, market shares, and changes in market shares, and not to rely only on the client's own data. Many companies feel that they know these data well (and many do), but the consultants must test internal data as rigorously as any other data, analysis, and concept brought to bear on the subject of study.

The strategy problem is too important to do less.

INDEX